REAL ESTATE DESK BOOK

FIFTH EDITION

IBP Research and Editorial Staff

Institute for Business Planning, Inc.
IBP Plaza, Englewood Cliffs, N.J. 07632

Fifth Edition
First Printing. . . .
February 1977

IBP Plaza, Englewood Cliffs, N. J. 07632

Library of Congress Catalog Card Number: 76-027989

HOW TO USE THIS DESK BOOK

This Desk Book has one prime objective: to help you make top money from real estate by tuning you into the big profits that can be made from the real estate industry. Whether you're a real estate investor, dealer, broker, salesman, developer or builder, mortgage lender, or otherwise connected with real estate in some way, even as a lessee, the Desk Book provides you with a portable collection of all the main moves open to you to increase your profits through your real estate activities. Here you are given quick access to the tried and tested money-making and tax-saving techniques used by the master builders of real estate fortunes, techniques that are being successfully used in today's real estate world and under the current tax law.

If you are to make really big money in real estate, you can't stand still. You must be sensitive to the underlying pressures, both economic and political, that produce legislative changes—changes in our tax laws and in our housing and urban development laws, for example. These in turn not only stimulate real estate activity but also require us to use the latest methods of accomplishing our goals.

To travel the road to wealth through real estate, you must know the real estate world of the 1970's. Use the Desk Book as your money-making guide through this world.

Use this book as a quick refresher, as a checklist of the possibilities to be explored, and as an idea tickler, bearing in mind that you are operating in a rapidly changing world and that final decisions and moves should not be made without checking the latest developments.

TABLE OF CONTENTS

APPENDIX (continued) Page

[¶100] UNIQUE PACKAGE OF TAX BENEFITS OFFERED BY REAL ESTATE

Real estate enjoys some unique tax advantages. Careful use of the tax angles available in real estate transactions can make a bad deal acceptable, a good deal excellent and turn a prime deal into a real bonanza.

[¶101] Twenty Tax Advantages in Real Estate

(1) Flexibility: Real estate can be purchased or rented, sold or leased, with different tax results. Real estate can be divided into different types of fees, leasehold, and mortgage investments, each tailored to the tax position of its owner.

(2) Deductibility of Losses: When sold at a loss, the loss may be fully deductible.

(3) Capital Gain Opportunities: When sold at a profit, part or all of the gain may qualify for favorable capital gain treatment.

(4) Rent Deductions: When leased, the cost of occupancy can be charged off fully.

(5) Favorable Tax Treatment of Security Deposit: A properly arranged security deposit isn't taxed until the end of the lease.

(6) Depreciation Deductions: When owned, much of the cost of the investment can be recovered tax free by depreciation deductions. This reduces the size of the investment and steps up the yield.

(7) Tax Advantages of Highly Leveraged Situations: Ownership can be financed in a way so that the owner may include the amount of non-recourse loans in the depreciable basis, that increases the owner's equity with tax-free funds.

(8) Tax Advantages of Sale-Leasebacks: The cost of land can be made tax deductible by a sale followed by leaseback for a long period. The investment in the building is recovered tax free through depreciation deductions.

(9) Opportunities for Tax-Free Improvements: The owner may get his property improved tax free by having his tenant make the improvements.

(10) Interest and Tax Deductions: The owner can elect to deduct or capitalize interest and taxes paid to carry unimproved property.

(11) Tax-Deductible Repairs: The owner can sometimes build up the value of his holdings by tax-deductible repair expenditures.

(12) Tax Savings from Choosing Best Form of Ownership: Ownership can be held in whatever entity—partnership, corporation, trust, or personal ownership—will best protect the income from tax. When held in corporate ownership, income can accumulate at lower tax rates than might apply if personally owned. The tax savings can be applied to build up equity and future capital gain by paying off mortgages and improving the property.

(13) Opportunities for Postponing Taxable Gain: Tax on the sale of real estate may be postponed by electing the installment method of sale, a deferred payment sale, or by using option agreements, executory contracts, conditional contracts, lease with purchase options, escrow arrangements and contingent price arrangements. When selling a portion of the land, retaining some rights (i.e., oil and mineral rights) may convert a sale into an easement so that the proceeds will go to reduce your basis rather than be taxed as a gain.

(14) Flexibility as to Taxable Gain: Even after an installment sale, we may be able to change our minds to have the gain taxed earlier by disposing of the installment obligations.

(15) Tax-Free Cash: On the sale of real estate, there are methods of getting cash in advance while deferring the taxability of gain. One way is to borrow on the obligation obtained on an installment sale of real estate, giving the installment notes as collateral.

(16) Tax-Free Swaps: Real estate held for investment can be built up in value and traded tax free for other real estate to be held for investment.

(17) Opportunities to Avoid Personal Holding Company Penalty: Rental income may be used to take a company out of the personal holding company category and thus avoid penalty tax.

(18) Capital Gain Opportunities from Leases: Leases can be canceled for money which is taxed at capital gain rates.

(19) Tax-Free Treatment of Condemnation Awards: Condemnation awards can be received without tax if reinvested in real estate.

(20) Tax-Free Sale of Home: A residence can be sold without capital gain tax if the proceeds are used to buy or build a new residence.

[¶102] Basic Tax Planning with Real Estate

Because real estate values tend to hold up, real estate investors have been able to trade ordinary depreciation deductions (which reduce ordinary income) for more favorable capital gain tax rates. The depreciation deductions taken during the time the property is held reduce the basis of the property to the owners. So, when they sell (assuming values have held up), they have a capital gain for the difference between the reduced basis and the selling price. This technique of converting ordinary deductions into capital gains may however, be limited by recapture provisions of the tax law.

[¶103] The Interplay of Depreciation and Mortgage Amortization

Real estate investors look at their return from real estate investments this way: How much am I earning on the cash I have invested? In arriving at this return, keep these factors in mind: (1) Depreciation is based on the full cost of the property—not only the cash paid. (2) Depreciation deductions require no cash outlay. (3) Mortgage amortization payments (the amount paid to reduce the mortgage principal) require cash outlays, but are not deductible for tax purposes.

As a result, where the depreciation deductions exceed the amortization payments, the difference is tax free to the investor. But where the amortization payments exceed the depreciation deductions, the difference is taxable income to the investor. (At this point, one may want to sell and get capital gain or seek refinancing to reduce the amortization payments.)

The interplay of depreciation and amortization is an important concept that is referred to throughout this book. A simple example will show how it works. Assume gross rents of $100,000; operating costs of $40,000 (including mortgage interest); depreciation of $10,000, and mortgage amortization of $6,000. Taxable income is $50,000 ($100,000 rents less $40,000 operating costs and $10,000 depreciation). However, the cash income is $54,000 ($100,000 rents less the $40,000 operating costs and $6,000 mortgage amortization). This $4,000 difference is the excess of depreciation over amortization, and is tax free. Conversely, if depreciation had amounted to $6,000 and the mortgage amortization amounted to $10,000, taxable income would be $54,000 and cash income would only be $50,000.

[¶104] Results of Various Real Estate Acquisition Methods

The method of acquisition has immediate and future tax consequences because it determines the basis for depreciation during ownership and the computation of gain or loss upon disposition. Here we analyze the methods of acquiring real estate and the tax consequences involved.

(1) Acquisition by purchase involves no immediate tax consequences. The cost of a purchase is a capital expenditure (Code §263). If acquired on or after March 1, 1913, the basis is cost (§1012).

(2) Acquisition by gift involves no immediate tax consequences. If acquired before January 1, 1921, unadjusted basis is fair market value at date of gift (§1015(c)). If acquired after December 31, 1920: (a) the basis for determining gain is the same as it would be in the hands of the donor, and (b) the basis for determining loss is the donor's basis or fair market value at date of gift, whichever is lower (§1015(a)).

Note: The gift tax the donor paid on the gift will step up the basis of the property. But the basis cannot be raised above its market value at the time of the gift.

(3) Acquisition from decedent by way of transfer at death involves no immediate tax consequences. The unadjusted basis is the fair market value at *date of death* or optional valuation date (six months after death) (Code §1014).

(4) Acquisition as compensation for services results in immediate taxable income to recipient (§61(a)(1)). The amount of this income is the fair market value of the property at the date of acquisition, that may be presumed to be the stipulated price of the services rendered (Reg. §1.161-2(d)). The unadjusted basis is the amount included in income.

(5) Acquisition as liquidating distribution from a corporation results in immediate tax consequences to the extent of capital gain or loss in the amount of the difference between the shareholder's adjusted basis in stock and fair market value of the real estate received in liquidation (§331). Special rules apply in a one-month liquidation.

(6) Acquisition as full or partial satisfaction of indebtedness may or may not involve immediate tax consequences. If the basis of the obligation is greater than the fair market value of the acquired real estate, the difference may be charged off as a bad debt (§166). If the fair market value of the property received exceeds the basis of the obligation, the difference may be taxed as capital gain. If the exchange is equal, no immediate tax consequences result.

(7) Acquisition of mortgaged realty may or may not involve immediate tax consequences:

(a) In a foreclosure situation if a third party bids in the property for less than the basis of the obligation, the mortgagee has a bad debt deduction for the difference between the obligation and amount received. If the mortgagee bids in the property for less than the obligation the bad debt deduction is the difference between the obligation and the bid price (Reg. §1.166-6). However, if the amount received or the bid price (presumed to be the fair market value) is greater than the obligation basis, the mortgagee has capital gain.

(b) In a voluntary conveyance situation, the fair market value of the property is considered payment of the unpaid balance of the obligation. If the property value is less than the basis of the obligation, the mortgagee receives a bad debt deduction for the difference, if such is proved worthless. If the property value is greater than the basis of the obligation, the mortgagee has ordinary income to the extent of delinquent interest, recovery of prior write-off, or collections over basis of note.

(8) Acquisition by repossession involves immediate tax consequences. Code §1038 limits the amount of realized gain on repossessions. Whenever a sale of real property creates an indebtedness to the seller which is secured by the real property sold, §1038 operates to limit taxable gain on repossession, regardless of whether the property is sold on an installment sale or on a deferred payment sale and whether or not, under local law, title had passed to the buyer. An indebtedness is secured by the property whenever seller has the right to take title or possession of the property or both if buyer defaults under the contract.

Under §1038, the gain on repossession is to be realized to the extent of collections made on the sale of the property, less amounts previously picked up as taxable income. However, the amount of income to be realized is not to exceed the total potential profit on the original sale reduced by income previously picked up and payments made by the seller on the repossession. What's more, the type of gain on repossession is the same as on the original sale (ordinary income, §1231 income, or capital gain).

The distinctions that previously existed, based on whether or not title passed, are eliminated. Also eliminated is the practice of using fair market value to measure gain on repossession.

So, it is not necessary for title to have passed to have a "sale" within the terms of §1038. The Section applies as long as the buyer has a contractual right to obtain possession of the property, so long as he performs his obligations under the contract and to obtain title on the completion of the contract (Reg. §1.1038-1(a)(2)).

Another requirement for §1038 to apply is that seller must reacquire the property in partial or full satisfaction of the debt. This reacquisition may come about by agreement or by process of law (e.g., voluntary conveyance, abandonment, foreclosure) (Reg. §1.1038-1(a)(3)).

(9) Acquisition through purchase of tax lien is a common transaction involving no immediate tax consequences. A tax lien bought at public auction is a purchase, and the bid price is treated as a capital expenditure (§263).

[¶200] HOW TO FIGURE TAX ON A SALE

The sale or exchange of real estate generally results in a realized gain or loss. Whether the gain or loss must be recognized for tax purposes depends on the nature of the transaction. The tax law specifically defers recognition on transactions such as like-kind exchanges, transfers to controlled corporations, and replacement of property subject to involuntary conversions. If gain or loss is recognized, whether you receive capital gain treatment or ordinary income treatment depends on the nature of the property and your status as investor or dealer. If capital gain treatment applies, whether you have short-term or long-term capital gain or loss depends on the holding period (i.e., more than six months for long-term treatment).

[¶201] Determining Your Gain or Loss

To determine amount of gain or loss, you must know your adjusted basis and the amount realized. If the amount realized exceeds the adjusted basis, you have a gain. If the amount realized is less than the adjusted basis, you have a loss.

Amount Realized: The amount realized on a sale for tax purposes includes the amount of cash received plus the fair market value of any other property you receive. Mortgages on the property which the purchaser either assumes or takes subject to are added to the sale price.

Adjusted Basis: This is the original cost of the property plus the value of any improvements put on the property by the seller minus depreciation taken by him. The manner in which the property was acquired will also affect its basis.

Selling Expenses: Expenses such as recording fees and transfer taxes, commissions and all the other expenses of the sale, including legal fees, reduce the sale price. In other words, if you realize a capital gain, the selling expenses reduce that gain—they are not deductible against ordinary income. A dealer in real estate, however, does deduct all his selling expenses as ordinary and necessary business expenses.

[¶202] Costs Involved in Acquisition

Acquiring title to realty involves various costs, and a question arises as to their deductibility. Generally, capital expenditures are not deductible

(§263), whereas trade or business expenses are deductible (§162). Thus, the cost of the property and the costs involved in acquiring the property or perfecting title are "capital expenditures" and as such are not deductible. They are added to basis. Included in this category are fees paid to surveyors, architects, lawyers, and legal fees involved in perfecting, defending or removing a cloud on title (*Louisiana Land & Exploration Co.,* 161 F.2d 842). But legal fees to protect income are deductible. Where a suit involves both, you have to prorate between the deductible and the nondeductible.

Improvements made to the property increase basis because they are not deductible. The big problem is determining when there is an improvement and when there is a repair.

[¶203] Figuring the Tax

After computing the gain or loss to be reported from the sale or exchange of a capital asset, the next step is to figure your tax.

(1) Regular Way: Gain or loss must be classified as short-term if the capital asset was held for six months or less and as long-term if the asset was held for more than six months. Next, any short-term gain is offset by any short-term loss and long-term gain is offset by any long-term loss to arrive at net amounts.

Short- and long-term gains must be included in your gross income (§61). If you have a net long-term capital gain that exceeds your net short-term capital loss, you deduct 50% of such amount from your gross income (§1202). You may deduct capital losses to the extent of capital gains and up to $1,000 of ordinary income with some limitations (§1211). Net short-term losses are first used to offset ordinary income on a dollar-for-dollar basis and then long-term losses are used to offset ordinary income on a 2-for-1 dollar basis subject to the $1,000 limitation (the counterpart of the favorable 50% capital gain deduction is this unfavorable long-term capital loss provision).

If you have losses left over in a taxable year, you may carry over to later years the excess amounts until exhausted. The losses retain their long- or short-term character. Short-term capital loss carryovers offset short-term capital gain before offsetting long-term gains, and long-term carryovers offset long-term capital gain before offsetting short-term capital gain in the succeeding year.

Caution: Any gain from a sale or exchange of personal-use real estate must be reported as capital gain, but losses from such property are deductible only if they involve an involuntary conversion.

(2) ***Alternative Method:*** If your net long-term capital gain is greater than your net short-term capital loss, the alternative method taxes the first $50,000 of such gain ($25,000 on separate returns) at a 25% rate and any balance at a higher rate. Generally, the alternative capital gain tax will be desirable if your tax rate is more than 50%. This is because up to the 50% tax rate, the regular capital gain method produces a tax rate of up to 25%, but at the 52%-70% tax rate the regular method produces a tax rate ranging from 26% to 35% (higher than the 25% alternative).

When do you reach the over-50% tax bracket? (1) If you are married and file a joint return or you're a surviving spouse your taxable income in excess of $52,000 is taxable at a rate ranging from 53% up to 70% on income in excess of $200,000. (2) If you file as head of a household your taxable income in excess of $38,000 will be taxable at a rate ranging from 51% up to 70% on income in excess of $180,000. (3) If you're unmarried and not a surviving spouse or the head of a household, income in excess of $38,000 is taxable at the rate of 55%, and you reach the 70% rate at the $100,000 level. (4) For married individuals filing separate returns, amounts in excess of $26,000 are taxable at the rate of 53% and the 70% rate is reached at the $100,000 level.

How to Figure Tax by the Alternative Method: If you have $50,000 or less of net long-term capital gains (after you've offset your capital losses) it's easy to figure the alternative tax. It's 25% of your capital gain. The rest of your income is taxed at the regular rates. If your capital gain is more than $50,000, the calculation gets a bit more complicated because you have to compute part of your tax under the normal capital gain method and part under the alternative method. Since the normal capital gain calculation will result in a tax on that income at one-half of your ordinary tax rate, you have to figure the difference between what you would have been taxed, had your entire capital gain been calculated under the normal method, and what it would have been had you used the normal method for the first $50,000. While the method may seem confusing, all you are really doing is finding the normal rate at which capital gains in excess of $50,000 are to be taxed, given your particular tax bracket.

Example: Assume you are filing a joint return and after deductions and exemptions you end up with income of $200,000, of which $100,000 is capital gain. Under the normal capital gain method of calculating, your tax would be $76,980. Under the alternative method it would be $73,880, for a tax savings of $3,100.

Alternative Method:

Steps		*Tax*
(1) Ordinary income of $100,000 after deductions		$45,180
(2) First $50,000 of net long-term capital gain (NLTCG) taxed at 25% rate		$12,500
(3) Tax on the remaining NLTCG ($50,000)		
(a) Tax on total ordinary income of $100,000 plus 1/2 of the total capital gain under normal method at ordinary rate (Tax on $150,000)	$76,980	
(b) Tax on ordinary income of $100,000 plus 1/2 of capital gain previously calculated under the alternative method at ordinary rate (Tax on $125,000)	$60,780	
(c) Now subtract (b) from (a) and you have the third element of your tax		$16,200
(4) Add the results of steps one, two, and three for your total alternative tax ($45,180 + $12,500 + $16,200)		$73,880

(3) Capital Gain Tax for Corporations: If a corporation has net long-term capital gains exceeding net short-term losses, the tax on such gains is figured both by the regular method and an alternative method to determine the smaller tax. The regular method requires figuring the tax on taxable income which includes net capital gain. In effect, the alternative method produces a 30% tax rate on the excess NLTCG (§1201(a)). However, if your corporation has an income of less than $25,000, it can still pay the 22% normal tax.

[¶204] Timing Techniques and Tax Strategy

The timing of capital gains realization, the acceleration or deferral of tax-preference income, the maximum tax on earned income, and the averaging of income assume tremendous importance in minimizing taxes and legitimately avoiding taxes.

Effect of Minimum Tax on Tax-Preference Income: A 10% tax is imposed on tax-preference income in excess of $30,000 received in one year, subject to a credit for regular taxes paid (§56-58).

Tax-preference income for individuals and corporations except as otherwise indicated includes the following:

(1) Depreciation on personal property subject to a net lease in excess of straight line (for individuals, Subchapter S corporations and personal holding companies);

(2) Accelerated depreciation on real property in excess of straight-line depreciation;

(3) Depreciation of housing rehabilitation expenditures in excess of straight-line depreciation;

(4) Amortization of pollution control equipment in excess of accelerated depreciation;

(5) Amortization of railroad rolling stock over accelerated depreciation;

(6) Tax benefits from qualified stock options;

(7) Depletion costs to the extent they exceed the cost or other basis of the property involved;

(8) One-half of capital gains;

(9) Amortization of childcare facilities over §167 depreciation.

Point at Which Minimum Tax Provision Begins to Operate: Regardless of the nature of the tax-preference income you have, you won't be affected by the minimum tax provision as long as the total amount of tax-preference income does not exceed $30,000 ($15,000 for husband and wife filing separate returns) plus the amount of your regular income taxes. If your tax-preference income does exceed that amount, you'll pay a 10% tax on the excess.

How Minimum Tax Provision Works: Suppose a real estate investor has preferential income amounting to $300,000. His regular federal income tax comes to $75,000. The amount of tax on the preferential income works out as follows: Subtract the sum of $30,000 (exemption) and $75,000 (regular tax) from $300,000, leaving a balance of $195,000, 10% of which would come to a tax of $19,500 to be added to regular taxes.

Deductions and Carryovers: No deductions are allowed for purposes of the minimum tax except that net operating losses are deductible. If there is an operating loss carryover, the minimum tax is deferred until it becomes clear that the carryover losses will be available to offset regular income. If the losses are not used to offset regular income, the minimum tax would, to a corresponding extent, never apply.

Subchapter S Corporations: Items of tax preference are apportioned among the shareholders of Subchapter S corporations, as losses are apportioned, and they are not treated as preferences of the corporation. But where capital gains are taxed to both the corporation and shareholder (under §1378), the capital gain tax preference is subject to the minimum tax at both the corporate and the individual level. In such case, the amount treated as capital gain by the shareholder is reduced by the tax imposed under §1378 (as under present law) and by the 10% minimum tax imposed at the corporate level.

Basis Adjustments: Tax paid on tax-preference items is not added to the property basis.

What to Do: Basically, your strategy will be to see that your tax-preference income does not exceed the $30,000 exemption plus your regular federal income tax liability so you can avoid the 10% minimum tax. To do this you could distribute property which generates tax-preference income among your family so that no member of the family is within the minimum tax provisions. If part of your income is from accelerated depreciation, you may want to switch to the straight-line method.

Maximum Tax on Earned Income: A maximum tax of 50% is available for earned taxable income (§1348). This ceiling applies to individuals filing as singles or heads of household with an earned taxable income exceeding $38,000 and to married individuals filing jointly or to a surviving spouse with an earned taxable income exceeding $52,000. A married taxpayer must file a joint return to qualify for the maximum tax provisions. You must also choose between the use of the maximum tax or income averaging, as you can't use both.

A series of computations are necessary to determine earned income and the maximum tax. The important thing to know for our purposes is that earned income is reduced dollar for dollar by any tax-preference income in excess of $30,000. This reduction is the greater of the tax preference for the current year or one-fifth (1/5) of the current year and the prior four years.

Income Averaging: If you have disproportionately large amounts of taxable income in one year, income averaging permits you to spread it over a five-year period at a lower effective tax rate. Generally, you may elect to income average if your averageable income (earned income plus capital gain) for the current year is more than 20% higher than the average income for the preceding four years. This averaging method eliminates the use of the alternative capital gain tax averaging.

If you have earned income in one year of, say, $80,000 where you can take advantage of the earned-income tax rate ceiling of 50% and you were able to throw $20,000 of that income into the following year, this would boost your taxes paid in the following year by $10,000 and would give you $10,000 more in nontaxable tax-preference income for that year. The shift in income wouldn't cost you any more in taxes because you were already at the ceiling rate. What's more, you would defer the payment of $10,000 in taxes for the year; and the use of that money for the year, even if invested in high-grade corporates of recent vintage, could produce $900 or so additional income before taxes.

Choosing Between Maximum Tax and Income Averaging: As mentioned, you must choose between the use of income averaging or the maximum tax provisions. If you have large potential or realized capital gains and have sufficient earnings to make you eligible for both the 50% ceiling on earnings and income averaging (capital gains included), your first question is which is worth more?

In making this decision, you have to take into account the fact that the untaxed portion of capital gains realized is treated as tax-preference income and that the amount of tax-preference income in excess of $30,000 reduces dollar for dollar the earned income entitled to the 50% ceiling. For example, if a married couple filing a joint return has income in excess of $52,000 and has tax-preference income in excess of $30,000 consisting of the untaxed half of capital gains (or other tax-preference income) in an amount sufficient to offset earned income to the point where the 50% ceiling is of no value, income averaging may prove to be a tax saver.

If our married couple has no tax-preference income problem, they should still determine whether income averaging is a better tax saver. Depending on the arithmetic in their case, they might give up the 50% ceiling in favor of income averaging or vice versa.

How the Effective Capital Gain Rate May Be Boosted: The interplay of these various provisions can work to boost what may be regarded as the effective capital gain rate well above the nominal maximum of 35% in some cases.

Let's say a real estate operator's ordinary income comes to $525,000. He has capital gains amounting to $1,050,000 and files a joint return. Assuming income averaging doesn't work in his situation, how would he make out under the other provisions?

He'd be in the 35% capital gain rate range for $1,000,000 of his gain and in the 25% rate on the other $50,000. His total capital gain tax would be $362,500.

The untaxed half of his capital gains would amount to $525,000, and this would be tax-preference income subject to the minimum tax reduced by the exemption of $30,000, plus the credit for regular taxes paid—$362,500 on capital gains and $320,980 on ordinary income. The result is that he would not be subject to the minimum tax.

But the $495,000 in excess tax-preference income would offset all but $30,000 of his earned income so that he would be without earned income subject to the 50% ceiling rate.

After deducting $25,000 for his itemized deductions he would have $500,000 subject to tax at regular rates. The tax on this sum would amount to $320,980, as we've already indicated. Were it not for the tax-preference offset against earned income, his taxes on his earned income would have been $216,030 or $104,950 less than the amount otherwise due.

Add this $104,950 to the $362,500 paid on what are strictly capital gains, and we see that the total amount paid as a result of the capital gains realized amounts to $467,450. This on capital gains of $1,050,000. This works out to what in effect, amounts to a capital gain rate of more than 44% or, to put it the other way, boosts the ceiling on earnings from 50% to 70%. Increase the capital gains and the earned income and the "effective" capital gain rate would be even higher.

[¶300] HOW TO DEFER THE TAX ON A SALE

Deferring a taxable gain frequently works out to our advantage. For example, we may incur serious tax penalties if we allow the profits on a sale to bunch up in one year. Other reasons for deferring a taxable gain include:

(1) Taking payments over a period of time may facilitate the sale and improve the price. If the tax can't be similarly deferred, we have created a cash liability against a paper profit.

(2) Deferment of a long-term capital gain may provide the opportunity to offset it with a loss realized in the future.

(3) If a profitable sale takes place in the year of an operating loss, we may want to push the gain ahead because we'd rather have it taxed at the favorable capital gain rate than used to reduce the amount of loss which can be carried back against a previous year's ordinary income.

(4) An individual will save tax by deferring gain to years when his tax bracket will be low.

Here are three methods of deferring tax on profit resulting from a sale:

(1) Electing the installment method under Code §453.

(2) Using a deferred payment sale not on the installment basis (any sale in which part or all of the purchase price is payable in a year subsequent to the year of sale).

(3) Making a contingent sale in which payment is made dependent on future profits or production.

[¶301] Installment Sales

This is the most commonly used method of deferring sales income. It is the easiest deferral technique to use because the law sets out definite rules that you have to follow. But it is very important to make sure you do follow the technical rules.

This method allows you to spread your profit over the installment payments made by the purchaser by treating a fixed percentage of each installment as profit on the sale. If the sale resulted in a capital gain, each installment is reported as a capital gain.

To qualify, the payments received in the year of sale (including installments) must not exceed 30% of the total selling price of the property (including mortgages which the purchaser assumes or takes subject to and without deducting the selling expenses).

Under the tax law, certain types of indebtedness are treated as payments received in the year of sale and taken into account in determining whether the 30% rule has been exceeded. Included are bonds or debentures with interest coupons attached, in registered form, payable on demand or in any other form designed to make it possible to trade them readily in an established securities market. Ordinary promissory notes are not treated as payments received in the year of sale, even though they may be assigned by one party to another party.

Installment Computation for Sale of Realty: Contract price is divided by total profit; the resulting percentage is the percent of each payment received that must be reported by the seller as income. Contract price is the entire amount the seller will receive (excluding payments on existing mortgages, except to the extent they exceed the seller's basis).

We assume a selling price of $25,000 and a cost basis of $15,000. The buyer assumes an existing $5,000 mortgage and gives his own mortgage for the balance due, payable over a 20-year period. Down payment is $5,000, and payments in the first year total $1,000, of which $600 represents interest. Thirty percent of the selling price of $25,000 would be $7,500. Since a total of only $6,000 was received in the year of sale (less than 30%), the sale qualifies for installment reporting.

Here is the computation for the first year.

Selling price	$25,000	
Cost basis	15,000	
Gain	$10,000	
Payments received		$6,000
Less interest (reported as ordinary income)		600
Principal amount received		$5,400
Selling price	$25,000	
Less mortgage assumed	5,000	
Contract price	$20,000	
Profit percentage ($10,000 ÷ $20,000)	50%	
Reportable gain (50% × $5,400)		$2,700

In subsequent years, 50% of each payment of principal on the remaining $14,600 due would be reported as capital gain.

If the taxpayer was on the accrual basis and did not use the installment sale method of reporting the gain, the reportable gain would be $10,000 instead of only $2,700. And if he was a cash-basis taxpayer and didn't use installment method reporting, his reportable gain could also be $10,000 or somewhat less if the buyer's mortgage was worth less than face value.

Election to use the installment method must be made on the tax return for the year of sale. You can't start with another method and later switch to the installment method. However, this doesn't affect your right of choice as to other transactions, in other years. You have a separate election for each transaction.

While the rule requiring that the election to use the installment method be made on the tax return for the year of sale seems simple enough, IRS and the courts have had differences of opinion as to which returns fall under this description. Here's a rundown of how the courts now stand on the various types of returns:

(1) Amended Returns: Installment sales can be reported on an amended return even though omitted from the original return (*Reaver*, 42 TC 72).

(2) Amended Return after Election of Deferred Sale: However, if the taxpayer elected to report a deferred sale on his original return, he cannot change his election on an amended return (*Mamula*, 41 TC 572).

(3) Return for Year in Which First Payment Made: If the sale takes place in one year but no payments are made until the following year, the sale must be reported on the return for the year of sale (*Ackerman*, 318 F.2d 402).

(4) Late Return Due to Negligence: If the return is filed late due to the taxpayer's negligence, he can still elect the installment method (*C'de Baca*, 326 F.2d 189).

(5) Late Return Due to Mistake: The Tax Court has held that if a late return is filed because the taxpayer erroneously believed it need not file a return, the taxpayer can still use the installment method of reporting (*McGillick Co.,* 42 TC 1059).

To determine the year of sale, look to execution of the deed; mere completion of the contract of sale doesn't complete the sale. Passing of the title to the real property is the important thing, and that doesn't occur until the closing or a few days thereafter. Normally, the initial payments for computing the 30% limitation are the payments in the year of closing.

The 30% test is to be met in the year of "sale or other disposition." In *Stuart*, TC Memo 1960-234, the Tax Court ruled that the signing of a binding executory contract was a "sale or other disposition" of property. However, the Third Circuit reversed on the ground that a contract is an option rather than a sale where the buyer can terminate the agreement by forfeiting the payments previously made (*Stuart*, 300 F.2d 872).

For a contract for the sale of real estate to be held a disposition of the property, it would have to require the buyer to accept title in any event and pay the purchase price. The seller would have to retain the right to enforce specific performance. Otherwise, you must consider the year of title passing as the year of the sale for installment reporting purposes.

Placing Mortgage on Property Before Sale Can Postpone Tax on Gain: As indicated above, you can't take a substantial down payment (i.e., more than 30%) and still use installment sale reporting. But there may be another way of postponing the gain where you want a larger portion of cash in the year of sale. If you put a mortgage on the property first, you can get more than 30% in the year of sale and pay no tax at all that year. You can still have your installment sale and pay your tax ratably over future years.

Assume you own a building with a basis of $60,000 and now worth $100,000. The building is unencumbered. You can sell it now for $50,000 cash and a $50,000 purchase-money mortgage. If you did, you could not report on the installment sale method since the $50,000 cash is more than 30% of the sales price.

Suppose, instead, you put a $50,000 mortgage on the building. You'd have your $50,000 in cash. Then you sell, subject to the first mortgage and take back a $50,000 purchase-money second mortgage. You would have received no sales proceeds in the year of sale, so you can report on the installment basis. And because you receive no sales proceeds, you'd have no tax to pay that year even though you have the $50,000 cash from the first mortgage.

There may be a few drawbacks to such an arrangement, while you avoid tax in the year of sale, larger portions of your subsequent collections are taxable. Of course, overall, the same total gain ($40,000) will be taxed. But your own financial picture will tell you how it should best be spread out.

Possibly a bigger drawback is the substituting of a second mortgage for a first mortgage. You may or may not be satisfied with such an arrangement, depending on the nature of the property and the likelihood that its value will fluctuate appreciably. For example, if the property was rented to a prime tenant under a long-term net lease, you might not be too concerned about having a second rather than a first mortgage.

[¶302] Imputed Interest on Installment Sales

Formerly, it was possible when making an installment sale of real estate to omit interest from the contract altogether. Instead of getting a specific amount of interest on the unpaid balance, the interest element in the deal was reflected in the purchase price. In that way, instead of getting fully taxed interest, you got additional, favorably taxed capital gains.

Now the law puts a damper on this technique in certain cases where the sale price exceeds $3,000 by imputing an interest character to a portion of each installment. The law calls it "unstated interest." The unstated interest is then taxable as ordinary income to the seller and is deductible by the buyer as an interest expense (§483).

[¶303] What Sales Are Covered

For a sale or exchange to be covered by the imputed interest rules, there must be a contract for the sale or exchange of property under which some or all of the payments are due more than one year after the date of the sale or exchange. Once this requirement is met, the rules can apply to all payments which are due more than six months after the date of sale or exchange.

The imputed interest rules apply to the seller only if some part of the gain from the sale or exchange of the property would be considered as gain from a capital asset or as gain from depreciable property. If the property is sold at a loss or if no gain is recognized, the rules will nevertheless apply if, had there been a gain, some part of it would have been considered as gain from a capital asset or from depreciable property. And the fact that gain is ordinary income because of the application of the depreciation recapture provisions (§1245, 1250) makes no difference.

[¶304] How to Determine Unstated Interest

Basically, the law provides that IRS is to set a proper rate at which interest is to be imputed (7%). IRS must also prescribe a second rate of interest that must be at least 1% below the rate at which interest is imputed (6%). If the rate of interest is either below the 6% rate or is not specified at all, then there is a "total unstated interest" and the rules apply. Thus, if a contract provides interest at 5% and since the IRS "higher" rate is 7%, the 5% would be disregarded and the amount of interest would be recalculated for this purpose using the 6% rate.

When, however, the contract calls for 6% interest the imputed interest rules *do not* apply. So, you can always pick up an additional 1% as capital gain instead of ordinary income by setting an interest rate in the contract that equals IRS's second—or lower—interest rate. (Presumably, the contract price will be adjusted accordingly.) On the other hand, of course, the buyer will be getting a smaller interest deduction. But that fact can also enter into the negotiations for the purchase price.

Amount of Unstated Interest: Once we determine that there is a total unstated interest, we have to determine its amount. This will then be apportioned equally to the installments under the contract. Here is how to determine the proportion of each payment considered interest:

(1) Determine the present value of each installment payment using the specified interest rate. This is done by discounting each payment from its due date back to the date of the sale or exchange. Thus, the present value of a payment is the amount which, if left at interest at the prescribed rate from the date of the sale to the due date of payment, would have increased to an amount equal to the amount of the payment.

Payments are to be discounted on the basis of six-month brackets from the nearest date which marks a six-month interval. Payments due not more than six months from sale are excluded; thus, their present value is 100%.

(2) Deduct the sum of all the present values from the sum of all the payments under the contract. The resulting figure is the total unstated interest under the contract.

(3) This amount is then spread pro rata over the total payments involved so that the same percentage of each payment is deemed to be imputed interest. Technically, this is done by applying a fraction to each payment, the numerator of which is total unstated interest under the contract as arrived at in Step (2) above and the denominator is the sum of all the payments to which the rules apply.

You can't avoid the application of these rules by paying with a note. The note will not be considered to be payment, and the rules will be applied to payments under the note.

Indefinite Amounts Due: Where some or all of the payments are indefinite in amount as of the time of sale, the unstated interest for each indefinite payment will be determined separately as received based on elapsed time between sale and receipt. This might be the case where payments are dependent in whole or part on future income derived from the property. A similar rule holds true there there is a change in the amount due under the contract. The unstated interest is recomputed at the time of the change.

[¶305] Imputed Interest Rules Can Endanger Installment Sale Reporting

In addition to its stated effect, the imputed interest rules can also have far-reaching side effects. *Reason:* Any amount treated as interest under this provision is treated as interest for *all* purposes. For example, in a typical installment sale, there's a 30% down payment in the year of sale. This is the maximum amount you can receive and still have the sale qualify for installment reporting. But if any parts of the installments due in future years are held to be interest payments because this new provision applies, this could reduce the selling price to a point where the down payment exceeds 30%. Then, the sale will not qualify as an installment sale, and the entire gain could be taxable in the year of sale.

[¶306] Deferred Sales

This method may be used where the seller receives only part of the sale price in the year of sale. If the purchaser's debt for the balance is not evidenced by a note but is merely in the contract of sale, then the courts say it has no fair market value. So, the seller is taxable on the sale only when the cash amounts he receives cumulatively exceed his basis in the property (*Ennis*, 17 TC 465, *aff'd* 6th Cir.).

But an arrangement such as this may be unsatisfactory; the seller ordinarily wants some sort of bond or note for protection. So, we usually use installment sale reporting. However, if the seller wants more than 30% of the sales price in the year of sale, the deferred sale method may still be available.

If the seller can show that the notes he receives are not worth their face value, he only picks up the cash received plus the fair market value of the notes as the amount received on the sale. Assume his basis is $10,000 and the sale price is $40,000 ($15,000 cash, subject to a $15,000 mortgage and $10,000 notes secured by a second mortgage). The seller may claim that he only has a gain in the year of sale of $25,000 by valuing the notes at only $5,000 or half of their face amounts.

You can use the deferred sales method whether you report for tax purposes on the cash or the accrual basis because the Regulations give you permission to do so (Reg. §1.453-6). But this rule does not apply to personal property. For example, if you sold a hotel and its furniture and equipment, you couldn't use the deferred sales method of reporting gain on the furniture and equipment if your regular accounting method is the accrual method. *Reason:* There's no provision for such treatment in the Regulations (*Castner,* 30 TC 1061).

Note that if you use the deferred sale method of reporting, you will not have capital gain on the deferred part even if you have a capital gain on the original sale. IRS and the Tax Court say that if the notes are worth less than face, you pick up the notes at their value and compute your capital gain or loss at that time. In later years when you realize more than the value you assigned to the notes, that realization does not come from a sale or exchange and hence must be reported as ordinary income (*Culbertson*, 14 TC 1421).

[¶307] Sale at a Contingent Price

This is a sale where the consideration received by the seller is incapable of valuation with the result that the transaction is not considered closed and no income is realized until the seller recovers his basis for the property. Any excess over basis is capital gain if the property qualifies as a capital asset. The classic case involved a consideration of 60¢ a ton on all iron ore mined by a corporation. The Court held that no valuation could be attached to this agreement since there were no maximum and minimum requirements as to the amount of ore to be mined (*Burnett v. Logan*, 283 US 404).

Similarly, the promise of a corporation to pay a percentage of its profits for a number of years was held to be indeterminate, with the result that the transaction was not considered closed (*Yerger*, 55 F. Supp. 521). The same result should follow where the consideration is contingent on net profits to be received from real property which is the subject of the sale. No gain will be realized until the seller's basis is recovered.

You'll get an argument from the Treasury on this, though. It insists there rarely is a situation where value is indeterminable (*Rev. Rul. 58-402,* CB 1958-2, 15).

[¶308] Placing the Property Under Option

This is another method of postponing tax. You get an option payment. Usually this provides for forfeiture of the option price if it is not exercised. If exercised, the option price is credited to the purchase price. Options are practically a down payment. But there is no income when they are received. Until the option period expires, you do not know how it will finally be applied. If it is forfeited, you then have ordinary income. If it is exercised, it is added to the sales price. But, a word of caution: You want to be sure the option contract states what will happen if it is forfeited and if it is exercised. Otherwise, you will be taxed as soon as you receive the option payment (Reg. §1.1234-1).

Or, you can lease properties with an option to buy. Here there is the option plus possession by the buyer during the option period. This method must be used with great caution. The courts will strike down disguised sales in the forms of leases with options to buy; e.g., where the option price is only nominal, or the rental price is larger than normal rentals for the type and value of the property involved.

If called a sale, the "purchaser-lessee" will have his "rental" payments treated as part payment of the purchase price. The purchaser will not be allowed a deduction for rent, but will be allowed a deduction for depreciation (*Chicago-Stoker Corp.,* 14 TC 441; *Rev. Rul. 55-540,* CB 1955-2, 39).

[¶309] Use an Escrow Arrangement

You can intentionally postpone delivery of title. In the case of real property, the sale usually occurs on the closing or settlement date. Receiving a down payment or earnest money does not of itself fix the date of sale. So, you will not be taxed at that time if title *or* possession does not pass. A true escrow arrangement, with some of the purchase price set aside to be paid over to the seller together with the balance of consideration at the closing date provided seller furnishes a marketable title and otherwise complies with the contract, will defer the tax on the entire transaction until the closing or settlement date (*Waggover,* 9 BTA 629; *Holden,* 6 BTA 605). But if you give possession to the buyer before title passage, chances are the sale for tax purposes took place when you gave possession (*Scruggs*, D. Ct. Okla.).

[¶310] Classification of Disposition

The tax consequences of the disposition of real estate are affected by the classification or type of realty involved.

*(1) **Disposition of Investment Realty:*** This is realty held primarily for investment, as differentiated from trade or business, residential, or dealer's realty. Investment realty is considered a capital asset (like securities held for investment), and gain or loss realized on disposition gives capital gain or loss.

*(2) **Disposition of Trade or Business Property:*** This is depreciable property used in a trade or business which has been held for more than six months and is neither property includible in the owner's inventory nor dealer's realty. Rental property may be classified as trade or business realty, as is realty purchased for such purpose but never so used, and even idle realty. But if the realty is incapable of being used in business because of zoning restrictions, it is not trade or business realty. A personal residence may become trade or business realty if converted to rental or income-producing use before its disposition. Trade or business realty is not a capital asset, and its sale or exchange produces either a gain taxable at capital gain rates or an ordinary loss which is fully deductible. Gains from the sales or exchanges of such property are offset against losses from similar sales or exchanges. The net gain is taxed as capital gain, but a net loss is fully deductible as an ordinary loss.

*(3) **Disposition of Residential Realty:*** This is property used as a personal residence. The sale, exchange, or other disposition of residential realty results either in taxable capital gain or nondeductible loss.

(4) Disposition of Dealer's Realty: This is realty held primarily for resale and includible in the owner's inventory. The dealer classification may be pinned to an owner who would not normally consider himself such —whether it will stick depends on the facts in each case, the owner's actions, etc. Dealer's realty is not a capital asset, and gains or losses resulting from sales or exchanges are ordinary gains (fully taxable as ordinary income) or ordinary, fully deductible losses.

[¶311] How to Avoid Dealer Treatment and Get Capital Gain On Real Property

Dealers in real estate are taxable as any other businessmen. However, dealers may also be investors as to some property. So, unless they exercise some ingenuity in segregating their assets, they have ordinary income whenever they sell property.

The Factors Involved: Although each case in this area depends on its own facts for the solution as to which category the property is in, there are various factors involved usually found by the courts to be significant. Bear in mind that all the factors are important, not merely the number of sales made.

Here are the factors considered:

(1) Degree of activity: The size and number of sales involved, the regularity and past activities are all considered (see *Robert E. Austin,* TC Memo 1958-71).

(2) The purpose for which the property was acquired and held: Even though the taxpayer has purchased for ultimate resale, this alone will not make him a dealer (see *Robert Thomas*, 254 F.2d 233, 1958). In almost every purchase of property, the taxpayer hopes for a rise in its market value and a resale if such a rise does occur. But, if the taxpayer acquires the property involuntarily, say by inheritance or as security for a debt, the argument that his purchase was incidental to a real estate business is not present as a factor.

Under Code §1221(1), you are entitled to capital gains instead of ordinary income when you sell a piece of property at a profit if the property is a capital asset. In defining "capital asset," §1221(1) says that the term does not include property held by the taxpayer primarily for sale to customers in the ordinary course of his trade or business. The United States Supreme Court has ruled that "primarily" as used in §1221(1) means "principally" or "of first importance" and not "substantially" (*Malat,* 383 US 569, *vac'g and rem'g* CA-9, 347 F. 2d 23). In reaching this determination, the High Court said that the purpose of §1221 is to differentiate between the "profits and losses arising from everyday operation of the business'' and the ''realization of appreciation in value accrued over a substantial period of time.'' Under this decision, you can get capital gain treatment even though you always intended to sell if the income projections from the property didn't stand up or if someone came along and made an offer for the property that was too attractive to turn down. However, to assure capital gains, your actions in relation to the property during the holding period must be in accordance with an investment purpose or, at least, consistent with that purpose.

(3) The existence of other income and full-time businesses: If this is so, it indicates that the taxpayer is devoting his time and efforts elsewhere, not to real estate—especially where real estate income is low compared with other income.

(4) The length of time the property is held: If the taxpayer sells shortly after the six-month holding period (necessary for long-term capital gains), it may indicate he is not investing in real estate on a long-term basis but is more interested in short-term sales to customers.

(5) The extent of sales activity by the owner: Hiring an office or a broker, advertising the property for sale, and spending money to achieve sales can indicate the existence of a real estate business. Note that acts done for him by a third party are attributable to the taxpayer.

(6) The owner's representations: Any actions on the owner's part connecting him with the real estate business are held against him. This could include holding himself out as a real estate man (either to the public or on his tax return) or joining a dealers' association.

(7) Rental property: If the taxpayer has held the property for years for its rental value, this indicates that although he is in a business of owning and renting property, he is not in the business of selling it. But rental of property is not necessarily inconsistent with holding it for sale if the renting is made to realize income while planning or trying to sell.

(8) Purchase of other property: If you purchase other real estate at the same time that you sell or soon afterwards, this may indicate that you are continuing a business rather than disposing of an investment.

(9) Subdividing and developing: Almost any activity on this score makes you subject to a claim that you are a dealer.

(10) Liquidation: If the taxpayer can show that he is merely liquidating an investment, then he may get capital gain treatment. But he will argue that in almost any case; and the analysis of the other factors above will, in reality, concern itself with whether the taxpayer was in the business of selling real estate or merely liquidating an investment in it. Yet, this ''liquidation of investment'' theory still has vitality and has been reaffirmed. See

Charles E. Tibbals, TC Memo 1958-44; *Altizer Coal Land Co.,* 31 TC 70; *Wm. T. Minor, Jr.,* TC Memo 1959-4. Even if the liquidation argument is a valid one, you have to be sure that the taxpayer has, by subdividing and improving to increase the profit on his sale, not gone beyond the steps necessary. See *S. G. Achong,* CA-9, 246 F.2d 445.

What You Should Do: From the time you start your investments in real estate, you must set up your activity so as to minimize any claim against you as a dealer. You should check over the factors outlined above to make sure you don't do anything harmful. Enter into fewer transactions which involve more money rather than many transactions involving less money in each; spread your gains over different years (to avoid too much gain from real estate in any one year); hold the property for long-term periods for rental income; refrain from purchases of new property at the same time you sell.

Problems of Real Estate Professionals: People connected with real estate in more than an investment capacity face greater problems than investors. To achieve capital gain treatment, they must do more than convince a court that they are not in a separate real estate business. They have to establish that their real estate "investment" activity is separate from their professional full-time activity in real estate.

Attorneys and Brokers: Lawyers, particularly those connected with real estate in the exercise of their profession, and brokers cannot hide behind their professional activities. Actually, you consider their real estate investment activities as you would those of any other businessman to see whether they are in a side business of dealing in real estate (*J. M. Philbin*, 26 TC 1159).

Dealers and Builders: These are people in a full- or part-time business of owning real estate for resale or of building it for purposes of sale. Dealers in real estate, unlike those in securities, are not allowed statutory rules for segregation of investments. But, it is possible for a real estate dealer to get capital gain treatment on his investment real estate. Of course, the fact that you are a dealer makes it harder, but if you can establish that the property is not the type of land you usually sell, if you hold it for a long period, and if you do not subdivide, then you may be able to get a capital gain. But the fight will be an uphill one (see *N. Linton Atkinson*, 31 TC 126).

Builders face a slightly different problem. They must establish that the property they build for investment is rental property. Here a long-term holding period is generally essential. But even this may not be enough. If you're in the business of constructing apartment houses for resale, then you may find it easier to establish "investment" status on a shopping center you erect and hold on to and which is adjacent to your housing project.

Applying the Dealer Investor Rule: As indicated above, you can be both a dealer and investor. IRS has actually ruled that you can subdivide part of a tract and sell lots (making you a dealer as to those) and still be an investor as to the remaining undivided tract (*Rev. Rul. 57-565,* CB 1957-2, 546).

Tax Alternatives You Might Consider: There are alternatives which you might try if you fear dealer treatment and want more than you could get from sale of the property as a whole in one transaction.

(1) Rent: If you sold a tract outright to another, he might have to obtain mortgage financing in order to purchase, or you might have to take a purchase-money mortgage. But, instead of that, consider renting on a long-term basis, say to a builder who will construct and then himself rent or sell the building. You will have ordinary income on the rental payments, but you've spread these payments over a long-term period and so may have lowered your tax bracket. Since your lessee gets a deduction for his rental payments, his ability to pay you may be better than if he purchased outright from you. You also have the land and building on expiration of the lease (this will not be income to you); and if you then sell, your long-term holding of the property may negate any argument that you are a dealer.

(2) Contingent Sale: You might be able to find a developer willing to gamble on his ability to resell who will purchase for a percentage of his resale price. Since you've sold the entire tract without any subdivision or development activity on your part, you'd think you were entitled to a capital gain. Actually, you may be walking a tightrope. Here it's important to avoid any trace of a joint venture between you and the developer. Since he's a dealer, if you were in a joint venture with him, you would be a dealer, too (see *Bauschard,* 31 TC 910, *aff'd* CA-6, 279 F.2d 115). Try to find an independent party with whom you've had no prior dealings in order to avoid the inference that you set up a joint venture when you purchased the property.

(3) Sale to Several Builders: Instead of subdividing and selling individual lots, with possible dealer treatment resulting from your subdivision activity, you might sell the tract in large parcels to a few builders. This way, you may get more than you could from one sale. Here your position is that you've had no subdivision or development activity (*McKay*, D.C., S.C., 1953). But this might boomerang since the act of dividing among the builders themselves has been considered a subdivision (*Yunker*, 26 TC 161). You may be able to get around this by getting the builders to form a partnership and then selling to the partnership.

(4) Use of a Corporation: Here you sell the property to your corporation. Although it will be a dealer, you hope to get a capital gain at the time of transfer and thus to have ordinary income only on the profit added to the property by the corporation's efforts. If you transfer the property to the corporation for its stock, then you want to have a taxable transaction and so do not want to be in control of it. The best method here is to join a developer and give 21% of either voting or nonvoting stock to an outsider.

Here there are several risks: If you plan to sell the stock of the corporation, you have a collapsible corporation problem and may have to hold on to the property for three years after you've acquired it or completed any construction. And if you sell depreciable property, §1239 provides that you will have ordinary income on sale to the corporation if you own 80% of it.

(5) Devise the Property: Finally, you could hold on to the property until your death. This means your heir will be liquidating property he involuntarily acquired. Also, he gets a basis in the property equal to its value at the time you die. So, he'd have no taxable gain on immediate sale.

[¶312] Sale of Trade or Business Property

Although items of trade or business property are not capital §1221 assets, under Code §1231 they are treated as such if held more than six months and all sales or exchanges of this type of property during the year result in a gain. If it nets out to a loss, you benefit again (taxwise, at any rate); the loss is an ordinary loss that goes to reduce income taxed at the ordinary (rather than the special capital gain) tax rates.

Because you apply capital gain treatment to the net figure of all gains and losses in this trade or business category, it is better to have all sales at a gain in one year and all sales at a loss in another year. That way, all the gains get the full benefit of the capital gain treatment and all the losses are free to offset ordinary income.

Here is an example showing you how separating the years of gain and loss can work out. Take an owner of two apartment houses. He can sell one at a profit of $100,000 and the other at a loss of $30,000. His other ordinary taxable income is $50,000 a year. If he sells the two houses in different years, he can end up with more money than if he sells both in the same year. Here's how to work out the figures:

Both houses sold in one year:

Ordinary income each year is $50,000. Tax (assuming a joint return) each year is $17,060.

Subtracting two years' taxes ($34,120) from two years' income ($100,000) gives a two-year, after-tax ordinary income of ... $ 65,880

Net capital gain of $70,000 is taxable at $18,270, giving an after-tax income of	51,730
Total two-year, after-tax income is	$117,610
One house sold in each year:	
In first year, the $50,000 ordinary income is reduced by the $30,000 loss on the house sold in first year.	
Tax on the remaining $20,000 is $4,380, giving an after-tax ordinary income of	$ 15,620
In second year, the other house is sold at $100,000 gain. Tax is $27,210 giving after-tax gain of	72,790
Ordinary income in second year is $50,000. Tax is $17,060, giving after-tax income of..	32,940
Total two-year, after-tax income is	$121,350

[¶313] Holding Period

Your holding period is extremely important whether you are selling a capital asset or trade or business property. It is the difference between getting long-term and short-term capital gain. To get long-term gain, you need a holding period of more than six months.

Measuring the Period: Your holding period begins the day after you acquire title to the property; it ends when you pass the title to your purchaser. But if you make an unconditional contract of sale, the purchaser cannot cancel the deal if title is not clear, and the purchaser takes possession of the property before title closing, then your holding period ends when he moves in.

Since a holding period normally doesn't end until title passes, you could put off the closing date until you are past the six-month mark.

If you took an option to purchase property and exercised it, you do not add the length of time you held the option to the time you owned the property when you determine your holding period. You must hold the property for more than six months after you exercised the option and acquired title if you want a long-term capital gain. Alternately, you also can get a long-term capital gain if you hold the option itself for more than six months and then sell it if the property itself would have been a capital asset had you owned it instead of the option. But make sure that the option you sell is the same as the option which you bought. Do not acquire title to the property and then give a new option. If you do that, you will be treated as having acquired the land and sold it immediately which would mean that you did not hold the property for more than six months.

[¶400] HOW TO AVOID TAX PENALTIES IN SALE OF CORPORATE REAL ESTATE

When your real estate is held in a corporation, selling it can involve a double tax. The corporation is taxed on the sale and you are taxed again when the sale proceeds are paid out to you by the corporation—as ordinary income if you get a dividend, as capital gain if you get a distribution in complete or partial liquidation of the corporation.

[¶401] How to Avoid Double Tax

Here are various methods of avoiding double taxation on the sale of corporate real estate:

(1) Sell Your Stock: If you sell your corporate stock, you get a capital gain. The buyer now owns the corporation and can liquidate it (if he wants the cost of his stock to become the new basis for the property purchased) or continue to run the corporation. Trouble is, most buyers worry about possible hidden liabilities in the corporation and so don't want to buy stock.

(2) Liquidate, Then Sell: If the property has a value of $100,000 and your basis for stock in the corporation is $10,000, on liquidation you'd get the property and have a $90,000 capital gain. If you immediately resold the property at $100,000, there'd be no additional gain because the basis of your property would be $100,000. The net result is one tax. The trouble here is that if you have a buyer lined up before the liquidation, IRS might succeed in arguing that there was really a sale by the corporation (with you acting as the corporation's agent to make the sale) and a distribution to you of the proceeds. Then, you'd have a double tax (see *Court Holding Co.*, 324 US 451; *Cumberland Public Service Co.*, 338 US 341).

(3) Use a Twelve-Month Liquidation: To avoid the problem of liquidations followed by sale, Congress provided a relief provision in §337. If the corporation adopts a plan of complete liquidation and actually liquidates within 12 months, then sales of property made by the corporation during that 12-month period are not taxable to the corporation. Thus, there's only one tax, a capital gain tax on distribution in liquidation. One drawback to §337 involves installment sales. If the corporation made an installment sale (as is most likely the case), when it distributes the installment obligations to you in liquidation, you have to pick up the value of those obligations immmediately in figuring your gain on liquidation, even though you may not be paid on the installment obligations for a number of years.

(4) Use a One-Month Liquidation: If a plan of liquidation is adopted and the entire liquidation occurs within one month, there is (with certain exceptions) no gain or loss recognized on the liquidation (§333). The basis for what you receive in the liquidation is the basis for your stock. When you subsequently sell what you got in liquidation, you pick up your gain or loss. This type of liquidation is useful where you want to make an installment sale. Selling after liquidating allows you to report the sale as an installment sale and spread the profit out over the period of collection. This Section has limited use, however: (1) If the corporation had any earnings or profits accumulated at the time of liquidation, you have ordinary income to the extent those earnings and profits don't exceed the gain on the liquidation; (2) if cash or securities acquired after 1953 are distributed in liquidation, any excess gain (not eaten up by the earnings and profits) is taxable as capital gain. So, as a practical matter, you'll use §333 when the corporation has no profits and no cash or securities.

[¶402] Collapsible Corporations

All the above rules go out the window if you have a collapsible corporation. Then, whether you sell your stock or you liquidate, you'll get ordinary income, not capital gain. And you can't look to the relief provisions of §333 or §337 because they don't apply where your corporation is collapsible.

In general, you have a collapsible corporation when it is formed or availed of principally for manufacture, construction, production, or purchase of property held less than three years and you have a view to selling the stock or liquidating the corporation before it realizes a substantial portion of the income to be derived from the property.

The courts have interpreted this section of the law to mean that even a permanent corporation (not one formed for only one project) can be formed or availed of for collapsible purposes. And the view to avoid ordinary income can arise at any time before the sale of the stock or liquidation, say some courts (*Burge*, 253 F.2d 765; *Glickman*, 256 F.2d 108). This goes farther than the Regulations, which say the view to sell must exist during the manufacture, production, construction, or purchase (Reg. §1.341-2(a)(3)). One case goes along with the Treasury, saying that if the sale occurs because of events occurring after construction is completed, there is no collapsible corporation (*Jacobson,* 281 F.2d 703).

Exceptions to the Collapsible Rules: Even if the corporation is collapsible, the stockholder still gets capital gain if he can come within any one of three exceptions:

5% Shareholder: Shareholders owning 5% or less of the stock of the corporation are exempted from the collapsible rules. But you are deemed to own the stock owned by your corporation, partnership, partner, trust, brother, sister, spouse, ancestor and descendants plus the spouse of a brother, sister or lineal descendant.

70% Rule: More than 70% of the gain realized in the taxable year of sale or liquidation must be attributable to the collapsible property. So, if 30% or more of the gain of the corporation is from noncollapsible property, you can get a capital gain.

Three-Year Rule: The collapsible rules do not convert into ordinary income gain realized after three years following the completion of the construction, manufacture, production, or purchase. So, for example, if the corporation purchases property, holds it for three years and the stock is then sold, the stockholder gets capital gain. This three-year period depends on the length of time the property is held by the corporation, not on the time that the stock of the corporation is held.

Special Relief Provisions: If the unrealized appreciation of "ordinary income" assets of a corporation is not more than 15% of the corporation's net worth (on a market value basis), you can in some cases collapse the corporation (before three years) and get capital gain. This results from a special relief provision (§341(e)). "Ordinary income" assets are those which, if sold by the corporation, would result in ordinary income. So, if the only assets the corporation holds are rental property, it would have no "ordinary income" assets because sale of those assets would result in capital gain. In such a case, you could collapse the corporation immediately and get capital gains. But, as usual, there are some drawbacks: If a shareholder owning more than 20% of the corporate stock is a dealer in the property held by the corporation, the corporate property then becomes "ordinary income" assets. So, as a general rule, this relief provision can apply only when there are no dealer-stockholders who own more than 20% of the stock.

Avoiding Collapsible Treatment: Various ways are available for avoiding the collapsible rules or at least avoiding their full impact. Some involve qualifying under the exceptions discussed above—e.g., waiting three years after the corporation acquires the property before selling your stock or liquidating. This is the most common method used. Others, discussed below, employ the exceptions or seek a happy compromise; more than capital gain tax is paid but less than the ordinary income tax rates.

Maybe You Should Be Willing to Pay Two Capital Gain Taxes: Suppose your corporation owns a building for only one year which would result in a profit of $65,000. If you are in a very high individual bracket, you might be willing to settle for a 55% tax by having the corporation sell the building, pay the 30% capital gain tax and then liquidate. You pay another 25% tax on liquidation (see *Rev. Rul. 58-241,* CB 1958-1, 179). The net effect of the two taxes is a 55% tax on the entire gain.

Subchapter S as a Means of Avoiding the Collapsible Corporation Problem: Since under Subchapter S the corporation is not taxable and capital gains are passed through to the stockholders as capital gains, a corporation could sell, say, an apartment house at a gain and pass the gain through to the stockholders as capital gain.

But the Treasury has provided in its Regulations that in determining whether the gain to the Subchapter S corporation is a capital gain (and so passed through to the stockholders as a capital gain), it will look to the stockholders' personal activities. If they are dealers, the Treasury will treat the corporate gain as ordinary income.

Using a Two-Shot Corporation to Avoid Collapsible Rules: With a two-shot corporation, you get a result somewhere between all capital gain and all ordinary income. Assume Jones and Smith each puts up half the necessary capital for half the stock of a newly formed corporation, J. S. Builders, Inc. J. S. buys two separate tracts of land and builds two apartment houses. Building No. 1 is completed first and is immediately sold at a $25,000 profit. Building No. 2 is completed shortly thereafter, and J. S. is liquidated.

When Building No. 1 was sold, the corporation had to pay a 22% tax on the $25,000, leaving $19,500. On liquidation, it distributed this $19,500 plus Building No. 2 which now had a value of $40,000 in excess of cost. So, on liquidation, Smith and Jones had a capital gain of $59,500. A 25% capital gain tax on that came to $14,875. Adding the $5,500 tax the corporation paid gives us a total tax of $20,375 on a profit of $65,000 ($25,000 realized by the corporation and $40,000 realizable on disposition of Building No. 2). This came to an effective rate of 31%, which was more than the maximum 25% capital gain rate but probably considerably less than the ordinary income rates which would apply to Smith and Jones.

Here is how the above two-shot deal avoids the restrictions in the collapsible corporation rules: The collapsible corporation rules do not apply unless more than 70% of the gain on the collapse of the corporation is attributable to the collapsible property (§341(d)(2)). In our case, the only collapsible property was Building No. 2. Since Building No. 1 was sold, all the income from that property was realized and that property or its proceeds were no longer collapsible property to our corporation. Of the total gain of $59,500, $40,000 was attributable to collapsible property (Building No. 2). But this amount is 67% of the total gain; so, the collapsible rules should not apply. An exception to the collapsible rules—the substantial realization rules—may let you out with a compromise between capital gain and ordinary income. This exception says that a corporation is not collapsible if the sale of the stock or the distribution to the stockholders does not take place before the corporation has realized a substantial part of the taxable income to be derived from the appreciated property.

The Tax Court has said that this exception means that you can escape collapsibility once a substantial amount has been realized. And realizing one-third of the potential realizable taxable income is substantial. The Fifth Circuit agreed with the Tax Court on both counts (*Kelley,* 293 F.2d 904). But IRS (despite its position in the Regs) and the Third Circuit (*Abbott,* 258 F. 2d 537) say that if there is a substantial amount still to be realized (even though a substantial amount has already been realized), the collapsible rules still apply. After the *Kelley* case, IRS reaffirmed its original position and refuses to follow *Kelley* (*Rev. Rul. 62-12,* CB 1962-1, 321).

Suppose your corporation buys a tract of land which it then subdivides. If it sold all the subdivisions, it would realize a pretax profit of $180,000. Instead, after the corporation has realized about $60,000 of profits, you sell your stock or liquidate the corporation and sell the land. Assuming you realize an additional $120,000 profit on the sale of the stock or the land, you will pay a total of about $64,500 in tax. The corporation will pay a tax of about $23,000 on its $60,000 profit (less if the $60,000 of income is spread over more than one year), leaving an after-tax profit of some $37,000. Add this to the $120,000 unrealized profit in the land, and you will have a $157,000 profit whether you sell the stock or liquidate and sell the land. Your capital gain tax will be $39,250, leaving you with a balance of $117,750. So, you and your corporation have paid a combined tax of $62,250 on a profit of $180,000. This is an effective tax of only 35%.

In one case, the Tax Court found that 23% realization was substantial (although there were indications that the realization may have been as high as 34%). The Court pointed out that in no case has more than 20% ever been found to be insubstantial (*Zongker,* 39 TC 1046, *aff'd,* CA-10, 334 F.2d 44).

You Can't Avoid Collapsible Corporation Rules by Making an Installment Sale: Suppose you make an installment sale of your stock. When the sale is made, the three-year period has not yet run. But by the time you collect future installments, it has run. Can you report your gain on the later installments as capital gain on the theory that by then more than three years have passed since the corporation acquired the property? No, says IRS. The test is: Did the three-year period run when the sale was made? If it didn't, all the gain, no matter when received, is taxable as ordinary income (*Rev. Rul. 60-68,* CB 1960-1, 151).

[¶500] HOW TO AVOID TAX ON SALE OF A RESIDENCE

If you sell your house and buy or build a new residence, you can escape tax on the gain by complying with the rules of §1034.

[¶501] Time Within Which to Buy or Build New Residence

If you buy a new home, the purchase must be accomplished and use made of the home within 18 months before or after the sale of the old residence. If you build yourself, you must begin construction within 18 months after the sale. However, you have up to 24 months after sale of the old residence to occupy the new one.

[¶502] Old and New Homes Must Be Principal Place of Residence

Gain on sale of the old residence will be recognized unless both homes (old and new) are your principal residences. Summer homes, for example, don't count.

The term ''residence'' includes a trailer, a co-op or condominium apartment or house, and a houseboat. Gain is not recognized if your wife owns the old and/or new residence or if you own them jointly. However, in such cases a consent must be signed in order to get tax-free treatment.

[¶503] Figuring Tax Under §1034

No tax is due on the transaction unless the ''adjusted sales price'' of your old home exceeds the ''cost'' of the new home. The ''adjusted sales price'' is arrived at by subtracting selling expenses such as commissions and expenses for work performed on the old residence in order to assist in the sale (so-called fix-up expenses) from the selling price of the old residence. Expenses to assist in the sale reduce sale prices for these purposes only if performed within 90 days before the sale and paid within 30 days after the sale. The ''cost'' of the new residence is what you actually paid for it plus brokers' commissions or other purchasing expenses. Mortgages are included in the sale and purchase prices.

If you exchange residences, the result is about the same. For an even exchange (no boot), there is no tax due and the new residence is given the same tax basis as the old. If you receive or give boot, certain adjustments have to be made. For example, if you receive $1,000 boot, the old residence cost $20,000, and value of the new is $25,000, your gain is $6,000 ($26,000 received minus cost of old residence). The transaction is treated as if you had sold the old residence for $26,000 and bought the new residence for $25,000. Therefore, $1,000 of the gain is recognized. If you had given $5,000 boot, there would be no gain and no tax since you would have received $25,000 (value of new home) and paid out $25,000 ($20,000 basis of old house plus $5,000 cash).

[¶504] Selling and Replacing the New Residence

Where you have sold your old residence and bought another without the recognition of gain, the same procedure may be repeated, but only if 18 months have elapsed between the two sets of transactions (§1034(d)). Involuntary sales during the period have no effect.

[¶505] Tax-Free Sales of Residences by Those Who Are 65 or Over

Taxpayers 65 or over before the date on which they sell or exchange their residences can elect to exclude from their gross income that portion of their gain that is attributable to the first $20,000 of the *adjusted sales price*. In order to be eligible for this treatment, the seller must have owned and used the property involved as his principal residence for five of the last eight years before the sale or exchange.

If the home sells for $20,000 or less, the entire gain is tax free. If the adjusted sale price is more than $20,000, you compare $20,000 to the total adjusted sale price to find what percentage of that adjusted sale price $20,000 is. Then you apply that same percentage to the total gain to find the tax-free portion.

Example: Say the adjusted sale price is $60,000; $20,000 is 33-1/3% of $60,000. If the total gain is $9,000, 33-1/3% of that, or $3,000, is a tax-free gain. The remaining $6,000 of gain is taxable.

Special Limitations and Requirements: This tax-free gain is available to a taxpayer and his spouse only once during their lifetimes. This rule applies even if the previous sale or exchange was made by you or your spouse before you were married.

If you and your spouse before your marriage each owned and used a separate residence and if after your marriage both residences are sold, whether or not in a single transaction, an election to exclude the gain may be made as to either residence (but not as to both) if the age, ownership, and use requirements are met.

Here is an example of what happens where there is a divorce and remarriage by one spouse:

Example: Assume that while A and B were married, A sold his separately owned residence and made an election to avoid the tax. Pursuant to the requirement (discussed below), B joined in such election. Subsequently, A and B are divorced and B marries C. While B and C are married, C sells his residence, C *is not entitled to make an election* since an election by B, his spouse, is in effect at the time of such sale.

To qualify for the tax-free exclusion, you must show ownership and use for 60 full months or for 1,825 days (365 × 5). Short, temporary absences for vacation or other seasonal absences (although accompanied with rental of the home) count as periods of use.

"Adjusted Sales Price" and the Tax-Free Gain: Determining the amount of gain on the sale or exchange of a residence which is excludable depends on the "adjusted sales price." Where the adjusted sales price is $20,000 or less, the entire gain may be excluded. Over that figure, only a portion of the gain may be excluded.

The "adjusted sales price" is arrived at by subtracting selling expenses, such as commissions, and expenses for work performed on the old residence in order to assist in the sale (so-called fix-up expenses), from the selling price of the old residence. Expenses to assist in the sale reduce sales price for these purposes only if performed within 90 days before the sale and paid within 30 days after the sale. Mortgages are included in the sales price.

So, for example, if you sell your principal residence for $30,400 and it costs you $400 to fix up the property for sale, the adjusted sales price is $30,000.

Special Situations: Here's how various special situations are handled in connection with the tax-free gain for persons 65 or over:

Property Held Jointly by Husband and Wife: If (1) a residence is held by a husband and wife as joint tenants, tenants by the entirety, or community property, (2) they file a joint return, and (3) either spouse satisfies all the requirements (i.e., age, ownership, and use of the residence), then both spouses are treated as satisfying all the requirements. Thus, although only one spouse meets the requirements, the tax-free gain will be available on the sale of the jointly owned property.

Property of Deceased Spouse: The holding period and use of a residence of a deceased spouse carry over to the surviving spouse if the deceased spouse met those requirements before death during the eight-year period before the sale by the survivor. These carryover rules don't apply, however, if the surviving spouse is married at the time of the sale or if an election made by the deceased spouse is in effect with respect to any other sale or exchange.

Tenant-Stockholder in a Cooperative: An individual who holds stock as a "tenant-stockholder" in a "cooperative housing corporation" can be eligible to make an election to get tax-free gain on the sale or exchange of his stock. The ownership requirements are applied to the holding of the stock and the use requirements are applied to the house or apartment which the individual was entitled to occupy because of such stock ownership.

So, if he owned thc stock and used the apartment or house as his principal residence for at least five of the eight years before the sale (and, of course, if he's 65 or over), he can elect to avoid tax on the gain on the sale of his stock within the $20,000 limitation.

Involuntary Conversions: Destruction, theft, seizure, requisition, or condemnation of property is treated as the sale of property for the purposes of this section. So, tax on the gains resulting from these involuntary conversions can be avoided if the age, use, and holding period requirements are met.

Property Used Only in Part as Principal Residence: Where you can satisfy the ownership and use requirements with respect to a portion of the property sold, then the law applies only to as much of the gain from the sale or exchange of the property as is attributable to that portion. For example, an attorney uses a portion of his principal residence as a law office for a period of more than three years out of the eight years preceding the sale of that residence. Then he cannot avoid the tax on as much of the gain as is allocable to the portion of the property used as a law office.

Determination of Marital Status: Marital status is determined on the date of the sale or exchange of the residence. An individual who on the date of the sale or exchange is legally separated from his spouse under a decree of divorce or of separate maintenance is not considered as married on that date.

Reinvestment of Taxable Portion of Gain: You can reinvest the proceeds from the sale of a residence or the amount realized in an involuntary conversion. If you meet the reinvestment rules (i.e., you reinvest at least the amount you realized), you avoid a tax on the gain.

Example: You are over 65, have owned your present residence for the last 15 years, and have used it as your principal residence during all that time. You sell the residence and the adjusted sale price is $50,000. Your gain is $15,000. Since $20,000 is 40% of the $50,000 adjusted sale price, you can elect to avoid tax on 40% of your $15,000 gain, or $6,000. The remaining $9,000 gain is taxable.

But you can avoid the tax on the $9,000 gain, too. If you reinvest the full adjusted sale price in a new residence within 18 months, you avoid the tax on the gain. Since, however, you elected to take $6,000 of the gain tax free, you need not reinvest the full adjusted sale price to avoid tax on the $9,000 portion of your gain. You can reinvest only $44,000 (the $50,000 sales price less the $6,000 gain you picked up tax free) and get the full $9,000 tax free. Of course, if you reinvest less than $44,000, then the difference between the amount you reinvest and $44,000 (but not more than $9,000) will be taxable. If, for example, you reinvest $40,000, you'll have $4,000 of taxable capital gain.

[¶600] EXCHANGING REAL ESTATE

More and more brokers and real estate men are becoming aware of the money-making advantages in exchanges of real estate properties, especially in view of the increased impact of capital gains under the tax law.

The exchange provides the real estate owner with a method of achieving some favorable tax results he might not otherwise get by selling his property outright. It also allows the owner to trade his property and receive a new one immediately. An owner who is interested in continuity can exchange for a new property throwing off an income instead of selling outright and then having to wait perhaps for months until a suitable replacement property can be found.

Finally, tax-free exchanges are an excellent way of solving the problems created by a tight-money market. If you want to sell your property, take out most of the value and reinvest in a new property, it will be hard to find a buyer who is able to put up just cash for the value of the property. And if your prospective buyer can't get a loan in order to pay you the full cash value of the property, you'd have to take back a purchase-money mortgage. Thus, while eventually (as the mortgage is paid off) you'll pull out your full equity from the old property, you may find yourself with insufficient immediate funds to reinvest in new property. But on a tax-free exchange, two potential sellers who are both locked in by a tight-money situation can pull out the full equity they have in a property by trading with each other because after the trade each has fully reinvested his previous equity.

All these factors add up to a new and fertile market for real estate investors interested in entering into swap deals and for brokers who are in a position to bring them about.

[¶601] The Tax Reasons for an Exchange

The most realistic reason why you may try to go into a tax-free exchange, particularly in view of the tax law, is the postponement of capital gains taxes on the appreciation in value of the property. If the property has risen in value or if property values have stayed constant and your basis has been reduced by depreciation deductions, you would have a capital gain on sale of the property. For example, say the property cost you $20,000 and you took $5,000 of depreciation. If you now sell for $25,000, you will have a $10,000 gain on sale. (Your basis is now $15,000 and you have received $25,000.) This gain will be taxed at capital gain rates unless you are a dealer in the property or the property is subject to §1250 which recaptures depreciation on the disposition of depreciable real property at a gain.

Thus, the owner of the property has a great incentive to find some method by which he can dispose of the property and yet not pay a tax on his capital gain. He would like to be able to reinvest the full value of the old property in the new property that he eventually will get. And he would like to raise his basis for the new property in order to take large depreciation deductions on the new property, particularly when he has used up his depreciation on the old property. A good solution to many of these problems is the tax-free exchange.

[¶602] How Tax-Free Exchanges Work

Section 1031 of the Internal Revenue Code provides that no gain or loss on an exchange is recognized if property held for productive use in a trade or business or for investment is exchanged solely for property of a like kind which also is going to be held for productive use in a trade or business or for investment. If real estate is exchanged, then the property received is considered of like kind as long as it is real estate (improved, unimproved, farmlands, etc.) and both the property given up and the property received are trade or business or investment properties and not held for resale or as a residence.

This test is applied separately to each of the parties to the exchange. Thus A may give B a hotel he held for rental purposes and receive investment farmland; A does not have any taxable gain. But if B's intention is to resell the hotel, then the hotel may be held for resale to customers by B, and so B can have a taxable exchange even though A does not have a taxable gain.

If you have a tax-free exchange, then the basis of the property you receive is the same as that of the property you transferred. You add the time you held the old property to the new one for purposes of your holding period for the new property.

Boot: If, in addition to real estate, you receive boot (nonqualified property such as stocks, cash, a residence), then gain is recognized to the extent of the boot. So, if you transfer investment real estate with a basis of $20,000 and worth $100,000 for investment real estate worth $80,000 and $20,000 cash, you have $80,000 gain, but only $20,000 of it, the boot, is taxable. Your basis for the new property is still $20,000 (the basis of the old property, decreased by the amount of the boot received and increased by the gain recognized on the exchange). If you transfer property subject to a mortgage, the amount of the mortgage debt is treated as cash received. But if you *transfer* cash in the exchange or take the new property subject to a mortgage, that increases your basis for the new property.

Mortgages on Both Sides: Suppose both parties exchange properties subject to mortgages. Then each receives boot in the amount of the mortgage on the property he trades away, but he is entitled to deduct from this boot the amount of the mortgage on the new property he gets for purposes of determining his gain presently recognized. So, assume D transfers an apartment house worth $200,000 but subject to a mortgage of $100,000 (his equity is $100,000) and with an adjusted basis of $50,000 for E's tract worth $250,000, which is subject to a mortgage of $175,000 (E's equity is $75,000) and $25,000 cash. E's basis in the tract is $25,000.

D has a gain of $150,000. He has received a tract of land worth $250,000, cash of $25,000 and has been relieved of a $100,000 mortgage. From this total of $375,000, he deducts his basis of $50,000 and the $175,000 mortgage to which he takes subject on the property he receives. This gives him a gain of $150,000. But this $150,000 gain is recognized only to the extent of the $25,000 cash since this is the only boot D has received. (The mortgage liability on the old property, $100,000, is offset by the mortgage of $175,000 on the tract.) D's basis for the new property is $125,000: his old basis of $50,000 plus $175,000 (the mortgage he takes subject to the new property) minus $100,000 (the mortgage on the property he transfers).

E has a $225,000 gain, computed as follows: He receives an apartment house worth $200,000 and is relieved of a $175,000 mortgage on his old property. From this $375,000 total is subtracted his basis of $25,000 for his old property, the $100,000 mortgage to which he is subject on the new house and the $25,000 cash he is paying out. His gain is $225,000.

But this gain is recognized only to the extent of $50,000. The boot he receives is $175,000, which is the mortgage on his old property. But he subtracts from this amount the mortgage on his new property ($100,000) and the cash he gives to D ($25,000). E's basis for the apartment house is $25,000: $25,000 (his old basis) plus $25,000 (cash he transferred) plus $100,000 (mortgage on his new property) plus the gain recognized to him ($50,000) minus $175,000 (mortgage on tract he transferred to D).

Formula for Finding Basis of New Property: To find your basis of the new property after you have traded your old property for it:

Start with:	Adjusted basis of your old property
Add:	Cash paid; Any other "boot" paid; Mortgage or trust deed assumed or taken subject to; Recognized gain
	Total

Subtract:	Mortgage or trust deed on old property assumed or taken subject to by the other party; Cash received; Any other "boot" received
Result is:	Basis for new property

[¶603] Increasing Your Depreciation on a Tax-Free Exchange

You may have held on to property for so long that there is no depreciation left. You can only depreciate that portion of the cost of your property which is attributable to the value of the building. You might want to acquire another property to start depreciating it; but remember, in a tax-free exchange, your basis for the new property ordinarily is only what your basis for the old property was. And if you sell the old property and reinvest the proceeds of the sale in the new property, you've raised the basis of the new property, since your basis in the new property will be its cost to you. But to do that, you will have to take a capital gain on the sale of the old property, and the tax will reduce the proceeds that you will have to buy the new property.

An owner of property on which there is no mortgage or a small mortgage, however, might be able to solve this problem by trading up for a property which is worth more if he takes the new property subject to a substantial mortgage. This is because his basis for the new property will be his old basis *plus* the difference between the old mortgage and the new one.

Take the case of an investor who owns a building outright which has a basis of only $10,000 in his hands. There is no mortgage on the property. Yet, the value of the property is now $150,000, and his total basis is $16,000—$10,000 attributable to the building and $6,000 to the land. He trades up for an apartment house valued at $450,000 which is subject to a mortgage of $300,000. Now, he has a total basis for the new property of $316,000. And because of a high building-to-land ratio in the new property, most of this basis is now available for depreciation. Yet, he did not have to pay any tax on the exchange.

This last factor—land-building ratio—is probably one of the prime movers in tax-free exchanges. Often, the holder of a piece of property may have run out of depreciation deductions because originally the land-building allocation was incorrect or unrealistic. By trading, he may begin to pick up depreciation deductions again, although he pays no capital gain tax on the exchange.

Consider This Illustration: Jones has land and a building worth

$150,000. He has a remaining basis of $50,000, all of it allocated to the land. He trades for another piece of property (land and building) worth $150,000. There's no taxable gain on the swap, and Jones's basis for the new property is $50,000. But he can show (from appraisals, tax bills, etc.) that 80% of the value is in the building and 20% in the land. So, he now has a $40,000 basis (80% of $50,000) for the new building and can recover that via depreciation.

[¶604] When and How to Avoid a Tax-Free Exchange

If you don't take over property which has a higher mortgage or you can't get a more favorable land-building ratio, you won't be able to raise your basis. Here, it may be worthwhile to pay the capital gain tax to raise your basis and then take higher depreciation deductions against ordinary income. This is something you must calculate in advance. Determine how much the money you use to pay the tax would be worth to you in after-tax yield if invested (after a tax-free exchange) and compare this with the tax savings you'd get from the higher depreciation deduction resulting from a taxable exchange. You will also want to have a taxable transaction if you want to realize a loss. To make the transaction taxable, sell to one party and buy from another in separate transactions.

[¶605] The Broker's Role in Property Swaps

In order to create "exchange situations," the real estate broker will have to use some time-tested rules. Essentially, what is necessary is an alertness to the methods of finding participants in an exchange transaction, getting them interested in an exchange, developing an exchange even when one of the parties wants cash, and taking advantage of the opportunities offered by cooperating with other brokers.

Setting Up the Deal: First, the broker should go over his own listings to see if two prospective sellers would be interested in an exchange. Often, the customers for a trade are parties who at first wanted to sell their properties. As an initial step, the broker should ask prospective clients listing property exactly what they plan to do with the proceeds of the sale. If they plan to reinvest in new property, you, the broker, may be able to work out an exchange.

If you have reached the point where you think you have a deal, it's important to set all the terms so that both parties can understand exactly what will happen. This means that you will have to be able to explain financing, cash requirements, etc. In this connection, make sure that the exchange is not based on cash values. Don't put a value on each property in the exchange contract. Instead, just mention the terms of the exchange; for example, one party is exchanging a building subject to a $50,000 mortgage for a building subject to a $30,000 mortgage and $5,000 cash. In this way, you will protect the parties from having the inflated valuation figures considered as actual value for estate and property taxes.

Three-Way Exchanges: Suppose an exchange would be accepted by one of the parties but the other party is interested only in cash on the sale. In such a case, the broker will try to work out an exchange and get cash to the party who wants it by setting up a three-way exchange. For example, Green has a property that White is willing to trade for, but Green does not want White's property. Here the broker gets Black, who is interested in buying White's property, into the deal. Green and White exchange properties, and then Green sells Black the property he got from White. Green has a taxable gain on the sale to Black. In arranging three-way exchanges, the broker has to be careful to distinguish a nontaxable exchange from a taxable purchase and sale.

Take the case where A wants to buy B's property for cash; B wants to exchange it for C's property; and C wants to sell for cash. There are three possible ways to effect the three-party transaction:

(1) B can sell to A for cash and then buy C's property.

(2) A can buy C's property and then exchange it for B's property.

(3) B can exchange properties with C, who then sells to A for cash.

Situation (1) is clearly a sale and purchase, and B (the only party who both starts and ends with a property) must pay tax on any gain realized on the sale to A.

Situations (2) and (3) both can qualify as tax-free exchanges provided the various steps are carried out in the right order. Situation (2) is illustrated by the *Alderson* case (317 F.2d 790); situation (3) is illustrated by the *Baird Publishing* case (39 TC 608).

The Alderson Exchange: This began as a straight cash sale from Alderson to Alloy. After the contract was made, Alderson found land (the Salinas property) which he wanted in exchange for his. So, the contract with Alloy was amended to provide that (1) Alloy would acquire the Salinas property and exchange it for Alderson's property and (2), if the exchange didn't take place before a given date, the original cash sale would be made.

Alderson's daughter, acting in his behalf, made the arrangements for transfer of the Salinas property to Alloy and deposited $19,000 as a down payment. This amount represented the difference between the price of the Salinas property and the price which Alloy had contracted to pay for the Alderson property. At simultaneous closings, Alloy took title to the Salinas property, paying the rest of the purchase price, and then exchanged it for Alderson's land.

The Tax Court held that this was really (1) a sale by Alderson to Alloy for cash and (2) a purchase by Alderson of the Salinas property for cash. The Ninth Circuit held just the opposite, that this was (1) a purchase by Alloy of the Salinas property for cash and (2) an exchange between Alloy and Alderson. The Tax Court based its decision primarily on the *method* used—namely, the negotiation for the Salinas property by Alderson (through his daughter) rather than by Alloy. The Ninth Circuit rejected this as being too narrow. It relied on *intention* and *legal obligation*. It found that Alderson's intent from the beginning was to transfer his property in a tax-free exchange if at all possible, and it gave this finding great weight. In addition, there never was a fixed obligation on the part of Alloy (once the original contract was amended) to pay cash; it merely had to exchange the Salinas property or pay cash. Since it did the former, it didn't have to do the latter. The Court also made clear that it is perfectly all right for one party to acquire property solely for the purposes of an exchange.

The Baird Exchange: Baird was a publisher occupying its own building. The Baptist School Board was anxious to buy the property to round out its holdings on the block. Baird refused to sell despite attractive offers on the specific ground that it did not want to incur the capital gain tax on the substantial profit it would realize. An enterprising real estate broker then proposed that he (the broker) construct a building and trade it for Baird's building, which would constitute a tax-free exchange. The broker could then sell to the School Board.

Baird agreed, and a contract was drawn giving the broker the right to sell the property subject to Baird's occupancy of it rent-free until the broker provided a substitute building, which was to be constructed subject to Baird's approval and within a reasonable time. A price of $50,000 was put on Baird's property; the difference between the cost of the building and the purchase price would be paid to Baird in cash.

Subsequently, the broker sold the property to the School Board for $60,000. The $50,000 price it owed to Baird was deposited in an escrow account. Of this amount, $33,000 was used to put up the new building and the remaining $17,000 was paid to Baird in cash. Baird's basis for the property exchanged was $2,000, so that the total gain was $48,000. Since boot is taxable up to the amount of gain realized, Baird reported as capital gain only the $17,000 received in cash.

Baird took the position that it had entered into an agreement with the broker to exchange properties and that it had no interest in what the broker would do with the property he received. The Treasury argued that the deal was really a cash sale between Baird (by the broker acting as its agent) and the School Board and that the broker then constructed a building for Baird. Therefore, argued the Treasury, the entire profit of $48,000 was taxable gain. The test applied by the Treasury in determining if a transaction is a cash sale or an exchange of property is as follows: In an exchange, no fixed money price or value is placed on either property. In a sale, there is either a money consideration or the equivalent in property. Since Baird had placed a fixed price on its property, this was a sale.

The Court, however, went along with Baird and found a true exchange for two reasons: First, Baird had consistently said the only acceptable deal would be one involving an exchange. Second, the relationship between Baird and the broker was not an agency one—that is, Baird did not in fact authorize the broker to sell the property on Baird's behalf. The agreement really was that Baird would sell its building to the broker in exchange for another building to be built by the broker. The broker was under no duty to account to Baird for the price it received for selling Baird's property to another.

The Court did not agree with the Treasury's test to distinguish a sale from an exchange. Giving dollar values to the respective properties does not always make the deal a cash sale. Dollar values are involved whenever "boot" is exchanged, and the statute permits this in a tax-free exchange.

Still another example of a three-way tax-free exchange occurred in *Mays*, 246 F. Supp. 375. In that case, W. A. Mays, a Texas cattle rancher, signed an agreement to transfer a ranch he owned in Texas and other real estate plus about $213,000 in cash to a charitable foundation in exchange for a New Mexico ranch owned by the foundation. The foundation wanted cash. Any profit it made on this deal was tax exempt, anyway. The exchange was conditioned on the foundation's finding a buyer for the property. So, the very same day, the foundation entered into an agreement with Agridustrial, a financing company 100%-owned by Mays and his family, to sell it the exchanged property for $500,000. IRS held that this was a taxable sale by taxpayer to his controlled corporation. IRS put a sale price of $500,000 on the New Mzxico ranch. This was the amount realized by the foundation for the Texas ranch, according to IRS. But the District Court sided with taxpayer. In holding the exchange tax free under §1031(a), the Court reasoned as follows: (1) Mays held the New Mexico ranch for use in his business of cattle raising, as he had done with his Texas ranch; (2) the corporate entity of Agridustrial Financing (the family corporation) should not be disregarded as it had been active for ten years and had substantial assets. Further, it could not be considered as a conduit for the exchange of the properties involved; (3) the facts indicated an exchange between taxpayer and foundation—not a sale to Agridustrial for cash.

The Court concluded that since the transactions had been executed in a legal manner and were not simulated, they should be given their normal effect. Therefore, this was a nontaxable exchange under §1031 and Mays realized no taxable gain.

Working Relationship Between Broker and Speculators or Syndicates: In order to make these three-way exchanges, brokers have found that it is a good thing to keep a working relationship with one or more speculators in the real estate community. For instance, one investor might own small houses and raw land which he wants to trade for an apartment house. The apartment house owner wants the small house but isn't interested in the land. Here, you can get the speculator to agree to take the land for a specified price, which will go to the apartment house owner. Some brokers, instead of just using a speculator, will have a working relationship with a syndicate, which will make cash offers for properties offered in a trade which the other party to the trade does not want.

Splitting Commissions: Many brokers who handle exchanges do so because of the cash benefits to them in getting two commissions, one for each property. Sometimes, brokers can increase their volume by being alert and willing to split fees with other brokers. One broker was told of a three-story brick building by another broker who had a listing to sell it for $60,000. At a meeting, another broker told him about a client who had three small houses and wanted to trade for a bigger one. Our broker worked out an exchange between the two owners, and the three brokers involved split the commissions three ways. So, our broker, by ingenuity, had created his commission without having a listing on either of the properties.

Interbroker Deals: Just how do brokers get together to talk about exchanges? Many communities have developed periodic meetings between exchange-oriented brokers. They have luncheons at which they discuss properties they want to exchange. And they will have an exchange bulletin for the listing of properties. Swapping clubs are particularly numerous in southern California, where property turnover is considerable. These clubs are also helpful in giving brokers opportunities to study trading techniques and methods. In Chicago, for example, there is the Realtor-Traders Club. The International Traders Club of the Brokers Institute of NAR provides a countrywide listing exchange for members of the Brokers Institute.

[¶700] SALE—LEASEBACKS

Sale-leaseback deals have become an established method of putting real estate on a tax deductible basis, releasing cash for other business purposes, and supplying good investment opportunities in real estate for institutional and other investors.

[¶701] How They Work

What's involved in a sale-leaseback is the sale of property by the owner to an investor with an agreement to lease back the property to the seller.

Often, the sale-leaseback accomplishes the equivalent of mortgage financing, but the seller of the property, since he is in the position of a lessee, is entitled to tax deductions for the rental payments that he makes to his purchaser. As in the case of a mortgage, the seller-lessee keeps the use of the property (although he will lose it when his lease expires) and pays a constant net rental which can be conceived of as representing both interest and mortgage amortization. But in the case of a mortgage, the owner only gets a tax deduction for the interest that he pays, not for mortgage amortization.

In a sale-leaseback, since the rentals paid to the purchaser are, in effect, equivalent to interest and amortization on a mortgage, mortgage payments are now put on a tax-deductible basis. This may more than compensate for the loss of the depreciation deduction by the seller.

The investor-purchaser owns the building and is entitled to depreciate it. He is fully taxable on the rent he receives, and part of his rent represents amortization of his investment. But his depreciation of the property may provide enough of a tax deduction to make up for this.

Nowadays, sale-leasebacks are often entered into with institutional, tax-exempt investors. But deals are still worked out even where the investor is not tax exempt, particularly where short-term leases and high building-to-land valuation ratios exist. In this way the investor shelters from taxation, by way of the depreciation deduction, most of the portion of his rent which represents amortization and recovers this "amortization" in a short period of time.

[¶702] Example of How Leasebacks Have Been Used

Sears, Roebuck & Company was one of the pioneers of the sale-leaseback. When it switched from an exclusively mail-order business to chain store retailing, it was faced with the problem of financing the needed sales outlets and the storage facilities servicing those outlets. It could have sold additional stock to the public. But since the retail stores would not return much income initially, that would have meant a substantial drop in the dividend policy consistently followed. Sale-leaseback was suggested as an alternative.

Sears, Roebuck would put up the stores and warehouses, sell them to an insurance company at cost, and then lease them back at a good rent under a long-term lease. In Sears' case, the sale-leaseback was a financing device. It still is used to finance, but higher taxes give a tax overtone.

[¶703] The Arithmetic of Sale-Leasebacks

Here's a typical example of a leaseback deal:

A corporation used a plant in its business which it owned for 15 years. The original cost was $1,000,000, of which $700,000 was allocated to the building and $300,000 to the land. It took $450,000 of depreciation so that its basis for the whole property was $550,000. In the sixteenth year, it decided to sell the property to an investor corporation if it could get a 15-year leaseback. The sale price was $750,000 with a net rental under the lease equivalent to a 15-year amortization of the $750,000 at 6% return—or a rental of $77,225. Assume that the investor corporation could allocate $500,000 of its purchase price to the building for depreciation purposes.

The Seller: The seller corporation had a $200,000 gain on the sale and so paid a capital gain tax of $60,000. If it had borrowed $700,000 (the net amount it got after the capital gain tax) a 5% interest (under the then current market), payable over 15 years on a constant payment basis, the yearly payment would have been $67,450. So, over the 15-year period, the seller would have paid a total of some $1,012,000 instead of some $1,158,000 (15 times $77,225) which it paid on the sale-leaseback. But, in the case of the mortgage, the seller only would get a tax deduction for the $312,000 interest it paid. This together with the $250,000 depreciation that the seller had left on the property would have meant a total tax deduction of $562,000, a saving of $269,760 at the 48% corporate rate. So, the mortgage would have cost the seller $742,240 ($1,012,000 minus the tax saving). But under the leaseback, the seller got a tax deduction for the entire rental paid, thus realizing a tax saving of $555,840 (48% of the entire 15-year rental), which would mean a cost to the seller for the leaseback of $602,160 ($1,158,000 minus $555,840). So, the sale-leaseback cost the seller $140,080 less than the mortgage would have cost.

The Buyer: The buyer under the sale-leaseback got a deduction over the 15-year period of the lease (assuming that was the remaining life of the building) of $500,000, the amount that it allocated to the building. This meant that $500,000 of the rent income was protected from tax. The tax on the remainder was $317,840. So, the net to the buyer on the sale-leaseback over the 15-year period was $840,160. If the buyer had taken a mortgage position in this or similar property for $750,000 at 5% interest (the prevailing rate at that time), it would have received $1,084,000 with $334,000, the interest, taxable to it (the remainder would have been mortgage amortization). This would have meant a total tax of $160,320 or a net after taxes to the buyer of $923,680. This was about $83,500 more than the amount the buyer would net in the case of the leaseback.

What the Figures Mean to the Seller: The seller paid $140,080 less (net after tax deduction) than it would have in the case of a mortgage. But, to get this, the seller gave up its ownership of the property at the end of the lease. The land was valued at $250,000. So, the seller actually appears to have lost about $110,000. But this is deceptive. Seller's building wears out at the end of the lease; and because of the favorable aspects of the deal to the buyer, it would be able at the time of the sale-leaseback to give the seller an option to renew for, say, another 10 or 15 years at a very low rental. Any improvements constructed by the seller during the renewal term would be depreciated by the seller. Also, the sale-leaseback provided the seller with the maximum amount of financing, since with property worth $750,000 it would be hard, due to legal limitations on the amount of the mortgage in relation to market value in most states and to the desire by mortgagees for protection, to get a mortgage for the full market value.

What the Figures Mean to the Buyer: In effect, the buyer had $83,500 of his investment left in the property at the end of the original lease term. But the buyer had gotten out its 5% yield plus the rest of his "principal" and would own property worth at least $250,000 if land values did not change. So, the buyer could afford to give the seller a renewal lease at a rental of only $6,640 a year and still get an 8% before-tax return on its $83,500. By this method, during the renewal term, the seller would have the land on a tax-deductible basis. And if the renewal lease was properly set up, any improvements, such as a new building erected by the seller, would not be income to the buyer. At the end of the renewal term or the original lease if the seller did not renew, the buyer still owned the land.

[¶704] Advantages and Disadvantages of Sale-Leasebacks to Seller-Lessees

Advantages: (1) The capital which would otherwise be tied up in the ownership of property is freed for use for other purposes. The seller-lessee can use the capital in his business for further operating capital, debt retirement, or investment purposes.

(2) Credit is less directly tied up than in borrowing, and the balance sheet looks more favorable. Since the property is no longer owned by the seller-lessee, its financial statement will contain no reference to a fixed asset; and since the fixed asset has been converted to cash, the seller-lessee's liquid position greatly enhances its borrowing capacity.

(3) Restrictive covenants of the loan type are seldom required in a sale-leaseback transaction.

(4) The seller-lessee occupies facilities that are tailored to its needs under the protection of a long-term lease at a fixed rental. A fixed rent, in the event of an inflationary period, means that the seller-lessee discharges his lease obligations with "cheap dollars." In addition, capital improvements built by the seller-lessee may be amortized over the period of the lease. Frequently, this results in an amortization in excess of depreciation because the lease term is so much less than the expected useful life of the improvement.

(5) The seller-lessee has the tax advantage of being able to deduct the amount of his rent payments from income. (The total amount of rent paid by the seller-lessee is a deductible item for income tax purposes.) This places the seller-lessee in the position of, in effect, being able to take depreciation deductions for the land without running the risk that the depreciation deductions will be questioned. The seller-lessee can be sure of his rent deductions provided the sale-leaseback was at arm's length.

(6) The annual return from the cash realized on the sale may more than compensate for the interest figured into the rent.

(7) The seller-lessee does not have to get the approval of its funding sources to make the deal as it would if it were borrowing money.

(8) If the seller-lessee reserves the right to sublet the premises, the seller-lessee may be in an extremely flexible position, since it may be able to secure other desirable quarters and still offset its financial obligations under the terms of the lease.

(9) All these advantages can add up to peace of mind to the seller-lessee, especially where the transaction solves a sticky financial problem for the company.

Disadvantages: (1) The seller undertakes the obligation of the lease. The lease usually is a long-term lease, for a fixed period of time, and at a specified amount of rent. The obligation to pay rent may become difficult under adverse business conditions. Usually the aggregate rental payments made over the primary lease term amount to at least the total value of the property.

(2) The seller-lessee usually gives up all right to the property when the

term of the lease is over. This means that it has to relocate or renegotiate for continued occupancy of the premises at that time. It also means that, if the value of the property increases, the seller-lessee does not get any benefit from that increase at the end of the lease. But a recapture or renewal provision giving the seller-lessee the right to reacquire the property either at the end or during the lease term may be included in a sale-leaseback agreement.

(3) If there is an unexpected need for major additions or improvements, the seller-lessee must either finance the cost or amortize it over the remaining period of the lease or negotiate with the buyer-lessor to have him finance it. If the latter path is followed, an increase in the rent can be expected.

(4) If the price paid by the buyer-lessor for the property is in excess of the adjusted cost basis of the property, the seller-lessee incurs an income tax liability which may not be offset by other aspects of his tax structure applicable to the year of sale.

[¶705] Advantages and Disadvantages of Sale-Leasebacks to Buyer-Lessor

Advantages: (1) The buyer-lessor gets a rental return from the property which is evenly spread over the term of the lease. (Interest on a mortgage is greater in the earlier years and so creates an unequal tax burden.) What's more, the rental return will be partially tax free because of the depreciation deductions available to the buyer. So the net rental may be greater than the net interest plus amortization of principal which would be received under a mortgage. The annual net yield may range from 5% to 10% or more before income taxes assuming there are no outstanding loans. Furthermore, the return is based on a relatively long and definite period of time and it enjoys a relatively high degree of safety.

(2) In the case of an institutional lender, the usual loan-to-value ratios don't apply; and, in effect, a 100% loan can be made. This widens the market for the institution's funds.

(3) When the lease is over, the buyer-lessor has full ownership and possession of the land and improvements remaining on it. So, if the value of the property has gone up, the buyer-lessor can take advantage of the increase in value at the end of the lease by rerenting the property at an increased rental or by selling the property at a price which reflects its increased value.

(4) If the buyer-lessor wants to dispose of his investment, it may be easier for him to sell the fee interest subject to the lease than to sell a mortgage. In addition, sale of §1231 property would create an ordinary loss while sale of a mortgage at a loss normally would create a capital loss.

(5) The buyer-lessor may have a relatively carefree investment. Indeed,

all management problems can be left to the lessee by a net lease. (But, if the lessee is a poor manager, this may reduce the lessor's security or the value of the property.)

(6) The buyer-lessor is provided with an offsetting tax benefit against all his earned income (including rent from the property) for the current year, since he is entitled to apply one of the available depreciation schedules to the real estate—except, of course, the land.

(7) If there is a loan against the property, the interest paid on this loan provides the buyer-lessor with an additional deduction against current income.

Disadvantages: (1) The buyer-lessor takes the risk that the seller-lessee may go broke and, as a result, he may lose rental income and may have to find a new tenant. Of course, the buyer-lessor goes into the deal because he has confidence in the seller-lessee's credit strength.

(2) The ownership of the property requires a certain amount of management from the buyer-lessor. How much, depends on the terms of the lease. Even though the lease requires a minimum of management duties, the buyer-lessor still must cope with some of the problems of ownership. For example, someone has to take care of things in case of condemnation, destruction of the premises, formation of a new assessment district, etc.

(3) The buyer-lessor takes the risk that the property will be less valuable when the lease is over than it was when the deal was made.

(4) The buyer-lessor takes the risk that his tax position may change.

[¶706] Using a Recapture Provision

One drawback in a leaseback arrangement is the fact that the seller will lose its property at the end of the lease term. To overcome this, either a recapture or a renewal provision may be included. A recapture provision gives the seller the right to reacquire the property either at the end of the lease term or during it at a price that may or may not be nominal.

If the recapture price is nominal, the courts don't consider the original transaction a sale. Their reasoning is that since the seller would always be ready to take its property back for nothing, it's the same as if there had never been a sale (*Jefferson Gas Coal Co.*, 16 BTA 1135).

Where the recapture price is substantial, the courts have more trouble in deciding whether there has been a genuine sale. They compare the option (recapture) price with the value of the property at the time for exercising the option. The more nearly the option price approaches the fair market value of the property at the time the option is to be exercised, the more likely the courts are to consider the leaseback a genuine rental arrangement.

Usually the lease either fixes the option price or the value of the property at the beginning of the lease term and provides that this figure less the rentals paid shall be the option price. Where the option price is stated in the lease, the court may look at the remaining useful life to determine value on the option date. For instance, the Tax Court disallowed deduction of the rentals on a five-year lease of property with a useful life ranging from 12 to 16 years. To the Court, a low option price for the property useful for 7 to 11 more years meant the lessee had retained a substantial equity on the original sale (*Judson Mills,* 11 TC 25).

More frequently, the option price is determined by subtracting the rentals from the value for the property stated in the lease. A provision that the option can be exercised at any point over the life of the lease may bring a variable option price into the picture. Where the option price isn't stated in the lease, the total number of interim rental payments before the option is exercised becomes important.

Generally, the deduction for rent can be supported if the rental payments are not materially larger than the depreciation charges. As the spread between the two becomes larger, it will become increasingly hard to sustain the rental deduction. When the rental payments substantially exceed depreciation, the inference is that the excess is being paid to acquire an equity which will be formally claimed by exercising the option (*Louis E. Whitham*, TC Memo 1953-87).

If the option price is fixed in the lease agreement, the seller has done about all it can do to protect the rental deduction if the price is a reasonable estimate of what the value will be on the option date, based on the facts at the time. If instead, the seller has elected merely to fix the present value of the property, the best protection is to tie the rental figure as nearly as possible to the depreciation.

A good number of sale-leasebacks shy away from the use of an option to repurchase by the seller. Here, the same problems are involved as in any lease-option arrangement. The Treasury will look to see if the option price is a reasonable estimate of what the value of the property will be on the option date. If it is less, the whole transaction may be considered a loan, just as a lease with an option to buy where the tenant has never owned the property will be considered a sale if the lessee acquires an equity in the property from the start of the lease.

[¶707] How to Get a Deductible Loss on a Sale-Leaseback

Suppose you sell your property at a loss and lease it back. You might go through the leaseback deal primarily to get the loss to offset other income. But if your leaseback is for more than 30 years, there's a good chance the

Treasury will say your loss is not deductible. *Reason:* A 30-year lease, according to IRS, is equal to ownership of the real estate (Reg. §1.1031(a)-1(c)). So, says the Treasury, you've exchanged one property for property of a like kind—a tax-free exchange under which a loss is not recognized even if you receive cash, too. The Tax Court and the Eighth Circuit have gone along with this argument (*Century Electric Co.*, 192 F.2d 155). But the Second Circuit has put a twist on this interpretation that can open the way to deductible losses.

First, says the Second Circuit, look to the cash received on the sale portion of the sale-leaseback deal. Was the cash received equal to the value of the property sold? If it was and if the rent under the leaseback was equal to the fair rental value of the property, then there was a sale, not an exchange. In other words, insofar as the parting with the property was concerned, the seller received full value when he received the cash. The lease portion of the deal was not in exchange for the property. So, the sale is treated separately and the loss is deductible. Since there is no exchange, says the Court, there is no need to determine whether the Regulations that say a 30-year lease is equal to ownership of the property are valid (*Jordan Marsh Co.*, 269 F.2d 453).

Caution: This is an important decision and can be very helpful where you can use a tax loss and still want to use the property. Bear in mind, however, the need for firmly establishing values. If it can be shown that the cash received was less than the value of the property or that the rentals were particularly favorable, it may still be established that there was an exchange for the lease plus cash. In which case, you can end up with a nondeductible loss. Note, too, that IRS announced it will not follow the *Jordan Marsh* decision (TIR 194, 12/18/59). Thus, IRS sticks to its position that where there is a sale-leaseback and the lease runs 30 years or more, there is a tax-free exchange of like-kind property.

Even in the case of a lease of less than 30 years, it is possible that a loss may be attacked by the Treasury as being a sham—i.e., the loss is artificial, being created by a low purchase price in order to obtain a favorable lease. So, to avoid attack, it is important to gear both sale price and rentals to fair market value.

[¶708] Special Forms of Sale-Leasebacks

New Construction: Here, a builder may arrange financing for a new plant that he is constructing for a business corporation by getting that corporation to agree to lease the property and by interesting an investor in the purchase of the property upon completion. In the meantime, the builder will obtain construction financing unless the investor is an insurance company or pension trust which can handle the financing from the commencement of construction.

Split Financing: One way for a real estate developer to achieve high-ratio financing for his project is to use "split" financing. The developer sells the fee (the land) to an institutional investor and the institutional investor leases the land back to the developer. Simultaneously, a leasehold mortgage loan is executed. The developer comes out with 100% financing on the value of the land and approximately 75% financing on the value of the buildings and improvements. Frequently, financing may approach 100% of the actual cost of the project. The institutional investor will want a kicker to increase its yield above the straight mortgage rate and to provide an inflation hedge. The kicker may be in the form of a participation (say, 2% or 3%) in the annual effective gross income from the project. Or it might take the form of a participation (say, somewhere from 10% to 20%) in the increases in gross income over a specified base figure. The base figure will usually be the projected gross income figure with an offset against the income increase by an amount equal to any tax increases. Another type of kicker might be a percentage of the net income from the project after debt service but before depreciation.

The ground lease may be written for a period anywhere from 30 to 50 years. Renewal options may extend the period up to, say, 99 years. The developer should give particular attention to the provisions of the ground lease as to repurchase and renewal options, rent increases, and reappraisals.

Options to repurchase may be set up with a formula for fixing the price or may call for an appraisal at the time of repurchase by recognized appraisers.

Pension Trusts: These organizations enjoy tax-exempt status. Until recently they were unwilling to enter leasebacks. Now sale-leasebacks are being used not only where the pension trust is an outsider but also where a corporation sells its property to its own pension trust and takes back a lease. In order to satisfy the Treasury, the deal must be one which involves a fair sale price and reasonable rentals. If the seller corporation pays too much by way of rent, this will be treated as additional contributions to the pension trust. So, in a year where the maximum permissible amount of contributions for tax purposes was made to the pension trust, any deduction for excess rent might be denied to the corporation. Also, rentals traced to borrowed funds of the pension trust will be treated, as in the case of charitable organizations, as unrelated business income not subject to the tax exemption.

Use of the Family: You may want to set up a sale-leaseback with a relative or perhaps with a trust that you set up for, say, your children. In this way, by means of the rent deduction, you can shift the income from the property to lower tax brackets. Also, the trust gets a stepped-up basis for the property. Here, too, you must be prepared to show that the property has been sold at a fair and reasonable price and that a reasonable rental is being charged. Otherwise, the sale-leaseback will either be voided for tax purposes or you will only be able to deduct the amount of rental which is reasonable. If you sell to related parties—a corporation of which you own 50% or more, a trust you set up, an exempt organization controlled by you, or your spouse, brothers, sisters, ancestors, or lineal descendents—any loss on the sale is disallowed. And where you sell depreciable property to a corporation of which you own 80% or more of the stock or to your spouse, you will have ordinary income on the sale.

[¶709] Sale-Leaseback With a Stockholder

Take a company that needs working capital. It has a plant that has considerably appreciated in value. One of its stockholders—rather than advance money as a loan—would be willing to buy the plant and lease it back to the company. That gives him a steady income via rent, enables the company to get its working capital, and puts the entire plant and land on a tax-deductible basis. Assuming reasonable rentals, the rent deal should stand up.

While such a deal has many attractions, you have to approach it carefully to avoid several hidden pitfalls.

Look Out for Unexpected Dividends: If the stockholder does not pay full value for the property, he may very well end up with a taxable dividend equal to the difference between his purchase price and the full value of the land and buildings (see Reg. §1.301-1(j)).

Don't Deal With 80% Stockholders: If the corporation is going to sell at a gain, it should avoid a sale to a stockholder who—together with his wife, minor children, and minor grandchildren—owns more than 80% of the corporation's stock. *Reason:* Gain on the sale of the buildings or other depreciable property will be ordinary income; gain on sale of land will still be capital gain (§1239).

Look Out for 50% Stockholders if You Have a Loss: Sometimes a sale-leaseback will be worthwhile to establish a loss on the sale that can be used to offset other corporate income. But look out on a sale to a more-than-50% stockholder. Losses on such sales are disallowed (§267).

Note, too, that constructive ownership of stock in this case is much broader than under the 80%-rule above. Brothers', sisters', parents', trusts', partnerships', and other corporations' holdings of the selling corporation's stock can be attributed to the purchasing stockholder.

[¶710] Other Factors That Can Cause Problems

A sale-leaseback usually involves a valuable property with a substantial amount of cash changing hands. No two are exactly alike except that all involve a number of factors that require intensive study and evaluation. A mistake cannot be easily remedied. Here are some of the factors that pose problems:

At what amount should the selling price be fixed? This means more than evaluating at current value. Both parties generally are tied to the property for a long period.

For economic and tax reasons, the seller may be reluctant to take a loss on sale, but a loss sale may be called for, considering the value of the property.

Amount of rental and length of the lease require evaluation. Change in economic circumstances, the neighborhood, or property values could hurt either party.

Comparison with other methods of financing is required by the seller. Even if a sale-leaseback as agreed on by the parties seems advantageous, it may not be advisable for a particular seller-tenant. Other methods of financing may offer greater benefits.

State law has to be considered. There may be:

(1) Restrictions on institutional purchases.

(2) Mortgage restrictions in such deals or the transaction may be considered a mortgage and a recording tax sought.

(3) Question of legal title if the seller has an option to repurchase.

The lease, aside from rental amount, length of time, and options, must include provisions covering:

(1) Effect of condemnation of property.

(2) Subleasing and tenant's primary obligation for rent.

(3) Building alterations and security to the landlord against loss.

(4) Repair covenants.

(5) Insurance coverage.

(6) Destruction of the property regardless of insurance coverage.

(7) Restoration of the property in case of casualty and use of insurance recovery.

(8) Default and escape clauses for both parties if one or the other fails to live up to the agreement.

These lease provisions are intimately tied to the original sale-leaseback factors. For instance, a purchaser buying at a high price but protected by a high rental might suffer serious loss if complete destruction of the property allowed the tenant to escape from the lease.

[¶711] When Is It Better to Own Than to Lease?

It's all a matter of arithmetic. On one hand, the corporation will be saving the net after-tax rent cost. On the other hand, it will have after-tax operating expenses and loss of income on the money invested in the plant. However, it will have an additional release of cash equal to the tax saving caused by the depreciation deduction. If the net costs of owning the building are less than the after-tax rent costs, the corporation will be ahead by switching to ownership. If the residual value of the property is added to the total of the cash saved during the life of the building, you have the total value of the plant as an investment.

Example: Assume a corporation pays rent of $100,000 a year. It can buy a plant with a 25-year life for $600,000. Land is worth $100,000; the building, $500,000. Realty taxes and other expenses would come to $30,000. If the corporation invested the $600,000 cash at 6%, it would make $36,000 a year—$17,280 after taxes, assuming a 48% corporate tax rate.

As a lessee, the corporation's after-tax cost of its rent was		$52,000
As owner, its after-tax expenses are	$15,600	
Its after-tax loss on investment of the cost of the plant is	17,280	32,880
So, its after-tax cash outlay as an owner is reduced by		$19,120
But, in addition, the depreciation deduction of $20,000 (4% of $500,000) reduces the income tax and releases additional cash of		10,000
That makes the total cash benefit, per year, to the corporation, as a result of owning instead of leasing, a total of		$29,120

On a 25-year basis, the savings will total $728,000. At the end of 25 years, however, the building (theoretically) is worthless—it has been completely depreciated. But it should be possible to determine what the building will be worth in 25 years—whether it will have some resale value, or whether land values will hold up enough to make demolition and reconstruction feasible.

In our example, we've used straight-line depreciation. Declining balance is more favorable in the early years. Under the tax law, new commercial real estate can be depreciated under the 150%-declining-balance method; for used commercial real estate, only straight-line depreciation is available. Using the declining-balance method, depreciation is reduced yearly and so is the cash benefit. (In the event of an early sale, the recapture provisions of the tax law would apply.)

The corporation might consider paying only partly in cash and giving a mortgage for the rest. Whether this is advisable depends on whether the company can earn more with the money it doesn't put into the building than it will pay for mortgage money.

[¶800] FINANCING

The mortgage is undoubtedly the best known and most widely used form of real estate financing. Since most properties are not bought for cash alone, almost every investor knows that he must find some outside source of financing. Initial steps required of the investor are knowledge of the types of mortgage loans which are made and familiarity with the institutions that are in the business of making them. In addition, the investor, to be sure of success, may have to consider and possibly use one of the various alternatives to outside mortgage financing which are in use throughout the real estate industry.

If the mortgage route is chosen, familiarity with the tax ramifications of mortgaging is necessary. There are many obvious tax and nontax advantages of mortgages. You can get property worth more for less cash. Yet you get your depreciation on the full value of the property—not just your equity. So, you can cut your taxable return from the property without cutting into the cash income. A rise in value belongs to you even though your equity in the property may be far less than the mortgage debt on it. But, by the same token, any decline in the property is your loss, not the mortgagee's.

Many technical points arise in connection with mortgages. Whether you are the mortgagor or mortgagee, you have to know the rules so that you can make the right moves to get the results you are after whether you are negotiating a mortgage loan, considering how to avoid foreclosure, or what to do should the mortgage be foreclosed.

Besides knowing the tax and business implications of mortgages to the real estate owner, the knowledgeable investor will also want to know the profit-making possibilities to be found in investment in mortgages. This involves knowledge of companies offering debentures, where guaranteed second mortgages can be obtained for outright ownership, and familiarity with a nonsyndicate investment plan used for participation by investors in second mortgages.

[¶801] Types of Mortgage Financing Used in Real Estate

Mortgages are the traditional form of financing real estate. The mortgagor-owner retains legal title but offers his land as security for a loan from the mortgagee-creditor. The cost of this mortgage financing depends on interest rates offset by tax deductions for interest. Besides the conventional first (or senior) mortgage for a term of years, there are interim financing or construction loans, project financing, and junior financing loans.

Interim or Construction Financing: This is the most pressing problem in the real estate financing field. In the past, construction financing was handled via temporary loans from banks and trust companies. The danger in this method is that the temporary loan may fall due before the project has been completed and permanently financed. Many lenders of the permanent mortgage type are now willing to advance money from time to time as the improvement goes up, thus, in effect, supplying the construction financing. The lender in such an arrangement will be sure to insist on a waiver of liens or proof that materialmen and contractors have been paid. The payments due under the mortgage commence when the building is occupied and income from the property becomes available. The mortgage is then amortized over a long period of time. This method obviates the need for temporary financing of improvements and facilitates matters by allowing the owner to obtain his financing at long-term mortgage rates. It also eliminates the commissions, service charges, and fees which are tied up with temporary financing. From the lender's viewpoint, this combined construction and permanent mortgage is riskier than a straight mortgage on a finished building. From a tax point of view, there may be advantages to builders who plan to sell the property in using the single mortgage.

Project Financing: This is a mortgage used to cover a tract of land on which a builder plans to develop a subdivision and build homes. At one time the builder had to supply his own cash and obtain temporary credit until the purchaser of the home could obtain permanent financing. Now, lenders will take a blanket mortgage on the project and advance money as the improvements are completed. Some mechanism by which parcels sold by the mortgagor can be released from the lien of the overriding mortgage by the payment of some proportional amount is necessary. The mortgage, for example, might contain a provision that the mortgagor can obtain releases for designated parcels by paying a sum that is in the same proportion that the area of the land released bears to the total area of land covered by the mortgage, multiplied by a designated percentage (125%, for example) of the original mortgage amount.

Junior Financing: Because the second mortgage is junior to the first mortgage (i.e., is paid off after the first mortgage on foreclosure), the risks in second mortgages are greater. As a result, second mortgage investors will normally demand and receive a healthy discount in addition to the maximum interest rate they are permitted to obtain under the usury laws of their state. (To find the yield on mortgages bought at a discount see the table at the back of this book.) The second mortgage is fairly prevalent as a purchase-money mortgage where the seller of the property takes part of his purchase price as a second mortgage in order to swing a deal and set up a favorable tax picture for himself.

[¶802] The Mortgagee's Lending Standards

Mortgage lending involves long-term credit on prime security; namely, real estate. Some institutions engaged in financing short-term business operations put their funds into liquid investments. Other institutions, such as insurance companies, mutual savings banks, mortgage banks, and savings and loan associations, go into mortgages on a long-term basis.

An essential element underlying a mortgage loan is the appraisal. The appraisal is the foundation on which the loan will be based. Proper appraisal procedure will involve some sort of risk rating of the property. Besides looking to the value of the property as security, the credit rating of the borrower will be considered as additional security for the loan. A standard requirement for most mortgage loans is that the borrower have a good credit rating.

Most lenders will require that the mortgage loan be amortized in full or in part during the term of the loan. In a self-liquidating mortgage, the entire indebtedness is paid off during the period of the mortgage loan. If the property is well maintained, deterioration in property value will occur at a slower rate than the mortgage payoff. As a result, the lender's risk in terms of the ratio of loan to value is constantly being reduced during the amortization period. For mortgage amortization tables, turn to the tables in the Appendix.

The mortgage lender makes the loan primarily for the yield on its investment. In addition, the investor wants to make certain that it is protected against loss of its investment. A correlation between these two variables occurs to the extent to which the return on investment is a function of the security risk and inherent market conditions. Security, in essence, is the absence of risk. Although no investment is totally secure, mortgages are regarded as relatively secure investments. The reason for this is that the mortgage lien is primary to the underlying security; namely the property, a concrete asset that can be seen and has value. The major factors that are analyzed by the lending institution and that are considered to affect the security of the mortgage are the following:

(1) The community and neighborhood.

(2) Building activity and projected growth.

(3) The actual site and the building on it, including condition of repair, cost of reproduction, and the suitability of the improvement.

(4) Loan-to-value ratio.

(5) The borrower's ability to pay.

(6) The income which the property throws off. With nonincome-producing properties, the borrower's ability to pay becomes even more vital. Income properties are generally valued on an income basis.

(7) Maintenance and operating expenses of the property. The mortgagee may want the right to enter the premises in order to inspect them to see that they are properly maintained.

(8) Amortization schedule of the mortgage and the date of maturity.

[¶803] Making the Most of Financing Opportunities

Whether you find yourself in a tight-money, high interest rate market or whether the money market is loosening up and interest rates are on the decline, or, indeed, in any type of money market, real estate brokers with a knowledge of the types of deals they can make with the different financing sources open to them are in a position to be of substantial service to their clients. By exercising a little ingenuity and by having a knowledge of both the common and off-beat financing sources as well as the alternatives to direct outside mortgage financing, a broker can make the most of any type of money market.

[¶804] What to Know About Lenders to Expedite Financing

Lenders may differ vastly in their tastes, policies, and practices, even in the same community. The type of deal that one lender will not touch may be another's meat. You can be a successful guide through this financial maze by informing yourself about the preferences, procedures, and practices of your local lenders.

Here is a rundown of the items of information you will need to check:

(1) What type of property will the lender consider? (2) What limitations exist as to the size of loans? (3) Does the lender limit its operations geographically? (4) What are the lender's loan-to-value limits? (5) What rate of interest does the lender charge? (6) For what terms (maturity and payment) will the lender make loans? (7) What charges will the lender make? (8) What is the lender's policy on escrows? (9) What is the lender's reputation for cooperation on removal of objections or defects? (10) Will the lender pay a finder's fee? (11) Does the lender make government-backed loans? (12) Does the lender make loans similar to government-backed loans? (13) What are the lender's practices as to commitments? (14) What is the lender's policy as to security? (15) What is the lender's policy as to appraisals?

[¶805] What to Know About the Borrower to Expedite Financing

When you approach a lender on a financing deal, he expects you to give him sufficient facts for him to evaluate your proposition. You should anticipate the questions that he will ask and be able to give him accurate answers. Your ability to give a prospective lender accurate, complete, and ready answers to his questions should go a long way in predisposing him in your favor. The following list contains points about the borrower that you should check:

(1) What are the borrower's cash resources? (2) How about the borrower's personal assets or financial status? (3) What is the borrower's income? (4) How about day-to-day expenses? (5) What are the borrower's fixed obligations? (6) How about the borrower's personal characteristics? (7) Can federal financing aids be looked to?

[¶806] Information You Should Have About the Seller and the Property

The following points regarding the seller and the property should be checked: (1) What are the seller's maximum and minimum terms? As to price? As to the cash he requires? (2) Seller's retention of interest in the property: Here the question is to what extent the seller will retain an interest in the property? For example, will he take back a purchase-money mortgage? (3) How much is the property worth? (4) How about the present financing structure of the property? (5) How about the location? (6) What are the age and size of the property? (7) What type of building is involved? (8) What is the physical condition of the property? Structural soundness? Improvements? (9) How does the property's durability stack up in relation to the term of the loan? (10) What are the operating costs? (11) How about income potential? (12) Are there tenants? If so, list the tenants and amount of rents. State the leases and expiration dates. (13) What are the possibilities of other uses for the property? (14) What is the state of the title to the property?

[¶807] Know the Main Financing Sources

Get to know and learn how to work with the main financing sources. Each of the main groups of lenders has different preferences as to the type of investments they will make and the terms they will consider. Knowing what these preferences are and their general policies and practices will be your key to open tight-money doors. Here is a rundown on the main financing sources.

Life Insurance Companies: Because of their broad investment powers and their huge resources, these are a good source for the financing of the large as well as the off-beat real estate transaction. They are the principal source for nonresidential mortgage financing, although some of the smaller companies will deal exclusively with one- to four-family homes.

Since the inflow of their investment funds is not subject to the same fluctuations that hit other lenders, they have more money to lend at all times. Also, they will usually lend over a wide geographic area, using local mortgage correspondents or branch offices. They will take more time than the other lenders in processing applications. The usual loan-to-value ratio that you can expect is 66-2/3%. You will seldom have to plan on the payment of discounts or "points."

Savings and Loan Associations: These are mostly cooperative institutions that seek to encourage thrift and to foster home ownership. They are, as a group, the biggest source of mortgage funds for the financing of residential homes. Their holdings constitute a great chunk of all outstanding mortgage loans in the one- to four-family-home category.

Savings and loan associations have billions of dollars in deposits and about 80 to 90% of their assets are invested in home mortgages. They have grown so important in the field of home financing that when tight-money periods cause shifts of deposits from savings and loans to higher yielding sources, the effect is felt throughout the home sales and construction industries.

Their usual loan limits are $40,000 with loan-to-value ratios of 90% on single-family residences. However, the average you will generally get will be closer to 70%. Most state savings and loans have lower loan limits than federal savings and loans.

Mutual Savings Banks: Although they exist in only several states, mainly in the northeastern part of the country, mutual savings banks are a very important national as well as local source of real estate financing. They are heavy lenders of government-insured loans. Most of them keep these, as well as their conventional lending, at the "bread-and-butter" level, that is, on one- and two-family houses. In fact, home mortgage loans constitute a substantial portion of their total combined assets. Some of the larger mutual savings banks in the major cities do concentrate their lending activities in multifamily residential, commercial, and industrial properties, but they are a large minority. The limited resources of the majority of the savings banks preclude the staffing of their mortgage departments with personnel and equipment that can handle a wide variety of loans.

You should try a savings bank particularly when you have an FHA or VA loan to arrange. On conventional loans, their loan ratios will vary, running between 60 and 90%. Of the institutional lenders, you will probably get your fastest processing of loans from savings banks.

Commercial Banks: Commercial banks are the primary source of temporary short-term construction loan financing. They also exert a strong influence in other phases of mortgage financing, particularly in states that do not have mutual savings banks. The large commercial banks play a big part in the financing of business and commercial properties, while some of the small ones will deal exclusively with residential property loans to individuals.

Commercial banks, like savings and loan associations and savings banks, are local organizations. In fact, they have even more ties to the local community, since their other activities bring them into extensive contact with a community's business affairs. Because of this, you will find that most commercial banks will confine their mortgage lending to a relatively narrow area around their home office.

Pension Funds: Although at present only a small percentage of the billions of dollars in pension funds are invested in mortgage loans, it is the opinion of most financing experts that this will ultimately be one of the best sources for real estate financing on all levels. The flow of the pension funds' incoming investment money is second only to life insurance companies.

However, the tremendous increase of the assets of pension funds and the need to diversify their investments are turning them more and more to the making of real estate mortgages. Their managers are becoming educated to the advantages of mortgage investments and are gaining experience and facilities for the origination and servicing of mortgage loans. It is expected that this trend will continue and that you will find them making all types of mortgage loans, conventional as well as government-insured.

Mortgage Companies: We more often describe the lending process of mortgage companies as "origination" of loans than the making of loans. This is because mortgage companies do not usually make loans to hold in their own portfolios. Since they operate mainly on funds that they borrow on a short-term basis, usually from commercial banks, they typically sell the mortgages as quickly as possible. However, during tight-money periods, they will make loans for their own portfolios instead of merely being originators or loan correspondents.

Mortgage companies are a good source for construction money and short-term loans. You should acquaint yourself with all the mortgage companies in your area and know their manner of operation. Because they have broad lending powers and do not have to account to directors or trustees, they can act quickly on your loan. Interest rates are high, and discounts and "points" are a standard part of their practice.

The Individual Lender: Individuals perform an important function in mortgage financing. Since the individual is using his own money rather than money belonging to someone else, he is often willing to accept a greater risk than a lending institution. The individual lender is important in areas where there is a marked deficiency of mortgage capital; and during periods when mortgage money is tight, he is especially useful.

The individual lender is not usually interested in long-term amortized loans. This type of loan does not give him the yield he ordinarily expects on his investments and requires accounting and bookkeeping that he usually does not want to bother with. He is interested in short-term loans of below five years in term. Individual investors are also the largest single source of second mortgage loans, which lending institutions are not permitted to make. He can also be used as a source for construction loans, generally for one-year periods, where the builder does not have a "take-out" for a permanent mortgage.

Almost every community has one or more individuals who will make mortgage loans. The alert broker will keep a list of these individuals in his area, will find out what type of mortgage investments they are interested in and will always keep them in mind when a hard-to-finance deal comes along. Of course, you can expect the highest interest rates from individuals and most certainly "points." In return, you get quick action, the possibility of getting finders' fees and the opportunity to swing many a deal in a tight-money market that would otherwise be lost.

[¶808] How to Approach the Main Financing Sources

Even in a tight-money market, your usual sources of financing will have mortgage money available and will be anxious to do business with any broker who approaches them properly and with the proper expectations. Although the following pointers on how to approach lenders are applicable at any time, they are particularly important during tight-money periods:

(1) Do some research on the type of loan each lender prefers. By being selective in picking the mortgage source you approach, you will be able to take dead aim and shoot your application to the source most likely to give the financial assistance you're looking for. This selective approach will also

get you quicker action on your loan and probably more money at lowest cost.

(2) When you approach a lender on a financing deal that you are working on, he is going to expect you to have certain facts for him to evaluate. You should anticipate the questions that will be asked and have accurate answers before you go to the lender. By following this practice you will always get fair consideration of your application; and, more than likely, your accurate, complete, and ready information will swing many a mortgage deal that would otherwise be turned down.

(3) Keep your estimates and expectations reasonable and on the conservative side. Don't get into the habit of asking for more than you would be willing to accept and then negotiating down to what you really need. The chances are that the lenders may not bother with an application at all if they feel it's out of line.

(4) Make timely applications. During periods of tight money, lenders will need more than their usual time to check out the application and to qualify your client. If you give them rush deals, it may result in no deal.

(5) Don't get the reputation of being a "loan shopper." It costs the lenders time and money to check out the application and the borrower. If they find that you are in the habit of placing the same application with a number of lenders at the same time, you may soon lose their cooperation. So, give one lender at a time an opportunity to make the loan; and you'll find that the lenders will do everything in their power to help you.

[¶809] Consider the Alternatives to Normal Outside Financing

Besides exploring all the usual sources of mortgage financing, periods of tight money should also be the time for you to learn about and use other financing techniques and the alternatives to normal outside financing. In the following paragraphs we consider some of the techniques that can be used at all times, and especially during tight-money periods, in financing both homes and commercial properties.

[¶810] How to Use Special Techniques in the Financing of Home Sales

(1) Use Purchase-Money or Second Mortgages: When you're handling a resale and can't arrange for a first mortgage loan needed to swing the deal, try to get the seller to take back a purchase-money mortgage or, at least, a purchase-money second mortgage. Property values go down when mortgage money becomes tight; so, the seller can possibly be convinced when you point out to him that he will probably get a higher price for the property if he is willing to take a purchase-money mortgage. He may also be able to get the tax benefits of installment sale reporting if no more than 30% of the sale price is received in the year of the sale. Also consider individual lenders as possible sources for second mortgages. And if, as sometimes happens, the money runs out when it becomes time to pay the brokerage commission, don't be afraid to take a second mortgage for your commission.

On New Homes: A builder who has the necessary cash can obtain conventional mortgages for a designated percentage of the purchase price and then finance thc balance via a second mortgage on the same terms as the first mortgage. The buyer is given the right to prepay the second mortgage. The builder can sell the second mortgage to a third party at a discount. Although he takes a loss on the discount, the builder may be able to make up for this by increasing the sale price.

If the builder holds on to the second mortgage, he may be able to defer some of his tax by way of an installment sale. He can do this if he can show that he has received no more than 30% of the sale price in the year of sale.

(2) Use Land Contracts: You should consider using a land contract where the buyer can only make a small down payment at present but expects some money in the near future. At that time, he'll be able to pay you enough money so that his equity in the property will qualify him for an outside mortgage, which he can use to pay you off and acquire title.

You may also be able to set up an installment sale to the buyer when using a land contract. Here's how it would work: The seller (or broker connected with the seller) would make some arrangement by which a lender would advance to the seller the cash needed for payment of the balance of the purchase price over an existing mortgage. The seller would have to pledge his own credit or collateral for this loan, as well as the land contract as additional security. The buyer moves in under the land contract after making a small down payment. Under the installment sale feature of the transaction, the buyer assumes the payments due under the seller's loan. The risk of default by the buyer can be covered; since the buyer does not get title to the property, he can be evicted in most states for nonpayment of the installments without the necessity of a complicated foreclosure proceeding. And the seller can provide that the payments on the installment contract are liquidated damages if the buyer defaults. As soon as the buyer is able to refinance, he can get an outside mortgage, pay off the seller, and get title to the property. Although FHA will not insure loans made under the installment plan (except in the case of relocation housing), you can use the installment on the balance of the purchase price on a home which has an existing FHA mortgage.

(3) Use the Special HUD Mortgage Programs: Besides the basic FHA home mortgage program, there are other specially designed HUD plans that you should be familiar with and utilize. Each of these programs contains features which make them attractive to lenders, as well as enabling certain borrowers in difficult financing situations to get home mortgages that may otherwise be unobtainable. Some of these home financing aids include special programs for disaster victims, servicemen, moderate-income and displaced families, and armed services civilian employees and on homes located in low-cost suburban areas and in urban renewal areas. Additionally, certain veterans and elderly persons can get special terms in the basic FHA program.

(4) Promoting Trade-Ins: In order to get a mortgage, ordinarily the buyer has to put up an adequate down payment. Also, many potential buyers who own their own homes want to be sure that they can sell them before they commit themselves to buy a new one. Using a trade-in plan can help a broker or builder solve both these problems. The buyer trades in his old home as his down payment on the new one. Typically, the seller signs a contract guaranteeing to purchase the old home at the time the purchaser takes title to the new one. The seller, through his broker as sales agent, makes an appraisal to see if the old house can be resold at the trade-in value placed on it. The broker gets a commission on the sale of the new house and another on the sale of the old house.

Brokers acting for builders assume responsibility for the sale of the old home. If the broker cannot sell the old house by the time title passes to the new one, then the broker takes it over, after deducting the amount of the commission he would have gotten had he sold the old house.

(5) Follow the Exchange Route: Homeowners and others who are in the market to buy but can't swing the deal because of a tight-money situation may be able to swap. By swapping properties, an owner can get the property he wants either without financing at all or with a minimum of financing.

For the broker, the swap offers a way of earning commissions where, otherwise, the inability to finance would kill the deal.

(6) Use a Share Collateral Mortgage: The share collateral mortgage is a specialty of savings and loan associations that can lend not only on the security of real estate but also on their own share accounts. They are especially useful in a situation where a buyer cannot come up with more than 10% for a down payment and no lender will offer to give a 90% conventional or an FHA or VA loan. Assume in this situation that an association would be willing to make an 80% loan. An agreement is then worked out by which the association will make a loan for the full 90% of the appraised value provided the seller will pledge the extra 10% to the association as additional collateral for the purchaser-mortgagor's performance.

Example: Assume a selling price of $10,000 and a willing buyer who is an acceptable mortgage risk but who has only $1,000 for a down payment. A savings and loan appraises the property and is willing to make an 80% conventional loan of $8,000. The real estate broker involved suggests to the seller that he can close the deal if the seller agrees to put up as collateral a $1,000 share collateral account with the mortgagee savings and loan. Under this agreement, the association then makes a loan for $9,000, based on 80% of the appraised value and 100% of the seller's share account. The agreement provides that the $1,000 will be released to the seller when the loan is reduced to a certain point. Until that time, the seller can collect dividends or can sell the account to another investor. Of course, the investor will be bound by the original collateral agreement.

(7) Use "Sweat" Equity: Builders can increase their sales, save on labor and overhead, save time, and reduce the number of call-backs with this approach—i.e., have the home purchaser do some of the work. In one such arrangement, the homes are definitely not shell houses. As soon as the builder completes his work the family can move in. The way the deal is set up, the work to be done by the purchaser is to be finished within a three-month period. There's a specific itemization of the "equity down payment" credits for each type of home sold. The type of work that has to be done and the amount of money allocated for each type of work along with the estimated cost of the materials are listed. The builder guarantees the lender satisfactory completion of the home, but in one development, with over 200 sales and each sale involving relatively large work equity the builder had only two instances in which some difficulty arose. What's more, in each instance the loan was recast, the sale remained firm and the builder did not suffer any additional cost.

(8) If You Can't Sell, Rent: If you're a broker, one way to cope with a tight-money market and continue to make money is to push rental housing. Many people who would otherwise buy homes may be looking to rent.

You can make money in this market by convincing homeowners to rent instead of sell. You can show them that they can get a substantial income from their properties while they wait for the market to change. In this way, you build up your own rental commissions while assuring yourself of future sales commissions when the money situation changes.

[¶811] How to Use Special Techniques in the Financing of Commercial Properties

(1) Ground Leasing: This alternative, in effect, makes the seller provide the financing; since, as lessor, he maintains his investment in the property. All the lessee has to raise is the yearly rent. Whether this will work depends on whether the prospective seller concludes that the property is a good long-term investment for the money he could have obtained on sale and on the buyer's willingness to settle for a long-term lease. The buyer gets the tax benefit of deducting his rent payments and, in effect, puts the land on a tax-deductible basis. The seller keeps his depreciation of the property.

Long-term leases as a financing device are a comparatively recent development in the real estate field. There are certain circumstances under which leasing is more attractive than debt financing. Here are some of the reasons for the rapidly expanding use of the lease as a financing device: (a) long-term leasing releases funds for other uses, such as expansion or working capital; (b) tax advantages are available under the leasing device that are not available under debt financing where ownership is retained; (c) long-term leasing makes borrowing easier; (d) leasing simplifies the capital structure and keeps the businessman out of the real estate business so that he can concentrate on his own line of business.

(2) Sale-Leasebacks: If additional capital is needed, it is possible to get the equivalent of a 100% mortgage through a sale-leaseback—whereas it is usually difficult to get more than 80% of the realty value through a mortgage. However, analysis might reveal that less capital is needed or that it is possible to raise the same amount through a first mortgage plus an unsecured loan for the balance. (Investors generally rely mainly on the credit of the seller-lessee in extending 100% credit.)

Here's another point to consider: In the event of a seller-lessee's bankruptcy, the Chandler Act limits the lessor's claim to one year's rental in the case of a general bankruptcy and three years' rental in the case of a reorganization. Thus a lessee in bankruptcy can generally reject a long-term lease. On the other hand, under first mortgage financing the creditor is a preferred creditor to the extent of the proceeds from the mortgaged realty and a general creditor to the extent of any deficiency. Although a lessor's rights are limited in the event of a lessee's bankruptcy, the lessor does own the premises. Furthermore, the possibility of a lessee's bankruptcy is remote, since the initial investment is made after careful investigation of the lessee's overall credit.

The leasing device simplifies the capital structure of the business in that the lease is not a "liability" in the legal sense of the term, so that the ratio of debt to capital is reduced. However, this simplification is superficial since the lease payments are in reality fixed obligations just as mortgage amortization payments would be fixed obligations. Besides, if the leased-back realty becomes unprofitable to the lessee, rental payments must continue—whereas it is possible to sell mortgaged property with the mortgage. But again, the effects of leasing or mortgaging are similar, since the lessee can sublet or can include a clause in the lease permitting him to reject the lease on payment of, say, one year's rental as liquidated damages.

Another point: Leasing as a financing device does not require the user to register with the Securities and Exchange Commission, as would be the case if preferred or common stock were issued to the public. However, privately placed issues need not be registered, so that the same advantage would be available if instead of leasing, the business would obtain a direct loan from the same institutional lender—which is often a possibility. Besides, debt financing makes available as much capital as is needed, whereas financing through a sale-leaseback involves sale of the whole pie or nothing. Leasing is generally more suited to the needs of chain stores which can build to their own requirements and sell and lease back each property as it becomes necessary to finance another development.

Here's when the leasing device is more attractive than debt financing: (a) The seller-lessee can sell the property at a *gain* which, at current values, exceeds the anticipated loss of anticipated residual values at lease termination; (b) the seller-lessee can realize an offsetting *loss* by entering into a sale-leaseback transaction; (c) the buyer-lessor can get a higher basis for depreciation of the property than the present owner; (d) the seller-lessee may find it more advantageous to write off the periodic rental payments as a business *deduction* than to own and depreciate the property; or (e) the buyer-lessor may realize a *larger return* than under debt financing. In any event, a careful analysis of the relative advantages and costs of leasing versus debt financing will determine the best method of financing under a given set of circumstances.

Here's how to weigh the cost of financing by debt or by lease:

Debt financing cost is the interest rate (compounded over the loan period according to actuarial tables), less tax deductions for interest and depreciation arising out of ownership.

Lease financing cost is the total rental, decreased or increased by the after-tax gain or loss realized on the sale (Code §1231), and further decreased by the tax deduction for the rental payments and then increased by the loss of the depreciation deduction and the anticipated residual value at termination of the lease.

Here's the kind of thinking that swings sale-leaseback deals:

The seller-lessee gets his money—often easier through leasing than through debt financing—which he can use to produce income to offset the financing costs. The rental payments are written off as a business deduction. Besides, the anticipated residual value might actually be less at the termination of the lease than is now expected—so that it might be better to sell now and take the present high valuation than speculate on future economic trends.

The buyer-lessor gets ownership of the property with the incidental tax benefit of depreciating the property at perhaps a higher basis than the seller-lessee would have available. The rentals return the lessor's investment plus an attractive rate of return, disregarding residual values. This more than offsets the fact that the rental payments are taxable as ordinary income to the lessor—whereas under debt financing only the interest, not the amortization of principal, would be taxable income. The lessee generally has the responsibility for managing the property so that the lessor has no expenses other than income taxes. Furthermore, the lessor bets that the anticipated residual value (a variable element) might actually be more at the termination of the lease than is now expected—so that it might be better to buy now and cash in if the market appreciates.

(3) Syndicate: This is pertinent to promoters in commercial and apartment house properties who raise the investment money they need by syndicating. If you are unable to get a mortgage on property your syndicate plans to acquire, consider syndicating for the full purchase price. Then, when you are later able to obtain the mortgage, you can distribute the proceeds as a partial return of investment to the participants.

[¶812] How Mortgages Figure in Buying and Selling Real Estate

Since the basis of real estate includes not only the cash paid but any purchase-money mortgages and any mortgages assumed or taken subject to (*Crane,* 331 US 1), depreciation is figured on the total. The interplay of this high depreciation deduction, deductible mortgage interest (which goes down each year with constant payment mortgages), and nondeductible mortgage amortization (which increases each year) determines to a great extent the desirability of a real estate investment. Thus, the consideration of these factors can enter into the calculations of both the prospective investor (looking to buy a property) and the present owner (deciding whether the time to sell has arrived or, perhaps, the time to refinance—or maybe both). For example, the present owner may deem it necessary to sell because his depreciation deductions are dropping and his nondeductible amortization is on the increase. Yet, a new buyer may be willing to take over the property because he will be paying a higher price than the seller's basis (since, we assume, values have held up). Although perhaps two-thirds of his purchase price is in the form of mortgages, he'll still get depreciation based on the higher value, and that may make the purchase a worthwhile investment for him.

Leverage is another factor influencing a buyer. If he can buy with very little cash and get most of the purchase price financed, he's in a position to cash in on any rise in value. The entire appreciation belongs to him even though his equity is relatively small. Of course, any decline in value is also borne only by him.

Placing mortgages on property before selling may facilitate sales in several ways: It may enable avoidance of tax in the year of sale and spread the income over a period of years where the installment sale rules might otherwise not apply. Or, a refinancing of an existing mortgage prior to sale may make the arithmetic attractive to the buyer without penalizing the seller and swing a deal that might otherwise have died.

How Leverage Affects the Investor: We get leverage when we are able to buy property—for income or to speculate on an increase in value—by paying only a portion of the price in our own cash. The balance is paid either by a purchase-money mortgage from the seller, by an obligation to make further payments pursuant to an installment contract, by borrowing on the security of the property, or by assuming or taking subject to a mortgage debt already existing against the property.

Here's what leverage can do *for* the investor:

(1) When the underlying property increases in value, the owner gets the full benefit even though he has put up only part of the price in cash. Thus, if he buys property for 25% in cash and 75% in a purchase-money mortgage and the property doubles in value, he quintuples his money, thus:

	Before	*After*
Value	$100,000	$200,000
Debt	75,000	75,000
Equity	25,000	125,000

(2) If income property yielding 11% is purchased for 25% cash and 75%

a purchase-money mortgage carrying 7% interest, we kick up the yield on equity from 11% to 23%. Here's how:

Cost	$100,000
Net income	$11,000 (11% on full value)
Interest	$5,250 (7% of $75,000 mortgage)
Net income	$5,750 (23% on cash investment of $25,000)

But here's what leverage can do *to* the investor:

(1) If the property loses in value, the debt remains fixed and the loss of value is taken in full out of the cash investment. Thus:

	Before	*After*
Value	$100,000	$80,000
Debt	75,000	75,000
Equity	25,000	5,000

(2) If the income falls off, the interest burden remains fixed and the loss is taken in full out of the net to the owner. Thus:

	Before	*After*
Income	$11,000	$7,770
Interest	5,250	5,250
Net	5,750	2,450

So, the heavier the mortgage, the greater the percentage gain to the owner when the property rises in value or income-producing power; also, the greater the loss when value or rent turns the other way.

When to Sell Your Property or Refinance Your Mortgage: At some point during your ownership of property, either refinancing or sale may become necessary. Even if your rents are fixed, lower depreciation deductions in the later years coupled with constant mortgage payments (in which tax-deductible interest decreases and nondeductible amortization increases each year) cut your after-tax return from the property.

If depreciation was à prime incentive for your buying the property, you might later consider selling it. But if you still consider the property a good economic investment, you'll have to seek refinancing in order to keep up your after-tax return.

For example, you bought land and building for $1,200,000, paying $200,000 cash and giving a 25-year $1,000,000 mortgage at, say, 5% (the then prevailing rate) payable in constant yearly amounts of $71,000. The land is valued at $450,000; the building, at $750,000. The rent roll is $140,000 a year with $49,000 expenses before mortgage payments.

Your actual cash return (before taxes) each year is $20,000 ($140,000 rent received less $49,000 expenses and $71,000 mortgage payments), or 10% on your cash investment. Your after-tax return is affected by the relationship between your depreciation deduction and your amortization and, of course, by your tax bracket. To the extent that depreciation (which reduces taxable income but requires no cash outlay) exceeds amortization (which requires a cash outlay but does not reduce taxable income), you have a tax-free return. If the balance is reversed, you'll be paying taxes on income in excess of your cash return. And that is the time you'll have to consider refinancing or sale.

Assuming the figures we set out above and 150%-declining-balance depreciation on a 25-year life, the depreciation deduction in the first year would be $45,000, which would be $24,000 in excess of your amortization payments, making the $20,000 cash return entirely tax free and giving you $4,000 of deductions to apply against other ordinary income. Thus, your after-tax yield on the $200,000 cash invested was 12%. By the seventh year, depreciation exceeded amortization by only $2,950, making $17,050 of the $20,000 cash return taxable. Assuming a 50% tax rate, the net-after-taxes became $11,475, for an after-tax yield of 5½%.

The time to sell or refinance your mortgage, depends on whether property values drop or continue to hold up and increase. Assume you could get the same $1,200,000 you paid. You decide to sell and take a capital gain rather than refinance. You'd have a capital gain of some $260,000. But that $260,000 is the amount of the depreciation you deducted over the seven-year period. And those depreciation deductions (in the 50% bracket) saved you $130,000 in taxes.

Having sold, you would be in a position to reinvest in new property and take advantage of the high depreciation in the early years, boosting your yield again to what it was several years before. And your buyer is willing to pay the price he is paying because he can start depreciation all over again based on his cost.

The capital gain tax you'd have to pay need not deter you from making the sale. Keeping your cash received in the year of sale to no more than $360,000 (30% of the sale price), you could spread your gain over a number of years by making an installment sale. At the time of the sale, your mortgage would have been reduced to $829,000. If the buyer were to take subject to that mortgage, you could take part of the remaining $371,000 sale price in cash and take back a purchase-money second mortgage—spreading your gain over the period of that second mortgage.

If you were not ready to sell, you might consider mortgage refinancing.

At the beginning of the eighth year, your unpaid principal would be $829,350. Assume you refinanced at that time and intended to hold on to the property two more years. We'll assume you could get a 20-year 5% (then current rate) mortgage. This works out to constant payments of $66,500 a year or $4,500 less than your payments under your old mortgage. Thus, your cash return before taxes would be boosted from $20,000 to $24,500 per year. In the eighth year, instead of having taxable income exceed cash return by $3,500, you'd actually get $4,125 of your $24,500 cash return tax free. In the ninth year, you'd get $1,150 tax free.

How Mortgage Refinancing Helps to Get More Cash on a Sale: An investor in real estate looks to his cash return in figuring how much cash he's willing to put up. Thus, if an investor feels he should get a 10% return on his investment, he's willing to put up $100,000 cash if he'll get back $10,000 a year in cash (i.e., gross rents less cash expenses, mortgage interest, and amortization but before depreciation or personal income taxes).

Because of the buyer's concern with his cash return, a seller may find it difficult to sell a property at the total asking price both parties consider to be a reflection of fair value (taking into account other factors in addition to return on cash; e.g., future value after expiration of present leases, ratio of gross rentals to total asking price, etc.).

For example, assume the buyer agrees that the fair value of the property (taking all factors into consideration) is $122,500. The unpaid balance on the existing mortgage on the property is $50,000. That means the buyer would have to pay $72,500 cash. But the building's net rents after expenses but before interest and amortization amount to $10,000 a year. Say, 5% interest and 2% amortization were called for. On a $75,000 mortgage (now reduced to $50,000), this would come to $5,250 a year, cutting the cash return to $4,750. So, the buyer would not put up more than $47,500 in cash. A second mortgage would increase the amortization and interest payments, cutting the buyer's cash yield still further.

As seller, try to refinance your mortgage. If property values have held up (as they apparently have, in view of the asking price the buyer is willing to meet), you might get a new $75,000 mortgage at the same total 7% output. (You might [depending on the current market] get a 6% mortgage with 1% amortization. The buyer shouldn't object; he still pays out 7%, cuts his amortization expense, and increases his deductible interest cost.) You then get $25,000 in cash through the refinancing, plus the buyer's $47,500. The buyer still gets the return he wanted on the cash he invested.

Consider Refinancing Even if Values Haven't Quite Held Up: Suppose you can't get the $75,000 mortgage and your original asking price is too high. Even if you only refinance for an amount equal to the unpaid balance of your original mortgage, you may still be able to get more cash on the sale.

If you can get a new mortgage for $50,000 (equal to the unpaid balance of the existing mortgage) at, say, 5% interest and 2% amortization, the 7% annual payout will be figured on $50,000 instead of the $75,000 original mortgage. That reduces your annual payout for interest and amortization from $5,250 to $3,500. This reduction increases the cash yield of the building by $1,750. Thus, the buyer should be willing to pay an additional $17,500 in cash (ten times extra cash return).

How Home Builders Use Second Mortgages to Sell Houses: Suppose a house should sell for $30,000. A buyer can put up $5,000, but a bank is willing to write only a $20,000 mortgage. That leaves a $5,000 gap which some builders have been filling by lending that $5,000 themselves on second mortgages.

A problem arises in reporting the income. The builder will receive that $5,000 over a period of years. Yet, if he can't report an installment sale, he's going to be taxed on the entire profit immediately.

To have an installment sale, he can't receive more than 30% of the sale price in the year of the sale. Usually, he'll get more than that; he'll get the $20,000 first mortgage money (lent by the bank to the home buyer) and use that to pay off his construction loans. So, he'd lose out on installment reporting.

What Some Builders Are Doing: Some builders have been able to get construction loans under which the mortgagee or lender agrees to modify and extend the loan on sale of the house. This provision, they hope, will make the construction loan a mortgage from the very beginning. So, the home buyer will be taking subject to or assuming that mortgage even though the terms are changed when the home buyer takes over the mortgage. Since taking over of an existing mortgage by the buyer does not count as proceeds received by the seller for installment sale purposes, the builders expect to be able to report on the installment basis.

The New York Court of Appeals has ruled that an extension agreement between a buyer and a mortgagee, substituting the buyer for the seller and extending the time for payment of the mortgage, is not a new mortgage for New York State mortgage tax purposes (*Suffolk County Federal Savings & Loan Association v. Bragalini*). Of course, IRS is not bound by this decision, but it and the courts may be influenced by it. On the other hand, IRS may argue that a new mortgage was created and, in effect, the builder received cash and then paid off his construction loan even though he, not the home buyer, got the mortgage (*Gallagher Realty Co.*, 4 BTA 219).

Can a Ground Lease Be Substituted for a Mortgage? A ground lease generally involves this kind of an arrangement: A builder acquires land, puts up a house and sells the house subject to a ground rent he puts on the land. The purchaser ends up with the title to the house and a long-term lease (often, renewable forever). Under Maryland law, the purchaser can, after the lease has run five years, acquire ownership of the land by paying an amount equal to the annual ground rent capitalized at, say, 6% (e.g., if the ground rent is $600 per year, he'd have to pay $10,000).

IRS takes the position that the capitalized amount of the ground rent should be included in the selling price received by the seller in the same way that a purchase-money mortgage would be included. The Tax Court doesn't agree. It holds that since the purchaser cannot be compelled to buy the land, this agreement actually is a lease not a mortgage (*Welsh Homes, Inc.*, 32 TC 239).

How These Ground Rents Benefit Sellers: Great flexibility is available. If a seller sold the property outright and invested the funds elsewhere, he'd pay an immediate tax on the gain (capital gain or ordinary income, depending on whether or not he was a dealer). He'd then pay an annual tax on the income from his new investment. If he considers the ground rent a good investment, he's able to get into that without first having to pay a tax on most of the gain on the sale, since the selling price of the house could be fixed to reflect only a small gain.

Of course, the parties might set up a mortgage as part of the purchase price instead of employing the ground rent set-up. But the seller would have to receive no more than 30% of the sale price in the year of sale in order to be able to spread his income via an installment sale. And if he wanted more than 30%, he'd have to pay a tax on his entire gain immediately. And the purchaser then owns the property with the seller's remedies for nonpayment of the mortgage possibly restricted to expensive and time-consuming procedures.

Under the Maryland ground rent set-up, of course, the seller can split off his investment. He can keep the sale price for the house fairly low, showing only a small gain—yet this could involve more than the 30% of the sale price that he could take under an installment sale. He could reinvest these proceeds and at the same time keep his investment in the land. And the house purchaser is a tenant, not a mortgagor. So, he can evict for nonpayment, usually a much simpler procedure than the mortgage foreclosure route.

What About Other States? You can probably get a similar set-up in states other than Maryland by drawing your contract to give similar results. The contract itself can give the purchaser-lessee the option to buy at a price determined by capitalizing the ground rent. But you have to be careful that the price at which the option can be exercised is not too low. Otherwise, IRS may say that you have a sale of the land at the time the option is given because it is almost a foregone conclusion that the buyer will exercise.

Tax Factors Affecting Mortgagors: Tax rules come into play at various times during which a property owner is subject to or obligated under a mortgage. Here is a rundown of the more important situations:

(1) Cost of Obtaining Mortgage: Expenses such as appraisal fees, title costs, loan commissions, and surveys are costs of obtaining a loan and are not added to the basis of the property involved. These costs are only deductible where business property is involved and must be prorated over the life of the mortgage.

(2) Treatment of Interest on Mortgage—Business Expense or Itemized Deduction? Tax treatment of mortgage interest paid is governed by use of the mortgage proceeds, not the nature of the pledged assets. Merely pledging business assets for a mortgage loan does not automatically mean that any interest paid thereon is a business expense (deductible, by an individual in addition to the standard deduction). The pivotal factor is whether the proceeds of the loan are used to earn business income. Where the interest is considered a personal expense, it is still deductible as an itemized deduction.

If a taxpayer is not personally liable on a mortgage, as long as he is the legal or equitable owner of the real estate, an interest deduction is still available if he makes payment (Reg. §1.163-1(b)).

(3) Deduction of Insurance Expense: Insurance premiums paid by a mortgagor in advance for more than one year on business property are only deductible on a pro rata basis over the period covered by the payment and are not deductible in total in the payment year. This rule applies both to cash and accrual taxpayers (but one Eighth Circuit opinion held otherwise for cash-basis taxpayers: *Waldheim Realty and Investment Co.*, 245 F.2d 823).

(4) Property Taxes Deductible by Mortgagor: This is so because the mortgagor holds the beneficial interest in the property. Where business or investment property is involved, a business deduction is allowed; otherwise, with reference to a personal residence, only an itemized deduction can be taken.

Where a reserve is built up by monthly deposits to cover property taxes, no deduction is allowed for a cash-basis mortgagor until the reserve is actually applied by the mortgagee for payment of such taxes. An accrual-basis mortgagor may elect to accrue the tax ratably over the period to which the tax relates (§461(c)).

(5) Premiums Paid for Mortgages: A premium paid by a mortgagor in obtaining a mortgage loan is treated as discount income to the mortgagee. Taxwise, both are treated as interest expense and income.

The mortgagor is entitled to a deduction for any premium paid to the mortgagee for making the loan (excess of mortgage over proceeds received). Where a mortgagor is on the cash basis and prepays the premium, it seems that he could take the entire prepayment as a current deduction. Where the premium is withheld from the loan, it is not considered paid but is subsequently deducted on a percentage basis when the loan is repaid, whether in installments or by partial payments. A mortgagor on the accrual basis must deduct the premium ratably over the period of the loan.

(6) Penalty for Prepayment Privilege: This penalty is considered interest and is deductible where business or investment property or a personal residence is involved (*Rev. Rul. 57-210,* CB 1957-1, 94, *revoking Rev. Rul. 55-12,* CB 1955-1, 259). It seems that the penalty payment would still be an interest deduction and not an expense of sale where the mortgagor agreed to sell the mortgaged property free and clear of encumbrances and paid off the mortgage in anticipation of the sale.

(7) Proceeds From Involuntarily Converted Property: When property is condemned or destroyed by fire or other casualty, condemnation proceeds or insurance proceeds received by the property owner in excess of his basis are not taxable to him if, within two years after the close of the year in which the conversion took place, he reinvests the proceeds in property of a like kind (§1033(a)). Where there is a mortgage, the mortgagee's interest may be paid to him directly and the mortgage thus paid off. The question then arises as to how much the mortgagor has to reinvest. Is it the entire proceeds (including the amount that went to satisfy the mortgage debt), or need he reinvest the net proceeds only? The courts are divided on this point. The Tax Court says only the net proceeds need be reinvested (*Fortee Properties, Inc.,* 19 TC 99; *Babcock,* 28 TC 781, *nonacq.,* CB 1959-1, 6). This disagrees with the Treasury's Regulations which would require the entire proceeds to be reinvested (Reg. §1.1033(a)-2(c)(11)). The Second and the Ninth Circuits split on this issue, the Second reversing the *Fortee* case (211 F.2d 915), and the Ninth affirming the *Babcock* decision (259 F.2d 689).

If you are personally liable on the mortgage, you would have to reinvest the entire proceeds because then it would be considered that you had received the entire amount and used the amount covering the mortgage to pay off your personal liability.

(8) Assignment of Rents: The mortgagor is still taxable on any income from the mortgaged property, which he may assign to meet payments of interest and principal due on the mortgage. The mortgagor is the owner of the property and he must account for all income from such property during the period of his ownership (*Horst,* 311 US 112). The ownership period terminates on subsequent sale of the property or expiration of a redemption period of a foreclosure.

(9) Gifts of Mortgaged Property: Where there is a gift of mortgaged property, a gift tax is imposed on the donor to the extent of the value of equity transferred. Such value is the fair market value of the property less any mortgage indebtedness attached to the property. The donee's basis for purposes of gain is the same as the donor's, increased by any gift tax paid. For loss it is the donor's basis or fair market value at the time of the gift whichever is lower (§1015(a)). Any subsequent payments made upon the mortgage by the donee will not affect basis.

Watch Out for These Mortgage Pitfalls: Transactions involving mortgages can prove to be very tricky. Often a seemingly harmless transaction can result in an unanticipated tax. Keep the following tax traps in mind in your mortgage dealings:

(1) Mortgage Money in Excess of Basis of Property: If you get a mortgage on your property that exceeds your basis, there is no taxable gain at that point (*Woodsam Associates, Inc.,* 198 F.2d 357). But if you should transfer the mortgaged property to a corporation tax free for stock (§351) or where the mortgagor is a corporation and the property is transferred in a tax-free separation (reorganization; §368(a)(1)(D)), the excess of the mortgage over the basis of the property is taxable to the transferor as capital gain or ordinary income, depending on the nature of the asset (§357(c)).

If a corporation distributes excess mortgage money to its stockholders and the mortgage is insured by FHA or another US governmental agency, distribution is ordinary income to the stockholders regardless of whether or not the corporation has any other earnings and profits (§312(j)).

When an FHA mortgage is taken over by a successor mortgagor, he may find that when the mortgage is paid and FHA makes a distribution to him of part or all of the insurance premiums paid to it on that mortgage, he will have ordinary income. Since the mortgage was in existence before he took it over and the previous mortgagor paid premiums, the amount he receives from the FHA may be more than the total premiums he actually paid. The excess over what he paid is taxable to him (*Rev. Rul. 58-380,* CB 1958-2, 490).

A mortgagor during the entire life of the mortgage would not have any income from the premium repayment by FHA since he cannot get back more than he paid. But if the premiums paid were deducted as a business expense (where the mortgage is on income-producing property), then the entire amount received from FHA is taxable (see *Rev. Rul. 56-302,* CB 1956-2, 19).

(2) Relationship Between Debtor and Creditor: Special problems can arise where the debtor and creditor are related—especially in the case of a

corporate mortgagor and a stockholder-mortgagee. A number of problems can present themselves: accrued interest not paid within 2½ months after the end of the mortgagor's tax year will not be deductible (§267(a)(2)(A)); interest may be deemed too high and unreasonable, hence a dividend distribution; the corporation may be considered "thinly" capitalized and debt (including mortgage debt) treated as stock; or there may be a question of the validity of the debt to begin with. Good records and evidence of bona fides should be maintained.

Where an interest deduction has been disallowed under the 2½-month rule, any subsequent payments of interest should be specifically identified as payments of current interest, otherwise the payment may be applied, under the first-in-first-out theory, as a payment of the prior unpaid interest, so that more than one interest deduction may be disallowed (*Lincoln Storage Warehouse,* 189 F.2d 337).

(3) Personal Holding Company Danger: Where the mortgagee is a corporation (more than 50% of which is owned by five or fewer individuals), check to see that its income, other than mortgage interest, does not come within the sphere of personal holding company income (§543) so that when added to the mortgage interest the total will not equal more than 60% of gross income (§542(a)). If it does, the corporation will be subject to the crushing personal holding company tax (§541).

(4) Contribution of Mortgaged Property to a Partnership: This may result in a taxable gain to the contributing partner as a portion of the mortgage debt is shifted over to the other partner or partners. Under the Code, any decrease in a partner's individual liability by reason of its assumption by the partnership is considered a cash distribution (§752(b)).

(5) Settlement of Mortgage Debt at a Discount: Where a mortgagee settles a mortgage debt for less than par, income may be realized by an individual mortgagor (to the extent of the forgiveness) whose mortgaged property was not business property. Where business property is involved or the mortgagor is a corporation, no income is recognized (§108) if taxpayer elects to reduce the basis of property he holds (§1017).

As to the mortgagee, if he receives less than the par value of the mortgage, the difference between basis and amount realized will be treated as a bad debt deduction, business or nonbusiness, as the case may be.

Mortgages Acquired at a Discount: Where the mortgagee acquires a mortgage for a sum below par and the mortgagor is not a corporation, any gain realized therefrom is ordinary income. The percentage of gain from each collection received must be reported. However, where the mortgagor is a corporation, gain is capital gain (to a nondealer mortgagee) unless the mortgage was originally issued at a discount. If there was an original issue discount, the mortgagee has ordinary income on each collection to the extent the gain is attributable to the period during which he held the mortgage (the gain over the original issue price is spread ratably over the life of the mortgage). The gain attributable to the period preceding his ownership of the mortgage would be capital gain (see §1232(a)(2)).

Where a mortgage is redeemed, sold or exchanged, the entire original issue discount will be taxed at ordinary rates, unless it can be shown that at the time of original issue of the mortgage there was no intention to redeem, sell or exchange before maturity (§1232(a)(2)).

[¶900] CONSUMER PROTECTION

In recent years we have witnessed the birth and development of a new field of law dealing with the protection of consumers. This new type of legislation extends into various fields, of which real estate is but one. Because it is important that everyone in the industry be aware of these important new laws, we are including material on them in the paragraphs that follow. Whether you are or represent a borrower or lender, it is necessary for you to familiarize yourself with the Fair Credit Reporting Act, the Equal Credit Opportunity Act, and the Truth in Lending Act, as well as the Real Estate Settlement Procedures Act.

[¶901] Truth in Lending

The federal Consumer Credit Protection Act was signed into law on May 29, 1968, and became effective on July 1, 1969. The Federal Reserve Board published its Regulation Z, which implements the Act, in February 1969. Subsequently it issued 31 interpretations to cover practices omitted from Regulation Z. Title I of the Act is also known as the federal Truth-in-Lending Law. The purpose of the Truth-in-Lending Law is to give a borrower full information as to all the financing costs that he is being required to pay so that he can readily compare the various credit terms that are available to him. Both civil and criminal liability may be imposed for violations.

The federal Truth-in-Lending Law was adopted for the protection of consumers. It covers a credit deal the subject of which is primarily for personal, family, household, or agricultural purposes for which a finance charge is or may be imposed or which, pursuant to an agreement, is or may be payable in more than four installments. The Law does not apply where credit is extended for business purposes or to corporations, organizations (including corporations, trusts, estates, partnerships, cooperatives, associations) or units of government.

A credit sale is one in which credit is extended or arranged by the seller. Creditors subject to the provisions of the Law include those who regularly extend credit and those who arrange for the extension of credit, e.g., banks, credit unions, finance companies, S & L's, life insurance companies, and mortgage brokers. It has been estimated that something like one million creditors will be affected by the Law. In addition, those in the business of buying mortgages may also find themselves vulnerable since a borrower may sue for noncompliance, not only the original lender, but also one purchasing the mortgage from the original lender, provided a continuing business relationship existed between them.

Real estate brokers, sellers, and builders are vulnerable under the Law, since deals made with them may be subject to cancellation and also because they may, under some circumstances, be considered creditors.

What Are Real Estate Transactions Within the Law: The federal Truth-in-Lending Law applies to a real estate transaction within its purview regardless of the amount involved. Real property, in this context, means property that is real property under the law of the state in which it is situated. A loan secured by fixtures may be a real estate deal within the meaning of the Law, depending on state law. An extension of credit in connection with which a security interest in real property is acquired is a real property transaction.

Refinancing: Refinancing deals may be subject to the disclosure provisions of the Law requiring that the total finance charge and the total dollar amount of all payments be stated. Subject to the same exemptions applicable to original mortgage loans, assumptions are subject to the Law when the mortgagee accepts the new purchaser in writing.

Some Exceptions: As already noted, the federal Truth-in-Lending Law does not apply where credit is extended for business purposes or to corporations, trusts, estates, partnerships, cooperatives, associations, or units of governments. In addition, certain real estate credit transactions, even though for personal or family purposes, are exempt from some provisions of the Law. Thus, for example, a homeowner who sells his home and takes back a mortgage is not subject to the Law, nor is a relative or friend, not in the credit business, who helps finance a home purchase.

But these exemptions don't apply to deals as to which the Law gives the borrower a right to cancel; for example, open-end and other advances as to which a residence is used as security in the extension of credit for consumer needs other than to finance the purchase of a home.

Some Loans Are Completely Exempt From All Disclosure Requirements: These include mortgage loans on single-family houses not to be occupied by the owner and to be used for investment and rental income; loans on any kind of property where the proceeds are to be used for investment purposes, including loans made to homeowners on their own homes to finance investment in a business; and any loan on a building consisting of several dwelling or business units, where the units other than the one occupied by the buyer are to be rented for profit.

Law May Not Apply in Some States: The Law does not apply in a state having a substantially similar law containing adequate provision for its enforcement, but what constitutes substantial similarity remains to be determined.

What Disclosures Must Be Made: A brief rundown on what the disclosure statement should contain includes the annual percentage rate; the number, amount, and due rates of payments; the method of figuring delinquency charges; a legal description of the property securing the loan; composition of the finance charge, and total amount of credit; and total dollar amount of finance charge and sum of all monthly payments (but not in case of first mortgage loan on home to finance its purchase or construction).

How Mortgages on Homes to Be Occupied by the Borrower Are Affected: With respect to first mortgages, the total annual interest rate will have to be stated. While the total dollar amount of financing costs over the life of the mortgage will not have to be stated as to purchase-money first mortgages, it will have to be disclosed as to other first mortgages. Purchase-money first mortgages against dwellings are also expressly excluded from a provision giving the consumer three days in which to cancel the deal. But first mortgages other than purchase-money mortgages are subject to the provision. Thus a first mortgage given on a home to a home repair concern would be subject to the provision.

With respect to second mortgages placed on homes, both the total annual interest rate and the total dollar amount of financing cost will have to be stated. In addition, the borrower will have three days in which to cancel the deal.

While a borrower can cancel all junior mortgages on his principal residence, he cannot cancel a purchase-money first mortgage to purchase a home in which he lives or expects to live; or a first mortgage in connection with the financing of the initial construction of his home or the permanent loan used to satisfy the construction loan, regardless of whether or not he previously owned the land on which the home is to be constructed; or a lien by reason of its subordination after its creation, if he could not cancel it when it was created; or an advance made for agricultural purposes (e.g., an open-end real estate mortgage); or a mortgage on a house not his principal residence.

Since the Law applies only to creditors who regularly extend or arrange for the extension of credit, it would seem that a purchase-money second mortgage given to a private home seller would not be subject to its provisions. On the other hand, a second mortgage given to a home-repair concern would be covered.

A borrower, who has the right to cancel, has the right to do so until midnight of the third business day following the consummation of the transaction or delivery of all material disclosures (including disclosure of the right to cancel without liability), whichever is later. On exercise of this right, any security interests created under the transaction are voided, the creditor must refund any advances, and the borrower must tender back any property or its reasonable value which he has received from the creditor.

How to Figure Amount of Finance Charge and Annual Percentage Rate: First, the amount of the finance charge is computed. In determining this amount, all charges payable directly or indirectly by the consumer and imposed directly or indirectly by the creditor are included. This means not only interest but also points or discounts, service charges, loan fees, time-price differentials, premiums or other charges for any guarantees or insurance, etc. But fees or premiums for title examination, title insurance, or for similar purposes; fees for preparation of deed, settlement statement, or other documents; escrow for future payments of taxes and insurance; fees for notarizing deeds and other documents; appraisal fees and credit reports need not be included, provided all such charges are itemized and disclosed and are bona fide, reasonable in amount, and not for the purpose of evading the Law.

Premiums paid for various other types of insurance may also be excluded from the computation as, for example, where the debtor is clearly informed of his right to choose where to buy the insurance. Premiums for insurance against default need not be included but only if they are not a factor in the creditor's approval of the credit and the borrower is so informed in writing and he indicates in writing that he wants the insurance and knows its cost. Also, premiums for insurance against property damage need not be included if the borrower is informed in writing of the cost of the insurance if obtained through the creditor and that he can pick his own insurer.

The annual percentage rate is arrived at by (1) taking the nominal annual percentage rate which will yield a sum equal to the amount of the finance charge when it is applied to the unpaid balances of the amount financed, calculated according to the actuarial method of allocating payments between the amount financed and the amount of the finance charge, each payment being applied first to the accumulated finance charge and the balance to the unpaid amount financed; or (2) the rate determined by any method prescribed by the Board of Governors of the Federal Reserve System as one that materially simplifies computation and still retains reasonable accuracy. The Regulation Z Annual Percentage Rate Tables produced by the Board of Governors of the Federal Reserve System may be used to determine the annual percentage rate. (Write to Board in Washington, D.C., 20551, or to Federal Reserve Banks.)

What an Advertisement for a Mortgage Loan Must Contain: Real estate advertisements that contain consumer credit information are subject to the provisions of the Law dealing with advertising. Thus, an advertisement may not state the rate of a finance charge unless it states it as an annual percentage rate, specifically using that term.

Generally, if an advertisement states the amount of down payment or mentions that no down payment is required or the amount of any installment payment, or the number of installments, or the period of repayment, or that there is no charge for credit, it must also set forth the cash price or the amount of the loan, the amount of down payment or that no down payment is required, the number, amount, and due dates or period of payments if credit is extended, except for total of payments covering residential purchase mortgages, and the amount of finance charge expressed as an annual percentage rate.

Liabilities for Noncompliance: Failure to comply with the federal Truth-in-Lending Law can result in both civil and criminal liability. An aggrieved customer can bring a legal action for a violation not only against the original creditor, where a security interest in real property is involved, but also against assignees of the original credit where the assignees were in a continuing business relationship with the original creditor either when the credit was extended or when the assignment was made. But where the assignment was involuntary, liability will not be imposed on the assignee.

Civil penalties may be imposed if a creditor cannot prove that a violation of the Law was unintentional or was the result of a bona fide error in procedures which, if not for the error, were proper.

Amount and Nature of Penalties Which May Be Imposed: The customer is given the right to sue for twice the amount of the finance charge and he can obtain not less than $100 nor more than $1,000 in addition to costs and attorney's fees in some cases. But he will not be relieved of liability for the debt itself.

The penalty will not be imposed when the creditor, within 15 days after discovering the error and before receiving written notice of the error or the institution of the action, notifies the customer of the error and makes the necessary adjustments to insure that he won't have to pay a finance charge in excess of the amount or percentage rate actually disclosed. For "willful and knowing failure to comply with any requirement" criminal liability may be imposed in the way of a fine of up to $5,000, a prison term of up to one year, or both. The U.S. Attorney General is given the authority to prosecute.

Evidence of compliance with the "truth" provisions of the Law should be preserved by creditors. They are required to make their records and proof of compliance available for inspection by the appropriate enforcement agency. Keep in mind that, subject to some exceptions, in an action or procedure against a creditor or its assignee, written acknowledgement of receipt by a person to whom a statement is required to be given is conclusive proof of delivery of the statement and, unless the violation appears on the face of the statement, of compliance with the Law.

What About Real Estate and Mortgage Brokers? The NAR advises that those REALTORS who own or operate separate, independent mortgage banking or lending facilities, and those who have a ''financial tie-in with the actual lender'' may be held responsible for compliance. Likewise, a real estate broker who prepares a contract of sale and who is aware of the credit terms of the sale may also be held responsible under the Law. Individual mortgage originators and those who occasionally extend credit under second mortgages may be held liable.

[¶902] Real Estate Settlement Procedures Act

Finding that significant reforms in the real estate settlement process were needed to insure that homeowners are provided with greater and more timely information on the nature and costs of the settlement process, Congress enacted the Real Estate Settlement Procedures Act of 1974. Under this Law, which became effective on June 20, 1975, lenders making federally related mortgage loans are required to disclose to buyers and sellers the various costs of settlement.

On January 2, 1976, President Ford signed into law the RESPA Amendments of 1975, the effect of which was to repeal and modify the controversial provisions of the original Act. The Amendments repealed §6 (advance disclosure and waiting period) and §7 (seller disclosure of previous selling price). The Amendments also did away with page 3 of settlement statement, which dealt with Truth-in-Lending. The following summarizes the provisions of RESPA, as per the 1975 Amendments.

Federally Related Mortgage Loans: The HUD Regulations issued pursuant to the '75 Amendments provide that RESPA applies to all federally related mortgage loans, which for definitional purposes means loans that meet the following requirements (and are not made to finance exempt transactions (see below)):

(1) The proceeds of the loan are used in whole or in part to finance the purchase by the borrower, or other transfer of title, of the mortgaged property;

(2) The loan is secured by a first lien or other first security interest covering real estate, including a fee simple, life estate, remainder interest, ground lease, or other long-term leasehold estate,

(i) Upon which there is located a structure designed principally for the occupancy of from 1 to 4 families; or

(ii) Upon which there is located a mobile home; or

(iii) Upon which a structure designed principally for the occupancy of from 1 to 4 families is to be constructed using proceeds of the loan; or

(iv) Upon which there will be placed a mobile home to be purchased using proceeds of the loan; or

(v) Which is a 1- to 4-family residential condominium unit (or the first lien covering a cooperative unit);

(3) The mortgaged property is located in a state; and

(4) The loan (i) is made by a lender meeting certain specified requirements, or (ii) is made in whole or in part, or insured, guaranteed, supplemented, or assisted in any way, by the Secretary or any other officer or agency of the Federal Government, or (iii) is made in connection with a housing or urban development program administered by the Secretary or other agency of the Federal Government, or (iv) is intended to be sold by the originating lender to the Federal National Mortgage Association (FNMA), the Government National Mortgage Association (GNMA), or the Federal Home Loan Mortgage Corporation (FHLMC), or to a financial institution which intends to sell the mortgage to FHLMC.

As used in the above definition, exempt transaction refers to the following:

(1) A loan to finance the purchase or transfer of a property of 25 or more acres;

(2) A home improvement loan, loan to refinance, or other loan where the proceeds are not used to finance the purchase or transfer of the property. Execution of an instrument creating a security interest is not considered to be a transfer of the property for purposes of this part;

(3) A loan to finance the purchase or transfer of a vacant lot, where no proceeds of the loan are to be used for the construction of a 1- to 4-family residential structure or for the purchase of a mobile home to be placed on the lot;

(4) An assumption, novation, or sale or transfer subject to a pre-existing loan, except the use of or conversion of a construction loan to a permanent mortgage loan to finance purchase by the first user;

(5) A construction loan, except where the construction loan is intended to be used as or converted to a permanent loan to finance purchase by the first user;

(6) A permanent loan the proceeds of which will be used to finance the construction of a 1- to 4-family structure, where the lot is already owned by the borrower or borrowers; or

(7) A loan to finance the purchase of a property where the primary purpose of the purchase is for resale.

Good Faith Estimates of Costs: Lenders of federally related mortgage loans are required to provide borrowers with copies of HUD's Special Information Booklet. The Special Information Booklet is to be given to the borrower on the day his loan application is made or it may be mailed to him within three business days after the lender receives his application. Along with the Information Booklet, the lender is to provide the borrower at the same time, with a good faith estimate (based upon the lender's experience, and information then available to the lender) of the following settlement charges (if a good faith estimate of a specific charge cannot be made, the lender is to provide a good faith estimate of the range of charges): (1) Title search; (2) Title examination; (3) Attorney's certificate of title; (4) Title insurance binder; (5) Attorney's fees; (6) Preparation of documents; (7) Survey; (8) Credit report; (9) Appraisal; (10) Pest and similar inspections; (11) Notary fees; (12) Closing fee; (13) Recording fees, stamps, and similar fees; (14) Transfer tax, mortgage tax, stamps, and similar fees; and (15) other settlement services.

Uniform Settlement Statement Form: Section 4 of RESPA requires the person conducting the settlement, whether or not he is the lender, to use the Uniform Settlement Statement (HUD Form 1). The Settlement Statement itemizes the various closing costs that are to be paid by the seller and the borrower, except those charges the parties have agreed to pay separately.

The borrower, if he so requests, may inspect the completed Uniform Settlement Statement during the day before settlement. Otherwise, the person conducting the settlement must make the statement available for the borrower's inspection not later than at settlement. The Statement is to be delivered or mailed to the borrower or seller at or before settlement.

The borrower may, however, waive his right to inspect the completed Uniform Settlement Statement, by executing, prior to settlement, a written waiver. In such a case the completed HUD Form 1 is to be mailed or delivered to the seller or borrower "at the earliest practicable date."

Title Insurance: A seller of real estate that will be financed by a federally related mortgage is prohibited from requiring, directly or indirectly, as a condition of sale that title insurance from a particular title company be purchased by the buyer. If a seller violates this provision of the Act, he will be liable to the buyer for a sum of money that is equal to three times all the charges made for such title insurance. This section has not been changed by the '75 Amendments.

Limitation on Escrow Accounts: Lenders are restricted as to the amount of advance deposits that they can require buyers to place in escrow accounts for the purpose of insuring payment of real estate taxes and insurance. Under the Act, borrowers may be required by lenders to place in escrow no more than the amounts due and payable at the time of settlement, plus one-twelfth of the estimated total amount that will be due during the first year after the closing. The Amendments revised this section to remove various technical deficiencies.

No Fee: RESPA §12 prohibits lenders from charging fees for the preparation or distribution of the statements required under RESPA or the Truth-in-Lending Act.

Prohibition Against Kickbacks and Unearned Fees: Section 8 of RESPA prohibits kickbacks and the splitting of unearned fees, stating: "(a) No person shall give and no person shall accept any fee, kickback, or thing of value pursuant to any agreement or understanding, oral or otherwise, that business incident to or part of a real estate settlement service involving a federally related mortgage loan shall be referred to any person.

"(b) No person shall give and no person shall accept any portion, split, or percentage of any charge made or received for the rendering of a real estate settlement service in connection with a transaction involving a federally related mortgage loan other than for services actually performed."

The Amendments specifically exempt from §8 "payments pursuant to cooperative brokerage and referral arrangements or agreements between real estate agents and brokers." Also exempted from the provision are fees paid to attorneys for services actually rendered, fees paid to title companies or their agents, and several other types of settlement related services.

Act's Relation to State Law: The Act does not exempt lenders from complying with any state law (i.e., does not override any state law) regarding settlement practices. However, if any state law is inconsistent with the Act (as determined by the Secretary of HUD), then the Act will override the state law, but only to the extent of the state law's inconsistency. If a state law is inconsistent with the Act but offers consumers greater protection than the Act, then the state law will override the Act.

[¶903] Fair Credit Reporting Act

Through an amendment to the Consumer Credit Reporting Act of 1970, the Fair Credit Reporting Act became effective on April 25, 1971. This Act provides that if a consumer (other than a corporation) is denied credit for personal, family, or household purposes or the charge for such credit is increased because of information obtained from a consumer reporting agency, the consumer must be advised why such action is being taken. The creditor using adverse information obtained from a consumer reporting agency must notify the consumer that he has a right to request the reasons why he has been denied credit or why the charge was increased if the consumer's request for such information is received within 60 days after he learns of the action.

The Act also provides the following: Only if the consumer is first notified may investigative reports be commenced, obsolete information may not be used, the consumer is entitled to know the "nature and substance" of information contained in his file (although he can't examine the file) and the consumer is entitled to include in his file a 100-word statement of his side of any dispute on file.

[¶904] Equal Credit Opportunity Act

On October 28, 1975, the Equal Credit Act and Regulation B implementing the Act became effective.

Regulation B (12 CFR 202), issued by the Board of Governors of the Federal Reserve System, applies to people who offer, extend, or arrange to extend credit. These extenders of credit are prohibited from discriminating on the basis of sex or marital status in any aspect of the credit transaction. This means that a creditor may not discourage an applicant from requesting credit based on his or her sex. The Law requires that applicants be furnished with a notice of their rights under the Equal Credit Opportunity Act, which they may keep.

Limitation: Regulation B sets forth some rules with regard to information that creditors may require of applicants. Here, briefly, are the restrictions on inquiries.

(1) The application form must be neutral as to sex. Terms such as Mr., Mrs., Ms, or Miss may be used, but the form must conspicuously state that the choice of using such designation is to be optional with the applicant.

(2) Creditors are restricted on questions about the applicant's marital status. If the creditor does inquire about the applicant's marital status, only the terms married, unmarried, or separated may be used.

(3) Creditors cannot inquire about birth control practices or the parties' intentions or capabilities with regard to childbearing.

(4) Information about the applicant's spouse or former spouse is restricted unless that spouse will be contractually liable on the account (indebtedness) or the applicant is relying on alimony, child support, or maintenance payments from a spouse or former spouse as a basis for repaying the loan. With

regard to this information, it must be pointed out that the creditor may not ask whether the applicant will rely on alimony, child support, or maintenance payments to repay the loan unless the applicant is first advised that he or she need not answer such a question, nor need he or she rely on such a source of income in his credit application.

Restrictions on Evaluation: Regulation B sets forth some restrictions with regard to the creditor's evaluation of the application:

(1) A creditor may not discount the income of an applicant or of an applicant's spouse on the basis of sex or marital status, nor may part-time income be discounted.

(2) A creditor may not take sex or marital status into account in a credit scoring system or other method of evaluating an application.

(3) In certain situations where a person applies for credit independently of his or her spouse or former spouse, the creditor may not consider any information that is unfavorable about the excluded spouse or former spouse if the applicant can show that such information does not relate to him or her.

(4) A creditor may not take into account, in scoring or evaluating an application, the fact that a telephone listing exists in the applicant's name, but a creditor may take into account the existence of a telephone in the applicant's home.

It should be pointed out that a creditor may require a married or separated applicant who applies for a mortgage or deed of trust to sign with his or her spouse on instruments that are necessary under state law to create a valid lien, pass clear title, waive inchoate rights to property, or assign earnings.

Denial of Application: The Regulation requires a creditor to promptly notify an applicant about its decision. If the application is denied, the applicant may request the creditor to tell him why. If the applicant requests the creditor to supply him with such information, the creditor must comply, even if the denial is for reasons other than sex or marital status. The creditor's statement may be in any form he chooses and may be in writing or oral.

Enforcement: The Act provides that a person injured because of a violation of the Equal Credit Opportunity Act may sue the creditor for actual damages. In addition, the aggrieved party may request punitive damages up to $10,000; if a class action is brought, the limit is $100,000 or 1% of the creditor's net worth, whichever is less. The person injured by a violation of the Act may bring an action to enjoin the violation. The statute of limitations for such actions is one year from the date of violation.

Prohibitions Extended by 1976 Amendments: Amendments to the Equal Credit Opportunity Act provide that as of March 23, 1974, it is illegal for lenders to discriminate against applicants for credit:

(1) On the basis of race, color, religion, national origin, sex or marital status, or age (provided the applicant has the capacity to contract);

(2) Because all or part of the applicant's income derives from any public assistance program; or

(3) Because the applicant has in good faith exercised any right under the Consumer Credit Protection Act.

[¶1000] GOVERNMENT PROGRAMS FOR FINANCING REAL ESTATE

There are many federal programs directly involved in financing or subsidizing real estate development. The creation of the cabinet-level Department of Housing & Urban Development as successor to the Housing & Home Finance Agency, reflected the growth of the trend in this direction. When Congress adopted the Housing & Urban Development Act of 1968, it set up the most comprehensive housing program this country has ever seen.

Later, housing acts have considerably liberalized many of the FHA programs, added new programs, and, in conjunction with the tax laws, hold out strong tax and financing incentives to the private sector to meet the growing need for apartments, particularly for low- and moderate-income families.

HUD-FHA insures mortgages on homes and on multifamily projects of rental housing, cooperative and condominium housing, housing for members of the Armed Services, and housing especially designed for elderly persons. It insures mortgages on both homes and multifamily housing in urban renewal areas, as well as mortgages on relocation housing for families moving from urban renewal areas or displaced by some kind of governmental action. FHA also insures loans for repairs and improvements to homes and other properties.

By insuring the mortgage, FHA protects the lender against loss. With this protection, the lender can accept a smaller down payment from the buyer and can allow him a longer time to repay the loan. The FHA limits the interest rate and other charges and it must determine as far as possible that the transaction is a sound one. The FHA (and also the VA) may adjust the interest rate ceiling according to market conditions.

HUD-FHA does not designate entire communities or areas as ineligible for participation in its mortgage insurance operations. Instead, eligibility is established in response to an application and compliance with prescribed eligibility standards and criteria. This is done on a case-by-case basis and places major emphasis on the eligibility of the property being examined. This policy permits use of all mortgage insurance programs in any area provided the individual transaction meets the eligibility requirements.

[¶1001] How to Check Out an FHA Submission

Regardless of what HUD program you happen to be interested in, you want to cut down on the time it takes to process your submission. If your submission gives all the required information in the proper form, this should help avoid unnecessary delays in processing. So, it's a good idea to review your submission to make sure it's as complete as possible. Here's a list of items that you should be especially careful to keep in mind.

(1) Make sure the application is accurate and complete and contains all required signatures.

(2) Make sure that exhibits contain all the necessary signatures.

(3) Are the proper supporting exhibits included where VA compliance inspections are involved?

(4) Do the correct address and legal description of the property appear on the application? Are the lot dimensions correct? How about recorded easements, liens, or other encumbrances?

(5) How about necessary supplemental exhibits?

(6) Be sure to review drawings and Form 2005 (description of materials) for completeness and signatures.

(7) State the section of the National Housing Act under which the application is submitted.

(8) Be sure to submit the required number of copies of forms and exhibits.

(9) Make sure that the plans and specifications coincide as to materials and construction methods.

(10) Where the plans or specifications show optional items, check to see whether the application indicates clearly which alternates apply.

(11) Are all critical points in the construction and all unusual combinations of materials described in detail?

(12) Are necessary sections through fireplaces and stairways properly shown?

(13) Make sure that all the heat loss calculations, which must be included with all the applications, are complete.

(14) Plot plans should comply with requirements as stated in FHA Minimum Property Standards.

(15) Has provision been made for exterior storage for tools, garden equipment, bicycles, etc.?

(16) Where dealing with a request for an increased commitment, make sure it includes supporting market data. Cite recent sales of comparable properties.

(17) Is the request for change signed?

(18) When necessary to describe the change, be sure that the description of materials and the drawings are included.

(19) How about combining the requests?

[¶1002] How FHA Estimates a Mortgage Application

In judging the feasibility of insuring a mortgage, FHA relates all the factors covered in three estimates which it makes with respect to ability to meet monthly payments on the mortgage. The three estimates are: (1) An estimate of dependable income—what you have as dependable, continuing income. (2) An estimate of prospective monthly housing expenses—what it will cost you to occupy the property. (3) An estimate of all debts, living costs, and other financial obligations.

Dependable Income: Since a long period of time is usually involved in paying off the mortgage obligation, the prospect of increasing your income above your regular salary is seldom a safe basis for determining the amount of housing expense you will be able to pay. A realistic estimate of your current dependable income is a sounder basis. In estimating dependable income, FHA screens out all income except that of a continuing nature.

Income derived from overtime work, from employment of members of the family, from return on a capital investment, from the renting of a room, or from the rendering of occasional personal services can rarely be viewed as dependable, continuing income. Salaries of working wives may be considered effective for this purpose when their employment has been established as a part of the family life. Ordinarily, it would not be reasonable to conclude that a wife's employment is a definite pattern of the family life if she has been married only a short time or has been employed only recently.

Housing Expenses: FHA compares your prospective housing expense with the housing expense you are used to paying. If the prospective expense is greater and you have been unable to save any money while paying the smaller amount there will be more risk in your undertaking the additional expense.

Debts, Living Costs, Etc.: In arriving at a conclusion as to what is a safe relationship between your prospective housing expense and your net effective income, FHA gives due consideration to the housing expenses normal for your income bracket and to your use of installment credit as reflected in the items on your family budget. The relation between your total financial obligations and your net effective income is also very important.

The only sure way of evaluating potential risk when you buy a home is to use good judgment—your own best judgment combined with the sound judgment furnished by experienced mortgage lenders and by the FHA.

[¶1003] Summary of Major HUD Programs

Here we give you a quick rundown of important HUD programs showing their nature and purpose.

Major HUD Programs

Project	*Section of the National Housing Act*	*Who Qualifies*	*Purpose*	*Limitations*
		Community Development Program		
Community Development Block Grants.	Title I.	State and local governments and units thereof; new community development and new community citizen's associations.	Localities have decision-making power over how and where grants will be spent. Community Development projects might include urban beautification; historic preservation, water, sewer, neighborhood facilities, urban renewal, open space conservation and recreational facilities.	Compliance with federal planning requirements and assistance programs.
		Single-Family Homes		
Property improvement and mobile home insurance.	Title I	HUD-approved private lending institutions that make qualified loans.	Improving property (i.e., repairs, alterations, and modernization of private residences, apartment buildings, certain commercial and farm buildings) and purchasing mobile home for buyer's residence.	Generally $10,000 limit; payment within 12 years, and maximum financing charge of 12% per annum.
Basic home mortgage insurance.	203 (b)	Homebuyer with income sufficient to meet mortgage payments.	Purchase of 1-4 family dwelling.	Loan-to-value ratios; payment within 30 or 35 years and in-

	National Housing Act			terest rate ceiling of 9-1/2% per annum.
Home mortgage insurance for disaster victims.	203(h)	Occupant-mortgagor whose home is destroyed in disaster.	Reconstruction or replacement of damaged home within declared disaster area.	Application must be made within one year of disaster (later if federal assistance still being extended). $14,000 limit, payment within 30-35 years and interest rate ceiling of 9-1/2% per annum.
Home mortgage insurance for outlying properties.	203(i)	Occupant or nonoccupant mortgagor.	Purchase of properties in rural areas or of farm housing situated on 5 or more acres of land next to highway.	Loan-to-value ratios, interest rate ceilings of 9-1/2% per annum and payment within 30 or 35 years.
Loan insurance for major home improvements.	203(k)	Owner or lessee with a 99-year lease or a lease expiring 10 years beyond mortgage maturity date.	Major improvements or alterations of structures containing 1-4 family units. Property must be 10-years old or if newer, improvements must be necessary to correct structural defects or to repair casualty damage.	Generally limit of $12,000; interest rate ceiling of 9-1/2% per annum and payment within lesser of 20 years or 3/4 of the remaining economic life.
Urban renewal mortgage insurance.	220	Occupant or nonoccupant mortgagor.	Purchase or rehabilitation of 1-11 family units in urban renewal, code enforcement, or natural disaster areas receiving federal assistance.	Loan-to-value ratio or statutory limits based on size of structure, interest rate ceiling of 9-1/2% per annum, and payment within 30 or 35 years.
Insured improvement loans in urban renewal areas	220(h)	Occupant or nonoccupant mortgagor.	Alterations, repairs, or improvements to structures with	Loan-to-value ratio or statutory maximum, interest rate

Project	*Section of the National Housing Act*	*Who Qualifies*	*Purpose*	*Limitations*
			1-11 family units in qualified urban areas.	ceiling of 9-1/2% per annum, and payment within lesser of 20 years or 3/4 of the remaining economic life.
Mortgage insurance for servicemen.	222	Buyer presently on active duty in the armed forces for more than two years.	Purchase of a single-family home as a residence.	Loan-to-value ratio in statutory maximum, interest rate ceiling of 9-1/2% per annum, and payment within lesser of 30-35 years or 3/4 of the remaining economic life.
Miscellaneous housing insurance.	223(e)	Mortgagors.	Extend insurance to mortgagors of properties disqualified from other programs because of location.	Discretionary with HUD, but generally subject to limits of the program disqualified because of location.
Mortgage insurance for experimental housing.	233	Mortgagor.	Construct or rehabilitate housing utilizing advanced technology or experimental neighborhood design.	Generally same limits as the programs that would otherwise apply.
Homeownership for lower income families. (Mortgage insurance plus mortgage payment subsidy.)	235	Low-income mortgagor.	Purchase of a single-family home as a residence. (No commitments are presently being issued.)	Low-income families only may qualify.
Home mortgage insurance, special credit risks.	237	Mortgagor ineligible for other income mortgage programs due to bad credit or income history.	Purchase of single-family residence.	Must become an acceptable risk when provided with credit and debt management counselling.
Purchase of fee simple title from lessors.	240	Lessee owning a home subject to a leasehold.	Purchasing a fee simple title from the lessor.	Loan-to-value ratio in statutory maximum, interest rate ceiling of 9-1/2% per annum,

				and payment within lesser of 20 years or 3/4 of the remaining economic life.
		Multifamily Programs		
Multifamily rental housing insurance.	207	Profit motivated corporations, trusts, partnerships, and individuals.	Development or rehabilitation of rental housing for moderate- and middle-income families. Must contain eight or more units.	Subject to the lesser of loan-to-value ratios or regulatory dollar limits per family unit and to a term limit that is the lesser of 40 years or 3/4 of the economic life.
Mobile home parks.	207	Individuals, partnerships, corporations, or any other approved legal entity.	Construct or rehabilitate mobile home parks. The real estate involved must be held in fee simple or under a long-term lease.	Subject to the lesser of the loan-to-value ratio or regulatory dollar limits and to a term limit of 40 years.
Rental housing for low- and moderate-income families.	221(d)(3)	Mortgagors (nonprofit, public, limited distribution entities, cooperative and investor sponsors, profit motivated, and public housing agencies)	Construct or rehabilitate de tached, semidetached, walk up, or elevator housing of fiv or more units.	Subject to the lesser of loan-to-value ratio or regulatory dollar limits per family unit and to a term limit that is the lesser of 40 years or 3/4 of the economic life. There are no limits as to tenant income but priority given to displaced families.
Mortgage insurance for moderate-income housing projects.	221(d)(4)	Individuals, partnerships, corporations, or other approved legal entity, excluding nonprofit, limited dividend, cooperative, and public mortgagors. (Developer may be	Construct or rehabilitate rental housing for moderate income families. Projects must have at least five residential units of detached, semi-detached, row, walk-up, or	Mortgages are subject to the lesser of loan-to-value ratio or regulatory dollar limits, and to a term of 40 years at the allowable interest rate. No income requirements for ten-

Project	*Section of the National Housing Act*	*Who Qualifies*	*Purpose*	*Limitations*
		entitled to the Builders' Profit and Risk Allowance).	elevator type multifamily units. The real estate involved must be held in fee simple or under a lease with a remaining period of 50 years or more.	ants, but priority given to persons displaced by urban renewal or other governmental action.
Mortgage insurance for buying or refinancing existing multifamily housing projects.	223(f)	Owners of multifamily housing projects. Financing also available for multifamily projects that were under construction before June 30, 1974, and completed by December 31, 1975.	Refinancing existing mortgages over a longer period of time and/or at a lower interest rate. Projects must have at least eight residential units and limited commercial area and income.	Subject to loan-to-value ratio, to a term limit that is the lesser of 35 years or 3/4 of remaining economic life, and to the prevailing maximum interest rate.
Housing mortgage insurance for the elderly.	231	Individuals, partnerships, corporations, public mortgagors, and other approved legal entities. (Developer may be entitled to the Builders' Profit and Risk Allowance.)	Construction or rehabilitation of rental housing for elderly or handicapped persons. Real estate involved must be held in fee simple or under a long term lease.	Subject to the lesser of loan-to-value ratio or regulatory dollar limits per family unit and to a term limit that is the lesser of 40 years or 3/4 of the economic life. There are no limits as to tenant income.
Nursing home and intermediate care facilities mortgage insurance.	232	Mortgagors.	Construct or rehabilitate a single health care facility or a combination of related facilities containing at least 20 beds. The mortgage amount includes the cost of equipment for operating the facility.	Projects are subject to the controlling state and federal licencing and operating standards. Subject to a limit of 90% of the value and to a term of 40 years.
Rental and cooperative housing for lower income families. (Mortgage insurance	236	Nonprofit organizations, cooperatives, limited dividend entities, or a builder-	Construction or rehabilitation of rental and cooperative housing for lower income families.	Subject to unit dollar limits and to a term limit that is the lesser of 40 years or 3/4 of the economic life.

plus mortgage payment subsidy).		seller mortgagor intending to sell the project to a nonprofit organization. (No new contract authority since Congress authorized $75 million in 1975.)		
Supplemental loans for project mortgage insurance.	241	Mortgagors insured under one of the HUD-FHA programs may apply for an additional insured loan.	Finance improvements or additions to the insured property (multifamily project, a nursing home, an intermediate care facility, or a group practice facility). Supplemental loans may also be used to purchase furniture and equipment for these facilities.	Subject to a dollar limit according to value of improvement and maximum mortgage amount and to a term not exceeding the existing mortgage.
Mortgage insurance for hospitals.	242	Profit and nonprofit organizations.	Construction and rehabilitation of hospital facilities and/or the purchase of major movable hospital equipment. Real estate involved must be held in fee simple or under a long-term lease.	Subject to limit of 90% of the replacement value, a term limit of 25 years and to the prevailing maximum interest rate. The hospital proposal must be approved by the Secretary of Health, Education and Welfare.
Group practice facilities.	Title XI	An organization willing to operate a facility on a nonprofit basis.	Construction or rehabilitation of facilities and/or the purchase of equipment for the group practice of medicine, dentistry, optometry, osteopathy, and/or podiatry. Real estate involved must be held in fee simple or under a long-term lease.	Subject to a limit of 90% of replacement value. HEW reviews the need for the facility, and the applicant must show inability to obtain a comparable uninsured loan.

Project	*Section of the National Housing Act*	*Who Qualifies*	*Purpose*	*Limitations*
Mortgage insurance for land development.	Title X	Private land developer.	The purchase of undeveloped acreage to be adapted to building and related sites. Real estate involved must be held in fee simple or under a long-term lease.	Subject to loan-to-value ratio, to a term of 10 years, and a 9-1/2% interest rate per annum.
		Condominium Programs		
Mortgage insurance for condominiums. Note: Units in a condominium may also qualify under §235 and §236.	234 and 221(i)	Developers constructing or rehabilitating a multifamily project. Buyers of units within a condomium project, covered by FHA insured mortgage.	The construction or rehabilitation of a multifamily project that will be set up as a condominium with family-unit ownership and the purchase of individual units.	Subject to loan-to-value ratios, payment within 40 years and prevailing approved interest rate.
		Cooperative Housing Programs		
Cooperative housing mortgage insurance.	213 and 221(d)(3)	Developers, a nonprofit cooperative ownership housing corporation or trust, and/or a nonprofit corporation or trust. Buyers of membership interests in such cooperatives.	The construction or rehabilitation of structures to be owned and operated as a cooperative. Supplementary cooperative loans are available to finance (a) improvements or repairs of cooperatives (b) community facilities to serve cooperative occupants (c) cooperative purchases and resales of memberships.	Subject to loan-to-value ratios, payment within 40 years and prevailing approved interest rate.
		Leasing		
Leased housing assistance payments program.	8	Private or public owners of single-family units, multi-	Housing assistance payments to subsidize the rental pay-	Housing Assistance Payments Contracts bind HUD to make

	National Housing Act			
		family apartments, congregate housing, and new mobile homes.	ments of low- and very low-income tenants.	the subsidy payments and may have a term up to five years and can be renewed three times for a total of 20 years.
		Industrialized Housing		
Industrialized Housing.	201 and 207(a) of NHA	Housing manufacturer.	Construction of industrialized housing which includes modular housing, panel-type construction and on-site fabrication.	The manufacturer must have independent funding to finance the costs of construction, because HUD cannot insure a construction loan until the unit is placed on the foundation at the building site. The manufacturer is subject to a series of inspections during the manufacturing stage and to various building codes affecting the site location.

[¶1004] Loans Backed by Veterans Administration

Various provisions making VA-backed loans quite attractive to lenders and to veterans have been adopted. For example, the interest rate ceiling on these loans can, by virtue of statute, be readily adjusted to meet the demands of the money market. The VA can give higher guarantees against losses than ever before. Also, qualified veterans can pay more than the appraised value of a home although the loan itself must not be greater than the VA's estimate of reasonable value.

Eligibility: To be entitled to participate in the GI home loan program, the borrower must be a World War II veteran, a veteran of the Korean Conflict, a widow of a World War II or Korean Conflict serviceman, or a Cold War Veteran. In addition, the borrower must meet the following eligibility requirements:

World War II Veterans: The eligilbility requirements for World War II veterans are:

(1) Active military or naval service on or after September 16, 1940, and prior to July 26, 1947.

(2) A discharge or separation under other than dishonorable conditions.

(3) At least 90 days' total service unless discharged earlier for a service-connected disability.

Amount of VA Guarantee or Insurance: The amount of guarantee or insurance benefits available under the VA-guaranteed home loan program for a particular loan is spoken of as the "entitlement." The maximum entitlement available for a home loan (including a farm home) is reduced by the amount of any guarantees used by the veteran for other purposes, such as, for example, a VA-guaranteed business loan.

"Double Veterans": Some men may be eligible to participate in the VA-guaranteed home loan program because they are veterans of both World War II and the Korean Conflict, or because of service in the Korean Conflict and Cold War service, or because of service in all three periods of conflict. In such a case, the veteran's present entitlement is determined by his latest period of eligible service, any entitlement remaining from a prior period of service being canceled out. Further, his present entitlement usually will be reduced by the amount of guarantee used in the prior entitlement if (1) the veteran still owns at the time of application the home for which he used the prior entitlement or (2) the VA incurred a loss that has not been repaid on a loan taken with the prior entitlement. In addition, under the Cold War classification, an individual who is eligible as a serviceman will not gain additional entitlement when he is released or separated from the service.

Under What Circumstances Can a Veteran's Entitlement Be Restored? A veteran who has used up his entitlement can have it restored under various circumstances: Where the property for which he made the loan has been destroyed or badly damaged by fire or other natural hazard. Where he has been forced to sell through no fault of his own, as where he has had to sell for reasons of health, condemnation by federal, state, or local government, or other compelling reasons. Where he has had to sell because he has obtained a new and better job in a different city (even though the job change was voluntary). Where he is on active duty and is compelled to sell because he has been transferred under military orders.

Veterans of the Korean Conflict: The eligibility requirements for veterans of the Korean Conflict period are:

(1) Discharge or separation under other than dishonorable conditions.

(2) Active military or naval service at any time on or after June 27, 1950, and prior to February 1, 1955.

(3) At least 90 days' total service unless discharged earlier for a service-connected disability.

The expiration of an eligible Korean Conflict veteran's entitlement is governed by the same formula that applies to eligible World War II veterans, i.e., ten years from discharge or release from active duty in the Korean Conflict, plus an additional period equal to one year for each three months of active duty in that conflict.

Cold War Veterans: Veterans who served on active duty for more than 180 days or were discharged for disability, any part of which occurred after January 31, 1955, and who were discharged or released under conditions other than dishonorable are eligible. Persons whose military service after January 31, 1955, consisted of "active duty for training," however, are not eligible.

Members of the U.S. armed forces who have served at least two years in active duty status, even though not discharged, are eligible while their service continues without breaks.

The conditions for having an entitlement restored are that the veteran has paid off the previous VA-loan and sold the property, or that he has sold his home to another veteran who took over the VA-loan, using his own entitlement. The VA will release a veteran when he sells his home to a person who is a good credit risk and who assumes liability for repaying the amount of the loan still outstanding.

Note: Under legislation passed in 1976, veterans who served between July 25, 1947 and June 27, 1950, are now eligible for home loans.

Lenders That Can Make VA-Backed Loans: A VA-backed home loan may be made by any recognized lender to which persons normally go to borrow money. The lender may be an individual lender, a mortgage bank, a commercial bank, a mutual savings bank, or a savings and loan association. Insurance companies, pension plans and trusts, and any other public or private lending source that is able to finance and service loans may also make such a loan. Lenders are divided by the VA into two classes: "supervised" and "nonsupervised."

Supervised Lenders: These are lenders that are subject to examination by a federal or state agency or that have been approved as FHA lenders. This type of lender can make a GI home loan that will be guaranteed by the VA without first getting the VA's approval. The lender simply closes the loan and reports it to the VA for guaranty after the loan proceeds have been disbursed.

Nonsupervised Lenders: All lenders that are not subject to examination by a federal or state authority or that have not been approved as FHA lenders are considered to be nonsupervised lenders. In order to make a loan that will receive a VA guarantee, this type of lender must proceed in the following manner: The lender must first file an application with the VA. If the VA finds that the loan is eligible for guarantee, it sends the lender a commitment. On receipt of the commitment, the lender closes the loan and reports it to the VA for guarantee.

General Terms and Requirements of VA-Backed Loans: *(1) Amount of Loan:* There is no limit on the amount of a VA-guaranteed home loan. This is a matter between the lender and the borrower. However, as already noted, the amount of the VA guarantee or insurance is subject to limitations.

(2) Interest Rate: The VA is authorized to set the same interest rate on GI home loans that the FHA permits under its home loan program.

(3) Down Payment, Maturity, and Prepayment Rights: VA home loans may be made for a maximum term of 25 years but in certain situations this may be extended to a maximum term of 30 years. The law does not require down payments. However, since VA-guaranteed home loans are made by private lenders, the amount of down payment and the length of the repayment period are matters to be agreed upon between the lender and the veteran. But, the veteran must be given the right to prepay the entire indebtedness at any time without a premium or fee and to make partial payments on principal in amounts of one installment or $100, whichever is less. The usual practice in cases of full prepayment, if not made on an installment due date, is to charge pro rata interest to date of prepayment. Partial payments of principal are accepted on due dates.

(4) Required VA Fee: A borrower who is a veteran must pay to the VA a

"one-shot" fee of $50 or one percent of the amount of the loan, whichever is greater. This fee must be paid in cash and may not be paid out of the proceeds of the loan.

(5) Allowable Closing Costs: Closing expenses may include title search and survey costs, appraisal and credit report fees, prorated insurance premiums, recording charges, taxes, and other prepaid items.

(6) Broker's Commissions: In no case may a brokerage or other fee be required of a veteran for obtaining a GI home loan.

(7) Taxes, Insurance, and Assessments: In addition to the monthly installments of principal and interest that are due under the loan, the borrower is required to make monthly payments to the VA for deposits sufficient to cover taxes, other insurance premiums, and assessments. The VA's regulations require borrowers to maintain insurance against fire and other hazards and, where necessary, flood insurance. The borrower is required to pay to the VA at closing what the VA estimates may be necessary as an initial deposit in his tax and insurance reserve account.

(8) Safeguards: A veteran's property must meet or exceed minimum requirements for planning, construction, and general acceptability, unless the home was completed at least a year before it was purchased with a GI loan. The VA may refuse to appraise any dwelling or housing project owned or built by anyone who has attempted to take unfair advantage of veterans or who has declined to sell a newly constructed home to an eligible veteran because of his race, color, creed, or national origin. Lenders who have declined to make a guaranteed or insured home loan to an eligible veteran because of the applicant's race, color, creed, or national origin may be suspended from participation in the VA loan program.

(9) Warranty: On new homes appraised by VA on or after October 1, 1954, builders are required to give veteran-purchasers a warranty that their homes have been constructed in "substantial conformity" with VA-approved plans and specifications.

(10) Certification: A veteran must certify that he intends to live in the home he is buying or improving with a GI loan, both at the time of application and at the time of closing the loan.

How a Resale Affects an Existing GI Loan: A veteran may sell a home purchased with a VA-backed loan to anyone, whether a veteran or nonveteran, without getting VA approval and without paying off the loan.

The buyer may take subject to the mortgage obligation or he may assume the obligation. If the buyer takes subject to the GI mortgage obligation, he is not personally liable on the debt, and the veteran remains liable. On the other hand, if the purchaser assumes the GI mortgage obligation, he becomes personally liable. In such case, the veteran also remains personally liable, unless the lender, with prior approval of the VA, consents to his release from liability.

[¶1005] Direct Loans to Veterans by the Veterans Administration

Under some circumstances, the VA may make direct loans to veterans. The veteran must live in a rural area, a small town (including a "satellite" town), or a city not near a large metropolitan area. The area in which the veteran lives must have been designated as a "housing credit shortage area." The purpose for the loan can be: (1) to buy or build a dwelling to be occupied by the veteran as his home, (2) to buy a farm on which there is a farm residence to be occupied by the veteran as his home, (3) to build on land owned by the veteran a farm residence to be occupied by the veteran as his home, or (4) to repair, alter, or improve a farm residence or other dwelling owned by the veteran and occupied by him as his home.

What Veteran Must Show: The veteran must be able to show that he can't get a loan from a private lender at a rate not in excess of the interest rate authorized for guaranteed home loans, that a loan is not available from the Secretary of Agriculture, and that the property is one for which a VA-guaranteed home loan can be made.

Commitments to Builders: The VA may make commitments to builders of homes in a direct loan area; that is, the VA may agree to reserve funds to make direct loans to veterans buying the homes. The commitments are for three months but may be extended to meet the needs in any particular case. The builder must pay a 2% nonrefundable fee for the commitment. The fee is based on the amount of funds reserved.

[¶1006] Payment of FHA Mortgage Insurance Premiums For Servicemen and Their Widows

A serviceman may buy a home subject to an existing FHA-insured mortgage, and the mortgage insurance premiums will be paid by the government. (Formerly, the government paid FHA mortgage insurance premiums only if a serviceman bought a home and had a new mortgage placed on it.)

In addition, the government will continue to pay the premiums on a mortgage for the widow of a serviceman who died in the service. Premium payments will be made for two years or until the house is sold, whichever comes first.

[¶1007] VA Loan Program for Mobile Homes And Mobile Home Lots

In order to be eligible for a mobile home loan, a veteran must have maximum home loan guaranty entitlement available for use. The VA may guarantee up to 50% of a loan for the purchase of a mobile home to be used as the borrower's principal dwelling. Here are the maximum permissible amounts and terms for mobile homes:

For single-width mobile home: $12,500 for 12 years and 32 days
For single-width mobile home and lot: $20,000 for 15 years and 32 days
For double-width mobile home: $20,000 for 20 years and 32 days
For double-width mobile home and lot: $27,500 for 20 years and 32 days
For mobile home lot: $7,500 for 12 years and 32 days

It should be pointed out that by using a mobile home loan guaranty a veteran does not give up his right to a guaranteed home loan after the mobile home loan is completely paid.

[¶1008] Farmers Home Administration

The Farmers Home Administration (FmHA), an agency within the Department of Agriculture, is the major provider of credit for rural Americans who cannot get credit from other sources at reasonable rates and terms. The agency operates under Title V of the Housing Act of 1949 (42 U.S.C. 1471).

Applications for loans are made at the agency's 1,750 local county offices, which are generally located in county seat towns. FmHA currently sponsors the following programs.

Home Loans: FmHA's basic home loan program is the §502 program, under which loans are made to families in small rural communities (populations under 20,000) for buying existing or new houses or for building, rehabilitating, or relocating single-family homes. Loan amounts include the cost of purchasing a "minimum but adequate site." In some cases the loan may also cover the price of a refrigerator, stove, washer, dryer, or the costs of water and sewage facilities.

There are no maximum mortgage amounts under the FmHA home loan program. Borrowers can get loans for up to 100% of the site's and home's FmHA appraised value. The maximum term on such loans is 33 years. However, loans are restricted by statute to amounts that are "necessary to provide adequate housing, modest in size, design, and cost." FmHA interprets this to mean that it will not ordinarily make loans on houses that contain more than 1,300 square feet.

Eligibility: In order to qualify for a §502 loan, an applicant must be without decent, safe, and sanitary housing. In addition, his income must be adequate to make payments on the house, insurance, taxes, and his other necessary living expenses.

Qualifying income levels for loans vary from one part of the country to another, and also vary from time to time. In 1974, the average adjusted income of a borrower under this program (calculated by deducting the following items from gross income: 5% of the total income, plus any temporary or unusual income, plus income of minors, and $300 per minor (dependent) living in the home) was $7,327. FmHA requires that half of its loans under this program go to low-income families—those whose adjusted incomes are less than $8,500, except in Hawaii and Guam where it is $10,700 and Alaska where it's $13,500.

Regulations under §502 require that FmHA make an appraisal "when a mortgage will be taken on real estate securing a loan of $5,000 or more." Where the loan is for more than $5,000 and scheduled to be repaid in a term exceeding 15 years, it must be secured by a mortgage.

Guaranteed Loans: Section 119 provides an FmHA mortgage insurance program in rural areas whereby FmHA insures mortgages made by private lenders to rural residents, despite their income levels. Applications are to be made to FmHA county offices. FmHA is now writing regulations for this program.

Rental Programs: Under §515, FmHA provides direct loans to sponsors for rural rental and cooperative housing occupied by eligible tenants. To be eligible, tenants must be 62 years or older or low- or moderate-income families.

Borrowers under the program may be nonprofit, profit-oriented, or "limited-profit" organizations. Borrowers are required to deposit rental income in special accounts and set up reserve funds. Profit-oriented sponsors are limited by FmHA as to how much rent they can charge tenants; limited-profit sponsors are allowed to realize up to an 8% return on their initial equity investment.

Nonprofit borrowers, cooperatives, and limited-profit borrowers can qualify for interest credits (FmHA's own interest subsidy or assistance program). Borrowers that are profit oriented are required to pay FmHA's regular loan interest rates. A borrower applying for §515 loan must show that it is not able to get credit from other sources "on terms and conditions that would enable the applicant to rent the units for amounts that are within the payment ability of eligible occupants."

The repayment period for all projects is 40 years, except projects for senior citizens where the repayment term may be as long as 50 years. Nonprofit borrowers may qualify for 100% financing from FmHA. Application is made through FmHA county offices.

Although FmHA has the authority to make loans for repairs and rehabilitation, it prefers to make loans for the construction of various types of multi-unit housing. In order to qualify, units in a project must be of modest cost, design, and size. It should be noted that loans under §515 may not be used for institutional purposes. Therefore, nursing homes will not qualify.

Condominium Loans: Under the Housing and Community Development Act of 1974, FmHA has the authority to make loans to low- and moderate-income people for the purpose of buying units in rural condominiums (§526). These loans may be made either to individuals or as blanket loans. The terms and conditions of such loans are the same as under §515.

Other FmHA Loan Programs: In addition to the above, FmHA administers some other programs relating to rural housing. These programs include the following: (1) Home repair loans (§504). These loans are available to qualified borrowers for making repairs that will make homes healthier and safer. The maximum loan rate is $5,000 and the interest rate is 1% for 20 years. (2) Disaster loans (§502). These 5% loans are available for repairing or replacing "rural" single-family homes that are destroyed by disasters (earthquakes, lightning, floods, fires, etc.), so long as the disaster was not a presidentially designated major disaster. (3) Site loans (§523 and §524). Nonprofit organizations may qualify for FmHA loans to help them finance the purchase and development of housing sites. Such sites must be sold to low- or moderate-income families or to nonprofit organizations. The repayment term is two years.

[¶1100] HOW TO OWN REAL ESTATE

In almost any new real estate venture, one of the first questions you'll be faced with is the form of business organization you should use.

The most frequent problem in this field involves a choice between a corporation or some form of "single tax" ownership (such as individual, tenancy in common or joint tenancy, partnership, or trust). When you use a corporation, there is a double tax on the income—once at the corporate level and again when it is distributed. To the extent the income can be paid out in salaries, double tax is avoided because the corporation is able to deduct salaries for tax purposes. Otherwise, the income has to be paid out in dividends (taxable at ordinary income rates) to the individual owners. Or, to the extent permitted by law, the income can be accumulated in the corporation, coming through to the individuals as capital gain when the corporation is liquidated or the stockholders sell their stock at prices reflecting the accumulated earnings.

What is involved here is a comparison between the individual tax rates of the participants against the corporate tax rate (to see if it pays to keep the income accumulating in the corporation). But in figuring the corporate tax, you must also add the tax that will be paid on terminating the corporation or selling the stock based on the accumulated income—payable at capital gain tax rate.

We must also consider the personal holding company penalty tax and how to avoid it by mixing realty with investments. Another consideration is the provision regarding the unreasonable accumulation of surplus when your corporate surplus exceeds $100,000. This might force you to pay out dividends and result in a double tax.

Another problem involves getting the corporate profits into the stockholders' hands at capital gain rates. That's usually done either by liquidating the corporation or selling the stock. But here, we have to watch out for the collapsible corporation rules that would convert this capital gain into ordinary income. What it usually requires is waiting three years after the corporation gets the property before selling the stock or liquidating—that avoids the collapsible rules.

In addition to the various considerations involving the basic taxable forms in which real estate can be held, the special problems of holding property by syndicates and by real estate investment trusts (REITs) are considered at ¶1200 and 1400.

[¶1101] How to Acquire Realty in Individual Form

There are four methods of acquiring real property in the individual form:

—Individual ownership —Tenancy in common

—Joint tenancy —Tenancy by the entirety

These forms of common ownership are ordinarily confined to small scale real estate businesses. They avoid double taxation, but they can create considerable management and control problems where a number of people are involved.

Individual Ownership: This type of ownership exists where a lone investor acquires the property solely in his or her own name and is taxed on the income just once. The net income from real estate is added to his other income and he pays a tax on the total. If he has losses, they reduce his other income. Broadly speaking, the individual may acquire:

(a) Complete ownership, called the fee simple.

(b) Ownership subject to a spouse's dower, curtesy, community, or statutory rights. Dower is a wife's right to a life estate in the husband's property after his death; curtesy is a husband's right to a life estate in the wife's property after her death; community rights are the rights each spouse has in the other's property; statutory rights are the rights of a spouse to a share in the other's estate.

(c) Ownership subject to a future reversionary interest.

Joint Tenancy: Where two or more individuals have the same ownership interest in a single parcel of realty (each owns all), with the right of survivorship (the survivor gets all), we have a joint tenancy. In most states there is a presumption that a tenancy in common is created when realty is acquired by two or more persons. (This presumption may be rebutted by stating in the deed that the acquisition is as joint tenants.) From an income tax standpoint, each joint tenant reports his own share of income and gain or loss; but if one pays more than his share of costs, he may take the full deduction. From a gift tax standpoint, if one joint tenant pays the entire cost, one-half of the cost is a taxable gift. However, the creation of a joint tenancy between husband and wife postpones the gift tax (unless an election is made immediately to tax it as a gift) until the joint tenancy is ended other than by death (Code §2515). (There is no gift tax if the joint tenants divide the proceeds in proportion to their contributions.)

As a practical matter, when a joint tenant dies, the entire value of the joint tenancy must be included in his estate unless it can be shown that part was contributed by the survivor. The survivor gets an increased tax basis for the portion of the real estate which is subject to the estate tax.

Tenancy in Common: There is a tenancy in common where two or more persons each has the same right to possession (there may be unequal shares of ownership), with no rights of survivorship (the interest of a deceased tenant in common passes as an asset to his estate). Both joint tenants and tenants in common may transfer their interests, but they cannot transfer a specific portion of the realty. Where a joint tenant transfers his interest, the transferee becomes a tenant in common with the remaining joint tenants; when a tenant in common transfers his interest, the transferee becomes a tenant in common with the other tenants in common. In most states, the presumption today is that a tenancy in common is created when realty is acquired by two or more persons. From an income tax standpoint, each tenant in common reports income and gain or loss according to his own share of ownership. From a gift tax standpoint, liability arises from the gift of an interest in a tenancy in common or if one tenant in common pays more than his share of costs. From an estate tax standpoint, the interest of a deceased tenant in common is taxed as part of his estate at its value at date of death or optional valuation date (Code §2040). The heirs get the interest in the realty at an income tax basis equal to the value used for estate tax purposes (Code §1014(b)).

Tenancy by the Entirety: This form of ownership exists where realty is owned by a husband and wife (provided they were married at the time of the acquisition) and carries the right of survivorship. In most states there is a presumption that a conveyance to a husband and wife creates a tenancy by the entirety. Both tenants together can end a tenancy by the entirety, but one cannot. From an income tax standpoint, married persons will normally file joint returns. If separate returns are filed, each tenant reports his own share of the income and gain or loss; but, if one paid more than his share of the costs, he may take the full deduction. State laws are controlling in determining the method of reporting income and gain or loss—some states follow the common law rule that a husband is entitled to all income from realty; others provide that income be divided between husband and wife. (Again, this is not important if the tenants file a joint return.) The same gift and estate tax rules that apply to a joint tenancy apply here.

[¶1102] How to Use Partnerships

This is the most common form of unincorporated business involving more than one individual. The most usual form is the general partnership which involves the combining of several individuals into one business. Each normally has a voice in management and each can bind the business by his acts.

For tax purposes, the partnership is a conduit. This means that in itself the partnership is not a taxpayer. It merely computes its income or loss, and then each partner reports on his own tax return his share of the partnership's profits or losses.

Each partner picks up his share in the tax year with or in which the partnership year ends. So, if both partnership and partners have the same tax years (e.g., the calendar year), the partners pick up their shares of the partnership's profits on their personal returns. Where the partnership and the partners have different taxable years, the partners pick up the profits in their taxable year in which the partnership year ended. For example, the partnership year ends January 31, 1976. Partners use calendar years. Each partner picks up his share of the entire partnership year's profits on his 1976 return—even though about eleven-twelfths of that partnership profit was earned in 1975. Keep in mind, however, that usually—in new partnerships, at any rate—partners and the partnership will have the same tax year. To have different tax years, you need a good business purpose and permission from the Treasury.

Partnership profits or losses retain their same nature when picked up by the partners. So, if the partnership has long-term capital gains, for example, each partner would pick up his share as a long-term capital gain.

The big advantage of the partnership—especially in real estate operations—is that only one tax is paid by the partners. The advantages of high depreciation, for example, are passed directly to the partners. Thus, where the cash profit is greater than the tax profit, the excess cash can be paid to each partner tax free. For example, gross rents might be $100,000. All cash expenses might be $50,000. Amortization payments may come to $10,000. And depreciation might be $20,000. The cash left is $40,000 ($100,000 gross rents less $50,000 expenses and $10,000 amortization). But the taxable profit is $30,000 ($100,000 less the $50,000 expenses and the $20,000 depreciation). So, while $40,000 may be distributed to the partners, they pay tax on only $30,000. On the other hand, if the property was held in a corporation, the corporation would have to pay a tax on $30,000. If it distributed any profits, they'd be taxed again in the individuals' hands.

Because of this advantage in partnerships, the Treasury looks at them very carefully to see if they are not set up so as really to resemble corporations. If that is so, the partnership may be taxed as an association (i.e., as a corporation).

Tax Factors in Partnerships: Here is a checklist of tax factors affecting the partnership form of business. These points should be borne in mind if you are considering forming a partnership.

(1) Capital Contributions: There is no gain or loss to the individual partners when they contribute cash or property to a partnership.

(2) Partnership Basis: If appreciated property is contributed to the partnership, the partner may be credited with its current value; but the tax basis for the property to the partnership is the same as the contributing partner's basis.

(3) Reallocating Deductions: With low depreciation deductions available to the partnership because of low basis of contributed property, the other partners (who may have contributed cash) suffer a tax detriment. But this can be made up to some extent by allocating a larger depreciation deduction to them and a smaller deduction to the partner contributing the property.

(4) Sale of Partnership Interest: A partner selling his interest gets capital gain or loss. Where the partnership basis is much lower than the values reflected in the sale price of the interest, the partnership can elect to boost the basis as to the new partner only.

(5) Partnership Losses: A partner's share of the partnership losses beyond his basis for his partnership interest is not deductible. To get full loss, you could make a contribution to capital before the end of the year and boost your basis.

(6) Death of a Partner: On the death of a partner, the distributive share of profit to date of death is included in the deceased partner's last tax return. If the partnership continues, the profit to the end of the partnership year will be picked up by his estate or other successor.

(7) Collapsible Partnership: If you sell your partnership interest or have it redeemed, you usually have capital gain. But where there are unrealized receivables or substantially appreciated inventory items (real estate would be inventory where the partnership or the partner was a dealer in real estate), to the extent you are paid for your share of these items, you have ordinary income. You don't have substantially appreciated inventory items unless (a) the appreciation is more than 20%, and (b) the value of the appreciated property is more than 10% of the value of all partnership property (other than money).

[¶1103] Family Partnerships

A genuine family partnership is treated like any other partnership. The usual family partnership is created by gift. This is okay if capital is a material income-producing factor in the partnership. With a service partnership (e.g., a real estate brokerage firm), you can't create a partnership interest by gift. The donee has to participate actively in the firm's operations to be recognized as a partner in a service partnership. Where a gift of a partnership interest is recognized, it does not matter that the donee is a minor or a trust. But the trust should be independent of the donor.

Sharing Partnership Income: Whether there has been a gift of a partnership interest or a sale to a member of the transferor-partner's immediate family, these rules apply for sharing the partnership's income:

(1) The donor or selling partner must first receive reasonable compensation for the services he gives to the partnership.

(2) The share of profit going to the new partner that is based on his share of the capital he now owns in the partnership cannot be greater than the proportionate shares of profit that are allocated to the other shares of capital owned by the other partners.

[¶1104] Limited Partnerships

You can create limited partnerships with anyone—even with members of a family:

Some partners must be general partners and, as such, subject to the liabilities under the law as to general partners.

Each limited partner can be entitled to a fixed percentage of the profits and losses from the operation of the business. The liability of each limited partner can be expressed not to exceed the value of his capital contribution.

General partners conduct the management of the business and are personally liable for the obligations of the partnership. As long as limited partners do not participate in the partnership's management, they are exempt from personal liability for the debts, obligations, and losses of the partnership.

On liquidation, the distributive shares of the partners can be in proportion to their partnership interests.

With the death of a limited partner, his executor or representative may have all his rights just as if he had survived and this may go on until the termination of the partnership.

The agreement should provide either that the partnership terminates on a general partner's death, bankruptcy, insanity, or transfer of his general interest or that the partnership may continue in such event only if all the general partners agree to a continuation. But there need be no effect on the life of the partnership if a limited partner goes bankrupt or becomes insane.

The agreement may fix the duration of the partnership. At the end of the agreed term, there must be either a dissolution or an agreement to go on.

Limited partnerships are most commonly used in real estate syndications. Here, we have to be careful that the partnership is not treated as an association (taxable as a corporation). Treasury Regulations now make it fairly simple to avoid association treatment.

[¶1105] Joint Ventures

The joint venture is a business form that is particularly adaptable for special-purpose investments and real estate projects that require large sums of capital and specialized experience. An experienced operator who is short of capital or doesn't want to risk all of his capital in one venture may use a joint venture arrangement to team up with one or more investors who have the necessary capital. The joint venture form is used most often in the building field. A particular project may be too big and the risks too great for a single general contractor or builder, or the combination of equipment and supervisory personnel may produce important savings in the costs of construction. Syndicates, for example, are a form of joint venture; and they are widely used for investment purposes.

Joint ventures are in many ways like partnerships, and they're treated as such for tax purposes. The main distinction between a joint venture and a partnership is that the joint venture is a special association for a specific enterprise or project—such as constructing or designing a building or large-scale land development—with no intention on the part of the associates to enter into a continuing partnership relationship or to assume partnership obligations and liabilities. Joint venturers can't represent their associates and incur liabilities on their part as freely and broadly as may partners.

A joint venture agreement should make it clear that there is an intent to associate as co-venturers for a defined purpose and should spell out a joint interest in the subject matter of the venture, a sharing of profits and losses, and a right to an accounting. The mere ownership of property as joint tenants or tenants in common won't result in a joint venture.

As already noted, a joint venture is ordinarily treated as a partnership for tax purposes. As with other entities taxed as partnerships, if there are too many corporate characteristics, the entity will be considered an association taxable as a corporation. Partnership treatment combines the advantage of an immediate write-off of losses with the elimination of the second tax at the corporate level. However, a corporation may offer other tax advantages which may, in a particular situation, outweigh the tax advantages of a partnership-joint venture arrangement, and, before deciding on either form, both forms should be considered.

A joint venture may be in the form of an association of individuals, partnerships, or corporations, or some combination of these. Some joint ventures actually incorporate, sometimes for tax reasons and sometimes to avoid unlimited liability exposure.

[¶1106] When to Use a Corporation

From an economic standpoint, the great appeal of the corporate form is the fact that the law treats it as an entity in itself, apart from its stockholders. The general advantages of the separate entity of the corporation can be summarized as follows:

(1) Continues until dissolved by law (unless certificate of incorporation limits the time).

(2) As separate entity, it can sue and be sued, hold and deal in property.

Code §351 permits the transfer of real estate by an individual to a newly organized corporation without recognition of gain if, immediately after the transfer, the individuals making the transfer own 80% of the value of all issued and outstanding stock. This will usually be the case, with the result that the desired goal can be achieved free of tax.

Where, in addition to receiving stock on the transfer, the individuals also receive money, gain would be recognized to the extent of the money received.

The assumption of any mortgage debt by the corporation or the mere acquisition of property subject to a mortgage is *not* treated as money received by the individuals unless it can be shown that the principal purpose of the assumption or acquisition was tax avoidance or that it had no bona fide business purpose (§357(b)).

(3) Stockholder has no individual liability; only his capital contribution is involved.

(4) Stock can ordinarily be sold or otherwise transferred at will.

(5) Capital can be raised by the sale of new stock, bonds, or other securities.

(6) Authority is centered in a board of directors which acts by majority agreement.

(7) As separate entity, it has credit possibility apart from stockholders; in close corporation, stock is available as collateral.

(8) Stockholders do not participate in management and professional managers are usually employed.

(9) A corporation is limited to the powers (express and implied) in its charter from the state.

In addition to these general economic and legal advantages, use of the corporate form involves a number of important tax considerations that must be taken into account in deciding what form of operation is best suited to your needs. For example:

(1) Corporate tax rate is 22% on first $25,000; 48% thereafter. This may be lower than personal rates.

(2) Income is taxed to corporation; stockholders are taxed only on dividends distributed to them, reduced by dividend exclusion and credit.

(3) Stockholders are not taxed on accumulations. However, penalty tax (§531) applies if purpose is to avoid the surtax and accumulation is beyond $150,000.

(4) A corporation may use the alternative computation for capital gains; but, unlike individuals, there is no deduction of 50% of the excess of long-term gain over short-term loss.

(5) The corporation takes a deduction for the funds it expends for its stockholder-employees for accumulation in pension or profit-sharing trusts or to pay medical expenses, group term insurance, wage continuation plans, and health and accident insurance. Within specified limits these benefits are not taxable to stockholder-employees.

(6) Compensation to officer and employee stockholders is subject to Social Security tax.

(7) Stockholder has freedom to assign his stock without consulting anyone; but earnings can't be separately assigned.

(8) Tax-exempt interest earned by a corporation is fully taxable income when distributed to the stockholders.

You also may be able, beyond accumulations, to get some money to the shareholders without a dividend tax by setting up part of your capitalization as debts to the stockholders. Interest to the stockholders would be taxable to them, but deductible to the corporation. Return of principal would not be income to the stockholder-creditors. But you have to be very careful here. Besides making sure that your securities have a fixed maturity date and all the other attributes of securities, you have to pass the thin corporation hurdle. If the capitalization of the corporation is inadequate, the securities will be treated as stock. You may have to show that the ''debt'' was to be repaid in any case and not, as stock is, put at the risk of the venture.

Dummy Corporation: If you use a corporation merely to hold title and make this clear, then you may be able to avoid taxation of the entity. Actually, this amounts to a form of single proprietorship. For example, you may have to set up a corporation in order to avoid personal liability on a mortgage. Or the corporation may perform the same function as a trust—i.e., up-hold title to property for the convenience of the owners without performing any business function with regard to the property. Be sure to have the stockholders and directors adopt a resolution that the corporation is a dummy and make sure the corporation has no activity at all.

Subchapter S Corporations: Subchapter S, §1371 to 1377 of the Code permits corporate stockholders to elect to be taxed directly, as if they were partners, rather than taxing the corporation. Hence, there is only a single tax. Generally, this provision is applicable to small-scale real estate corporations which do not have much rental income.

For a corporation to be eligible for treatment as a Subchapter S corporation it must meet all the following requirements: (1) be a domestic corporation; (2) not be a member of a parent-subsidiary affiliated group; (3) have no more than ten stockholders; (4) have only individuals or estates as stockholders; (5) have no nonresident alien stockholders; (6) have only one class of stock; (7) derive no more than 80% of its gross receipts from sources outside the United States; (8) derive no more than 20% of its gross receipts from "passive investment income" (personal holding company-type income, e.g., rents, royalties, etc.).

For Subchapter S purposes, the shareholders of the corporation are the beneficial owners of the corporate stock and not merely the owners of record (*Harold Kean*, 51 TC 337; *Kates,* TC Memo 1968-264). The question of "beneficial ownership" may be raised to make the Subchapter S election void. For this reason, it might be a good idea to enter into a shareholders' agreement providing: (1) that the record owner is the real owner of the stock and that no other person owns any interest whatsoever in the shares purchased by the shareholder; (2) that the shareholder will not pledge the securities as a loan without first informing the other shareholders (lenders can be "beneficial owners"); (3) that in the event the election is lost because of the failure of any one stockholder to reveal beneficial interests in his stock, he will reimburse the other stockholders to the extent of the loss of the tax benefits they would have received had the election been valid.

Using a Subchapter S Corporation to Split Income: A Subchapter S corporation can act as an income-splitting device because it permits a division of ownership between a father and his minor children. This reduces taxable income because of additional standard deductions and personal exemptions. In addition, a taxable income is split among several taxpayers.

How a Builder Can Use Subchapter S: Suppose Builder anticipated income of $25,000 from his real estate operations. He has never incorporated because the standard corporation might create a double tax liability. He could avoid the double tax problem by using a Subchapter S corporation which would be treated as a partnership for tax purposes, but he has never seen any advantage to this.

Key to Tax Savings: Now assume he organized a Subchapter S corporation with himself and his three minor children as stockholders, the children's stock to be held under a custodial arrangement. The primary tax saving arises because Builder is entitled to claim his children as dependents as long as they are under 19 or are full-time students, even though they have income in excess of their personal exemption. The children in turn are entitled to claim their own personal exemptions in their own returns.

Be Sure to Achieve Economic Reality: The Tax Court has held that the use of a Subchapter S corporation to split income would be recognized only where the deal had economic reality (*Duarte,* 44 TC 193).

What to Do: If you make stock transfers in Subchapter S situations, make sure you cross all the t's and dot all the i's. If there are distributions to stockholders, make sure all the transferees get their shares. Where minors are involved and custodianships are set up, make sure the custodian sets up bank accounts for the minors and the distributions are deposited in those accounts. Pay taxes due for the minors from these accounts. Have the custodian exercise his right to vote in the corporation by appearing in person at the corporation's annual meeting or exercising a proxy. In short, do all that any stockholder can do in any corporation.

However, even absent these purposes, where the mortgage debt exceeds the transferors' basis for the property, the transferors are subject to tax on the transfer to the extent of such excess. If the property was a capital asset, the gain would be capital gain (§357(c)).

In a tax-free incorporation, the basis of the stock received is the same as that of the property transferred. And the corporation's basis for depreciation is your basis before the transfer.

There may be some situations in which you would want to have a taxable transaction to raise the basis of the property in the hands of the corporation at the cost of a capital gain tax to you. You can set up a taxable transaction by giving 21% of the stock of the corporation to an outsider in exchange for services. But you also have to watch out for §1239, which converts any gain on the sale of depreciable real estate by an individual to his controlled corporation from capital gain into ordinary income. Section 1239 will not apply so long as an outsider (not your wife, minor child, or minor grandchild) owns 20% or more of the outstanding stock of the corporation.

[¶1107] Tax Factors to Consider Before Incorporating

In addition to these general economic and legal advantages, use of the corporate form involves a number of important tax considerations that must be taken into account in deciding what form of operation is best suited to your needs. For example:

(1) Corporations take their own deduction for charitable contributions, but the rate is only 5%.

(2) The corporation takes a deduction for funds it expends for its

stockholder-employees for accumulation in pension or profit-sharing trusts or to pay for medical expenses, group term insurance, wage continuation plans, and health and accident insurance. These benefits are not taxable to the stockholder-employees, within specified limits.

(3) Compensation to officers and employee stockholders is subject to Social Security tax.

(4) Stockholders have freedom to assign their stock without consulting anyone, but earnings can't be assigned separately from the stock.

(5) Income is taxed to the corporation; stockholders are taxed only on dividends distributed to them, reduced by the dividend exclusion and credit.

(6) Stockholders are not taxed on accumulations. However, a penalty tax (§531) may apply if the purpose is to avoid taxation and the accumulation is beyond $150,000.

(7) A corporation uses the alternative computation for capital gains; but, unlike that for individuals, there's no deduction of 50% of the excess of long-term gain over short-term loss (§1201).

(8) Exempt interest distributed by a corporation would be fully taxable income to the stockholders.

(9) Death benefits up to $5,000 can be received tax free by stockholder-employees' beneficiaries (§101).

(10) Corporations are subject to various state taxes, although deductibility of these on the federal return lessens cost.

(11) After the 22% and 48% corporate rates are reached, the corporation is at least a temporary tax shelter.

(12) In the corporate form, a capital gain tax is paid when appreciation in value is received by liquidation or sale of stock. If stock is held until death and then sold by the family, the beneficiaries receive a stepped-up basis that reduces the capital gain tax.

You also may be able, beyond accumulations, to get some money to the shareholders without a dividend tax. This is done by setting up part of your capitalization as debts to the stockholders. Interest to the stockholders would be taxable to them but deductible to the corporation. Return of principal would not be income to the stockholder-creditors. But you have to be very careful here. Besides making sure that your securities have a fixed maturity date and all the other attributes of securities, you have to pass the thin-corporation hurdle. If the capitalization of the corporation is inadequate, the securities will be treated as stock. You may have to show that the "debt" was to be repaid in any case and not, as stock is, put at the risk of the venture.

[¶1108] Particular Problems of Corporate Ownership

(1) Tax Rates: The real rate advantage in corporate ownership lies in the writing off of the mortgage principal. More of the earnings will be left after tax at the 48% corporate rate than after tax at an individual rate of, let's say, 70%. More earnings left mean more earnings to apply to amortization. This means a faster amortization and a smaller total interest bill, all without extra expense to the investor.

(2) Accumulated Earnings Tax: As we've already shown, corporations are taxed at the rate of 22% on the first $25,000 of taxable income and at 48% on taxable income in excess of $25,000. The lower rate on the first $25,000 is the so-called surtax exemption. If income is paid out in the form of a dividend, tax is imposed not only at the corporate level but also at the individual level. If paid out in the form of salary and the amount is not unreasonable, tax is payable only at the individual level; and the amount of this salary is deductible as an ordinary expense of the corporation. If the corporation accumulates earnings instead of paying them out, it becomes subject to a penalty tax on earnings unreasonably accumulated if the accumulation exceeds $150,000.

(3) Loss Offset: Sometimes it's anticipated that a real estate investment will show a loss, especially in the first years of operation. If the property is acquired by a corporation owning other properties, the corporation can use the loss to offset other income. Unless such a situation exists, however, losses won't pay off in a corporation except as carryovers to offset future income. If the property is acquired in the individual form, the loss can be used to offset the individual's other income. Thus, an individual might be able to lower his tax bracket by acquiring the property in his own name. The corporate loss may, however, be available to the individual stockholders if the corporation is eligible to elect Subchapter S.

(4) Unimproved Realty: Real estate is often acquired for purposes of development. Ownership under the corporate form lends itself more readily to the qualification as "property used in the trade or business" (Code §1231) than does individual ownership. The special rules for determining capital gains and losses for business property may make it advisable to keep ownership of business property out of an individual taxpayer's hands.

(5) Dealers: The profits of a dealer who holds real estate primarily for sale to customers is taxed at ordinary income rates rather than at capital gain

rates. When a dealer buys realty for investment purposes, he must separate his investment property from his other holdings in order to receive capital gain treatment on a subsequent resale of his investment property. If the dealer is a corporation, investment property might be acquired in the individual form; if the dealer is an individual, investment property might be acquired in the corporate form.

(6) Personal Holding Company: If there is a danger that a corporation might be classified as a "personal holding company," it might be better to avoid the corporate form. Undistributed personal holding company income is subject to a 70% tax, in addition to other taxes (Code §541). Any corporation can fall prey if (1) 60% of its adjusted ordinary gross income is personal holding company income and (2) at any time during the last half of its taxable year more than 50% in the value of its outstanding stock is owned by not more than five individuals (Code §542(a)). Note that intent is not a factor; if the conditions are met, the tax will be imposed—even if the shareholders were not seeking to avoid any tax.

How to Avoid Personal Holding Company Penalty: Formerly, you could avoid the PHC penalty by making sure that at least 50% of your gross income came from rents. Now, you first have to reduce both your gross income and your rent income by depreciation, taxes, and interest on the rental property before applying the 50% test. Even if you meet the 50% test, you can "shelter" only other personal holding company income (that is, interest, dividends, royalties, etc.) to the extent of 10% of ordinary gross income. What's more, if more than 60% of a corporation's gross is passive income, such as dividends and interest, it is a personal holding company.

Thus, a corporation that derives most of its income from rent, such as one that owns an office building, will not have any personal holding company income. But if rental income is only a substantial part of the corporation's income, the corporation must be careful that adjusted rental income combined with other personal holding company income does not exceed 60% of adjusted ordinary gross income.

Example (1): Beta Corporation has $30,000 rental income, $20,000 dividend income, and $10,000 interest income, for a total gross income of $60,000. Beta has $10,000 in expenses related to the rental income (depreciation, etc.), giving it an adjusted ordinary gross income of $50,000 and adjusted rental income of $20,000. Since the adjusted rental income is only 40% of adjusted ordinary income, it constitutes personal holding company income. When taken together with the other personal holding company income, 100% of Beta's adjusted ordinary gross income is personal holding company income and subject to the 70% tax if not distributed.

Example (2): Same facts as Example (1), except now $45,000 of Beta's gross income is from rents and $15,000 is from dividends and interest. The adjusted rental income is now $35,000, which is more than 50% of Beta's $50,000 adjusted ordinary gross income. However, Beta's $15,000 dividend and interest income is more than 10% of its $60,000 ordinary gross income. Thus, the rental income still constitutes personal holding company income. Beta can avoid this result very simply by paying a dividend of $9,000. This will leave only $6,000 in undistributed dividends, and the 10% test will be met.

(7) Collapsible Corporation: If you want to sell your corporate business (either by selling your stock or liquidating), you may end up with ordinary income instead of your expected capital gain if the corporation has held its property less than three years. That's the collapsible corporation rule. Where almost all the corporate property would give it a capital gain on sale (i.e., it's real or depreciable property used in the corporation's trade or business), then the collapsible rules can be avoided even though the three years have not elapsed—unless some of the substantial stockholders are also real estate dealers (see §341(c)).

(8) Management Compensation: The corporate form may be justified if a low-bracket taxpayer manages the realty and draws a salary for his services. For example, a man might have two sons managing the property, each drawing a $15,000 salary. The salaries eat up the $30,000 earnings, so the corporate tax is diminished. The earnings (in the form of salaries) are taxed only at the sons' lower brackets. By this method, you withdraw corporate earnings at only an individual tax since the corporation gets a deduction for salaries paid. But you will have to show that the compensation is reasonable in amount and for actual services. For the method of finding the "best" salary for tax purposes, see page 509.

[¶1109] How and Where to Use a Land Trust In Holding Property

The land trust form of holding property has been used principally in Illinois. There is no particular reason why the use of this form has been confined to Illinois. It could probably be used in many other states. Under this arrangement, record title is held by a trustee. As a matter of public record, the trustee has full powers to deal with the real estate. At the same time, all the rights of ownership are exercisable by the owner-beneficiary through the trust agreement. This is accomplished by giving the trustee, by means of a deed in trust, full powers to deal with the title in the property, when, actually, his powers are restricted by a trust agreement which is executed prior to or at the time the deed is given. This trust agreement gives the beneficiary complete power of management and control and permits him to direct the trustee in his dealings with the property. Third parties do not have an opportunity to look into the terms of the nonrecorded trust agreement.

The trustee's interest is considered a real property interest, while the beneficiary's interest is deemed to be personal property.

The land trust provides an inexpensive method of eliminating many problems involved in the acquisition and holding of real property. Among the advantages of land trusts are the following:

(1) Provides a means of preventing disclosure of true owner. Record title is held by the trustee (often a corporate trustee). Illustrative of a circumstance in which it is advantageous that public records not reveal ultimate ownership is the assembling of a parcel in several stages. The owner can carry on negotiations more effectively where his identity and ultimate purpose are not known.

(2) Acts as a shield against encumbrances that might be put on the property if it were held by the individual.

(3) Provides for flexibility of management.

(4) Allows simplicity in conveyance. A deed from the beneficiary is not necessary.

(5) Avoids personal liability on mortgage loans. The trustee executes the mortgage without any assumption of personal liability by himself or by the beneficiary.

(6) Simplifies ownership by several persons. The trustee alone executes all the instruments. Obtaining signatures of absent owners and spouses is eliminated. In the same way, complications are avoided if an owner should become incompetent or bankrupt.

(7) Avoids legal complication on the death of the owner. Probate can be avoided as a provision can be inserted in the trust agreement for the succession of ownership on the beneficiary's death.

[¶1200] SYNDICATION OF REAL ESTATE

Syndicates allow the public to invest in high-yield real estate enterprises that would otherwise be beyond the means of all but wealthy investors. The investor gets the benefit of the knowledge of the professional operator who forms the syndicate, and this includes the latter's ability to find, organize, and close a deal. Syndicates permit the investor to stay away from the problems of managing the property; the promoter handles the matters of books, operations, accounting, etc. Ordinarily, the investor receives part of his yield as a tax-free cash return. Frequently, high paper "losses" generated by the enterprise in its early years serve to shelter the income of investors from other sources.

Syndicators who buy income-producing property, package it and sell pieces to the little man are prime prospects for the broker who lists commercial, office, apartment, and other income-producing real estate.

[¶1201] Setting Up the Syndicate

Here are some general guide posts followed by most promoters in working out their arrangements:

(1) Analysis: The syndicator will determine how much he can make from a property before purchasing it. Assume that a syndicate is looking for a 10 to 15% return on its cash equity investment. It should count on purchasing its property for about ten times net earnings. Net earnings for this purpose are defined as "earnings before depreciation and income taxes but after debt amortization."

On this basis, let's assume you're interested in an apartment building with a 30-year remaining life, a $35,000-a-year rent roll, maintenance and operating expenses of $18,000 and an outstanding $120,000, 5%, 30-year mortgage calling for annual amortization payments of $4,000 a year. "Net earnings" are $35,000 minus $18,000 expenses, $6,000 interest and $4,000 amortization, or $7,000 before depreciation and income taxes. So, you should pay about 10 times this or $70,000 cash.

Your taxable income, excluding the depreciation deduction, is $35,000 minus $18,000 expenses and $6,000 mortgage interest, or $11,000. Assume 80% of the purchase price of $190,000 or ($152,000) is allocable to the building. You'll want to start out using a declining-balance depreciation method, which is most favorable in the early years. In the first year, declining balance (which for an existing apartment building gives 125% of straight-line depreciation) amounts to $6,232.

Since your depreciation deduction is $6,232, taxable income in the first year is reduced to $4,738 of the $7,000 cash return you receive. To the extent your bargaining power is strong and you think you can get more than 10%, you'll offer less cash. Or perhaps you may try to make part of your payments in a purchase-money second mortgage, thereby increasing your yield on cash invested.

(2) Financing: Study the financing necessary on the property for the desired yield to the syndicate investors. Find out if you can obtain this financing before you contract to buy the property. If there is an existing mortgage, see if you should and can refinance.

(3) Management: Make sure of the details for supervision. If a limited partnership is to be formed, who will handle the management of the building for the general partners? Or, if you are going to set up a joint venture or general partnership with a net lease, who will be the lessee and who will manage for the lessee? The degree of management, continuity of life, etc., will be determined to some extent by the form of ownership used. See later discussion under each form of ownership.

(4) Purchase: At this point, the syndicator will contract to purchase the property, even before he actually sets up the syndicate. You need some binding commitment from the seller in order to interest prospective investors.

(5) SEC Requirements: Before you actually make an offering of syndicate shares, you may have to comply with applicable regulations of the Securities and Exchange Commission, by filing necessary registration statements. Exemptions from registration apply to: (a) offerings where less than $500,000 is involved, (b) intrastate offerings solely to residents of the state where the issuer is organized and does business, (c) private offerings as defined in Rule 146, and (d) special small offerings of Rule 240.

Failure to comply with SEC requirements may subject you to civil and penal liabilities and no offering should be made until you have received competent legal advice. You also have to consider any applicable state laws applying specifically to syndicate offerings (as in New York, for example) or to security offerings generally.

(6) Forming the Syndicate: From the very beginning, of course, you've decided on the form of ownership. But this is the point at which to set up

your syndicate. Comply with necessary state filing requirements when, for example, you set up a partnership. Then assign your contract to purchase the property to the syndicate. At this point, the only partners in the syndicate are ordinarily the promoter and his associates. The next step will be solicitation of investors. If a large-scale syndicate is involved, you'll make a public offering. You'll probably send the investors a prospectus containing information about the building and its financial set-up, the partnership itself and the promoters. You'll also include a form of offer to purchase a participation interest in the syndicate.

(7) The Syndicator's Share: You should plan this aspect from the very beginning and include it in the partnership agreement. If the syndicator takes his compensation as a percentage of the partnership, he has ordinary income at that point unless he can show the Treasury that he has received the partnership share in exchange for his contribution of his contract right to buy the property, rather than for his services in forming the partnership. But if he limits his rights to a percentage of profits, then he avoids a tax at formation of the partnership.

[¶1202] Information Syndicators Will Want From Brokers

The following is a list of factors that a corporate buyer or syndicator should know before buying income-producing property.

[¶1202.1] Tenancy

General Background: You want to know what the expenses and obligations of the landlord are under the tenants' leases.

Renewals: What percentage of the tenants can renew their leases?

Cancellation Risks: You want to find out if there are any major cancellation clauses in any of the leases. A syndicator will also want to know if there are any outstanding rights in the tenants to cancel, not in the leases, but in separate written agreements.

Credit Risks: Your interest is in the general background of the tenant. Is he on the way down? What is his credit rating?

Expiration Date: When do the leases expire?

Fire and Condemnation Clauses: What are the tenants' rights and obligations under these clauses?

Lease Deposits: Are there any deposits by tenants under present leases?

[¶1202.2] Mortgage Status

General Background: Your interest is in the term of the mortgage, its original placement date, schedule of payments, interest on unpaid balance. This becomes important at the time that mortgage amortization becomes greater than depreciation, since at that point investors would be paying a tax on more than they earn.

Balloon Payments: Is a large part of the mortgage due in one lump sum at the end of the mortgage term?

Fire and Condemnation Clauses: What are the rights of the mortgagee in case of either occurrence?

Tenancy: Does the mortgage require any special type of tenancy by lessees? Are there any construction or alteration clauses in the mortgage?

[¶1202.3] Tax Assessments

Rate Curve: Not only the present rate but also a projected rate curve for the future is necessary, since realty tax assessments and rates are among the expenses which figure in the analysis of net income.

Present Assessment: You want to know the ratio of land-to-building value in order to help determine the probable amount of depreciation allowed on the building.

Possible Change? Here you project the possible change of assessment in relationship to either a higher selling price or to area equilization trends.

[¶1202.4] Service Contracts

This is an analysis of service contracts, involving the following:

Possible Savings: Perhaps by use of the building's own crew.

Comparison: Other standard properties and their labor costs are detailed.

Projection: Possible rise in future service costs.

[¶1202.5] Income and Operation

General: You want a comparison with standard properties and the projection of savings or increases.

Union Contracts: Analysis of costs.

Possible Increase or Decrease in Rents: This is vital to the syndicator; he wants to make sure that he can continue to pay the promised return even if rents decrease or vacancies occur.

Depreciation: Depreciation minus mortgage amortization tells you how much of your cash-flow is tax free. If depreciation is involved you want to know the availability of declining-balance depreciation and the possibility of a switch to it if it is not presently in use.

[¶1203] What to Look for Before Investing in a Real Estate Syndicate

Here we give you a nine-point checklist of what a potential investor in a real estate syndicate should consider and look into before making his investment, in addition to having his attorney and accountant check the validity of the offering. The checklist was created by Attorney R. A. McNeil, chairman of the California Real Estate Association's Real Estate Syndication Division.

(1) Economic Soundness: Is the investment a sound one even without any unusual tax shelter?

(2) Financial Resources: Will the project stand on its own financial resources under any reasonable change in economic conditions? Have strong cash reserves been provided?

(3) Syndicators' Background: Do the syndicators have substantial and successful experience in syndication?

(4) Syndicators' Financial Resources: What are the financial resources of the syndicators themselves? Are they personally involved or only corporately?

(5) General Partner's Background: How capable and experienced is the general partner in improving the value of the building through proper management over a five- to seven-year period?

(6) Vacancies and Replacements: Have the projections adequately provided for vacancies and replacements?

(7) Investors' Liability: Are the limited partners (the investors) liable for additional financial contributions to the partnership?

(8) Projections: Are the projections economically realistic?

(9) Offering: Has the offering received a real estate securities permit?

[¶1204] Limited Partnership Syndicate Taking Advantage of Tax Shelter in Low- and Moderate-Income Rental Housing

The Tax Reform Act favors apartment buildings and makes this type of investment a great tax shelter. Investments in apartment buildings are often set up in the form of limited partnerships for two good reasons: (1) During the period of construction and in the early years of operation when there are "losses," the partnership form permits the passthrough of the losses to the investors who can offset other income and save taxes. (2) When the loss period is over, the partnership form avoids the double taxation inherent in the corporate form. There is no tax at the partnership level as in the corporate set-up—only a single tax at the investor level.

We put the term "losses" in quotes because, of course, as in any real estate deal where depreciation is an element of the "loss," it's only a paper or tax loss. In fact, all the time the property is being depreciated for tax purposes, it may in actuality be increasing in value. And, of course, the tax "loss" will keep money in the investor's pocket which he would otherwise have to pay to IRS. The higher the investor's tax bracket, the more money he saves.

A private offering may be made of limited partnership interests specifying the total dollar amount of the partnership interests, the number of units offered, and the dollar amount of each unit. A rundown will be given on the project, financing, building and manager, architect, the general partners and their contributions, the limited partners and their contributions, and allocation of benefits and liabilities. A description of the proposed offering will be given including projections of tax benefits, a schedule of income and expense items, and other pertinent data.

Accelerated Depreciation: The availability of accelerated depreciation is the big thing in these deals. On new projects, 200%-declining-balance is still available. Thus, if you use a 33-1/3 year life and 200%-declining-balance depreciation, the partnership gets and passes through to the investors as a depreciation deduction in the very first year, 6% of the entire cost of the building. This is so even though the building is 90% or more financed with borrowed money so that the 6% may actually represent 50% or more of your equity investment.

Special Benefits in Low- and Moderate-Income Housing: The tax shelter in real estate deals may be offset by the recapture of faster than straight-line depreciation as ordinary income when you sell or dispose of the property in certain ways. Prior to tax reform, there was no recapture on any real estate deal if you had held the property for at least ten years. Tax reform removed the ten-year limitation on recapture as to all real estate except federally or municipally assisted low- and moderate-income rental housing. This, of course, offers additional incentive for investing in low- and moderate-income housing.

Equity Buildup: The investor not only gets the tax shelter, but he's building up equity, too. The mortgage is being amortized, the land value figures to increase, and, as we've suggested, the building itself, despite depreciation for tax purposes, may indeed be expected to appreciate in value.

High Leverage Made Higher: Apartment houses have high loan value, and federally and municipally assisted low- and moderate-income deals have the highest loan values and so the highest leverage. The loan may, in some cases, be as high as 95% of the recognized cost of the project.

On top of that, the deal may be structured so that the investor can finance as much as half of his investment.

[¶1205] The Syndicate Manager's Share

Proper syndicate operation does not require that the syndicate operator take part in the deal with his own funds. As a rule, however, syndicate managers profit by sharing in the yield of a property without investing any money of their own. There are several ways of accomplishing this.

For example, a syndicate manager may buy or contract to buy a building for $1,000,000 cash over existing mortgages. He knows from studying the structure's operating figures that the property yields 14% a year, or $140,000, after operating expenses. He then sells the property to investors for $1,200,000, dividing the cost into participation units of a predetermined size—$12,000 each, for example. The syndicate members will then share the $140,000 yield; a $12,000 unit will earn $1,400 a year. This is a return of 11.7% on the investment.

Another method is for the syndicate manager to acquire the same property with $1,000,000 cash and distribute units among investors in such a way as to have some units left for himself. In the example given, a division into 120 units may be required. One hundred of them would be sold to investors at $10,000 apiece, the twenty others being held by the syndicate manager at no cost to himself. On distribution of profits, however, all 120 units receive equal shares, thereby giving the investors the same return of about 11.7%.

Under still another method, the syndicate manager buys the property and resells it to the syndicate without a markup. Only after the cash down payment is recovered through accrued profits is the syndicate manager or operator entitled to an extra share of future capital proceeds from the holding. This is usually done in cases where the syndicate manager or operator is part of the syndicate.

Methods of participation by the syndicator are varied. In some cases, the syndicator will take a 10 to 15% interest for his work. Assuming that the money necessary is $85,000, he will set up a syndicate for $100,000, put himself in for 15% or $15,000 and will participate in all the returns as though he had actually placed his own money in the enterprise. There are other cases where the syndicator will take a one-third interest subordinated to the original investment, first pay out, say, 10 to 12% to those who put in their money and then take 5 to 6% of the income for himself. In the event of sale, the monies invested are paid back first. After this is done, the syndicator receives his proportionate interest.

In other instances, the syndicator may participate as broker, as lessee, as provider of secondary financing, as lessor, or as manager. Sometimes he shares in the benefits of refinancing, in increased returns, in capital appreciation, or in all three.

The Tax Problems: From a tax point of view, it's essential for the syndicator to plan his share of the deal from the very beginning. If the syndicator takes a percentage of the partnership as compensation for his services, he has ordinary income at that point unless he can convince the Internal Revenue Service that he has received his partnership share in exchange for his contribution of a contract right to buy the property. A partnership interest is ordinary income when it is received in exchange for services; it is a capital asset when received in exchange for property and the partnership interest is not taxable on receipt in such a case. So, by acquiring a contract right to buy the property and transferring the right to the partnership in exchange for his partnership interest, the syndicator will attempt to show that the partnership interest has been received in exchange for the contract right. If the partnership interest is a capital asset in the hands of the syndicator, he can hold it for the necessary six-month period and then sell it at a capital gain.

Even if the syndicator's partnership interest is received in exchange for his services, and so is compensation, he avoids a tax on formation of the partnership if he limits his rights to a percentage of profits. Another alternative would be to limit his right to withdraw his capital interest until termination. If the partnership agreement is silent, the syndicator will share in important depreciation deductions to the extent he shares in profits and losses, even though he may have contributed nothing but his contract right.

[¶1206] How to Buy and Sell a Syndicate Share

There are firms that specialize in sales and resales of syndicate shares. These firms maintain listings of syndicate shares that are offered for sale and of requests for purchase of particular shares. The fee for resale of a share is 5% of the selling price and is ordinarily paid by the seller. At present, most shares in syndicates are resold at par. Eventually, the existence of greater activity in the resale field may create fluctuations in prices to reflect supply and demand.

Problems on Purchase: The initial problem to consider when buying a partnership share is whether the syndicate itself forbids resale of syndicate shares. A clause prohibiting resale might have been inserted as a means of guarding against taxation as an association. Or, the seller may have to offer the share to the other participants or to the syndicate itself before selling to an outsider. If this is so, make sure that this provision has been complied with before you buy.

Caution: One of the main inducements for ownership of syndicate shares is the favorable tax picture produced by depreciation, which a participant in a partnership, trust, or tenancy in common takes as a deduction against part of syndicate earnings. But if you purchase a share that has been offered for resale, you may not have the same tax basis for purposes of depreciation that your seller had.

If you pay par for a partnership interest, you may be paying considerably more than the undepreciated portion of the syndicate property allocable to your share in the syndicate. This is so because the syndicate has been taking depreciation deductions when you were not a syndicate member. For example, Jones becomes a member when the syndicate is formed. He pays $10,000 for his share. The syndicate takes 150%-declining-balance depreciation. Assume Jones's share of the first-year depreciation is $480. After three years, Jones sells his share to Smith at par. Although Smith paid $10,000 for his share, the depreciation allocable to him in the fourth year that the syndicate has held the building is down to about $400.

[¶1207] Standards for Operating as a Real Estate Syndicator

(1) The principal consideration of every syndicator should be to protect the interest of the investing public.

(2) Full and truthful disclosure of all material facts should be made to all investors. A written prospectus or brochure, in clear factual language, should be made available to every prospective investor and should fairly and

honestly set forth the material facts respecting the investment, including without limitation:

(a) A full and accurate description of the property.

(b) A statement of estimated income and expense.

(c) Complete information on mortgages and other liens against the property stating by whom held, terms of payment, maturity, etc.

(d) A statement of any interest, direct or indirect, owned by the syndicator in the property being offered.

(e) The syndicate managers and any other persons who will direct the affairs of the syndicate should be identified and brief resumes of their experience in the real estate field should be set forth.

(f) Projections, if any, into the future should be clearly identified as estimates by the syndicators and stated as such.

(g) A statement of all compensation and profit, direct or indirect, of any nature, paid or to be paid to any of the syndicate managers or to any other person who will direct the affairs of the syndicate.

(h) A statement of the amount of compensation, if any, paid or to be paid for the management of the property or for the management of the syndicate.

(i) If the property is under contract, the salient terms and conditions of the contract of purchase.

(3) Participants should be given all necessary protection for funds deposited with the investment managers. Such funds should be deposited in a special account and should not be commingled with the syndicator's personal funds.

(4) False, misleading or exaggerated claims or statements in advertisements or other publicity are expressly condemned.

(5) The purchase contract and all other documents in connection therewith, pertinent to the transaction, that are in the possession of the syndicate manager should be made available for inspection by prospective participants.

(6) In all their dealings with each other and with the public in general, syndicators should maintain the highest standards of honesty, frankness, fair dealing, and dignity.

(7) The foregoing basic code of ethics may be clarified, supplemented or amended from time to time.

[¶1208] Corpnership: Tax Benefits of Limited Partnership With Advantages of Corporate Attributes

A vast $80,000,000-plus real estate investment enterprise was launched in the form of a limited partnership giving investors reasonable assurance of continuity of life, limited liability, and free transferability of interests. The set-up is backed by a private IRS ruling that the enterprise will be taxed as a partnership, not as a corporation.

This enterprise offers investors substantially all the advantages of investment in a corporate enterprise without the disadvantage of double taxation. What's more, it offers participation to tens of thousands of investors in a giant real estate enterprise, rivaling in size some of our corporate giants. An examination of the prospectus shows a very carefully thought out plan for dealing with those troublesome areas that might make the partnership taxable as a corporation:

Continuity of Life: On the death of a general partner or the sale of his interest, the partnership is terminated; but the remaining general partners will form a new partnership to continue the business. Two of the four general partners are corporations, presumably perpetual in existence. A further provision in the partnership agreement provides for termination on December 31, 2069, unless the general partners by unanimous vote decide to terminate earlier.

Centralization of Management: Reg. §301.7701-2(c) says that centralized management does not generally exist in a limited partnership subject to the Uniform Limited Partnership Act or a similar law but that centralized management can exist if substantially all the interests in the partnership are owned by the limited partner. The latter is not the case with this limited partnership, and so it appears that this element is missing.

Limited Liability: The individual general partners or associates are personally liable and have substantial assets. The corporations which are general partners also appear to have substantial assets. Hence, the limited liability characteristic of a corporation is missing.

Transferability of Interests: The offering consists of 81,700 units of $1,000 9% junior mortgage bonds and 10 participation interests representing undivided economic interests in the limited partnership interest held by the one initial limited partner. Holders of participation interests are not limited partners nor otherwise members of the partnership.

It is contemplated that there will be a public market for the participation interests and that they will be freely transferable. This, however, would not be true of the limited partnership interest as such. So, the corporate characteristic of free transferability of interests is also lacking.

[¶1300] JOINT VENTURE SYNDICATES

In setting up a real estate syndicate, we want to preserve for the investors the tax advantages that lie in the property—the right to make the best use of depreciation charges by offsetting depreciation against income from the property and the benefit of only a single tax on the income from the property.

The partnership form is used in real estate syndicates because, when properly set up, it avoids double taxation and passes the high depreciation deductions directly through to the individual investors. In order to facilitate the operation of the partnership, the syndicator will try to give it some of the powers and characteristics of a corporation. But, too many corporate characteristics in the partnership might result in taxation as a corporation. The general rule has always been that the Treasury will treat an organization as an association and tax it as a corporation if it more nearly resembles a corporation than a partnership.

What is desired is a syndicate with some of the characteristics of a corporation that is still not taxable as an association. Treasury Regulations spell out when an unincorporated group is a partnership and when it is a corporation for tax purposes.

[¶1301] Treasury Rules Allow Partnership Treatment

Frequently, to facilitate the operation of a partnership-syndicate, the syndicator will try to give it some of the characteristics of a corporation. But he has to be careful—if the partnership shows too many corporate characteristics it will be taxed as if it were a corporation.

Reg. §301.7701 sets forth the following six corporate characteristics, that are to be used in determining whether an unincorporated group is a partnership or an association for tax purposes:

(1) Associates.

(2) An objective to carry on a business and divide the profits from it.

(3) Continuity of the life of the entity on the death, insanity, bankruptcy, retirement, resignation, or expulsion of any member.

(4) Centralization of management.

(5) Limited liability.

(6) Transferability of interests.

As a practical matter, the first two characteristics are present in both corporations and partnerships, so the Treasury is concerned with only the last four characteristics. The Regulations (§301.7701-2(a)(3)) say that an organization will not be taxable as an association unless it has more corporate than noncorporate characteristics. So, if there are no other significant factors aside from the four corporate characteristics (continuity, centralized management, limited liability, and transferability of interest), your partnership is taxable as a partnership and not as a corporation unless it has more than two of these characteristics present.

[¶1302] The Corporate Characteristics Applicable to Partnerships

Before we weigh the various characteristics, let's first examine each and see when the Regs say a characteristic is present.

Continuity of Life: To avoid continuity of life, the withdrawal of a member (by death, insanity, bankruptcy, retirement, resignation, or expulsion) should cause a dissolution.

If the organization is to continue for a stated time (or until the end of a particular project) and there is no provision for prior termination—either at death, insanity, etc., or at will of any partner—there is continuity. But, if despite the agreement, state law allows any partner to dissolve the partnership at will, there is no continuity.

Limited partnership law, or the agreement, often provides that the retirement, death, or insanity of a general partner of a limited partnership causes a dissolution of the partnership unless the remaining general partners agree to continue the partnership, or unless all remaining partners agree to continue. In these circumstances, there is no continuity of life (Reg. §301.7701-2(b)). The Regulations go even further and say that a general partnership subject to a law corresponding to the Uniform Partnership Act and a limited partnership subject to a law corresponding to the Uniform Limited Partnership Act both lack continuity of life. This means that a limited partnership can provide for continuation on the death of a general partner by agreement of the remaining general partners and still avoid continuity of life for tax purposes.

Centralized Management: This corporate characteristic exists if any person or group of less than all the members has continuing and exclusive authority to make independent business decisions for the organization. In order for there to be centralization, these decisions must be necessary for the conduct of the business and not subject to ratification by the other members. But the Regulations say that a general partnership cannot have centralized management, since the act of any partner within the scope of business binds all the partners. Even if the partners in a general partnership agree that their management powers will be centralized in a few of them, this agreement would not be binding on outsiders who have no notice of it.

A large-scale limited partnership will still have centralized management. The Regulations (§301.7701-2(c)) say that limited partnerships subject to a statute corresponding to the Uniform Limited Partnership Act generally do not have centralized management, but that centralized management does exist in such a limited partnership if substantially all the interests in the partnership are owned by the limited partners. This means that a small-scale limited partnership might not have centralized management but a large-scale limited partnership will.

Limited Liability: In order for the corporate characteristic of limited liability to be absent, at least one of the general partners has to have personal liability. The Regulations (§301.7701-2(d)) say that the general partner in a limited partnership does not have personal liability *only* when he has no substantial assets *and* is also merely a dummy acting as agent for the limited partners. Even if he has no substantial assets (other than his interest in the partnership), he still has personal liability if he is not a dummy. It makes no difference whether the personally liable partners contributed services or capital to the partnership for their interests in it.

Transferability of Interest: Transferability exists if all those members owning substantially all the interests in the organization have the power to substitute an outsider for themselves. For there to be transferability, they must possess this power without the consent of the other members. Also they have to be able to give their transferee all the attributes of their position in the organization. So transferability does not exist if a member can assign only his right to share in the profits and not his right to participate in the management of the organization. And transferability does not exist if under state law a transfer of a member's interest results in dissolution of the old organization and formation of a new one.

[¶1303] The Main Impact of the Regulations on Associations

A limited partnership formed under the Uniform Limited Partnership Act will not have continuity; and, unless the general partners have no substantial assets and are dummies, it also will not have limited liability. So right there two corporate characteristics are absent; and, ordinarily, at most, only centralized management and free transferability would be present. In that case, under the Regulations, your organization would be taxable as a partnership. If there is any fear that the general partners might be considered dummies, you could tie up transferability to ensure that two corporate characteristics (namely, continuity and transferability) would be absent. In any event, if a real estate limited partnership is set up under the Uniform Limited Partnership Law, you are fairly sure of getting partnership treatment for tax purposes.

[¶1304] Trusts

To avoid being taxable as an association, a trust must show that there are no associates or the trust was not formed to carry on a business and divide its profit (§301.7701-2(a)(2)). (The other four corporate characteristics are present in just about all trusts.)

In the ordinary syndicate situation, where promoters solicit investment in an enterprise, it is pretty clear that there are associates. And you're going to have a difficult time showing there is no conduct of a business. So it will be very hard to operate a syndicate as a trust, unless the trust can qualify for treatment as a real estate investment trust.

[¶1400] REAL ESTATE INVESTMENT TRUSTS

Back in September 1960, a law was adopted that provides for real estate investments trusts (REITs) to be treated much the same way as mutual funds are treated for tax purposes. Under this set-up, if a qualified REIT annually distributes at least 90% of its ordinary taxable income to its shareholders, it pays no federal tax on the income it distributes—this includes capital gains that are passed through by it. The shareholder, for his part, pays tax on the cash he receives from the REIT at capital gain rates on the capital gains distributed, none at all on any distribution that does not constitute taxable income or capital gains, and at his normal income tax rate for that part of the distribution that constitutes ordinary income.

[¶1401] Advantages Offered by REITs to Their Investors

REITs enable small investors to get the tax and economic advantages that might otherwise be available only to large real estate investors. REITs spread the risk among many investors and provide diversification (as to type and location) of investments and professional management. By pooling the resources of many individuals, they enable investors to finance projects they could not undertake singly. REITs also provide liquidity by establishing a market for their shares.

Proper use of a REIT means that you can set up an organization with the attributes of a corporation (centralized management, limited liability, continuity of interest, and transferability of shares) and, at the same time, get single-tax treatment for the beneficiaries of the trust, similar to the tax treatment given to partners in a large-scale partnership (except that losses cannot be passed through to the beneficiaries).

The market value of the properties that a REIT carries in its portfolio usually will not reflect the accelerated depreciation that the REIT takes for these properties. So the REIT can make substantial distributions to its shareholders out of its net cash flow. Given professional and skilled management, the investments made by a REIT should perform on a relatively high level. Since REITs have a good deal of flexibility in timing their sales, they're in a position to select the most favorable time to sell. (A REIT must hold a real estate asset for four years or more before selling in order to get capital gain treatment. Thereafter, it can sell at any time.)

How REIT Shareholders Get Favorable Tax Treatment: Since, as stated above, a qualified REIT gets "conduit" tax treatment only if it annually distributes at least 90% of its ordinary taxable income to its shareholders, an investment in a REIT is attractive to one looking for current income. In effect, REIT shareholders benefit from all the tax shelter that real estate offers, including deductions for interest payments, depreciation, and operating expenses; and when they get their annual cash distribution, only a small part of it might be taxable as ordinary income. The rest may come to them tax free as a return of capital or part tax free and part taxable at capital gain rates.

A REIT may designate as "capital gains distribution" only the excess of its net long-term capital gains over its net short-term capital losses, so that every distribution of this kind is long term. The shareholder may report it as a long-term gain without regard to his individual holding period. Shareholders are not allowed any deductions, credits, or exclusions for these distributions.

Shareholders are treated almost the same as real estate partners, with one important difference: Partners can pick up their shares of a partnership tax loss to the extent of their respective bases. But losses of a REIT are not distributed to its shareholders, and it can have no operating loss carryover.

Late Dividends: A REIT may meet the 90% rule by distributing some of the dividends to the shareholders in its next taxable year provided it declares a dividend before the time for filing its return for a taxable year. It must then distribute the amount of the dividend to shareholders in the 12-month period following the close of its taxable year but not later than the date of the first regular dividend payment of the next taxable year.

[¶1402] How Equity and Mortgage REITs Operate

REITs are unincorporated associations that operate in the business trust form. They own real estate, interests in real estate, or mortgages. Some REITs are "equity" trusts that invest directly in real estate and derive their income from rentals. Other REITs are "mortgage" trusts that are specifically organized to deal in debt paper. Some REITs engage in both types of operation.

Equity REITs concentrate on quality real estate for long-term investment. They invest in properties that offer the advantage of leases to prime tenants that contain escalation provisions. Their holdings may include prime shopping centers, apartment houses, modern office buildings, and industrial buildings with prime tenants in first-class industrial parks. Their primary source of income is from rents.

Mortgage REITs can and do finance every step of a real estate enterprise, including the acquisition and development of land, construction and completion of buildings. This "one-stop" financing gives them the opportunity to make interim or construction loans from which they get high interest rates and a relatively fast turnover. Mortgage REITs have no trouble complying with the asset tests because the Regulations provide that mortgages, including trust deeds, qualify as "real estate assets." Similarly, with the exception of interim-purchase mortgages, interest received on mortgages is eligible under the 75% income test.

A Mortgage REIT may invest in the following types of mortgages: (1) residential mortgages, (2) commercial mortgages, (3) construction and development loans, (4) interim-purchase mortgages, and (5) mortgages purchased at a discount.

How REITs Are Used as Real Estate Mutual Funds: The most obvious use of a REIT is as a mutual fund for real estate. The purpose is (1) to earn immediate income and (2) to benefit from gradual appreciation in the value of the holdings. REITs, because of their passive nature, are not geared to the "special situation" type of property that syndicators look for, where aggressive management and know-how can mean a sharp increase in income and market value. And because the trust can't pass losses through to its shareholders nor carry them forward itself, the "tax loss" property offers it no great advantage.

[¶1403] Taxation of the Trust Income

As already pointed out, a REIT is treated as a corporation and is subject to the corporate income tax rates unless it annually distributes 90% or more of its ordinary income. Then, as a qualified REIT, it only pays a tax on the income it retains and does not distribute as dividends. If it distributes all of its income, it pays no tax. While the trust pays tax at the favorable capital gain rate on long-term capital gains, a qualified REIT avoids tax to the extent it distributes the capital gains to the beneficiaries.

Beneficiaries: The ordinary income of the trust that is distributed to beneficiaries is taxable to them as ordinary income. Beneficiaries are not allowed any deductions, credits, or exclusions for these dividends received. Long-term capital gain dividends received by beneficiaries are taxed to them as capital gains.

[¶1404] How to Organize a Real Estate Investment Trust

To be entitled to obtain the special "conduit" tax treatment afforded to REITs, a REIT must comply with all the statutory requirements:

(1) Unincorporated Trust or Association: It must be a common-law

business trust, having all the attributes of a corporation. It cannot be either a corporation or a limited partnership.

(2) At Least 100 Beneficial Owners: It must have at least 100 beneficial owners. Owners can include individuals, trusts, estates, partnerships, and corporations.

(3) Transferable Shares: Ownership of a REIT must be evidenced by transferable shares or by transferable certificates of beneficial ownership.

(4) Management by Trustees: The trustees may be individuals or corporations and may hold property in their own name or in the name of a nominee. The trustees must hold legal title to the trust property and have continuing and exclusive authority over management of the trust's properties and affairs.

(5) Association Taxable as a Corporation Except for REIT Provisions: A corporation cannot qualify as a REIT. On the other hand, a REIT cannot qualify unless it would (apart from the REIT provisions) be considered as if it were a corporation for tax purposes under Reg. §301.7701-2.

(6) No Active Business Enterprise: A REIT is a public investment vehicle and is not intended to participate actively in business. Consequently, it must limit itself to a passive position. A REIT cannot hold property primarily for sale to customers in the ordinary course of trade or business. In addition, less than 30% of the annual gross income of a REIT may be derived from sales of securities held for less than six months and sales of real estate held for less than four years (except for involuntary conversions).

(7) Personal Holding Company Limitation: A REIT cannot be more than 50% owned by five or fewer individuals. A trust cannot qualify as a REIT if it is a personal holding company.

(8) Election: A trust must elect to be treated as a REIT on its tax return for the first taxable year in which it wants the treatment, even though it may have otherwise qualified for a prior year. An election once made is irrevocable for all succeeding taxable years. If an electing REIT does not distribute 90% of its ordinary income or does not comply with the other requirements, it will be taxed for that year as a corporation.

(9) Distribution of Income: A REIT must distribute annually to its shareholders at least 90% of its ordinary taxable income. The trust then pays a tax only on the income that it retains. If it distributes all its income, it pays no tax. To the extent that it distributes capital gains to its shareholders, no tax is payable by the trust. On retained long-term capital gains, it pays the capital gain tax.

[¶1500] THE PUBLIC REAL ESTATE CORPORATION

One of the important developments in real estate syndication involves the switch from limited partnership syndicates to public corporations. Some switchovers have involved nationally known real estate syndicators. For example, each of two prominent real estate syndicators independently set up a corporation and made public offerings of the corporate stock. In each case, the new corporation took over the properties of various limited partnership syndicates which had been organized by the syndicators. Essentially, both of these syndicators used a similar method in setting up their corporations. How this type of switchover works out taxwise depends on whether the individual involved is an investor in the partnership, a promoter, or a prospective investor; what he is looking for and what his own situation (aside from this real estate investment) adds up to.

One syndicator (K) used the following approach in acquiring the partnerships' properties: The stock offering was made directly to limited partners in the seven partnerships which were involved, with the intention of acquiring at least 51% of the investment of the limited partners in each of the partnerships. In all the syndicates, at least 51% of the partnership shares were turned over to the Corporation. The K partnerships have continued to exist, with K Corporation maintaining the position of a holder of capital units.

Each limited partner who accepted the offer received stock in exchange for his interest. After these exchanges, the Corporation anticipated that the limited partners would own at least 80% of the combined voting power of all classes of stock entitled to vote. On this basis, the exchanges would be tax free to the investors in the limited partnerships who agreed to take stock for their interests.

Although there was no step-up in basis, the Corporation expected its depreciation and leasehold amortization deductions to be high enough to exceed taxable income for a few years. Depreciation deductions available in the early years of ownership of the property added to the interest deductions on the mortgage and the operating expenses can create a loss for tax purposes. But, on a cash-income-less-cash-outgo basis, there can be a cash profit available to distribute to stockholders. This is so because while depreciation reduces taxable income, it does not require a payout of cash.

While ordinarily corporate earnings are subject to a double tax, first on the corporate level and then when they are distributed to the shareholders, this is true only if the corporation itself has earnings. If a corporation is set up and does not have any earnings and profits, then not only is the corporation free of any tax, but in addition the stockholders are not taxable on any distributions to them by the corporation. But they must reduce their basis for their stock.

If the corporation's tax deductions exceed its income, then it has an operating loss carryover that it can apply against the three prior years' profits and any excess against the five years following the year of loss. If in one of these later years the corporation makes a profit, it can reduce this profit by the loss carried over from the previous year. If money is distributed to the stockholders in a profit year, however, it is taxable to them to the extent that there were corporate profits that year.

[¶1501] Nontax Reasons for Using a Corporation

There may be many attractive features to syndication through incorporation:

(1) Diversification: When an investor goes into a one-partnership-type syndicate, there is usually one property involved. Thus, the success or failure of his investment is tied to just one property. The public corporation, however, owns various properties both as to type and location and provides some hedge against a few bad properties. The good ones help hold up the not-so-good ones, in much the same way that the advantages of diversification are achieved in securities investment through mutual funds.

(2) Liquidity: Owners of publicly traded stocks will probably find them easier to sell than partnership interests.

(3) Stock Market Climate: The availability of investments in real estate in the form of stock may force prices up due to the pressure of investment money willing to discount future earnings.

(4) Estate Planning: Valuation of traded stocks will probably be a lot easier than interests in partnerships. Furthermore, the division of evidences of ownership into smaller units (i.e., shares of stock) makes it simpler to make gifts, including gifts to minors via the custodian laws that many states have.

[¶1502] Advantages for the Promoter

A promoter in a syndication via a publicly traded corporation can enjoy all the benefits listed above for the investor. In addition, there may be these additional benefits to the promoter.

(1) Control: He can get voting control by using two classes of stock. Or he can acquire practical voting control although he does not own anywhere near 51% of the stock.

(2) Raising Capital: Raising a lot of money from many investors in the stock market may be easier than selling more expensive partnership interests to fewer investors.

(3) Limited Liability: Promoters using limited partnerships are usually the general partners in those partnerships and thus have unlimited liability. In a corporation, a promoter enjoys the benefits of limited liability.

(4) Fringe Benefits: As a corporate employee, the promoter is in a position to get various employee fringe benefits: participation in deferred compensation arrangements, pension and profit-sharing plans, stock options, medical and health insurance, group life insurance.

[¶1600] COOPERATIVES

There is a healthy market for existing as well as newly constructed cooperative apartments. The key to a successful cooperative apartment project is the tenant. Ownership of stock in a cooperative corporation gives him the pride of owning his own home. Taxwise, the tenant gets a deduction for his proportionate share of the taxes and interest paid by the cooperative corporation. The tax deduction reduces his net yearly "rent" and often makes the cooperative apartment an economical investment—the rent saving each year can be conceived of as yield on the amount of money spent to purchase the apartment.

For the developer of the property or the broker who undertakes to execute the cooperative plan, care and attention to the provisions of the tax law which afford favorable tax treatment to cooperatives is necessary. The owner of the property has yet another problem—selling the apartment house to the cooperative corporation (which he has set up) in a way calculated, if possible, to achieve a capital gain rather than ordinary income tax. In addition, there are some practical business and legal problems in setting up the cooperative corporation.

For the broker who sells the individual apartments to prospective tenants, there are some time-tested methods by which the inherent investment aspects of a cooperative purchase can be emphasized. New finance plans can be utilized to facilitate cooperative apartment sales.

Finally, care should be taken from the outset in making sure that the cooperative set-up affords all possible protection to the tenant-stockholder in relation to the amount of his gain on resale of his apartment and his liabilities to outside parties.

Three important ways of creating successful cooperative apartment developments are:

(1) The conversion of existing apartments to cooperatives. Here, individual apartments are sold to tenants. The owner liquidates his equity at a profit. The tenant gets reduced monthly charges and tax benefits.

(2) Building FHA cooperative apartments. Here, the profit is made on the land and the construction. The promoter and builder get high-ratio financing.

(3) Building cooperative apartments with conventional financing.

[¶1601] Big Appeal in Cooperative Housing

The tax-deductible features of a housing co-op, are, of course, a major inducement for becoming a tenant cooperator. The tax benefits to the tenant cooperator can be very substantial, especially when compared with what would be achieved from the same amount of money invested in stocks and bonds, the income from which (dividends and interest) are subject to income tax. This comparison of after-tax return is the most pertinent reason for the popularity of cooperative housing among widows, pensioners, and others living on invested capital, as well as among the wealthy. In addition, even for middle- and low-income people, features of cooperative housing constitute an incentive. The higher the tax bracket, of course, the greater the tax savings. So, a taxpayer in a higher bracket, paying more rent, would save even more tax dollars. At the same time, part of the rent money is increasing equity by reducing the mortgage; and, in addition, the property should be appreciating in value.

[¶1602] Qualifying for Tax Deductions

The man who rents his home or apartment gets no deduction for the rent, but the man who owns stock in a cooperative apartment or housing corporation deducts his proportionate share of the interest and real estate taxes paid by the corporation. This proportionate share is based on the proportion of the total stock he owns; and the interest that is deductible can relate to any debt incurred by the corporation to acquire, construct, alter, rehabilitate, or maintain the building and land.

The cooperative must be bona fide; that is, the stockholder's ownership must give him the right to live in an apartment or house on the property owned or leased by the corporation. He needn't actually live there, but he must have the right to do so if he wants to.

The following requirements must be met:

(a) Stockholders are entitled to no distribution other than out of corporate earnings and profits (except on liquidation).

(b) Stockholders are the source of 80% of the corporation's gross income for the taxable year in which the deduction is taken.

(c) Only one class of stock outstanding: the stock issued to the tenant-stockholders.

As to the last requirement, an exception is made in favor of governmental agencies and entities; and under this exception stock owned and apartments leased by governmental entities and agencies authorized to acquire shares of stock in cooperative housing corporations in order to provide housing facilities are not taken into account. Included within the meaning of the exception are shares of stock owned and apartments leased by the United States or any of its possessions, a state or any political subdivision, or any agency or instrumentality of the foregoing, empowered to acquire shares in a cooperative housing corporation for the purpose of providing housing facilities.

As a convenience, a tenant-stockholder may pay the corporation a lump sum periodically to cover interest, taxes, maintenance, overhead, and amortization payments on the mortgage. He is allowed to compute the portion of the payment allocable to interest and taxes, and deduct it. This is a helpful exception to the general rule that interest must be segregated in order to be deductible. The basis used for the computation is the corporation's total expenses. From that, the tenant-stockholder computes his own share of the interest and taxes. This illustration will show how it's done. Assume the tenant-stockholder owns 10% of the stock and is in a 70% tax bracket. At the beginning of the year, he pays the corporation $1,600 as his share of the estimated expenses of $16,000 for the year. The actual expenses turn out to be only $15,000. Our tenant-stockholder's share is reduced to $1,500. The extra $100 is either refunded to him or he leaves it with the corporation as an installment on his share of next year's expenses.

Here's the way he computes his deduction.

Corporation's Expenses During the Year

Interest	$ 5,500	
Real estate taxes	5,000	
Maintenance	3,500	
General overhead	1,000	
Total	$15,000	
Tenant's share of total (1/10)		$1,500.00
His share of interest (1/10 of $5,500)	$ 550	
His share of taxes (1/10 of $5,000)	500	
Total deduction	$ 1,050	
Tax saving (70% of $1,050)		$ 735.00
Tenant's net cost for the year		$ 765.00

How about housing corporations that change to cooperative ownership during the year? Does the 80% requirement apply to the entire year or only to the portion after the change? IRS has ruled that the 80% requirement applies to the entire year (*Rev. Rul. 55-556*, CB 1955-2, 57).

[¶1603] How to Cooperate an Apartment House And Get a Capital Gain

If the owner sells the individual apartments, he risks ordinary income treatment on his gain, for he holds them for sale to customers in the ordinary course of business from the time that he adopts the plan of cooperation. But if he sells to a cooperative corporation composed of the new purchasers of the apartments who are the corporation's stockholders, then assuming he was not previously a dealer, it would seem that he has held the property for rental purposes up to the time of sale. So, by dealing with the cooperative corporation from its formation (as the representative of the purchasers), the seller probably preserves the character of his property as rental property to the time of sale. So, he should get a capital gain.

[¶1604] How to Organize a Cooperative

The first step is to be sure that the construction costs or the selling price is fair and reasonable in comparison with the market value of comparable land and comparable building costs. Then a decision must be reached as to the amount of mortgage that will be placed on the property at the time it is taken over by the cooperative corporation. The terms of the mortgage should be the most advantageous that are feasible in the current market. The difference between the mortgage and the selling price is the equity. This is spread over the various apartment units in the building to establish a purchase price for each unit. A proper apportionment of stock is essential because the number of shares of stock allocated to a particular living unit will not only establish its purchase price but also the ratio of the annual maintenance charges of the apartment to the total maintenance costs of all the units in the building. The usual method of apportioning stock to apartments is to place a schedule of rental values on the various living units and use this as a basis for apportioning the stock.

It is then necessary to estimate the operating expenses for the cooperative corporation, and to itemize this estimate in detail with proper allowance for all charges that can prudently be anticipated. Real estate taxes must be estimated. Mortgage interest and amortization requirements should also be adequately accounted for. A reserve for contingencies and possible increases should be estimated and added. From the estimate of expenses, deduct an estimate for any income that may be realized by the building. The net figure is then divided by the number of shares issued by the cooperative corporation to provide an estimate of the annual maintenance charges for each unit.

The next step is to sign up purchasers for the cooperative apartments. They are offered a purchase agreement outlining the apartment selected, the number of shares, total purchase price, and method of payment. They are also given a proprietary lease. These leases have become pretty well standardized. The lease provides that there should be no assignment or subletting without the written consent of the cooperative management. It limits the tenant's liability for the principal of the mortgage.

[¶1605] The Cooperative Plan

The scheme for the organization of the cooperative, the sale of property to it, and the sale of the stock and lease to the stockholder-tenants will be outlined in a plan. The plan is simply a framework for the overall arrangement. It is followed by a charter and bylaws for the cooperative corporation, the proprietary lease to the tenant-stockholders, a management agreement, and a subscription agreement with the individual tenant-stockholders.

The Charter: The charter will state that the purpose of the corporation is to provide homes for tenant-stockholders who will be entitled to a proprietary lease. The corporation should be given the power to buy, sell, hold, lease, and mortgage real estate. In addition, the specific building which will be purchased and cooperated is mentioned. The charter also fixes the number of directors, the actual number depending on state law.

Bylaws: The bylaws approve the proprietary lease form, authorize the fixing of an annual maintenance charge by the directors, and provide for voting by the stockholders. The provisions which should be included are a provision that the directors can adopt and amend house rules, requirements regarding assignment of leases or subleases, provisions for amendment of the bylaws.

The Proprietary Lease: In this lease, the tenant agrees to pay his proportionate share of the expenses of the corporation, to be based on the number of shares he holds. Provisions in the lease include a limit on the maintenance charge per share. Changes must be approved by the stockholders. The tenant, pursuant to this lease, will have the obligation of repairing his own apartment (including maintenance, redecorating, and painting). The lease will normally provide that it cannot be assigned or sublet without the approval of the board of directors or the other stockholders, and a statement that the tenant will not be obligated to pay rent until the building is ready for actual occupancy.

Independent Counsel: Because the seller of the building is in a dual position, since he also forms the cooperative corporation, full disclosure of all of the deals of the transaction in the cooperative plan is essential. As a further protection against the charge of self-dealing, the seller will want to obtain independent counsel to represent the cooperative corporation.

Unsold Units: In many cases, the seller will not be able to obtain 100% sale of stock in the cooperative by the time the property is actually sold to the cooperative. In such a case, the seller will take back the lease and stock of the unsold apartments and sell them later. The seller should provide in the cooperative's bylaws for a sale by him without advance approval or alternatively for his representation on the board of directors. This will protect him against being tied up by the cooperative when he starts to sell the remaining shares.

[¶1606] What Makes an Apartment Cooperative Salable

(1) The operating cost or monthly maintenance charge should be 40% below the rental value of each unit. This discount includes about 15% to cover those items of maintenance usually included in rents but now borne by the cooperative owners such as decorating, shades, refrigerator, and stove maintenance. It includes 25% of the monthly rent, which in a conventional building becomes profit or dividend to the equity owner.

(2) Most mortgagees limit their mortgages to 66% of the appraised value. If the appraised value of the actual cost of land and completed building and the broker's commission plus working capital and other initial expenses are added, a total selling price results of which 50% to 60% is represented by mortgage and the balance is equity. In new buildings, the mortgage share may be higher than 60%. In FHA projects, the mortgage is usually 80%.

(3) Working capital should be reserved at either 5% of total capital or three to six month's operating expenses.

The expenses of a property may be something like this:

(1) Mortgage charges ....20% of total expenses
(2) Real estate taxes...................................20% of total expenses
(3) Payroll ....40% of total expenses
(4) All other expenses ....20% of total expenses

(Of course these ratios or costs will vary widely because of particular circumstances in each building.)

Relating these major items to a tenant-cooperator's rent—let us assume it is at an annual rate of $3,000—this tenant-cooperator pays annually:

(1)	$ 600	for mortgage charges
(2)	600	for real estate taxes
(3)	1,200	for building payroll
(4)	600	for all other operating expenses
	$3,000	

[¶1607] How to Promote a Cooperative

Where new buildings are being constructed for sale to cooperative owners, the promoters must put up sufficient cash which, when added to the available first mortgage financing, will complete the construction. Then, as they sell off the units, they can collect cash from the buyers of the apartments and tack on a second mortgage for part of their profit.

The cash can be cut down by making advance sales of cooperatives and offering some kind of a concession to the buyer for putting up some of his cash in advance. Cash required can be reduced further if the land owner will wait for his money until construction is completed or put up his land on a long-term lease. Further cash reductions are accomplished by getting builders, architects, and others rendering professional services to take their payment when the job is completed.

To get buyers to put up cash in advance and get the land owner and those rendering professional services to wait for their cash, it is necessary to show that the project is assured completion by virtue of purchase and mortgage financing commitments, plus a bond of completion or performance bond, executed by the contractor and the surety company in favor of the promoter.

Payment of selling costs can also be deferred until construction funds are received.

With these measures, the cash required to promote a new cooperative can be reduced to a surprisingly small amount.

[¶1608] How Finance Plan Helps to Sell Cooperative Apartments

Helping co-op apartment buyers finance their down payments helps to sell co-op apartments. Under one plan, purchasers of co-op apartments obtain the equivalent of second mortgage financing for their apartments. In effect, the sponsor of the cooperative takes back a second mortgage on the buyer's individual apartment. The buyer uses the proceeds of the second mortgage in order to buy the stock, representing the apartment, from the cooperative corporation. The buyer does not have to give the sponsor a mortgage bond but instead deposits the cooperative stock with the sponsor until the debt is paid off. This does not affect the buyer's right to the proprietary lease nor his voting rights in the cooperative.

This set-up solves the problems of a sponsor who wants to extend credit to some buyers to facilitate sales but wants to allow those who want to purchase their apartments outright to do so. A second mortgage covering the entire property would not help, since it would affect those purchasers who have not borrowed money from the sponsor. So the new plan acts as a mortgage only on the individual apartment of the borrower. The buyer pays back the mortgage by increasing his monthly carrying charge payment until amortization is completed.

Taxwise, the buyer can deduct interest paid to the sponsor.

[¶1609] Managing a Cooperative

Tenant-owners in a cooperative apartment building take a very real interest in the operation of the property: For this reason, in addition to the usual management functions, there is an opportunity for the co-op manager to perform the following special services for the corporation and for the tenant-stockholders:

(1) Director and Stockholder Meetings: Call meetings by preparing and mailing proper notices of meetings and proxies; arrange for physical set-up at place of meetings; provide minutes of meetings and special reports.

(2) Disbursements: Make all disbursements for the corporation including taxes, amortization, mortgage, interest, repairs, fuel, supplies, electricity, and insurance premiums.

(3) Financial Reports and Tax Returns: Obtain from the corporation's accountants and furnish to directors periodic financial statements and tax returns; before annual stockholders' meeting send financial statement and report of operations to each stockholder.

(4) Transfer of Apartments: Handle sale of apartments by acting as transfer agent for stock and proprietary leases and keep records of changes in stockholders. Interview prospective purchasers and sublessees and obtain references. Submit references and managing agent's recommendation to the board of directors for consent to the transfer.

(5) Financing of Improvements: Make recommendations and suggest arrangements for financing of building improvements and modifications of mortgage financing that will result in savings to the corporation.

(6) Estimated Income and Expenses: Prepare budget of estimated income and expenses so that the board of directors can set annual maintenance charges.

(7) Prepare and Present Bills: Bill and collect maintenance charges from tenant-stockholders.

(8) Tax Assessments: Advise board of any changes in assessed value for real estate tax and make recommendations as to action to reduce excessive valuation.

(9) Building Appearance and Decorating: Keep up standards of appearance and good housekeeping.

(10) Check Insurance Coverage: Maintain and review records of insurance coverage to protect corporation's position as to amount and form of coverage.

(11) Savings from Trade Discounts: Get corporation and tenant-stockholders benefit of trade discounts resulting from volume purchasing of supplies, equipment, and painting.

[¶1610] The Cooperative Tenant

Stepping Up Stock Basis: Tenant-stockholders are permitted to deduct for tax purposes the amount of their monthly carrying charges equal to their proportionate shares of the co-op's real estate taxes and mortgage interest. The balance of the monthly charges is not deductible. But a portion of the balance of that carrying charge could increase the tenant-stockholder's basis for his co-op stock (thus cutting down on any taxable gain when he sells). To get this step-up in basis, the proprietary lease has to provide that the portion of the carrying charge that is to be applied by the co-op to pay off the principal on its mortgage should not be credited to the co-op's income but should be credited to its paid-in surplus. In such case, the amount so designated has been held to be a contribution by the tenant-stockholder to his corporation's capital, stepping up his basis for his stock. The co-op, too, benefits. The contribution to capital is eliminated from its income and it may very well have no taxable income at all.

How Co-op Tenants Avoid Personal Liability on the Co-op's Mortgage: Since the cooperative's mortgage has been given by the corporation, the stockholder-tenants are protected against personal liability. But should some of the tenants default in paying their assessments, the remaining tenants can be forced by the cooperative through higher assessments to pay a greater part of the mortgage amortization.

Solution: Give each tenant the right to terminate his proprietary lease on short notice even if he cannot find a buyer for his stock. So, if assessments become too high, a tenant-stockholder can always get out. It is provisions of this type in cooperative leases that have helped to sell cooperative apartments.

How to Avoid Gain on Residence Sale by Reinvesting in Co-op Apartment: When you sell your residence, you can avoid a tax on the gain if you reinvest the adjusted sale price in a new residence within 18 months of the sale of your old one. Purchase of a co-op apartment is considered the purchase of a new residence.

But there's the question of how much you have invested in the co-op. Is your investment only what you paid for your co-op stock? If so, chances are you have invested considerably less than the sale price of your old residence. Then, part or all of the gain on the residence would be taxable. Or does the investment in the co-op also include your share of the mortgage on the co-op property? Then, you may very well have invested as much as the sale price of your residence. Where your share of the mortgage is allocated to you by the co-op, that mortgage share is part of the price you paid for the co-op, says the Treasury (*Rev. Rul. 60-76,* CB 1960-1, 296).

[¶1700] CONDOMINIUMS

In a condominium, each condominium unit is individually owned, and the common elements of the building on which each condominium unit depends are jointly owned. A condominium thus permits ownership of a specified *horizontal layer* of air space and adds a third dimension to land conveyance and ownership. Because condominium ownership has certain definite advantages over cooperative ownership, it makes a great market for builders.

Condominiums may be commercial or residential. The condominium form of ownership may be used for high-rise apartment buildings, garden apartments, townhouse developments, detached single-family homes, office buildings, industrial plants and industrial parks, buildings of mixed uses (i.e., apartment and office), recreational developments, etc.

[¶1701] How to Set Up a Condominium

(1) Creating the Condominium: A condominium is created by the declaration of condominium, which is a binding contract among the owner or co-owners of the property. The declaration must be in the form of a deed, duly executed. This is the "master deed" and binds the present owners and all future owners. (However, unanimous agreement by all co-owners can restore the property to its original status.) The master deed may be executed even though the building has not yet been constructed. It is then recorded, along with a complete description of the building, a detailed plan of each condominium unit, a description of the common elements of the building (that is, everything except the individual condominium unit that is of common use or necessary to its existence, upkeep, and safety), and certain other information.

(2) Selling the Condominium Units: The owners then may sell individual condominium units in the building. A purchaser may be one or more individuals, a corporation, or any other entity capable of holding property. The purchaser owns his individual condominium unit. He may mortgage it, bequeath it, or resell it (although it may have to be offered first to the other apartment owners). He receives a deed which can be recorded as a deed of real property. Taxes are assessed against each apartment separately. The purchaser also is a joint owner of the common elements in the building, including the land, the foundations and roof, the basement and heating plant, the hallways, lobby, stairways, elevators, etc. It is this joint ownership, or "condominium," that makes possible individual ownership of "subdivided space." This joint ownership differs from the more familiar tenancy in common and joint tenancy because the latter can be partitioned by any joint owner by a court proceeding. Obviously, partition of the common elements of a building is impossible. (It is conceivable, however, that formal agreements among the owners not to seek partition may be held void under the local rule against perpetuities.)

(3) Operating and Administering the Condominium: Each condominium unit owner is liable only for his own taxes and mortgage. However, maintenance costs for the common elements are necessarily a joint obligation. The percentage contribution of each owner is fixed in the master deed and is based on the relation between the value of his apartment to the whole. This value cannot be changed thereafter without the unanimous consent of all. Of course, this does not affect the actual value of the condominium unit for purposes of resale, etc. The owner's obligation to contribute toward maintenance cannot be avoided by his abandonment of the condominium unit nor "waiver" of his right to use the common elements. As long as he owns his condominium unit his liability remains and may be enforced by legal action.

To provide for "harmonious living," a typical statute sets forth certain rules for the government of the building. These are usually supplemented with bylaws or other agreements which bind the owners in the same manner as restrictive covenants in the deeds. The statute provides that a quorum for meetings shall be 51% of the ownership. Approval for alterations and improvements in the building must be by majority vote. Once approved, they are paid for in accordance with the formula set forth in the master deed. Amendments to the bylaws require a 75% vote.

Although there is no need for restrictions on the sale or lease of individual condominium units to set up the condominium, the owners will usually want assurance that sales and leases will be made only with financially responsible persons or persons meeting other standards that may be established. In such case, prior approval of the association of owners may be required, or (in the case of sales) the association may be given the right of first refusal. The validity and scope of these restrictions will depend on local law.

(4) Is Specific Legislation Necessary for a Condominium? There are three elements that are necessary for the proper establishment of a condominium. To the extent they are not already present in a particular jurisdiction, special legislation may be needed.

First, the jurisdiction must recognize the division of ownership on a condominium basis, i.e., division into "space lots." In some jurisdictions, the ownership of air space is valid provided the space can be reduced to possession. This, of course, the condominium unit owner can do since he is a joint owner of the structural and foundation elements of the building which permit occupancy of a "space lot." In addition, it must be possible to measure the air space. This can usually be done in one of three ways: (1) land and space survey—measure the distance above the ground to establish height, and measure the distances between the condominium unit walls and identifiable points on the ground as in an ordinary deed; (2) subdivision plat—record a subdivision plat of air space and indicate each apartment by numbering the plat; (3) floor plan—show the location of the building by a survey and attach floor plans giving the specifications of each condominium unit.

Secondly, the state must permit the recording of instruments creating and mortgaging condominium apartments.

Furthermore, taxes should be assessed separately against each individual condominium unit (except for the taxes on the common elements in the building). If this were done and all taxes were assessed against the building as a single unit, failure of a condominium unit owner to contribute his share would add materially to the obligations of the remaining owners. This is what condominium seeks to avoid.

[¶1702] Condominium Compared With Cooperative

In a condominium, each condominium unit is individually owned. In a cooperative, the building is owned by the cooperative corporation and the ownership of shares in the corporation carries with it the right to a proprietary lease of an apartment or other space (e.g., office, single-family residence, etc.). The advantages or disadvantages of cooperatives and condominiums stem from this basic difference.

Financing: In a cooperative, a single mortgage is taken out with the entire building as security. Each shareholder is responsible for his share of amortization and interest just as for his share of maintenance costs. If one shareholder defaults, the rest must make up his share. In such a case, the corporation can evict the one defaulting and resell or rent his apartment, etc. This normally will be adequate to cover his liability. However, during an economic depression, numerous defaults combined with a lessened demand could result in substantial losses for cooperative owners.

In a condominium, on the other hand, there is no mortgage against the entire building. Instead, each purchaser of a condominium unit arranges his own financing. He can, if he wishes, pay all cash. Or he can obtain a mortgage on his individual unit. Even assuming his individual mortgage is equal in amount to the cooperative owner's proportionate share of the single building mortgage, the condominium owner need not worry about his obligation increasing because of the defaults of others. It is true that the cooperative owner can limit any possible loss to his investment (plus any obligations under his lease) by abandoning the apartment. The condominium owner, on the other hand, remains personally liable on his mortgage. Nevertheless, many persons no doubt prefer to carry their own independent obligations.

What's more, financing a condominium will probably be easier because many small loans replace a single large one. So, a lending institution may be able to finance a condominium although not a cooperative because of the limit placed on its authority to lend money on the security of a mortgage. Some lending institutions are limited to lending no more than 70% of value on apartment houses, while they may lend up to 90% on one-family homes. If the 90% limit is applied to condominiums, much higher overall mortgages will be available.

One of the problems in cooperative financing is that after a few years and as the building mortgage is amortized, the cooperative owner increases his equity. If he then wants to sell, the buyer either has to make a large cash payment or the seller has to take payments in installments. While financing which is equivalent to a second mortgage may be available to solve this problem, the condomium offers a simpler answer—the original mortgage need only be refinanced by the buyer.

GI Insurance: GI insurance, as well as FHA insurance, is available for the purchase of condominium units.

Unrestricted Use and Ownership of the Apartment: The cooperative "owner" actually has a landlord—the cooperative corporation—which ordinarily imposes restrictions on the use of the apartment or other unit, permissible alterations, etc. In many cases, transfer of the stock (and the apartment or other unit) to another requires approval of the board of directors. Many persons find this irksome, and want to feel as if they truly are property owners. For them, condominium may be the answer. While there are also rules in a condominium, they are fewer and less burdensome, more like rules adopted by a group of private owners for their mutual benefit. Above all, restrictions on resale are less strict and may require only that the remaining owners be permitted a first refusal at the price the seller can get from an outsider.

Income Tax Position: This is substantially the same for both. A condominium owner can deduct his interest and taxes (just as a cooperative tenant deducts his share of the co-op's interest and taxes).

[¶1703] Converting Rental Apartments To Condominium Ownership

The owner of an apartment building might want to convert to condominium ownership when his depreciation deductions have reached a point at which they no longer provide him with the tax shelter he requires and he wants to pull out his equity. He might be at a point at which an increase in rentals would be indicated but an increase is not practicable because of the risk of substantially increased vacancies and tenant turnover. Other reasons for conversion might be that attempts to sell the building turned up no purchasers or that the work necessary to bring the building up to snuff is too costly.

What the Owner Gains: Among the most important benefits that the owner obtains when he successfully converts to condominium ownership are:

(1) A much larger return than the current value of the existing mortgage and his equity;

(2) A great opportunity to free funds for new investments;

(3) Long-term capital gain rather than receiving rental income as ordinary income;

(4) Offering dwelling units in a market in which prospective purchasers find it difficult to obtain suitable housing.

How the Lender Benefits: A lending institution that has held the mortgage on the property for a substantial length of time may find the interest rate unfavorable in the current market. With a successful conversion, the loan can be repaid before maturity, and the lending institution can reinvest the money at current rates. Also it has a chance to invest in condominium-unit mortgage loans which have proven their soundness through the years.

[¶1800] DEPRECIATION

In any consideration of real estate, whether of the tax or financial aspects, depreciation and amortization play vitally important roles. Often, the difference between a profitable or nonprofitable transaction is due to the interplay of these two elements.

Depreciation provides a tax-free return of your investment. To the extent that depreciation exceeds amortization payments, you have a tax-free cash flow. That is why in appraising a real estate investment, in setting up financing, in building, in leasing, and in selecting the depreciation method to be used, it is essential that these elements be carefully scrutinized.

While the 1969 tax law cut down on the right to take accelerated depreciation and tightened up the depreciation recapture rules in certain real estate areas, the tax benefits of real estate depreciation continue to be of great importance to real estate investors. In the following material, you will find out just how tax shelter is obtained through depreciation deductions that real estate investments throw off.

[¶1801] What Kind of Property Is Depreciable?

Generally, depreciable property is property used in trade or business or held for the production of income, which is subject to physical decay or obsolescence and has a definite useful life. It isn't necessary that the asset is earning income or bringing in money as long as it is used in a trade or business or held for the production of income (*Hardwick Realty Co.*, 7 BTA 1108). Holding a single piece of rental property is enough to give you a depreciation deduction.

You cannot take a deduction for personal assets—a personal residence, for example. But property can be used for a dual purpose. For instance, suppose a building has two apartments. You rent one apartment to a tenant and occupy the other as your residence. You can take a depreciation deduction for the half that is used in business (i.e., rented to a tenant) but not for the residential half.

Land is not depreciable (*Hawkins,* TC Memo 1955-110). So, when you buy improved property, you have to allocate your purchase price among the land and the buildings and other improvements.

Former Residence: What was formerly your personal residence can be converted into income-producing property. In *Smith*, TC Memo 1967-28, the taxpayers permanently abandoned their residence and offered it for sale but made no attempt to rent it. They not only took depreciation deductions, but also deductions for repair and maintenance expenses. The Tax Court okayed the deductions.

Realizing that the *Smith* case was subject to abuse, the Tax Court in 1970 created a new test. The Court held that neither mere rental offers nor the listing of a home for sale was the sole factor for determining whether the conversion occurred (*Newcombe,* 54 TC 1298, 1970). Instead, the Court weighed several factors (including rental offers and listing the house for sale) to determine the taxpayer's intention. Why intention? The Court was looking to see if in light of all the surrounding facts and circumstances it was the taxpayer's intention that his vacated home be held for the production of income; i.e., did he expect a profit (not merely a recoupment of his original investment) to result from his post-conversion holding of the property? See also *Lowry,* DC N.H., 384 F.Supp. 287, 1974.

Vacant Building: Under Code §167(a)(2), property held for gain from its disposition is depreciable, as is property held for the purpose of producing recurring income (*Mitchell,* 47 TC 120). So a vacant building bought as an investment but never rented, never producing income, and then sold at an attractive price is depreciable during the period you own it.

[¶1802] Depreciation of Land Preparation Costs

Under a Revenue Ruling (*Rev. Rul. 74-265*, CB 1974-1, 56), you are allowed a depreciation allowance for some of your land preparation costs. Here's how the rule works.

As you know, Code §167 permits a depreciation allowance for the exhaustion of and wear and tear on property held for the production of income. Usually this does not cover deductions for the land itself but is restricted to improvements to the land, such as buildings (Reg. §1.167(a)-(2)).

IRS has ruled that it can determine that land adjacent to buildings may have a useful life. How is this determined? If the replacement of your buildings will require the physical destruction of your land preparation immediately adjacent to those buildings, you may treat that land preparation, consisting of the shrubbery and ornamental trees, as depreciable property under Code §167. However, the balance of the landscaping—clearing and grading, topsoil, seeding, and planting shrubbery and ornamental trees around the boundaries of your land—will not be affected by replacement of the buildings. The cost of landscaping these areas will not be subject to the depreciation allowance. Instead, the cost of this land preparation is added to your basis.

Land not adjacent to a building is unaffected by the building's life so that it does not have a determinable life. As a result, a depreciation allowance for the preparation of such land is not applicable.

Land adjacent to a building will be destroyed when the building is replaced. The preparation of such adjacent land has a useful life contemporaneous with the building's and may therefore be depreciated for tax purposes.

In *Aurora Village Shopping Center, Inc.*, TC Memo 1970-39, the Tax Court ruled that some of the grading costs incurred by the taxpayer were depreciable but it disallowed others. Here's why.

Necessity for Supporting Allocation of Costs Between Land and Buildings: Aurora's architect, in planning a shopping center, recommended that the plateau of the building site be raised to make the shopping center more conspicuous to passing traffic. The architect also recommended that the grading of the parking area be no greater than 3% to avoid discomfort to female patrons. It cost Aurora about $52,000 to get these jobs done. Aurora allocated $42,000 of this amount to its depreciable basis of the building. IRS allowed only $21,000 of this amount, and the Tax Court agreed with IRS. The Court stated that Aurora had grading costs that were attributable to building costs but that Aurora also had costs attributable to the cost of land. Although Aurora relied on an accountant to make the allocation, the accountant did not testify, and no reason was given for his absence. Neither did anyone else who could shed some light on the allocation testify. So the Court had no basis for making an allocation more favorable than that made by IRS.

What to Do: To sustain your allocation of grading costs between land and buildings, you must show that the costs you allocate to the buildings are directly associated with them. While you can prevail where the grading is necessary for the proper setting of the buildings, you must prove your case. The burden will be on you if you're put to the test. You can't leave the court in a position in which it has no basis for making an estimate as to which costs are attributable to buildings and which to the land.

In the *Aurora* case, the taxpayer might have been able to sustain its allocation or at least a larger portion of its allocation had it come prepared to prove its case.

[¶1803] Who Can Take a Depreciation Deduction?

The person who takes the economic loss because of the decrease in value is the one entitled to take the depreciation deduction. Normally, that means the owner of the property. For this there must be a capital investment. (See

Atlantic Coast Line Ry. Co., 31 BTA 730.) Bare legal title alone is not sufficient. Depreciation is dependent on real investment. (See *Gladding Dry Goods Co.,* 2 BTA 336.)

A lessee would be entitled to the depreciation deduction, as opposed to the owner of bare legal title; the lessor, where the rental payments were in effect payments of the purchase price (*Rev. Rul. 55-25,* CB 1955-1, 283). Property that does not cost anything has no basis and, therefore, does not result in any depreciation deduction (*Detroit Edison Co. v. Comm.,* 319 US 98). This would also apply where property is contributed to a corporation by persons who do not make the contribution in the capacity of stockholders. That property has a zero basis (§362(c)).

A depreciation deduction may be claimed by any person or taxable entity owning a capital interest in property. These are individuals, whether citizens or aliens, residents or nonresidents; corporations, whether domestic or foreign; partnerships and joint ventures; fiduciaries and beneficiaries of estates and trusts; heirs, legatees and devisees; life tenants; and any other entities that are subject to tax (Reg. §1.167).

Where the owner of depreciable property dies, the allocable portion of depreciation for the taxable year, computed on the basis of the number of months to the date of his death, is taken by his executor or administrator on his final return. The deceased's estate computes the depreciation from the date of death and uses a new basis for such computation: the value of the property at the date of death or, if elected, the alternate valuation (§1014(a)).

A life tenant is entitled to the deduction as if he were the absolute owner of the property (Reg. §1.167(h)-1(a)). After the death of the life tenant, the deduction, if any, is allowed to the remainderman.

[¶1804] Elements of Depreciation

Before you can determine the amount of your depreciation deduction, you must know the following three elements: (1) the method of depreciation that you will use, (2) the amount you can recover (depreciable basis), and (3) the period over which you can take deductions (useful life).

(1) Depreciation Methods: There are several methods by which to calculate the depreciation deduction. Sometimes the rate at which you take depreciation deductions can vary considerably from one method to another. The accelerated depreciation methods, of course, permit the fastest recovery of cost.

(2) How Much You Can Recover: The amount recoverable through depreciation usually is what you pay for the property (cost) reduced by the amount that you estimate you will realize on disposition of the property (salvage). Where the property is tangible personal property which is eligible for the 20% first-year writeoff, this too has to be deducted from the cost to arrive at the amount recoverable.

(3) Useful Life: The last element is useful life, the period over which you can take depreciation deductions. The length of the depreciation period will have the greatest effect on the amount of your annual depreciation deductions. This usually is the area where disputes with IRS arise.

Back in 1942, IRS issued Bulletin F which listed the useful lives of various types of assets. These guidelines were used until 1962 when IRS, in *Rev. Proc. 62-21,* issued depreciation guidelines. *Rev. Proc. 62-21* replaced the item-by-item listing of Bulletin F with broad classes of assets which had shorter lives than those listed in Bulletin F.

IRS used the reserve ratio test to check up on the useful lives claimed by taxpayers. The test was rather complicated and had the effect of discouraging use of the guidelines. As a result of difficulties arising out of using the reserve ratio test, IRS adopted the Asset Depreciation Range (ADR) system. The Revenue Act of 1971 authorized a new class life system which combined the provisions of the ADR system with parts of the guidelines.

For determining an asset's useful life, you can now elect to use the class life system or you can use depreciation rates based on all the facts and circumstances surrounding your situation. Useful lives under ADR are set forth in the Appendix.

[¶1805] Depreciation Methods

Straight-Line Depreciation: With this method, the depreciation expense is the same from period to period. The formula followed for this method is:

$$\frac{\text{(Cost—Salvage Value)}}{\text{Estimated Life}} = \text{Depreciation Expense}$$

For example, if the improvement costs $20,000, has a salvage value of $200, and an estimated life of 20 years, the depreciation expense for the year would be computed as follows:

$$\frac{(\$20{,}000–200)}{20} = \$990$$

The straight-line method is essentially an accounting concept which, to a great extent, is based on a conjecture that the depreciation will be at a constant rate throughout the estimated life. Despite this unscientific approach in a scientific world, the straight-line method is followed by many taxpayers and is recognized as a method of depreciation by the Internal Revenue Service. This method of depreciation is available for all new or used property.

Declining-Balance Depreciation: Under this method, the amount of depreciation expense decreases from period to period. It is favored by economists because it takes note of the fact that real depreciation in value is greatest in the first year and becomes progressively less as the asset ages. Therefore, the largest depreciation deduction is taken in the first year. The amount then declines steeply over succeeding years until the final years of estimated useful life when the depreciation charge becomes relatively small. This method of depreciation can be used only with respect to new residential rental properties.

While the true declining-balance method requires the application of a complex formula, if you are going to use the maximum declining-balance depreciation (i.e., the 200% method), you need not go through these mathematical computations. Just: (1) determine the straight-line percentage rate; (2) double it; (3) apply it to your full basis (undiminished by salvage value) to get your first year's deduction. In the second year, (1) reduce your basis by the previous year's depreciation deduction; (2) apply the same percentage rate to the new basis you arrived at in step (1). In the third year and later years, repeat the same process.

Sum-of-the-Years'-Digits Depreciation: Here, diminishing rates, expressed fractionally, are applied to the total depreciable value. Determination of the fractional rate to be used each year may be made as follows:

(a) Obtain the sum of the years' digits. On a ten-year life, add this way: 1 + 2 + 3 + 4 + 5 + 6 + 7 + 8 + 9 + 10 = 55.

(b) The first year's depreciation will be 10/55 × $10,000; the second year's depreciation will be 9/55 × $10,000; the third year's depreciation will be 8/55 × $10,000; and so on.

This method is permitted by the Internal Revenue Service only on property acquired and first put into use after 1953. Here's how it works:

Assume: Cost, $10,600; salvage value, $600; life, 10 years.

Year	*Depreciation*
1st	$ 1,818.18
2nd	1,636.36
3rd	1,454.55
4th	1,272.73
5th	1,090.94
6th	909.09
7th	727.27
8th	545.45
9th	363.64
10th	181.82
	$10,000.00

Under this method, the asset is depreciated over the estimated life, and in the first three years more of the cost is recovered than with the 200%-declining-balance method. All of the cost of the asset is recovered over its useful life, but this is not so in the declining-balance method. The sum-of-the-years'-digits method will give a more rapid return of capital than the percentage declining-balance method.

[¶1806] Depreciation Available for Different Types of Property

Here is a rundown on the different methods of depreciation available with respect to different types of real estate where the depreciation rules set up by the Tax Reform Act of 1969 apply:

(1) Straight-Line: This method of depreciation is available for all types of new and used properties.

(2) 125%-Declining-Balance: This depreciation method is available for (a) used real property acquired before July 25, 1969, and (b) used residential rental property acquired after July 24, 1969, with a useful life of 20 years or more.

(3) 150%-Declining-Balance: This method is the fastest available for (a) used real property acquired before July 25, 1969, and (b) new nonresidential rental properties constructed after July 24, 1969.

(4) Sum-of-the-Years'-Digits: This method of depreciation is available only for (a) new real estate constructed before July 25, 1969, and (b) new residential rental properties.

(5) 200%-Declining-Balance: This depreciation method is available only for (a) new real estate constructed before July 25, 1969, and (b) new residential rental properties.

(6) Straight-Line Using Short Useful Life: This method of depreciation is available only for rehabilitation expenses for low- or moderate-income residential rental properties. Expenditures are depreciated on a straight-line basis using a 60-month useful life.

When to Use Composite or Separate Depreciation: Depreciation on real estate may be either composite or separate. Composite depreciation calls for the application of an average rate that takes into consideration all the elements in the building—such as heating plant, elevators, etc. Separate depreciation requires each piece of equipment to be depreciated separately and, therefore, may permit higher deductions during the earlier years in the high tax period where short-lived elements represent an amount of the total cost. Otherwise, it is generally to the taxpayer's advantage to adopt composite depreciation.

In composite depreciation, the expense is computed by averaging the depreciation rate and applying it against the cost in the asset account, as follows:

Items	*Cost*	*Rate %*	*If Computed by Individual Asset*
Building	$30,000	4	$1,200
Machinery #1	2,000	5	100
Machinery #2	2,000	10	200
Machinery #3	1,000	5	50
Machinery #4	5,000	10	500
	$40,000	34*	$2,050

*Weighted average rate of depreciation is 5.1%
Average Rate × Cost = Depreciation
5.1% × $40,000 = $2,040 Annual Write-off

What Is New Residential Rental Property Within Meaning of Depreciation Rules? New residential rental property is residential rental property with respect to which the taxpayer is the first user. At least 80% of the gross rental income from the property in the taxable year must be rental income from dwelling units. While a "dwelling unit" can be a house or apartment used to provide living accommodations in a building or structure, a unit in a hotel, motel or other establishment, more than one-half the units of which are used on a transient basis, is not a dwelling unit. For purposes of the 80% test, if part of the building is occupied by the taxpayer, the gross rental income includes the rental value of that portion of the building. Interest subsidy payments under the FHA §221(d)(3) and 236 programs are not included in gross income for this purpose.

The property may be situated within the U.S. or any of its possessions or in a foreign country if that country's laws provide a method of depreciation for the property which is comparable to the 200%-declining-balance or the sum-of-the-years'-digits method. In the event such a method is provided and it results in a depreciation allowance which is greater than that under the 150%-declining-balance method but less than the fastest method available under Code §167, the depreciation deduction is limited to that provided by the foreign country's law.

[¶1807] Comparison of Different Depreciation Methods

Here's how straight-line, declining-balance, sum-of-the-years'-digits, and declining-balance with a switch to straight-line depreciation methods work on a piece of property with a ten-year life, assuming a $10,000 cost and no salvage value.

Year	*Straight-Line*	*Declining-Balance*	*Sum-of-Digits*	*Declining-Balance Switch to Straight-Line*
1st	$ 1,000	$ 2,000	$ 1,818	$ 2,000
2nd	1,000	1,600	1,636	1,600
3rd	1,000	1,280	1,455	1,280
4th	1,000	1,024	1,273	1,024
5th	1,000	819	1,091	819
6th	1,000	655	909	655
7th	1,000	524	727	655
8th	1,000	420	545	655
9th	1,000	336	364	655
10th	1,000	268	182	655
	$10,000	$ 8,926	$10,000	$ 9,998

[¶1808] Which Form of Accelerated Depreciation Should You Use?

Let's assume that, after due consideration, you've definitely decided to adopt one of the accelerated methods of depreciation. Which form of accelerated depreciation should you use?

If you are the first user of new residential rental real property, you are allowed to use either the 200%-declining-balance or sum-of-the-years'-digits method of figuring depreciation. Either method will return your basis much faster than the conventional straight-line method.

Consider these rules when you pick your method. Then pick the method that fits your requirements:

(1) Depreciation in the first two years will be greater under the 200%-declining-balance method than under the sum-of-the-years'-digits method. By the third year, the digits method will catch up. Thereafter, the digits method will pull ahead.

(2) At halfway mark in the property's life, you'll have recovered about two-thirds your cost under the 200%-declining-balance method; about three-quarters, under the digits method.

[¶1809] Switching Depreciation Method

You can always switch from a declining-balance to the straight-line depreciation method and get automatic approval of the switch. (You'd usually switch near the halfway mark because then you'd get bigger deductions under straight-line.) To get automatic approval of the switch, you must file Form 3115 within the first 90 days of the taxable year in which you want the change to become effective and, in addition, meet other conditions. You won't be able to switch where you have entered into an agreement with the Commissioner prohibiting such a switch.

How to Figure When Switch Should Be Made: The depreciation rate to be used on the declining-balance method and on the straight-line method should be determined when the asset is first acquired. The time of the switch from the declining-balance method to the straight-line method should be carefully ascertained. Safeguards should be posted so that the change is made during the proper year, otherwise the asset will not be exhausted over its estimated life.

[¶1810] Depreciation Rates

Agreement Covering Depreciation Allowance: Written agreements as to useful life and depreciation rates may be made between the taxpayer and IRS and are binding on both parties unless new facts can be shown justifying a change. Any such change would be prospective only and would not affect previous taxable years (§167(d)). In the absence of an agreement to the contrary, the taxpayer has the privilege, as indicated, of switching at any time from the double-declining-balance to the straight-line method (§167(e)). Unless there is "clear and convincing basis for a change" from the amount of deduction taken by a taxpayer, the Internal Revenue Service will not question a depreciation allowance (*Rev. Rul. 53-90,* CB 1953-1, 43). Application for agreement is made to the director for the district in which your return is required to be filed.

[¶1811] Basis for Depreciation and Salvage Value

The basis for depreciation (i.e., the capital amount on which you figure your deductions) is the adjusted basis (under §1011) for the purpose of determining the gain or loss on the sale or other disposition of the property (§167(g)). Normally, this means your basis is what you paid for the property. But where you have trade exchanges, gifts, and other forms of acquisitions, there are special rules.

To the original basis for the property, from time to time should be added the cost of improvements, additions, and betterments. Any deductible loss or damage from casualty must be subtracted.

Where both depreciable property and nondepreciable property (such as land and buildings) are acquired for a lump sum, the basis for depreciation of the depreciable property is its proportionate part of the total cost, based on the ratio of the total cost to total value at the time of purchase (Reg. §1.167(a)-5).

A mortgage on the property at the time of acquisition does not reduce the basis; it is immaterial whether the property was taken subject to the mortgage or the mortgage was assumed. If property is repossessed because of default by the purchaser, the allowance for depreciation after the repossession should be computed upon cost at time of repossession, not upon original cost (*Crane*, 331 US 1).

If property that is used for personal reasons, such as a personal residence, is converted to rental property, the basis for depreciation is its fair market value at the time it was converted or its adjusted basis on that date, whichever is less (Reg. §1.167(f)-1). The same basis would be used for computing any gain or loss on the sale of property that was converted from residential to rental property before its sale (Reg. §1.165-3(b)).

Example: Johnson purchased a residence in 1965 for $25,000. Of this amount, $15,000 was allocable to the building. The property was used as residence until 1/1/74, at which time it was converted to rental property. Its fair market value on that date was $22,000, of which $12,000 was allocable to the building; and its estimated life was 20 years. The basis for depreciation starting on 1/1/74 is $12,000, the amount then allocable to the building which is less than $15,000, the cost of the building; the annual amount deductible for depreciation on the straight-line basis is $600, one-twentieth of $12,000. The basis to be used for the entire property in computing gain or loss on a subsequent sale would be $22,000, not $25,000.

A careful ledger should be kept of all construction costs, such as direct labor, manufacturing overhead, etc., so that a depreciation basis can be computed. If due to the construction of the asset there are assessments against the company or taxpayer, the amount of the assessment increases the basis.

All charges are to be included in determining basis. Freight charges, cost of installation, and special lines and services all go into determining the cost of the asset. However, on property which was not used in a trade or business but is converted to business use, the basis for depreciation is the fair market value at the time of the conversion or the cost of the property, whichever is lower.

If you act as your own builder or general contractor in putting up your own building or a capital improvement, you don't get a depreciation deduction on your equipment used on the job. The depreciation allocable to that job is added to the cost of your improvement (*Rev. Rul. 59-380,* CB 1959-2, 87).

Salvage Value: Salvage value must be taken into account in computing the annual allowance under all but the declining-balance method of depreciation. Salvage value is the net amount realizable from the sale of an asset, the usefulness of which has been exhausted, over and above the cost of dismantling or removing (Reg. §1.167(a)-1(c)). Furthermore, in no event can an asset (or account) be depreciated below a reasonable salvage value (Reg. §1.167(b)-2; *Massey,* 364 US 92). Use a realistic value, taking into consideration your use of the property, your retirement and maintenance practice, and the proceeds which experience has indicated you can expect. Junk or scrap value can be used only if your policy is to use depreciable property for its full serviceable life (*Special Ruling*, 5/18/55). At one time it was thought that the concept of salvage value did not apply to real estate; but in a series of cases, beginning with *Casey*, 38 TC 357, and *Grace,* TC Memo 1961-252, the Tax Court held otherwise.

The reason for not deducting salvage from basis where declining-balance depreciation is used is that this method will leave an undepreciated balance at the end of the estimated useful life. This amount is the salvage value, bearing in mind the requirement that it must be reasonable.

To the extent salvage eventually realized exceeds the estimate which was used in computing the basis for depreciation, the excess is §1231 income (long-term capital gain) in the year of realization. If it is less than the estimate or if the declining-balance method was used so there is an unrecovered basis at the end of the useful life, the unrecovered amount is a fully deductible loss when the asset is sold or abandoned.

Where you switch from declining-balance to straight-line, estimated salvage must be subtracted from unrecovered basis, to which the straight-line method is thereafter applied (Reg. §1.167(e)-1(b)).

Either salvage or net salvage may be used in determining depreciation.

[¶1812] Trap in First-User Rule

Under a provision of the 1969 Tax Reform Act, when property that was not depreciable at the time of original use becomes depreciable property after 7/24/69, it cannot be treated as new property, the original use of which began with the taxpayer. Therefore, the taxpayer cannot use the fastest methods of accelerated depreciation with respect to the property if it is residential rental property or the 150%-declining-balance method if it is new nonresidential rental property (Code §167(j)(6)(B)).

Even before the adoption of the 1969 tax law, the right to use accelerated depreciation was limited to property not previously used by someone other than the taxpayer who claimed the deduction (§167(c)).

Here's an example of how you can run into this tax trap and how to avoid it:

Assume you have started a new business. Like many others, you use the sole proprietorship form of business so that the expected initial losses can be set off against personal income. When the profits start coming in, you incorporate the business in order to protect those profits from the individual income tax rates. The incorporation, of course, is tax free (§351).

If you want the corporation to get the benefit of accelerated depreciation, don't acquire depreciable property for the business while you are operating it as a sole proprietorship. A corporation that receives depreciable property in a tax-free exchange isn't the "first user" of the property as required by §167. Consequently, the corporation won't be entitled to accelerated depreciation (*Rev. Rul. 56-256,* CB 1956-2, 129; Reg. §1.167(c)(6)).

It might be well to protect yourself either by renting instead of buying during the proprietorship period or by foregoing the proprietorship entirely and incorporating immediately. If you are reasonably well satisfied that profits will be coming along fairly early in the operation, immediate incorporation won't hurt; the initial losses can be taken care of through carryovers.

[¶1813] Special First-Year Depreciation Allowance

There is a special 20% first-year depreciation allowance which applies only to tangible personal property. However, it is frequently available to real estate investors, for example, where a real estate operation requires a significant expenditure for personal property items, as in the case of a motel. Also, IRS treats certain items as personal property even though they are deemed fixtures and part of the real estate under local law. Typical examples are refrigerators and individual air conditioners.

The first-year allowance permits you to write off as much as $2,000 ($4,000 on a joint return) in addition to regular depreciation in the year the personal property is acquired (§179). This is based on a 20% deduction on a maximum annual investment of $10,000 ($20,000 on a joint return).

The effect of the 20% first-year writeoff when used with 200%-declining-balance depreciation is to step up the recovery of investment by about 10% over the first half of the life of the property. Under the 200%-declining-balance method, about 65% of cost is recovered in the first half of the life of the asset. Adding the 20% first-year writeoff, the recovery over the first half of the life of the property is boosted to about 72%. With the sum-of-the-years'-digits method, the first half of the useful life recovery is boosted from about 73% to about 79%.

The immediate 20% writeoff is available on the purchase of both new and secondhand property. You still get your ordinary depreciation deduction on the balance of the cost.

The first-year writeoff plus the 150%-declining-balance method can give better results than the 200%-declining-balance or the digits methods (without the first-year writeoff) on property with an equal useful life.

Here are some *technical rules* you have to follow to be eligible for the special 20% first-year writeoff:

(1) The property you buy has to have a useful life of at least 6 years.

(2) The property has to have been bought after 1957.

(3) You cannot buy property from a related interest between whom losses are disallowed, e.g., a corporation in which you own 50% or more of the stock; a partnership in which you own a more-than-50% interest (nor can the partnership or corporation buy from you); a trust of which you are the grantor or beneficiary; certain relatives. As to relatives, however, the prohibition applies only to transactions between spouses, ancestors, and lineal descendants (e.g., parents, children, and grandchildren). So you can make

purchases from a brother or sister and from in-laws. Note too that when applying the constructive ownership rules to find if you own 50% of the stock of a corporation, for example, holdings of spouse, ancestors, and lineal descendants are the only relatives' holdings that count.

(4) The property can't be purchased from a corporation with which the purchaser files a consolidated return. The entire group filing a consolidated return is entitled to only one 20% deduction.

(5) The first-year writeoff does not apply to property received by gift or inheritance.

(6) If you trade in property as part of your purchase, that part of the basis of the new property which is a carryover of the basis of the traded-in property does not count in applying the 20% writeoff. For example, assume you buy a new machine for $10,000, paying $7,000 in cash and trading in your old machine. If the old machine had a basis to you of $1,500, your basis for the new machine is $8,500. But your 20% writeoff applies only to $7,000, giving a $1,400 first-year writeoff.

(7) Where partnerships are concerned, the amount that can be written off under first-year depreciation is up to 20% of the cost of the property but not to exceed $10,000 ($20,000 if married and filing a joint return) for each partner (Reg. §1.179-2(d)).

[¶1814] Class Life System (ADR)

The Revenue Act of 1971 established a "Class Life System" which does five things: (1) Authorizes IRS to accept depreciation based on lives for business equipment acquired after 1970 that are not more than 20% shorter nor 20% longer than the "guideline lives" fixed by the Treasury in July 1962. (2) Provides for a half-year averaging convention as exemplified by the following alternative methods: (a) all eligible property obtained during the taxable year is deemed to be acquired at midyear or (b) each asset placed in service during the first half of the taxable year is deemed to be acquired on the first day of the same year, while each asset placed in service in the second half of the year is deemed to be acquired on the first day of the next taxable year. (3) Permits a deduction for expenditures for repair and maintenance based on a percentage of the assets in a guideline class on which depreciation under the Class Life System is elected. It will not be necessary to prove that such expenditures do not have to be capitalized. (4) Sets up an Office of Industrial Economics which will analyze the annual information submitted by taxpayers using the Class Life System and constantly revise the guideline classes, guideline lives, and repair allowances and set up new guidelines and allowances where appropriate. (5) Reserve ratio test is no longer used.

How to Decide Whether to Adopt System: To determine whether it pays to sell or trade in your old equipment and buy new in order to get the higher depreciation under the Class Life System, take a careful look at the arithmetic. How much depreciation are you getting out of the old? How much will you get with the new? How much is any loss on the sale of the old worth? What are the estimated expenses with the old? With the new? What are the estimated cost savings, if any, through the higher efficiency of the new, etc.?

The approach will be different depending on whether or not the tax basis of the old equipment is higher than its present value. If it's not and you trade it in on the new equipment, you avoid the recapture of the gain as ordinary income under §1245—the gain carries over to the new equipment and is not realized until the new property is sold.

On the other hand, if the basis is higher than the present value and you trade in the property, you can't claim the loss, so that you'd be looking to sell the property in order to realize the loss (and to avoid having IRS look on it as a trade-in anyhow, the sale should be to a third party).

Gauging the Savings in Purchase of Used Equipment: Under the Class Life System, you have to be extra careful in situations where you buy relatively small quantities of used equipment along with more substantial purchases of new equipment. The danger is that if the System is elected, it will apply to both used and new assets. The result could be that the used equipment would be subject to the same useful life range as the new equipment; whereas, as used equipment it actually has a shorter useful life. However, there's an exception if the used assets exceed 10% of the total basis of all assets placed in service in the year. In such case, lives for used assets may be determined without regard to the new asset depreciation ranges.

[¶1815] Special Five-Year Depreciation for Rehabilitation Expenditures

Under Code §167(k), capital expenditures made for the rehabilitation of existing buildings used for low- and moderate-income rental housing can be depreciated on a straight-line basis over a 60-month period if the additions or improvements have a useful life of five years or more. This five-year writeoff gives the investor in rehabilitated housing great tax shelter.

As to qualified property for which rehabilitation expenditures were made before January 1, 1976, an election can be made to compute depreciation by using straight-line depreciation, a useful life of 60 months, and no salvage value in lieu of any other method. If an election is properly made and in effect to use this method as to any portion of the basis of property, no deduction for depreciation or amortization will be allowed as to that portion of the basis of the property under any other provision of the Code. Thus, for example, the additional first-year depreciation allowance for small businesses permitted under §170 would not be available as to that portion of the basis of property for which a proper election was in effect.

In addition, if the expenditures were pursuant to a contract entered into before December 31, 1974 and incurred before January 1, 1978, then such expenditures qualify for §167(k) treatment. Once the election is made, you get the full 60 months to depreciate. (It should be noted that this extension reflects congressional concern and further extensions may occur in the future.) To determine whether rehabilitation expenditures are incurred before the deadline, each dwelling unit will be considered separately. Regardless of the method of accounting used by the taxpayer as to other items of income and expense, an expenditure is incurred for the purposes of the election on the date that expenditure would be considered incurred under the accrual method of accounting.

Election by Partnership: An election to use the 60-month depreciation as to property held by a partnership must be made by the partnership (§703(b)).

Excess Depreciation as Item of Tax Preference: Under Code §57, the amount by which the depreciation deduction taken for a taxable year using the 60-month useful life exceeds the amount of the depreciation deduction which would have been allowable for the taxable year if the taxpayer had depreciated the property under the straight-line method for each taxable year of its useful life (determined without regard to the 60-month useful life provided for by §167(k)) for which the taxpayer has held the property constitutes an item of tax preference subject to the minimum tax on tax-preference income.

Recapture of Excess Depreciation: Additional depreciation of rehabilitation expenditures after one year after they were incurred is subject to recapture to the extent that they exceed the amount of depreciation adjustments which would result from straight-line depreciation without regard to the 60-month useful life (§1245 and 1250).

Expenditures for Which Special Five-Year Tax Writeoff Is Available: Expenditures for which the special 60-month depreciation is available include amounts chargeable to a capital account for depreciable property with a useful life of five years or more, in connection with the rehabilitation of an existing building for low- and moderate-income rental housing. Expenditures do not qualify unless, following the completion of rehabilitation, the dwelling unit is held for occupancy on a rental basis by tenants meeting the income requirements set up for this type of housing.

Expenditures incurred to purchase land, the existing building, or any interest in the building (e.g., a leasehold interest) do not qualify. Likewise, expenditures attributable to a commercial unit (e.g., a grocery store) do not qualify. But an expenditure need not actually be made on a dwelling unit or a building provided it is incurred in connection with the rehabilitation of an existing building and is not attributable to a commercial unit. So, for example, expenditures to pave a parking lot for use by the tenants might qualify. Such expenditures must meet the requirements set up as to minimum and maximum amounts of rehabilitation expenditures that may be taken into account.

New Construction: Expenditures for new construction do not qualify. But expenditures may qualify if the foundation and outer walls of the existing building are retained. Other relevant factors in making the determination may include the amount paid to acquire the existing building and the amount of material remaining for the existing building. The question will be determined as one of fact.

Enlargement of Existing Buildings: Expenditures for the enlargement of the total area occupied by the dwelling units in a rehabilitated building do not qualify. But expenditures for the construction of a related facility, such as a garage, sidewalk, or parking lot, may qualify.

What Is Low- and Moderate-Income Rental Housing for Which Rehabilitation Expenditures May Qualify for 60-Month Writeoff? In this context, "low-income rental housing" refers to any dwelling unit in a building which is held for occupancy by families and individuals of "low or moderate" income. If a dwelling unit fails to qualify as low-income rental housing at any time during the 60-month election period, the election is considered revoked by the taxpayer as to that unit. If a dwelling unit is rented for one or more periods during the taxable year beginning after the date the property attributable to rehabilitation expenditures allocated to such unit is placed in service, the dwelling unit will be considered low-income rental housing only if it is occupied by families and individuals of low or moderate income during each such period. If a dwelling unit is rented for some period during the taxable year beginning after the date the property attributable to rehabilitation expenditures allocated to such unit is placed in service, the dwelling unit will be considered low-income rental housing only if, at all times during that period, the rental at which the unit is offered indicates that the unit is held for occupancy by families and individuals of low or moderate income. Generally, if the rental at which the unit is offered does not exceed 30% of the low- or moderate-income level for the number of persons occupying comparable units, the unit will be considered low-income rental housing.

What Is a Dwelling Unit for Purposes of 60-Month Writeoff? The term "dwelling unit" means a house or an apartment used to provide living accommodations in a building or structure and containing the usual facilities found in a principal place of residence (e.g., kitchen and sleeping accommodations). A unit in a hotel, motel, inn, or other establishment more than half of the dwelling units in which are used on a transient basis does not qualify. Generally, a unit will be considered used on a transient basis if the normal rental term is less than 30 days.

Maximum and Minimum Amounts of Rehabilitation Expenditures That May Qualify: The amount of rehabilitation expenditures that may be taken into account as to any dwelling unit is subject to the following limitations. In the case of a partnership, the limitations apply to the partnership, not to the individual partners. The taxpayer must maintain detailed records which permit specific identification of the rehabilitation expenditures paid or incurred as to each dwelling unit:

Minimum Amount: The taxpayer must pay or incur rehabilitation expenditures of more than $3,000 as to any dwelling unit over a period of two consecutive years in order to qualify.

Maximum Amount: The maximum amount of expenditures as to any dwelling unit which may be taken into account is $15,000. Property attributable to amounts in excess can be depreciated according to the usual methods. All amounts as to which a property election has been filed are taken into account, including expenditures covered by an election which has been revoked.

Allocations Rules: Expenditures attributable to more than one dwelling unit will be allocated among those individual dwelling units in the same ratio as the area of each such dwelling unit bears to the total area of all dwelling units to which the expenditures are attributable. Expenditures for related facilities attributable solely to dwelling units, such as parking facilities for tenant use, are to be allocated among the dwelling units to which they relate in the manner described. Expenditures for commercial units or for related facilities attributable solely to commercial units are not to be allocated to dwelling units. Expenditures for common areas such as stairways, halls, and entranceways are to be allocated among the particular dwelling and non-dwelling units to which they relate.

How to Make the Election to Take the 60-Month Writeoff: An election under §167(k) to take the special five-year depreciation is made by attaching a statement to the income tax return filed for the first taxable year in which you compute the depreciation deduction using a 60-month useful life.

An information statement should be attached to the income tax return filed for each subsequent taxable year in which you compute depreciation. The 60-month election period begins with the date the property is placed in service, unless you adopt an averaging convention in accordance with Reg. §1.167(a)-10(b), which permits the use of some other date.

Generally, no election may be made until all conditions and limitations have been met. But, if the amount expended does not exceed the minimum amount of $3,000 per unit in the taxable year in which the property is placed in service and in the immediately preceding taxable year, you can make the election for the taxable year in which the property is placed in service by filing the election in the prescribed time and manner by enclosing a separate written statement showing an intent to fulfill the $3,000 minimum in the succeeding taxable year. Provision is also made for making the election by filing an amended return.

When Election Must Be Filed: The election must be filed no later than the time prescribed by law (including extensions thereof) for filing the taxpayer's return for the taxable year in which the property is placed in service provided the expenditures meet the statutory requirements in that year, taking into account expenditures of the preceding taxable year for purposes of the $3,000 minimum amount limitation.

The statement required for subsequent years must be filed no later than the time prescribed by law (including extensions thereof) for filing the return for such subsequent years. If the taxpayer does not file a timely return for the year in which the property is placed in service, the election should be filed at the time the taxpayer files his first return for such year.

If the taxpayer fails to make an election within the prescribed time, no election may be made as to such property by filing an amended return or in any other manner.

If an election is filed with an amended return, it must be filed no later than the time prescribed for filing a return for the first taxable year following the year in which the property is placed in service.

The election may be made for any taxable year ending after July 24, 1969, even though the prescribed period for filing an election for such taxable year has expired. The provisions dealing with the time for making an election apply for purposes of determining the beginning of the 60-month election period.

If the taxpayer is permitted to revoke an election as to any property within the 90-day period, the taxpayer may adopt any method of depreciation permitted for such property, beginning with the date the property was placed in service, using the estimated useful life of the property on such date and determined without regard to the provisions permitting the 60-month writeoff.

When Election May Be Revoked: An election may be revoked by the taxpayer at any time prior to the time prescribed by law (including extensions thereof) for filing a tax return for the last taxable year in which any portion of the 60-month election period falls.

The revocation of an election does not affect taxable years for which a tax return was filed computing a depreciation deduction. A revocation is effective on the date specified by the taxpayer. Once an election is revoked, it may not be reinstated.

Failure to Meet Requirements as Revocation of Election; Effect of Revocation: An election is considered revoked if at any time during the taxable year (1) the unit is rented to a person or persons outside the definition of low or moderate income, (2) such unit is not held for occupancy by families and individuals of low or moderate income, (3) more than half the dwelling units in the building are rented on a transient basis, or (4) expenditures which are required in order to meet the $3,000-minimum-amount limitation for the preceding taxable year are insufficient.

The revocation is deemed to occur on the first day during the taxable year that the dwelling unit does not meet the requirements. Revocation of an election does not affect prior taxable years for which a tax return computing a depreciation deduction was filed if all the conditions were met for those years. Once an election is considered revoked, it may not be reinstated.

Effect of the Revocation: The taxpayer may not compute the depreciation deduction using the 60-month useful life for any portion of any taxable year beginning after the date on which a revocation is effective. The depreciation deduction allowed for the taxable year in which a revocation is effective is the amount the deduction would have been for that year if no revocation had occurred, multiplied by a fraction consisting of (1) the number of days in the taxable year prior to the date of the revocation over (2) the number of days of the 60-month period which fall within such year. Taxpayer will continue to use straight-line depreciation using the estimated remaining useful life and salvage value of the property, determined without regard to the provisions of §167(k) which permits the 60-month writeoff as of the date the revocation is deemed to occur. If a taxpayer wants to adopt another method of depreciation following a revocation of an election, the new method of depreciation would be a change in the method of accounting requiring consent of IRS (§446(e)). Generally, the straight-line method of depreciation, using the property's remaining useful life determined without regard to the provisions permitting a 60-month writeoff, will be the only method which will be accepted following a revocation.

[¶1816] Depreciation of Leaseholds

If instead of purchasing a fee interest in a parcel of real estate, the buyer were to purchase a leasehold interest—that is, purchase for a stated sum of money a lease on the particular piece of property which permits subleasing to other tenants—a reasonable allowance for exhaustion is permitted. This simply consists of an aliquot part of the cost of the lease based on the term of the lease (see *Minneapolis Security Bldg. Corp.,* 38 BTA 120).

Where an owner of improved property leases it to another person, he is nevertheless entitled to take a deduction for depreciation of the property. However, where, by the lease terms, the lessee is required to return the property at the end of the term in as good a condition as it was at the beginning of the term, it is doubtful that the lessor-owner can take any deductions for depreciation as he will not have suffered any economic loss (*G. C. M. 11933,* CB XII-2, 52). Of course, neither can the lessee take any deduction for depreciation although he can deduct the cost of restoring the property to its original state in the year of restoration (*O. D. 516,* CB 2, 112).

Where the lessee improves the property during the term of his lease, he is permitted either to (1) amortize the cost of the improvements over the term of the lease or (2), if the useful life of the improvements is less than the remaining term of the lease, depreciate the improvements over such useful life.

The accelerated methods of depreciating property cannot be used if the cost of the improvements is amortized over the term of the lease, since the accelerated methods are only available when the deduction is for depreciation not *amortization in lieu of depreciation* (Reg. §1.167(a)-4). The deduction for amortization of the leasehold improvement is similar to a deduction for depreciation on the straight-line method, using the term of the lease as the life of the property.

[¶1817] Accounting for Depreciation

In accounting for depreciation, a credit to a depreciation reserve account is preferred over a direct deduction from book value (but this isn't mandatory). The allowance must be returned and recorded either for specific asset items or for groups of assets, the groups being so arranged that the same depreciation factors apply to all assets in the group.

Each individual item may be accounted for separately, or two or more assets may be combined in a single account (Reg. §1.167(a)-7). Various combinations are permitted, such as:

(1) Group or Component Account. Assets similar in kind, with approximately the same useful lives.

(2) Classified Account: Assets segregated according to use, without regard to useful life, e.g., machinery and equipment, furniture and fixtures, transportation equipment.

(3) Composite Account: Assets included in same account, regardless of their character or useful lives, e.g., all assets used in a business can be included in a single account.

Group, classified or composite accounts can be further broken down on the basis of location, dates of acquisition, cost, character, use, etc.

For classified or composite accounts, average useful life and rate are redetermined whenever additions, retirements, or replacements substantially alter the relative proportion of types of assets in the accounts (Reg. §1.167(a)-7(d)).

You can have as many depreciation accounts as you wish (Reg. §1.167(a)-7(c)). Depreciation allowances are computed separately for each account.

Depreciation schedules filed with the tax return should show the accumulated reserves, computed in accordance with the allowances for tax purposes.

You Cannot Accumulate Your Depreciation Deductions: Depreciation is an annual deduction. You should deduct the proper depreciation allowance each year since you cannot increase your depreciation deduction later by failing to take the deduction in earlier years. (See Reg. §1.167(a)-10(a); *Young,* TC Memo 1957-222.) Of course, the fact that you did not depreciate in a previous year will not prevent you from taking the proper depreciation deduction in a later year.

Example: Gray should depreciate $5,000 on his building in 1976. He fails to do this. In 1977, he again can depreciate $5,000 on the building. This time, he does so. However, he cannot get the deduction in 1977 that he should have taken in 1976.

If You Buy or Sell Depreciable Property During the Year: If you buy or sell a depreciable asset during the taxable year, you can only deduct a part of its annual depreciation allowance.

Example: Green bought a depreciable building for $10,000 on April 1 of a year. He is a calendar-year taxpayer. The building's useful life is 20 years. Assume no salvage value. Annual depreciation allowance would be $500. But Green only held the asset for three-fourths of the year. So, he is only entitled to take $375 for that year.

Averaging Convention Methods: Where there is a multiple asset account, you can determine depreciation on an average balance unless the result is a material distortion of the depreciation deduction for a particular year. This is called the averaging convention.

You can assume that all additions and retirements occur uniformly throughout the year. The depreciation rate is applied to the average of the beginning and ending balances in the asset account for the tax year.

Under another method, you can assume that all additions and retirements during the first half of the year were made on the first day of the year and all additions and retirements during the second half of the year were made on the first day of the following year. Thus, a full year's depreciation is taken on additions in the first half of the year and retirements in the second half of the year. On the other hand, no depreciation is taken on additions in the second half of the year and on retirements in the first half of the year (Reg. §1.167(a)-10).

[¶1818] Recapture of Depreciation as Ordinary Income

Back in 1964, Congress enacted Code §1250, which recaptures depreciation on the sale of depreciable real property at a gain. In other words, to the extent that the gain reflects previously deducted depreciation, the gain is ordinary income. Any remaining gain is normally capital gain. The Code also provides for depreciation recapture covering depreciable personal property (i.e., nonreal estate property) (§1245).

Before the adoption of the 1969 Tax Reform Act, real estate depreciation recapture applied to all types of real estate in a uniform manner; and, if the real estate was held onto for 21 months, the proportion of ''additional'' depreciation which was recapturable as ordinary income was reduced by 1% per month for each full month thereafter the property was held. Thus, real estate depreciation was phased out gradually; and if you held on to the property long enough, you could realize all your gain as capital gain and none of it would be treated as ordinary income.

The 1969 Tax Reform Act changed this picture. Real estate depreciation recapture no longer applies across the board in a uniform manner to all types of properties. Indeed, with some real estate—all depreciable real estate other than residential rental properties—there's 100% recapture no matter how long you hold on to the property. The material below contains a detailed rundown on how the 1969 depreciation recapture provisions work and how to deal with them to lessen their impact as much as possible.

[¶1819] Property Subject to Depreciation Recapture

Depreciation recapture applies in the following ways.

Commercial, Industrial, and Office Buildings: Under the 1969 law, 100% of the excess of accelerated over straight-line depreciation is subject to recapture with respect to all properties other than residential rental properties, including commercial, industrial, and office buildings. This rule applies to depreciation for periods subsequent to December 31, 1969, with respect to properties acquired before December 31, 1969, as well as to properties acquired after that date, except as noted above.

Example: Your gain on a sale of an office building is $15,000. Additional depreciation after 1969 is $1,500 and for earlier periods additional depreciation was $3,000. Your holding period is 30 months. All the additional post-1969 depreciation ($1,500) is recaptured as ordinary income. As to depreciation taken in the pre-1970 years, 90% (120 months–30 months) of the $3,000 additional depreciation gives you $2,700 recaptured as ordinary income. The way it works out is that $4,200 of the $15,000 gain is recaptured as ordinary income; the rest is capital gain.

Residential Rental Properties: The entire excess of accelerated over straight-line as to new residential properties is recaptured as ordinary income if the property is disposed of within 100 months. Thereafter, the amount recaptured as ordinary income is reduced by 1% for each month. The result is that if the property is sold after a holding period of 16 years and 8 months, the entire gain on the sale will be long-term capital gain. The same rule applies in the case of rehabilitated expenditures for low- and moderate-income rental housing.

Government-assisted low- and moderate-income rental properties are subject to the recapture rules in effect before the 1969 tax law.

[¶1820] Depreciation Recapture Rules Introduced By the 1969 Tax Law

The Tax Reform Act of 1969 strongly favors investments in residential rental properties, not only by permitting the fastest methods of accelerated depreciation with respect to such properties while limiting other new properties to the 150%-declining-balance method, it also favors residential rental properties by applying softer depreciation recapture rules to them. Here's how the depreciation recapture rules introduced by the 1969 tax law shape up.

Under the provisions of §1250 as amended in 1969, accelerated depreciation taken in excess of allowable straight-line depreciation with respect to all forms of depreciable real estate except residential rental property is subject to recapture as ordinary income to the extent of gain resulting from the sale. As to residential rental property, a 1%-per-month reduction in the amount subject to recapture is allowed after the property has been held for 100 full months. As to government-assisted residential rental properties, the more liberal pre-1969 recapture rules apply. As to property, the sale of which was subject to a binding contract in existence before July 26, 1969, the earlier recapture provisions (discussed below) still apply even though the transfer took place after that date.

[¶1821] Pre-1969 Depreciation Recapture Provisions May Still Apply

The 1969 tax law provides for the application of the earlier and more liberal depreciation recapture provisions to property the sale of which was subject to a building contract in existence before July 26, 1969, even though the actual transfer took place after that date. They also apply to federally assisted projects (e.g., FHA §221(d)(3) and §236 programs) and to other publicly assisted housing programs under which the investor's return is limited. Also, since the 1969 depreciation recapture rules apply only to depreciation taken after December 31, 1969, depreciation taken before that date is subject to recapture under the earlier rules.

How Pre-1969 Real Estate Depreciation Recapture Works: "Additional" depreciation taken after 1963 is subject to recapture as follows:

(1) If real estate is sold when it has been held not more than one year, any realized gain is taxable as ordinary income to the extent of all depreciation taken by or allowed to the seller.

(2) If sold in the first eight months of the second year—i.e., the 13th through the 20th month of the holding period—gain is taxable as ordinary income to the extent of additional depreciation. Additional depreciation is the difference between the depreciation actually taken or allowed (e.g., some form of accelerated depreciation) and the straight-line rate of depreciation for that period.

(3) If sold at the end of the 21st full month of ownership or thereafter, the proportion of additional depreciation which is to be treated as ordinary

income is diminished by 1% per full month after excluding the first 20 months. Thus, at the end of 10 years of ownership, no ordinary income would result on the sale. This works out because from the 21st month through the 120th (the end of 10 years) is a period of 100 months. Reducing the additional depreciation subject to recapture by 1% per month for 100 months brings us to a point, at the end of the 100 months, where no part of the additional depreciation is subject to recapture.

Note: We are dealing with "full" months in applying these rules. So, if property was sold after being held, say, 20 months and 25 days, the entire additional depreciation could be recovered as ordinary income (i.e., the rules in (2), above, rather than the rule in (3), above). Similarly, if property was sold after being held 30 months and 20 days, 90% of the additional depreciation could be taxable as ordinary income. Since 30 months is 10 more months than 20 months, the amount of additional depreciation subject to ordinary income is reduced by 10% (1% for each full month; the 20 days don't count).

Example: Suppose a low-income apartment building was constructed in 1969 for $300,000 and depreciated according to the double-declining-balance method. Assume $50,000 is allocated to land and $250,000 to the building, and a 50-year life is used. At the end of 4 years (48 full months), it is sold for $350,000. The seller's gain would be taxed as follows:

Selling price		$350,000
Original cost	$300,000	
Depreciation taken	37,663	
Basis		262,337
Gain		$ 87,663
Depreciation taken	$ 37,663	
Depreciation on straight-line basis (2% a year for 4 years)	20,000	
Additional depreciation subject to recapture	$ 17,663	
Percent recaptured (48th full month)	72%	
Amount recaptured (ordinary income)		12,717
Amount taxable as capital gain		$ 74,946

Of course, in any case where the total gain is less than the depreciation subject to recapture, the full gain is taxable as ordinary income—but no additional amount is taxable.

[¶1822] Figuring Amount of Additional Depreciation

If a useful life (or salvage value) was used in determining your depreciation for any taxable year, that life (or value) is used in determining the straight-line depreciation for that period. However, a method of depreciation might have been used as to which a useful life was not taken into account—for example, the units-of-production method. Or, you may have used a method as to which salvage value was not taken into account—for example, the declining-balance method or the amortization of a leasehold improvement over the term of a lease. In these situations, for the purpose of determining the straight-line depreciation for the applicable period, you use the useful life or salvage value which would have been proper if depreciation had actually been determined under the straight-line method. For this purpose, useful life or salvage value is determined by taking into account for each taxable year the same facts and circumstances as would have been taken into account if you had used such method.

Example: On January 1, 1976, a calendar-year taxpayer sells real estate which he purchased for $10,000 on January 1, 1974. Throughout the period he held the property, he computed depreciation under the 200%-declining-balance method and used a useful life of 30 years. Salvage value was not taken into account. If he had computed depreciation under the straight-line method he would have used a salvage value of $1,000. The depreciation on the property under both methods is as follows:

Year	Declining-balance	Straight-line
1974	$ 667	$ 300
1975	622	300
1976	581	300
Total depreciation	$1,870	$ 900

The additional depreciation for the property is $970, that is, the depreciation actually deducted minus the depreciation which would have resulted for that period under the straight-line method ($900).

[¶1823] Amount of Recapture Where Property Consists of Separate Elements

Where property made up of separate elements is sold or disposed of, special rules are provided for figuring the amount of depreciation recapture.

Under these rules, where real estate has been improved or has had different parts of the property added or put into service before the completion of the entire property, the property is divided into separate elements. When the property or any element is sold or disposed of, each separate element is treated as a separate property; and you figure the recapture based on the depreciation attributable to that element, using a separate holding period for that element. Under the law (§1250(f)), effective for taxable years ending after 7/24/69, you figure the amount of recapture attributable to any element as follows:

The amount of depreciation recaptured as ordinary income attributable to any element is the sum of (1) the amount (if any) determined by multiplying (a) the amount which bears the same ratio to the lower of the gain or the additional post-1969 depreciation on the entire property as the additional post-1969 depreciation for that element bears to the additional post-1969 depreciation for all elements by (b) the applicable percentage for such element plus (2) the amount (if any) determined by multiplying (a) the amount which bears the same ratio to the lower of the additional pre-1970 depreciation on the whole property or the excess of the gain over the additional post-1969 depreciation, as the additional pre-1970 depreciation for such element bears to the additional pre-1970 depreciation for all elements, by (b) the applicable percentage for such element. You make your determinations as to any element as if the element were a separate property as follows:

(A)		(B)		(C)		(D)
Additional post-1969 depreciation for the element	÷	Additional post-1969 depreciation for all elements	×	Lower of gain (under post-1969 rules) or additional post-1969 depreciation on whole property	×	Applicable percentage for the element (under applicable percentage rules for post-1969 depreciation)

Plus

(E)		(F)		(G)		(H)
Additional pre-1970 depreciation for the element	÷	Additional pre-1970 depreciation on all elements	×	Lower of additional pre-1970 depreciation on whole property or excess of gain over additional post-1969 depreciation on whole property	×	Applicable percentage for the element (determined under applicable percentage rules for pre-1970 depreciation)

Example: You sell real estate for $90,000. Adjusted basis is $37,500. Additional post-1969 depreciation comes to $6,000. Additional pre-1970 depreciation is $24,000. Gain is $52,500. Excess of gain over post-1969 depreciation is $46,500. The property is made up of three elements (I, II, III). The additional post-1969 and pre-1970 depreciation and applicable percentage for each element, determined as if each element were a separate property, are:

Post-1969 Depreciation

Element	*Additional Depreciation*	*Applicable Percentage*
I	$3,000	80
II	1,500	100
III	1,500	100
Total	$6,000	

The amount of gain for each element of property of post-1969 depreciation is figured as follows:

I	$3,000/$6,000	×	$6,000	×	80%	=	$2,400
II	$1,500/$6,000	×	$6,000	×	100%	=	$1,500
III	$1,500/$6,000	×	$6,000	×	100%	=	$1,500
	Total Amount Recaptured						$5,400

Pre-1970 Depreciation

Element	*Additional Depreciation*	*Applicable Percentage*
I	$15,000	50
II	4,500	80
III	4,500	60
	$24,000	

The amount of gain for each element of property of pre-1970 depreciation is figured as follows:

I	$15,000/$24,000	×	$24,000	×	50%	=	$ 7,500
II	$ 4,500/$24,000	×	$24,000	×	80%	=	$ 3,600
III	$ 4,500/$24,000	×	$24,000	×	60%	=	$ 2,700
	Total Amount Recaptured						$13,800

Total amount of post-1969 and pre-1970 depreciation recapture comes to:

Element	*Post-1969 Depreciation*	*Pre-1970 Depreciation*	*Total*
I	$2,400	$ 7,500	$ 9,900
II	1,500	3,600	5,100
III	1,500	2,700	4,200
Total	$5,400	$13,800	$19,200

How "Substantial Improvements" Affect Depreciation Recapture Under Pre-1969 Tax Law Rules: The rules discussed above apply with respect to taxable years ending after 7/24/69. Under the earlier rules, property is divided into the following elements (if they exist as to a particular property) and depreciation recapture as ordinary income is figured separately for each element: (a) each separate improvement, (b) each unit of a property placed in service before the property itself was completed, and (c) the remaining property after (a) and (b) have been separated from it.

Step One: For each taxable year of ownership, add together all amounts added to the capital account in that year for improvements made after acquisition or completion of the property. See if the total for the year exceeds the greater of $2,000 or 1% of the basis of the property at the beginning of the year (unadjusted for any depreciation deductions taken by you). If it does not, this year need not be considered in any further calculations. If the improvements for the year do exceed the greater of the above two amounts, then go on to step two.

Step Two: Determine if during any three-year period of your ownership, improvements which must be considered under Step One total an amount which exceeds the greatest of: (i) 25% of the adjusted basis of the property, (ii) 10% of the basis of the property unadjusted for prior depreciation taken by you, or (iii) $5,000. The basis under (i) and (ii) is as of the beginning of the three-year period or the beginning of your holding period of the property, whichever is later. If improvements during any three-year period do exceed the greatest of the above, then each improvement added during the period is a "separate improvement."

How the Rule Is Applied: If a property has separate elements, then the recapture formula must be applied separately to each such separate element. This is done by determining the additional depreciation for each element and then treating a percentage of that depreciation as ordinary income according to the length of time the separate element was held. If the gain on the entire transaction is less than the total of additional depreciation, the amount of gain allocable to each separate element is in the same proportion as the additional depreciation of that element bears to the total amount of additional depreciation.

Example: Suppose you bought a parcel of vacant land for $10,000 and held it for seven years, during which time you made no improvements and, of course, took no depreciation. In the eighth year, you added a $5,000 improvement and began to depreciate on the double-declining method. In the tenth year, you added another improvement costing $2,500 and similarly depreciate it. In the eleventh year, you sold for $25,000.

For purpose of the recapture rule, you would have "substantially improved property" because in a 36-month period you added improvements costing a total amount greater than 25% of the adjusted basis of the property, 10% of the unadjusted basis, or $5,000. So after you sold, you must treat separately the original vacant land and each of the two improvements. The land was not depreciable, and so no recapture was involved. The $5,000 improvement was held for 36 months prior to the sale, so some proportion of the additional depreciation over straight-line depreciation will be recaptured. If the sale was in the 20th month after the improvement was constructed, the proportion of additional depreciation recaptured would be 84% (since each month after the 20th dropped the recapture percentage by one point).

In the case of the second improvement of $2,500, if the sale took place within one year of its construction, the entire depreciation deduction for that year (including the straight-line amount) would be recaptured at ordinary income rates.

[¶1824] Special Holding Period Rules

To determine the percentage of additional depreciation that can be taxed as ordinary income, you must use special holding period rules set forth in §1250. In all other respects, as in determining the amount of straight-line depreciation, the usual holding rules set forth in §1223 apply. (Keep in mind that, while as to all real estate other than residential rental property, the 1969 tax law provides for 100% recapture of excess depreciation regardless of how long the property has been held, as to residential rental properties, there is a gradual phaseout of recapture after the property has been held for the specified time). These rules are as follows:

(1) For property acquired by the taxpayer, the holding period begins on the day after the date of acquisition. (2) For property constructed, reconstructed, or erected by the taxpayer, the holding period begins on the first day of the month in which the property is placed in service (i.e., used in a trade or business, or for the production of income, or for personal use). (3) For property where the basis is transferred from the former owner because it

was acquired by gift or in a tax-free transaction, the holding period of the new owner includes that of the former owner. (4) For property acquired in exchange for a principal residence and where recapture didn't apply, the holding period of the new property includes the holding period of the former property.

[¶1825] Reducing or Postponing Depreciation Recapture

The effect of the stiff recapture provisions introduced by the Tax Reform Act of 1969 can be softened by using various techniques for postponing gain such as, for example, installment sales, tax-free exchanges, and refinancing.

If you hold your real estate long enough before disposing of it, you may be able to come out without any depreciation recapture and still benefit from the tax advantages of accelerated depreciation in the early years of your holding. As to depreciation taken after 1963 and before 1970, after you've held any depreciable property more than 20 months, the amount of excess depreciation subject to recapture is reduced by 1% for each full month. So, no pre-1970 depreciation is recaptured if you hold the property for 10 full years.

As to depreciation taken after 1969 with respect to government-assisted residential rental property (e.g., FHA §221(d)(3) and 236 programs) acquired before 1976, the amount of excess depreciation subject to recapture is reduced by 1% per full month in excess of 20 months. At the end of 10 years, there's no recapture. A simple rule applies to other types of depreciable real estate which you dispose of after 1969 but pursuant to a binding contract in effect on July 24, 1969.

As to residential rental housing (other than government-assisted housing or for low- or moderate-income rental housing) that qualifies for the five-year writeoff, the amount of post-1969 excess depreciation subject to recapture is reduced by 1% per month after 100 months. If you hold the property for over 16 years and 8 months, there's no recapture.

Here we give you a rundown on some of the important ways open to real estate men to ease the bite of or postpone depreciation recapture.

(1) Tax-Free Exchanges: Tax-free exchanges of like-kind property can be used to unlock your "locked in" position, since you postpone the tax on your gain and, consequently, the effect of the recapture provisions. You may want to trade up your property and finance the difference between your equity in your old property and the value of the new.

(2) Refinancing: Another avenue that you might consider is the advisability of refinancing. Refinancing can help you raise the cash necessary for another investment, get the benefits of interest deductions, and, at the same time, retain the benefits of accelerated depreciation.

(3) Income Averaging: The 1969 tax law liberalizes the old income-averaging provision in two basic ways that can help real estate investors as well as other investors: (1) It lowers from 33-1/3% to 20% the percentage by which an individual's income must increase over the four-year base period before the averaging provision becomes available. (2) It extends income averaging to long-term capital gains.

If you elect to use income averaging (1) you can't use the alternative capital gain rate, nor (2) the 50% maximum tax on earned income. As to the first limitation, it is now 25% on the first $50,000 of capital gains and up to 35% on the excess.

What it all comes down to is that, before you elect to use income averaging, you will have to do some arithmetic to figure out how much you will gain by income averaging and how much you will lose, if anything, by the loss of the alternative capital gain rate and the earned-income ceiling.

(4) Sale After End of Holding Period: If you sell when the holding period is exactly one year or less, the entire depreciation (including straight-line) can be recaptured as ordinary income. If the holding period is one year and one day, only as much of the depreciation as exceeds straight-line is recapturable as ordinary income. As to residential rental property, there is a phaseout of recapture; and for each full month in excess of 100 months, the recapture is reduced by 1%. What is required here is a full month; part of a month doesn't count. Keep in mind that a sale of real estate generally is considered to occur on the day of the closing, i.e., the day when title passes.

Low- and Moderate-Income Rental Housing: When you invest in federally assisted low- and moderate-income rental housing (FHA §221(d)(3) and 236 programs) or in other publicly assisted housing programs, the pre-1969 recapture rules apply (but the sale may be a tax-free sale to tenants or occupants or to a tax-exempt organization). The pre-1969 recapture rules apply provided the property is constructed, reconstructed, or acquired before January 1, 1976. Under these rules, depreciation is recaptured in full if the sale occurs in the first twelve months and there is a phaseout of the recapture of the excess of acceleration over straight-line depreciation after 20 months. The recapture is reduced at the rate of 1% per month until 120 months, after which no recapture applies.

Sale During the 20-Month Holding Period: Keep the *full-month* concept in mind. For each full month of holding period in excess of 20, you knock off an additional 1% from the amount of additional depreciation (i.e., excess of accelerated over straight-line depreciation) that's subject to recapture at ordinary income rates. Here too timing becomes important. For example, if you acquire property on the 16th of the month, each full month of ownership will end on the 16th of succeeding months. So, if you are setting a closing date near the middle of the month when you dispose of the property, make sure it is the 16th or later. Otherwise, 1% of the additional depreciation that you could otherwise pick up at capital gain rates will become ordinary income.

Where construction is nearing completion and the end of the month is approaching, it may be worthwhile to push hard to put the property into service before the end of the month. If you do, you pick up almost a whole month in holding period because your holding period then starts on the first day of the month. That speeds up the completion of the first year's holding period if there's going to be an early sale; it gets you past the 20-month holding period, after which less than the full additional depreciation is subject to recapture; or it gives you an additional edge of 1% reduction in additional depreciation subject to recapture when you dispose of the property sometime after you've held it for a period that exceeds 20 months.

(5) Should You Make a Gift or Let the Property Pass by Inheritance? Here are the factors to consider:

(a) The gift tax is three-fourths of the estate tax.

(b) Making a lifetime gift gets the property and the gift tax paid on it out of the estate (the estate tax paid on property in the estate does not reduce the estate subject to tax).

(c) Making a lifetime gift gets the income from the property into the hands of the donee (whose income tax bracket is presumably lower than the donor's).

(d) A lifetime gift does not result in §1250 (depreciation recapture) income. But the donee takes the donor's basis for the property; so, on a subsequent disposition, the donee may realize §1250 income. And the donor's holding period is "tacked on" to the donee's holding period.

(e) When property passes on death, there is no §1250 income realized. Furthermore, the beneficiary who receives the property gets a basis for it that is equal to the market value at the time of death. And any potential §1250 income that was present when the decedent held the property disappears. A new holding period begins to run.

In each case, you'll have to analyze these factors in view of your own situation. But keep this in mind: Where other indications point to a lifetime gift, the potential §1250 income to the donee need not always be a deterrent. Remember that your holding period before the gift carries over to him. So, if he holds the property for some time thereafter (especially where you already had a substantial holding period), he will be approaching the 10-year limit. And the potential ordinary income on recapture keeps diminishing.

On the other hand, if you let the property pass by inheritance, while the potential §1250 income that built up in your hands disappears at death, the one who gets your property starts a new holding period and new potential §1250 income. And it will take him a longer time to reach a point where he is approaching the 10-year safety area or an area where the percentage of additional depreciation subject to recapture becomes minimal.

(6) Purchase of Stock Versus Sale of Assets: Of course, there are many considerations that come up in determining whether or not to operate a business in corporate or unincorporated form. If you incorporate and subsequently sell stock rather than assets, you avoid any impact of §1250.

Purchase of Assets Rather Than Stock: On the other side of the coin, we have the tax considerations of the purchaser. Before the 1969 tax law, where asset values had appreciated, a corporate purchaser could buy stock rather than assets and within two years liquidate the purchased corporation. Under §334(b)(2), the basis of the assets acquired in the liquidation would be stepped up to the price paid for the stock. The purchaser in many cases is willing to buy stock. But under §1250, the corporation being liquidated will have to pick up as taxable income as much of the §1250 profit as is equal to the difference between its basis and the market value of the assets (as reflected by the purchase price paid for the stock) at the time of liquidation.

If assets rather than stock are sold, the sellers will have to pick up the §1250 gain—either in a 12-month liquidation (§337) or via an ordinary liquidation followed by a sale of the assets. In either case, the corporation being liquidated will pick up the §1250 gain—in a 12-month liquidation, when it sells the assets within the 12-month period; in an ordinary liquidation, when it distributes the assets. In the second situation, we have to worry about *Court Holding Company* (324 US 331, 33 AFTR 593 [1945]). Under that case, the stockholders of the seller must be able to show that they negotiated on their own behalf (not the corporation's) when they sold the property received in liquidation. Otherwise, the entire gain (not only the recaptured depreciation) can be taxable to the corporation.

(7) Sale of Depreciable Real Estate Used in Business: Since the sale of a §1231 asset might very well result in ordinary income under §1250, timing a sale in a year to coincide with the availability of an ordinary loss may be desirable, since the loss will offset ordinary income to the extent that §1250 applies to the sale of §1231 assets.

[¶1826] Recapture Rules Apply in Unexpected Situations

Just as in the case of §1245 (recapture of depreciation of personal property), §1250 affecting real estate is broad enough to cover more than sales and exchanges; it can even create taxable situations where otherwise the transaction would be tax free. Generally, §1250 applies to sales and exchanges and other dispositions subject to a number of exceptions and modifications, the more important of which are as follows:

Gifts are not taxable events—but the recapture potential in the hands of the donor is transferred to the donee. So, when the donee disposed of the property, he could have ordinary income based on excess depreciation taken by the donor. But, the donor's holding period is tacked on to the donee's period. So, if they had a combined holding period of more than 10 years, there'd be no depreciation recapture.

Transfers at death are not taxable events. And since the recipient takes as his basis the fair market value of the property at the time of the decedent's death, there is no transferred basis, and the law forgives the ordinary income potential that arose from depreciation taken by the decedent.

Charitable contributions of real property have to be reduced by the amount that would have been taxable income under the recapture rules had the property been sold at market value.

Tax-free incorporations, etc. (§351); reorganizations (§361); and liquidations of subsidiaries (§332) do not give rise to taxable events except to the extent of "boot."

Distributions to partners by a partnership generally do not create a taxable event for depreciation recapture. But the potential ordinary income in the distribution will carry over to the partner to be applied when he disposes of the property.

Corporate distributions normally not taxable to the corporation can be taxable to it to the extent that the depreciation recapture provisions apply. The situations involved are: (1) distributions of dividends in kind, (2) distributions in partial or complete liquidation, and (3) sales made by corporation during the course of a 12-month (§337) liquidation.

Disposition of a principal residence does not create any recapture problem, whether or not the residence is sold for cash or exchanged for other property. For purposes of this exception, "principal residence" has two meanings: (1) it may be a principal residence as defined in §1034 which permits tax-free exchanges, or (2) it may be a principal residence as defined in §121 which refers to a residence of a person attaining the age of 65 before he disposes of a house which he has owned and used as his principal residence for five out of the past eight years.

Like-kind exchanges and involuntary conversions where proceeds are reinvested under the tax-deferral rules do not give rise to taxable events under the recapture section except, generally, to the extent that gain would be recognized under the like-kind or involuntary conversion rules. There are two important cases, however, where otherwise unrecognized gain is subject to recapture: (1) Where the owner of converted property uses the money obtained from the conversion to buy stock to acquire control of a corporation owning property similar or related in service or use to the converted property. Although under §1033(a)(3)(A) this use of the funds creates no taxable gain, §1250 says gain to the extent of the funds so used is subject to recapture. (2) Where the properties received in the tax-free exchange consist partly of §1250 property and partly of other property (e.g., vacant land), as much of the gain as exceeds the fair market value or cost of the §1250 property received is subject to recapture.

Sales during a 12-month liquidation period are generally tax free. But to the extent of ordinary income potential in the property sold, the corporation will be taxable under the rules of §1250. If the company takes back installment notes and thus delays reporting the gain, when the notes are distributed to the stockholders in the liquidation, the corporation will have to pick up the same amount of ordinary income that it would have realized had it sold the notes.

[¶1900] INVESTMENT TAX CREDIT*

The 1971 Revenue Act restored, with some modifications, a credit against tax equal to 7% of the investment in most depreciable business property other than buildings or their structural components. The credit offsets dollar for dollar the buyer's tax without affecting his basis for purposes of depreciation or his right to take accelerated depreciation. It applies to property acquired after 8/15/71, or acquired after 3/31/71 and before 8/16/71 if ordered after 3/31/71. Where property is constructed or erected by the taxpayer, the credit applies to property whose construction was begun after 3/31/71 or was completed after 8/15/71. If construction was begun before 4/1/71, only the construction costs incurred after 8/15/71 are eligible for the credit. You get the full credit subject to the limitations discussed below in the year in which the property is put into service—even if on the last day.

[¶1901] Property Qualifying for the Credit

To qualify for the credit, the investment must be in property that is (1) depreciable property, (2) having a useful life of at least three years, and (3) tangible property which is (a) personal property; or (b) property used as an integral part of manufacturing, production, or extraction *or* of furnishing transportation, communications, electrical energy, gas, water or sewage disposal services, or that consists of a research or bulk storage facility for fungibles used in connection therewith; or (c) elevators and escalators if construction, reconstruction, or erection is completed by a taxpayer after June 30, 1963 *or* if acquired after that date and original use commences with taxpayer after that date.

Structural Components of a Building: There is no definition of structural components of a building in the law. However, under the Regulations (§1.48-1(e)(2)), structural components that do not qualify for the credit include, for example, such parts of a building as walls, partitions, floors and ceilings, as well as any permanent coverings therefor such as paneling or tiling, and other components relating to the operation and maintenance of a building. The term "building" does not include such structures as oil and gas storage tanks, grain storage bins, silos, fractionating towers, blast furnaces, coke ovens, brick kilns, and coal tipples (so-called "special purpose" buildings).

*For 1975 and 1976, the tax credit was 10% and the limit for investment in used property was increased to $100,000.

Lodging Facilities: Property that is used predominantly to furnish lodging or in connection therewith generally does not qualify for the investment credit. But it can qualify if it is a nonlodging commercial facility that is available to nonlodgers on the same basis as to lodgers or is used by a hotel or motel where the predominant portion of the accommodations is used by transients. ''Predominant portion'' and ''transients'' are the key words. IRS says that ''predominant portion'' means ''more than one-half'' and that accommodations will be considered used on a transient basis if the rental period is normally less than 30 days.

[¶1902] Qualified Investments

The credit is 7% of the qualified investment—subject to the various limitations discussed below. To have a qualified investment there must be an acquisition of property that qualifies for the credit. The amount of the qualified investment also depends on whether the investment is in brand-new or second-hand property.

Used v. New Property: If the acquired property is new, there's no limitation on how much you can invest in one year and still be eligible for the credit (subject, of course, to the other limitations).

If the property is used, however, you can include as qualified investment property only purchases up to $50,000 in one year. If you buy more than $50,000 worth of property in one year, you can select whichever items you wish to designate (within the $50,000 limitation) as qualifying property.

Placed in Service: Property is eligible for the investment credit in the year in which it is placed in service. According to the Regulations (§1.46-3) property is placed in service when it becomes depreciable or when it is in a condition or state of readiness or availability for a specifically assigned function (whether or not in your business), whichever occurs earlier. Thus, a certain amount of flexibility is possible in the case of used property by controlling these factors in order to stay within the $50,000 annual limitation.

Thus, if depreciation is deferred to the following year because of an averaging convention or because of the method of depreciation used (e.g., completed contract, unit of production, retirement), nevertheless, the credit is available in the earlier year if the property is placed in a condition of readiness for a specific function in that year.

How Much Is Your Investment? With new property, the amount of your investment is basis. So, if you trade in old property for new, you take the basis for the old plus any additional amount you pay and figure the credit on the total. If you trade in a machine on which you claimed a credit in the past, there may be a recapture of part of the previous credit. With acquisitions of used assets, the basis of your credit is cost, not basis. On a trade-in, the only part that would qualify for the credit is the cash you pay in addition to the trade-in. What's more, if used assets are acquired to replace other property that was disposed of (in a transaction that's not a tax-free trade-in), the cost of the acquired property has to be reduced by the basis of the disposed-of property.

If the recapture rules apply on a disposition of property to make way for replacement of used property, then the cost of the acquired used property is not reduced by the basis of the disposed-of property.

Included in basis (or cost for used property) are all items properly included in your basis for depreciation (Reg. §1.46-3(c)(1)).

[¶1903] Tax Liability Limitations on Investment Credit

The credit is applied in full against your tax liability up to $25,000 in any taxable year. The credit can never exceed the tax liability. But if your tax liability exceeds $25,000, any remaining credit can only be applied against one-half of the excess. Any unused credit is available as a carryback for three years and then as a carryforward for five years.

In the case of married taxpayers, the $25,000 figure is cut to $12,500 on a separate return. There is an exception, however, where your spouse makes no investments that would qualify for the credit and has no credit carryovers to that year. But in making this determination, IRS will consider that your wife made a qualifying investment even if she is only an indirect beneficiary of the credit.

[¶1904] Casualty Loss Limitations on Investment Credit

Another limitation covers reinvestment of casualty insurance proceeds. If property is stolen or destroyed or damaged by fire, storm, shipwreck, or other casualty, the amount spent on replacement property must be reduced by any insurance recovery or the adjusted basis of the destroyed property, whichever is smaller.

[¶1905] Recapture of Investment Credit

If you dispose of an asset before the useful life on which the credit was figured has run out, you have to refigure the credit (§47). Any excess credit you took is added to your current tax.

Suppose you buy an asset for $6,000. Its useful life is ten years. Your credit is $420 (7% of $6,000). But in the sixth year you sell. That entitles you to a credit of only two-thirds of cost ($4,000). Your credit is $280 (7% of $4,000) rather than $420. The $140 difference is added to your tax in the year of sale.

The recapture rules apply when you dispose of the asset. A disposition includes a sale, trade-in, exchange, gift, distribution, involuntary conversion, casualty, theft, in-kind dividend or contribution to a corporation, contribution to a partnership or a sale by a partner or Subchapter S stockholder of his interest in the firm.

Occurrences Triggering Recapture of Investment Credit: Here are some prime instances:

(1) Cessation: The asset ceases to be §38 property. For example, a business asset is switched to personal use or the percentage of use of an asset between personal and business changes after the year the credit was taken.

(2) Property Destroyed by Casualty: Recapture applies if §38 property is disposed of or otherwise ceases to be qualified due to its destruction or damage by casualty or theft. However, qualified replacement property may get the investment credit.

(3) Lease of Property: While mere leasing of an asset escapes recapture, a lease treated as a sale will not. Also, leased property ceases to be §38 property to the lessor if, after the credit year, it doesn't qualify as such in the hands of the lessor, lessee, or sublessee (Reg. §1.47-2(b)(1)). Further, recapture may occur in a sale-leaseback subject to certain exceptions.

(4) Corporate Liquidations: Recapture can be triggered by corporate distributions in liquidation, sale by a corporation in a "tax-free" §337 liquidation and also in a §333 (one-month) liquidation where the sole shareholder continues to use the property in business (*Rev. Rul. 73-515,* CB 1973-2, 7).

(5) Subchapter S Corporations, Partnerships, Estates: Recapture applies in cases of contributions of property to Subchapter S corporations or to certain partnerships, sales of stock by a Subchapter S corporation, sale of a partnership interest, or sale by a beneficiary of an interest in a trust or estate. A corporation electing under Subchapter S may trigger recapture.

Exceptions to Recapture: Some principal examples include:

(1) Death Transfers: There's no recapture when an asset is transferred because of the death of an individual taxpayer or in the case of a death transfer of a partner's interest or of the stock of a Subchapter S corporation or even in a joint tenancy to the surviving owner.

(2) Corporate Transfers in Tax-Free Reorganization: This takes place in

a tax-free reorganization or liquidation (§381(a)) if the acquiring corporation succeeds to the tax attributes of the transferor corporation.

(3) Change in the Form of Conducting Business: Recapture is avoided where a proprietorship or partnership is changed to a corporation provided the transferor retains a substantial interest in the firm. Shareholders retaining substantial interests in a corporation while others sell all their stock are not subjected to recapture.

(4) Reselection of Used Property: The $50,000 limit on used §38 property can be bypassed on early disposition by reselecting excess used property for the earlier year to take the place of the disposed property.

[¶1906] Availability of Investment Credit to Noncorporate Lessors

The credit is not available to noncorporate lessors (included in this category are Subchapter S corporations) unless they are manufacturers or producers or lease on a short-term basis. A lease is considered short term if it satisfies two conditions: (1) the term of the lease must be less than 50% of the useful life (that is, the life allowable for credit and depreciation purposes) of the property subject to the lease and (2) for the first 12 months after transfer of the property to the lessee, the sum of the deductions allowable to the lessor with respect to the leased property must exceed 15% of the rental income produced by the property during such 12-month period. To qualify for the credit, the lease must have been entered into after September 22, 1971. Where the lessor is a partnership which has a corporate partner, the corporate partner will not be denied the credit otherwise allowable to it.

[¶1907] Investment Credit on Leased Property

A lessor of *new* property can elect to pass the credit through to the lessee under certain conditions discussed below. This can be a valuable sales tool in the hands of companies that engage in equipment leasing. The tax advantage can make the difference to a lessee in determining whether to lease or buy. The lessor must make a timely election, however, by filing *with the lessee* a signed statement that contains the consent of the lessee and certain other information. The statement must be filed on or before the due date (including any extensions) for the lessee's return in the year that possession of the property is transferred to the lessee. Once the election statement is filed with the lessee, the election is irrevocable.

The property must qualify in the hands of the lessor as new property eligible for the credit. It must also be such that it would have qualified for the credit as new property if it had been acquired by the lessee. Thus, the lessee must have been the original user of the property. A lessee is the original user as long as he is the first person to use the property for its intended function. Thus storage, testing, or previous attempts at leasing by the lessor will not preclude the lessee from being treated as the original user.

Reconditioned property will not qualify for the passthrough of the credit since it is not new property. Property that has been reconstructed by the lessor is new property in his hands and will qualify for the credit without regard to the lease. However, IRS says that *neither reconditioned nor reconstructed property* will qualify for the passthrough of credit to the lessee because the lessee is not the original user of the property.

All other limitations on eligibility apply to both lessor and lessee. The useful life limitation, that is, of course, the life used for depreciation, is applied to the property in the hands of the lessor.

General Election: Lessors who engage in numerous leasing transactions with a single lessee can make a *general election* covering all their transactions with a particular lessee. The election must be filed on or before the due date (including any extensions) for the lessee's tax return in the year of possession under the lease of the first property that is eligible for the general election. And once filed as to that property, it is irrevocable as to all transfers under lease to that lessee during that entire taxable year (of that lessee).

How It Works: As to leased property where the lessor elects to pass the credit through to the lessee, the credit is based on the fair market value of the property as of the date when possession of the property is transferred to the lessee. However, in the case of leases between corporations, both of which are members of the same affiliated group, the credit is based on the lessor's basis. These rules apply to leases entered into after November 8, 1971.

The full investment credit on new property may be passed through to the lessee subject to the following limitation: the property may not have a class life of more than 14 years and be leased for less than 80% of its class life (except in the case of a "net lease," which would not be subject to the above limitation). Where the limitation applies, the lessor can pass through to the first lessee of the property only that portion of the credit that the period of the lease bears to the class life of the property. The portion of the credit that cannot then be passed through to the lessee can be taken by the lessor. Since the entire credit is available in the year the property is placed in service, the result may be a tax saving in the first year that exceeds that year's expenditure. Recapture can apply, however.

[¶1908] Carryover of Unused Credits

To the extent that a credit cannot be used in the current year because of the tax liability limitation, it can be carried back for three years and then carried forward five years. The unused credit is applied to the earliest year first and then in order to subsequent years until exhausted. There is a specific order of priority as follows: Pre-1971 carryovers are first applied until exhausted (pre-1971 carryovers can be carried over for ten years), then the regular credits for the tax year, and, lastly, post-1970 carryovers, but all only to the extent that the maximum credit amount allowable for the tax year is not exceeded. In addition, the 20% limitation on post-1968 carryovers is abolished for years after 1972.

[¶1909] Method of Accounting

Taxpayers, for purposes of reporting to federal agencies and making financial reports subject to regulation by federal agencies, can account for the tax benefit of the investment credit either currently in the year in which the credit is taken as a tax deduction or ratably over the life of the asset. This includes not only reports made to the federal government but also reporting to stockholders to the extent any federal agency has the authority to specify the method of reporting. The method used must be consistently followed unless permission to change is obtained.

[¶2000] DEMOLITION LOSSES

Generally speaking, a loss due to the voluntary demolition or removal of a building or machinery is deductible as an ordinary loss (Reg. §1.165-1).There are certain wrinkles to this rule with respect to the demolition of old buildings. Where the demolition occurs as a result of a plan or intention formed subsequent to the acquisition of the buildings demolished, the loss is fully deductible as long as incurred in a trade or business or in a transaction entered into for profit (Reg. §1.165-3(b)). But where the intent to demolish was formed at the time of purchase, the ''loss'' on the old building (its undepreciated basis) plus the cost of demolition may not be deducted, but must (with one exception) be allocated to the *land* only as part of its cost basis. This is true even though the intention is not to demolish immediately and any demolition originally planned is subsequently deferred or abandoned.

[¶2001] Recovery of Depreciation

One exception relates to old buildings that are used in a trade or business or for the production of income. A portion of the basis of the property may be allocated to such buildings and depreciated over the period during which they are so used or held. In no event, however, can the portion allocated exceed the present value of the right to receive rentals from the buildings during the remaining period of their intended use. Naturally, the fact that the taxpayer *intends to demolish* the buildings must be taken into consideration in making the allocation (Reg. §1.165-3(a)(2)). Any portion of the basis of the buildings which has not been recovered through depreciation or otherwise at the time of the demolition is allowable as a deduction.

[¶2002] Intent to Demolish

An intention to demolish is evidenced by all the surrounding facts and circumstances but may be suggested by any of the following:

(1) Only a short interval between purchase and demolition.

(2) Prohibitive remodeling costs.

(3) Zoning or other regulations which prohibit the economic use to which the building would have to be put.

(4) General unsuitability for taxpayer's business.

Countering factors include:

(1) Substantial improvements after acquisition.

(2) Prolonged use after acquisition.

(3) Suitability of building as investment asset.

(4) A substantial change in the building or the taxpayer's business after acquisition which then makes demolition desirable (Reg. §1.165-3(c)).

If the building is removed to place the land in a condition desired by a prospective or present lessee, the capitalized costs are treated as part of the cost of obtaining the lease, amortizable over the lease term (*Wm. Ward,* 7 BTA 1107 (*acq.*); Reg. §1.165-3(d)).

[¶2003] Transfer from Controlled Corporation

Here is something to watch for when you transfer property into or out of a wholly owned corporation: Assume your corporation acquires a building without any intention to demolish it. Later, you decide to demolish. But, first, you transfer the property out of the corporation into individual ownership. Then, you demolish. You may lose the demolition loss because the transfer of the property from your corporation to you was an acquisition; therefore, you acquired the property after you intended to demolish it (*Newark Amusement Corp.,* TC Memo 1960-137).

[¶2100] CASUALTY LOSSES

A loss on business or nonbusiness property that results from an accident, fire, storm, drought, theft, shipwreck, or other casualty can be deducted. Such losses are commonly referred to as casualty losses. They are not limited to losses that are incurred in a trade or business or a transaction entered into for profit. An individual can deduct casualty losses that occur to his home if he itemizes his deductions. Even if you can't use the full deduction in the current year, there is still the possibility of getting all of the benefit over the years. Since casualty losses are subject to the net operating loss carryover provisions, any part of the loss not used one year can be carried back three years and, if there is still a balance, ahead for five years. The deduction and the carryover are available to an individual, a married couple, or an estate or trust. Members of a partnership share casualty losses. A corporation does not have to rely on the casualty loss. It is entitled to deduct all its losses in any event.

[¶2101] What Is a Casualty Loss?

The categories set out in the Code are fire, storm, shipwreck, theft, or other casualty. In *Matheson,* 54 F.2d 537, a casualty was defined as "an event due to some sudden, unexpected or unusual cause." But in *Heyn,* 46 TC 302, the Tax Court ruled that you can get the deduction although the loss may have been foreseeable and even preventable by the exercise of due care.

Casualty losses do not include losses due to progressive deterioration of property through a steadily operating cause (*Fay,* 120 F.2d 153; *Durden,* 3 TC 1; *Rev. Rul. 79,* CB 1953-1, 41).

The deductible loss is limited to property. If you pay damages for personal injuries to others, you cannot take a casualty loss deduction (*Mulholland,* 16 BTA 1331).

If your property loses value because it is in or near a disaster area, you cannot take a deduction for that loss. The loss must occur in relation to your property, not someone else's. See *Stoll,* 5 TCM 731.

The expenses incident to a casualty, such as the cost of moving or rental of temporary living accommodations, are not allowed as a casualty loss deduction.

Deductible Casualty Losses: Losses due to bomb damage (*IT 3519,* CB 1941-2, 96. See *Ebner,* TC Memo 1958-108). Losses to home caused by a sudden settling of the land due to excessive rainfall (note this is not erosion) (*Hester,* TC Memo 1954-176). Losses of trees due to drought (*Buttram v.*

Jones, 87 F. Supp. 322). Losses due to an earthquake (*A.R.R. 4725,* CB III-1, 143). Losses due to fire (§165(c)(3)). Losses due to shipwreck (§165(c)(3)). Losses due to storm (§165(c)(3)). Damage to a grain mill by unusual river ice formation (*Stewart City Mills,* 44 BTA 173). Losses due to a mine cave-in (*Rev. Rul. 55-327,* CB 1955-1, 25). Losses due to a deep sinking of land caused by a subterranean disturbance (*Grant,* 30 BTA 1028). Losses caused by vandalism (*Banigan,* 10 TCM 561). Losses due to a quarry blast (*Durden,* 3 TC 1). Losses due to "sonic boom" when an airplane breaks the sound barrier (*Rev. Rul. 59-344,* CB 1959-2, 74). Losses due to termite destruction if the attack is sudden. The important concept is suddenness (*Rosenberg,* 198 F.2d 46; *Buist,* 164 F. Supp. 218; compare *Rogers,* 120 F.2d 244). Although there was previous termite damage and it was stopped, later termite damage revealed in annual inspection is deductible as being sudden (*Kilroe,* 32 TC 1304). Losses due to landslide (*Heyn,* 46 TC 302).

Disallowed Casualty Losses: Damage to property of another (*Stoll,* 5 TCM 731. See also *West,* 163 F. Supp. 739). Cost of defending a damage suit (*Oransky,* 1 BTA 1239). Erosion loss (*Texas and Pacific Ry. Co.,* TC Memo 1943-507). Loss caused by moths (*Rev. Rul. 55-327,* CB 1955-1, 25). Wrongful seizures of property (*Hughes* 1 BTA 944). Loss of trees resulting from Dutch elm and other diseases (*IRS Field Release No. 56,* August 5, 1957). Damage done by rats (*Banigan,* 10 TCM 561).

[¶2102] Deductible Casualty Loss Without Damage to Property

The District Court in *Stowers* (169 F. Supp. 246) held that one can get a casualty loss deduction even if his property is not damaged. In that case, there was a sudden cave-in of land near the taxpayer's residence. As a result, the street was closed, and the taxpayer lost access to his own house. That was enough to create a casualty loss, said the Court.

The Treasury admitted that since the property's access (except for a rear entrance served by a small alley) was cut off, its value was reduced by some $7,000. But it had disallowed the deduction because there was no physical damage to the property itself. The Court disagreed, and held that loss of use is sufficient to give the deduction.

Not all cases arising from indirect property damage have been resolved as favorably to taxpayers, however. In *Kamanski v Commissioner,* (CA-9, 477 F.2d 452, *aff'g* TC Memo 1970-352), a homeowner whose property was not directly injured by a landslide which destroyed the surrounding neighborhood claimed he was entitled to a casualty loss deduction. The Tax Court disallowed the loss, saying it was a personal loss, not a casualty loss. The Ninth Circuit affirmed, stating that the loss claimed was based on market predictions, not on the damage actually caused by the casualty and that therefore the loss claim must wait until such time as the loss is actually incurred—not on the present predicted loss.

[¶2103] Computing the Amount of Your Casualty Loss

The method of computing a casualty loss is the same regardless of whether the loss was incurred in a trade or business or in any transaction entered into for profit (Reg. §1.165-7(a)(1)).

Personal Casualty Loss: The amount of the deduction for any casualty under Code §165(c)(3) is the lesser of two figures: (a) the difference between the value of the property before the casualty and after the casualty (including any salvage) or (b) the amount of the adjusted basis of the property. Your adjusted basis for personal property will probably be your cost plus your additions to the property, since you are not allowed a depreciation deduction for such property.

The lesser of these figures must then be reduced by insurance payments you receive and the $100 floor imposed by the tax law. No matter which figure you use, you must deduct this compensation whether it is insurance, relief from disaster agencies or the Red Cross, or any other compensation. You do not have to reduce for food, medical supplies, or other forms of subsistence which are not replacements of lost property.

Business Property: IRS's position on the treatment of casualty losses to business property is revealed in its Regulations (Reg. §1.165-7(a)).

Under IRS Regulations, losses to business property are required to be computed in the same manner as losses for nonbusiness property are computed. The amount of the deduction, therefore, is the lesser of: (a) the difference between the fair market value of the property before and after the casualty or (b) the adjusted basis of the property. This lesser amount is further reduced by any insurance received. But, if the property is fully destroyed and the fair market value is less than basis, you can deduct basis.

Trees and Shrubs: If buildings, trees, or shrubs are integral parts of your property not used in a trade or business, you compute the loss caused by damage by computing what happened to your entire property (Reg. §1.165-7(b)(2)(ii)).

[¶2104] How to Determine the Decrease in Value

The difference between the value of the property immediately before and immediately after the casualty is usually the key to how much you can deduct. It becomes a matter of proof. With considerable amounts involved, the best bet is to use competent appraisers (Reg. §1.165-7(a)(2)).

The costs of repairing, replacing, or cleaning will not be a deduction. However, where the repairs do nothing more than restore the property to its pre-casualty condition, the cost of repairs may be accepted instead of an appraisal in determining the amount of the loss (Reg. §1.165-7(a)(2)(ii)). In many cases, this is the practical solution accepted by the courts. See *Harmon,* 13 TC 373; *Jenard,* TC Memo 1961-70.

[¶2105] Insurance Exceeds Basis

If your compensation payments (insurance, etc.) are more than the adjusted basis of the property destroyed, you have a gain rather than a loss. However, if you purchase within a specified time either a replacement property or the controlling interest in a corporation owning such property, you can put off your gain (§1033). Your cost of the new property must equal or exceed the amount received on the old.

[¶2106] When You Deduct Your Loss

A casualty loss is deductible in the year it occurs. The deduction should be taken in that year and not in any other year whether or not the damages are actually repaired or replaced that year. The loss must be fixed by an identifiable event which occurred in the year deduction is taken (Reg. §1.165-1(d)(1)).

If in the year in which the casualty occurred, there is a claim for reimbursement (e.g., insurance) and there is a reasonable prospect of recovery, you cannot deduct that portion of the loss for which you may be reimbursed until it becomes reasonably certain that reimbursement will not be received (Reg. §1.165-1(d)(2)(i)). The loss, then, will only be deductible in the taxable year in which the claim is adjudicated or otherwise settled (Reg. §1.165(d)-(2)(iii)). If a loss is deducted in one year and a reimbursement is received in a later year, no recomputation of tax is made for the prior year; the reimbursement is included in the year received and is treated as a recovery of an amount previously deducted (Reg. §1.165(d)(2)(iii)).

[¶2107] Proof of Loss

You must be able to prove your loss to obtain a deduction. You should be prepared to show: (1) the nature of the casualty and when it occurred; (2) that the loss was the direct result of the casualty; (3) that you were the owner of the property; (4) the cost or other adjusted basis of the property, evidenced by purchase contract or a comparable instrument. Note that you must also show improvements; (5) depreciation allowed or allowable; (6) values before and after the casualty; (7) the amount of insurance or other compensation received or recoverable, including the value of repairs, restoration, or cleaning up provided without cost by disaster agencies.

[¶2108] Your Casualty Loss May Have to Be Set Off Against Capital Gains

Generally, your casualty loss will be an ordinary loss offsetting ordinary income. However, if your casualty loss involves property held for more than six months and you have other gains or losses from the disposition of property used in your trade or business and held for more than six months, you may have to offset capital gains with your casualty loss. Where the aggregate of these gains exceeds the aggregate of the losses, including casualty losses, you get capital gain treatment for the net gain (§1231).

In short, Code §1231 gives the taxpayer a break on some gains that would otherwise be ordinary income by giving them capital gain treatment. But, in figuring the amount of gain to be taxed at capital gain rates, you must include certain losses. Only the excess gain will be given capital gain treatment. This has certain disadvantages. Although you wish to have the gain taxed at capital rates, you do not want to have your losses set off that way. Rather, you want your losses to become a deduction against ordinary income. Casualty losses are among the losses that must be set off against the §1231 gains. Of course, if there are no §1231 gains, casualty losses are set off against ordinary income. So, if you have a casualty loss, you should try to avoid a §1231 gain in the same year.

There is an exception to this rule, however: If your casualty loss is completely uninsured, it will not have to be set off against the §1231 gains. In such a case, you can have your cake and eat it, too. Even though your §1231 gains exceed your §1231 losses (including casualty losses), if the casualty loss is completely uninsured, you can get your capital gain on the §1231 gain and take an ordinary loss on your uninsured casualty loss.

IRS says this exception does not apply to casualty losses for capital assets not *connected with a trade or business or held for the production of income*. One court disagrees with IRS and would treat residential property the same as business property (*Maurer*, 284 F.2d 122). But IRS announced it will not follow this case (*TIR-304*, 2/16/61).

[¶2109] Adjustment of Basis After Casualty

You must adjust the basis of your property after the casualty loss, so that on a subsequent sale your gain or loss can be computed. Also, for depreciation purposes, you must adjust your basis (*IRS Pub. 155, Rev. 1/58*).

You adjust your basis by taking your old basis and adding any taxable gain. Then you subtract the total of your insurance or other compensation and your casualty loss.

[¶2110] If Casualty Loss Exceeds Income for the Year

It is possible that if you have a substantial casualty loss, it may exceed your income for the year. If so, you can treat the excess casualty loss as a net operating loss and carry it back and forward to other tax years.

[¶2200] DEDUCTING REAL ESTATE TAXES

Normally, real estate taxes are deductible for federal income tax purposes.

If a piece of property is sold during the year, the tax deduction is apportioned between the buyer and the seller. The period up to the date of the sale is apportioned to the seller; the period after that date, to the buyer (§164(d)).

Example: Allen sells Green a parcel of land on June 1. Allen gets a deduction for five-twelfths of the property tax. Green can claim a deduction for seven-twelfths of the tax.

[¶2201] When You Get a Deduction for Real Estate Taxes

If you sell or buy property, you will have to know not only what property taxes to deduct but when to deduct them.

If you are on the accrual basis and no election to accrue has been made and you are either buying or selling a parcel of real estate the following rules apply:

(1) If the other party to the transaction (buyer or seller) held the property when the tax became a lien or the other party became personally liable, your share of the deduction accrues on the date of the sale.

(2) If not, the general rule applies and the deduction accrues on the lien date.

If you are on the cash basis the following rules apply:

(1) If the other party to the transaction (buyer or seller) held the property when the tax became a lien or the other party became personally liable, it is assumed that your share of the tax was paid on the date of sale (regardless of when actually paid).

(2) If not, the general rule applies and you deduct your share of the tax when actually paid.

Example: In County of White, the real property tax year is the calendar year. The real property tax is a personal liability of the owner of the real property on June 30 of the current year but is not payable until February 28 of the following year. Doe, a cash-basis taxpayer who had owned property in White County on January 1, sells his property to Roe on May 30. Roe retains ownership of the property for the balance of the year. A tax equal to 149/365 for January 1 to May 29 is imposed on Doe and is considered paid on the date of sale. Doe may deduct in the year the sale occurs (or year he actually pays). Roe is charged a tax equal to 216/365 for May 30 until December 31. He may deduct in the tax year when he actually pays the tax.

Example: In Brown County, the real property tax year is the calendar year. The real property tax becomes a lien on January 1 and is payable on April 30. It is not treated as a personal liability of the owner. Smith, a cash-basis taxpayer, is the owner of the property on January 1 and pays the real property tax on April 30. On May 1 Smith sells the real property to Jones. Jones retains the property until September 1 when he sells it to Brown. Smith pays a real property tax equal to 120/365 for January 1 to April 30. He may deduct only in the year the tax was actually paid. Jones pays to the extent of 123/365 for May 1 until August 31 and is considered to have paid on the date of sale. He may deduct the tax in the year of sale or the year when actually paid. Brown pays to the extent of 122/365 for September 1 through December 31. He is also considered to have paid on the date of sale and can deduct in the year of sale or in taxable year when tax is actually paid.

Example: In Green County, the real property tax year is the calendar year. The tax becomes a lien on June 30 and is payable on September 1. Lake, who is on the cash basis and owned the real property on January 1, sells it to Rivers on July 15. The tax is imposed on Lake to the extent of 195/365 for January 1 through July 14. He may deduct in his taxable year when the sale occurs or when the tax is actually paid. Rivers pays to the extent of 170/365 for July 15 through December 31. He may also deduct in his taxable year when the sale occurs or when he actually pays the tax.

[¶2202] Accruing Real Estate Taxes

An accrual-basis taxpayer can elect to accrue real property taxes over the period of time to which these taxes relate (§461). But he must elect to do so. If the taxpayer does not elect, the property taxes accrue according to the state or local law—at some definite moment, usually when the tax becomes a lien or when personal liability arises.

[¶2203] Checklist of Deductibility of Real Estate Taxes in Special Situations

□ ***Tenancy in Common:*** If you are a tenant in common, you can only deduct your proportionate share of the taxes even if you pay the entire tax.

☐ ***Tenancy by the Entirety:*** Either tenant can take the deduction if he pays the tax (*Nicodemus,* 26 BTA 125, *acq.*).

☐ ***Joint Tenancy:*** The one who pays the tax, as in tenancy by the entirety, can take the deduction.

☐ ***Mortgagees:*** If you are a mortgagee, you cannot deduct taxes you pay on the property for periods prior to your acquiring title to the property. If the taxes are paid before foreclosure, they represent an additional loan on the property. If they are paid after foreclosure, they represent additional cost of the property (*Schieffelin,* 44 BTA 137).

☐ ***Back Taxes Paid by a Buyer:*** A buyer of real property gets no deduction for any back taxes he pays. The sum he pays is added to the purchase price (Reg. §1.164-6).

[¶2204] Local Benefit Taxes

No deduction is allowed for taxes assessed against local benefits if they tend to increase the value of the property assessed (Code §164(c)). These taxes, which increase the value of your land, can be added to the cost of the property. There are two important exceptions to the rule of nondeductibility in this area:

(1) You can deduct the part of the tax which goes toward maintenance and interest charges with respect to the benefit. But you, the taxpayer, must show the allocation.

(2) Taxes levied by a special taxing district are deductible. However, the special district must cover the whole of at least one county and at least 1,000 people must be subject to the taxes levied by that district. Also, in order to get the deduction, the district must levy its assessments annually at a uniform rate on the same assessed value of real estate as is used for purposes of the real property tax generally.

It is important for you to remember that where both nondeductible special assessments and deductible general taxes are levied, you must make an allocation. Otherwise, you won't get any deduction (*Roper,* 7 BTA 1112).

[¶2205] Capitalizing Real Estate Taxes

Taxes that are ordinarily deductible, like interest and other carrying charges on property, may be capitalized by the taxpayer. Capitalization increases the basis of the property. The taxpayer must elect to capitalize.

Once an election to capitalize a charge on a piece of property is made, charges of the same type must be capitalized in later years also. There is an exception with respect to taxes and other carrying charges on unimproved and unproductive real property. Here, you can elect for each given year without regard to past years.

The election to capitalize comes in very handy if you have little or no income for the year and own unproductive real property. Since you get no benefit through the deduction, the capitalization may work out better. Boosting your basis will cut down on any future gain or increase a future loss.

[¶2300] LOCAL PROPERTY TAXES AND HOW TO REDUCE THEM

Taxes levied against real property are a primary source of government revenue in every American community. Once levied against real estate, taxes become a lien and may be enforced by the sale of the property or some interest in it. A determination of the tax burden that a piece of real estate will have to carry is a primary element in determining its desirability for acquisition and its value. Since real property tax rates vary from year to year and assessing practices may be changed from time to time, the tax burden that a parcel of real estate will be required to carry in the future can only be an estimate.

To arrive at a tax rate a local government takes these steps: (1) sets a budget (the amount of money it will have to raise), (2) determines the total valuation of taxable property within its confines, and (3) arrives at the tax rate by dividing the amount to be raised by taxation by the total assessed valuation. The tax rate applied to the value of a particular parcel of real estate as determined by assessment gives the amount of taxes that will be charged to it. Thus, we see that the budget or, over the long term, whether local government is economical or extravagant will determine the real estate tax burden. Whether a particular piece of real estate carries a fair share of that burden will depend on how it is valued by the assessing authorities..

[¶2301] Assessment Methods

Various methods of appraisal are used to determine assessed valuation. Some communities take assessed property at a fraction of its current market value. Others take the value to be the amount for which the property would sell at a forced sale. Others assess property at its full market value. Full market value assessment is being used by more and more communities.

The assessor usually separates the value of land and buildings. Land values are set on the basis of the value of a typical lot—one of a size which is standard or common in laying out land in the community. Using this standard as a base, the assessor tries to value odd-size lots and special-location lots in relationship to that standard. Depending on prevailing subdivision practices in the development of the community, the standard lot will usually have a 20- to 50-foot width and a 100- to 125-foot depth. One method of determining variations from a standard 100-foot depth lot is the 4-3-2-1 depth rule which determines variations for lots having less depth or more depth than 100 feet in this way:

Depth of Lot in Feet	*Percent of Standard Lot Value*	*Depth of Lot in Feet*	*Percent of Standard Lot Value*
25	40	125	109
50	70	150	117
75	90	175	124
100	100	200	130

In valuing buildings the assessor must consider age, depreciation, type, size and character, suitability to the location, and various other factors. Most assessors start out with cost per foot of cubical content or cost per square foot of floor space. This rule of thumb will vary with different types of buildings—loft, factory, fireproof, nonfireproof, elevator and walk-up apartments, office buildings of various heights, etc. The size of the building is determined, and the appropriate square foot or cubic foot factor is applied to arrive at an estimate of the replacement cost of the building. Then, based on age, an allowance is made for accrued depreciation. Assessors also consider the rent a building is able to produce. In fact, many assessors treat this as the paramount factor on the basis that an improved piece of real estate is never worth more than its capitalized rental value unless the value of the land alone is greater. In some communities, land increases in value while buildings almost always decline. Thus, sometimes buildings are only valued at the amount they add to the value of the land, and this may decline until it becomes a nominal amount.

The important thing about assessment is that it be equitable. All parcels of real property should be treated in substantially the same way. The assessed value should impose on each parcel of real estate a portion of the community tax burden which is no greater than the ratio that the true value of the particular piece of real estate bears to the total value of all the real estate in the community. This objective is never fully achieved. Reassessment cannot be carried out as rapidly as values change and as new buildings are added to the total real estate in a community. For this reason, there must be procedures by which taxpayers can have their assessments reviewed if they think they are being asked to carry a greater share of the community tax burden than is proper or fair.

To estimate the future tax burden on a piece of property, it is necessary to understand the assessing practices used by local authorities. This information can best be obtained from a responsible official in the local assessing office.

[¶2302] Reduction of Real Estate Taxes

Wherever a taxpayer feels that his real property has be(ssed too high, local law affords him an opportunity to petition for a r)n of the assessment. Such a proceeding is usually initiated by makingest with an application for correction to the taxing authority itself. Onl- such an application is denied, either in whole or in part, may a]ding for judicial review of the assessment be initiated. When tax officrn down the property owner's protest, this action is usually subject tew by a court in an appeals proceeding. This is a proceeding whereb tax officials are called on to produce their records and to certify them court so that the court may determine whether the officials have proceeccording to the principles of law that they are required to follow in the pe\ance of their assessing duties.

Local tax authorities usually have forms of application tc used in asking for a review of an assessment.

If an application of protest is rejected, the next step is to initia)roceeding in the appropriate court to review the final assessment. Tgrounds upon which an assessment may be reduced usually are these: (1)rvaluation, (2) inequality, (3) illegality.

Overvaluation can be established by showing that the assessn of real property has been set at a sum which is higher than the full and market value of the property.

Inequality, which somewhat overlaps overvaluation, can be eblished by showing that the assessment was made at a proportionately hig valuation than the assessment of real estate of like character in the samrea. To obtain relief it usually is necessary to show that the assessment out of proportion as compared with valuations in the municipality genelly. To prove inequality, it is necessary to examine a considerable number oparcels of real estate for the purpose of comparing the market values f these properties with their assessed valuation and ascertain the ratio of ssessed value to market value in each instance. You have a case of inequali if such a study shows that the ratio of assessed values to market values gerally is substantially lower than the ratio between the assessed value and th market value of your property.

Illegality exists when the assessment has been levied in an irregilar manner or on a basis erroneous in law or in fact other than an error in the evaluation itself. An example of an illegal assessment is the inclusion on the tax roles of an assessment of a parcel of real estate which is legally exempt from taxation.

To seek a reduction of a real estate assessment, take these steps: (1)

Examine th or's report. If this is predicated on some error of fact, such as an i t description of the property, an incorrect statement of its actual incon xpenses, or any other error concerning the property itself, submit pro he correct facts. (2) Find out what the property cost. Compare th l cost of the property with the assessment. If the purchase price is sub lly below the assessed value that is to be challenged and the date of se is not too remote from the tax date, this comparison will be relevant g as it can be established that the property was purchased in an arm's-l transaction. (3) Study the records of income received from the propert the expense of operation over several years prior to the tax date. The g capacity of income property is the most significant single factor in d ining its market value for purposes of seeking reduction of a tax assess (4) Make a comparison of sales prices and assessed valuations and timates of market value and assessed valuations for other comparab perties in the area. This kind of a comparison will have been made by s, and so a great deal of the necessary information may be obtained at way rather than through the laborious, costly method of getting ap als on a large number of properties. (5) Consult experts. The testimony xpert witnesses is usually the most important proof in court proceedin o seek reduction of real estate taxes. You may want to use the testimony a building expert as well as a real estate expert. The real estate expert wi estify as to sales of comparable property and to the value the property uld bring in the market place. The building expert would testify as to the nd structural value or reproduction cost, less depreciation of the building.

[¶2400] HOW TO CONTRACT FOR THE SALE OF REAL ESTATE

The essential elements in the sale and purchase of real estate converge in the contract of sale (purchase and sale agreement). There must be a meeting of the minds on the essential substantive and dollar-and-cents elements that have to be reflected in the contract. Here we will list the elements that must be negotiated and pinned down to consummate the sale of real estate.

The law requires that a contract for the sale of real estate be in writing. A lot of arrangements are necessary before transfer of the title to real estate can be accomplished with the assurance that all the parties know what they are doing. The buyer must have time to ascertain if the seller is in fact the owner of the real estate and that there are no defects in his title. Before paying the purchase price, the buyer will want to have the seller's title examined and will want to see evidence that the title is good. The contract of sale has to specify the type of title the buyer will get, how he is to be assured that he is getting the kind of title agreed on, and what is to happen if defects in the title are discovered. While all this is being checked and worked out, the contract of sale nails the seller so that he can't turn around and deal with somebody who offers a higher price. It also prevents the buyer from changing his mind as long as the seller can deliver the kind of title he promises. In addition, the contract of sale must deal with insurance policies, leases, chattels, mortgages and other items that are related to the real estate. All this has to be set forth clearly and exactly in the contract of sale. In an installment contract, it its essential to spell out how and when future installment payments are to be paid and what happens if they are not.

The contract must definitely identify the real estate that is being sold and specify what furniture and other personal property go with the real estate. Usually, all fixtures automatically go with the real estate. In the absence of a specific provision, the buyer is not entitled to any personal property associated with the real estate that is not a fixture.

To be enforceable, the contract must be complete. All the terms must be settled with none left to be determined by future negotiations. For example, failure to specify when a purchase-money mortgage would fall due made a contract unenforceable.

Specify the type of deed to be given. In most states if the contract is silent, the seller is required only to give a quitclaim deed. In some states where the contract is silent, the seller has to give a warranty deed. The buyer should try to commit the seller to give him a warrant deed.

[¶2401] Marketable Title

Unless the contract makes specific exceptions, the seller is required to convey a marketable title—free from defects, free from doubt, one that will assure the buyer that he can hold and use the real estate free of conflicting claims to possession and of litigation. The buyer should have reasonable assurance that he will be able to sell the land without encountering any difficulty that would minimize its value. The buyer does not have to take the real estate if it is subject to any mortgages, liens, easements, restrictions, leases and tenancies, and encroachments unless the contract specifies the existence of these limitations on the title that the buyer will receive. Substantial existing violations of zoning or building ordinances render a title unmarketable, but the prudent buyer will have the contract of sale specify that the seller will deliver the property free from all violations of zoning and building ordinances.

The kind of title that a seller must deliver depends on the terms and provisions of the contract of sale. If the contract is silent, the seller must deliver marketable title free from encumbrances. If the contract requires the seller to deliver title "free from all defects or encumbrances," the buyer may be able to reject title if there is even a trivial encroachment or a beneficial easement. Usually, the seller lists in his contract the encumbrances that exist; and the buyer agrees to take title subject to these encumbrances, such as building restrictions, existing mortgages, etc. If the contract says that the contract will be subject to a lot of general language such as "conditions and restrictions of records, easements, existing tenancies, any state of facts which an accurate survey may show" etc., the seller can probably get away with delivering what he has; and the buyer is left holding the bag.

One practical way for seller and buyer to make definite the kind of title they are talking about is to check the examination of title made at the time the seller acquired the property. If the restrictions that then existed are satisfactory to the buyer, the seller can commit to deliver a title subject only to the limitations existing when he acquired the property. Another way is for the contract to require the seller to deliver a marketable title and a policy of title insurance. This permits the buyer to walk out on a contract if a title is not marketable or if title insurance is not forthcoming. If the contract merely requires the seller to furnish title insurance, then the buyer is required to take title even if it is technically unmarketable as long as a title company will issue insurance. This a title company will sometimes do on the basis that there is little business risk in a technical defect which may render the title less than fully marketable.

In order to avoid being tied up in delays attendant to clearing a defective title, the buyer may want to fix a time for delivery of the deed and have the contract provide that time is of the essence. Then, if the seller does not have good title at the time fixed for delivering the deed, the buyer can relieve himself of the obligations of the contract.

The buyer should insist that the contract specify the kind of evidence of good title that the seller will be required to produce, i.e., title insurance, abstracts, certificate of title, etc. He should require that the evidence of title show the condition of the title as of the date on which the deed is delivered rather than the date of contract. The contract should give the seller a reasonable time to furnish the buyer with evidence of title; the buyer a reasonable time to examine such evidence and point out any defects; then, the seller a further reasonable time to eliminate or cure any such defects; and a further time within which the buyer can decide to accept or reject a title still carrying a defect which the seller has been unable to cure.

[¶2402] Deposits

When the buyer makes a deposit or a down payment on the contract, that money applies as part payment of the purchase price if he conforms. If he defaults, the deposit can be retained by the seller. This should be specifically covered by the contract. The seller should, to protect himself, require a large enough deposit to cover the broker's commission, expense of title search, and compensation for his loss of time and loss of opportunity to sell elsewhere if the buyer should default. If the seller can't deliver clear title, then the buyer is entitled to his deposit back.

[¶2403] Mortgages

If the buyer is to take the property subject to an existing mortgage, the contract should so state. It should specify whether the buyer is assuming an existing mortgage or merely taking subject to the mortgage. If the buyer is giving a purchase-money mortgage as part of the payment, the contract should spell out the interest rates, maturity, amortization payments, the form of mortgage, and other details.

[¶2404] Contingencies and Loss

The buyer's obligation may be made subject to contingencies such as his ability to get a mortgage, zoning variance, etc. It is important that the contract spell out the kind of mortgage, the kind of variance, who has the responsibility for getting the mortgage or variance, the time within which the contingency is to be satisfied, and when the deal is to be terminated if the contingency has not been satisfied by that time. Specify who is to carry the risk of loss and damage to the property, the right of the buyer to cancel the deal if there is a substantial loss, his right to insurance money if he does not back out, etc.

[¶2405] Survey

If the buyer wants the seller to provide a survey at the seller's expense, the contract should so provide. The time for delivery of the survey should be specified. The contract should require the survey to be satisfactory to the buyer's lawyer, and a time should be fixed for the buyer to raise objections based on the survey.

The survey should be verified with local ordinances, private covenants and restrictions, party wall agreements, and setback requirements.

[¶2406] Protecting the Buyer Where Survey Not Available

The risk of violations, encumbrances, and restrictions can be put on the seller by inserting these provisions in the contract:

(1) Subject to local zoning and setback ordinances that are not violated by the present structure.

(2) Subject to the state of facts an accurate survey would show provided they do not render the title unmarketable.

(3) Subject to covenants and restrictions of record not rendering title unmarketable or revertible.

[¶2407] Outstanding Leases and Lease Provisions

If the purchaser is buying income-producing property as an investment, his attorney will want to examine the leases and check the rentals in those leases against the rental information that has been furnished by the seller. The attorney will also want to look for lease provisions that include many unusual clauses, particularly those that concern the landlord's obligations to make repairs and the tenants' rights to cancel or renew. Clauses that concern damage or destruction to the premises, either by casualty or fire or taking through eminent domain, will require an intensive scrutiny.

[¶2408] Limitations as to Use

The purchaser's attorney will examine the type, area restrictions, and use restrictions imposed on the property either by government regulation or by private covenant. In order to protect his client, he may require a provision that the purchaser will not have to buy the property if its intended use is prohibited by such restrictions. The seller of the property will usually not object to this type of a provision unless market conditions are in his favor and he feels that the tying up of the property during the contract period will unfavorably affect the value of the property. A possible compromise might be the requirement that the purchaser must acquire the necessary knowledge about existing regulations and covenants within a certain amount of time after the contract of sale has been entered into. Typically, this type of provision will give an option to the purchaser to terminate the contract if there is any prohibition on the particular use he intends to put the property to during the specified period of time.

[¶2409] Zoning

The seller will ordinarily provide a warranty that existing structures on the property are not in violation of any zoning regulations and ordinances. If the purchaser plans to change the existing use of the property, this warranty is not enough for him. The same considerations will also apply to a purchaser who is acquiring vacant land on which he plans to erect a building that he will devote to a particular use. Here the purchaser will insist on a repetition by the seller that the purchaser's contemplated use of the land will not violate zoning regulations and ordinances. The seller, of course, may not be willing to go that far in his assurances. The ultimate disposition of this problem depends on the parties' bargaining positions.

[¶2410] Performance Time

The seller may want the proceeds of the sale of the property on a particular day, since he may intend either to enter a new venture or to discharge an obligation. In such circumstances, he may want to make time for performance under the contract *of the essence*. Under a "time of the essence" arrangement, seller's obligation to convey the property to the purchaser will be relieved by the purchaser's failure to meet the payments on the specific day. In addition, the seller may have a suit for damages against the purchaser. The purchaser's attorney may insist that if time is of the essence, it should be so for both parties. However, the seller has a good argument against that type of arrangement, since generally the purchaser's only obligation is to pay cash on the day of title closing. The seller has numerous obligations, since he must clear up the property before conveying it to the purchaser. As a possible compromise, the parties may agree thwt time for performance is of the essence for both parties but that the purchaser will notify the seller in writing a specified number of days before the date set for the closing of title of all objections to the seller's title. This provision allows the seller to clear up those objections.

[¶2411] Purchase-Money Mortgage

Sellers often take back a purchase-money second mortgage as part of their purchase price for the property. Here, the seller will want to be assured that the purchaser will not milk the property by collecting rents for a certain number of months and then default on the mortgages. The solution is to prepare a timetable that integrates principal and interest payments on the purchase-money mortgage with the other obligations of the purchaser (including water charges, taxes, and interest and principal on the first mortgage). Such a timetable assures that the purchaser is obligated to make payments for these different items in different months. This means that the seller can soon find out if the purchaser has defaulted on his obligations.

Another provision the seller will want is one protecting against a default in the payment of principal or interest on the purchase-money mortgage, or on the payment of principal or interest on any other mortgage, or on the payment of taxes, water rates, or assessment. This provision gives the seller, at his option, the right to accelerate all the principal amount of the purchase-money mortgage on default of any one of the above-named obligations by the purchaser.

[¶2412] Personal Property

When a purchaser acquires a building, he ordinarily expects to acquire title to the property within that building; for example, gas ranges and refrigerators in an apartment house. But gas ranges and refrigerators are usually considered to be personal property and will not be included in the sale of real estate unless there is an express provision covering them. It is very important, therefore, for the purchaser's attorney to state all the personal property included in the sale. The best practice is the requirement of a bill of sale from the seller covering personal property. The purchaser will also want to be assured that the personal property is free of all liens and encumbrances.

[¶2413] Sales Contract Checklist

The basic realty contract is the blueprint for the deal that establishes the rights of the parties. If the contract is faulty or incomplete, the prospects of a satisfactory closing are not favorable. The objective in the sales contract, as indicated above, is to spell out fully and fairly the rights of the parties. The following is a proposed guide or a checklist for a sales contract. This guide is not recommended for any particular jurisdiction, since real property conditions vary from state to state. Instead it is an indication of some of the more common problems which occur in most jurisdictions to which the attorneys will devote their attention. In most states, the contract is prepared by the attorney for the seller. Usually, the contract has already been drawn and prepared before the parties come together for the signing of the contract.

(1) Date of the contract.

(2) Names and addresses (full) of seller and purchaser.

(3) Description of the property (usually the description in the prior deed is used).

(4) Purchase-price clause. This clause includes the actual purchase price; the down payment; whether it is to be made in cash or by a check subject to collection; the amount payable on the closing of title (by cash or by certified check); and the balance of purchase price by taking subject to an existing mortgage and/or a purchase-money mortgage. Provisions may also be made for assumption by the purchaser of the existing mortgage.

(5) Survey. Provide that the sale is subject to a specific survey if there is one or that the sale is subject to any state of facts an accurate survey might show if there is none.

(6) Other provisions to which the sale is subject:

Zoning ordinances
Easements
Party wall agreements
Encroachments
Restrictive covenants of record
License agreements
Tenancies—outstanding leases to be inspected by purchaser
Mortgages
Beam rights
Other liens

(7) Purchase-money mortgage. Provisions here include the amount and how it will be amortized, the due date, the interest rate and how it is payable, the type of mortgage form to be used, subordination to a first mortgage if there is one, who shall draw the bond and mortgage (ordinarily by the attorney for the seller at the expense of the purchaser) and also who shall pay recording fees, mortgage recording taxes, etc.

(8) Possession. Decide whether purchaser should be permitted to enter possession of premises before closing of title and, if so, provide in the contract.

(9) Title. What kind of title should the contract call for and what kind of title evidence will be adequate? What kind of deed is to be given? What happens if the property is damaged before closing? Decide whether protec-

tive clause should provide for submitting of any objections before the closing of title.

(10) Remedies in case of default.

(11) Personal property clause.

(12) Specify the time and place of closing of title.

(13) Broker. Insert the broker's name and specify his commission rights, when, and who will pay.

(14) Items to be apportioned. Assessments, lease defaults, rents, taxes, insurance.

(15) Taxes and other liens. Consider including a clause that they will not be an objection to title and may be paid out of the purchase price at the closing of title.

(16) Consider clause that the purchaser is buying the premises "as is," has inspected them and there is no warranty as to physical condition.

[¶2414] Purchaser's Considerations

The following items are especially for the consideration of the purchaser's attorney:

(1) Find out the nature of covenants and restrictions to which the sale is subject. Add the following: "Provided the present structure does not violate same."

(2) Make sure of the identity of the owner of the property before the contract is signed. Find out if the seller is competent to pass good title (age, marital status, and dower rights).

(3) Have the down payment held in escrow if there is any doubt as to whether the seller has title or is financially responsible.

(4) If the sale is subject to easements or encroachments or is subject to any state of facts an accurate survey may show, add "provided same does not render title unmarketable."

(5) Get contiguity clause if there is more than one lot.

(6) Prepayment clause for the purchaser if there is a purchase-money bond and mortgage.

(7) Examine leases, survey (if the seller has one), and copy of seller's previous abstracts or title company reports.

(8) Terms to be performed after the delivery of the deed need the following clause: "This clause shall survive the delivery of the deed."

(9) If the sale is subject to zoning ordinances, add a provision that the same must not be violated by the present structure.

(10) Get written authority to make searches for departmental building violations.

[¶2500] CLOSING THE TITLE

This is where the deed and final evidence of good title are delivered, the money is paid, the mortgages are executed, and charges against the property are prorated.

The buyer should get the deed; a title report or policy or other evidence of good title; a bill of sale of any personal property going with the real estate; a receipt for the purchase price he paid; a survey of the property; insurance policies and assignments thereof; a statement from the mortgagee of the amount due on any existing mortgage; release and satisfaction of any mortgage or other lien paid but not yet recorded; leases and assignments thereof; letter by seller telling tenants to pay future rents to buyer; letter by seller advising managing agent of the sale and the termination of his authority; statement by seller as to rents paid and due; receipts for taxes, water, gas, electricity; special assessments; assessment of any service contracts and building maintenance guarantees; seller's affidavit of title security deposits and tenants' consent to transfer if required; social security and payroll data on building employees; keys to the building.

The seller receives the balance of the purchase price including any purchase-money mortgage and notes. He will want evidence of fire insurance protection if he has a continuous mortgage interest.

[¶2501] After the Closing

The buyer should record his deed and any releases obtained at the closing. The seller should record any purchase-money mortgage. The seller should notify the managing agent and employees that he is no longer responsible for their compensation. The buyer should arrange for necessary services, get the consent of the insurance company to assignment of policies, get any new insurance necessary, and have water, gas, electric, and tax bills changed to his name.

[¶2502] Title Closing Checklist

If the preliminary work is done well, the physical act of title closing can be accomplished with dispatch. In order to do this, however, all the documents (deeds, bills of sale, mortgages, bonds, assignments, etc.) must be ready and checked in advance. The actual formal closing then consists of an exchange of documents and checks.

(1) Verifying title. The seller's attorney will want to check title and

remove any possible objections. The following considerations should be covered:

(a) Make certain that title evidence has been brought up to date and is in the form agreed on in the contract. Resolve position as to exceptions and encumbrances (that is, whether or not material; check the survey if one is required by contract). Have building plans and specifications available.

(b) Is title insurance in the agreed amount and form?

(c) Does deed conform to contract requirements (marital status of seller, acknowledgment, legal description, and local tax stamps, if required)? The deed should specify that the conveyance is subject to exceptions, liens, encumbrances, restrictions, and reservations provided for in the contract. Otherwise, seller will be warranting a better title than he has.

(d) Title affidavits to cover period between title evidence and the closing.

(e) Affidavits to clear up objections revealed by abstract and covering mechanics' liens.

(f) For new construction obtain proper waivers, contractor's statements, and architect's certificate.

(g) Obtain bill of sale covering any personal property included.

(2) Amount of unpaid taxes, liens, assessments, water, sewage charges, etc., on the property should be ascertained.

(3) Get statement of amount due on existing mortgages showing unpaid principal and interest, rate of interest, and date of maturity.

(4) Produce the following:

(a) Policies of insurance to be transferred.

(b) Schedule of rents.

(c) Deed from predecessor-title.

(d) Vault permits.

(e) Power of attorney.

(5) Deed should include the following:

(a) Full name and address of seller and purchaser.

(b) Description of property (same as in contract of sale unless there has been a new survey).

(c) Covenants and warranties provided for in contract of sale.

(d) Special clauses in contract of sale.

(e) Exceptions, restrictions, easements, etc., provided in contract of sale.

(f) Description of mortgages, both the mortgages to which the purchaser is taking subject and those which the purchaser is assuming. Also, recital of purchase-money mortgage if there is one.

(6) Additional papers:

(a) Satisfaction, release, or discharge of liens.

(b) Purchase-money bond and mortgage.
(c) Bill of sale of personal property included in the sale.
(d) Letter of introduction to tenants.
(e) Satisfaction of judgments.
(f) Authorization of sale by corporation if owner is corporation.

(7) Prepare statement showing all apportionment of:
(a) Taxes.
(b) Electric, gas, and water charges.
(c) Rents as adjusted, for prepaid and accrued rent.
(d) Salaries.
(e) Services, such as exterminator.

(8) Have the deed signed, sealed, and executed by the parties necessary to convey good title. Acknowledgments of signatures required. Affix appropriate local revenue stamps (if required), prepare proper closing statement and then record purchase-money mortgages.

[¶2503] Purchaser's Considerations

The purchaser's attorney should do the following:

(1) Get affidavit of title.

(2) Obtain letter of introduction to tenants.

(3) Check violations of building regulations, any dwelling laws, health and fire agencies. Determine whether there is a certificate of occupancy outstanding.

(4) Look for chattel mortgages or conditional sales contracts on personal property if the latter is included for sale.

(5) Examine mortgages and satisfactions of record.

(6) Look at existing leases.

(7) Check town, city, village, and school taxes, water and sewerage rates, assessments.

(8) Check to see if state franchise taxes have been paid if corporations are involved.

(9) Look for assessments and vault permits.

(10) See that the premises comply with zoning rules and restrictive covenants.

(11) Find out who is in possession and whether they are entitled to be.

(12) Check for licenses and permits for signs on the street.

(13) Find out if state and federal estate taxes have been paid. Does a state transfer tax have to be paid?

(14) Inspect the premises.

(15) Check the age and competency of the seller.

(16) Look at insurance policies and assignments of service contracts.

(17) Check contiguity clause if more than one lot is involved.

(18) Get acknowledgment of seller's signature; check title company report; record power of attorney if any; obtain state revenue stamps (if required).

(19) Record deed, have endorsements on transfer of ownership on insurance policies and prepare closing statement.

[¶2504] The Closing Statement

The contract of sale should provide for the adjustment of costs and income. If it does not, local custom does. Rents up to the time of closing are credited to the seller, and costs are charged against him. Any costs already paid beyond the closing date are credited to the seller.

Items customarily credited to seller are: (1) purchase price, (2) unearned insurance premiums, (3) unexpired portion of service contracts paid in advance, (4) unexpired portion of water tax, (5) fuel on hand, (6) supplies, and (7) delinquent rents.

Items customarily credited to buyer are: (1) initial deposit or payment, (2) current balance on existing mortgages, (3) unpaid taxes for prior years and pro rata portion of taxes for current year, (4) special assessments due and unpaid, (5) amounts due for electricity, gas, and water based on meter readings, (6) accrued wages, (7) prepaid rents, and (8) tenant's cash security deposits.

The seller pays for revenue stamps on the deed (if required by state law); the buyer pays for recording unless the contract provides otherwise. A sample closing statement appears on the following page.

Form of Closing Statement

DUE SELLER		CREDITS TO PURCHASER	
Purchase price	$	Deposit (earnest money)	$
1st Mortgage		1st Mortgage	
Int. on 1st Mortgage		Int. on 1st Mortgage	
Accrued Int. $___@___%		Accrued Int. $___@___%	
from______to__________		from______to__________	
2nd Mortgage		2nd Mortgage	
Int. on 2nd Mortgage		Int. on 2nd Mortgage	
Accrued Int. $___@___%		Accrued Int. $___@___%	
from______to__________		from______to__________	
3rd Mortgage		3rd Mortgage	
Int. on 3rd Mortgage		Int. on 3rd Mortgage	
Accrued Int. $___@___%		Accrued Int. $___@___%	
from______to__________		from______to__________	
Rents		Rents	
Comm. on Rents collected		Comm. on Rents collected	
Unearned Insurance Premiums:		Cash and/or Securities deposited by tenants	
(details opposite)			
Fire			
Plate Glass			
Liability			
Rent			
Boiler			
Tornado			
Water Taxes		Water Taxes	
Electric Light		Electric Light	
Electric Power		Electric Power	
Gas		Gas	
Coal		Coal	
Supplies on hand			
General Taxes for year_____		General Taxes for year_____	
General Taxes as prorated for year		General Taxes as prorated for year	
Special Assessments		Special Assessments	
Janitor and other wages		Janitor and other wages	

Form of Closing Statment (continued)

DUE SELLER			CREDITS TO PURCHASER		
Advertising—accrued and unpaid			Advertising		
Service Contracts			Service Contracts		
Ash Removal			Ash Removal		
Roach Exterminator			Roach Exterminator		
Elevator			Elevator		
Survey			Survey		
Miscellaneous			Miscellaneous		
Escrow Fee			Escrow Fee		
Abstract			Abstract		
Guarantee Policy			Guarantee Policy		
Recording Fees			Recording Fees		
Mtge. cost or premium			Mtge. cost or premium		
Drawing Title papers			Purchase-money notes (to be secured by mortgage or trust deed)		
Attorneys' fees			Attorneys' fees		
Federal Income Tax			Federal Income Tax		
Normal Income Tax			Normal Income Tax		
State Taxes			State Taxes		
AMOUNT DUE SELLER	$		AMOUNT OF CREDIT TO PURCHASER	$	

[¶2505] Customs in Respect to Title Closings

Recommended by The Real Estate Board of New York, Inc.

I. All adjustments of interests, rents, taxes, water rates, sewer rents, and insurance premiums shall be made as of the day immediately preceding the day on which title is closed.

II. (a) Equitable adjustment should be made of obligations arising under the "job security" of apartment house superintendents and resident managers under the provisions applicable thereto in the agreement with Local Union No. 219 of the Building Service Employees' International Union.

(b) Equitable adjustment should be made of accrued vacations of building service employees under the provisions applicable thereto in the agreement with Local Union No. 32-B.

III. Interest, taxes, water rates, sewer rents, and insurance shall be computed by the 360-day method, each month representing 1/12 of the annual charge and each day 1/30 of the monthly charge.

IV. Rent shall be computed on the basis of the days in the particular month in which title is closed.

V. Where the period for which the computation of interest, taxes, water rates, sewer rents, and insurance is to be made is more than one month, the elapsed time shall be computed by full months and by the actual number of days in excess of such full months.

VI. Where the period for which the computation of interest, taxes, water rates, sewer rents, and insurance is to be made is less than one month, the actual number of days shall be counted, excluding the first day and including the last.

Note: These rules mean that the seller shall be charged with interest, taxes, water rates, sewer rents, and insurance to and including the day immediately preceding the day on which title is closed and that the purchaser shall bear these items from the day on which title is closed and receive the rents for that day. This has always been the practice when title is closed on the first day of the month and the purpose of these rules is to apply the same practice to closings occurring during the month.

For example: A title closes on June 4. Mortgage interest was paid to but not including March 15. The second half of the taxes has been paid. Insurance has been paid to June 15. Rent has been collected for the month of June. The computation would be as follows:

Allow purchaser: Interest from March 15 to June 3 both inclusive–2 months 20 days.

Rent from June 3 to June 30–27 days.

Allow seller: Insurance premium from June 3 to June 15–12 days.
Taxes from June 3 to June 30–27 days.

VII. When the time for closing a title is adjourned without any specific provisions as to adjustments, all adjustments shall be made as of the day prior to the adjourned date and the seller shall not be entitled to interest from the original date on the unpaid balance of the purchase price or on any purchase-money mortgages.

VIII. When the time for closing a title is adjourned under a stipulation that all adjustments are to be made as of original date, the seller shall be entitled to interest at the legal rate on the unpaid balance of the purchase price which is to be paid on closing and interest on the amount of any purchase-money mortgage at the rate provided in the contract to be paid on such mortgage, from the original date set for closing title.

IX. Whenever the contract provides that taxes are to be apportioned, this shall be deemed to include water charges and sewer rents.

X. Even if no reference is made in the contract to the liability of purchaser to pay recording tax on a purchase-money mortgage and revenue stamps on a purchase-money bond, the purchaser shall nevertheless be deemed under obligation to pay the same.

XI. If the contract provides that one of the parties is to pay for drawing papers and no charge is stated in the contract, the charge shall be as follows:

A Deed	$________
A Bond and Mortgage	________
A Satisfaction Piece	________
An Assignment of Mortgage	________
A Release of Part of Mortgaged Premises	________

[¶2506] Escrow Closing

In some areas, sales are closed in escrow. An escrow is "the deposit by the vendor of his deed with a third party to be delivered over to the purchaser upon payment of the purchase price." That third party is the escrowee. Escrows provide a mechanism to insure safety and convenience in carrying out the provisions of previously executed real estate sales contracts. In some cases, however, there is no written contract, the escrow agreement being the sole contract between the parties.

Most of the matters mentioned in the checklist for real estate closings are applicable when the deal is closed through an escrow. The mechanical details of the closing, however, are turned over to the escrowee.

Among the many advantages of escrows are the following: The escrowee assumes responsibility for the many ministerial tasks involved in a closing; the danger of title defects arising between the effective date of title evidence and the date of the deed is avoided; the possibility that the deal may fail is decreased; liens and encumbrances may be cleared through the escrow without danger to the buyer.

[¶2507] Contents of Escrow Agreement

(1) Documents to be deposited by seller, such as deed, insurance policies, separate assignments of insurance policies, leases, assignments of leases, abstract or other evidence of title, tax bills, cancelled mortgage notes, notice to tenants to pay rent to buyer, and service contracts.

(2) Deposits to be made by buyer, such as purchase price and purchase-money mortgage, if any.

(3) When deed is to be recorded: immediately, after buyer's check clears, or after seller furnishes evidence of good title at date of contract.

(4) Objections to which buyer agrees to take subject.

(5) Type of evidence of title to be furnished.

(6) Time allowed seller to clear defects in title.

(7) How and when purchase price is to be disbursed, with directions as to what items are to be prorated or apportioned if escrow holder is to do the prorating.

(8) Directions to deliver deed, leases, insurance policies, assignments of policy, and service contracts to buyer when title shows clear.

(9) Return of deposits to the respective parties where title cannot be cleared.

(10) Reconveyance by buyer to seller if deed to buyer has been recorded immediately on signing of escrow agreement and examination of title thereafter discloses seller's title was defective and cannot be cured.

(11) Payment of escrow, title and recording charges, broker's commission, and attorney's fees.

[¶2600] TITLE STANDARDS AND TITLE INSURANCE

Much of the real estate business revolves around the legal concept of title. Title gives the holder all the elements that constitute ownership—exclusive possession and the right to call on the force of law to take possession, use, and exclude others. Every prudent buyer and lender will insist that the seller or mortgagor have good title. The mere execution of a deed is not satisfactory proof of clear title. In real estate, there is no deal unless the owner can produce evidence of clear title or obstacles to clear title are either (1) eliminated prior to closing or (2) anticipated and specifically excepted by buyer or lender at the time the deal was made. Such exceptions must be reflected in the contract of sale or commitment of mortgage.

Good title is evidenced by abstracts and opinion of title, by certificate of title, by title insurance and, in only a few localities, by a Torrens certificate. The title insurance method is predominant in urban localities and is growing. The abstract and opinion method prevails in the Middle West outside the cities and the certificate of title is used in the South and in some rural areas in the East.

An abstract is a history of the title to the property. It is made up of the material portions of every instrument or record that affects the title. The abstracter certifies as to what records he has examined and those he has not. After the abstract has been compiled and certified, it is then necessary to have it examined and evaluated by a competent attorney so that he can give an opinion as to the title. When the certificate of title is used, an attorney searches the public records and issues a certificate that expresses his opinion of the title he has examined.

Even a perfect abstract or opinion or certificate of title does not furnish protection against hidden defects. Here are some: forged deeds, unknown heirs, errors by recorders or by courts, incompetence of parties executing instruments vital to the chain of title, deeds that are defective because of failure of delivery or lapse of power of attorney, and false statements made to close title, such as that a grantor is single when his wife may assert an interest in the property. Title insurance protects a property owner against such hidden defects and also against litigation that, however unwarranted, may attack a perfectly good title and cause cost and trouble to the holder of record title.

[¶2601] Title Insurance

Title insurance is a contract of indemnity against loss or damage arising out of defects in or lien on the title to real property. Some companies expressly guarantee a marketable title. Others guarantee against any loss occasioned by defects of title.

Title insurance covers the insured against financial loss that may arise as a result of unknown defects in the title to property covered by the insurance. The policy does not cover loss resulting from any known defects in the title. The policy will list known defects and expressly provide that it is not indemnifying any loss resulting from the defects so specified.

A title insurer's liability is dependent on the terms of the policy. The rule of liberal construction in favor of the insured that obtains in respect to insurance policies generally applies equally to policies of title insurance, and the general rule that an express exception excludes the implication of other similar exceptions is likewise applicable. An exception will not be given a broader effect than the language requires. In case of ambiguity or uncertainty, exceptions are strictly construed against the insurer and in favor of the insured.

The measure of recovery under a title insurance policy is ordinarily the amount of the actual loss or damage sustained, limited to the face amount of the policy. By negligence, the insurer, however, can incur liability for amounts in excess of the face of the policy.

Like other types of insurance, false or fraudulent representations made by the insured to the insurer may void liability unless the falsity is known to the insurer at the time the policy is issued.

[¶2602] Types of Title Policies

There are two general types of title insurance policies: owner's policies, sometimes called fee policies, and mortgagee policies, sometimes called loan policies.

Owner's Policy: This type of policy is generally used in insuring all estates of ownership, occupancy, and possession, including leaseholds. There are some estates or interests, however, that the common form of owner's policy does not fit. Some local companies have a separate form of leasehold policy, and some have owner's policy forms that insure only the record title. In areas in which so-called land purchase contracts are in vogue, there is a form of policy that insures the contract purchaser against loss or damage arising from defects in or liens on the title of the vendor. While varying to some extent in phraseology, the owner's policy forms of most companies afford substantially the same coverage.

Mortgagee Policy: This policy is used to insure estates or interests held by lenders as a pledge or security for the payment of a debt. Such estates or interests exist in many different forms, depending largely on the laws and customs of the individual state. Mortgages, deeds in trust, and loan deeds are the most common types.

The coverage of mortgagees' policies is designed to meet the security needs of mortgage lenders. This coverage, while entirely consistent with sound underwriting principles, is broader than that of standard owners' policies. The basic differences between the two are:

(1) Liability under a mortgage policy is reduced as payments on the mortgage are made and terminates on satisfaction of the debt; whereas liability under an owner's policy is perpetual and indeterminate.

(2) There is a theoretical salvage value in the equity between the amount of the mortgage debt and the actual value of the property.

(3) The estate or interest of a security holder is not transferred with the frequency of an estate of ownership, and the nuisance element of petty claims is thereby minimized.

Loss payable under a mortgage policy is automatically transferred to the assignee of the debt and security. In the event of foreclosure and purchase by the holder of the security, the policy automatically becomes an owner's policy. It insures the purchaser, as owner of the fee, against loss or damage arising out of matters existing prior to the effective date of the policy.

[¶2603] Title Insurance Procedure

The person about to acquire property applies to a title insurance company. He agrees to pay a specified fee for the company's examination of the title. The company obligates itself to make an examination of the record title and to insure against undiscovered defects but not against defects or encumbrances that the examination discloses.

The Title Report: The applicant should get a title report when the examination has been completed. This report describes the property, sets forth the name of the record owner, and lists all objections to title, i.e., defects and encumbrances on the record. This tells the applicant the exact state of the title. It permits a seller to set forth appropriate exceptions in the contract of sale. It tells a buyer what encumbrances and defects exist over and above any that may have been provided for in the contract of sale. The buyer or lender has to require the owner to clear up all defects and encumbrances not agreed on before paying the money and accepting the deed or mortgage. After objections not agreed on have been removed, title is ready for closing. The title company now prepares to issue its policy of title insurance subject to any exceptions that it finds necessary and subject to which the new owner is prepared to accept the property.

The Title Policy: The title insurance policy is usually made up of four parts: agreement of insurance, a description of what is insured, a schedule of exceptions, and the conditions of the policy.

The insurance agreement undertakes to indemnify and save harmless the named assured and transferees of the policy with the assets of the company against all loss and damage (usually not exceeding a specified amount) that the assured may sustain by reason of defects or unmarketability of title to the described interest in property or because of liens or encumbrances as of the date of the policy. The indemnity excepts loss from (a) judgments against or defects, liens, and encumbrances created by the act of or with the privity of the assured and (b) items listed in the schedule of exceptions or excepted by the conditions of the policy.

The policy describes the interest of the assured in the property, the instrument by which he acquired his title and the property itself.

The schedule of exceptions sets forth a detailed list of any and all encumbrances or defects against which the policy does not insure. Usual exceptions are the rights of parties in possession, any state of facts that an accurate survey would disclose, etc.

The conditions of the policy specify the terms of the company's liability, its obligations to defend the insured at its own cost in all actions based on claim of title or encumbrance prior to the date of the policy. If the insured contracts to sell and the buyer rejects title for some defect not excepted in the policy, the title insurance company reserves the option of paying the loss or bringing an action to determine the validity of the defect. Other conditions of the policy are provisions for arbitration of certain disputes, right of subrogation, and right to take the property when the full amount insured for has been paid to indemnify a loss.

[¶2604] Title Standards

Title standards crystalize the practices of conveyances and declare the answers to questions or the solutions to problems involved in the process of title examination. Their purposes are perhaps best indicated from this quote taken from the foreword to the *Standard for Title Examination* issued by the Committee on Real Property Law of the New York State Bar Association:

"The purpose of the standards was to eliminate the countless cases where one attorney who had approved a title was met by a difference of opinion by the attorney for the subsequent purchaser with a different attitude towards some of the questions involved. Whether a title was considered marketable or not depended a great deal on the technical interpretation by one attorney as opposed to another and hair-splitting for one reason or another has resulted in rejections and litigation of titles and in unnecessary delay and cost to attorneys and clients alike.

"With the adoption of the uniform standards, it is felt that many technical objections will be disregarded by attorneys who will look upon these questions in the same light. These standards are fundamental in character, and have been consciously formulated on that basis so as to avoid, at the beginning, a wide difference of opinion which would hinder their general acceptance."

[¶2605] New York State Standards

The New York standards, which follow, are typical of state title standards:

STANDARDS FOR TITLE EXAMINATION

1. Action—Lost Papers

Objection should not be made to a title derived through an action or proceeding conducted more than thirty years prior to the examination date because of inability to find certain pleadings, orders, decrees, or judgments on file in the office of the clerk of the court in which the action or proceeding was conducted, provided:

(a) That the clerk's register or other index shows that the missing pleading, order, decree or judgment was filed in said office or

(b) That the conveyance given pursuant to the judgment or final decree in such action or proceeding recites the making or granting of the missing pleading, order, decree or judgment.

2. Acknowledgments

Objections shall not be made because of any defect or invalidity in acknowledgments after the acknowledged document has been recorded or filed for fifteen years.

3. Affidavits by Interested Parties

Affidavits made by interested parties are acceptable provided the affidavit shows proper circumstances under which, and proper means through which, the affiant has knowledge of the facts included therein.

4. Ancient Mortgages

All mortgages appearing of record for more than fifty years need not be discharged by appropriate proceeding provided proof of nonpayment of principal or interest for at least six years last past is obtained, except that mortgages which have apparently merged with the fee need not be discharged if followed by a deed executed by the owner in which the interest merged, which deed has been of record for at least twenty years.

5. Breaks in Chain of Title

Title affecting improved or cultivated land, as distinguished from wild land, should not be rejected because of any break or hiatus in the chain of title which occurred over eighty years prior to the examination date.

6. Commitments Under Mental Hygiene Law

Where a person previously committed under the provisions of the Mental Hygiene Law has been discharged as recovered by the superintendent of the state hospital to which such commitment was made, a court order declaring such person sane and competent to manage his person and affairs shall be deemed to be adequate proof of competency.

7. Chancery Actions

The regularity of the proceedings in actions conducted in the Court of Chancery will be presumed.

8. Corporation Deed

A. If a deed is dated and recorded before the certificate of incorporation of the grantee is filed and a confirmatory deed is obtained from the grantor to the corporation after the filing of the certificate, the deeds will be passed as such without any further requirement of consent from stockholders of the grantee.

B. If a deed is dated before the certificate of incorporation of the grantee is filed and the deed is recorded on the same day as the certificate is filed or on a later day, the deed will be passed as such without further requirement.

C. A deed from a corporation to a grantee who from the record appears to be an officer, director, or stockholder of the grantor corporation or a grantee obviously related to such a person may be passed without question where the title has reached a purchaser for value. The same rule may be applied to a conveyance from a corporation to a corporate grantee having interlocking directors or stockholders.

9. Corporation—Filing Certificate

Where a corporation is out of title more than twenty years, no proof beyond proof of its incorporation need be required.

10. Corporate Names—Variations

Objection should not be made where the name of a corporation appearing in the chain of title prior to the examination date is substantially the same as the name appearing in the certificate of incorporation.

11. Delivery

Where there is a time lapse between the date of a deed and the date of its recording, no objection will be raised where the deed has been on record for more than fifteen (15) years. If the deed has been on record for fifteen (15) years or less, the period search in the Surrogate's office would be run against the grantor from the date of the instrument to the date of recording in the county where the grantor resides and in the county where the property is situated. If no death was found then the question would be passed unless the grantee, or some one connected with him, was still in title and more definite information could therefore be obtained, or unless knowledge of the death of the grantor is definitely known.

The question of delivery should not be raised where the interval between the date of the deed and the recording date thereof was less than thirty (30) days unless there was affirmative knowledge of the death of the grantor prior to recording. Under this 30-day period no Surrogate's search will be made.

12. Dower

Release of dower shall not be required where a period of thirty-three years or more has elapsed since the conveyance, descent or other disposition of the property, wherein the possibility of an outstanding dower interest became apparent.

13. Discharge of Encumbrances

In the event that an encumbrance is recorded, the purpose of which is to correct a prior encumbrance, and a subsequent release of satisfaction is recorded releasing or satisfying one encumbrance but not specifically releasing or satisfying the other, such a release or satisfaction is sufficient to release or satisfy both.

14. Discharge of Mortgage—Clerical Error

Objection should not be made in respect to a discharge of mortgage recorded more than fifteen years prior to the examination date because of clerical errors or omissions in the instrument of discharge, provided that the mortgage is reasonably identified.

15. Revenue Stamps

The omission of state revenue stamps on a deed does not affect the marketability of the title of the premises therein described.

16. Fiduciaries—Nominal Consideration

Objection shall not be made on the ground of the recital of a nominal consideration in a deed given by an executor or other fiduciary after the expiration of twenty years from the recording of such deed.

17. Inheritance by Surviving Spouse

If there is an estate where the surviving spouse would take the first $10,000.00, a proceeding for leave to sell or an accounting proceeding will be required despite the fact that the estate may appear to be well below the $10,000.00 limit because of the possibility of undisclosed or undiscovered assets.

18. Names

A. Objection should not be made where there is a variance of initial between the names of successive grantees and grantors in the chain of title more than twenty years prior to the examination date.

B. All common abbreviations are acceptable as sufficiently establishing the identity of parties. Also, variations in names which are clearly covered by the doctrine of "Idem Sonans" should not be the subject of title requirements.

19. Open Lis Pendes

If no judgment has been entered, a lis pendes will be disregarded if the mortgage has been satisfied.

20. Posthumous—Afterborn Children

When the record fails to show whether or not any child of a decedent was born after the death of the decedent or after the date of the decedent's will, and reasonable effort is made to determine the above, the question may be disregarded if 30 years have elapsed since the date of the death of the decedent and the estate is out of title.

21. Proof of Heirship

In the absence of recitals in conveyances described in Section 379 of the Civil Practice Act, the following will be accepted as proof of devolution of title by descent:

(a) When a deed from the supposed heirs of a former owner who died intestate has been recorded for more than 15 years and the only proof that such grantors are the only heirs is contained in a statement in the transfer or estate tax petition by a person who under ordinary circumstances would be presumed to know the heirs of the decedent to the effect that they are the only persons interested in the estate of the decedent, further proof will not be required.

22. Signing of Record

Objection shall not be made solely on the ground that the record is not signed, in respect to any instrument which has been recorded for more than twenty years.

23. State Sales for Taxes

State sales for taxes, conducted prior to 1900 may be disregarded provided that proof by affidavit is furnished showing adverse possession against said tax title for a period of thirty years, unless the title search discloses a chain of title by deed beginning with a conveyance given pursuant to such sale and extending to a time less than fifty years prior to the examination date.

24. Survivorship

The following will be accepted as proof of death and of the survivorship of a joint tenant or a tenant by the entirety:

(a) A transfer tax return made by a relative of the blood or by affinity or by the surviving joint tenant or tenant by the entirety.

25. Unrecorded Mortgage

Recital of an unrecorded mortgage in a deed of record for 20 years or more may be passed on proof that for 6 years or more last passed no principal or interest has been paid or demanded and no knowledge was had by the owner during that period of said unrecorded mortgage. However, where such recital is contained in the last deed of record, the above is not applied.

[¶2700] APPRAISALS OF REAL ESTATE

An appraisal is an estimate and opinion as to value. Values of real property cannot be determined or established by appraisal, they can only be estimated.

The purpose of an appraisal is to determine the market value of the real estate being appraised. The American Institute of Real Estate Appraisers' handbook defines market value as the highest price, estimated in terms of money, that the property will bring if exposed for sale in the open market, allowing a reasonable time to find a purchaser who buys with knowledge of all the uses to which it is adapted and for which it is capable of being used.

Professional Appraisals: The services of a skilled professional real estate appraiser are frequently desirable and even essential for any of the following purposes:

(1) To assess property for purposes of local real estate taxes.

(2) To review and contest an assessment in order to reduce the burden of real estate taxes.

(3) To determine income tax liability in a taxable exchange or in a liquidation of a corporation owning real estate.

(4) To determine inheritance and estate tax liability when real estate was owned by a decedent at the time of his death.

(5) To determine gift tax liability when real estate is the medium of a taxable gift.

(6) To determine whether a proposed purchase or sale is at a fair or attractive price.

(7) To determine whether a piece of real estate constitutes adequate security for a loan.

(8) As a basis for offering investors an interest in real estate through syndication or participation in a public corporation or real estate investment trust.

(9) To establish replacement costs less physical deterioration in order to determine how much fire and casualty insurance should cover a specific piece of real estate. An appraisal may also be needed to establish proof of loss or the basis for settlement in cases of partial or total loss under insurance contracts.

(10) To estimate damages that are adequate but not in excess of fair compensation in negotiating a condemnation award or seeking the determination of fair compensation for condemned property in court.

A professional appraiser might be a member of any of the following societies: American Institute of Real Estate Appraisers, American Society of

Appraisers; The American Society of Farm Managers and Rural Appraisers, the National Association of Independent Fee Appraisers, and The Society of Real Estate Appraisers. These societies promulgate high standards of professional ethics to which their members must conform. Their members must also demonstrate their professional skills and expertise. For these reasons, appraisals made by professional appraisers are very useful and carry due weight, not only with the investing public, but also before governmental agencies and the courts.

[¶2701] Methods of Appraisal

There are three approaches to appraising real estate: (1) the market data or sales price approach, (2) the income or earnings approach, and (3) the cost approach.

The Sales Approach: The method of determining value by comparative sales is probably the most widely used of the three approaches. Its successful application depends on the accurate collection and tabulation of a considerable amount of information and on the exercise of good judgment in the selection and screening of the properties to be compared with the property that is being valued. Adjustments must be made to actual sales to reflect any change in general market prices between the time of the sale and the time of appraisal. Great care must be exercised in separating authentic information from hearsay. Don't depend on revenue stamps, asking prices, and neighborhood gossip. Confine sales used as a basis of comparison to those in which verification of price can be obtained from buyers, sellers, or brokers who are usually cooperative when properly approached.

The Income Approach: Two steps are involved in arriving at value through the income approach: (1) Estimate the net income to be derived from the property. This means estimating gross income and deducting estimated expenses. (2) Select the capitalization rate that is appropriate.

Another method frequently used is to multiply gross income or net income by figures that are considered appropriate. For example, small apartments may be selling at seven times gross income. Single-family residences may be selling at 120 times monthly rental value.

The Cost Method: In this method, the cost of reproducing the buildings is added to the value of the land and a discount is then applied for the depreciation and deterioration that the buildings have suffered.

In using this method, reproduction cost usually is determined by finding the average cost per square foot of floor space or cubic foot of contents for buildings of similar construction and size and applying this average cost to the dimensions of the building under appraisal. Land value is determined by comparison with sales of comparable property. Then a deduction is made based on amount of depreciation, functional obsolescence (inability to perform adequately the function for which the building should be used), and economic obsolescence (all unfavorable economic influences on the value of competing properties).

The significance of the cost approach is that it develops the upper or maximum limit of fair market value.

[¶2702] Correlation of the Three Approaches

In most appraisals at least two approaches are used, usually the market data or sales approach and the replacement cost approach. Primary weight is usually given to the market data or comparative sales approach. The earnings approach should also be used where the net income of a property can be estimated with accuracy and appears reasonably stable over a period of years. The final appraisal should represent a judgment giving such account to the value arrived at under each of the three approaches used as seems appropriate to the appraiser in all the circumstances.

In this last step of the valuation process, the appraiser correlates the preliminary figures arrived at by applying the cost approach, the comparative sales approach, and capitalized income approach. He does not merely divide the sum of these estimates by three to arrive at his final valuation. He takes the spread between the minimum and maximum figures and weighs the adjustment in favor of that approach which appears to have the greatest reliability and relevance in the case of the particular property. Generally, the cost approach becomes a guide to the upper limit of fair market value. In many types of properties, particularly agricultural properties, the earnings approach is usually the lowest limit of fair market value.

How to Use Appraisals to Establish Value for Tax Purposes: Having a professional appraiser determine the value of your property can be very useful when you have to establish that value for tax purposes. But, it is equally important that you can show the basis for the appraisal, otherwise it won't carry much weight.

This is illustrated by *Coddington,* TC Memo 1960-95. In Court, three appraisers testified. Each had appraised the building in question. Two had come up with a $645,000 value and testified for the taxpayers. Trouble was, however, neither had a written report, neither indicated how he arrived at his value, nor what methods he employed. So, the Court gave little weight to their testimony. On the other hand, a third appraiser, testifying for the

Treasury, had a written report and showed in detail how he arrived at his valuation. The Court accepted his valuation—$661,500—as the proper value.

Here are the items contained in the appraiser's report that impressed the Court: a picture of the building, a survey plat showing the dimensions of the land involved and of the building thereon, a detailed description of each floor of the building and of the facilities thereon, and a schedule which showed the amounts of the total income, expenses of operation, and net income for the year. The appraisal report also contained the appraiser's computation of value by different methods.

[¶2703] Rules of Professional Ethics of American Institute of Real Estate Appraisers of the National Association of Realtors

Article I—Fees

SECTION 1. It is unethical for an appraiser to accept an engagement to appraise a property if his employment or fee is contingent upon his reporting a predetermined or specified amount of value, or is otherwise contingent upon any finding to be reported.

SECTION 2. It is unethical for an appraiser retained in cases where monetary damages are involved to make his compensation contingent upon the amount of, or to fix his compensation as a percentage of, the damages which may be agreed upon or finally decreed.

Article II—Commissions and Favors

SECTION 1. It is unethical for an appraiser to accept any commission, favor, or emolument in connection with the appraising of a property other than a fair professional fee for the responsibility entailed and the work and expense involved.

Article III—Disinterested Appraisals

SECTION 1. It is unethical for an appraiser to issue an appraisal report if he is acting or intending to act in the capacity of broker, loan broker, or manager, or if he has an ownership, contemplated future ownership, or any other interest in connection with the property appraised unless such interest or interests be fully disclosed in the appraisal certificate.

Article IV—Hypothetical Appraisals

SECTION 1. It is unethical for an appraiser to issue an appraisal report in which the reported valuation is based upon predicated rentals and expenses unless he describes in detail in his report the basis for his predication.

In particular, it is unethical for an appraiser to certify a valuation predicated upon assumed rentals and expenses which he does not feel certain are highly probable of achievement under ordinary competent management.

SECTION 2. It is unethical for an appraiser to issue an unqualified appraisal report on an investment property which does not reflect the effects of existing leases upon the value of the property.

SECTION 3. It is unethical for an appraiser to issue an appraisal report in which the reported value is based upon the completion of public or private improvements which are not assured unless he clearly states that the appraisal is made on that hypothesis. In any event, he must state in his report the conditions with regards to such improvements which he assumes in determining the value reported.

SECTION 4. It is unethical for an appraiser to issue an appraisal report in which the reported value is based upon the assumed absence of any legal restriction unless such assumption is reasonable or in accord with legal opinion accepted by the appraiser, and unless the legal authority and his opinion are quoted in the appraisal certificate, and it is expressly stated that the appraisal is contingent on such lawful restriction being changed or absent in accordance with the assumption.

Article V—Fractional Appraisals[1]

SECTION 1. It is unethical for an appraiser to issue an appraisal report on only a part of a whole property unless he specifically states that it is a fractional appraisal and as such can be used only in a manner consistent with such limitations.

SECTION 2. In appraising the security for a loan, it is unethical for an appraiser to issue a certificate covering anything less than all of the property designated as security for the loan unless conditions and limitations of the use of the report are clearly stated.

---

[1]It is not intended that anything in Articles V and VI shall be construed to prevent an appraiser from preparing and presenting fractional appraisals or summation appraisals where such appraisals are required for rate making, cost accounting, and other special purposes, where the concept of cost independent from value may be appropriately involved.

SECTION 3. In appraising the security for a leasehold loan, it is unethical for an appraiser to issue a certificate of value of the improvement only, omitting the value of the leasehold, which latter may be positive, zero, or negative.

Article VI—Summation Appraisals[1]

SECTION 1. It is unethical for an appraiser to issue an appraisal report on a property in which the total reported value is derived by adding together the values of fractional parts of the property, unless the limitations are clearly stated or other and conclusive evidence is given that this result equals the total value of the property considered as a whole.

Article VII—Economic Probabilities and Value of Property

SECTION 1. It is unethical for an appraiser to issue an appraisal report on a construction project which does not give the appraiser's opinion on the economic soundness of the project.

SECTION 2. It is unethical for an appraiser to issue an appraisal report on a construction project without also reporting his estimate of the reasonably expected earnings of the project and an opinion as to the reasonable time required to attain normal occupancy.

Article VIII—Duty to Hold Findings Confidential

SECTION 1. It is the duty of an appraiser to hold as confidential the results and other findings of his appraisal until released from his obligation by the client or by due process of law.

Article IX—Expert Testimony

SECTION 1. In giving testimony as to the value of real property in any court or before any other legally constituted tribunal, an appraiser may follow rules of procedure as to appraisal method legally binding in that jurisdiction even though such rules may be at variance with the provisions of these Rules of Professional Ethics.

---

[1]It is not intended that anything in Articles V and VI shall be construed to prevent an appraiser from preparing and presenting fractional appraisals or summation appraisals where such appraisals are required for rate making, cost accounting, and other special purposes, where the concept of cost independent from value may be appropriately involved.

SECTION 2. When a member accepts employment to make a real estate appraisal or employment to testify as to the value of real estate before a court of law, the appraiser will complete an adequate written appraisal of the property, signed by him, and retain a copy thereof in his files which shall be delivered to the Governing Council or the Professional Ethics Committee on request for the purposes of any investigation of the professional conduct of the member.

Article X—Contents of Appraisal Reports

SECTION 1. It is unethical for an appraiser to omit any of the following from his appraisal report:

a. An unequivocal and reasonably complete description of the property appraised.

b. A statement of any contingent conditions upon which this appraisal has been based. For example: (1) the validity of legal, engineering, or auditing opinions used; (2) the completion of projected public or private improvements; (3) that management is assumed to be competent and the ownership to be in responsible hands.

c. The date or time at which the value obtains.

d. The amount of the value.

e. A statement that the appraiser has no present or contemplated future interest in the property appraised; or a statement disclosing all such interests which the appraiser may have in the property appraised.

f. In case the property appraised is a fractional part of the property of a type covered by these Rules of Professional Ethics, a statement that the value reported is invalidated if used in making a summation appraisal of the property as a whole unless conditions and limitations of the use of the report are clearly stated.

SECTION 2. It is recommended that each appraisal report should contain a statement or certificate, substantially in the following form:

> "I (We), the undersigned do hereby certify that to the best of my (our) knowledge and belief the statements and opinions contained in this appraisal are correct, subject to the limiting conditions herein set forth; also, that this appraisal has been made in conformity with the Rules of Professional Ethics of the American Institute of Real Estate Appraisers of the National Association of Real Estate Boards."

Article XI—Advertising

SECTION 1. It is unethical for a member of the Institute to advertise his professional attainments or services except in a dignified manner in keeping with high professional standards.

Public notices preferably should be limited to an advertisement of the name, professional titles including M.A.I. (Member of the American Institute of Real Estate Appraisers of the National Association of Realtors), class of service, and address of the advertiser without any other qualifying word or letters; or in the case of announcement of change of address, the plain statement of the fact for the publication of which the announcement purports to be made.

Cards permitted by this rule when appearing in newspapers shall not exceed two columns in width and three inches in depth; when appearing in magazines, directories, and similar publications, cards shall not exceed one fourth of a page in size. This Rule shall not be construed to inhibit the proper and professional dissemination of impersonal information among a member's own clients or personal associates or the properly restricted circulation of bulletins containing professional information.

SECTION 2. It is ethical, however, for an appraiser of the Institute to carry an announcement in a classified directory, as follows: "JOHN DOE, M.A.I., *Address, Telephone Number*" under the subdivision *REAL ESTATE APPRAISALS*.

Article XII—Relations With the Institute and Fellow Members

SECTION 1. No member shall conduct himself in such manner as to prejudice his professional status or the reputation of the Institute.

SECTION 2. Any oral or written statement by any member with reference to his affiliation with the Institute that is not specific and exact shall be construed to be professional misconduct and subject to immediate disciplinary action.

SECTION 3. It is unethical for any member to injure falsely or maliciously, directly or indirectly, the professional reputation, prospects, or business of another member.

SECTION 4. It is unethical for any member to accept an appraisal assignment without having had previous experience and/or general knowledge of such character as to qualify him to accept such an assignment unless either:

a. He has associated with him in the making of the appraisal an appraiser who has had experience in the valuation of the type of property under appraisement, or

b. Unless the facts are fully disclosed to the client.

[¶2800] CONDEMNATIONS

Condemnation, the taking of property by eminent domain, is the right by which the government or others acting under its authority acquires private property for public use upon the payment of reasonable compensation and with or without the consent of the owner. The Fifth Amendment to the Constitution of the United States reads: "No person shall be deprived of life, liberty or property without due process of law; nor shall private property be taken for public use without just compensation."

The Constitution and the state and federal statutes implementing it do not define the meaning of "just compensation," with the result that the courts have been free to construe its meaning by reference to the common law and to their own standards. As the Court indicated in the case *Olson v. United States,* 292 US 246:

"Just compensation includes all elements of value that inhere in the property, but it does not exceed market value fairly determined. The sum required to be paid the owner does not depend upon the uses to which he has devoted his land, but is to be arrived at upon just consideration of all the uses for which it is suitable. The highest and most profitable use for which the property is adaptable and needed, or likely to be needed in the reasonably near future is to be considered, not necessarily as the measure of value, but to the full extent that the prospect of demand for such use affects the market value while the property is privately held."

The Supreme Court of the United States in *U.S. v. Miller,* 317 US 369, stated that just compensation is to be determined by equitable principles and its measure varies with facts. The Court said as follows:

"It is conceivable that an owner's indemnity should be measured in various ways depending upon the circumstances of each case and that no general formula should be used for the purpose. In an effort, however, to find some practical standard, the courts early adopted, and have retained, the concept of market value. The owner has been said to be entitled to the 'value,' 'the market value,' and the 'fair market value' of what is taken. The term 'fair' hardly adds anything to the phrase 'market value' which denotes what it fairly may be believed that a purchaser in fair market conditions would have given, or, more concisely, market value fairly determined."

[¶2801] Methods of Condemnation

There are two broad methods of condemnation—administrative and judicial.

Procedurally, the administrative method is quite simple. The condemnor files with the appropriate public official the designated papers (plot of land and description of the contemplated improvement) and tenders to the landowner or deposits in court an award of compensation. At this juncture in the proceedings, title and right to possession vest in the condemnor. In the event the landowner desires to contest the right to take the property or the amount of compensation, he must assume the burden of commencing court proceedings to determine these issues. The essence of the method is the ex parte vesting of title and right to possession in the condemnor at the inception of the action.

The judicial approach requires a taking to be instituted by a petition in the courts requesting that the right to take and compensation due the affected landowner be determined. Notice of the commencement of the condemnation proceedings is served on the property owner. The details vary from jurisdiction to jurisdiction; but, generally, a preliminary estimate of damages is made by court-appointed viewers, assessors, or commissioners with recourse eventually to a jury. Title vests after the entry of an order of condemnation and payment of the award. There is a wide variance from state to state concerning the time a condemnor may first take possession of the property and devote it to public use.

[¶2802] Partial Takings

When the taking involves the entire property, just compensation is an estimate of the market value of all the property as of the date of taking. Where there is a partial taking, there are two rules applied in different jurisdictions: (1) The measure of compensation is the market value of the part taken plus the difference in the market value of the remainder before and after the taking. (2) The measure of compensation is the difference between the value of the entire parcel before the taking and the value of the remainder after the taking.

How to Handle a Partial Condemnation: It is not unusual to have only part of your property condemned. That may leave you with remaining property that you can no longer use for your present business or investment purposes. You can sell the balance of your property and reinvest the combined condemnation and sales proceeds in a new property of like kind. You avoid any tax on any gain on the condemnation and sale that way. IRS agreed to follow a Tax Court decision which allowed the avoidance of tax on gain on the sale of the remaining property (*Rev. Rul. 59-361,* CB 1959-2, 183).

The property condemned need not be physically attached to the remaining property—as long as you used the two properties as one economic unit and can't use the remaining property without the condemned part. For example, in one Tax Court case (*Masser,* 30 TC 741), the owner of a freight terminal used the lots he owned across the street to store his semitrailers when not in use. Because they were nearby, he could move the semitrailers into the terminal and unload freight from them into delivery trucks. When the lots were taken by condemnation, the lack of the nearby parking area made it impossible to continue operating the freight terminal. So, the taxpayer sold the freight terminal and used the proceeds from that sale and from the condemnation to buy a new terminal with adjacent parking facilities. The Tax Court treated both condemnation and sale together as an involuntary conversion and allowed the avoidance of tax by reinvestment.

IRS indicates the same principle would also apply where part of a golf course is condemned and the remaining part is sold because it can no longer be used as a golf course.

Of course, in each case, you'd first have to show you could not replace the condemned portion with equally suitable property before you'd be allowed to treat the sale of the remaining property as an involuntary conversion.

[¶2803] Severance Damages

Severance damage is any loss in value of the remaining property of an owner caused by the taking of part of his real estate. It is not a part of the value of the land to be taken but a measure of the reduction in value as a result of a partial taking of real property. Severance damages are recognized only when identity of ownership and unity of use with respect to parts taken and parts remaining exist. These damages result when a partial taking lowers the highest and best use or otherwise limits the use of the remainder.

Estimates of severance damages are developed by use of what is known as the "before" and "after" appraisal method. For example, the "before" (before a taking) fair market value of the fee of an entire farm of 400 acres at $200 per acre is $80,000. The part to be acquired by the government, in fee, for example, is 200 acres with a fair market value of $40,000 at $200 per acre. Simple arithmetic would indicate that the value to the owner of the 200 acres left to be $40,000. Such, however, is not necessarily the case. The "after" appraisal (appraisal of the remainder left to the owner) may indicate a fair market value in fee of, say, $35,000, reflecting a severance damage of $5,000. This damage may have occurred from any one or more of several causes. The owner may have been left with surplus buildings, originally designed to service 400 acres, on his remaining 200 acres, which leaves him with decidedly overimproved farmland. In another case, the damage could be occasioned by the fact that so much of his land was taken that the remainder was appreciably limited as an economic farming unit due to its size, irregular boundary, etc. This example may be illustrated as follows:

Before appraisal, fair market value of entire farm, 400 acres @ $200 per acre	$80,000
After appraisal, fair market value of 200 acres left to owner (the remainder) @ $175 per acre	35,000
	$45,000
Fair market value, appraisal of part to be taken, 200 acres @ $200 per acre	40,000
The difference, severance damages	$ 5,000

As shown in the preceding example, three distinct appraisals are required: the entire property before the taking, the part to be taken, and the remainder. Some courts have held that only two steps are essential, viz., the value before and the value after the taking.

Severance Value in Condemnation Proceedings: On occasion, however, when the state or municipality condemns property, it splits the amount awarded into two parts, one for the value of the property taken over by it and the other as a "severance" damage to the property retained. If this is done, the part awarded for "severance" damage does not enter into the computation of any gain on the condemned property. The "severance" award is then compared with the cost or other basis of the retained property. In the event the "severance" damages do not exceed such costs (or other basis), the only effect is to reduce the basis of the retained property. On the other hand, if this type of damage is greater than the basis of the retained property, it is taxable gain to the extent of the excess.

[¶2804] How to Avoid Income Taxes on Gains in Condemnations

Where property is destroyed or condemned and you have a resulting gain or loss because you receive insurance or condemnation proceeds in excess of or less than your basis, you have the equivalent of an exchange. Your gain or loss is capital or ordinary, depending on the nature of your property.

Under §1033, you can avoid any tax on the gain on an involuntary conversion by reinvesting the proceeds in property that is similar or related in use to the converted property. Where the converted property is real property used in a business or held for investment, you can reinvest in property of a like kind. "Like kind" has been given a broader interpretation than "similar or related in use." Thus, under the like-kind rule, you can reinvest in unimproved property although the property converted was improved.

All you need do to avoid tax on the gain is to replace the converted property within a period running from the earliest date of threat or imminence of the conversion to two years after the tax year in which the gain is realized. If you need more time, you can apply for an extension.

A conflict has arisen in this situation: Suppose the state condemns your property, giving you an award of $200,000. At that time, your basis is $80,000; but there's a $50,000 mortgage on the property. Instead of paying the $200,000, the state pays you $150,000 and pays the mortgagee the $50,000 to wipe out the mortgage debt. How much do you have to reinvest in similar property to avoid tax on the gain—$150,000 or $200,000? The Tax Court and the Ninth Circuit say $150,000 if you're not personally liable on the mortgage (*Babcock,* 259 F.2d 689). This disagrees with IRS and the Second Circuit which require the $200,000 to be reinvested (Reg. §1.1033(a)-2(c)(11); *Fortee,* 211 F.2d 915).

If you're personally liable on the mortgage, you'd have to reinvest the $200,000 because then it would be considered that you had received the $200,000 and used $50,000 to pay off your liability.

When Do You Have a Threat of Condemnation? Knowing when a condemnation is threatened or imminent is very important for tax purposes. It starts the period during which you can invest in like-kind property and avoid a tax on any gain on the condemnation. Thus, you can anticipate the actual condemnation and get your new property before you get the condemnation award. In addition, gain realized on a *sale* made under the "threat of, or imminence of" condemnation may also be reinvested tax free or, if not reinvested, is eligible for capital gain treatment if the sale was of §1231 property. At one time, IRS held that no threat occurred until a public body having the authority to comdemn land indicated by public resolution or act that specifically designated land would be condemned (*Rev. Rul. 58-557,* CB 1958-2, 402). Now, however, IRS has changed its tune. It agrees that a threat exists when a property owner learns through a newspaper or other news medium of a decision to acquire his property. However, he must obtain confirmation of his news item from a government representative of the body involved. And he must have reasonable grounds to believe this (*Rev. Rul. 63-221,* CB 1963-2, 332).

A sale made under threat of condemnation may be made either to the condemning authority or to a third party. Although §1033 doesn't specifically authorize private sales, the Fifth Circuit has approved such a rule (*Creative Solutions,* 320 F.2d 809), and IRS apparently has gone along by failing to raise the issue in a case involving this type of situation (*Kress & Co.,* 40 TC 142).

Involuntary Conversions Let You Swap Capital Gains for Ordinary Deductions: You are usually tempted to avoid tax on the gain by reinvesting the proceeds in property of a like kind. But if you elect to pay the tax, that may mean you can get the advantage of swapping capital gains for ordinary deductions.

How It Works: If you elect to avoid the tax, your basis for your new property is the basis you had for your old property. So your depreciation deductions on your new property (the ordinary deductions) are very small. On the other hand, if you paid the capital gain tax and reinvested the proceeds, your basis for your new property would be what you paid for it. So, you'd be getting larger depreciation deductions.

[¶2900] PROPERTY INSURANCE

Ownership, lessee, and mortgagee interests in real estate should be protected from three kinds of loss: (1) direct damage to the property, (2) consequential loss resulting from damage to the property, and (3) liability for damage suffered by others on the property.

The manager, the owner, the lessee, and the mortgagee must see that the property is covered by types of policies in amounts that will fully protect his interest from loss. The best way to do that is to get a good insurance agent to analyze the risks in the property and submit recommendations. He can tell you not only the kind of policies and the amounts to carry but also suggest steps, such as sprinkler installation, to reduce insurance costs.

Then, it's up to the interested parties to make sure that the policies are taken out and kept in force by continued payment of premiums and by meeting all the conditions of the policies.

[¶2901] Fire Insurance

A fire insurance policy is a contract of indemnity. Its objective is to put the insured in the same position he was before the fire—no profit, no loss. Standard forms of policy are required by the different states. They are similar in basic provisions. The standard form usually covers against all direct losses by fire or lightning.

Special forms are attached to the basic policy to adapt it to the specific kind of property to be insured. There are special forms for dwellings and apartment, office, and loft buildings. There are mercantile and manufacturing forms. There are forms for buildings only, for contents only, and for buildings and contents. The builders' risk form is designed to cover properties during the course of construction.

Endorsements—Extended Coverages: The fire policy may be extended to cover these additional perils: windstorm and hail, explosion, riot and civil commotion, loss by aircraft and vehicles, smoke, earthquake, vandalism and malicious mischief, sprinkler leakage, sprinkler leakage liability, residents' glass loss, boiler explosion, theft, flood and wave wash. These additional coverages can be obtained by specific endorsements reading into the policy the specified source of damage, i.e., "explosion," wherever "fire" appears in the policy. All risk policies and broad form endorsements have been developed to combine many coverages into a single policy or a single endorsement. To illustrate, the "additional extended coverage endorsement" covers direct loss resulting from:

(1) Accidental discharge, leakage or overflow of water or steam from within a plumbing, heating, or air-conditioning system or a domestic appliance;

(2) Sudden and accidental tearing asunder, cracking, burning, or bulging of a steam or hot water heating or storage system;

(3) Vandalism and malicious mischief;

(4) Vehicles owned or operated by the insured or a tenant;

(5) Fall of trees;

(6) Objects falling from the weight of ice, snow, or sleet;

(7) Freezing of plumbing, heating and air-conditioning systems, and domestic appliances;

(8) Collapse of buildings;

(9) Landslide;

(10) Breakage of glass.

An important extension of coverage is replacement cost coverage on buildings. With this type of coverage, the insurance will cover the repair of a building without deduction for depreciation. If the amount of insurance is 80% or more of the full replacement cost of the building, the full amount of the cost of repair or replacement is payable without deduction for depreciation. Such replacement cost is paid only if repair or replacement is made. If the insured wants to take a cash settlement, he doesn't get more than the actual cash value after deduction for depreciation.

Fire Rates: There are different types of rates—minimum or class rates and specific rates. Minimum-rated risks give the same rates to whole groups of buildings of similar construction and hazard—brick dwellings, in a certain area, frame dwellings, apartment buildings, certain store buildings. These rates are the lowest available unless the rate for the whole class is reduced. Other buildings such as mercantile and manufacturing structures are specifically rated. A schedule is made up to reflect the occupancy and condition of the building, and a rate is set based on the conditions and degree of hazard indicated by the schedule. The owners of a substantial building should have this schedule reviewed by an insurance professional to see whether the rate set is justified by the condition and whether application for a lower rate should be made on the ground that certain types of occupancy or certain conditions of maintenance or structure or certain deficiencies in management have been eliminated. A study of existing physical conditions should be made to determine whether sprinklers or fireproofing or other fire protection devices or physical alterations would produce a saving in applicable insurance rates which would justify the cost of installation.

[¶2902] Insurance Valuations

Insurable value is actual replacement cost new on the date of the loss, less physical depreciation. In the absence of the special extra premium endorsement which eliminates the adjustment for depreciation, this insurable value or actual cash value of the property is the only basis recognized by insurance companies in adjusting losses.

Because of the fluctuation in construction and other costs over the years, the insurable value should be checked periodically and the amount of insurance adjusted accordingly. Ideally, a reliable appraisal should be made by a competent appraisal firm or, alternatively, when only insurance on the building is involved, by a competent architect, engineer, or contractor. Once made, an appraisal may be used for many years simply by adjusting material and labor cost components and depreciation. Some insurance companies, through their engineers, give their clients opinions of value to guide them in the amount of insurance to be placed, but these opinions are informal and are practically never a guarantee that at the time of loss the insurance company will agree to the stated valuation.

Co-insurance: In fire-resistive buildings and in areas having fire protection, most fires do not result in total destruction. In order to distribute equitably the cost of insurance in proportion to the total existent hazard as between individual property owners, insurance companies have attached to their policies a co-insurance or contribution clause.

An owner who has a policy with a contribution clause and who carries an amount of insurance less than the required percentage will find himself underinsured at the time of loss and will suffer a penalty whether his loss is only partial or total. One of the most misunderstood provisions of an insurance policy is the co-insurance or contribution clause, but the following illustration may clarify its operation. An insurance company will pay the owner only its pro rata share of a loss on the basis of the ratio of the amount of actual coverage to the required coverage. In the case of underinsurance, the owner is a "co-insurer" or contributor with the insurance company. For example, a building having an insurable value of $100,000 is insured against fire under a policy bearing the 80% contribution clause. The owner should, therefore, carry at least $80,000 insurance. If he does carry $80,000, he meets the requirement of the contribution clause, and any fire loss he sustains will be paid in full to the limit of his policy.

On the other hand, if the same owner carries only $40,000, he is carrying only half the required amount. Under these circumstances, if he sustains a loss, he will be paid only half of the loss, but the insurance company will not pay more than the limit of its policy, namely $40,000. In this example if he sustains a loss of $1,000, he will collect only $500 and will have to contribute or absorb the other $500. Here's a formula to work with:

$$\frac{\text{Actual amount of coverage}}{\text{Minimum required under co-insurance clause}} = \times \text{ Actual loss} = \text{Insured's recovery}$$

Since the contribution clause can inflict severe penalties for underinsurance, many prudent owners carry more insurance than is required by the contribution clause. For example, their policies may contain the 80% clause, yet they may carry 85% insurance to insurable value. This is relatively inexpensive and leaves a margin for error or for a future increase in value.

The existence of a contribution clause makes it especially important that the insurable value of the property be accurately determined and that it include all property insured by the policy.

Whatever the insurance policy covers should be taken into account as respects valuation and amount of insurance, since at the time of loss the insurance company will include all values when ascertaining that the contribution clause has been complied with.

Vacancy: The standard fire policy provides for suspension of the insurance "while a described building whether intended for occupancy by owner or tenant is vacant or unoccupied beyond a period of sixty consecutive days." Unoccupancy means devoid of human habitation; vacancy means absence of habitation and furnishings. If vacancy or unoccupancy is likely to extend beyond 60 days, the insurance company should be notified and a Vacancy and Unoccupancy Permit may be attached to the policy.

[¶2903] What to Do If You Have a Loss

The standard fire insurance policy requires that the insured shall:

(1) Give immediate written notice to each company of any loss;

(2) Protect the property from further damage;

(3) Forthwith separate the damaged and undamaged personal property and put it in the best possible order;

(4) Furnish a complete inventory of the destroyed, damaged, and undamaged property showing in detail quantities, costs, actual cash value, and amount of loss claim; and

(5) Within 60 days after loss, unless such time is extended in writing by the company, render to the company a proof of loss.

Among other requirements in connection with the proof of loss, the insured may be required to provide verified plans and specifications of the building, fixtures, or machinery destroyed or damaged.

Furthermore, neglect by the insured to use all reasonable means to save and preserve the property at and after a loss or when the property is endangered by fire in neighboring premises will relieve the insurance company of liability.

It is important, therefore, to notify each company or its agent immediately on the occurrence of a fire or damage by any other peril insured and, even though the company does not send an adjuster immediately, to preserve the property against further damage and take just as good care of it as though no insurance existed.

[¶2904] Consequential Loss Coverage

A fire or other peril may cause a financial loss other than that resulting from the direct destruction of the property. Such losses are called "consequential losses." These include losses resulting from the loss of use of the property destroyed, such as interruption of business, and property loss from indirect connection with the hazard rather than from direct destruction. The main types of insurance against consequential losses are these:

(1) Business interruption insurance.

(2) Contingent business interruption insurance that covers losses resulting from the interruption, not of the insured's business, but of a supplier or some other activity on which the continued conduct of the business is dependent.

(3) Extra expense insurance that covers the cost of emergency operation by newspapers, banks, and other types of businesses which cannot afford to have their operations interrupted.

(4) Rent and rental value insurance that covers the loss of rents during the time when a building has become unusable because of fire or other insured peril.

(5) Delayed profits insurance which covers loss of profits that might result from a delay in the completion of a project.

(6) Profits and commission insurance that covers profits on finished goods when sales will be lost as a result of the destruction of goods. This is appropriate for seasonal goods, specially built machinery, etc.

(7) Leasehold insurance that is designed to cover a tenant's financial loss if he has a lease more financially advantageous to him than he could secure at the time of the loss and the lease is cancelled because of the loss.

(8) Excess rental value insurance that covers the difference between the current rental value of the property and what the landlord is receiving from

the tenant under the lease where the tenant or the landlord may cancel the lease following a specific percentage of damage to the property. It is the reverse of the leasehold interest insurance.

[¶2905] Public Liability

Owners of property are subject to certain legal liabilities for the safety of those using the property as occupants, visitors, and even passersby. Poor lighting, structural defects, wet floors, failure to remove ice, and hundreds of other conditions and circumstances have resulted in suits and judgments against property owners.

A number of contracts protect the insured against direct legal liability for the alleged negligent condition causing the accident. The Comprehensive Personal Liability Policy; Owners', Landlords', and Tenants' Public Liability coverage; and Contractors' and Manufacturers' Public Liability coverage are policies covering direct legal liability. The Owners' and Contractors' Protective Public Liability policy is an illustration of the protective type of liability policy covering against indirect liability. This policy, for instance, will protect the contractor against claims that may be brought against him for damage for which a subcontractor is directly responsible.

Make sure that the policy covers not only the owner, but its officers, employees, and managing agent.

[¶2906] What Amounts of Liability Insurance?

The limits or amounts of liability insurance to be carried are always determined on the basis of judgment on the part of the owner. The size of a building and the number of tenants are not necessarily the determining factor. Serious accidents can occur in small buildings as well as large. The extent of injuries need bear no relationship whatever to the size or value of the building nor to the financial responsibility of the owner. In all cases, the owner has to decide on limits which he feels will adequately cover him under any circumstances. Although the limit of recovery of damages for accidental death is determined by law in many states, no limit is placed on recovery for temporary or permanent disability; and since juries are inclined to give extremely liberal awards in personal injury suits, most owners in recent years have substantially increased their limits of insurance. The added premium cost of the higher limits is reasonable enough to warrant the placement of higher amounts than may be normally considered necessary.

Limits are generally expressed as $50/100 or $50,000/100,000, each meaning the same thing; namely, up to $50,000 available for the payment of a claim for injuries to one person hurt in one accident and if more than one person is injured, up to $100,000 limited to $50,000 for any one person. As indicated, a series of accidents is fully covered, with the limits applying separately to each; and no reduction in the amount of coverage occurs by reason of payment of claims.

[¶3000] BROKERAGE

Brokers are involved in almost every type of real estate transaction, including sales, leasing, and mortgaging. Certain specialized rules have evolved concerning the broker and his relationship to the parties to the transaction. Individual states prescribe qualifications for a real estate broker, which usually include an examination evidencing knowledge of a wide range of papers, instruments, and real estate investment economics.

In order to be entitled to a commission for his services, the broker has to show employment by the party from whom he expects payment. Some sort of contract arrangement has to be shown, and in some states a written contract is necessary. Besides showing the existence of the contract, the broker's right to a commission will depend on whether he has satisfied the terms of the contract. These arrangements can vary from open listings to exclusive agencies, exclusive rights to sell, and conditional contracts. Under any one of these contracts, the broker's employment may be limited to a definite period of time. If this is so, his performance will have to be completed (or in some cases at least started) during that period. If no time is specified, the brokerage contract has to be performed within a reasonable time.

In litigation on the broker's claim, he has to establish that the deal between buyer and seller was actually consummated or that he produced a buyer ready, able, and willing to buy. In addition, he must show that there was a meeting of the minds and that the broker was the procuring cause of the sale. And in any deal, the broker has certain specified duties of loyalty to the person who hired him.

Tax laws permit brokers to combine in a corporation and still be taxable as a partnership. They can use pretax dollars for the purchase of life insurance and shares in mutual funds, for the payment of medical expenses, premiums on health and accident insurance, and for profit-sharing and pension plans.

[¶3001] Functions of the Broker

Real estate brokers are those who help and guide others in the acquisition, leasing, mortgaging, and sale of real estate. Real estate brokerage has become a highly specialized field within the real estate business. In many states, the broker is considered an intermediary between seller and buyer. In a few, he is considered to act as the agent of just one of the parties. The relationship formed with the party for whom the broker is an agent is almost universally considered to be a fiduciary relationship—confidential in nature.

Employment: To be entitled to compensation for his services, the broker must be able to show that he was employed by one of the parties to the transaction. Failure to insure that this employment actually exists has led many brokers to the law courts. For example, a broker who brings a prospective purchaser to the owner of property is not entitled to commission even if the deal goes through unless the seller has made some sort of request for the broker's services. Normally, this introduction of a buyer (or tenant) to seller (or landlord) does not create employment of the broker even though the property actually is sold (or leased). What is likely in this case is that a court will find that the owner has merely consented to sell his property or lease it to the purchaser whom the broker has convinced to buy it. So the first point for any broker to remember when setting up a deal is that compensation depends on the existence of a contractual relationship between the broker and one of the parties.

Written Contract: Generally, a written contract which is definite and complete in detail as to the terms of the broker's employment is desirable. Some states will require this contract to be in writing in order for the broker to assure any rights against his principal (the person who hired him). This contract should contain the names of the parties; a description of the property; the price, conditions, and terms of the prospective transaction; purpose of the agreement; the date; the length of time the employment will continue and rate of compensation and when it is payable. Mention is ordinarily made of existing encumbrances on the property and how they will be disposed of. There usually is a provision for termination of the employment contract by means of a revocation.

Contracts with Corporations: A broker who undertakes to sell property for a corporation must make sure that the officer who has employed him has the authority to make such a contract. A corporation acts through certain designated officials who have been authorized by the corporation. All the officers of the corporation usually do not possess this power, and the authority to sell property or to purchase it is generally not given to minor officials or to directors of a corporation (unless the directors happen to be major officers).

Commissions: The compensation that a broker receives for the services he has performed usually is a percentage of the amount involved in the transaction. The percentage, or rate, is up to the broker and his principal. But almost all real estate boards prescribe certain rates that are suggested to brokers to charge in given transactions. Here, the broker and principal can usually contract for any rate of commission, whether more or less than the amount suggested by the real estate board. But if no rate is fixed, the rate set up by the board will probably control as a matter of custom. Some states have provisions which affect the payment of the commission. The license of New York State, for example, denies a commission to anyone who is not licensed to practice as a real estate broker or salesman. It also prevents a broker from splitting his commission with any person unless that person is a licensed real estate broker, salesman, or a broker engaged in the real estate brokerage business in another state.

Loyalty: If the broker acts as agent for both buyer and seller he has an obligation to reveal that fact to both of them. The broker also has a duty not to reveal any secret information to prospective buyers, such as the fact that the seller will actually take less than the listed price. If the broker fraudulently buys the property from his employer without the latter's knowledge and resells it at a profit, he is liable to his employer. Any breach of loyalty will result in the forfeiting of the broker's commission.

[¶3002] Qualifications for Brokers

License laws of the individual states set up qualifications for real estate brokers consisting of experience and knowledge of the negotiations and conduct of real estate transactions. Some states go so far as to require a bond from the broker assuring faithful performance of his duties. Most jurisdictions in their licensing of the broker, require a knowledge of real estate papers and instruments (deeds, bonds, mortgages, leases, contracts), locations, trends, rentals, general real estate values, and appraisals.

The following list outlines the requirements for the licensing of brokers and salesmen in each state. For more information about a particular jurisdiction's requirements write to the address listed for that state.

ALABAMA

Real Estate Commission
State of Alabama
562 State Office Building
Montgomery, Alabama 36130

		Salesman	Broker
Age:		—	—
Minimum Requirements:		H.S. diploma *plus* 45 hrs. appr. R.E. courses	2 yrs. lic. sales *or* equiv., and appr. R.E. course
Fees:	*Test:*	$50	$50
	License:	$25	$25
Test Schedule:		Monthly	Monthly

ALASKA

Division of Occupational Licensing
Alaska Dept. of Commerce
Pouch D, Juneau, Alaska 99811

		Salesman	Broker
Age:		19	19
Minimum Requirements:		None	2 years (24 months) continuous active experience as salesman
Fees:	*Test:*	$50	$50
	License:	$50	$50
Test Schedule:		January, April, July, October	Same

ARIZONA

Arizona Real Estate Department
1645 W. Jefferson Street
Phoenix, Arizona 85507

		Salesman	*Broker*
Age:		18	21
Minimum Requirements:		45 hrs. appr. R.E. course completed in Arizona	3 yrs. active lic. sales out of last 5 yrs. *plus* 90 hrs. R.E. courses, appr. compl. in Arizona
Fees:	*Test:*	$25	$50
	License:	$25	$50
	Recovery Fund:	$10	$10
Test Schedule:		Monthly	Monthly

ARKANSAS

Arkansas Real Estate Commission
1311 West Second Street
P.O. Box 3173
Little Rock, Arkansas 72201

		Salesman	*Broker*
Age:		18	18
Minimum Requirements:		30 hrs. within 1 yr. of passing exam	2 yrs. lic. sales (out of last 4 yrs.) *plus* 30 class hrs. appr. R.E. course *or* 90 hrs. appr. R.E. course
Fees:	*Test:*	$15	$15
	License:	$10	$40
Test Schedule:		Every other month, begin Feb.	Every other month begin Jan. (except Nov.)

CALIFORNIA

Department of Real Estate
State of California
714 P Street
Sacramento, California 95814

		Salesman	*Broker*
Age:		18	18
Minimum Requirements:		—	2 yrs. lic. sales full-time *plus* 6 appr. college courses in R.E. law, practice, finance & appraisal
Fees:	*Test:*	$10	$25
	License:	$45 (4 yrs.)	$75 (4 yrs.)
Test Schedule:		Weekly	6 × yearly

COLORADO

Colorado Real Estate Commission
110 State Services Building
1525 Sherman Street
Denver, Colorado 80203

		Salesman	*Broker*
Age:		18	21
Minimum Requirements:		24 classroom hrs. R.E. practice, 24 classroom hrs. R.E. law	2 yrs. lic. sales full time *plus* 24 classroom hrs. appr. courses
Fees:	*Test:*	$10	$15
	License:	$10	$20
Test Schedule:		Monthly except Dec.	Monthly except Dec.

IDAHO

Idaho Real Estate Commission
State Capitol Building
Boise, Idaho 83720

		Salesman	*Broker*
Age:		18	18
Minimum Requirements:		H.S. diploma or equiv.; 30 class hrs. appr. R.E. course	2 yrs. lic. sales *plus* 70 class hrs. appr. R.E. courses
Fees:	*Test:*	$25	$25
	License:	$30	$30
	Recovery Fund:	$10	$10
Test Schedule:		Monthly	Quarterly

ILLINOIS

Dept. of Registration & Education
Springfield, Illinois 62786

		Salesman	*Broker*
Age:		21 (may be waived to 18)	21
Minimum Requirements:		H.S. diploma or equiv.; 30 hrs. appr. R.E. courses	1 yr. lic. sales *plus* 90 hrs. appr. R.E. courses; *or* B.A. appr. college
Fees:	*Test:*	$15 (+$10 processing fee)	$30 (+$20 processing fee)
	License:	$5 (1 yr.)	$20 (2 yr.)
Test Schedule:		Monthly	Monthly

INDIANA

Indiana Real Estate Commission
1022 State Office Building
100 N. Senate Ave.
Indianapolis, Indiana 46204

		Salesman	*Broker*
Age:		18	18
Minimum Requirements:		H.S. or equiv. *plus* appr. R.E. Salesmen's Course.	H. S. or equiv.; 2 yrs. lic. sales; *or* B.A. degree
Fees:	*Test:*	$20	$30
	License:	$10 (2 yr.)	$20 (2 yr.)
Test Schedule:		Feb., July, Sept.	Feb., July, Sept.

IOWA

Iowa Real Estate Commission
1223 East Court Ave.
Des Moines, Iowa 50319

		Salesman	*Broker*
Age:		18	18
Minimum Requirements:		30 hrs. during first 12 months of license	1 yr. lic. sales
Fees:	*Test:*	$10	$10
	License:	$10	$20
Test Schedule:		Monthly except Nov. & Dec.	Monthly except Nov. & Dec.

KANSAS

Kansas Real Estate Commission
Room 1212
535 Kansas Avenue
Topeka, Kansas 66603

		Salesman	*Broker*
Age:		18	18
Minimum Requirements:		H.S. diploma or equiv.	2 yrs. lic. sales within preceding 5 yrs.
Fees:	*Test:*	$10	$15
	License:	$15	$25
Test Schedule:		Twice monthly	Twice monthly

KENTUCKY

Kentucky Real Estate Commission
100 E. Liberty St.
Louisville, Kentucky 40202

		Salesman	*Broker*
Age:		18	18
Minimum Requirements:		H.S. or equiv.	30 classroom hrs. appr. R.E. courses
Fees:	*Test:*	$25	$25
	License:	$10 (first year)	$10
	Recovery Fund:	$5 (renewal)	
		$30 (first year)	Same
		$20 (renewal)	Same
Test Schedule:		Every other month starting in Jan.	Every other month starting in Jan.

CONNECTICUT

Connecticut Real Estate Commission
90 Washington Street
Hartford, Connecticut 06115

		Salesman	*Broker*
Age:		None	18
Minimum Requirements:		30 Hrs. R.E. Principles & Practices course or equiv. exp. or ed.	2 yrs. lic. sales and 30 hrs. R.E. P&P; *plus* 30 hrs. appraisal and 30 hrs. appr. add'l course.
Fees:	*Test:*	$10	$15
	License:	$75 (1st yr.) $75 (renewal)	$150 (1st yr.) $100 (renewal)
Test Schedule:		Twice monthly approx.	Same as sales.

DELAWARE

Delaware Real Estate Commission
Div. of Business & Occupational Regulations
Dept. of Administrative Services
State House Annex
Capital Square
Dover, Delaware 19901

		Salesman	*Broker*
Age:		None stated	None stated
Minimum Requirements:		75 class hrs. appr. course R.E. practice	5 yrs. lic. sales *plus* list 30 completed sales within 5 yrs., and 32 hrs. R.E. Law appr. course
Fees:	*Test:*	$15	$15
	License:	$10	$25
	(State Tax):	$50	$50
Test Schedule:		Monthly	Monthly

DISTRICT OF COLUMBIA

Real Estate Commission of the District of Columbia
Department of Economic Development
614 H Street, N.W.
Washington, D.C. 20001

		Salesman	*Broker*
Age:		21	21
Minimum Requirements:		None	None
Fees:	*Test:*	$10	$30 (inc. appl.)
	License:	$10	$10
Test Schedule:		Monthly	Monthly

FLORIDA

Florida Real Estate Commission
2699 Lee Rd.
Winter Park, Florida 32789

	Salesman	*Broker*
Age:	18	18
Minimum Requirements:	Course 1, R.E. Principles & Practice, appr., U. of Fla. or equiv.	Course II, Advanced R.E. course appr., U. of Fla. or equiv.
Fees: Test:	$25	$50
License:	$10	$20
Test Schedule:	Twice Monthly	Twice Monthly

GEORGIA

Georgia Real Estate Commission
166 Pryor St. S.W.
Atlanta, Georgia 30303

	Salesman	*Broker*
Age:	18	18
Minimum Requirements:	High School diploma	H.S. plus 60 class hours appr. course, *or* 15 credit hours at a college or university.
Fees: Test:	$25	$25
License:	$15	$50
Test Schedule:	6 × yrly.	3 × yrly.

HAWAII

Professional & Vocational Licensing Div.
Dept. of Regulatory Agencies
State of Hawaii
P.O. Box 3469
Honolulu, Hawaii 96801

		Salesman	*Broker*
Age:		18	18
Minimum Requirements:		Appr. sales R.E. course or equiv.	2 yrs. lic. sales *plus* appr. Broker course
Fees:	*Test:*	$25	$25
	License:	$50	$50
	Recovery fund:	$50	$50
Test Schedule:		3 × yrly.	3 × yrly.

Uses ETS

LOUISIANA

Real Estate Commission
Dept. of Occupational Standards
P.O. Box 44095 State Capitol
Baton Rouge, Louisiana 70804

		Salesman	*Broker*
Age:		18	21
Minimum Requirements:		30 hrs. R.E. appr. course	1 yr. sales *plus* 90 hrs. R.E. Broker course appr.
Fees:	*Test:*	$10	$10
	License:	$25 (first yr.) $15 (renewal)	$100 (first yr.) $25 (renewal)
Test Schedule:		Monthly except Dec. & Jan.	Monthly except Dec. & Jan.

MAINE

Real Estate Commission
Capitol Shopping Center
Western Avenue
Augusta, Maine 04330

	Salesman	*Broker*
Age:	18	18
Minimum Requirements:	H. S. diploma or equiv.	H.S. or equiv. *plus* 1 yr. lic. sales or appr. R.E. courses
Fees: Test:	$35	$40
License:	$20 (2 yrs.)	$30 (2 yrs.)
Test Schedule:	6 × yrly.	6 × yrly.

MARYLAND

Maryland Real Estate Commission
Dept. of Licensing and Regulation
1 South Calvert Street
Baltimore, Maryland 21202

	Salesman	*Broker*
Age:	18	18
Minimum Requirements:	36 hr. course, Basic R.E. Principles & Practices	3 yrs. lic. sales *plus* 6 semester credit hours, *or* graduate, Realtors' Institute
Fees: Test:	$5	$10
License:	$20 (2 yr.)	$70 (2 yr.)
Test Schedule:	Monthly	Monthly

MASSACHUSETTS

The Commonwealth of Massachusetts
Bd. of Registration of Brokers & Salesmen
State Office Building
100 Cambridge Street
Boston, Massachusetts 02202

		Salesman	*Broker*
Age:		18	21
Minimum Requirements:		None	None
Fees:	*Test:*	$8 (waived for vets)	$15 (waived for vets)
	License:	$20 (2 yr.) $15 (renewal)	$35 (2 yr.) $25 (renewal)
Test Schedule:		Monthly except Dec.	Monthly except Dec.

MICHIGAN

Michigan Dept. of Licensing & Regulation
1033 S. Washington Avenue
Lansing, Michigan 48926

		Salesman	*Broker*
Age:		18	18
Minimum Requirements:		30 clock hours if applicant fails first exam	3 yrs. in R.E. (2 as lic. sls.); *plus* 90 clock hrs. R.E. courses
Fees:	*Test:*	$5	$5
	License:	$25	$30
Test Schedule:		Monthly	Monthly

MINNESOTA

Commissioner of Securities
Department of Commerce
State of Minnesota
Metro Square Building, 5th Floor
St. Paul, Minnesota 55101

		Salesman	*Broker*
Age:		18	18
Minimum Requirements:		90 hrs.	2 yrs. lic. sls. or equiv.
Fees:	*Test:*	$10	$10
	License:	$25 (1st yr.) $10 (renewal)	$50 (1st yr.) $25 (renewal)
Test Schedule:		Weekly	Weekly

MISSISSIPPI

Mississippi Real Estate Commission
Busby Building
754 North President
Jackson, Mississippi 39202

		Salesman	*Broker*
Age:		18	21
Minimum Requirements:		—	Lic. R.E. sales 1 yr.
Fees:	*Test:*	$30	$30
	License:	$15	$20
Test Schedule:		At least 4 × yearly	At least 4 × yearly

MISSOURI

Missouri Real Estate Commission
3523 North Ten Mile Drive
P.O. Box 1339
Jefferson City, Missouri 65101

		Salesman	*Broker*
Age:		21	21
Minimum Requirements:		32 hrs. R.E. Basic course, appr.	1 yr. active lic. R.E. sales *or* 32 hrs. Advanced course, appr.
Fees:	*Test:*	$16	$33
	License:	$3.75	$7.50
Test Schedule:		7 × yrly.	Jan., Apr., July, and Oct. 4 × yrly.

MONTANA

Montana Real Estate Commission
La Londe Building
42½ North Main Street
Helena, Montana 59601

		Salesman	*Broker*
Age:		18	18
Minimum Requirements:		2 yrs. H.S.	H.S. diploma *plus* 2 yrs. active lic. sales.
Fees:	*Test:*	$50	$50
	License:	$25	$50
Test Schedule:		Jan., Mar., May, July, Sept., Nov.	Jan., Mar., May, July, Sept., Nov.

NEBRASKA

Nebraska Real Estate Commission
600 S. 11th Street Suite 200
Lincoln, Nebraska 68509

		Salesman	*Broker*
Age:		19	19
Minimum Requirements:		H.S. diploma *or* equiv.	2 yrs. lic. sales *plus* 60 class hrs. *or* equiv. appr.
Fees:	*Test:*	$25 *plus* $25 for investigation	$25 *plus* $25 for investigation
	License:	$15	$30
Test Schedule:		10 × yrly.	10 × yrly.

NEVADA

Administrator
Real Estate Division
Department of Commerce
201 S. Fall Street Rm. 129
Carson City, Nevada 89701

		Salesman	*Broker*
Age:		18	18
Minimum Requirements:		75 classroom hrs. Appr. R.E. courses	2 yrs. active lic. sales *plus* appr. R.E. courses
Fees:	*Test:*	$40	$40
	License:	$25	$40
	Recovery Fund:	$15	$15
Test Schedule:		Minimum every 2 months	Same

NEW HAMPSHIRE

New Hampshire Real Estate Commission
3 Capital Street
Concord, New Hampshire 03301

		Salesman	*Broker*
Age:		18	18
Minimum Requirements:		—	1 yr. active lic. sales *or* part-time 2000 hrs.
Fees:	*Test:*	$15	$15
	License:	$15 (2 yr.) $10 (2 yr. renewal)	$25 (2 yr.) $20 (2 yr. renewal)
Test Schedule:		Feb., May, Aug., and Nov.	Feb., May, Aug., and Nov.

NEW JERSEY

New Jersey Real Estate Commission
Dept. of Insurance
P.O. Box 1510
201 East State Street
Trenton, New Jersey 08625

		Salesman	*Broker*
Age:		18	20
Minimum Requirements:		8th Grade *plus* 30 hrs. appr. R.E. courses	H.S. diploma, and 2 yrs. lic. sales *plus* 42 hrs. appr. R.E. Broker course
Fees:	*Test:*	$10	$10
	License:	$15	$30
	Registration:	$9	$9
Test Schedule:		Monthly, except Dec.	Same

NEW MEXICO

New Mexico Real Estate Commission
Suite 608
600 Second N.W.
Albuquerque, New Mexico 87102

		Salesman	Broker
Age:		18	18
Minimum Requirements:		—	1 yr. lic. sales *or* 60 hrs. appr. R.E. courses *or* 1 yr. equiv. exp. *or* current broker lic. from reciprocating state
Fees:	*Test:*	$10	$10
	License:	$10	$25
Test Schedule:		Weekly: Tues.-Fri.	Twice a month, except Dec. & Jan.

NEW YORK

Secretary of State
Department of State
Division of Licensing Services
270 Broadway
New York, New York 10007

		Salesman	Broker
Age:		18	21
Minimum Requirements:		—	1 yr. lic. sales *or* 2 yrs. related business exper. *plus* 45 hrs. appr. R.E. courses
Fees:	*Test:*	—	—
	License:	$10 (2 yr.)	$50 (2 yr.)
Test Schedule:		Weekly	Monthly

NORTH CAROLINA

North Carolina Real Estate Licensing Board
P.O. Box 266
Raleigh, North Carolina 27602

		Salesman	*Broker*
Age:		No specification	18
Minimum Requirements:		30 hrs. appr. R.E. courses *or* equiv. exp.	12 months lic. sales *or* equiv. (appr. combination experience & educ. considered equiv.)
Fees:	*Test:*	$15 (exam & license)	$25 (exam & license)
	License:	$10 (Renewal)	$10 (Renewal)
Test Schedule:		Monthly, except Dec.	Monthly, except Dec.

NORTH DAKOTA

North Dakota Real Estate Commission
P.O. Box 727
Bismarck, North Dakota 58501

		Salesman	*Broker*
Age:		18	18
Minimum Requirements:		—	1 yr. lic. sales
Fees:	*Test:*	$30 (incl. appl.)	$35 (incl. appl.)
	License:	$20	$30
Test Schedule:		Monthly, except Dec.	Monthly, except Dec.

OHIO

Department of Commerce
Division of Real Estate
180 East Broad Street
Columbus, Ohio 43215

		Salesman	*Broker*
Age:		18	20
Minimum Requirements:		H.S. diploma 30 hrs., R.E. Law 30 hrs. R.E. Practice	2 yrs. lic. sales *plus* 30 hrs. R.E. Law, 30 hrs. R.E. Practice, 30 hrs. R.E. Appraisal, & 30 hrs. R.E. Finance
Fees:	*Test:*	$27	$47
	License:	$7	$12
	Recovery Fund:	$10	$20
Test Schedule:		Twice monthly	Monthly

OKLAHOMA

Oklahoma Real Estate Commission
4040 North Lincoln Blvd.
Oklahoma City, Oklahoma 73105

		Salesman	*Broker*
Age:		18	18
Minimum Requirements:		30 clock hrs. appr. R.E. course	One yr. registered sales, *plus* two 30 clock hrs. appr. courses.
Fees:	*Test:*	$10	$15
	License:	$5	$12
Test Schedule:		150 × yrly.	50 × yrly.

OREGON

Department of Commerce
Real Estate Division
158 12th Street N.E.
Salem, Oregon 97310

		Salesman	*Broker*
Age:		18	18
Minimum Requirements:		H.S. diploma *or* equiv.	3 yrs. lic. sales *plus* 9 credit hrs. (3 each: R.E. Law, R.E. Finance, and R.E. Practice.)
Fees:	*Test:*	$25	$25
	License:	$60 (2 yrs.)	$75 (2 yrs.)
Test Schedule:		Every 70 days	Every 70 days

PENNSYLVANIA

Commissioner of Professional
& Occupational Affairs
State Real Estate Commission
Commonwealth of Pennsylvania
Box 2649
Harrisburg, Pennsylvania 17120

		Salesman	*Broker*
Age:		18	21
Minimum Requirements:		4 credits R.E. study	3 yrs. lic. sales *plus* 16 credits appr. R.E. course
Fees:	*Test:*	$5	$10
	License:	$5 (2 yr.)	$10 (2 yr.)
Test Schedule:		2nd Sat., each Feb., May, Aug., Nov.	Same dates as sales

RHODE ISLAND

State of Rhode Island
Department of Business Regulation
Real Estate Division
169 Weybosset Street
Providence, Rhode Island 02903

		Salesman	*Broker*
Age:		18	18
Minimum Requirements:		—	1 yr. full time sales *or* 90 hrs. appr. courses
Fees:	*Test:*	$10	$10
	License:	$50	$50
Test Schedule:		Biweekly	Biweekly

SOUTH CAROLINA

South Carolina Real Estate Commission
900 Elmwood Avenue
Columbia, South Carolina 29201

		Salesman	*Broker*
Age:		18	21
Minimum Requirements:		—	2 yrs. lic. sales *or* 60 hrs. appr. R.E. courses *or* appr. business exper. as equiv.
Fees:	*Test:*	—	$25
	License:	temporary $10 permanent $25	$25
Test Schedule:		Monthly	Monthly

SOUTH DAKOTA

South Dakota Real Estate Commission
P.O. Box 638
Pierre, South Dakota 57501

		Salesman	*Broker*
Age:		18	18
Minimum Requirements:		30 hrs. appr. R.E. courses	2 yrs. Lic. sales *plus* 90 hrs. appr. courses
Fees:	*Test:*	$50	$50
	License:	No additional fee	No additional fee
Test Schedule:		Jan., Apr., July, and Oct.	Jan., Apr., July, and Oct.

TENNESSEE

Tennessee Real Estate Commission
556 Capitol Hill Bldg.
Nashville, Tennessee 37219

		Salesman	*Broker*
Age:		Information not available	
Minimum Requirements:			
Fees:	*Test:*		
	License:		
Test Schedule:			

TEXAS

Texas Real Estate Commission
P.O. Box 12188
Capitol Station
Austin, Texas 78711

	Salesman	*Broker*
Age:	18	18
Minimum Requirements:	30 classroom hrs. appr. courses	2 yrs. lic. sales *plus* 180 hrs. appr. R.E. courses
Fees: Test:	$5	$5
License:	$20	$40
Test Schedule:	22 times per month	10 times per month

UTAH

Real Estate Division
Dept. of Business Regulation
State of Utah
330 East Fourth South Street
Salt Lake City, Utah 84111

	Salesman	*Broker*
Age:	18	21
Minimum Requirements:	H.S. diploma *plus* 30 hrs. appr. R.E. courses	3 yrs. active lic. sales *plus* 90 hrs. appr. R.E. courses
Fees: Test:	$15	$25
License:	$15 $12 (renewal)	$40 $25 (renewal)
Test Schedule:	1st Tues. of each month	Every 3 months

VERMONT

Vermont Real Estate Commission
7 East State Street
Montpelier, Vermont 05602

		Salesman	*Broker*
Age:		18	18
Minimum Requirements:		H.S. diploma *or* equiv.	1 yr. lic. sales *or* R.E. courses appr.
Fees:	*Test:*	$25	$25
	License:	$15	$15
Test Schedule:		4 × yrly.	4 × yrly.

VIRGINIA

Virginia Real Estate Commission
P.O. Box 1-X
Richmond, Virginia 23202

		Salesman	*Broker*
Age:		No specification	18
Minimum Requirements:		Appr. R.E. Courses	1 yr. lic. active sales 3 semester hrs. to 7/77 6 semester hrs. to 7/79 9 semester hrs. to 7/81 12 semester hrs. — in appr. R.E. courses
Fees:	*Test:*	$25	$25
	License:	$30 (2 yr.)	$50 (2 yr.)
Test Schedule:		Monthly, except Dec.	6 × yrly. Odd-numbered months

WASHINGTON

Washington Real Estate Commission
Dept. of Motor Vehicles
P.O. Box 247, Highway-Licenses Bldg.
Olympia, Washington 98504

		Salesman	*Broker*
Age:		18	18
Minimum Requirements:		H.S. diploma or equiv.	2 yrs. lic. active sales *plus* 90 hrs. appr. R.E. courses
Fees:	*Test:*	$15	$25
	License:	$15	$25
Test Schedule:		6 × yrly.	3 × yrly.

WEST VIRGINIA

West Virginia Real Estate Commission
402 State Office Bldg. No. 3
1800 East Washington Street
Charleston, West Virginia 25305

		Salesman	*Broker*
Age:		18	18
Minimum Requirements:		—	2 yrs lic. active sales *or* equiv. R.E. exper.
Fees:	*Test:*	—	—
	License:	$25	$50
Test Schedule:		2 days per month	2 days per month

WISCONSIN

Department of Regulation & Licensing
Real Estate Examining Board
State of Wisconsin
819 North 6th Street
Milwaukee, Wisconsin 53203

		Salesman	*Broker*
Age:		18	18
Minimum Requirements:		—	—
Fees:	*Test:*	$20	$25
	License:	$15	$20
Test Schedule:		Approx. 4 × yrly.	Approx. 4 × yrly.

WYOMING

Real Estate Commission of Wyoming
2219 Carey Avenue
Cheyenne, Wyoming 82002

		Salesman	*Broker*
Age:		19	19
Minimum Requirements:		—	2 yrs. lic. sales *or* degree in R.E.
Fees:	*Test:*	$15	$15
	License:	$25	$35
Test Schedule:		4 × yrly. Jan., Apr., July, Oct.	4 × yrly. Jan., Apr., July, Oct.

[¶3003] Different Types of Listing Arrangements

Open Listing: An open listing arrangement is one whereby the owner reserves the right either to sell the property himself or to hire other brokers. Ordinarily, the owner can hire more than one broker to sell the property unless a specific agreement to the contrary is made. Almost all informal listing arrangements that are verbally entered into are open listings. Even under these arrangements, when the property has been listed with several brokers for sale and none of them has an exclusive right to sell the property, the broker who first finds a buyer ready, able, and willing is nevertheless entitled to the commission.

Under an open listing arrangement, the broker may engage in negotiations with a prospective purchaser, and the sale may ultimately be closed by the owner of the property or perhaps by another broker. To protect himself against this possibility—namely, that he will produce a prospective purchaser, that negotiations will temporarily break off, and that someone else will resume them—the broker in an open listing contract should avail himself of a protective provision. The listing contract should provide that the broker will be entitled to commission if the property is sold to any person with whom the broker negotiated within a specific period of time.

Exclusive Agency: Under this arrangement, the broker is assured that no other broker will be hired as long as his employment continues (usually for a specified period of time). Often an exclusive agency will be created by a provision in the listing contract that the owner will pay a commission to the broker if the property is sold by the broker or by "any other person" during the specified period of employment. This exclusive agency does not prevent the owner himself from exerting his own individual efforts in selling the property. In that eventuality, the exclusive agency will end, and the owner will not be liable for any commission.

Exclusive Right to Sell: The exclusive right to sell provides that the broker will receive commission in any case where the property is sold: by another broker, by the owner, or by anyone else. So even if the owner makes the sale himself through his own effort he has to pay the broker. This exclusive right to sell consequently gives the broker even more rights than he would get under an exclusive agency. But to take advantage of this, the broker has to make sure that his contract with the owner specifically spells out the nature of the broker's exclusive sale right.

Multiple Listing: This is a means by which brokers combine their efforts to sell properties listed with any member of a broker's pool. The broker who has obtained the listing gives a copy of it to all the members of the pool. If any member besides the original broker sells the property, the commission is divided between that broker and the original broker. Usually, the pool agreement will provide that no member will try to get the listing for himself after the original broker's listing has expired.

[¶3004] Duration of Employment

No Specified Time: If no time is specified for performance of the employment contract, it has to be performed "within a reasonable time." What is a reasonable time will be determined from all of the facts of the particular transaction. If the broker continues to work on the deal after a reasonable time has elapsed and finds a willing, able, and ready buyer, the seller can still refuse to sell and does not have to pay a commission. The owner can revoke the listing even during the reasonable time period at any time before the broker has found a buyer. The owner can even do this while the broker is negotiating with a prospect if the negotiations have not been substantially completed. But this revocation has to be in good faith—the owner has to have decided to withdraw the property from sale. This general rule which is found in most jurisdictions will give way in a case where the listing involves a situation where it is anticipated that the broker will incur unusual expenses. And in some states a broker will be allowed a reasonable length of time to complete his work if he has put in some time and effort before the owner has revoked.

Fixed Time: If the employment is limited to a definite period of time, it will expire at the end of that period. But if the owner has waived this time limit and accepted the services of the broker, the courts will treat the contract of employment as if it were in force. In such case, if the broker has performed his services, he will be entitled to the commission. Or, if the expiration of the specified listing time is due to the fault of the owner, in bad faith, the broker will be entitled to collect if he has found a ready, able, and willing buyer. This would be the case when the owner postponed an agreement with the buyer until the expiration of the time period in order to divest the broker of his right to a commission. So, also, if negotiations were begun during the specified time and continued after expiration, the seller would be deemed to have waived the time limit. Some contracts will provide for a fixed period of time, say 60 days with automatic renewals for 60-day periods until the owner serves a termination notice on the broker. Many states will consider this an open listing during the extended period.

In some states, if the listing contract specifies a fixed period of time, the owner can revoke the employment only until the agent has put in money and effort. Thereafter, the broker is considered to have begun performance of his contract and will be entitled to a commission if he finds a buyer ready, able, and willing to buy within the specified employment period.

Finally, there are some brokerage contracts in which the broker promises to perform certain specified acts, such as advertising in a specified paper once every week. Here the exclusive agency cannot be terminated and will be in effect until the time set for expiration; the owner has an enforceable right to make the broker advertise; conversely, the broker has an enforceable right to an exclusive agency for the entire period specified.

[¶3005] Protection of the Broker's Right to Commission

The broker's right to a commission will depend on the type of contract he has made with the seller (who ordinarily would be his principal). The general type of arrangement can vary from an open listing to an exclusive agency or an exclusive right to sell. Somewhere in between is the conditional agency, where the owner of the property conditions his liability for commission on some specific event or perhaps on the ultimate closing of the deal.

[¶3006] Practical Considerations in Drawing Up Brokerage Agreements

(1) Is the agency to be exclusive or nonexclusive? If exclusive, has a time period been set? Distinguish between an exclusive agency and an exclusive sale.

(2) Does the broker's commission depend on consummation of the sale or on merely finding a willing and able buyer?

(3) Should the exclusive broker be made to cooperate with other brokers? Does the broker have authority to sell or merely authority to procure a buyer or negotiate once a prospect is found? Does he have authority to exchange?

(4) What is the owner's right to withdraw the property from the market? Is the agent entitled to the commission payable out of the down payment on the purchase price or only at the time of closing?

(5) Is the commission payable in a lump sum or installments?

(6) Specify the rate of commission.

(7) Should the broker assume any obligations for advertising the property or are these costs and other out-of-pocket expenses to be absorbed by the owner?

(8) Check to see whether the broker should conduct the transaction on an undisclosed-principal basis, remembering that, if nondisclosure is de-

sired, the broker will be liable and committed as a principal. Is this personal liability covered by an adequate agreement running between the broker and his undisclosed principal? The broker should be protected against disaffirmance of the transaction consummated by a clear statement of his authority, the terms on which he can negotiate, the representations he can make, and the discretion given.

(9) Has a loyalty clause been inserted where the broker or agent has been entrusted with confidential reports, financial statements, and similar data? What penalty is imposed for nondisclosure, self-dealing, and double employment?

(10) Check to make sure that the broker or agent is duly licensed to handle the transaction under local law.

(11) Has misrepresentation been guarded against by setting forth a clear description of property to be handled by the broker? An indemnity clause may be advisable where the broker has wide authority in the transaction without prior approval from the owner.

[¶3007] Tax Considerations in Drawing Up Brokerage Agreements

(1) Taxability of Commissions: The money earned by and payable to a broker is taxable like any other compensation.

(2) Deferral of Tax: If the brokerage agreement specifies that the commission is to be payable over a period of years subsequent to the consummation of the transaction, the income will be deferred for tax purposes so that it will not be taxed until the payments are received by a broker who is on the cash basis. Keep in mind, too, that the income-averaging provisions of Code §1301-1305 can remove the prohibitive tax bite on bunched income and may make deferral unnecessary.

(3) Equity Interest for Broker: Frequently, a broker will try to convert his commission into an equity participation in the property that is sold or to form a syndicate to acquire the property. The value of his equity in the property or in the syndicate will be taxed to him as ordinary compensation. In a partnership, if he's given either a profits-only interest or a capital interest that cannot be drawn out until the termination, he can avoid immediate compensation income for his share in the syndicate.

[¶3008] When Is the Commission Earned?

Unless the owner has set some additional condition in hiring him, the broker is entitled to his commission when he can show the following:

(1) The broker's services were performed during the specified time of the agency.

(2) The deal was consummated (if that was a condition of the broker's rights to a commission).

(3) The broker produced a buyer ready, able, and willing to buy.

(4) There was a meeting of minds between the two parties.

(5) The broker was the procuring cause.

Conditions: The owner to protect himself may provide in the contract of employment that the payment of compensation to the broker will occur only if some specified event is satisfied. So the contract can provide that the commission will be paid if the contract to sell the property is valid and enforceable, or if the broker obtains a purchaser at the specified price, or if the purchaser pays the purchase price agreed upon to the seller and takes title in accordance with the terms of the contract. One condition frequently in use is a specification in the listing contract that the owner will pay a commission "only on the completion of the transfer of the property and the owner shall not be liable for, and will not pay, nor be required to pay, a commission unless, and until the transaction is finally completed." In this type of setup the broker does not earn his commission when he finds a buyer ready, able, and willing to buy. The payment of the commission will depend on the closing of the deal and the full payment of the purchase price to the owner. So if the transaction does not close, the broker loses his commission. Even under this type of arrangement, however, if the deal fails to go through due to the owner's fault and the seller's refusal to complete the sale is in bad faith, the broker will get his commission. What is necessary for recovery by the broker here is that the owner by his own act has prevented closing or has made the property unmarketable.

Ready, Able, and Willing: In order for a broker to be entitled to his commission the purchaser must be "ready, able, and willing" to satisfy the conditions that have been specified by the owner. Even if the broker has brought the parties together and they make a different contract from the one that the broker was employed to obtain, the broker will still be entitled to compensation. "Ready" means that the buyer will execute a contract of sale. "Able" means that the buyer will be able to get up the necessary funds to close the deal within the time required. He must have the money to meet the cash payment and be financially able to meet later installments. "Willingness" is the voluntary act of the purchaser without any compulsion or coercion. Under these definitions, a purchaser who is insolvent and who has failed to deposit a required security is not ready, able, and willing.

Meeting of the Minds: The parties have to agree on all the terms of the transaction of sale. This will include, among other things, the purchase price, the amount of the purchase-money mortgage, the date, time, and place of taking title, form of deed, adjustments, cancellation provisions on default, and the physical condition of the property and subject clauses as to liens, encroachments, assessments, covenants, leases, etc. But an agreement between the parties on terms that are different from those that were originally given to the broker will not prevent the broker from obtaining his commission if he was the procuring cause of the buyer and if negotiations that he began ended in an executed contract. But if the parties negotiate on different terms than those given to the broker and do not reach agreement, the broker has no rights.

Consummation of the Transaction: This will be important where the broker's right to a commission has been conditioned on the final conclusion of the transaction. Here, again, if the deal goes through, the broker is entitled to his commission even if the parties have changed the terms from those which were originally given to the broker. Or, if the deal does not go through because of default on the part of the owner, in bad faith, the broker is entitled to his commission. In an exclusive agency or an open listing where the broker's right to a commission has not been conditioned upon the final conclusion of the transaction, the broker will get his commission even if the purchaser fails to carry out the deal after having made a valid contract.

Procuring Cause: The broker has to show that his efforts were the primary and direct cause of the consummation of the transaction. For example, if someone finds out that the property is for sale and purchases it without ever meeting, talking to, or having any business with the broker, the broker is not the procuring cause of the sale. But if the broker had an exclusive right to sell, procuring cause would not enter into the brokerage situation and he would be entitled to his commission regardless of how the sale took place. In the case of an exclusive agency, the broker gets his commission even if the employer hired another broker who actually sold the property, since here the owner broke a contract he made to sell only through this broker.

To establish that he was the procuring cause, the broker can show that he advertised the property, that he introduced the parties, that he was the first to call the purchaser's attention to the property, and that he was continuously engaged in the transaction by correspondence or conversations.

If several brokers were involved and there was a disagreement among the parties after the first broker brought them together and later a second broker came in and got the parties to agree, the second broker is the procuring cause. However, the first broker is a procuring cause if he brought about a substantial agreement and the second broker worked out the details.

[¶3009] National Association of Realtors Multiple Listing Policy

Under the multiple listing policy of the National Association of Realtors, a multiple listing service must not (1) fix, control, recommend, suggest, or maintain commission rates or fees for services to be rendered by members; (2) fix, control, recommend, suggest, or maintain any percentage division of commission or fees between cooperating members or nonmembers; (3) require financial support of multiple listing service operations by any formula based on commission or sale price; (4) require or use any form which establishes or implies the existence of any contractual relationship between the multiple listing service and the client (buyer or seller); (5) make any rule relating to the posting or use of signs; (6) make any rule prohibiting or discouraging cooperation with nonmembers; (7) limit or interfere with the terms of the relationship between a member and his salesmen (Interpretations 16 and 17); (8) prohibit or discourage any member from political participation or activity; (9) make any rule granting blanket consent to a selling member to negotiate with the seller (owner) (Interpretation 10); (10) make any rule regulating the advertising or promotion of any listing; (11) prohibit or discourage a member from accepting a listing from a seller (owner) preferring to give "office exclusive"; (12) adopt any rule denying a listing member from controlling the posting of "sold signs"; (13) refuse any exclusive listing submitted by a member on the basis of the quality or price of the listing; (14) adopt rules authorizing the modification or change of any listing without the express, written permission of the listing member.

In addition, the multiple listing policy provides that Realtors who are members of a multiple listing service which is not affiliated with or owned by a Board of Realtors shall not recognize or adhere to any multiple listing service rule which is contrary to this policy.

[¶3010] National Association of Realtors, Code of Ethics

Part I
Relations to the Public

ARTICLE 1.

The Realtor should keep himself informed as to movements affecting real estate in his community, state, and the nation, so that he may be able to contribute to public thinking on matters of taxation, legislation, land use, city planning, and other questions affecting property interests.

ARTICLE 2.

It is the duty of the Realtor to be well informed on current market conditions in order to be in a position to advise his clients as to the fair market price.

ARTICLE 3.

It is the duty of the Realtor to protect the public against fraud, misrepresentation, or unethical practices in the real estate field. He should endeavor to help stamp out or prevent arising in his community, any practices which could be damaging to the public or to the dignity and integrity of the real estate profession. If there be a board or commission in the state, charged with the duty of regulating the practices of brokers and salesmen, the Realtor should lend every help to such body, cooperate with it, and report violations of proper practice.

ARTICLE 4.

The Realtor should ascertain all pertinent facts concerning every property for which he accepts the agency, so that he may fulfill his obligation to avoid error, exaggeration, misrepresentation, or concealment of pertinent facts.

ARTICLE 5.

The Realtor should not be instrumental in introducing into a neighborhood a character of property or use which will clearly be detrimental to property values in that neighborhood.

ARTICLE 6.

The Realtor should not be a party to the naming of a false consideration in a deed, unless it be the naming of an obviously nominal consideration.

ARTICLE 7.

The Realtor should not engage in activities that constitute the practice of law and should recommend that title be examined and legal counsel be obtained when the interest of either party requires it.

ARTICLE 8.

The Realtor should keep in a special bank account, separated from his own funds, monies coming into his hands in trust for other persons, such as escrows, trust funds, client's monies, and other like items.

ARTICLE 9.

The Realtor in his advertising should be especially careful to present a true picture and should not advertise without disclosing his name or his firm name, nor permit his salesmen to use individual names or telephone numbers, unless the salesman's connection with the Realtor is obvious in the advertisement.

ARTICLE 10.

The Realtor, for the protection of all parties with whom he deals, should see that financial obligations and commitments regarding real estate transactions are in writing, expressing the exact agreement of the parties; and that copies of such agreements, at the time they are executed, are placed in the hands of all parties involved.

Part II
Relations to the Client

ARTICLE 11.

In accepting employment as an agent, the Realtor pledges himself to protect and promote the interests of the client. This obligation of absolute fidelity to the client's interest is primary, and does not relieve the Realtor from the obligation of dealing fairly with all parties to the transaction.

ARTICLE 12.

In justice to those who place their interests in his hands, the Realtor should endeavor always to be informed regarding the law, proposed legislation, legal orders issued, and other essential facts and public policies which affect those interests.

ARTICLE 13.

Since the Realtor is representing one or another party to a transaction, he should not accept compensation from more than one party without the full knowledge of all parties to the transaction.

ARTICLE 14.

The Realtor should not acquire an interest in or buy for himself, his firm or any member thereof, or a corporation in which he has an interest, property listed with him, or his company or firm, without making his true position known to the listing owner. In selling property owned by him, or in which he has some ownership interest, the exact facts should be revealed to the purchaser.

ARTICLE 15.

The exclusive listing of property should be urged and practiced by the Realtor as a means of preventing dissension and misunderstanding and of assuring better service to the owner.

ARTICLE 16.

When acting as agent in the management of property, the Realtor should not accept any commission, rebate, or profit on expenditures made for an owner, without the owner's knowledge and consent.

ARTICLE 17.

The Realtor should charge for his services only such fees as are fair and reasonable, and in accordance with local practice in similar transactions.

ARTICLE 18.

When asked to make a formal appraisal of real property, the Realtor should not render an opinion without careful and thorough analysis and interpretation of all factors affecting the value of the property. His counsel constitutes a professional service for which he should make a fair charge.

The Realtor should not undertake to make an appraisal or render an opinion of value on any property where he has a present or contemplated interest unless such interest is specifically disclosed in the appraisal report. Under no circumstances should he undertake to make a formal appraisal when his employment or fee is contingent upon the amount of his appraisal.

The Realtor should not undertake to make an appraisal that is outside the field of his experience unless he obtains the assistance of a Realtor or appraiser familiar with such types of property, or unless the facts are fully disclosed to the client.

ARTICLE 19.

The Realtor should not submit or advertise property without authority, and in any offering, the price quoted should not be other than that agreed upon with the owners as the offering price.

ARTICLE 20.

In the event that more than one formal offer on a specific property is made before the owner has accepted a proposal, all written offers should be presented to the owner for his decision.

Part III
Relations to His Fellow-Realtor

ARTICLE 21.

The Realtor should seek no unfair advantage over his fellow-Realtors and should willingly share with them the lessons of his experience and study.

ARTICLE 22.

The Realtor should so conduct his business as to avoid controversies with his fellow-Realtors; but, in the event of a controversy between Realtors who are members of the same real estate board, such controversy should be submitted for arbitration in accordance with regulations of their board and not to a suit at law. The decision in such arbitration should be accepted as final and binding.

ARTICLE 23.

Controversies between Realtors who are not members of the same real estate board should be submitted to an arbitration board consisting of one arbitrator chosen by each Realtor from the real estate board to which he belongs. One other member, or a sufficient number of members to make an odd number, should be selected by the arbitrators thus chosen.

ARTICLE 24.

When the Realtor is charged with unethical practice, he should voluntarily place all pertinent facts before the proper tribunal of the real estate board of which he is a member, for investigation and judgment.

ARTICLE 25.

The Realtor should never publicly criticize a competitor, nor volunteer an opinion of a competitor's transaction. If his opinion is sought, it should be rendered with strict professional integrity and courtesy.

ARTICLE 26.

When the Realtor accepts a listing from another broker, the agency of the broker who offers the listing should be respected until it has expired and the property has come to the attention of the accepting Realtor from a different source, or until the owner, without solicitation, offers to list with the accepting Realtor unless contrary to the rules of the local real estate board; furthermore, such a listing should not be passed on to a third broker without the consent of the listing broker.

ARTICLE 27.

The Realtor should cooperate with other Realtors on property listed, sharing commissions on an agreed basis. Negotiations concerning property listed exclusively with one Realtor should be carried on with the listing broker, not with the owner, except with the consent of the listing Realtor.

ARTICLE 28.

The Realtor should not solicit the services of an employee or salesman in the organization of a fellow-Realtor without the knowledge of the employer.

ARTICLE 29.

Signs giving notice of property for sale, rent, lease, or exchange should not be placed on any property by more than one Realtor, and then only if authorized by the owner, except as the property is listed with and authorization given to more than one Realtor.

ARTICLE 30.

In the best interest of society, of his associates, and of his own business, the Realtor should be loyal to the real estate board of his community and active in its work.

Conclusion

The term Realtor has come to connote competence, fair dealing, and high integrity resulting from adherence to a lofty ideal of moral conduct in business relations. No inducement of profit and no instructions from clients ever can justify departure from this ideal, or from the injunctions of this Code.

[¶3100] LEASING

Here, we set forth the main considerations that should be reflected in negotiating a lease of property.

[¶3101] What Kind of Rent?

We have these possibilities:

(1) *Flat rental* calling for a uniform rate throughout the term.

(2) *A step-up lease* that provides for a gradually increased amount of rent, to step up at specified intervals.

(3) *Net lease* where the tenant agrees to pay a fixed rent plus all the expenses of carrying the property, i.e., real estate taxes, fire, public liability, and other hazard insurance, repairs, etc. (Keep in mind that under the tax law, interest payments incurred by individuals, Subchapter S corporations, and holding companies for an investment in property leased under a net lease come within the provisions under which excess investment interest incurred by individuals, partners, and members of Subchapter S corporations, but not regular corporations is treated as tax-preference income and is subject to a limitation on its deductibility.)

(4) *Expense participating lease* where the tenant pays a fixed basic rent and a specified portion of the real estate taxes, insurance, and repairs other than those of a structural nature that would normally fall on the landlord.

(5) *Escalator lease* where the tenant assumes the obligation to meet all or a specified proportion of increases in taxes and other operating costs.

(6) *Re-evaluation lease* that calls for an appraisal of the property and a fixing of the rent as a percentage of the reappraised value at specified intervals.

(7) *Cost-of-living lease* where the initial rent is fixed and revised upward or downward at specified intervals depending on the fluctuation of the dollar as revealed by price indices or other agreed measures of the degree of inflation or deflation that has occurred.

[¶3102] Percentage Leases

Percentage leases usually provide for a minimum fixed rent plus a percentage of the tenant's gross income over and above this minimum.

The types of percentage leases are:

(1) Fixed minimum rent with percentage of gross added to minimum.

(2) Fixed minimum rent with additional rent based on percentage of gross

being payable only after the applicable percentage applying to the gross has earned the minimum.

(3) Percentage lease with no minimum.

(4) Minimum rent plus the percentage with a maximum rent that the percentage may produce.

Where the percentage is the most important part of the deal, it is usual to have a clause giving the landlord the right to cancel after a specified period of time if the tenant's business fails to attain an agreed on minimum volume of sales. This minimum volume may be stepped up periodically. The tenant may be given the right to keep the lease in force by paying the rental that would have been produced by the stipulated minimum volume. The tenant is sometimes given the right to cancel if his volume fails to attain a stated minimum.

[¶3103] Security Deposits

Here are the main security devices that landlords use to obtain protection against a tenant's abandonment of the property, nonpayment of rent, or other default.

(1) The tenant is required to deposit money or securities with the landlord. Should interest be paid to the tenant on this deposit? If the tenant abandons the property or is evicted for a default in rent, the lease provision authorizes the landlord to relet the premises and to collect any damages out of this security deposit.

(2) The tenant makes a security deposit and the lease provides that the amount so deposited is to be retained by the landlord as liquidated damages if the tenant abandons or defaults.

(3) The tenant is required to pay a bonus for obtaining a lease, and the landlord is entitled to this money whether or not the tenant fulfills his obligation under the lease. Sometimes the tenant is given credit for this bonus by reduced rentals at the end of the lease term.

(4) The lease requires the tenant to pay the last several months' rent in advance. If the tenant abandons the premises or is evicted for default in rent, the lease permits the landlord to retain the advance rents.

[¶3104] Tax Consequences to Landlord of Payments, Deposits, Improvements, and Alterations

Advance Rents and Security Deposits: A cash-basis lessor reports taxable income from rents and advance rentals in the year of receipt. An accrual-basis lessor also reports such income when received (Reg. §1.61-8(b)).

Example: Smith entered into a lease with Jones, the lessee. The lease is to run for 10 years. The yearly rental is $2,000. On signing the lease, Jones pays Smith $4,000—two years' rent. The $4,000 is income to Smith in the year received (signing of lease). The fact that Smith is an accrual-basis taxpayer does not change the results.

Note that an amount paid by the buyer for assignment of a lease is income to the seller in the year received. It is deemed an advance rental, the parties being lessor and lessee (*Rev. Rul. 57-537,* CB 1957-2, 52).

Bonuses, like advance rentals, are includible in the lessor's income in the year received, regardless of his method of accounting. See *Pembroke*, 70 F.2d 850.

A contingency providing for the refund of the advance rental on certain conditions will not mean any different treatment to the landlord. He still must include the advance rental when received (*New Capital Hotel, Inc.,* 28 TC 706).

A security deposit, unlike an advance rental, is not taxable on receipt. This is so even though the money is deposited with the lessor who has temporary use of it (*Mantell,* 17 TC 1143). Of course, a security deposit will become income if and when appropriated by the lessor because of rent default or for some other reason.

The difference between an advance rental and a security deposit is essentially this: An advance rental is money that belongs to the landlord. It's his to do with as he wishes. A security deposit, on the other hand, is not the landlord's property. It is like money in trust to be paid to the landlord only on certain conditions such as a default in rent. That is why escrow arrangements are often used in this area. If the security money is given to the landlord, he acts as a fiduciary and must account to the tenant. He (the landlord) does not own these funds.

While the landlord may be able to get the interest that the security money earns, this interest is taxable to him even though the security deposit itself is not taxable income to him. In some states there are statutes which expressly make the landlord a trustee of the security deposit and make him accountable for the interest earned on the security.

If you wish to get security deposit treatment, avoid provisions which apply the security deposit to the last month's rent. This is simply an advance rental (*August,* 17 TC 1165).

Payments to Acquire a Leasehold: Generally, the problem of handling the costs involved in acquiring leaseholds is that of the tenant, but it can also apply to the landlord. This is especially true in arrangements involving ground leases or where the landlord is both lessee and lessor under a subleasing agreement.

In amortizing costs of acquiring leases where there are renewal options, the costs can be spread over the life of the original lease where 75% or more of the cost is attributable to the unexpired lease period (exclusive of the renewal periods). Suppose, however, that the lease has been renewed or can reasonably be expected to be renewed. Then, the renewal period will be taken into account even though the 75%-test is met (§178).

Net Lease Payments: Generally, if the lessee pays the expenses of his landlord, such payments are considered rent and income to the landlord (Reg. §1.61-8(c)). There is, in effect, a washout if the tenant pays these expenses. For instance, suppose the tenant paid $5,000 in real estate taxes for you, as per the lease. You get this $5,000 in your rental income, but it is deductible by you as an expense (taxes). You are deemed to have received the money as rent and then paid your tax bill. So, the result is a washout.

How to Handle Improvements: Another phase of the lessor's tax problems deals with improvements. Improvements made by the lessor are generally capital expenditures and not deductible (§263(a)). It may be advisable to have the lessee make the improvement in return for a smaller rent. Improvements by the lessee are not included in the lessor's taxable income if they are not rent (§109), nor is the lessor's basis affected thereby (§1019). In this way, the lessor realizes no income when the improvement is made, nor does he realize income at the termination of the lease (§109). At the same time, the rental value may subsequently increase as a result of the improvement. On subsequent sale, any gain resulting directly from the lessee's improvement will be taxable at more favorable capital gain rates. The rental should be reasonable rather than no rent or radically reduced rent, and there should be no intimation in the lease that the lessee's improvement will be considered rent—otherwise the lessee's improvement may be construed as immediately taxable income to the lessor as rent paid in kind (*IT 4009,* CB 1950-1, 13).

Whether improvements are deemed rent is up to the intent of the parties. If they intended that the lessee's improvements shall be in lieu of rent or as a substitute for rent, it will be rental income to the lessor. Their intent will be seen from the terms of the lease and the surrounding circumstances.

Depreciating Improvements: Depreciation on improvements poses another problem. The lessor depreciates improvements existing when the lease was entered into, as well as improvements made by the lessee as a condition of the lease (*Alaska Realty Co.,* CA-6, 141 F.2d 675). But the lessee depreciates improvements he makes on his own. Neither the lessor nor the lessee may depreciate improvements made by the lessee pursuant to a requirement that the lessee return the realty unimpaired and in its original condition (*Georgia Ry. & El. Co.*, CA-5, 77 F.2d 897, *Cert. den.* 296 US 601), but the lessee is entitled to a deduction for the expense of making the restoration improvements in the taxable year that the expense was either incurred or paid (*Frank & Seder Co.,* CA-3, 44 F.2d 147). However, the lessor can get the depreciation deduction during the lease term to offset rent income by providing in the lease that the lessee return the property in its original condition *except for ordinary wear and tear or exhaustion.*

Lease with Option to Purchase: At the very outset, a lease containing an option to purchase must be scrutinized with great care. While the lease may describe the tenant's payments as rent, the details of the transaction may indicate they are really installments paid on a deferred purchase of the property. The law permits rentals to be deducted only if they are paid for property to which the taxpayer has not taken or is not taking title, or in which he has no equity (Code §162; *Berry*, 52 TCM 271). If it is a purchase, the tenant must capitalize the payments and take deductions in the form of depreciation.

Similarly, under a deferred purchase, the lessor doesn't get rent income but a return of capital and capital gain or loss (unless he is a dealer in which event he has ordinary income or loss).

Example: Evans, who is not a dealer, enters into a 10-year lease with an option-to-purchase agreement with Black, the lessee. The rent is $10,000 a year. At the end of the tenth year, Black has the option of buying the property for $5,000. Evans's adjusted basis for the property is $60,000. A court may find that this is not a lease with an option but an installment sale. The $105,000 is not rental income to Evans. $60,000 is a return of capital. $45,000 is capital gain.

There is no statutory provision to tell you when a lease with an option to purchase becomes an installment sale. However, the cases in the field give you some rules of thumb. The important considerations are the amount of rent called for in relation to the fair rental value of the property and a comparison of the "rent" with the option purchase price. See *Berry,* 52 TCM 271; *Haggard,* 241 F.2d 288.

Some examples of lease-option arrangements that were deemed sales include: a rental of $680,000 payable over a 68-year period with an option to buy for $10 at the end of the lease term (*Oesterreich*, CA-9, 226 F. 2d 798, 1955; *Wilshire Holding*, 288 F. 2d 799); a 10-year lease calling for annual rent of $19,000 with an option to purchase at the end of the lease at $75,000—the annual "rent" being more than 25% of the "purchase" price, the Court concluded a sale was intended (*Elliot*, CA-9, 262 F.2d 383, 1959).

But the Ninth Circuit now agrees that in such a lease-option agreement not all the "rent" is necessarily payment of principal. Part may be interest on the unpaid balance of principal. In the *Wilshire* case, the Ninth Circuit determined that the maximum interest rate allowed by the state—12% —should be used to find what part of the rental paid was really interest.

Payments for Cancellation of a Lease: If the tenant pays a lump sum to the landlord in order to cancel the lease, the payment is a deductible expense in the year paid. The landlord must report the payment as ordinary income in the year received, since it is regarded as rent (Reg. §1.61-8(b); *Hort*, 313 US 28).

Where there is a security deposit and the landlord receives that in payment for canceling the lease, the security deposit will generally be discounted for tax purposes (*Bradford Hotel Operating Co.,* 244 F. 2d 876). For instance, suppose that in 1974 the landlord-taxpayer and the lessee enter into a lease for 35 years. The security deposit given to the landlord is $250,000. At the end of three years, in 1977, the lessee decides to cancel the lease. The landlord-taxpayer and the lessee enter into an agreement whereby the lessee will receive $65,000 of the $250,000 which was to be repaid the tenant at the conclusion of 35 years. The agreement provides that the payment of $65,000 will release the landlord from any further repayment of the security deposit. The remaining $185,000 which goes to the landlord is not all taxable income in 1977, but merely the present value in 1977 of the $185,000 due in 2009.

Landlord's Waiver of Rent for Cancellation of Lease: If the landlord makes a cash payment to the tenant in order to cancel the lease and obtain immediate possession of the property, the payment is not immediately deductible but must be amortized. If the landlord waives rent that is past due and unpaid, this is treated the same as if the rent had been collected and then a cash payment had been made to the tenant (*Cosmopolitan Corp.,* TC Memo 1959-122). The tenant is entitled to treat payments for cancellation of a lease as capital gain, taxable in the year of receipt (§1241). The period over which the landlord must amortize the cancellation payments will depend on his intention when he makes the payment and on what he actually ends up doing with the property.

Landlord's Own Use: If the landlord cancels the lease so he can use the property himself, then he amortizes the cancellation payment over the unexpired term of the lease (see *Berger,* 7 TC 1339).

New Building: If the landlord demolishes the old building and puts up a new one that he rents to a new tenant, then the courts disagree over the period during which the cancellation payments must be deducted. Ordinarily, taxpayers have been required to amortize the cancellation payment over the life of the new building (since the old lease is canceled with a view to its construction) rather than over the remaining years of the canceled lease. But the *Cosmopolitan* case, supra, said that the cancellation payment should be deducted over the life of the 50-year lease given on the new building. The old lease was canceled and the land was leased to a new tenant who then put up a new building. But in a case where the owner maintains control of the new building and makes leases with different tenants, it is hard to see this case applying. He'd probably have to amortize over the life of the new building.

New Lease: If instead of constructing a new building the owner makes a new long-term lease, his cancellation payments are probably deductible over the term of the new lease, rather than the shorter, unexpired term of the old lease.

How to Handle Rent-Free and Bargain-Rental Apartments: Giving an apartment rent free or at a bargain rent can create tax problems for both landlord and tenant. So, you have to plan carefully to get the tax results you want.

When There's a Gift: When an apartment is given rent free (especially when the building is owned by an individual and the apartment is given to a relative), the landlord can lose a portion of his deduction for maintenance and operating costs of his building. *Reason:* The Treasury says he's no longer in the business of renting as to the apartment occupied rent free. So a proportionate part of his expenses is disallowed (see *Walet, Jr.*, 31 TC 461, *aff'd* CA-5, 272 F.2d 694, 1960).

Apartment as Compensation: If you can show that the use of the apartment is given as compensation for services rendered, the landlord does not lose any part of his maintenance and operating expenses. The landlord probably has rental income equal to the rental value of the apartment and an offsetting deduction for compensation paid; so, there's a washout. The tenant, of course, has compensation income. But within a family, if the tenant's tax bracket is lower than the landlord's, this could be a method to shift income.

Stockholder-Tenants: Where a corporation owns the building and a stockholder lives in one of the apartments at a bargain rental, the courts have looked to see if the stockholder performs services. If he does, the difference between the going rental for a similar apartment and lesser rental paid by the stockholder is taxed as compensation (*Peacock,* 256 F.2d 160; *Richards,* 111 F.2d 376; *Chandler*, 119 F.2d 623; *Dean*, 187 F.2d 1019).

Where there is no compensation, the courts have never said there was a dividend. But the Treasury has taken that position. It says the bargain portion of the rent is a dividend where the apartment is occupied by a stockholder (*Rev. Rul. 58-1*, CB 1958-1, 173).

[¶3105] Tax Consequences to Tenant of Payments, Deposits, Improvements, and Alterations

Lessee's Deductions: Periodic rent payments made by the lessee for business property are fully deductible (§162(a)(3)). This is subject to the general limitation that all business expenses must be "ordinary and necessary expenditures" (Reg. §1.162-1(a)). Rent for a private residence is not deductible; but if a professional man actually uses part of his residence as an office, he may deduct the portion of his rent that is attributable to his office (Reg. §1.262-1(b)(3)).

When Can You Deduct Rent? Only that part of the rent allocable to the year is deductible. This is true for both cash-basis and accrual-basis taxpayers. This means that you cannot prepay rent and take the entire deduction in the year of payment (*Baton Coal*, 19 BTA 169).

Example: Smith, a cash-basis taxpayer, has a 10-year lease calling for rent of $5,000 a year. In 1975, the first year of the lease, Smith has a particularly high income for the year, so he prepays five years' rent ($25,000). He may only deduct $5,000 in that year. The rest must be deducted ratably over the next four years.

A Payment by the Tenant May or May Not Be Rent for Tax Deduction Purposes: If the lease calls for you to pay the taxes (or other expenses) on the property, the taxes that you pay are deductible as rent (Reg. §1.162-11). Taxes are deductible in the year paid as a current business expense, but payments for local improvements are amortized over the lease period (*IT 2164*, CB IV-1, 34).

If both the lessee and the lessor are corporations, federal income taxes paid by the lessee for the lessor are not deductible if the lease was entered into before January 1, 1954, or is a renewal or continuation pursuant to an option contained in such a lease on December 31, 1953. Not only are the taxes paid by the lessee for the lessor not deductible, they are also not deductible by the lessee nor taxable to the lessor (§110).

If you pay part or all of your rent in property, the amount deductible is the fair market value of the property.

Payment in Services: You can pay your rent in services, and can deduct the amount of rental agreed on if it is reasonable. (The value of such services is included in your gross income.)

Prepayments Made by the Lessee of Business Property: Regardless of whether the lessor treats these as advance rentals or security deposits, they are capitalized by the lessee and deducted in the years to which they apply (*Boston & Providence R. Corp.*, CA-1, 37 F.2d 670). Similarly, the lessee capitalizes bonus payments and amortizes the deduction over the remaining lease period (Reg. §1.162-11). This applies to bonuses paid by the lessee for modifications or extensions of the lease. A bonus to cancel the lease is deductible in full in the year of payment as a current business expense. On the other hand, a bonus paid by the lessor to the lessee for the surrender of the lease is treated as a capital gain by the lessee.

Improvements: Improvements made by the lessee are not deductible since they are considered capital expenditures. The lessee recovers his improvement expenses by amortizing them over their useful lives or over the lease period, whichever is shorter (Reg. §1.167(a)(4)). In some cases, however, improvements made by a tenant instead of paying rent may be deducted by the tenant. It depends on the intent of the parties (*IT 4009,* CB 1950-1, 13).

Renewal periods are to be taken into account in determining the period over which amortization is to take place if the initial term of the lease remaining upon the completion of the improvements is less than 60% of the useful life of the improvements. Even if you do not meet the 60% rule, you can still amortize over the initial term if you can establish that, as of the taxable year of the improvements, it is more probable that the lease will not be renewed than that it will (§178(a)).

Example: You put up a building on property you lease. The building has a 35-year life. The lease has 21 years to run, with a renewal option of 10 years. Since the 21-year original term is 60% of the 35-year life of the building, you can write off your building cost over 21 years, unless there is a reasonable certainty you'll renew the lease.

Example: You put up an improvement with a 30-year life on a leasehold having a remaining term of 15 years with a 20-year renewal period. The 15-year remaining term is only 50% of the life of the improvement. So, you have to use the combined terms of the lease (35 years) in your computation. Since the building's life of 30 years is less than the combined term, you depreciate over the 30-year period. However, you can still use the 15-year period if you can prove it is more probable that you will not renew the lease than that you will.

If the lessor and lessee are related persons, the improvements must be amortized over their remaining useful life without regard to the terms of the lease (§178(b)).

Related persons include:

(1) Spouse, ancestors, and lineal descendants.

(2) An individual and a corporation, more than 80% of the stock of which is owned by that individual.

(3) Two corporations if more than 80% of the stock of each is owned by the same individual and one of the corporations is a personal holding company or a foreign personal holding company.

(4) A grantor and a fiduciary of any trust.

(5) A fiduciary of a trust and a fiduciary of another trust if the same person is a grantor of both trusts.

(6) A fiduciary and beneficiary of the same trust.

(7) A fiduciary of a trust and a beneficiary of another trust if the same person is a grantor of both trusts.

(8) A fiduciary of a trust and a corporation if more than 80% of the stock of the corporation is owned by the trust or by the grantor of the trust.

(9) A person and a tax-exempt organization (one qualifying under §501) if the person controls the organization or members of his family do.

(10) Corporations of an affiliated group which are eligible for filing a consolidated return.

Maintenance by the Lessee: Occasionally, a lease will require the lessee to replace, repair, or otherwise maintain leased furnishings and equipment. This kind of clause is most prevalent with hotels. You can deduct the cost of replacements as a current expense if the replaced items have relatively short lives and similar expenditures can be expected in subsequent years of the lease (*Illinois Central Ry.*, 90 F.2d 458).

Cost of Acquiring a Lease: The cost of acquiring a lease is to be amortized over the life of the lease. Prior to July 29, 1958, the amortization was to take place over the life of the lease regardless of any renewal period unless it was probable that the lease would be renewed (Reg. §1.162-11).

If you obtained your lease after July 28, 1958, and if less than 75% of the cost is attributable to the initial term of the lease remaining on the date of acquisition, you must take into account the renewal period as well as the remaining initial period for the purposes of amortization (§178(a)). This rule will not apply if you can show that it is more probable than not that the lease will not be renewed.

Example: You pay $10,000 to acquire a lease for 20 years with two options to renew for 5 years each. Of the cost $8,000 is allocable to acquiring the original 20-year term. You can write the $10,000 off over the 20-year period, unless there is a reasonable certainty that you will renew.

Example: Same as above, but only $7,000 is paid for the original 20-year term. You have to write off the $10,000 over the full possible 30-year term, unless you can show that it is more probable that you will not renew than you will.

Amount Paid by Lessee for Cancellation of a Lease: If you pay a sum to your lessor to cancel your lease, this amount will be a deductible expense in the year paid (*Denholm and McKay Co.,* 2 BTA 444).

Excessive Rents: You can lease property from a member of your family or a corporation that you control and will be able to deduct the rent you pay. However, if the rent is excessive, as much of the rent as is excessive (beyond what another would pay) will be disallowed. In *Jolly's Motor Livery Co.,* TC Memo 1957-231, the Tax Court disallowed part of the rent paid by a corporation to the controlling stockholder's son. The rent was disallowed to the extent that it was unreasonable. See also *Kamen Soap Products Co.,* TC Memo 1956-157, and *Utter McKinley Mortuaries,* 225 F.2d 870. Note, however, that where there is no evidence of a gift or a dividend, rent is paid or incurred during the taxable year and there is an arm's-length transaction, the rent deduction is not limited to a reasonable allowance (*Imerman,* 7 TC 1030). When rent is based on a percentage of profits, it is deductible if the percentage was reasonable when the lease was entered into even if the amount paid in any one year might not be reasonable if that year stood by itself (*Brown Printing Co.,* 255 F.2d 436, 1958).

How to Get Capital Gain on Sale of Lease: When a lease is sold back to the lessor or to a third party, you get a capital gain. Suppose, however, it's the sublessee who pays for the lease transfer to the lessor. Then, said the Tax Court, the payment is really a settlement of rent due under the sublease and taxable as ordinary income. But the Ninth Circuit reversed that case and allows capital gain (*Metropolitan Building Co.,* 282 F.2d 592).

Make Sure You Assign the Lease–Not Sublet–If You Want a Capital Gain: Many people who own profitable leases sell to get some of their future income as capital gain.

If you assign the lease and step out of the picture entirely, what you receive for selling the lease is taxable as capital gain. But if you merely sublet—even for the balance of term of the lease—what you receive is rent and fully taxable as ordinary income.

For example, in a Tax Court case, the lessee agreed to sublet the premises for the balance of the lease term. A new agreement among all three parties requiring the sublessee to make monthly payments to landlord (equivalent approximately to the rent originally called for) and additional payments to the lessee was drawn up. The monthly payments alone distinguish this case from cases where lump-sum payments were held to be capital gain, said the Tax Court. In addition, there was no indication that the landlord released the lessee from any liability as tenant under the original lease. Also, the lessee retained the right of re-entry should the sublessee break any conditions of the new agreement. All these circumstances point to a sublease, not a sale of the lease. Hence, payments received are taxable as rent (*Voloudakis,* 29 TC 1101).

The case was appealed to the Ninth Circuit and that Court agreed (274 F.2d 209) with the Tax Court.

[¶3106] Chart Showing Tax Consequences to Landlord and Tenant of Important Lease Provisions

Here, we give you a handy chart from which you can tell at a glance what the tax consequences both to landlord and tenant of payments, deposits, improvements, and alterations by landlord and tenant are.

	Effect on Landlord	*Effect on Tenant*
Deposit of security by tenant	No immediate tax effect on landlord or tenant if deposit is properly restricted. If forfeited, it is treated for tax purposes the same as a payment of the obligation for which it is forfeited would have been treated.	
Payment by tenant to renew	Rental income to landlord.	Cost of renewed lease amortizable by tenant over life of lease.
Payment by tenant to modify	Rental income to landlord.	Cost of modified lease amortizable by tenant over life of lease.
Payment of broker's commission by tenant	None.	Amount amortizable by tenant over life of lease. In case of premature cancellation of lease, amount not recovered deductible in year of cancellation.

	Effect on Landlord	*Effect on Tenant*
Payment of broker's commission by landlord	Amount amortizable by landlord over life of lease. If lease prematurely canceled, amount not recovered deductible in year of cancellation.	None.
Payment of bonus by tenant to landlord for lease	Taxable when received by landlord as additional rental income.	Amortizable by tenant over life of lease.
Advanced payment of rent by tenant	Additional rental income to landlord.	Amortizable by tenant over life of lease.
Payment by landlord to cancel	Amortizable over life of lease. If made for purpose of selling premises, amount of payment is added to basis of property for purpose of figuring gain on sale.	Amount is received by tenant as realized on sale or exchange of lease and reportable as capital gain.
Payment by tenant to cancel	Additional rental income to landlord.	Deductible by tenant as rent.
Payment of taxes, interest, insurance, and operating costs by tenant	Additional rental income to landlord.	Deductible as rent by tenant.
Payment of special assessments on property by tenant	Additional rental income to landlord.	Deductible by tenant over life of lease.
Payment of debt against property by tenant	Additional rental income to landlord.	Deductible as rent payment by tenant when paid.

	Effect on Landlord	*Effect on Tenant*
Capital alterations to premises by tenant	If intended as rent, it is rental income to landlord when improvements are made.	Deductible by tenant as rent when improvements are made.
Alteration of premises by landlord for tenant	Landlord can take depreciation deductions for improvements. Cost is amortizable by landlord over life of lease if improvements are suitable only for tenant.	None.
Installation of trade fixtures by tenant	None.	Tenant may take depreciation deductions over useful life of trade fixtures.
Permanent improvements by tenant not intended as rent	Not income to landlord when improvements are made or when lease terminates.	Tenant may take depreciation deductions over useful life of improvements or over life of lease whichever is shorter.
Restoration of premises by tenant at end of lease term	Landlord cannot deduct depreciation in improvements to leasehold unless agreement provides that tenant's duty to restore does not include restoration made necessary by ordinary wear and tear.	Cost is deductible by tenant when restoration is made.

[¶3200] PROPERTY MANAGEMENT

Real estate management, simply defined, is the effort of the owner or his agent to maximize the income from property by (1) preserving the physical desirability of the property (checking for ways to prevent economic depreciation, studying and anticipating functional obsolescence, being alert to interior and exterior maintenance needs) and (2) maintaining high standards of service to tenants (being conscious of tenant and public goodwill, valuing the reputation and appearance of a building, being alert to extending services that will be appreciated by tenants).

[¶3201] Important Management Duties

(1) Planning the rent schedule. (2) Finding tenants who can meet the schedule. (3) Qualifying the tenants by a thorough credit investigation. (4) Preparing the lease and having it executed. (5) Preparing specifications for decorating, securing estimates, awarding the contract, and supervising the work. (6) Hiring, instructing and maintaining satisfactory personnel to staff the building. (7) Purchasing all supplies necessary for the operation of the building. (8) Auditing and paying bills. (9) Advertising and publicizing vacant space through selected media and broker lists. (10) Planning alterations and modernizing programs. (11) Inspecting vacant space frequently and periodically. (12) Keeping abreast of the times and posted on competitive market conditions. (13) Maintaining a complete system of records available for immediate reference. (14) Preparing accurate and periodic statements and a complete accounting of all funds handled. (15) Paying insurance premiums and taxes and recommending tax appeals when warranted.

[¶3202] How to Maximize Your Rental Returns

The major aim in managing investment property is to fill the space with desirable tenants who will pay the highest possible rents. Securing maximum rents is the result of careful planning. A leasing program requires decisions on the following matters: (1) what rents to charge; (2) the terms of the lease; (3) the selection of tenants; (4) means of obtaining tenants —advertising, brokers, etc.; and (5) means of insuring tenant goodwill.

You must watch costs. If too much is spent on advertising and other sales costs, the net return from the property is reduced. The problem is to sell skillfully.

[¶3203] How to Determine the Rent Schedule

In preparing a rent schedule, the first step is to ascertain the competitive situation. This involves a survey of the area which makes up your zone of competition to find out (a) how much space is vacant; (b) the rentals being charged; (c) terms of leases and concessions allowed to tenants. In making comparisons, be sure to take into consideration any differences (for better or worse) between other space and your own. This includes such things as age of the building, any prestige element, distance to transportation, and so forth.

After making the survey, you then select a ''base rate floor''—often the middle floor of your building. The square foot rental, or rent per room, for this space is fixed on the basis of your analysis of the market. Rentals for all other space in the building are then determined as a percentage of the base floor rate. For example, each higher floor might be increased 1%, with a further premium for corner suites or other desirable features. In this way, a rental schedule for the entire building is established.

[¶3204] How to Direct Your Efforts in Maintaining Income

(1) Preserve the physical desirability of the property: Check for the possibilities to cure depreciation; study and anticipate functional obsolescence; be alert to interior and exterior maintenance needs.

(2) Stress servicing of tenants: This function of management is vital. Service has to be good to attract tenants and you have to keep it that way to hold them. Be conscious of tenant and public goodwill; value reputation and appearance of the building; handle deliveries and visitor contacts with patience; in an apartment house, for example, within cost limitation, provide trouble-free heat, water, light and power, telephone and gas; be alert to extend those services that will be well received by tenants.

[¶3205] How to Meet the Rental Market

The manager, under the owner's guidance and authority, must constantly adapt his rents and the money he spends to operate and improve the property to the local demand for space. His compromise with the market will be some combination of these steps: (1) obtaining additional capital with which to make the property more productive; (2) adding certain tenant services to be rendered at a profit; (3) convincing the owner that he should be satisfied with a smaller return on his investment; (4) withdrawing certain services no longer required by the tenants; (5) lowering the maintenance standards; (6)

changing the character of tenantry; (7) developing a better balanced rental schedule through the base-rate method, thereby decreasing the percentage of vacancies in certain locations.

[¶3206] How to Choose a Property Manager

Many property owners make it a practice to use a professional property manager to handle all their investment real estate. A manager works on a commission basis, figured on a percentage of gross income plus an additional percentage for obtaining tenants.

The professional organization of management men is the Institute of Real Estate Management. Those meeting its requirements and accepted to membership are authorized to identify themselves by the designation CPM, meaning "Certified Property Manager."

The Institute also has a procedure for designating as an "Accredited Management Organization" those management agencies which meet its established standards of ability and integrity.

[¶3207] Management Agreement Checklist

The terms of a management contract should be reduced to writing and spelled out in sufficient detail so that the understanding of the parties is made clear and costly disputes are avoided. The actual terms of the contract will, of course, depend on a variety of factors including the number and the type of properties which are the subject of the contract and the fee or commission the manager is to receive for his services. The following basic points are applicable to all management contracts:

(1) Term of Management Agreement: Original contract should be drawn for one or more years, as can be agreed on, and the original contract should provide for a continuance thereafter from month to month. The original contract period goes by quickly, and rather than take the natural easy way out and operate thereafter without a contract, which is not advisable, continuance on a month-to-month basis is a sound procedure to follow.

(2) State Specific Services in Detail: The contract should state in detail the specific services to be rendered. Items to be covered are: (a) The Agent agrees to use due diligence in the management of the property and agrees to furnish the services of his organization for the renting, leasing, operating, and managing of the property; (b) the agreement states which employees the Agent shall provide. There then can be no question as to payment of and control over wages for the various employees. The Agent should be responsible for the acts of his own employees; (c) The Agent should be given authority to make contracts for electricity, gas, fuel, water, telephone, window cleaning, ash or rubbish hauling and such other services as the Agent shall deem advisable.

*(3) **Special Bank Account:*** Provide that all monies shall be deposited in a special trust bank account selected by the Owner, separate from the Agent's personal account and that the Agent shall not be responsible for acts, bankruptcy, or failure of the banking institution. The Agent's employees who handle or are responsible for the Owner's monies shall be bonded by a fidelity bond.

*(4) **Expenditures by Agent:*** Limit authorization of the Agent as to expenditures he can make without the consent of the Owner, except in cases of emergency, or monthly, or recurring operating charges. This is important because it gives confidence to the Owner in the knowledge that the Agent will be required to consult him before making large expenditures. The amount stated as the limit which the Agent can spend without specific consent will vary with the size of the property and the degree of control the Owner wants to retain over the property.

*(5) **Maintaining Records and Furnishing Statements:*** The Agent shall maintain proper records and furnish such statements as may be required by the Owner as to all collections and disbursements. The Agent shall, on or before the 10th day of each month, render to the Owner a statement, in such form as shall be required, of the operations for the preceding month accompanied by a remittance of the balance owing by the Agent to the Owner. The Agent should see that statements go out at the agreed time. This gives the Owner confidence and makes it easier to secure the Owner's signature when renewal time comes. In the event the disbursements are in excess of the rents collected by the Agent the Owner should pay such excess promptly upon demand of the Agent.

*(6) **Assistance in Reducing Tax Assessments:*** Agent shall check assessments and render the Owner assistance in reducing tax assessments. Have it clear whether a charge is to be made for this service.

*(7) **Agent Cooperation with Other Brokers:*** Provide that Agent will cooperate with other brokers. This assures the Owner that he will get the broadest possible market and that he will not be responsible for two commissions if an outside broker finds a tenant for vacant space.

*(8) **Insurance Should Also Protect Agent:*** Provide adequate public liability, elevator liability, workmen's compensation, and steam boiler insurance with policies which shall, to the extent possible, protect the Agent as well as the Owner. It costs the Owner nothing to have the Agent's name included in the policy. In most cases, if suit is instituted, the Agent is joined as a party defendant.

*(9) **Payment for Advertising:*** The agreement should clearly state who is to pay for various types of advertising. The Owner should not be charged for institutional type advertising. However, the Agent should undertake the basic obligation to advertise the availability for rental of the premises and to display signs thereon.

*(10) **Reports on Rental Market:*** To make certain that your lease terms are attractive the manager should maintain and report information as to the following: (a) customary duration of leases in area; (b) the prevailing practices in granting concession; (c) prevailing rentals.

[¶3208] Code of Professional Ethics for Institute of Real Estate Management

PREAMBLE

The objective of this Professional Code is the continuing enhancement of professional performance by Certified Property Managers through acceptance and conformance with those procedures that are the necessary elements of a mutually beneficial relationship between the Certified Property Manager, his fellow CPMs, his fellow Realtors, his clients, his employers, and the public at large.

A CPM shall be bound by the following professional Pledge:

"I pledge myself to the advancement of professional property management through the mutual efforts of members of the Institute of Real Estate Management and by any other proper means available to me.

"I pledge myself to seek and maintain an equitable, honorable and cooperative association with fellow members of the Institute and with all others who may become a part of my business and professional life.

"I pledge myself to place honesty, integrity and industriousness above all else; to pursue my gainful efforts with diligent study and dedication to the end that service to my clients shall always be maintained at the highest possible level.

"I pledge myself to comply with the principles and declarations of the Institute of Real Estate Management as set forth in its Bylaws, Regulations and this Code of Professional Ethics."

ARTICLE I

The Code of Ethics of the National Association of Real Estate Boards as in effect from time to time is incorporated into this code by reference.

ARTICLE II

A CPM shall not use or permit the use of the CPM designation in any manner that shall adversely affect the objectives or high purposes of the Institute of Real Estate Management.

ARTICLE III

A CPM shall not make, or authorize, or otherwise encourage any oral or written statements of a derogatory nature concerning another CPM or his business practices.

ARTICLE IV

Section 1: A CPM shall neither in his own behalf nor for others solicit the services of any employee known to be under the supervision of another CPM without prior knowledge by the other member.

Section 2: A CPM shall not offer his services to the client of another CPM whose services have heretofore been satisfactory, by basing his solicitation on the inducement of a reduced management fee.

ARTICLE V

A CPM shall not accept association with or employment by an individual, partnership, group or other organization unless to the best of his knowledge and belief such organization complies with all applicable governmental laws, ordinances, rules and regulations and with this code of professional ethics.

ARTICLE VI

A CPM shall at all times be loyal to his clients, and shall be diligent in the maintenance and protection of their reputations and properties.

ARTICLE VII

A CPM shall not represent divergent or conflicting interests, nor engage in any activity reasonably calculated to be contrary to the best interests of his client or client's property unless the clients have been previously notified.

ARTICLE VIII

A CPM shall not receive directly or indirectly any rebate, fee, commission, discount or other benefit, whether monetary or otherwise, without the full knowledge and prior consent of the client concerned.

ARTICLE IX

A CPM shall not disclose to a third party confidential information concerning the business or personal affairs of his clients without prior authorization, except upon legal demands by competent governmental authority.

ARTICLE X

A CPM shall keep his clients currently advised in all matters concerning their respective properties or welfare. A CPM shall cause to be furnished to each client at agreed intervals a complete regular accounting in respect to the operation of that client's properties.

ARTICLE XI

A CPM shall exert due diligence for the protection of clients' funds against all foreseeable contigencies. The deposit of such funds in account with a reputable banking institute shall constitute due diligence.

ARTICLE XII

A CPM shall at all times keep and maintain accurate accounting records, properly marked for identification concerning the properties managed for each client, and such records shall be available for inspection at all reasonable times by each respective client.

ARTICLE XIII

The interpretation of compliance with this professional code is the responsibility of the Ethics and Discipline Committee of the Institute of Real Estate Management. Disciplinary action for violation of any portion of this code shall be instituted by the Governing Council of IREM in accordance with rules and regulations established by that Governing Council and approved by the membership.

[¶3300] LAND DEVELOPMENT

The acquisition, subdivision, improvement, and sale of land are fraught with difficult, practical, legal, and tax problems. Picking the right land is the first problem.

[¶3301] Location

Upper-priced subdivisions can usually be found on the outer ring of the city. Ordinarily, successive developments have occurred beyond existing ones. You will therefore find that, as a practical matter, any high-priced residential development must be built in the same direction as existing developments.

Even after you have chosen a desirable location, your problems are far from solved. The price of land has risen to high levels, and many owners are unwilling to part with this basic commodity. Many developers, to solve this problem, form some sort of a partnership to develop the land with the present owner. The developer undertakes the responsibility for plotting, developing, and promoting the subdivision. The landowner contributes the property to the partnership (or perhaps a corporation formed by both parties), and the landowner gets a fixed price for the property plus a percentage of the sale price of each lot. This type of system prevents high land costs from making the development of the property prohibitive.

Locating Near Favorable Adjacent Land Uses: The use to which the surrounding property is put can sometimes make the difference between success or failure for the subdivision:

A subdivision located directly on a heavily traveled main route will mean that prospective owners of single-family houses will be discouraged from locating in the subdivision. But, this type of location might be ideal for a garden-type apartment development.

A nearby, closely grouped shopping center might be much better for the subdivision than commercial properties located along the highway near the houses.

Adjacent industrial uses can automatically lower the value of the houses to be sold.

Railroads, cemeteries, and industrial uses that produce smoke, fumes, or odors from nearby plants can all have an adverse effect on the subdivision. But some industrial parks which have open, landscaped areas and favorable architectural factors are popular and may have a positive rather than a negative effect on adjacent residential properties.

Distances: The *Community Builders' Handbook,* published by the Urban Land Institute, Washington, D. C., sets out some handy rules of thumb regarding distances to various facilities to be used in picking a subdivision site. It has been found that certain maximum distances for either walking or driving are demanded by most home buyers.

Maximum Distances From the Home	Walking	Transportation
Neighborhood Shopping Center	½-¾ miles	
Community or Regional Shopping Center		3-4 miles
Recreation Facilities		3-4 miles
Public School	½-1 mile	
High School	2 miles	
Churches		3-4 miles
Work		45 min.

[¶3302] Community Facilities

As the chart above indicates, certain facilities must be within walking distance of the subdivision. These usually include stores and schools. In addition, any prospective buyer will look for the location of nearby churches, recreational facilities, etc.

Schools: Elementary schools nearby are a must for any new residential development, since a family with children of school age is a basic consumer of a new home. A developer will find it best to have an existing elementary school within about a half mile of his project. A distance of one mile from the elementary school is usually considered the outer distance possible. But, property located immediately next to school grounds is sometimes considered undesirable for homes because of the noise. If the developer must of necessity have some homes located near the school, he should try to provide at least ample screening by planting shrubbery.

Churches: Here the important problems are location near the subdivision, good access from the street, and adequate facilities for parking automobiles. If a development is going to be constructed near an existing church, it is usually a good idea either to sell or to give to the church some of the land in order to enlarge facilities for off-street parking if this appears necessary. Access to the parking area should be directly from a major or at least secondary street.

Recreational Facilities: In a large subdivision, developers have found that an allocation of about 5% of the area of the project can be dedicated to park or recreational use (in addition to play lots for children). This will normally apply to a subdivision of at least 35 acres. Of course, as the size of the subdivision decreases, it becomes harder for the developer to dedicate enough acreage for park and recreational use. It has been found that building values will rise from 15 to 20% when the property is located in the vicinity of park and recreation areas.

[¶3303] Site Analysis

Developers often make the mistake of failing to select a subdivision site which has the most favorable topographical features that are possible. An initial step along these lines is a topographic survey of the site before you buy it. Your subsequent lot and street development expenses will to a large extent depend on the basic information that you get from the topographic survey. Purchasing a site in spite of predictable defects in the land (such as the need for excessive clearing, lot grading, sewer and water extension, and poor drainage and soil conditions) usually means that a bargain on the surface can turn out to be a very costly venture.

The tract should be in as compact a shape as possible, with regular boundaries. If this is not the case, there may be a serious waste of land. Slopes are usually preferable to either very steep or flat land. You should avoid fills and cuts that require either retaining walls, steps, or steep banks. Normally, if the site has any substantial land which slopes over 9 or 10%, development costs will be very high. In that type of situation, you might still consider using the site for garden apartments or large single-family detached homes. This is because higher density in apartments allows a greater cost of development per acre, and single-family detached homes on large lots usually need a minimum of change in the slope of the land. Wooded areas are usually costly to clear but can be adapted to single-family developments located on large lots where you can leave most of the trees untouched. You should particularly avoid swampy areas, low ground, trash fills, and tracts which have rights of way or easements cutting through them.

After a site has been selected, the job of sital analysis is not over. Ingenuity is necessary in order to fit the subdivision plan to the actual topography. You must locate your streets in order to get a minimum amount of grading and earth moving. You should avoid heavy fills wherever there are going to be roadways, underground facilities, or sidewalks. Often, you will have to subordinate a desire for straight streets laid out at right angles to the economic benefits involved in curving streets in order to fit existing topography.

[¶3304] Utilities

Every developer will check for the availability of an adequate public water supply, sanitary sewers, and gas and electricity service. If these cannot be easily obtained, the site usually should be abandoned. You will have to check elevation of the site to make sure that gravity will facilitate distribution of waste material into the sewer. Electricity can usually be extended to your site without much difficulty. Obtaining a site adjacent to public water mains and sanitary sewers helps an operator avoid many difficult problems.

Often the developer may have to install water and sewer lines to make his subdivisions salable. Allocating the costs to the various subdivided tracts so that the developer can recover his costs (even where it is possible that under his arrangement with the water company he might get his money back) has been approved by the Treasury.

[¶3305] Checklist for Subdivision Site Analysis

Here is a handy list of items you will want to be sure to consider in analyzing a site and comparing it with other sites in which you may be interested.

Location

Direction from the city
Type of surrounding developments (low, medium, or high income)
Distance from major employment centers and travel time
Distance from central business district via designated favorable route
Public transportation—quality
Highway approaches and automobile access
Fares to employment and business center

Community Facilities

Shopping center and stores: size; distance; type; new center possible
Churches: denominations and numbers; distance
Recreation facilities: parks; playgrounds; other
Schools: distance; number of nursery, elementary, high

Adjoining Land Uses

General: zoning; subdivision regulation; any private covenants

Industrials, smoke, noise
Airports—distances from subdivision
Nearby thoroughfares
Surrounding developments—type and quality

Topography and Quality

Hilly, rolling or level
Amount of land over 8% elevation—highest, lowest, and average
Existing streets—above or below grade
Any heavy grading needed for either lots or streets
Type of soil
Any swamp areas
Rock outcrop
Any heavy woods, scrub, or open land

Sewers

Connections
Distance, size and invert of nearest main
Any independent system necessary
Septic tanks or cesspools

Water Supply

Any public water supply connections
Distance and size of nearest mains
Any independent system necessary
Individual wells possible

Raw Land

Price per acre
Total cost

Conclusion

Type of Development Indicated:

☐ Single family, separate
☐ Row
☐ Group
☐ Garden apartments

Some Specifics:

☐ Small shopping center to be put up
☐ Any large lots required
☐ Market demand
☐ Indicated uses permitted by zoning and covenants
☐ Price range of the land

[¶3306] Economics of Developing Raw Acreage

Rule of Five for Subdivisions: The "rule of five" is used to determine subdivision costs. The general rule of thumb for relating the expenses for developing unimproved acreages into residential subdivisions is along the following lines:

20%—Land Cost . . . 1/5

Anticipated selling prices after improving, including installation of utilities, public sidewalks, and street surfacing, should be equal to or exceed five times the raw land cost.

40%—Risk Factor . . . 2/5

Administrative costs, advertising, sales commission, cushion, and profit are in this portion.

20%—Improvements . . . 1/5

Engineering, legal fees, grading, utilities, and street surfacing are in this fifth.

20%—Miscellaneous . . . 1/5

This fifth is applied to interest and/or carrying charges and to the "cats and dogs" left unsold after the 3-, 5-, or 10-year objective liquidating period.

100%—Final selling price . . . 5/5

[¶3307] How to Acquire Land for Development

Land and housing development is a large-scale operation. The acquisition and the improvement of land are requiring increasingly large amounts of capital. These two trends call for methods of land acquisition which give the developer access to and control over a large enough tract to make development economical to him without requiring him to put up all the capital necessary to acquire such a tract in one bite. From the landowner's point of view, to dispose of a large tract at a good price, he should look for a formula which will encourage the developer to commit improvement, development, and advertising money which will build future value into the entire tract and surrounding acreage. A large landowner can afford to set a relatively low price on original acreage if he gets a developer to commit himself to carrying through the costly pioneering.

These requirements are met by techniques like these:

(a) Purchase contracts covering relatively long periods of time;

(b) Successive options granted to developers, sometimes at successively higher prices;

(c) Release clauses which commit the developer to release from the lien of the purchase-money mortgage any acreage which he needs to carry out his development plan;

(d) Modest carrying charges on long-term purchase commitments or to keep options in force, and modest payments to get land released from the lien of purchase-money mortgages taken by the landowner.

In *Community Builders' Handbook,* published by Urban Land Institute, Washington, D. C., David Bohannon, large-scale California developer, has suggested this method of land assemblage:

(1) The developer sets up a master plan which sets forth the general scheme of development and submits it for the approval of the owner.

(2) Developer and owner enter into an agreement setting forth the acreage prices for the entire property.

(3) Owner and developer agree on the number of years over which the full development is to be completed.

(4) To protect the owner against freezing of his property, the developer firmly commits to buy a predetermined number of acres each year.

(5) If the developer fails to meet this schedule, the owner is released from his commitment.

(6) The developer can buy any amount of acreage he desires in any year.

(7) If he develops an amount of acreage over and beyond the minimum requirement, he is permitted to apply the excess purchase to cover his minimum requirements for future years.

Another approach is for the developer to share the net profits from the land development with the landowner. This is done by a land development agreement in which the developer agrees to perform the platting, the laying out, the installation of lot improvements, and the promotion of the subdivision. The landowner agrees to accept a percentage of the sale price of each lot with a fixed minimum guaranteed. For example, *Community Builders' Handbook* cites one program in which the developer agreed to pay net to the landowner 25% of the sale price of each lot sold with a minimum price specified for each lot.

In all these approaches, it is important to protect the landowner from having his land cluttered up with liens left by a subdivider who goes broke. We have these approaches to solving that problem:

(1) Make the developer create a substantial cushion by cash payments, sewer and street installation, and other improvements, the completion of which can be bonded.

(2) Confine the developer or subdivider to a small tract of land at a time and give him "rolling options" to acquire additional pieces. The developer buys one parcel and agrees to exercise options to buy additional parcels at intervals over a period of time. Failure to keep up with this purchase program results in loss of future options. Under this program the subdivider can

quit at any time; but while he continues, he has control over and access to additional land without subjecting the plan to liens.

(3) The seller of a large tract can take a purchase-money mortgage which will give him priority over any creditors of the developer. To permit the developer to construct buildings with mortgage money, the purchase-money mortgage must contain either a partial release clause which will release particular lots on the blanket mortgage on receipt of specified payments, or a subordination clause obligating the mortgagee to execute the subordination agreements which will put the purchase-money mortgage behind specified construction mortgages as they are executed. This latter method is less desirable to the landowner because it pushes his purchase-money mortgage back to the status of a second mortgage so that the lender putting up the building money can get the first mortgage which he will insist on.

(4) Another method is for the landowner and subdivider to deed the land to a bank in trust. The purchase contract becomes a part of the trust agreement. Individual mortgages are signed by the trustee who has clear title to the land and can give first mortgages. When a sale is made, the buyer gets his deed from the trustee. Payments by the subdivider on this contract are made to the trustee who forwards them to the landowner. If the subdivider defaults in payments, the trustee then deeds any unsold land back to the landowner.

[¶3308] Land Acquisition Checklist

(1) Check local zoning and building ordinances to see:

Type of building allowed.

Lot size required.

Setback lines required on front, rear, and side lines.

Building area required and bulk and height allowed.

Construction requirements.

Use limitation.

Will the present or future uses permitted by zoning ordinances impair the attractiveness of your development and thus impede mortgage financing?

(2) Inspect the land itself to see:

Does water from adjoining sites drain into the one you are considering?

When you develop, will you increase the flow of drainage water going onto other land? If so, how will you control?

Make soil test to see if you will need deep footing or encounter rock problems.

How will sewerage be handled?

Are there any power or sewer lines cutting underground through the land?

Are there any streams or water flow problems?
How will you make road connections?

(3) Study the neighborhood to see:
Are school facilities adequate and accessible? What about buses and rail transportation?
How far away are shopping facilities?
Is garbage removal a problem? Are police and fire protection available?
Are park, hospital, and church facilities available?
What are the financial structure and the tax burden of the community?

(4) Discuss your proposed development with local planning authorities, get their thinking and suggestions informally. Find out what they require along these lines.
Location and width of streets.
Grading and paving of streets. At whose expense?
Curbs, gutters, and sidewalks. At whose expense?
Water and other utilities.
How are fire hydrants, street lighting, and street signs to be installed?
Will you have to dedicate any land for public use?
Sump or other drainage requirements.
What kind of a bond will be required to secure the completion of improvements which you are required to make?

(5) Talk to the local FHA officials and get their ideas. Congress has authorized various programs in areas of land development and new communities development.

(6) Talk to mortgage sources to get their thinking on your plan, their evaluation of the neighborhood, and their ideas on the kind of improvements that will prove most profitable and most mortgagable.

(7) Get a good survey of the land if you decide to go ahead. Next, talk to your lawyer about the contract of sale and terms of purchase. Discuss with him the kind of contingencies to put in the contract. You should try to make your obligation contingent on getting any required zoning change, mortgage finance approved by the FHA, and the mortgage lender and local planning authorities to approve the subdivision plat. Have your lawyer evaluate all restrictions and easements to which the seller wants you to take subject. Make your obligation contingent on the approval of any which would block your development plans.

(8) Talk to your title insurance company. You will want to have the title that you are acquiring insured and may want to make a wholesale deal for title policies covering the houses or other improvements that you plan to construct.

(9) Talk to your insurance broker to make sure that you have public liability insurance coverage from the time you acquire title and protection from liabilities and other risks involved in any construction you contemplate.

[¶3309] The Developer's Tax Problems

A project may take as little as two or three years to complete and consists of three natural stages: (1) the acquisition and development of land into lots, (2) the home building, and (3) the ultimate sale of the residence (and lots) to the home owners. Because of this natural division, the venture readily lends itself to the use of multiple corporations. And this can give you a big tax advantage—the spreading of profits over three (and sometimes more) corporations can keep all the income taxed at 22% instead of having a good part taxed at 48%. But you will have to be careful to set up genuine entities, not merely go through the motions of operating tax-saving corporations to get IRS's approval. However, as can be seen later, the choice of entity may be dictated by other circumstances.

As a general rule, you can expect that the sale of subdivided real estate will result in ordinary income since, most likely, you, the seller, will be treated as a dealer—that is, engaged in the business of selling real estate. But for a fortunate few, there is a relief provision. By meeting the technical requirements of §1237, it is possible for an individual (and, to a more limited extent, a corporation) to get capital gain treatment. However, there is one other way of obtaining capital gain. That's where you can show that you are not acting as a real estate dealer. But this is difficult, indeed. There are no clearly defined rules or guidelines, and we can only look to the actual cases of realtors who succeeded in convincing the courts that they were merely holding the property for investment which thus entitled them to capital gain treatment.

[¶3310] How to Choose Form of Business

There is no standard choice of the type of entity to be used for a residential subdivision. Custom hasn't dictated that corporations are the only thing to use, or partnerships, or proprietorships. A variety of all three may be found in use in the typical subdivision.

Operations are sometimes conducted entirely by a single individual, corporation, or partnership. Or there may be a combination of several individuals, corporations, and partnerships involved, each owning and operating a portion of the entire project. Sometimes, you will find a single partnership at the top, comprising as its partners a number of individuals, corporations, and other partnerships. Other partnerships may be stockholders in the corporations, and other corporations may be members of member partnerships.

If there has not been complete advance planning before the land is purchased, taking title in the name of an individual or partnership may provide more flexibility of organization. If the land is held unimproved for several years, it may increase in value; and the profit made on the sale to a corporation will result in capital gain treatment. Once title is recorded in a corporate name, however, a tax-free transfer of part of the land to a controlled corporation created for this purpose may result in the disallowance of the surtax credit under §1551 and the accumulated earnings credit.

As will be seen, the number of variations that can be used successfully is almost limitless.

Remember, whatever the arrangement, the key to success on the tax front is having real entities performing real functions.

[¶3311] How a Developer Computes His Income

This is a problem of great consequence. Since the developer has to some extent an election to capitalize or deduct taxes and carrying charges before he makes the election, he should know what method will benefit him the most. Also, it may be difficult in many cases to determine which expenditures must be capitalized and how much can be deducted annually against income.

Cost of Land: Where building lots contained in a given tract of land are sold before the contemplated development work is fully completed, the gain should be determined on the basis of the cost of the land plus actual and estimated future expenditures or the development of the property in accordance with the terms of the contract of sale (*Mackey,* 11 BTA 596, *acq.*). However, any unexpended estimated cost at the end of the project will naturally reduce the cost of sales.

Here is a sample of the items included in the cost of land:

(1) The original acquisition costs, e.g., purchase price, closing cost, attorneys' fees.

(2) Improvements, e.g., construction of roads, streets, sewers, water and electric lines.

Furthermore, IRS has approved boosting land costs by a developer where he bears the cost of installing water lines in order to induce prospective purchasers to buy lots. An arrangement was made with the water company which called for the developer to pay the water company a fixed sum. The water company agreed to pay the installation cost to the developer based on 6% of the gross annual receipts from the sale of the water to residents of a subdivision.

Although there may be a repayment of the installation costs to the developer, IRS agrees that the developer can add a pro rata share of the cost of installing the water line as part of the cost of the lots he sells. He can also include the cost of the water meter. This is so, says IRS, because payment to the water company is unconditional. He may never get back some of his installation costs—for example, if all the lots are not sold or if houses are not constructed on the lots and so water is not purchased (*Rev. Rul. 60-3,* CB 1960-1, 284).

Sometimes builders or subdividers find it necessary to lay down sewage disposal systems where septic tanks cannot be used. They treat the costs involved as an increase in the basis of the land sold and, in this way, try to deduct their costs. IRS, however, has met this treatment with resistance and has usually maintained that the builder or his controlled corporation has retained rights of ownership in the sewage system and, therefore, is not entitled to any deduction. The Tax Court allowed the deduction where the builder formed a corporation to run the sewage disposal plant. He then constructed a plant and collecting lines for the corporation. The corporation then transferred it back to the builder as trustee for the benefit of the various lot owners who would be serviced by the sewage collection system. In these circumstances, the Tax Court is convinced the sewage system was constructed to induce and make possible the sale of the lots and that the subdividers did not retain full ownership in the sewage system. Since extensive beneficial rights were transferred to the lot owners, the subdivider was permitted to add the sewage system's cost to his basis for the lots sold. (*Estate of Collins,* 31 TC 238).

Nondeductible Costs: If the developer donates land to form a country club adjacent to his subdivision and such land enhances the value of the subdivision, he cannot claim a charitable deduction for the value of the property donated. The cost of the donated property is to be treated as part of the cost of the lot sold (*Country Club Estates,* 22 TC 1283, *acq.* CB 1955-1, 4). Similar treatment is given land turned over to water, sewer, or electric companies for rights of way and to land and streets deeded to a locality to obtain government maintenance.

If the subdivision is to be developed by sections rather than all at about the same time, an apportionment should be made on the ratio of the sale price of the various lots or divided equally over the number of lots to be sold if the cost is to be apportioned ratably.

Elections Available: The subdivider may elect to include taxes and carrying charges in his land costs if they otherwise would be deductible. Some of the items that may be capitalized are:

(1) In the case of unimproved and unproductive real property, annual taxes, interest on a mortgage, and other carrying charges.

(2) In the case of real property whether improved or unimproved and whether productive or unproductive, all necessary expenditures for the development of the property or for the construction of improvements but only up to the time the development or construction work has been completed. This includes interest on a loan to provide funds for the venture and all payroll taxes and state use or sales taxes (or other similar taxes) paid on materials used in such development or construction work (Reg. §1.266-1(b)).

Where a portion of a development has been completed, it is necessary to allocate the above charges between the developed section which must be expensed and the undeveloped section which still may be capitalized.

The election to capitalize is exercised by attaching a statement to the income tax return listing those charges to be included in the land costs.

[¶3312] How to Get Capital Gains on Subdivision Sales

If you own a large tract of land and subdivide it and sell lots, chances are you are going to run into a Treasury claim that you are holding the property for sale in the ordinary course of business. So, the gain on the sale of the lots, as the Treasury sees it, would be ordinary income.

Of course, if you are a dealer, there's no question: You have ordinary income. Where you bought the land as an investment and find that the only way you can liquidate your investment is by subdividing, you may convince a court you are not holding the property for sale to customers in your business.

Even if you cannot establish that you are merely liquidating an investment, you can still get almost all your gain as capital gain (if you're not incorporated) if you can come within the rules of §1237.

What You Should Know About §1237: This Section lays down specific rules for keeping your sales out of the dealer category and achieving the capital gain rate. It does not apply to losses. The capital gain rate is available if three conditions are met:

(1) You were not otherwise a dealer during the taxable year of sale and

never held the subdivided tract or any part thereof as a dealer primarily for sale to customers. Also, you cannot have held any other real property as a dealer in the year of sale.

(2) No substantial improvements increasing the value of the property were made by you or related entities. Neither could such improvements be made by a lessee if the improvement constituted income to you, nor by a governmental body if the improvement constituted an addition to your basis for the property.

(3) You held the subdivided realty for at least five years, unless the property was inherited.

What Is a Substantial Improvement? As indicated above, you cannot make substantial improvements to the property if you want §1237 to apply. According to the Regulations, an improvement that does not increase the value of a lot by more than 10% is not substantial. Only those lots in the tract increased by more than 10% in value may lose §1237 treatment. Shopping centers, other commercial or residential buildings, hard surface roads, or utilities such as sewers, water, gas, or electric lines are substantial improvements. But temporary field offices, gravel roads, surveying, filling, draining, leveling, and clearing operations are not substantial.

Necessary Improvements: Even if an improvement would be considered substantial under the above rules, it still does not knock out §1237 treatment if the improvement is necessary. It's necessary if all the following conditions are met:

(1) You held the lot for at least 10 years.

(2) The improvement is a water, sewer, or drainage facility or a road.

(3) You can show that the property would not have otherwise been marketable at the prevailing local price for similar building sites.

(4) You elect neither to deduct the expense nor add it to the basis of any lot sold for purposes of determining how much your gain is. This results in the loss of any tax benefit for these expenses.

Here's an example of when a substantial improvement can become a necessary improvement. Suppose you donate to your city a strip of land that is part of your undeveloped tract in order to allow the city to extend a street into your property. This may result in a city special assessment for paving expenses. This assessment would be for a substantial improvement to the retained land and you would add the assessment to the basis of that land. But you can make it a necessary improvement and still come within the rules of §1237 by electing not to add the assessment to your basis (*Rev. Rul. 59-30*, CB 1959-1, 161).

How to Time Your Sales: Assuming all the conditions of §1237 are satisfied, all gain on sale of the lots in a tract is capital gain until the year in which the sixth lot is sold. From then on, gain to the extent of 5% of selling price less selling expenses is ordinary income, only the remainder is capital gain. Selling expenses are deductible only to the extent they reduce ordinary income; any balance of selling expenses reduces the amount realized as capital gain. After five years without a sale, the remaining lots become a new tract, and you can start the count of the first five sales over again.

For example, you sold five lots back in 1973 for $10,000 each. You then sold one lot in 1974 for $10,000. If your basis for each lot was $8,000 and your selling expenses for each was $300, you'd have $1,700 capital gain on each lot sold in 1973. In 1974, your total gain was $1,700 but 5% of your selling price (or $500) was subject to ordinary income treatment. Since you had $300 selling expenses, you had only $200 ordinary income. Your capital gain on lot six was thus $1,500. If you had sold the six lots all in 1973, you'd have $200 ordinary income on each, since each lot would be sold in the year in which the sixth lot was sold. In any event, if you discontinued sales after 1973, you could have sold five more lots in 1979 without any ordinary income if §1237 applied.

Capital Gain Outside the Requirements of §1237: Failure to meet the requirements of §1237 doesn't mean there will be no possibility of your obtaining the benefit of the capital gain rate. However, to get the favorable rate, you will have to produce strong evidence that you were not acting as a real estate dealer in making the sales. See *Edward Industries,* TC Memo 1974-120.

[¶3400] ZONING AND OTHER RESTRICTIONS

The value of real estate and the use to which it can be put may be limited by zoning ordinances, private restrictions, and covenants embodied in deeds, or by ordinances and practices of public authorities requiring the owner to spend substantial sums on improvement or conditions precedent to developing and using real estate. To deal intelligently in real estate, it is essential to know how to determine and evaluate the status of property with respect to the zoning and other restrictions that may affect its use and the community facilities to which the owner will have to contribute in order to develop it.

[¶3401] Zoning

The general purposes of zoning are to control and order the future growth of an area in accordance with a comprehensive plan. The power to zone stems from the inherent police power vested in the state, and this power can be delegated to local communities by proper enabling statutes or constitutional authorization. Regulations can be sustained if they promote public safety and general welfare in accordance with a well-considered and comprehensive plan. Zoning regulations are invalid if it can be established that they are arbitrary or confiscatory. There is no clear-cut line that separates arbitrary and capricious zoning from proper and legal zoning. The courts decide the propriety of zoning on a case-by-case basis and depend on the factual background. Zoning restrictions have been upset on the basis of undue hardship to the owner, failure of the zoning requirement to serve an adequate public purpose, the fact that the zoning regulations will permit a use which would be just as harmful to the purported public purpose of the general plan as would the proposed use, lack of a sensible relationship between the loss of value inflicted on the property owner and the injury to public purpose if he were allowed to develop the property in the most economic manner available, and discrimination against a particular piece of property.

[¶3402] Types of Zoning Control

Zoning ordinances accomplish their purpose by dividing property into districts and specifying or limiting the use to which property in those districts can be put and by setting restrictions and requirements on the improvement and use of land. There are three main types of control:

(1) Control of use by specifying the particular type of activity which may be carried on in a building on the property, i.e., residential (single-family or multi-family dwellings specified), commercial, light manufacturing, unrestricted, etc.

(2) Control of height and area by specifying the number of stories permitted or height in feet or both; by fixing a minimum front, side, and rear yard setback of buildings; by limiting the percentage of a lot that may be covered by a building; by fixing the minimum size of dwellings; by limiting the relationship of height to width of streets.

(3) Control of population density by specifying a maximum number of families per acre, a minimum lot area for a family to be housed, the number of square feet of open space required, a maximum number of families that may be permitted to occupy a given area.

[¶3403] Variances

In some instances a property owner is forced, out of necessity, to use his land in a manner that is prohibited by the zoning ordinance. Under circumstances where a strict application of the ordinance will in effect deny the owner beneficial use of his property, he may apply to the board of adjustment or the board of appeals for a variance. This administrative board has the authority to allow the owner to deviate from the provisions of the ordinance where strict compliance would cause him to suffer unnecessary hardships or practical difficulties. Pursuant to judicial interpretation, there are several requirements that must be met in order for a variance to be granted.

(1) The unnecessary hardship must be unique to the owner's particular property. A showing of a condition that affects all property in the district will not suffice. An undue hardship justifying a variance would arise in the situation where a person owns property that is so irregular that if all the restrictions of the ordinance were observed it would not be possible to construct a building on the lot. In this case, the ordinance, if strictly applied, would amount to a confiscation, so that a variance to alleviate the unnecessary hardship is justified.

(2) Within the context of variances, unnecessary hardship means that if an owner is made to comply with the ordinance, the property will not yield a reasonable return or the owner will not be able to make a reasonable use of his property. Merely showing that one can make more money by using his land in a different way will not be a sufficient basis for unnecessary hardship.

(3) The hardship claimed may not be created by the landowner. It should

be noted that the purchase of a lot that is subject to the restrictions sought to be varied will not in and of itself constitute a self-created hardship.

(4) A variance may be granted only if the new use will not change the essential character of the neighborhood or zoning district in which the lot is located. The board must also be assured that the use it will be permitting will not impair the appropriate use or development of adjacent property, and that such use will not be detrimental to public health, safety, morals, or general welfare.

[¶3404] Amending a Zoning Ordinance

Often when an existing zoning ordinance will not permit a desired use, the owner of the property will apply for, or urge, an amendment of the zoning ordinance to permit him to use the property as he desires. For instance, suppose you own a large tract of land that is zoned for residential use but allows only one house per acre. You want to build a planned unit development (PUD) on the parcel. As you know, a PUD, by definition, achieves an efficient use of land by having within the PUD district a mix of commercial, residential, and sometimes industrial uses. Since most zoning ordinances do not provide for such districts, more often than not you'll have to apply for a change of zone to allow you to construct your project.

The procedure in applying for a change of zone is as follows:

Application: An application can generally be made by the owner to the local legislative body responsible for zoning, usually the town or city council or board. (It should be noted that while most enabling acts delegate the power to amend to legislative bodies, it can be vested in another agency of the municipality. In Connecticut and Georgia, for example, statutes delegate the power to amend to the zoning commission.) This application generally requires information as to the reason for the desired change, the character of the area, maps showing neighboring properties, etc. A map showing the neighbors who must be notified about the application may also be required.

Planning Board Review: Usually the town board or other appropriate legislative body will refer the application for amendment of the zoning ordinance to the planning board for review by that body. As an advisory agency of the town board, the planning board's function in this area is to review the application and, in so doing, to insure that any zoning changes will be in keeping with the comprehensive plan of the town. The legislative body (in this discussion, the town board) may not delegate to the planning board the power to amend a zoning ordinance, since an amendment is clearly a legislative function. Under many zoning regulations, the legislative body may not hold a public hearing to effect a zoning change until it has received the planning board's report.

Notices: Notices of the public hearing concerning a pending application must be published in official newspapers of general circulation. In addition, neighbors are given notice of the application. Under some zoning ordinances, consent must be obtained from a specified percentage of neighbors or the application will not be heard.

Evidence indicating that the required procedures to give the neighbors notice have been complied with may have to be presented to the zoning authority.

Public Hearing: Under most enabling acts, the legislative body must hold a public hearing before amending a zoning ordinance. However, you should note that in many states it does not have to hold a public hearing in order to lawfully refuse to amend a zoning ordinance. In other words, the town board must hold a public hearing before it may change the status quo; but if the board chooses to maintain the status quo by denying the application, it may do so without a public hearing.

In applying for a change in zone, the applicant is generally arguing that the amendment would aid the development of the community. However, if he is arguing that the existing ordinance is unreasonable or that he has no reasonable use under the existing ordinance, he will have to prove his case at the time of the application.

The applicant and/or his attorney will generally apply in favor of the application. Because the project, which now hinges on zoning, has required a great deal of time and money to plan, you may want to use some of your project consultants when making your presentation to the town board. A professionally executed presentation, complete with reports, slides, and maps, will usually help your cause. Here's a rundown on how your presentation should go:

(1) Attorney: Your attorney should be your first speaker. It is his job to introduce the project formally and state to the board what it is that you are requesting. Remember, you are making a presentation within a legal framework, and it is your lawyer's function to state for the record precisely what it is that you are seeking. (It's a good idea to have a court reporter on hand so that there will be a record to which the parties can refer should litigation follow.)

Because your attorney may be the most articulate member of your presentation team, you may want him to act as your spokesman throughout the entire presentation; i.e., after his introductory remarks he will introduce each consultant, entertain questions from the floor, and make closing remarks.

(2) Planning Consultant: Rather than using your lawyer, you may wish to have a planning consultant lead the presentation. The planning firm will probably subcontract the consultants and is most familiar with their reports. The choice of spokesman is yours.

The planning consultant (and all other consultants) should try to avoid going into great detail and using technical language when making his presentation. Remember, you're making your presentation to laymen who most likely don't know a great deal about planning terms.

It is the job of the planning consultant to lay out by words, maps, and slides your development plans. While his presentation should not be flashy, it should be professional and impressive. He should be able to create a visual impression of what the project will look like, its size, features, etc. It is his job to create a framework within which, and in support of which, your other consultants can speak.

(3) Market Feasibility Report: The local zoning authorities should be shown that there is a local or regional demand for the type housing or commercial space that you are proposing. It's the function of your market analyst to point this out by showing such things as existing housing costs, local and regional income levels, housing demand, employment centers and commuting time to them from your project, and the like.

(4) Water Supply and Sewerage Report: A representative of the engineering firm hired to design your water supply and sewerage systems should be on hand to present your proposals for solving problems in these areas. Be sure to coach this person so that he is sure to avoid using technical terms wherever possible.

(5) Traffic Report: People are always concerned with how much additional traffic a project will generate and whether this increase in traffic will require the construction of new roads. Therefore, your traffic consultant's report will be very important. He must demonstrate by using slides or charts how the existing and proposed roads accommodate the present levels of traffic and how the traffic generated by your project will affect the projected peak-hour volumes. Your consultant should be prepared to meet with local opposition to his projections, so it's a good idea to have him carefully substantiate all projections in his written report.

(6) Economic Impact Report: This is the report that people are usually most eager to hear, because this is the one that hits them in their pocketbooks. Your consultant's report should describe when taxes will increase or decrease and stabilize and the amount of any increase or decrease. Because his figures will be closely questioned, the consultant should be prepared to give a brief description of how he arrived at his calculations.

(7) Environmental Report: Your environmental consultant will describe the property as it presently exists and show how it is suitable for development according to your plans. He should use slides showing the land in its natural state and emphasize certain features with maps or drawings; i.e., for topography, he can use an elevation map. Emphasis should be placed on such things as soil conditions, vegetation, wildlife, water analysis, and the like.

The environmental consultant should, after describing the natural conditions and showing why the site is suitable for development, discuss the impact that your project will have on the surrounding environment. This report can emphasize that you will maintain a certain percentage of your project as open space (always a good selling point).

(8) Geological Report: If you've hired a geologist, you'll want him to talk about the site's soil, rock formations, and topography from a building feasibility point of view. He should discuss the types of soil and drainage features, as well as describing the depth of bedrock. Often this report and the environmental report will overlap; however, the geologist's report is much more detailed. You'd be surprised at how many people are interested in what he'll say.

(9) Question-and-Answer Period: Because these presentations tend to be rather lengthy and everyone gets tired, it's a good idea to cut down on time as much as possible. Rather than have the officials question each consultant at the end of his presentation, it's a good idea to have a question-and-answer period at the end of the presentation if the board to which you are making the presentation will allow this. Your spokesman may be able to answer many of the questions. Those that he can't, he can pass along to the appropriate consultant.

You may wish to speak. If so, you should decide with your team when it is the most appropriate time for your remarks. It may work out well if you speak immediately before or after the question-and-answer period, so that the board will have an opportunity to question you freely.

(10) Summary: The presentation spokesman should make the closing remarks in a brief and polite manner. Remember, any official who wants more information can always check his copy of the consultant's written report.

Decision: Following the above presentation, the body authorized to make this legislative decision will vote, based on the foregoing, on whether or not it should amend the zoning ordinance. Usually a majority vote is all that is required. However, in most jurisdictions following the Standard State Zoning Enabling Act, provision is made for the filing of a protest petition by local affected citizens. Under this scheme, if the owners of 20% or more of either the area or the lots included in the proposed change or closely behind or opposite the area to be affected file a protest petition, the amendment cannot be effective unless three-fourths of the members of the town board vote affirmatively to amend the ordinance.

[¶3405] Impact of Zoning on Title

A zoning ordinance is not in and of itself an encumbrance on real property, and it does not render title unmarketable. However, violation of a zoning ordinance, subjecting the owner of the property to possible penalties and either removal or relocation of the building, does make title unmarketable. A change in zoning restrictions between the time of contract and the time of the closing has been held not to justify the buyer rejecting title in the absence of a specific condition to that effect in the contract. The best procedure for a buyer is to have the contract of sale contain a representation by the seller that the property may be used for a specifically identified purpose. This representation should survive the delivery of the deed. In the case of vacant land, the contract is sometimes made subject to obtaining a zoning variance and other approvals necessary to permit the contemplated improvements. Sometimes the buyer gets a proviso that the zoning will not be changed between the date of contract and the date of closing and even for a sufficient time after the closing to permit the purchaser to commence construction which would give him a vested right and protect him against future changes.

[¶3406] How Zoning Can Result in Financial Loss

Zoning violations and zoning changes can result in unmarketability and financial loss. Here are things to watch for:

(1) Selling the wrong amount of land or not buying enough land may make it impossible to comply with the restrictions governing height, area, and bulk. The value of property owned may thus be impaired or it may be necessary to acquire adjoining property at considerable cost.

(2) Changes in use of buildings subsequent to the issuance of a certificate of occupancy or the enlargement and relocation of buildings may constitute a zoning violation which would make title unmarketable or impair value.

(3) Building permits or certificates of occupancy can be revoked on the basis that they were issued through fraud, mistake, or without authority.

(4) A variance or special exception permit may be subject to a time limitation or other conditions set forth in the resolution granting it and may be declared illegal on appeal. Also, a variance may lapse or be nullified by changes in zoning prior to the beginning of construction.

(5) When a district is zoned, existing buildings not conforming to the newly established zoning requirements are allowed to continue as legal nonconforming buildings or uses. However, this kind of legal nonconforming use may be nullified by voluntary abandonment, discontinuance of the nonconforming use, provisions for amortizing and outlawing nonconforming uses over a period of time, or destruction of buildings. Recent zoning involving substantial downgrading or upgrading may be the subject of legal attack from surrounding owners. Their success could result in loss to a buyer or mortgagee who relied on the change in zoning in acquiring the property.

These possibilities emphasize the importance of a thorough investigation of the zoning status of property before acquiring it. This can be accomplished by a check of the zoning map, discussion with local planning and building authorities, study of the minutes and resolutions in which any variances were granted and, in a complex situation, by getting an opinion from a lawyer, engineer, or architect throughly familiar with local zoning practices.

[¶3407] How to Attack the Zoning Powers

In exercising zoning powers, the authorities must avoid certain pitfalls. Unless these powers are used correctly and for proper community purposes only, the zoning ordinance may be set aside by the courts. In addition, in preparing and passing a zoning ordinance and in amending or changing it, the zoning enabling act should be complied with.

Zoning must serve a public purpose that touches and affects health, safety, morals, or the general welfare (i.e., a purpose within the so-called "police" power). The zoning regulations must be uniform within each district. They may differ from district to district, but those within a district must apply uniformly to each class or kind of property. Since zoning powers may be used only in the interest of public health, safety, morals, or the general welfare, zoning regulations, many of which are combined in zoning ordinances, must promote one or more of these public ends. The various regulations must be combined into a whole, in accordance with a comprehensive plan for the community.

State and local government zoning power must be applied within the framework of the guarantees of the United States Constitution and the various state constitutions. The principal constitutional tests are as follows:

Is the Ordinance Arbitrary? A zoning ordinance may be struck down as being an unconstitutional exercise of the zoning power where a court is convinced that the ordinance involves a mere arbitrary exercise of the zoning power, and does not bear a substantial relation to the public health, safety, morals, or general welfare of the community.

Is the Ordinance Confiscatory? A zoning ordinance will also be struck down as unconstitutional if it is confiscatory. The Constitution of the United States guarantees that no person will be deprived of his property without due process of law. Where a zoning ordinance deprives the owner of the entire use value of his property, it has often been held by the courts that the owner is being deprived of his property without due process of law. What's more, it is not always necessary to show that the owner has been deprived of the entire use value of his property—some courts have held that a zoning ordinance which permanently restricts the use of land so that it cannot be used profitably for any reasonable purpose goes beyond the permissible bounds of zoning and becomes confiscatory. However, a zoning ordinance will not be declared invalid merely because it deprives the owner of the highest and best use of the property.

Is the Ordinance Discriminatory? A zoning ordinance will also be held invalid if it can be shown to be discriminatory or exclusionary. The Constitution affords each citizen equal protection of the law. Discriminatory zoning ordinances have been held to violate this constitutional protection.

If the person attacking the validity of a zoning ordinance can show that there is no basic police power reason for the imposition of the boundary lines between zoning districts, the courts may find the ordinance unconstitutional. Similarly, a zoning ordinance which discriminates between various uses without reasonable basis is discriminatory and invalid.

Zoning and Eminent Domain: The state or the local government generally has the power to acquire property by condemnation or eminent domain. But the acquisition must be for a public use and the state or local government must compensate the owner for the value of the property taken. A local government cannot use its zoning authority as a means to acquire property for public purposes.

The uses to which property may be put cannot be restricted to public purposes by zoning. To do this would constitute taking property without due process of law and without compensating the owner, in violation of the constitutional protection. Zoning cannot be used as a means of reducing the cost of condemnation. For example, a city cannot validly enact an ordinance providing that certain property owned by a private person can be used only for a public housing development sponsored by its housing authority.

Does the Ordinance Amount to Spot Zoning? A zoning ordinance should fit in with a comprehensive plan designed to protect the public health, safety, and welfare. Often zoning ordinances are attacked on the basis that they represent spot zoning—zoning of a particular parcel without extending the benefits of the zoning change to neighboring similar parcels.

Spot zoning has been defined as the process of singling out a small parcel of land for a use classification totally different from that of the surrounding property for the benefit of owners of that area and to the detriment of other owners. The spot zoning attack is one which must be carefully avoided by the authorities in dealing with a zoning ordinance which has been frequently amended.

[¶3408] Protective Covenants

Protective covenants, sometimes called private deed restrictions or restrictive covenants, are contracts made between private parties to constitute an agreement as to the way in which land may be used. Their purpose is to protect and preserve the character and integrity of the area covered by these covenants. Protective covenants should not be confused with race restrictions that have been held unconstitutional by the United States Supreme Court. Restrictions may be applied individually to each lot or parcel as it is sold or they may be declared and applied simultaneously to all of the property in a development. The best way of controlling use and development is by blanket restrictions that are recorded with the plot of subdivision with each lot or parcel to which the restrictions apply enumerated.

Protective restrictions established by declaration or by covenants in deeds will usually undertake to impose the same kind of limitations as zoning regulations—use, lot, and building size; setbacks; etc.

Deed restrictions may be enforced by any owner of land included in the common plan; but a court can, on application, set them aside when conditions have changed sufficiently.

[¶3409] TDR: An Alternative to Zoning

Preserving open space has become a topic of intense interest to many municipalities. Because you are actively engaged in the real estate industry, it is important that you be aware of emerging trends and new concepts in local governmental treatment of open space. Over the past few years, transferring development rights has evolved as a land-use planning tool. Some observers feel that eventually TDR may replace conventional zoning in many communities.

Transferring development rights is a system predicated on the fact that ownership of property carries with it a bundle of rights—a fact familiar to most real estate people. TDR recognizes that these rights can be separated and sold individually. One such right, and perhaps the most valuable one, is the owner's right to develop his land.

The TDR system operates by allowing the transfer of development rights from open space property to land where greater density is permitted. By using this system, a community can protect or preserve a designated area and in turn guide the orderly growth of another area. The property owner retains all his rights except those development rights that he has transferred, for which he is adequately compensated.

One of the most innovative TDR proposals has been developed by a committee of faculty members of Rutgers University and members of the New Jersey Department of Community Affairs. Here's how such a system as envisioned by the committee, would work.

The first step is for the local government to prepare a land-use plan. This plan should indicate the percentage of undeveloped land within the municipality, designating such land as open space to be preserved, and specify developable land and its acceptable uses. The municipality adopting such a TDR system must either enact or amend a zoning law to provide for the system.

The planning board would then determine the number of development rights necessary for a housing unit to be developed within the developable district. Then, the planning board could figure the total number of development rights that would be necessary for developing the community in conformity with the land-use plan.

Next, the municipality would issue certificates of development rights (these certificates would be recorded) to owners of undeveloped land. An owner of property that has been designated as open space to be preserved would receive a certain number of certificates representing the percentage of assessed value of his land to the total assessed value of undeveloped land within the designated open space preservation area.

If a person owning land within the developable district of the community (as per the land-use plan) wants to increase the density of his land, he would have to buy a certain number of certificates representing the necessary development rights. The owner of the undeveloped land, by selling his development rights, permanently transfers his right to develop his land in exchange for payment from the developer. This exchange is accomplished without the municipality incurring capital costs. (Note: Under this scheme, the development rights would be recorded and taxed as real property.)

Although TDR is a relatively new land-use concept, it is growing in popularity, and real estate people would do well to be informed about it. TDR has been used for landmark preservation in Chicago and New York.

Other jurisdictions, such as Puerto Rico; Fairfax County, Virginia; Sonoma County, California; Maryland; St. George, Vermont; and Southampton, New York, are working on proposals or have adopted and are using TDR systems to achieve various land-use planning goals.

If you're interested in learning more about this emerging land-use tool, see the January 1975 issue of Urban Land (Vol. 34 No. 1). In this fine publication, the Urban Land Institute fully explores and explains how the transfer of development rights works.

[¶3410] Community Requirements

In addition to zoning, the landowner in an urban community will experience increasing regulation of his rights to use land. His basic right to exercise dominion over property he acquires has to be balanced against the increasingly exercised right of the state to regulate the use of property and the conduct of business. Before land can be developed, many local communities are:

(1) Specifying minimum lot size and minimum housing area.

(2) Requiring the builder to construct drainage and streets and even sewer facilities.

(3) Imposing special assessments or other fees for permission to build.

(4) Requiring dedication of part of land for school, park, or other public use as a condition for recording plat.

[¶3411] Environmental Restrictions

Recently, Americans have awakened to the environmental havoc which this country has experienced in the past two decades. As a result, we are increasingly concerned not only with the present condition of the environment, but, almost more importantly, with how we can presently work toward bettering the future condition of our environment. Much of the federal environmental legislation, from the National Environmental Policy Act (NEPA) on down, mentions Congress's concern with the environment as it will presently affect the future.

Due to the plethora of environmental legislation now directly and indirectly affecting land usage in this country, it has become necessary for all those engaged in the real estate industry to become familiar with environmental laws and regulations, as such regulations will condition the development of land.

Environmental Impact: Under the National Environmental Policy Act, an environmental impact statement is required for all "major federal actions significantly affecting the quality of the human environment.'' If you own a piece of real estate that you want to develop, you will most likely find that during the course of development you will need to obtain a federal permit. For example, suppose your project calls for some construction along the banks or in the body of a river over which the Army Corps of Engineers has jurisdiction. Well, the Corps of Engineers, in granting you a permit to construct along the banks of the river, may be involving itself in a major federal action that significantly affects the environment, so that an environmental impact statement will be necessary. In addition, if you want to receive federal funding for your project, the governmental agency providing you with funds may be required to prepare an environmental impact statement.

Applicants for federal permits or funding are not required to prepare the environmental impact statement. The statement is to be prepared by the federal agency responsible for the appropriate funding or licensing. However, along with your project application, you should submit an environmental impact assessment setting forth necessary data and information to assist the agency. Usually, the government agency with which you are dealing will give you an outline of what you are to indicate in your environmental impact assessment.

It's a good idea to prepare your environmental assessment early in the planning process. This assessment is to be written objectively so that it will be of assistance to the federal agency that will prepare the environmental impact statement. In this assessment, you should include alternatives and allow for flexibility in making later choices. Do your best to foresee and meet as many environmental objections as possible before submitting the statement to the agency. Also, it is advisable to delete from your assessment anything that cannot be supported by expert testimony. Be prepared for a good deal of paper work as well as public relations work where public hearings will be conducted.

State Environmental Policy Acts: In additon to NEPA, the federal act, many developers may have to comply with state-enacted ''little NEPAs.'' Developers should check the ''little NEPAs'' in the following areas: Arizona, California, Connecticut, Delaware, Hawaii, Massachusetts, Michigan, Montana, Nevada, New Mexico, New York, North Carolina, Puerto Rico, Texas, Virginia, Washington, and Wisconsin.

Spelling Out Environmental Impact: Environmental impact, within the meaning of the federal and state statutes, occurs at the design, construction, and operational stages of the project.

Design and Planning Impact: Here we're dealing with the impact on the social and economic characteristics of nearby areas by reason of uncertainty; the impact on planning and providing public services; the effect of the acquisition and condemnation of the property required for, or affected by, the project; and the effect of the dislocation of families and businesses.

Construction Impact: Here we're dealing with the displacement of people; soil erosion; disturbance of natural drainage; noise; interference with the water table; water and air pollution; effect on parks, recreational areas, historic sites, wildlife habitats, esthetics (including the impact of construction activity and destruction of, or interference with, scenic values); the effect of ancillary activities, including earth disposal and acquisition of fill and gravel; safety hazards; and the commitment of resources to construction.

Operation Impact: At the operational stage, we're dealing with a direct impact in terms of air, water, and noise pollution; an increase in the demand for, and use of, such resources as water and energy; and social, economic, esthetic, and ecological (animal and plant life) impact.

At the operational stage, we're also dealing with what might be called indirect impacts including the impact on the use of contiguous lands; on patterns of regional development; on the demand for housing and public facilities; on the use of nearby woodlands, parks, recreational areas, and other environmental amenities; of additional or improved transportation facilities on already congested areas; of the usefulness of the project for different economic and ethnic groups and what problems and solutions result; of increased mobility on life-styles; and the effect and impact of improved transportation and related technological development.

How Environmental Impact Statements Are Processed: Under NEPA, the following procedure applies: An environmental assessment, as described above is submitted to the appropriate federal agency along with the project application. The statement is submitted by the private firm or individual or by the municipal or state agency that is involved. The federal agency then drafts an impact statement which it circulates among the appropriate governmental bodies, private institutions, and individuals for review and for their comments. Public hearings may then be conducted. (In some cases, public hearings are required.) Then a final statement is formally issued and made available to the public. Formal approval of the project will be given, denied, or suspended, depending on whether the impact on the environment is favorable or unfavorable.

GLOSSARY OF REAL ESTATE TERMS

The majority of the following definitions and explanations of real estate terms have been made available by the Mortgage Bankers Association of America, through their publication *Mortgage Banking Terms–A Working Glossary* and are printed here with the permission of the MBA.

Abstract of Title: A written history of the title transactions or conditions bearing on the title to a designated parcel of land. It covers the period from the original source of title to the present, and summarizes all subsequent instruments of public record by setting forth their material parts.

Acceleration Clause: A common provision of a mortgage and note providing that the entire principal shall become immediately due and payable in the event of default. Without this clause, the mortgagee may have to file separate foreclosure suits as each installment of the mortgage debt falls due and is in default.

Accrued Interest: The interest earned for the period of time that has elapsed since interest was last paid.

Acknowledgment: A formal declaration, attached to or a part of an instrument, made before a duly authorized officer (usually a notary public) by the person who has executed the instrument, the execution being a free act and deed. (See affidavit.)

Addendum: An addition to a written document. Addenda is the plural.

Add on Interest: The full amount of interest calculated on the original principal for the term of a loan. It is added to the principal thereby becoming a part of the face amount of the promissory note.

Advance: In real estate, a partial disbursement of funds under a note. Most often used in connection with construction lending.

Adverse Possession: The right by which someone occupying a piece of land might acquire title against the real owner, if the occupant's possession has been actual, continuous, hostile, visible, and distinct for a statutory period.

Affidavit: A sworn statement in writing before a proper official, usually a notary. (See acknowledgment.)

After-Acquired Property: The property a debtor acquires as security after the execution of a mortgage or other form of indebtedness that additionally secures the indebtedness. If the mortgage note contains a statement on after-acquired property it is said to have an "after-acquired clause."

Agent: One who legally represents another, called a principal, from whom authority has been derived.

Air Rights: The ownership of the right to use, control, or occupy the air space over a designated property.

Alienation: To transfer the title to real property from one person to another.

Alienation Clause: A special type of acceleration clause that demands payment of the entire loan balance upon sale or other transfer of the title.

Allotment: The funds allocated for the purchase of mortgages within a specified time by a permanent investor with whom a mortgage loan originator has a relationship but does not have a specific contract in the form of a commitment. The allotment may state the investor requirements as to processing, the term of the loan, and/or underwriting standards.

Amenity: An aspect of a property that enhances its value. Off-street reserved parking within a condominium community, the nearness of good public transportation, tennis courts, or a swimming pool are examples.

American Land Title Association (ALTA): A national association of title insurance companies, abstractors, and attorneys, specializing in real property law. The association speaks for the title insurance and abstracting industry and establishes standard procedures and title policy forms.

Amortization: Gradual debt reduction. Normally, the reduction is made according to a predetermined schedule for installment payments.

Amortization Schedule: A table showing the amounts of principal and interest due at regular intervals and the unpaid balance of the loan after each payment is made.

Annual Mortgagor Statement: A report by the lender or servicing agent to the mortgagor telling what taxes and interest were paid during the year, and how much principal balance remains.

Apportionment: A prorated division and distribution of prepaid or accrued taxes, prepaid insurance premiums, prepaid rents and other income and expenses. Apportionment usually occurs when a property is sold, and is the manner of determining the amounts due to and from the party.

Appraisal: A report setting forth an opinion or estimate of value. The process by which this estimate is obtained.

Appraised Value: An opinion of value reached by an appraiser based upon knowledge, experience, and a study of pertinent data.

Appraiser: One qualified by education, training, and experience to estimate the value of real and personal property. The estimate is based on a process in which the appraiser judges the facts discovered in an investigation of the property. (See MAI, SREA.)

Appreciation: An increase in value, the opposite of depreciation.

Appurtenance: Anything—concrete or abstract—attached to the land and thus part of the property, such as a barn, garage, or an easement.

Assessed Valuation: The value that a taxing authority places upon real or personal property for the purposes of taxation.

Assignment: The transfer of a right of contract from one person (assignor) to another (assignee).

Assignment of Leases: The absolute or conditional transfer of the rights of either party to a lease.

Assignment of Mortgage: A document that evidences a transfer of ownership of a mortgage from one party to another.

Assignment of Rents: An agreement signed between the property owner and mortgagee specifically fixing the rights and obligations of each under a lease affecting the property.

Associate Broker: A person who has qualified as a real estate broker but works for a principal broker licensed in the state.

Assumption Fee: The fee paid to a lender (usually by the purchaser of real property) resulting from the assumption of a mortgage.

Assumption of Mortgage: Assumption by a purchaser of the primary liability for payment of an existing mortgage or deed of trust. The seller remains secondarily liable unless specifically released by the lender.

Attornment (Attorn):The act of a tenant agreeing to become the tenant of a new landlord and to regard him as the new owner of the premises and to pay rent to him.

Auction: A method of selling real or personal property. An auctioneer asks for bids and, upon receipt of the highest bid, completes the sale.

Automated Mortgage Market Information Network (AMMINET): A nationwide electronic quotation system designed for listing Veterans Administration, Federal Housing Administration, conventional single-family and multi-family loans, and Government National Mortgage Association securities. The system can be expanded to include commercial property loans and mortgage participations. The network handles buy and sell offers that participating subscribers enter into the system through their own terminals. It was developed by the Federal Home Loan Mortgage Corporation (FHLMC) and is operated by a non-profit corporation whose directors are selected from several national trade associations.

Average (Rate of Return): The return on an investment calculated by averaging the total cash flow over the years during which the cash flow is received by the investor.

Balloon Mortgage: A mortgage with periodic installments of principal and interest that do not fully amortize the loan. The balance of the mortgage is due in a lump sum at the end of the term.

Bank, Mutual Savings: State chartered financial institutions that invest mainly in mortgages.

Bankrupt: A person, firm or corporation, who, through a court proceeding, is relieved from the payment of all debts after the surrender of all assets to a court-appointed trustee, for the protection of creditors.

Base Rent: The minimum fixed guaranteed rent in a commercial property lease.

Basic Rent: The rent charged in a subsidized housing project and computed on the basis of a maximum subsidy.

Betterment: An improvement that increases property value as distinguished from repairs or replacements that simply maintain value.

Bill of Sale: A document in writing that transfers title to personal property.

Binder, Real Estate: A preliminary agreement between a buyer and seller in which the basic price and terms of a real estate contract are included. The final contract is then prepared and signed by both parties. In some instances, the term refers to the actual sales contract.

Blanket Mortgage: A lien on more than one parcel or unit of land, frequently incurred by subdividers or developers who have purchased a single tract of land for the purpose of dividing it into smaller parcels for sale or development. Also called blanket trust deed.

Blighted Area: A declining area in which property values are adversely affected by destructive natural or economic forces, such as encroachments, inharmonious property usages, changing social and economic neighborhoods, or rapidly depreciating buildings.

Bona Fide: In good faith, without fraud.

Bond: An interest-bearing certificate of debt with a maturity date. An obligation of government or business corporation. A real estate bond is a written obligation usually secured by a mortgage or a trust deed.

Book Value: The capitalized cost of an asset less depreciation taken for accounting purposes based upon the method used for the computation of depreciation over the useful life of the asset. Also, the actual value of an asset after the deduction of depreciation and all liabilities is the net book value.

Break-Even Point: In residential or commercial property, the figure at which occupancy income is equal to all required expenses and debt service.

Building Code: The local regulations that control design, construction, and materials used in construction. Building codes are based on safety and health standards.

Buy-Sell Agreement: An agreement entered into by an interim and a permanent lender for the sale and assignment of the mortgage to the permanent lender when a building has been completed. Often the mortgagor is a party to this agreement on the theory that the mortgagor should have a contractual right to insist that the permanent lender buy the mortgage.

Call Provision: In the mortgage or deed of trust, a clause giving the mortgagee or beneficiary the right to accelerate payment of the mortgage debt in full on a certain date or on the happening of specified conditions.

Capitalization: The process of converting into present value a series of anticipated future installments of net income, by discounting them into a present worth using a specific desired rate of earnings.

Capitalization (as applied to appraisal): The process of ascertaining the magnitude, worth, or value of capital goods through the use of a rate that is believed to represent the proper relationship between capital goods or property and the net income it produces.

Capitalization Rate: The rate which is believed to represent the proper relationship between real property and the net income it produces.

Carrying Charges: Costs incurred by a developer or builder. Principally, interest on land and construction loans and property taxes to cover expenses until the point of sale.

Cash Flow: The spendable income from an investment after subtracting from gross income all operating expenses, loan payments, and the allowance for the income tax attributed to the income. The amount of cash derived over a certain measured period of time from the operation of income-producing property after debt services and operating expenses, but before depreciation and income taxes.

Certificate of Occupancy: Written authorization given by a local municipality that allows a newly completed, or substantially completed structure to be inhabited.

Certificate of Title: A statement furnished by an abstract or title company or attorney to a client stating that the title to a piece of property is legally vested in the present owner.

Chain of Title: The history of all the documents transferring title to a parcel of real property, starting with the earliest existing document and ending with the most recent.

Chattel: Personal property.

Closing: The conclusion or consummation of a transaction. In real estate, closing includes the delivery of a deed, financial adjustments, the signing of notes, and the disbursements of funds necessary to the sale or loan transaction.

Closing Costs (borrower's): Money paid by the borrower to effect the closing of a mortgage loan. This normally includes an origination fee, title insurance, survey, attorney's fees, and such prepaid items as taxes and insurance escrow payments.

Closing Statement: A financial disclosure giving an account of all funds received and expected at the closing, including the escrow deposits for taxes, hazard insurance, and mortgage insurance for the escrow account.

Cluster Zoning: A zoning procedure where there is a prescribed amount of residential or unit density for an entire area. The developer is permitted to concentrate or disperse the density within the area in accordance with flexible site planning criteria.

CMB: Certified Mortgage Banker. A professional designation of the mortgage banking industry.

Collateral: Property pledged as security for a debt, such as the real estate securing a mortgage.

Commercial Paper: Short-term unsecured notes that are sold to meet short-term capital needs.

Commission: An agent's compensation (fee) for negotiating a real estate or loan transaction, often expressed as a percentage of the sales price or mortgage amount.

Commitment (builder): An agreement by a lender to provide long-term financing to a builder, secured by an existing or proposed building. The commitment usually provides for the substitution of a to-be-approved owner-occupant at a higher loan amount than committed to the builder.

Commitment Fee: Any fee paid by a potential borrower to a potential lender for the lender's promise to lend money at a specified date in the future. The lender may or may not expect to fund the commitment.

Common Areas: Land or improvements for the benefit of all tenants and property owners. Shopping center parking lots and residential parks and playgrounds are generally common areas. All the space within a development that can be used by all the tenants in that development. (See condominium and planned unit developments.)

Community Associations Institute (CAI): The CAI is an independent, non-profit research and educational organization formed in 1973 to develop and distribute the most advanced and effective guidance for the creation, financing, operation, and maintainence of the common facilities and services in condominiums, townhouse projects, planned unit developments, and open space communities.

Community Property: In some states, a form of ownership under which property acquired during a marriage is presumed to be owned jointly unless acquired as separate property of either spouse.

Completion Bond: A bond furnished by a contractor to guarantee completion of construction.

Condemnation: Taking private property under the right of eminent domain for public use with compensation to the owner.

Condition Precedent: A condition that must occur before some action or other thing may follow.

Conditional Sales Contract: A contract for the sale and delivery of property to a buyer, with the seller retaining the title thereof until the conditions have been fulfilled. (See sales contract.)

Conditions and Restrictions: A common term used to designate restrictions on the use of land and providing penalties for failure to comply. Commonly used by land subdividers on newly plotted areas.

Condominium: A form of ownership of real property. The purchaser receives title to a particular unit and a proportionate interest in certain common areas. A condominium generally defines each unit as a separately owned space to the interior surfaces of the perimeter walls, floors, and ceilings.

Title to the common areas is in terms of percentages and refers to the entire project less the separately owned units.

Consideration: The required element in all contracts by which a legal right or promise is exchanged for the act or promise of another person.

Constant: The percentage of the original loan paid in equal annual payments that provide for interest and principal reduction over the life of the loan.

Construction Contract: An agreement between a general contractor and an owner-developer stating the specific duties the general contractor will perform according to blueprints and specifications at a stipulated price and terms of payment.

Construction Loan Agreement: A written agreement between a lender and a builder and/or borrower in which the specific terms and conditions of a construction loan, including the schedule of payments, are spelled out.

Contiguous: Adjoining.

Contract of Sale: A contract between a purchaser and a seller of real property to convey a title after certain conditions have been met and payments have been made. (See sales contract.)

Conventional Loan: A mortgage loan neither insured by FHA nor guaranteed by VA. (See insured loan and guaranteed loan.)

Convey: The act of transferring title to another.

Conveyance: The document, such as deed, lease, or mortgage, used to effect a transfer.

Cooperative: A form of multiple ownership of real estate in which a corporation or business trust entity holds title to a property and grants the occupancy rights to particular apartments or units to shareholders by means of proprietary leases or similar arrangements.

Corporation: A body of persons granted a charter legally recognizing them as a separate entity (legal person) having its own rights, privileges, and liabilities distinct from those of its members.

Correspondent: A mortgage banker who services mortgage loans as a representative or agent for the owner of the mortgage or investor. Also applies to the mortgage banker's role as originator of mortgage loans for an investor.

Cost Approach to Value: A method in which the value of a property is derived by estimating the replacement cost of the improvement, deducting therefrom the estimated depreciation, then adding the value of the land as estimated by use of the market data approach. Also called physical indication of value.

Cost-Plus Contract: A construction contract in which the contract price is equal to the cost of construction plus a profit allowance to the builder; as opposed to a fixed price contract.

Covenant: A legally enforceable promise or restriction in a mortgage. For example, the borrower may covenant to keep the property in good repair and adequately insured against fire and other casualties. The breach of a covenant in a mortgage usually creates a default as defined by the mortgage and can be the basis for foreclosure. (See restrictive covenant.)

Credit Report: A report to a prospective lender on the credit standing of a prospective borrower, used to help determine credit worthiness.

Debt Coverage Ratio: The ratio of effective annual net income to annual debt service.

Debt Service: The periodic payment of principal and interest earned on mortgage loans.

Dedication: The granting of land by the owner for some public use and its acceptance for such use by authorized public officials.

Deed: A written document by which the ownership of land is transferred from one party to another.

Deed of Trust: In some states, the document used in place of a mortgage. A type of security instrument conveying title in trust to a third party covering a particular piece of property. It is used to secure the payment of a note. A conveyance of the title land to a trustee as collateral security for the payment of a debt with the condition that the trustee shall reconvey the title upon the payment of the debt, and with power of the trustee to sell the land and pay the debt in the event of a default on the part of the debtor.

Deed Restriction: A limitation placed in a deed limiting or restricting the use of the real property.

Default: A breach or nonperformance of the terms of a note or the covenants of a mortgage.

Defeasance Clause: The clause in a mortgage that gives the mortgagor the right to redeem property upon the payment to the mortgagee of the obligation due.

Delinquent: The status of a mortgage with a payment past due.

Delivery: The legal, final, and absolute transfer of a deed from seller to buyer in such a manner that it cannot be recalled by the seller. A necessary requisite to the transfer of title. In mortgage banking, the physical delivery of loan documents to an investor or agent in conformance with the commitment.

Density: The ratio between the total land area and the number of residential or commercial structures to be placed upon it. Local ordinances usually regulate density.

Deposit: (1) A sum of money given to bind a sale of real estate, or (2) a sum of money given to assure payment or an advance of funds in the processing of a loan. Also known as earnest money.

Depreciation: A loss of value in real property brought about by age, physical deterioration, or functional or economic obsolescence. Broadly, a loss in value from any cause. The opposite of appreciation.

Depreciation Allowance: The accounting charge made to allow for the fact that the asset may become economically obsolete before its physical deterioration. The purpose is to write off the original cost by distributing it over the estimated useful life of the asset. It appears in both the profit and loss statement and the balance sheet.

Deviated Rate: In hazard insurance, a premium rate established by reduction of the bureau (or standard) rate. It may often be 10 to 15 percent less than the bureau rate.

Direct Reduction Mortgage: A mortgage that requires a fixed payment of principal each period. The total payment will vary, as the interest portion will reduce with each payment.

Disbursements: The payment of monies on a previously agreed to basis. Used to describe construction loan draws.

Discount: The sale of a note for less than its face value. The opposite of a premium.

Down Payment: The difference between the sale price of real estate and the mortgage amount.

Earnest Money: See deposit.

Easement: Right or interest in the land of another entitling the holder to a specific limited use, privilege, or benefit such as laying a sewer, putting up electric power lines, or crossing the property.

Economic Life: The estimated period of time during which a property can be utilized profitably.

Effective Rate: The actual rate of return to the investor. It may vary from the contract rate for a variety of reasons. Also called yield. (See yield.)

Egress: To go out. It is used with the word ingress to describe the right of access to land.

Eminent Domain: The right of a government to take private property for public use upon payment of its fair value. It is the basis for condemnation proceedings. (See condemnation.)

Encroachment: An improvement that intrudes illegally upon another's property.

Encumbrance: Anything that affects or limits the fee simple title to property, such as mortgages, leases, easements, or restrictions.

Environmental Impact Statement (EIS): A statement required by many federal, state, and local environmental and land use laws. It contains an analysis of the impact that a proposed change may have on the environment of a specific geographic region. It examines a wide variety of physical, social, and economic conditions that would be affected by the proposed development. The analysis covers effects that cannot be avoided, alternatives to the proposed change, short-term vs. long-term uses and long-term productivity, irreversible commitments of resources, and the benefits to be derived.

Environmental Protection Agency (EPA): Regulatory agency created to coordinate governmental efforts to protect the environment by abating and controlling pollution on a systematic basis. EPA is primarily responsible for administrating laws regarding air, noise, and water quality.

Equity: In real estate, the difference between fair market value and current indebtedness, usually referring to the owner's interest.

Equity of Redemption: The common law right to redeem property during the foreclosure period. In some states the mortgagor has a statutory right to redeem property after a foreclosure sale.

Equity Participation: Partial ownership of income property, given by the owner to the lender, as part of the consideration for making the loan.

Escalator Clause: A clause providing for the upward or downward adjustment of rent payments to cover specified contingencies, such as the provision in a lease to provide for increases in property tax and operating expenses.

Escrow: A transaction in which a third party, acting as the agent for the buyer and the seller, carries out instructions of both and assumes the responsibilities of handling all the paperwork and disbursement of funds.

Escrow Account: The segregated trust account in which escrow funds are held.

Escrow Agent: The person or organization having a fiduciary responsibility to both the buyer and seller (or lender and borrower) to see that the terms of the purchase/sale (or loan) are carried out. Synonyms: escrow company and escrow depository. (See closing statement.)

Escrow Contract: A three-party agreement of the buyer, seller, and the escrow holder specifying the rights and duties of each.

Escrow Costs: All of the costs to the buyer and seller individually that are associated with the purchase, sale, or financing of real property. These include, but are not limited to, prorating of agreed items such as taxes and rents, the cost of title insurance policies, the cost of credit reports, recording fees and escrow fees. Synonyms: closing costs, settlement costs.

Escrow Overage or Shortage: The difference, determined by escrow analysis, between escrow funds on deposit and escrow funds required.

Escrow Payment: That portion of a mortgagor's monthly payments held in trust by the lender to pay for taxes, hazard insurance, mortgage insurance, lease payments, and other items as they become due. Known as impounds in some states.

Eviction: The lawful expulsion of an occupant from real property.

Exclusive Listing: A written contract giving one licensed real estate agent the exclusive right to sell a property for a specified time, but reserving the owner's right to sell the property alone without the payment of a commission.

Exclusive Right to Sell: The same as exclusive listing, but the owner agrees to pay a full commission to the broker even though the owner may sell the property.

Exculpatory Clause: A clause in a contract holding one party harmless in the event of some default. For example, the provision in a note that the debtor will not be held personally liable in the event of a default.

Execute: To complete, finish, or in real estate deeds, to sign, seal, and deliver.

Exempt Property: Real estate that is not subject to property taxation. Religious, educational, and charitable organizations generally hold exempt property.

Fair Market Value: The price at which property is transferred between a willing buyer and a willing seller, each of whom has a reasonable knowledge of all pertinent facts and neither being under any compulsion to buy or sell.

Fannie Mae: Nickname of Federal National Mortgage Association.

Farmers Home Administration (FmHA): A government agency established under the Farmers Home Administration Act of 1946 to provide financing to farmers and other qualified borrowers who are unable to obtain loans elsewhere.

Feasibility Study: A study or analysis that determines whether a real estate project, proposed or existing, successfully meets desired objectives.

Federal Home Loan Bank Board (FHLBB): A regulatory and supervisory agency for federally chartered savings institutions. It oversees the operations of the Federal Savings and Loan Insurance Corporation and the Federal Home Loan Mortgage Corporation.

Federal Home Loan Mortgage Corporation (FHLMC): A private corporation authorized by Congress. It sells participation sales certificates secured by pools of conventional mortgage loans, their principal and interest guaranteed by the federal government through the FHLMC. It also sells Government National Mortgage Association bonds to raise funds to finance the purchase of mortgages. Popularly known as Freddie Mac.

Federal Housing Administration (FHA): A division of the Department of Housing and Urban Development. Its main activity is the insuring of residential mortgage loans made by private lenders. It sets standards for construction and underwriting. FHA does not lend money, nor plan, nor construct housing.

Federal National Mortgage Association (FNMA): A tax paying corporation created by Congress to support the secondary mortgage market. It purchases and sells residential mortgages insured by FHA or guaranteed by VA, as well as conventional home mortgages.

Fee Simple: The greatest possible interest a person can have in real estate.

Fiduciary: A person in a position of trust and confidence for another.

Financing Package: The total of all financial interest in a project. It may include mortgages, partnerships, joint venture capital interests, stock ownership, or any financial arrangement used to carry a project to completion.

First Mortgage: A real estate loan that creates a primary lien against real property.

Fiscal Year: Any 12-month period used for financial reporting and preparation of balance sheets, profit and loss statements, and other financial summations.

Fixture: Personal property that becomes real property upon being attached to real estate.

FNMA: See Federal National Mortgage Association.

Foreclosure: An authorized procedure taken by a mortgagee or lender, under the terms of a mortgage or deed of trust for the purpose of having the property applied to the payment of a defaulted debt. (See equity of redemption.)

Franchise: The authorization to do business using the name and operating methods of another. In income property lending, a franchise may have value as an additional security. It may also be assigned to the lender.

Front-End Money: Funds required to start a development and generally advanced by the developer or equity owner as a capital contribution to the project.

Future Advance: Disbursement of funds subsequent to the execution of a mortgage. Obligatory future advances are found in construction loans and normally take preference over another encumbrance which is recorded prior to disbursing the next construction loan advances. Optional future advances are found in open-end mortgages and do not take preference over another encumbrance recorded prior to the disbursement of the advance.

Gap Financing: An interim loan given to finance the difference between the floor loan and the maximum permanent loan as committed.

G. I. Loan: Colloquial term given to a mortgage loan guaranteed by the Veterans Administration.

Government National Mortgage Association (GNMA): On September 1, 1968, Congress enacted legislation to partition FNMA into two continuing corporate entities. GNMA has assumed responsibility for the special assistance loan program and the management and liquidation function of the older FNMA. Also, GNMA administers the mortgage-backed securities program which channels new sources of funds into residential financing through the sale of privately issued securities carrying a GNMA guaranty.

GNMA Mortgage-Backed Securities: Securities, guaranteed by GNMA, that are issued by mortgage bankers, commercial banks, savings and loan associations, savings banks, and other institutions. The GNMA security holder is protected by the "full faith and credit of the U.S." GNMA securities are backed by FHA, VA, or Farmers Home Administration mortgages.

Graduated Lease: A lease providing for a variable rental rate sometimes set forth in the lease, sometimes determined by a reappraisal using a predetermined formula.

Grantee: The person to whom an interest in real property is conveyed.

Grantor: The person conveying an interest in real property.

Gross Leaseable Area: The total floor area designated for tenant occupancy and on which tenants pay rent. Usually used in describing property used for retail sale establishments. (See net rentable area.)

Ground Lease: Contract for the rental of land, usually on a long-term basis.

Ground Rent: The earnings of improved property allocated to the ground itself after allowance is made for earnings of the improvement. Also, payment for the use of land in accordance with the terms of a ground lease.

Guaranteed Loan: A loan guaranteed by VA, the Farmers Home Administration, or any other interested party.

Hard Dollars: Cash money given in exchange for an equity position in a transaction for real property. (See soft dollars.)

Hazard Insurance: A contract whereby an insurer, for a premium, undertakes to compensate the insured for loss on a specific property due to certain hazards.

Hereditaments: Things that are capable of being inherited. Hereditaments are either corporeal (tangible objects) or incorporeal (intangibles, such as property rights).

Highest and Best Use: The available present use or series of future uses that will produce the highest present property value and develop a site to its full economic potential.

Holdover Tenant: A tenant who remains in possession of leased property after the expiration of the lease term.

Homeowners Association: An organization of homeowners residing within a particular development whose major purpose is to maintain and provide community facilities and services for the common enjoyment of the residents.

Homeowners Policy: A multiple peril policy commonly called "package policy." It is available to owners of private dwellings and covers the dwelling and contents in the case of fire or wind damage, theft, liability for property damage, and personal liability.

Housing Code: Local standards that ensure that maintenance and improvements of housing meets accepted standards and is adequate for occupancy.

HUD: The Department of Housing and Urban Development, established by the Housing and Urban Development Act of 1965 to supersede the Housing and Home Finance Agency. It is responsible for the implementation and administration of government housing and urban development programs. The broad range of programs includes community planning and development, housing production and mortgage credit (FHA), equal opportunity in housing, research, and technology.

Immediate Purchase Contract (FNMA): An offer of a mortgage by a seller to FNMA for immediate purchase on an over-the-counter basis.

Improvements: Those additions to raw land that normally increase its value, such as buildings, streets, and sewers.

Income Approach to Value: The appraisal technique used to estimate real property value by capitalizing net income. (See capitalization.)

Income Property: Real estate developed or improved to produce income.

Ingress: To go in, to enter. Used with egress, to describe the right of access to land.

Inspection Certificate: Certification by a correspondent or designated agent that a property has been inspected and is accurately represented in a submission. A certificate is sometimes accepted in lieu of a survey.

Installment: The regular periodic payment that a borrower agrees to make to the mortgagee.

Institutional Lender: A financial institution that invests in mortgages and carries them in its own portfolio. Mutual savings banks, life insurance companies, commercial banks, pension and trust funds, and savings and loan associations are examples.

Insurable Title: A title on which a title insuring company is willing to issue its policy of insurance.

Insurance: A contract for indemnification against loss.

Interest: Consideration in the form of money paid for the use of money, usually expressed as an annual percentage. Also, a right, share, or title in property.

Interest Factor: The decimal equivalent for an interest rate on a unit amount for a period of time. Computed by interest rate ÷ basic year × days accrued.

Interim Financing: Financing during the time from project commencement to closing of a permanent loan, usually in the form of a construction loan and/or development loan.

Involuntary Lien: A lien imposed against property without consent of an owner. Examples include taxes, special assessments, federal income tax liens, judgment liens, mechanics' liens, and materials liens.

Joint Tenancy: An equal undivided ownership of property by two or more persons, the survivors to take the interest upon the death of any one of them.

Joint Venture: An association between two or more parties to own and/or develop real estate. It may take a variety of legal forms including partnership, tenancy in common, or a corporation. It is formed for a specific purpose and duration.

Junior Mortgage: A lien that is subsequent to the claims of the holder of a prior (senior) mortgage. (See subordinate.)

Kicker: A term describing any benefit to a lender above ordinary interest payments. It may be an equity in a property or a participation in the income stream.

Land Bank: Land purchased and held for future development.

Land Loan: A loan for the acquisition of land to be held in anticipation of zoning and until plans are drawn and construction financing can be obtained.

Late Charge: An additional charge a borrower is required to pay as penalty for failure to pay a regular installment when due.

Lease: A written document containing the conditions under which the possession and use of real and/or personal property are given by the owner to another for a stated period and for a stated consideration.

Leasehold: An estate or interest in an estate in real property held by virtue of a lease.

Leasehold Mortgage: A loan to a lessee secured by a leasehold interest in a property.

Legal Description: A property description recognized by law, which is sufficient to locate and identify the property without oral testimony.

Lessee (tenant): One holding rights of possession and use of property under terms of a lease.

Lessor (landlord): One who leases property to a lessee.

Letter of Credit: A letter authorizing a person or company to draw on a bank or stating that the bank will honor their credit up to the stated amount.

Level Payment Mortgage: A mortgage that provides for a constant, fixed payment at periodic intervals during its term. Part of each payment is credited to interest with the balance of the payment used to reduce the principal.

Leverage: The use of borrowed money to increase one's return on cash investment. For leverage to be profitable, the rate of return on the investment must be higher than the cost of the money borrowed (interest plus amortization).

Lien: A legal hold or claim of one person on the property of another as security for a debt or charge. The right given by law to satisfy debt.

Life Estate: An individual's right to use and occupy property for life without the right to pass the property to another in his or her will.

Limited Partnership: A partnership that consists of one or more general partners who are fully liable and one or more limited partners who are liable only for the amount of their investment.

Lis Pendens: A notice recorded in the official records of a county to indicate that there is a pending suit affecting the lands within that jurisdiction.

Listing: A written authorization to sell or lease real estate. (See exclusive right to sell.)

Loan Guaranty Certificate: A certificate issued to a lending institution by the Veterans Administration indicating the percentage of the loan that is guaranteed.

Loan-to-Value Ratio: The relationship between the amount of the mortgage loan and the appraised value of the security, expressed as a percentage of the appraised value.

Local Housing Authority (LHA): A city agency that monitors and implements community housing development needs. Local agencies do not necessarily possess renewal or redevelopment authority.

MAI (Member, Appraisal Institute): The highest professional designation awarded by the American Institute of Real Estate Appraisers.

Marketable Title: A title that may not be completely clear, but has only minor objections that a well-informed and prudent buyer of real estate would accept. (See clear title.)

Market Approach to Value: In appraising, the market value estimate is predicated upon actual prices paid in market transactions. It is a process of correlation and analysis of similar recently sold properties. The reliability of this technique is dependent upon (a) the degree of comparability of each property with the subject property, (b) the time of sale, (c) the verification of the sale dates, (d) the absence of unusual conditions affecting the sale, and (e) the terms of the sale.

Market Value: The highest price that a buyer, willing but not compelled to buy, would pay, and the lowest a seller, willing but not compelled to sell, would accept.

Maturity: The terminating or due date of a note, time draft, acceptance, bill of exchange, or bond. The date a time instrument of indebtedness becomes due and payable.

Mechanics' Lien: A lien allowed by statute to contractors, laborers, and suppliers on buildings or other structures upon which work has been performed or for which materials were supplied. (See notice of completion.)

Merchantable Title: A title that a court of equity considers so clear that it will force acceptance of it by a purchaser. (See marketable title.)

Modular House: A factory assembled residence built in units or sections, transported to a permanent site and erected on a foundation. The term excludes mobile homes.

Moratorium: A period during which a borrower is granted the right to delay fulfillment of an obligation.

Mortgage: A conveyance of an interest in real property given as security for the payment of a debt. (See deed of trust.)

Mortgage-Backed Securities: Bond-type investment securities representing an undivided interest in a pool of mortgages or trust deeds. Income from the underlying mortgage is used to pay off the securities. (See GNMA mortgage-backed securities.)

Mortgage Banker: A firm or individual active in the field of mortgage banking. Mortgage bankers, as local representatives of regional or national institutional lenders, act as correspondents between lenders and borrowers.

Mortgage Banking: The packaging of mortgage loans secured by real property to be sold to a permanent investor with servicing retained for the life of the loan for a fee. The origination, sale, and servicing of mortgage loans by a firm or individual. The investor-correspondent system is the foundation of the mortgage banking industry.

Mortgage Broker: A broker who brings the borrower and lender together, receiving a commission. A mortgage broker does not retain servicing.

Mortgage Discount: The difference between the principal amount of a mortgage and the amount it actually sells for. Sometimes called points, loan brokerage fee, or new loan fee. The discount is computed on the amount of the loan, not the sales price.

Mortgagee: A person or firm to whom property is conveyed as security for a loan made by such person or firm (a creditor).

Mortgagee in Possession: A mortgagee who, by virtue of a default under the terms of a mortgage, has obtained possession but not ownership of the property.

Mortgage Insurance: A type of term life insurance often bought by mortgagors. The amount of coverage decreases as the mortgage balance declines. In the event that the borrower dies while the policy is in force, the debt is automatically satisfied by insurance proceeds.

Mortgage Insurance Premium (MIP): The consideration paid by a mortgagor for mortgage insurance either to FHA or a private mortgage insurance (PMI) company. On the FHA loan, the payment is one-half of one percent annually on the declining balance of the mortgage. It is a part of the regular monthly payment and is used by FHA to meet operating expenses and provide loss reserves.

Mortgage Note: A written promise to pay a sum of money at a stated interest rate during a specified term. It is secured by a mortgage.

Mortgagor: One who borrows money, giving as security a mortgage or deed of trust on real property (a debtor).

Multiple Listing: A listing, usually an exclusive right to sell, taken by a member of an organization composed of real estate brokers.

Negative Cash Flow: Cash expenditures of an income-producing property in excess of the cash receipts.

Net Income: The difference between effective gross income (property) and the expenses including taxes and insurance. The term is qualified as net income before depreciation and debt service.

Net Lease: A lease calling for the lessee to pay all fixed and variable expenses associated with the property. Also known as a pure net lease, as opposed to a gross lease. The terms net net and net net net are ill-defined and should be avoided.

Net Rate: The rate of interest remitted to an investor by a correspondent after deducting a servicing fee from the gross interest rate.

Net Rentable Area: The actual square footage of a building that can be rented. Halls, lobbies, stairways, elevator shafts, maintenance areas, and the like are not included.

Net Spendable: The amount of cash that remains from the gross income after deducting operating expenses, principal and interest payments, and income taxes.

Net Yield: That part of gross yield that remains after the deductions of all costs, such as servicing, and any reserves for losses.

Non-Recourse Note: A debt instrument giving the lender no recourse to the borrower. The lender must rely solely on the property for repayment.

Notary: One authorized by the state to take acknowledgments and give oaths.

Occupancy Rate: The percentage of space or units which are leased or occupied.

Open-End Mortgage: A mortgage with a provision that the outstanding loan amount may be increased upon mutual agreement of the lender and the borrower. (See future advance.)

Operating Expenses: Generally regarded as all expenses of a property with the exception of real estate taxes, depreciation, interest, and amortization.

Option: A contract agreement granting a right to purchase, sell, or otherwise contract for the use of a property at a stated price during a stated period of time.

Origination Fee: A fee or charge for the work involved in the evaluation, preparation, and submission of a proposed mortgage loan.

Package Loan: Interim and take-out loan made by the same investor, as in construction lending.

Package Mortgage: A mortgage or deed of trust including items that are technically chattels, such as appliances, carpeting, and drapery.

Par: The principal amount of a mortgage with no premium or discount.

Partial Payment: In loan collection, less than the full payment due, usually not credited until the balance is received.

Participation Loan: (1) A mortgage made by one lender in which one or more other lenders own a part interest; (2) A mortgage originated by two or more lenders.

Pension Fund: An institution that holds assets invested in long-term mortgages and high-grade stocks and bonds having acceptable yields and security. The purpose of a pension fund is to accumulate funds to hold and invest in such a manner that it will provide retirement income to individuals on an agreed upon plan.

Percentage Lease: A lease in which a percentage of the tenant's gross business receipts constitutes the rent. Although a straight percentage lease is occasionally encountered, most percentage leases contain a provision for a minimum rent amount.

Percolation Test: A test given to soil to determine its water seepage capacity when the use of a septic tank is being considered.

Perfecting Title: The elimination of any claims against a title.

Permanent Loan: A long-term loan or mortgage that is fully amortized and extended for a period of not less than ten years.

Personal Liability: Personal liability arises when the borrower's assets are pledged or subject to claim in addition to a primary security.

Personal Property: Any property that is not real property. State laws vary on the definition of personal property.

Physical Approach to Value: An appraisal method whereby property value is derived by estimating the replacement cost of improvements, less estimated depreciation, plus estimated land value by use of market data. (See market approach to value.)

Planned Unit Development (PUD): (1) A comprehensive development plan for a large land area. It usually includes residences, roads, schools, recreational facilities, and service areas plus commercial, office, and industrial areas; (2) A subdivision having lots or areas owned in common and reserved for the use of some or all of the owners of the separately owned lots.

Plat (plot): A map representing a piece of land subdivided into lots with streets, boundaries, easements, and dimensions shown thereon. It is usually recorded and made a part of the public record.

Point: An amount equal to 1 percent of the principal amount of an investment or note. Loan discount points are a one-time charge assessed at closing by the lender to increase the yield on the mortgage loan to a competitive position.

Police Power: That right by which the state or other governmental authority may take, condemn, destroy, impair the value of, limit the use of, or otherwise invade property rights. It must be affirmatively shown that the property was taken to protect the public health, public morals, public safety, or the general welfare.

Preliminary Title Report: A title search by a title company prior to issuance of a title binder or commitment to insure.

Premises: A defined portion of land and the improvements thereon as usually described in a deed, deed of trust, or a mortgage.

Premium: The amount, often stated as a percentage, paid in addition to the face value of a note or bond. Also, the charge for insurance coverage.

Prepayment Fee: A consideration paid to the mortgagee for the prepayment privilege. Also known as prepayment penalty or reinvestment fee.

Prepayment Privilege: The right given a borrower to pay all or part of a debt prior to its maturity. The mortgagee cannot be compelled to accept any payment other than those originally agreed to.

Primary Financing: A loan secured by a first mortgage or trust deed on real property. (See secondary financing.)

Prime Tenant: A tenant, or related group of tenants, that is the largest single occupant of a building. Such occupancy is generally for 25% or more of the aggregate square footage.

Priority: As applied to claims against property, the status of being prior or having precedence over other claims. Priority is usually established by filing or recordation in point of time, but may be established by statute or agreement.

Private Mortgage Insurance (PMI): Insurance written by a private company protecting the mortgage lender against loss occasioned by a mortgage default.

Processing: The preparation of a mortgage loan application and supporting documents for consideration by a lender or insurer.

Prorate: To allocate proportionate shares of income (such as rents) or of an obligation (such as taxes and insurance premiums), paid or due, between seller and buyer at closing.

Prospectus: A proposal or offering in conjunction with the sale of improved or unimproved property that outlines all aspects of the offer. Regulations of the Securities and Exchange Commission require many real estate offerings to be described by a detailed prospectus.

Purchase-Money Mortgage: A mortgage given by the purchaser of real property to the seller as part of the consideration in the sales transaction.

Quiet Enjoyment: The right of an owner to the use of property without interference of possession.

Quitclaim Deed: A deed that transfers only such interest, title, or right a grantor may have at the time the conveyance is executed.

Real Estate Investment Trust (REIT): A trust established for the benefit of a group of real estate investors and managed by one or more trustees who hold title to the assets for the trust and control its acquisitions and investments. A major REIT advantage is that no federal income tax is paid if certain qualifications are met. The REIT is designed to provide an opportunity for large-scale public participation in real estate investment.

Real Estate Syndicate: A group of investors who pool funds for investment in real property.

Real Property: Land and appurtenances, including anything of a permanent nature such as structures, trees, minerals, and the interest, benefits, and inherent rights thereof.

Realtor: A real estate broker or an associate holding active membership in a local real estate board affiliated with the National Association of Realtors.

Recapture: An owner's recovery of money invested in real estate, usually referring to a depreciation allowance.

Recourse Note: A debt instrument under which the lender can take action against the borrower or endorser personally, in addition to foreclosure.

Redemption Period: The time allowed by law in some states during which a mortgagor may buy back property by paying the amount owed on a foreclosed mortgage, including interest and fees. (See equity of redemption.)

Refinancing: The repayment of a debt from the proceeds of a new loan using the same property as security.

REIT: See real estate investment trust.

Release Clause: A stipulation in the mortgage or deed of trust that a portion of the security may be released from the lien if certain conditions are met.

Rent: Consideration paid for use or occupancy of property, buildings, or dwelling units.

Rental Requirement: A condition in the commitment letter stipulating that a specific number of units must be rented at a minimum rental rate before the entire loan amount will be funded.

Rent-Up Period: The time after construction that a rental property requires to achieve projected stabilized income and occupancy levels.

Restrictive Covenant: A clause in a deed limiting use of the property conveyed for a certain period of time.

Return on Equity: The ratio of cash flow after debt service to the difference between the value of property and the total financing.

Reversion: A right to future possession retained by an owner at the time of a transfer of an owner's interest in real property.

Right of Survivorship: In joint tenancy, the right of survivors to acquire the interest of a deceased joint tenant.

Right of Way: A privilege operating as an easement upon land, whereby a land owner, by grant or agreement, gives another the right to pass over land. (See easement.)

Riparian Rights: The right of owners to the water and land below the high water mark. These rights vary according to state law.

Sale-Leaseback: A technique in which a seller deeds property to a buyer for a consideration and the buyer simultaneously leases the property back to the seller, usually on a long-term basis.

Sales Contract: A deliberate written agreement between competent parties stating terms and conditions of a sale.

Sandwich Lease: A lease in which the "sandwich party" is a lessee, paying rent on a leasehold interest to one party, and also is a lessor, collecting rents from another party or parties. Usually the owner of the sandwich lease is neither the fee owner nor the user of the property.

Satisfaction of Mortgage: The recordable instrument given by the lender to evidence payment in full of the mortgage debt. Sometimes known as a release deed.

Savings and Loan Association: A mutual or stock association chartered and regulated by either the federal government or a state. They accept time deposits and lend funds primarily on residential real estate.

Secondary Financing: Financing real estate with a loan, or loans, that are subordinate to a first mortgage or first trust deed.

Secondary Mortgage Market: An unorganized market where existing mortgages are bought and sold. It contrasts with the primary mortgage market where mortgages are originated.

Secured Party: The party holding a security interest or lien; may be referred to as the mortgagee, the conditional seller, or the pledgee.

Security: The collateral given, deposited, or pledged to secure the fulfillment of an obligation or the payment of a debt.

Security Agreement: An agreement between a secured party and a debtor creating a security interest.

Settlement Costs: See closing costs.

Shopping Centers: The type of shopping center is determined by its major tenant or tenants. Neither site area nor building size determine the type. Neighborhood Center provides for the sale of convenience goods and personal service for the day-to-day living needs of the immediate neighborhood. It is built around a supermarket as the principal tenant. Community Center provides, in addition to convenience goods, a wider range of wearing apparel, hardware, and appliances. It is built around a variety store or junior department store as the major tenant. Regional Center provides for a full range of general merchandise including apparel, furniture, and home furnishings in full depth. It is built around one or more department stores.

Soft Costs: Architectural, engineering, and legal fees as distinguished from land and construction costs.

Soft Dollars: The amount invested in the development or purchase of a property that is immediately deductible for tax purposes, such as prepaid interest and fees. (See hard dollars.)

Special Assessment District: Any governmental subdivision having the power to tax and improve property within its jurisdiction. Also known as a Special Improvement District.

Special Warranty Deed: A deed containing a covenant whereby the grantor agrees to protect the grantee against any claims arising during the grantor's period of ownership.

SREA: The designation of an appraiser who is a member of the Society of Real Estate Appraisers. The designations are: Senior Residential Appraiser (SRA), Senior Real Property Appraiser (SRPA), and Senior Real Estate Analyst (SREA).

Standby Commitment: A commitment to purchase a loan or loans with specified terms, both parties understanding that delivery is not likely, unless circumstances warrant. The commitment is issued for a fee with willingness to fund in the event that a permanent loan is not obtained. Such commitments are typically used to enable the borrower to obtain construction financing at a lower cost on the assumption that permanent financing of the project will be available on more favorable terms when the improvements are completed and the project is generating income.

Standby Fee: The fee charged by an investor for a standby commitment. The fee is earned upon issuance and acceptance of the commitment.

Starts: A term commonly used to indicate the number of residential units begun within a stated period of time.

Statute of Frauds: A state law requiring certain contracts to be in writing. In real estate, a contract for the sale of land must be in writing to be enforceable.

Statute of Limitations: A law that limits the length of time within which a lawsuit must be commenced or the right to sue is lost. It varies from state to state.

Step-Down-Lease: A lease calling for one initial rent followed by a decrease in rent over stated periods.

Step-Up-Lease: A lease calling for one initial rent followed by an increase in rent over stated periods.

Subcontractor: The person or company under contract to perform work for a developer or general contractor.

Subdivision: Improved or unimproved land divided into a number of parcels for the purpose of sale, lease, or financing, immediate or future.

Subject to Mortgage: When the purchaser buys subject to a mortgage but does not endorse the same or assume to pay the mortgage, the purchaser cannot be held for any deficiency if the mortgage is foreclosed and the property sold for an amount not sufficient to cover the note. (See assumption of mortgage.)

Sublease: A lease executed by a lessee to a third person for a term no longer than the remaining portion of the original lease.

Subordinate: To make subject to, or junior to.

Subordination: The act of a party acknowledging, by written recorded instrument, that a debt due is inferior to the interest of another in the same property. Subordination may apply not only to mortgages, but to leases, real estate rights, and any other types of debt instruments.

Subordination Clause: That clause in a deed of trust that effects the subordination.

Survey: A measurement of land, prepared by a registered land surveyor, showing the location of the land with reference to known points, its dimensions, and the location and dimensions of any improvements.

Sweat Equity: Equity created in a property by the performance of work or labor by the purchaser or borrower. It directly increases the value of the property.

Takedown: The act of a borrower in drawing needed funds against a previously made loan commitment. The advance of money by a lender to a borrower under a loan agreement, loan commitment, or line of credit.

Takeout Commitment: A promise to make a loan at a future specified time. It is most commonly used to designate a higher cost, shorter term, back-up commitment as a support for construction financing until a suitable permanent loan can be secured.

Takeout Loan: A first mortgage loan that is committed and expected to be made upon completion of a specific real estate project. (See permanent loan.)

Tandem Plan: A mortgage assistance program whereby GNMA agrees to purchase qualified FHA and VA mortgages at prices favorable to sellers and at terms attractive to low and moderate income home buyers. The mortgages purchased by GNMA are accumulated and periodically sold at auction as either GNMA securities or whole mortgages.

Tenancy at Will: A holding of real estate that can be terminated at the will of either the lessor or the lessee, usually with notice.

Tenancy by Entirety: The joint ownership of property by a husband and wife where both are viewed as one person under common law that provides for the right of survivorship.

Tenancy in Common: In law, the type of tenancy or estate created when real or personal property is granted, devised, or bequeathed to two or more persons, in the absence of express words creating a joint tenancy. There is no right of survivorship. (See joint tenancy.)

Tenant: One who is not the owner but occupies real property under consent of the owner and in subordination to the owner's title. The tenant is entitled to exclusive possession, use and enjoyment of the property, usually for a rent specified in the lease.

Term Mortgage: A loan having a specified term, usually not over five years, during which interest is paid but the principal is not reduced. The entire loan is due and payable at the end of its term.

Time Is of the Essence: The inclusion of this phrase in a contract means that performance within a specified time is a material element of the transaction.

Title: The evidence of the right to or ownership in property. In the case of real estate, the documentary evidence of ownership is the title deed which specifies in whom the legal estate is vested and the history of ownership and transfers. Title may be acquired through purchase, inheritance, devise, gift, or through foreclosure of a mortgage.

Title I: The section of the FHA insurance program primarily for home improvements.

Title Defect: Any legal right held by others to claim property or to make demands upon an owner.

Title Search: An examination of public records, laws, and court decisions to disclose the past and current facts regarding ownership of real estate.

Townhouse: A residential unit on a small lot which has coincidental exterior limits with other similar units. Title to the unit and its lot is vested in the individual buyer with a fractional interest in common areas, if any.

Triple A Tenant: A prime tenant who has the highest credit rating.

Turnkey Leasing: The leasing to a housing authority for use by low-income tenants of completed housing constructed by private sponsors.

Turnkey Project: One in which a builder-contractor-developer contracts with a government or approved private agency to construct and deliver a completed facility that includes all items necessary for occupancy.

Unencumbered Property· A property that is free and clear.

Urban Land Institute (ULI): The Urban Land Institute is an independent, nonprofit research and educational organization incorporated in 1936 to improve the quality and standards of land use and development. It conducts practical research in the various fields of real estate knowledge, identifies and interprets land use trends in relation to changing needs, and disseminates information to promote orderly and efficient land use.

Usury: Charging more than the legal rate of interest for the use of money.

Usury Ceiling: A maximum legal rate, established by state law, of interest that may be charged for the use of money. The ceiling may vary depending on the nature or type of the loan.

VA: See Veterans Administration.

Vacancy Factor: A percentage rate expressing the loss from gross rental income due to vacancy and collection losses.

Valuation: See appraisal.

Variable Rate Mortgage: A mortgage agreement that allows for adjustment of the interest rate in keeping with a fluctuating market and terms agreed upon in the note.

Variance: An approved special charge in construction codes, zoning requirements, or other property use restrictions.

Vendee: The party to whom personal or real property is sold.

Vendor: The seller of personal or real property.

Vendor's Lien: An unpaid seller's right to a prior lien on property until the purchase price has been recovered.

Veterans Administration (VA): An independent agency of the federal government created by the Servicemen's Readjustment Act of 1944 to administer a variety of benefit programs designed to facilitate the adjustment of returning veterans to civilian life. The VA home loan guaranty program is designed to encourage lenders to offer long-term, low-down payment mortgages to eligible veterans by guaranteeing the lender against loss.

Warehousing: The borrowing of funds by a mortgage banker on a short-term basis at a commercial bank using permanent mortgage loans as collateral. This form of interim financing is used until the mortgages are sold to a permanent investor.

Warranty Deed: A deed in which the grantor or seller warrants or guarantees that good title is being conveyed, as opposed to a quitclaim deed that contains no representation or warranty as to the quality of title being conveyed.

Wrap-Around: A mortgage which secures a debt which includes the balance due on an existing senior mortgage and an additional amount advanced by the wrap-around mortgagee. The wrap-around mortgagee thereafter makes the amortizing payments on the senior mortgage. An example: A landowner has a mortgage securing a debt with an outstanding balance of $3,000,000. A lender now advances the same mortgagor a new $1,500,000 and undertakes to make the remaining payments due on the $3,000,000 debt and takes a $4,500,000 wrap-around junior mortgage on the real estate to secure the total indebtedness.

Yield: In real estate, the term refers to the effective annual amount of income which is being accrued on an investment. Expressed as a percentage of the price originally paid.

Zoning: The act of town, city, or county authorities specifying the type of use to which property may be put in specific areas.

Zoning Ordinance: The regulations of a municipality for controlling the character and use of property.

Depreciation

Here is a rundown on the different methods of depreciation available with respect to various types of real estate where the depreciation rules set up by the Tax Reform Act of 1969 apply:

(1) Straight-Line: This method of depreciation is available for all types of new and used properties.

(2) 125%-Declining-Balance: This depreciation method is available for (a) used real property acquired before July 25, 1969, and (b) used residential rental property acquired after July 24, 1969, with a useful life of 20 years or more.

(3) 150%-Declining-Balance: This method is the fastest available for (a) used real property acquired before July 25, 1969, and (b) new nonresidential rental properties constructed after July 24, 1969.

(4) Sum-of-the-Years-Digits: This method of depreciation is available only for (a) new real estate constructed before July 25, 1969, and (b) new residential rental properties.

(5) 200%-Declining-Balance: This depreciation method is available only for (a) new real estate constructed before July 25, 1969, and (b) new residential rental properties.

(6) Straight-Line Using Short Useful Life: This method of depreciation is available only for rehabilitation expenses for low- or moderate-income residential rental properties. Expenditures are depreciated on a straight-line basis using a 60-month useful life.

The following tables give the straight-line; the 200%-, 150%- and the 125%-declining-balance; and sum-of-the-years'-digits annual depreciation amounts and cumulative totals for assets having useful lives of from 3 to 50 years.

Computing Depreciation

Straight-Line: The cost or other basis of the asset is reduced by the anticipated salvage value. The remainder is then divided by the remaining useful life to find the annual straight-line deduction.

200%-Declining-Balance: The straight-line rate is first determined by dividing the useful life into 100. For example, if the useful life is 10 years, the straight-line rate is 10% (100 divided by 10). This rate is then doubled. The doubled rate is applied to the cost for the first year. The second year, the doubled rate is applied to the remaining (or declining) cost. This process is repeated each year.

At any time when the *remaining balance* divided by the *remaining useful life* (straight-line) gives a larger deduction than would result from continuing to apply the 200%-declining-balance rate against the declining balance, you can shift to straight-line. For example, with an asset having a useful life of 20 years, the 200%-declining-balance rate is 10%. If the asset cost $100, $68.62 will have been recovered via depreciation after 11 years, leaving a balance of $31.38. If we continue to apply the 10% rate, the 12th year's depreciation will be $3.14 (10% of $31.38). But if we used straight-line, dividing the remaining balance of $31.38 by the remaining useful life of 9 years, the result would be an annual depreciation for the last 9 years of $3.49.

In computing 200%-declining-balance, you need not consider salvage in determining the annual deductions. But, you cannot depreciate below the salvage value. When you switch to straight-line, you must take salvage into account in computing the straight-line deductions.

150%-Declining-Balance: You determine the straight-line rate as above. Then, multiply it by 1.5.

125%-Declining-Balance: First, determine the straight-line rate. Then multiply it by 1.25.

Sum-of-the-Years'-Digits: Total the years that make up the useful life. For example, if the useful life is 5 years, add together 1, 2, 3, 4 and 5, for a total of 15. Then, the first year's depreciation is 5/15 of your cost, say, $1,500, or $500. The second year, deduct 4/15 of $1,500, then 3/15 of $1,500, etc. Alternatively, starting with the second year, you can reduce the denominator by the previous year's numerator and apply the fraction to the reduced balance. Thus, in the second year, you'd take 4/10 of $1,000 and in the third year, 3/6 of $600. You cannot switch to straight-line without permission.

First-Year Depreciation

Personal tangible property (i.e., non-real estate items) get a special first-year writeoff under the tax law. Twenty percent of the cost up to $10,000 ($20,000 on a joint return) can be written off immediately. Then, the balance of the cost is subject to depreciation under the usual rules. Thus, if an asset costs $10,000, $2,000 is written off in the year of acquisition. The cost then becomes $8,000, and that is subject to depreciation under any approved method from the time of acquisition as if the original cost were $8,000.

Comparative Depreciation Tables

The following tables show the annual and cumulative depreciation for various useful lives under the straight-line, 200%-declining-balance, 150%-declining-balance, 125%-declining-balance,* and sum-of-the-years-digits methods. *All amounts are expressed as percentages of the basis of the property at the time the useful life begins.*

Year	*Straight-Line*		*200%-Declining-Balance*		*150%-Declining-Balance*		*Sum-of-Digits*	
	Annual %	*Cum.* %	*Annual* %	*Cum.* %	*Annual* %	*Cum.* %	*Annual* %	*Cum.* %
				3-Year Life				
1	33.33	33.33	66.66	66.66	50.00	50.00	50.00	50.00
2	33,33	66.66	22.22	88.88	25.00	75.00	33.33	83.33
3	33.34	100.00	7.41	96.29	12.50	87.50	16.67	100.00
				4-Year Life				
1	25.00	25.00	50.00	50.00	37.50	37.50	40.00	40.00
2	25.00	50.00	25.00	75.00	23.44	60.94	30.00	70.00
3	25.00	75.00	12.50	87.50	14.65	75.59	20.00	90.00
4	25.00	100.00	6.25	93.75	9.15	84.74	10.00	100.00
				5-Year Life				
1	20.00	20.00	40.00	40.00	30.00	30.00	33.33	33.33
2	20.00	40.00	24.00	64.00	21.00	51.00	26.67	60.00
3	20.00	60.00	14.40	78.40	14.70	65.70	20.00	80.00
4	20.00	80.00	8.64	87.04	10.29	75.99	13.33	93.33
5	20.00	100.00	5.18	92.22	7.20	83.19	6.67	100.00
				6-Year Life				
1	16.67	16.67	33.34	33.34	25.00	25.00	28.57	28.57
2	16.67	33.34	22.22	55.56	18.75	43.75	23.81	52.38
3	16.66	50.00	14.81	70.37	14.06	57.81	19.05	71.43
4	16.67	66.67	9.87	80.24	10.55	68.36	14.29	85.72
5	16.67	83.34	6.58	86.82	7.91	76.27	9.52	95.24
6	16.66	100.00	4.39	91.21	5.93	82.20	4.76	100.00
				7-Year Life				
1	14.28	14.28	28.57	28.57	21.43	21.43	25.00	25.00
2	14.28	28.56	20.41	48.98	16.83	38.26	21.43	46.43
3	14.29	42.85	14.58	63.56	13.23	51.49	17.86	64.29
4	14.29	57.14	10.41	73.97	10.40	61.89	14.29	78.58
5	14.29	71.43	7.44	81.41	8.17	70.06	10.71	89.29
6	14.29	85.72	5.31	86.72	6.42	76.48	7.14	96.43
7	14.28	100.00	3.79	90.51	5.04	81.52	3.57	100.00
				8-Year Life				
1	12.50	12.50	25.00	25.00	18.75	18.75	22.22	22.22
2	12.50	25.00	18.75	43.75	15.23	33.98	19.44	41.66
3	12.50	37.50	14.06	57.81	12.38	46.36	16.67	58.33
4	12.50	50.00	10.55	68.36	10.06	56.42	13.89	72.22
5	12.50	62.50	7.91	76.27	8.17	64.59	11.11	83.33
6	12.50	75.00	5.93	82.20	6.64	71.23	8.33	91.66
7	12.50	87.50	4.45	86.65	5.39	76.62	5.56	97.22
8	12.50	100.00	3.34	89.99	4.38	81.00	2.78	100.00

*Available for used residential real estate acquired after 7/24/69 and having useful life of 20 years or more when acquired. (See following page.)

Comparative Depreciation Tables *(continued)*

Year	*Straight-Line* Annual %	*Straight-Line* Cum. %	*200%-Declining-Balance* Annual %	*200%-Declining-Balance* Cum. %	*150%-Declining-Balance* Annual %	*150%-Declining-Balance* Cum. %	*125%-Declining-Balance* * Annual %	*125%-Declining-Balance* * Cum. %	*Sum-of-Digits* Annual %	*Sum-of-Digits* Cum. %
					9-Year Life					
1	11.11	11.11	22.22	22.22	16.67	16.67			20.00	20.00
2	11.11	22.22	17.28	39.50	13.89	30.56			17.78	37.78
3	11.11	33.33	13.44	52.94	11.57	42.13			15.56	53.34
4	11.11	44.44	10.45	63.39	9.65	51.78			13.33	66.67
5	11.11	55.55	8.13	71.52	8.04	59.82			11.11	77.78
6	11.11	66.66	6.32	77.84	6.70	66.52			8.89	86.67
7	11.11	77.77	4.92	82.76	5.58	72.10			6.67	93.34
8	11.11	88.88	3.83	86.59	4.65	76.75			4.44	97.78
9	11.12	100.00	2.98	89.57	3.88	80.63			2.22	100.00
					10-Year Life					
1	10.00	10.00	20.00	20.00	15.00	15.00			18.18	18.18
2	10.00	20.00	16.00	36.00	12.75	27.75			16.37	34.55
3	10.00	30.00	12.80	48.80	10.84	38.59			14.56	49.09
4	10.00	40.00	10.24	59.04	9.21	47.80			12.73	61.82
5	10.00	50.00	8.19	67.23	7.83	55.63			10.91	72.73
6	10.00	60.00	6.56	73.79	6.66	62.29			9.09	81.82
7	10.00	70.00	5.24	79.03	5.66	67.95			7.27	89.09
8	10.00	80.00	4.19	83.22	4.81	72.76			5.46	94.55
9	10.00	90.00	3.36	86.58	4.09	76.85			3.63	98.18
10	10.00	100.00	2.68	89.26	3.47	80.32			1.82	100.00
					15-Year Life					
1	6.67	6.67	13.33	13.33	10.00	10.00			12.50	12.50
2	6.66	13.33	11.56	24.89	9.00	19.00			11.67	24.17
3	6.67	20.00	10.01	34.90	8.10	27.10			10.83	35.00
4	6.67	26.67	8.68	43.58	7.29	34.39			10.00	45.00
5	6.66	33.33	7.53	51.11	6.56	40.95			9.17	54.17
6	6.67	40.00	6.51	57.62	5.90	46.85			8.33	62.50
7	6.67	46.67	5.65	63.27	5.32	52.17			7.50	70.00
8	6.66	53.33	4.90	68.17	4.78	56.95			6.67	76.67
9	6.67	60.00	4.25	72.42	4.30	61.25			5.83	82.50
10	6.67	66.67	3.67	76.09	3.88	65.13			5.00	87.50
11	6.66	73.33	3.19	79.28	3.49	68.62			4.17	91.67
12	6.67	80.00	2.76	82.04	3.14	71.76			3.33	95.00
13	6.67	86.67	2.40	84.44	2.82	74.58			2.50	97.50
14	6.66	93.33	2.07	86.51	2.54	77.12			1.67	99.17
15	6.67	100.00	1.80	88.31	2.29	79.41			.83	100.00

*Available for used residential real estate acquired after 7/24/69 and having useful life of 20 years or more when acquired. (See following page.)

Comparative Depreciation Tables *(continued)*

Year	*Straight-Line* Annual %	*Straight-Line* Cum. %	*200%-Declining-Balance* Annual %	*200%-Declining-Balance* Cum. %	*150%-Declining-Balance* Annual %	*150%-Declining-Balance* Cum. %	*125%-Declining-Balance** Annual %	*125%-Declining-Balance** Cum. %	*Sum-of-Digits* Annual %	*Sum-of-Digits* Cum. %
20-Year Life										
1	5.00	5.00	10.00	10.00	7.50	7.50	6.25	6.25	9.52	9.52
2	5.00	10.00	9.00	19.00	6.94	14.44	5.86	12.11	9.05	18.57
3	5.00	15.00	8.10	27.10	6.42	20.86	5.49	17.60	8.57	27.14
4	5.00	20.00	7.29	34.39	5.94	26.80	5.15	22.75	8.10	35.24
5	5.00	25.00	6.56	40.95	5.49	32.29	4.83	27.58	7.62	42.86
6	5.00	30.00	5.91	46.86	5.08	37.37	4.53	32.11	7.14	50.00
7	5.00	35.00	5.31	52.17	4.70	42.07	4.24	36.35	6.67	56.67
8	5.00	40.00	4.78	56.95	4.35	46.42	3.98	40.33	6.19	62.86
9	5.00	45.00	4.31	61.26	4.02	50.44	3.73	44.06	5.71	68.57
10	5.00	50.00	3.87	65.13	3.71	54.15	3.50	47.55	5.24	73.81
11	5.00	55.00	3.49	68.62	3.44	57.59	3.28	50.83	4.76	78.57
12	5.00	60.00	3.14	71.76	3.18	60.77	3.07	53.90	4.29	82.86
13	5.00	65.00	2.82	74.58	2.94	63.71	2.88	56.79	3.81	86.67
14	5.00	70.00	2.54	77.12	2.72	66.43	2.70	59.49	3.33	90.00
15	5.00	75.00	2.29	79.41	2.52	68.95	2.53	62.02	2.86	92.86
16	5.00	80.00	2.06	81.47	2.33	71.28	2.37	64.39	2.38	95.24
17	5.00	85.00	1.85	83.32	2.15	73.43	2.23	66.62	1.90	97.14
18	5.00	90.00	1.67	84.99	1.99	75.42	2.09	68.70	1.43	98.57
19	5.00	95.00	1.50	86.49	1.84	77.26	1.96	70.66	.95	99.52
20	5.00	100.00	1.35	87.84	1.70	78.96	1.83	72.49	.48	100.00
25-Year Life										
1	4.00	4.00	8.00	8.00	6.00	6.00	5.00	5.00	7.69	7.69
2	4.00	8.00	7.36	15.36	5.64	11.64	4.75	9.75	7.39	15.08
3	4.00	12.00	6.77	22.13	5.30	16.94	4.51	14.26	7.07	22.15
4	4.00	16.00	6.23	28.36	4.98	21.92	4.29	18.55	6.77	28.92
5	4.00	20.00	5.73	34.09	4.68	26.60	4.07	22.62	6.47	35.39
6	4.00	24.00	5.27	39.36	4.40	31.00	3.87	26.49	6.15	41.54
7	4.00	28.00	4.86	44.22	4.14	35.14	3.68	30.17	5.85	47.39
8	4.00	32.00	4.46	48.68	3.89	39.03	3.49	33.66	5.53	52.92
9	4.00	36.00	4.10	52.78	3.66	42.69	3.32	36.98	5.23	58.15
10	4.00	40.00	3.78	56.56	3.43	46.12	3.15	40.13	4.93	63.08
11	4.00	44.00	3.48	60.04	3.23	49.35	2.99	43.12	4.61	67.69
12	4.00	48.00	3.19	63.23	3.03	52.38	2.84	45.96	4.31	72.00
13	4.00	52.00	2.94	66.17	2.86	55.24	2.70	48.67	4.00	76.00
14	4.00	56.00	2.71	68.88	2.68	57.92	2.57	51.23	3.69	79.69
15	4.00	60.00	2.49	71.37	2.52	60.44	2.44	53.67	3.39	83.08
16	4.00	64.00	2.29	73.66	2.37	62.81	2.32	55.99	3.07	86.15
17	4.00	68.00	2.11	75.77	2.23	65.04	2.20	58.19	2.77	88.92
18	4.00	72.00	1.94	77.71	2.10	67.14	2.09	60.28	2.47	91.39
19	4.00	76.00	1.78	79.49	1.97	69.11	1.99	62.26	2.15	93.54
20	4.00	80.00	1.64	81.13	1.85	70.96	1.89	64.15	1.85	95.39

*Available for used residential real estate acquired after 7/24/69 and having useful life of 20 years or more when acquired. (See following page.)

Comparative Depreciation Tables *(continued)*

Year	*Straight-Line* Annual %	*Straight-Line* Cum. %	*200%-Declining-Balance* Annual %	*200%-Declining-Balance* Cum. %	*150%-Declining-Balance* Annual %	*150%-Declining-Balance* Cum. %	*125%-Declining-Balance* Annual %	*125%-Declining-Balance* Cum. %	*Sum-of-Digits* Annual %	*Sum-of-Digits* Cum. %
					25-Year Life *(continued)*					
21	4.00	84.00	1.51	82.64	1.74	72.70	1.79	65.94	1.53	96.92
22	4.00	88.00	1.39	84.03	1.64	74.34	1.70	67.65	1.23	98.15
23	4.00	92.00	1.28	85.31	1.54	75.88	1.62	69.26	.93	99.08
24	4.00	96.00	1.17	86.48	1.45	77.33	1.54	70.80	.61	99.69
25	4.00	100.00	1.08	87.56	1.36	78.69	1.46	72.26	.31	100.00
					30-Year Life					
1	3.33	3.33	6.67	6.67	5.00	5.00	4.16	4.16	6.45	6.45
2	3.34	6.67	6.22	12.89	4.75	9.75	3.99	8.16	6.24	12.69
3	3.33	10.00	5.81	18.70	4.51	14.26	3.83	11.99	6.02	18.71
4	3.33	13.33	5.42	24.12	4.29	18.55	3.67	15.65	5.81	24.52
5	3.34	16.67	5.06	29.18	4.07	22.62	3.51	19.17	5.59	30.11
6	3.33	20.00	4.72	33.90	3.87	26.49	3.37	22.54	5.37	35.48
7	3.33	23.33	4.40	38.30	3.68	30.17	3.23	25.76	5.17	40.65
8	3.34	26.67	4.12	42.42	3.49	33.66	3.09	28.86	4.94	45.59
9	3.33	30.00	3.84	46.26	3.32	36.98	2.96	31.82	4.73	50.32
10	3.33	33.33	3.58	49.84	3.15	40.13	2.84	34.66	4.52	54.84
11	3.34	36.67	3.34	53.18	2.99	43.12	2.72	37.38	4.30	59.14
12	3.33	40.00	3.12	56.30	2.84	45.96	2.61	39.99	4.09	63.23
13	3.33	43.33	2.92	59.22	2.70	48.66	2.50	42.49	3.87	67.10
14	3.34	46.67	2.72	61.94	2.57	51.23	2.40	44.89	3.65	70.75
15	3.33	50.00	2.53	64.47	2.44	53.67	2.30	47.19	3.44	74.19
16	3.33	53.33	2.37	66.84	2.32	55.99	2.20	49.39	3.23	77.42
17	3.34	56.67	2.21	69.05	2.20	58.19	2.11	51.50	3.01	80.43
18	3.33	60.00	2.07	71.12	2.09	60.28	2.02	53.52	2.80	83.23
19	3.33	63.33	1.92	73.04	1.99	62.27	1.94	55.45	2.58	85.81
20	3.34	66.67	1.80	74.84	1.89	64.16	1.86	57.31	2.36	88.17
21	3.33	70.00	1.68	76.52	1.80	65.96	1.78	59.09	2.15	90.32
22	3.33	73.33	1.56	78.08	1.70	67.66	1.70	60.79	1.94	92.26
23	3.34	76.67	1.46	79.54	1.62	69.28	1.63	62.43	1.72	93.98
24	3.33	80.00	1.37	80.91	1.54	70.82	1.57	63.99	1.61	95.49
25	3.33	83.33	1.27	82.18	1.46	72.28	1.50	65.49	1.29	96.78
26	3.34	86.67	1.19	83.37	1.39	73.67	1.44	66.93	1.07	97.85
27	3.33	90.00	1.11	84.48	1.32	74.99	1.38	68.31	.86	98.71
28	3.33	93.33	1.03	85.51	1.25	76.24	1.32	69.63	.65	99.36
29	3.34	96.67	.97	86.48	1.19	77.43	1.27	70.89	.43	99.79
30	3.33	100.00	.90	87.38	1.13	78.56	1.21	72.11	.21	100.00
					33-1/3 Year Life					
1	3.00	3.00	6.00	6.00	4.50	4.50	3.75	3.75	5.82	5.82
2	3.00	6.00	5.64	11.64	4.30	8.80	3.61	7.36	5.65	11.47
3	3.00	9.00	5.30	16.94	4.10	12.90	3.47	10.83	5.47	16.95
4	3.00	12.00	4.98	21.93	3.92	16.82	3.34	14.18	5.30	22.25
5	3.00	15.00	4.68	26.61	3.74	20.56	3.22	17.40	5.17	27.37

Comparative Depreciation Tables *(continued)*

Year	Straight-Line		200%-Declining-Balance		150%-Declining-Balance		125%-Declining-Balance		Sum-of-Digits	
	Annual %	Cum. %	Annual %	Cum. %	Annual %	Cum. %	Annual %	Cum. %	Annual %	Cum. %
33-1/3 Year Life *(continued)*										
6	3.00	18.00	4.40	31.00	3.57	24.14	3.10	20.49	4.95	32.32
7	3.00	21.00	4.14	35.15	3.41	27.55	2.98	23.47	4.76	37.10
8	3.00	24.00	3.89	39.03	3.16	30.81	2.87	26.34	4.60	41.70
9	3.00	27.00	3.66	42.70	3.11	33.93	2.76	29.11	4.43	46.13
10	3.00	30.00	3.44	46.14	2.97	36.90	2.66	31.77	4.25	50.38
11	3.00	33.00	3.23	49.37	2.84	39.74	2.56	34.32	4.08	54.46
12	3.00	36.00	3.04	52.41	2.71	42.45	2.46	36.79	3.90	58.36
13	3.00	39.00	2.86	55.26	2.59	45.04	2.37	39.16	3.73	62.10
14	3.00	42.00	2.68	57.95	2.47	47.51	2.28	41.44	3.55	65.64
15	3.00	45.00	2.52	60.47	2.36	49.88	2.20	43.63	3.38	69.02
16	3.00	48.00	2.37	62.84	2.26	52.13	2.11	45.75	3.20	72.22
17	3.00	51.00	2.23	65.07	2.15	54.29	2.03	47.78	3.03	75.25
18	3.00	54.00	2.10	67.17	2.06	56.34	1.95	49.74	2.85	78.10
19	3.00	57.00	1.97	69.14	1.96	58.31	1.88	51.63	2.68	80.78
20	3.00	60.00	1.85	71.00	1.88	60.18	1.81	53.44	2.50	83.28
21	3.00	63.00	1.74	72.73	1.79	61.97	1.75	55.19	2.33	85.61
22	3.00	66.00	1.64	74.37	1.71	63.69	1.68	56.87	2.15	87.77
23	3.00	69.00	1.54	75.90	1.63	65.32	1.62	58.48	1.98	89.75
24	3.00	72.00	1.45	77.35	1.56	66.88	1.56	60.04	1.81	91.56
25	3.00	75.00	1.36	78.71	1.49	68.37	1.50	61.54	1.63	93.19
26	3.00	78.00	1.28	79.99	1.42	69.79	1.44	62.98	1.46	94.64
27	3.00	81.00	1.20	81.19	1.36	71.15	1.39	64.37	1.28	95.92
28	3.00	84.00	1.13	82.32	1.30	72.45	1.34	65.71	1.11	97.03
29	3.00	87.00	1.06	83.38	1.24	73.69	1.29	66.99	.93	97.96
30	3.00	90.00	1.00	84.37	1.18	74.88	1.24	68.23	.76	98.72
31	3.00	93.00	.94	85.31	1.13	76.01	1.19	69.42	.58	99.30
32	3.00	96.00	.88	86.19	1.08	77.09	1.15	70.57	.41	99.71
33	3.00	99.00	.93	87.02	1.03	78.12	1.10	71.67	.23	99.94
33⅓	1.00	100.00	.26	87.28	.33	78.45	.35	71.95	.06	100.00
35-Year Life										
1	2.86	2.86	5.71	5.71	4.29	4.29	3.57	3.57	5.56	5.56
2	2.86	5.72	5.38	11.09	4.10	8.39	3.44	7.02	5.40	10.96
3	2.85	8.57	5.07	16.16	3.93	12.32	3.32	10.34	5.24	16.20
4	2.86	11.43	4.78	20.94	3.76	16.08	3.20	13.54	5.08	21.28
5	2.86	14.29	4.51	25.45	3.60	19.68	3.09	16.63	4.92	26.20
6	2.85	17.14	4.25	29.70	3.44	23.12	2.98	19.60	4.76	30.96
7	2.86	20.00	4.01	33.71	3.29	26.41	2.87	22.48	4.60	35.56
8	2.86	22.86	3.78	37.49	3.15	29.56	2.77	25.24	4.44	40.00
9	2.85	25.71	3.56	41.05	3.02	32.58	2.67	27.91	4.29	44.29
10	2.86	28.57	3.36	44.41	2.89	35.47	2.57	30.49	4.13	48.42

Comparative Depreciation Tables *(continued)*

Year	Straight-Line		200%-Declining-Balance		150%-Declining-Balance		125%-Declining-Balance		Sum-of-Digits	
	Annual %	Cum. %	Annual %	Cum. %	Annual %	Cum. %	Annual %	Cum. %	Annual %	Cum. %
	35-Year Life *(continued)*									
11	2.86	31.43	3.17	47.58	2.77	38.24	2.48	32.97	3.97	52.39
12	2.85	34.28	2.99	50.57	2.65	40.89	2.39	35.36	3.81	56.20
13	2.86	37.14	2.82	53.39	2.53	43.42	2.31	37.67	3.65	59.85
14	2.86	40.00	2.66	56.05	2.42	45.84	2.23	39.90	3.49	63.34
15	2.85	42.85	2.51	58.56	2.32	48.16	2.15	42.05	3.33	66.67
16	2.86	45.71	2.37	60.93	2.22	50.38	2.07	44.12	3.18	69.85
17	2.86	48.57	2.23	63.16	2.13	52.51	2.00	46.11	3.02	72.87
18	2.85	51.42	2.10	65.26	2.03	54.54	1.92	48.04	2.86	75.73
19	2.86	54.28	1.98	67.24	1.95	56.49	1.86	49.89	2.70	78.43
20	2.86	57.14	1.87	69.11	1.86	58.35	1.79	51.68	2.54	80.97
21	2.86	60.00	1.76	70.87	1.79	60.14	1.73	53.41	2.38	83.35
22	2.86	62.86	1.66	72.53	1.71	61.85	1.66	55.07	2.22	85.57
23	2.86	65.72	1.57	74.10	1.64	63.49	1.60	56.68	2.06	87.63
24	2.85	68.57	1.48	75.58	1.56	65.05	1.55	58.22	1.90	89.53
25	2.86	71.43	1.40	76.98	1.50	66.55	1.49	59.72	1.75	91.28
26	2.86	74.29	1.32	78.30	1.43	67.98	1.44	61.15	1.59	92.87
27	2.85	77.14	1.24	79.54	1.37	69.35	1.39	62.54	1.43	94.30
28	2.86	80.00	1.17	80.71	1.31	70.66	1.34	63.88	1.27	95.57
29	2.86	82.86	1.10	81.81	1.26	71.92	1.29	65.17	1.11	96.68
30	2.85	85.71	1.04	82.85	1.20	73.12	1.24	66.41	.95	97.63
31	2.86	88.57	.98	83.83	1.15	74.27	1.20	67.61	.79	98.42
32	2.86	91.43	.92	84.75	1.10	75.37	1.16	68.77	.63	99.05
33	2.85	94.28	.87	85.62	1.06	76.43	1.12	69.88	.47	99.52
34	2.86	97.14	.82	86.44	1.01	77.44	1.08	70.96	.32	99.84
35	2.86	100.00	.77	87.21	.97	78.41	1.04	72.00	.16	100.00
	40-Year Life									
1	2.50	2.50	5.00	5.00	3.75	3.75	3.13	3.13	4.88	4.88
2	2.50	5.00	4.75	9.75	3.61	7.36	3.03	6.15	4.75	9.63
3	2.50	7.50	4.51	14.26	3.47	10.83	2.93	9.09	4.64	14.27
4	2.50	10.00	4.29	18.55	3.34	14.17	2.84	11.93	4.51	18.78
5	2.50	12.50	4.07	22.62	3.22	17.39	2.75	14.68	4.39	23.17
6	2.50	15.00	3.87	26.49	3.10	20.49	2.67	17.34	4.27	27.44
7	2.50	17.50	3.68	30.17	2.98	23.47	2.58	19.93	4.14	31.58
8	2.50	20.00	3.49	33.66	2.87	26.34	2.50	22.43	4.03	35.61
9	2.50	22.50	3.32	36.98	2.76	29.10	2.42	24.85	3.90	39.51
10	2.50	25.00	3.15	40.13	2.66	31.76	2.35	27.20	3.78	43.29
11	2.50	27.50	2.99	43.12	2.56	34.32	2.27	29.48	3.66	46.95
12	2.50	30.00	2.84	45.96	2.46	36.78	2.20	31.68	3.54	50.49
13	2.50	32.50	2.71	48.67	2.37	39.15	2.13	33.82	3.41	53.90
14	2.50	35.00	2.56	51.23	2.28	41.43	2.07	35.88	3.29	57.19
15	2.50	37.50	2.44	53.67	2.20	43.63	2.00	37.89	3.18	60.37

Comparative Depreciation Tables *(continued)*

Year	Straight-Line		200%-Declining-Balance		150%-Declining-Balance		125%-Declining-Balance		Sum-of-Digits	
	Annual %	Cum. %	Annual %	Cum. %	Annual %	Cum. %	Annual %	Cum. %	Annual %	Cum. %
40-Year Life *(continued)*										
16	2.50	40.00	2.32	55.99	2.11	45.74	1.94	39.83	3.04	63.41
17	2.50	42.50	2.20	58.19	2.03	47.77	1.88	41.71	2.93	66.34
18	2.50	45.00	2.09	60.28	1.96	49.73	1.82	43.53	2.81	69.15
19	2.50	47.50	1.99	62.27	1.88	51.61	1.76	45.30	2.68	71.83
20	2.50	50.00	1.88	64.15	1.81	53.42	1.71	47.01	2.56	74.39
21	2.50	52.50	1.79	65.94	1.75	55.17	1.66	48.66	2.44	76.83
22	2.50	55.00	1.71	67.65	1.68	56.85	1.60	50.27	2.32	79.15
23	2.50	57.50	1.62	69.27	1.62	58.47	1.55	51.82	2.19	81.34
24	2.50	60.00	1.53	70.80	1.56	60.03	1.51	53.33	2.07	83.41
25	2.50	62.50	1.46	72.26	1.50	61.53	1.46	54.78	1.94	85.37
26	2.50	65.00	1.39	73.65	1.44	62.97	1.41	56.20	1.82	87.19
27	2.50	67.50	1.32	74.97	1.39	64.36	1.37	57.57	1.71	88.90
28	2.50	70.00	1.25	76.22	1.34	65.70	1.33	58.89	1.59	90.49
29	2.50	72.50	1.19	77.41	1.29	66.99	1.28	60.18	1.46	91.95
30	2.50	75.00	1.13	78.54	1.24	68.23	1.24	61.42	1.34	93.29
31	2.50	77.50	1.07	79.61	1.19	69.42	1.21	62.63	1.22	94.51
32	2.50	80.00	1.02	80.63	1.15	70.57	1.17	63.79	1.10	95.61
33	2.50	82.50	.97	81.60	1.10	71.67	1.13	64.93	.98	96.58
34	2.50	85.00	.92	85.52	1.06	72.73	1.10	66.02	.86	97.44
35	2.50	87.50	.87	83.39	1.02	73.75	1.06	67.08	.73	98.17
36	2.50	90.00	.83	84.22	.98	74.73	1.03	68.11	.61	98.78
37	2.50	92.50	.79	85.01	.95	75.68	1.00	69.11	.49	99.27
38	2.50	95.00	.75	85.76	.91	76.59	.97	70.07	.36	99.63
39	2.50	97.50	.71	86.47	.88	77.47	.94	71.01	.25	99.88
40	2.50	100.00	.68	87.15	.85	78.32	.91	71.92	.12	100.00
45-Year Life										
1	2.22	2.22	4.44	4.44	3.33	3.33	2.78	2.78	4.35	4.35
2	2.22	4.44	4.24	8.68	3.22	6.55	2.70	5.48	4.25	8.60
3	2.22	6.66	4.05	12.73	3.12	9.67	2.63	8.10	4.15	12.75
4	2.23	8.89	3.87	16.60	3.01	12.68	2.55	10.66	4.06	16.81
5	2.22	11.11	3.70	20.30	2.91	15.59	2.48	13.14	3.96	20.77
6	2.22	13.33	3.54	23.84	2.81	18.40	2.41	15.55	3.86	24.63
7	2.22	15.55	3.38	27.22	2.72	21.12	2.35	17.90	3.77	28.40
8	2.23	17.78	3.23	30.45	2.63	23.75	2.28	20.18	3.67	32.07
9	2.22	20.00	3.09	33.54	2.54	26.29	2.22	22.40	3.57	35.64
10	2.22	22.22	2.95	36.49	2.46	28.75	2.16	24.55	3.48	39.12
11	2.22	24.44	2.82	39.31	2.38	31.13	2.10	26.65	3.38	42.50
12	2.23	26.67	2.69	42.00	2.30	33.43	2.04	28.68	3.28	45.78
13	2.22	28.89	2.57	44.57	2.22	35.65	1.98	30.67	3.19	48.97
14	2.22	31.11	2.46	47.03	2.15	37.80	1.93	32.59	3.09	52.06
15	2.22	33.33	2.35	49.38	2.07	39.87	1.87	34.46	3.00	55.06

Comparative Depreciation Tables *(continued)*

Year	*Straight-Line*		*200%-Declining-Balance*		*150%-Declining-Balance*		*125%-Declining-Balance*		*Sum-of-Digits*	
	Annual %	*Cum.* %	*Annual* %	*Cum.* %	*Annual* %	*Cum.* %	*Annual* %	*Cum.* %	*Annual* %	*Cum.* %
					45-Year Life *(continued)*					
16	2.23	35.56	2.25	51.63	2.00	41.87	1.82	36.28	2.90	57.96
17	2.22	37.78	2.15	53.78	1.94	43.81	1.77	38.05	2.80	60.76
18	2.22	40.00	2.05	55.83	1.87	45.68	1.72	39.77	2.70	63.46
19	2.22	42.22	1.96	57.79	1.81	47.49	1.67	41.45	2.61	66.07
20	2.23	44.45	1.87	59.66	1.75	49.24	1.63	43.07	2.51	68.58
21	2.22	46.67	1.79	61.45	1.69	50.93	1.58	44.66	2.42	71.00
22	2.22	48.89	1.71	63.16	1.64	52.57	1.54	46.19	2.32	73.32
23	2.22	51.11	1.63	64.79	1.58	54.15	1.49	47.69	2.22	75.54
24	2.23	53.34	1.56	66.35	1.53	55.68	1.45	49.14	2.13	77.67
25	2.22	55.56	1.49	67.84	1.48	57.16	1.41	50.55	2.03	79.70
26	2.22	57.78	1.42	69.26	1.43	58.59	1.37	51.93	1.93	81.63
27	2.22	60.00	1.36	70.62	1.38	59.97	1.34	53.26	1.84	83.47
28	2.23	62.23	1.30	71.92	1.33	61.30	1.30	54.56	1.74	85.21
29	2.22	64.45	1.24	73.16	1.29	62.59	1.26	55.82	1.64	86.85
30	2.22	66.67	1.18	74.34	1.25	63.84	1.23	57.05	1.55	88.40
31	2.22	68.89	1.13	75.47	1.21	65.05	1.19	58.24	1.45	89.85
32	2.23	71.12	1.08	76.55	1.17	66.22	1.16	59.40	1.35	91.20
33	2.22	73.34	1.03	77.58	1.13	67.35	1.13	60.53	1.26	92.46
34	2.22	75.56	.98	78.56	1.09	68.44	1.10	61.63	1.16	93.62
35	2.22	77.78	.94	79.50	1.05	69.49	1.07	62.69	1.06	94.68
36	2.22	80.00	.90	80.40	1.02	70.51	1.04	63.73	.97	95.65
37	2.23	82.23	.86	81.26	.98	71.49	1.01	64.74	.87	96.52
38	2.22	84.45	.82	82.08	.95	72.44	.98	65.72	.77	97.29
39	2.22	86.67	.78	82.86	.92	73.36	.95	66.67	.68	97.97
40	2.22	88.89	.75	83.61	.89	74.25	.93	67.59	.58	98.55
41	2.23	91.12	.72	84.33	.86	75.11	.90	68.49	.48	99.03
42	2.22	93.34	.69	85.02	.83	75.94	.88	69.37	.39	99.42
43	2.22	95.56	.66	85.68	.80	76.74	.85	70.22	.29	99.71
44	2.22	97.78	.63	86.31	.78	77.52	.83	71.05	.19	99.90
45	2.22	100.00	.60	86.91	.75	78.27	.80	71.85	.10	100.00
					50-Year Life					
1	2.00	2.00	4.00	4.00	3.00	3.00	2.50	2.50	3.92	3.92
2	2.00	4.00	3.84	7.84	2.91	5.91	2.44	4.94	3.85	7.77
3	2.00	6.00	3.69	11.53	2.82	8.73	2.38	7.31	3.76	11.53
4	2.00	8.00	3.54	15.07	2.74	11.47	2.32	9.63	3.69	15.22
5	2.00	10.00	3.39	18.46	2.66	14.13	2.26	11.89	3.60	18.82
6	2.00	12.00	3.26	21.72	2.58	16.71	2.20	14.09	3.53	22.35
7	2.00	14.00	3.14	24.86	2.50	19.21	2.15	16.24	3.45	25.80
8	2.00	16.00	3.00	27.86	2.42	21.63	2.09	18.33	3.38	29.18
9	2.00	18.00	2.89	30.75	2.35	23.98	2.04	20.38	3.29	32.47
10	2.00	20.00	2.77	33.52	2.28	26.26	1.99	22.37	3.22	35.69

Comparative Depreciation Tables *(continued)*

Year	Straight-Line Annual %	Straight-Line Cum. %	200%-Declining-Balance Annual %	200%-Declining-Balance Cum. %	150%-Declining-Balance Annual %	150%-Declining-Balance Cum. %	125%-Declining-Balance Annual %	125%-Declining-Balance Cum. %	Sum-of-Digits Annual %	Sum-of-Digits Cum. %
50-Year Life *(continued)*										
11	2.00	22.00	2.66	36.18	2.21	28.47	1.94	24.31	3.15	38.82
12	2.00	24.00	2.55	38.73	2.15	30.62	1.89	26.20	3.06	41.88
13	2.00	26.00	2.45	41.18	2.08	32.70	1.84	28.05	2.98	44.86
14	2.00	28.00	2.35	43.53	2.02	34.72	1.80	29.84	2.91	47.77
15	2.00	30.00	2.26	45.79	1.96	36.68	1.75	31.60	2.82	50.59
16	2.00	32.00	2.17	47.96	1.90	38.58	1.71	33.31	2.74	53.33
17	2.00	34.00	2.08	50.04	1.84	40.42	1.67	34.98	2.67	56.00
18	2.00	36.00	2.00	52.04	1.79	42.21	1.63	36.60	2.59	58.59
19	2.00	38.00	1.92	53.96	1.73	43.94	1.58	38.19	2.51	61.10
20	2.00	40.00	1.84	55.80	1.68	45.62	1.55	39.73	2.43	63.53
21	2.00	42.00	1.77	57.57	1.63	47.25	1.51	41.24	2.35	65.88
22	2.00	44.00	1.70	59.27	1.58	48.83	1.47	42.71	2.28	68.16
23	2.00	46.00	1.62	60.89	1.53	50.36	1.43	44.14	2.19	70.35
24	2.00	48.00	1.57	62.46	1.49	51.85	1.40	45.54	2.12	72.47
25	2.00	50.00	1.50	63.96	1.44	53.29	1.36	46.90	2.04	74.51
26	2.00	52.00	1.44	65.40	1.40	54.69	1.33	48.23	1.96	76.47
27	2.00	54.00	1.39	66.79	1.36	56.05	1.29	49.52	1.87	78.35
28	2.00	56.00	1.33	68.12	1.32	57.37	1.26	50.78	1.81	80.16
29	2.00	58.00	1.27	69.39	1.28	58.64	1.23	52.01	1.72	81.88
30	2.00	60.00	1.22	70.61	1.24	59.89	1.20	53.21	1.65	83.53
31	2.00	62.00	1.18	71.79	1.20	61.09	1.17	54.38	1.57	85.10
32	2.00	64.00	1.13	72.92	1.17	62.26	1.14	55.52	1.49	86.59
33	2.00	66.00	1.08	74.00	1.13	63.39	1.11	56.63	1.41	88.00
34	2.00	68.00	1.04	75.04	1.10	64.49	1.08	57.72	1.33	89.33
35	2.00	70.00	1.00	76.04	1.07	65.56	1.06	58.78	1.26	90.59
36	2.00	72.00	.96	77.00	1.03	66.59	1.03	59.81	1.18	91.77
37	2.00	74.00	.92	77.92	1.00	67.59	1.00	60.81	1.09	92.86
38	2.00	76.00	.88	78.80	.97	68.56	.98	61.79	1.02	93.88
39	2.00	78.00	.85	79.65	.94	69.50	.96	62.75	.94	94.82
40	2.00	80.00	.81	80.46	.92	70.42	.93	63.68	.87	95.69
41	2.00	82.00	.78	81.24	.89	71.31	.91	64.58	.78	96.47
42	2.00	84.00	.75	81.99	.86	72.17	.89	65.47	.71	97.18
43	2.00	86.00	.72	82.71	.84	73.01	.86	66.33	.62	97.80
44	2.00	88.00	.69	83.40	.81	73.82	.84	67.18	.55	98.35
45	2.00	90.00	.67	84.07	.79	74.61	.82	68.00	.47	98.82
46	2.00	92.00	.64	84.71	.76	75.37	.80	68.80	.40	99.22
47	2.00	94.00	.61	85.32	.74	76.11	.78	69.58	.31	99.53
48	2.00	96.00	.59	85.90	.72	76.83	.76	70.34	.24	99.77
49	2.00	98.00	.57	86.47	.70	77.53	.74	71.08	.15	99.92
50	2.00	100.00	.54	87.01	.67	78.20	.72	71.80	.08	100.00

ADR Classes and Guidelines

Asset guide-line class	*Description of assets included*	*Asset depreciation range (in years)* Lower limit	Asset guide-line period	Upper limit	*Annual asset guide-line repair allow-ance percent-age*
00.0	Depreciable Assets Used in All Business Activities, Except as Noted:				
00.2	Transportation Equipment:				
00.21	Aircraft (airframes and engines) except aircraft of air transportation companies	5	6	7	14.0
00.22	Automobiles, taxis	2.5	3	3.5	16.5
00.23	Buses	7	9	11.0	11.5
00.24	General purpose trucks, including concrete ready-mix trucks and ore trucks for use over-the-road:				
00.241	Light (actual unloaded weight less than 13,000 pounds)	3	4	5	16.5
00.242	Heavy (actual unloaded weight 13,000 pounds or more)	5	6	7	10.0
00.25	Railroad cars and locomotives, except those owned by railroad transportation companies	12	15	18	8.0
00.26	Tractor units used over-the-road	3	4	5	16.5
00.27	Trailers and trailer-mounted containers	5	6	7	10.0
00.28	Vessels, barges, tugs, and similar water transportation equipment, except those used in marine contract construction	14.5	18	21.5	6.0
00.3	Land Improvements:[1]				
	Improvements directly to or added to land that are more often than not directly related to one or another of the specific classes of economic activity specified below. Includes only those depreciable land improvements which have a limited period of use in the trade or business, the length of which can be reasonably estimated for the particular improvement. That is, general grading of land, such as in the case of cemeteries, golf courses and general site grading and leveling costs not directly related to buildings or other structural improvements to be added, are not depreciable or included in this class, but such costs are added to the cost basis of the land.				
	Includes paved surfaces such as sidewalks and roads, canals, waterways, drainage facilities and sewers; wharves and docks; bridges; all fences except those included in specific classes described below (i.e., farm and railroad fences); landscaping, shrubbery and similar improvements; radio and television transmitting towers, and other inherently permanent physical structures added to land except buildings and their structural components.				

[1]This class is established for a three-year transition period in accordance with Section 109(e)(1) of the Revenue Act of 1971 (P.O. 92-178, I.R.B. 1972-3, 14) and will be in effect for the period beginning January 1, 1971 and ending January 1, 1974 or at such earlier date as of which asset classes incorporating the assets herein described are represcribed or modified.

ADR Classes and Guidelines *(continued)*

Asset guide-line class	*Description of assets included*	*Asset depreciation range (in years)* Lower limit	*Asset guide-line period*	*Upper limit*	*Annual asset guide-line repair allow-ance percent-age*
	Excludes land improvements of electric, gas, steam and water utilities; telephone and telegraph companies; and pipeline, water and rail carriers which are assets covered by asset guideline classes specific to their respective classes of economic activity		20		
01.0 to 79.0	Depreciable Assets Used in the Following Activities:[2]				
01.0	Agriculture:				
	Includes only such assets as are identified below and that are used in the production of crops or plants, vines and trees (including forestry); the keeping, grazing, or feeding of livestock for animal products (including serums), for animals increase, or value increase; the operation of dry lot or farm dairies, nurseries, greenhouses, sod farms, mushroom cellars, cranberry bogs, apiaries, and fur farms; the production of bulb, flower, and vegetable seed crops; and the performance of agricultural, animal husbandry and horticultural services.				
01.1	Machinery and equipment, including grain bins and fences but no other land improvements	8	10	12	11.0
01.2	Animals:				
01.21	Cattle, breeding or dairy	5.5	7	8.5	
01.22	Horses, breeding or work	8	10	12	
01.23	Hogs, breeding	2.5	3	3.5	
01.24	Sheep and goats, breeding	4	5	6	
01.3	Farm buildings	20	25	30.0	5.0
10.0	Mining:				
	Includes assets used in the mining and quarrying of metallic and non-metallic minerals (including sand, gravel, stone, and clay) and the milling beneficiation and other primary preparation of such materials	8	10	12	6.5
13.0	Petroleum and natural gas production and related activities:				
13.1	Drilling of oil and gas wells:				
	Includes assets used in the drilling of onshore oil and gas wells on a contract, fee or other basis and the provision of geophysical and other exploration services; and the provision of such oil and gas field services as				

[2] All asset classes defined below include subsidiary assets within the meaning of Section 109(e)(2) of the Revenue Act of 1971 whenever such assets are used in the economic activities specified. However, in accordance with the provisions of that section of the Act, during the period beginning on January 1, 1971 and ending January 1, 1974 or such earlier date as of which asset classes incorporating the subsidiary assets are represcribed or modified, taxpayers may exclude from an election all subsidiary assets in a specified class provided that at least 3 percent of all the assets placed in service in the class during the taxable year subsidiary assets. See Section 1.167(a)-11(b)(5)(vii) for application of 3 percent test.

ADR Classes and Guidelines *(continued)*

Asset guide-line class	*Description of assets included*	*Asset depreciation range (in years)* Lower limit	Asset guide-line period	Upper limit	*Annual asset guide-line repair allow-ance percent-age*
	chemical treatment, plugging and abandoning of wells and cementing or perforating well casings; but not including assets used in the performance of any of these activities and services by integrated petroleum and natural gas producers for their own account	5	6	7	10.0
13.2	Exploration for petroleum and natural gas deposits: Includes assets used for drilling of wells and production of petroleum and natural gas, including gathering pipelines and related storage facilities, when these are related activities undertaken by petroleum and natural gas producers	11	14	17	4.5
13.3	Petroleum refining: Includes assets used for the distillation, fractionation, and catalytic cracking of crude petroleum into gasoline and its other components	13	16	19	7.0
13.4	Marketing of petroleum and petroleum products: Includes assets used in marketing, such as related storage facilities and complete service stations, but not including any of these facilities related to petroleum and natural gas trunk pipelines	13	16	19	4.0
15.0	Contract construction: Includes such assets used by general building, special trade, heavy construction and marine contractors; does not include assets used by companies in performing construction services on their own account.				
15.1	Contract construction other than marine	4	5	6	12.5
15.2	Marine contract construction .... Includes floating, self-propelled and other drilling platforms used in offshore drilling for oil and gas.	9.5	12	14.5	5.0
20.0	Manufacture of foods and beverages for human consumption, and certain related products, such as manufactured ice, chewing gum, vegetable and animal fats and oils, and prepared feeds for animals and fowls:				
20.1	Grain and grain mill products: Includes assets used in the production of flours, cereals, livestock feeds, and other grain and grain mill products	13.5	17	20.5	6.0
20.2	Sugar and sugar products: Includes assets used in the production of raw sugar, syrup or finished sugar from sugar cane or sugar beets	14.5	18	21.5	4.5
20.3	Vegetable oils and vegetable oil products: Includes assets used in the production of oil from vegetable materials and the manufacture of related vegetable oil products	14.5	18	21.5	3.5

ADR Classes and Guidelines *(continued)*

Asset guideline class	Description of assets included	Asset depreciation range (in years): Lower limit	Asset guideline period	Upper limit	Annual asset guideline repair allowance percentage
20.4	All other food and kindred products: Includes assets used in the production of foods, beverages and related production not included in classes 20.1, 20.2 and 20.3	9.5	12	14.5	5.5
20.5	Manufacture of food and beverages—special handling devices: Includes assets defined as specialized materials handling devices such as returnable pellets, pelletized containers, and fish processing equipment including boxes, baskets, carts, and flaking trays used in activities as defined in classes 20.1, 20.2, 20.3, 20.4. Special handling devices are specifically designed for the handling of particular products and have no significant utilitarian value and cannot be adapted to further or different use after changes or improvements are made in the design of the particular product handled by the special devices. Does not include general purpose small tools such as wrenches and drills, both hand and power-driven, and other general purpose equipment such as conveyors, transfer equipment, and materials handling devices	3	4	5	20.0
21.0	Manufacture of tobacco and tobacco products: Includes assets used in the production of cigarettes, cigars, smoking and chewing tobacco, snuff and other tobacco products	12	15	18	5.0
22.0	Manufacture of textile mill products:				
22.1	Knitwear and knit products: Includes assets used in the production of knit fabrics, knit apparel, and yarns processed for knitting, such as boarding machines, dryers, knitting machines, loopers, warpers, winders, seaming machines, twisting machines, twist setting machines, texturizing machines, and collection system equipment	7	9	11	7.0
22.2	Textile mill products, except knitwear: Includes assets used in the production of spun yarn and woven or non-woven fabrics, mattresses, carpets, rugs, pads, sheets, and of other products of natural or synthetic fibers, such as preparatory equipment for fibers, and machinery for carding, combing, drawing, roving, spinning, twisting, warping, winding, slashing, and weaving	11	14	17	4.5
22.3	Finishing and dyeing: Includes assets used in the finishing and dyeing of				

ADR Classes and Guidelines *(continued)*

Asset guide-line class	Description of assets included	Asset depreciation range (in years) Lower limit	Asset guide-line period	Upper limit	Annual asset guide-line repair allow-ance percent-age
	natural and synthetic fibers, yarns, fabrics including knit materials, and knit apparel, such as assets used for washing, bleaching, finishing, printing and dyeing, and drying	9.5	12	14.5	5.5
23.0	Manufacture of apparel and other finished products: Includes assets used in the production of clothing and fabricated textile products by the cutting and sewing of woven fabrics, other textile products and furs; but does not include assets used in the manufacture of apparel from rubber and leather	7	9	11	7.0
24.0	Manufacture of lumber and wood products:				
24.1	Cutting of timber: Includes logging machinery and equipment and road building equipment used by logging and sawmill operators and pulp manufacturers on their own account	5	6	7	10.0
24.2	Sawing of dimensional stock from logs: Includes machinery and equipment installed in permanent or well-established sawmills	8	10	12	6.5
24.3	Sawing of dimensional stock from logs: Includes machinery and equipment installed in sawmills characterized by temporary foundations and a lack, or minimum amount, of lumber-handling, drying, and residue disposal equipment and facilities	5	6	7	10.0
24.4	Manufacture of lumber, wood products, and furniture: Includes assets used in the production of plywood, hardboard, flooring, veneers, furniture and other wood products, including the treatment of poles and timber	8	10	12	6.5
26.0	Manufacture of paper and allied products:				
26.1	Manufacture of pulps from wood and other cellulose fibers and rags: Includes assets used in the manufacture of paper and paperboard, but does not include the assets used in pulpwood logging nor the manufacture of hardboard	13	16	19	4.5
26.2	Manufacture of paper and paperboard: Includes assets used in the production of converted products such as paper coated off the paper machines, paper bags, paper boxes, and envelopes	9.5	12	14.5	5.5
27.0	Printing, publishing and allied industries: Includes assets used in printing by one or more of the common processes, such as letterpress, lithography, gravure, or screen; the performance of services for the printing				

ADR Classes and Guidelines *(continued)*

Asset guide-line class	*Description of assets included*	*Asset depreciation range (in years)* Lower limit	Asset guide-line period	Upper limit	*Annual asset guide-line repair allow-ance percent-age*
	trade, such as bookbinding, typesetting, engraving, photoengraving, and electrotyping; and the publication of newspapers, books, and periodicals, whether or not carried out in conjunction with printing	9	11	13	5.5
28.0	Manufacture of chemicals and allied products: Includes assets used in the manufacture of basis chemicals such as acids, alkalies, salts, and organic and inorganic chemicals; chemical products to be used in further manufacture, such as synthetic fibers and plastics materials, including petro-chemical processing beyond that which is ordinarily a part of petroleum refining; and finished chemical products, such as pharmaceuticals, cosmetics, soaps, fertilizers, paints and varnishes, explosives, and compressed and liquified gases. Does not include assets used in the manufacture of finished rubber and plastic products or in the production of natural gas products, butane, propane, and byproducts of natural gas production plants ..	9	11	13	5.5
30.0	Manufacture of rubber and plastics products:				
30.1	Manufacture of rubber products: Includes assets used for the production of products from natural, synthetic, or reclaimed rubber, gutta percha, balata, or gutta siak, such as tires, tubes, rubber footwear, mechanical rubber goods, heels and soles, flooring, and rubber sundries; and in the recapping, retreading, and rebuilding of tires	11	14	17	5.0
30.11	Manufacture of rubber products—special tools and devices: Includes assets defined as special tools, such as jigs, dies, mandrels, molds, lasts, patterns, specialty containers, pallets, shells and tire molds and accessory parts such as rings and insert plates used in activities as defined in Class 30.1. Does not include tire building drums and accessory parts and general purpose small tools such as wrenches and drills, both power and hand-driven, and other general purpose equipment such as conveyors and transfer equipment	3	4	5	
30.2	Manufacture of miscellaneous finished plastics products: Includes assets used in the manufacture of plastics products and the molding of primary plastics for the trade. Does not include assets used in the manufacture of basic plastics materials nor the manufacture of phonograph records	9	11	13	5.5

ADR Classes and Guidelines *(continued)*

Asset guide-line class	*Description of assets included*	*Asset depreciation range (in years)* Lower limit	*Asset guide-line period*	*Upper limit*	*Annual asset guide-line repair allow-ance percent-age*
30.21	Manufacture of miscellaneous finished plastic products—special tools: Includes assets defined as special tools such as jigs, dies, fixtures, molds, patterns, gauges, and specialty transfer and shipping devices, used in activities as defined in Class 30.2. Special tools are specifically designed for the production or processing of particular parts and have no significant utilitarian value and cannot be adapted to further or different use after changes or improvements are made in the model design of the particular part produced by the special tools. Does not include general purpose small tools, such as wrenches and drills, both hand and power-driven, and other general purpose equipment such as conveyors, transfer equipment, and materials handling devices	3	3.5	4	5.5
31.0	Manufacture of leather: Includes assets used in the tanning, currying, and finishing of hides and skins; the processing of fur pelts; and the manufacture of finished leather products, such as footwear, belting, apparel, luggage and similar leather goods	9	11	13	5.5
32.0	Manufacture of stone, clay, glass, and concrete products:				
32.1	Manufacture of glass products: Includes assets used in the production of flat, blown, or pressed products of glass, such as float and window and window glass, glass containers, glassware, and fiberglass. Does not include assets used in the manufacture of lenses	11	14	17	12.0[6]
32.11	Manufacture of glass products—special tools: Includes assets defined as special tools such as molds, patterns, pallets, and specialty transfer and shipping devices such as steel racks to transport automotive glass, used in activities as defined in Class 32.1. Special tools are specifically designed for the production or processing of particular parts and have no significant utilitarian value and cannot be adapted to further or different use after changes or improvements are made in the model design of the particular part produced by the special tools. Does not include general purpose small tools such as wrenches and drills, both hand power-driven, and other general purpose equipment such as conveyors, transfer equipment, and materials handling devices	2	2.5	3	10.0

ADR Classes and Guidelines *(continued)*

Asset guide-line class	*Description of assets included*	*Asset depreciation range (in years)* Lower limit	*Asset guide-line period*	*Upper limit*	*Annual asset guide-line repair allow-ance percent-age*
32.2	Manufacture of cement: Includes assets used in the production of cement, but does not include any assets used in the manufacture of concrete and concrete products nor in any mining or extraction process	16	20	24	3.0
32.3	Manufacture of other stone and clay products: Includes assets used in the manufacture of products from materials in the form of clay and stone, such as brick, tile and pipe; pottery and related products, such as vitreous-china, plumbing fixtures, earthenware and ceramic insulating materials; and also includes assets used in manufacture of concrete and concrete products. Does not include assets used in any mining or extraction processes.	12	15	18	4.5
	Includes assets used in the smelting and refining of ferrous and nonferrous metals from ore, pig, or scrap, the rolling, drawing, and alloying of ferrous and nonferrous metals; the manufacture of castings, forgings, and other basic products of ferrous and nonferrous metals; and the manufacture of nails, spikes, structural shapes, tubing, and wire and cable.				
33.0	Manufacture of primary metals: Includes assets used in the smelting and refining of ferrous and nonferrous metals from ore, pig, or scrap, the rolling, drawing, and alloying of ferrous and nonferrous metals; the manufacture of castings, forgings, and other basic products of ferrous and nonferrous metals; and the manufacture of nails, spikes, structural shapes, tubing, and wire and cable.				
33.1	Ferrous metals	14.5	18	21.5	8.0
33.11	Ferrous metals—special tools: Includes assets defined as special tools such as dies, jigs, molds, patterns, fixtures, gauges, and drawings concerning such special tools used in the activities as defined in Class 33.1, Ferrous metals. Special tools are specifically designed for the production or processing of particular products or parts and have no significant utilitarian value and cannot be adapted to further or different use after changes or improvements are made in the model design of the particular part produced by the special tools. Does not include general purpose small tools, such as wrenches and drills, both hand and power-driven, and other general pur-				

ADR Classes and Guidelines *(continued)*

Asset guide-line class	Description of assets included	Asset depreciation range (in years) Lower limit	Asset guide-line period	Upper limit	Annual asset guide-line repair allow-ance percent-age
	pose equipment such as conveyors, transfer equipment, and materials handling devices. Rolls, mandrels and refractories are not included in Class 33.11 but are included in Class 33.1	5	6.5	8	4.0
33.2	Nonferrous metals	11	14	17	4.5
33.21	Nonferrous metals—special tools: Includes assets defined as special tools such as dies, jigs, molds, patterns, fixtures, gauges, and drawings concerning such special tools used in the activities as defined in Class 33.2. Nonferrous metals. Special tools are specifically designed for the production or processing of particular products or parts and have no significant utilitarian value and cannot be adapted to further or different use after changes or improvements are made in the model design of the particular part produced by the special tools. Does not include general purpose small tools such as wrenches and drills, both hand and power-driven, and other general purpose equipment such as conveyors, transfer equipment, and materials handling devices. Rolls, mandrels and refractories are not included in Class 33.21 but are included in Class 33.2	5	6.5	8	4
34.0	Manufacture of fabricated metal products: Includes assets used in the production of metal cans, tinware, nonelectric heating apparatus, fabricated structural metal products, metal stampings and other ferrous and nonferrous metal and wire products not elsewhere classified	9.5	12	14.5	6.0
34.01	Manufacture of fabricated metal products—special tools: Includes assets defined as special tools such as dies, jigs, molds, patterns, fixtures, gauges, and returnable containers and drawings concerning such special tools used in the activities as defined in Class 34.0. Special tools are specifically designed for the production or processing of particular machine components, products or parts, and have no significant utilitarian value and cannot be adapted to further or different use after changes or improvements are made in the model design of the particular part produced by the special tools. Does not include general purpose small tools such as wrenches and drills, both hand and power-driven, and other general purpose equipment such as conveyors, transfer equipment, and materials handling devices	2.5	3.0	3.5	3.5

ADR Classes and Guidelines *(continued)*

Asset guide-line class	Description of assets included	Asset depreciation range (in years) Lower limit	Asset guide-line period	Upper limit	Annual asset guide-line repair allow-ance percent-age
35.0	Manufacture of machinery, except electrical and transportation equipment:				
35.1	Manufacture of metalworking machinery: Includes assets used in the production of metal cutting and forming machines, special dies, tools, jigs and fixtures, and machine tool accessories	9.5	12	14.5	5.5
35.11	Manufacture of metalworking machinery—special tools: Includes assets defined as special tools, such as jigs, dies, fixtures, molds, patterns, gauges, and specialty transfer and shipping devices, used in activities as defined in Class 35.1. Special tools are specifically designed for the production or processing of particular machine components and have no significant utilitarian value and cannot be adapted to further or different use after changes or improvements are made in the model design of the particular part produced by the special tools. Does not include general purpose small tools such as wrenches and drills, both hand and power-driven, and other general purpose equipment such as conveyors, transfer equipment, and materials handling devices	5	6	7	12.5
35.2	Manufacture of other machines: Includes assets used in the production of such machinery as engines and turbines; farm machinery, construction, and mining machinery; general and special industrial machines including office machines and non-electronic computing equipment; miscellaneous machines except electrical equipment and transportation equipment	9.5	12	14.5	5.5
35.21	Manufacture of other machines—special tools: Includes assets defined as special tools, such as jigs, dies, fixtures, molds, patterns, gauges, and specialty transfer and shipping devices, used in activities as defined in Class 35.2. Special tools are specifically designed for the production or processing of particular machine components and have no significant utilitarian value and cannot be adapted to further or different use after changes or improvements are made in the model design or the particular part produced by the special tools. Does not include general purpose small tools such as wrenches and drills, both hand and power-driven, and other general purpose equipment such as conveyors, transfer equipment, and materials handling devices	5	6.5	8	12.5

ADR Classes and Guidelines *(continued)*

Asset guideline class	Description of assets included	Asset depreciation range (in years): Lower limit	Asset guideline period	Upper limit	Annual asset guideline repair allowance percentage
36.0	Manufacture of electrical machinery, equipment, and supplies: Includes assets used in the production of machinery, apparatus, and supplies for the generation, storage, transmission, transformation, and utilization of electrical energy.				
36.1	Manufacture of electrical equipment: Includes assets used in the production of such machinery as electric test and distributing equipment, electrical industrial apparatus, household appliances, electric lighting and wiring equipment; electronic components and accessories, phonograph records, storage batteries and ignition systems	9.5	12	14.5	5.5
36.11	Manufacture of electrical equipment—special tools: Includes assets defined as special tools such as jigs, dies, molds, patterns, fixtures, gauges, returnable containers, and specialty transfer devices used in activities as defined in Class 36.1. Special tools are specifically designed for the production or processing of particular machine components, products or parts, and have no significant utilitarian value and cannot be adapted to further or different use after changes or improvements are made in the model design of the particular part produced by the special tools. Does not include general purpose small tools such as wrenches and drills, both hand and power-driven and other general purpose equipment such as conveyors, transfer equipment, and materials handling devices	4	5	6	
36.2	Manufacture of electronic products: Includes assets used in the production of electronic detection, guidance, control, radiation, computation, test and navigation equipment and the components thereof. Does not include the assets of manufacturers engaged only in the purchase and assembly of components	6.5	8	9.5	7.5
37.0	Manufacture of transportation equipment: Includes assets used in the production of such machinery as vehicles and equipment for the transportation of passengers and cargo.				
37.1	Manufacture of motor vehicles:				
37.11	Motor vehicle manufacturing assets: Includes assets used in the manufacture and assembly of finished automobiles, trucks, trailers, motor homes, and buses. Does not include assets used in mining,				

ADR Classes and Guidelines *(continued)*

Asset guide-line class	Description of assets included	Asset depreciation range (in years): Lower limit	Asset guide-line period	Upper limit	Annual asset guide-line repair allow-ance percent-age
	printing and publishing, production of primary metals, electricity, or steam, or the manufacture of glass, industrial chemicals, batteries, or rubber products, which are classified elsewhere. Includes assets used in manufacturing activities elsewhere classified other than those excluded above,[4] where such activities are incidental to and an integral part of the manufacture and assembly of finished motor vehicles such as the manufacture of parts and subassemblies of fabricated metal products, electrical equipment, textiles, plastics, leather, and foundry and forging operations	9.5	12	14.5	9.5
	Activities will be considered incidental to the manufacture and assembly of finished motor vehicles only if 75 percent or more of the value of the products produced under one roof are used for the manufacture and assembly of finished motor vehicles. Parts which are produced as a normal replacement stock complement in connection with the manufacture and assembly of finished motor vehicles are considered used for the manufacture and assembly of finished motor vehicles. Does not include assets used in the manufacture of component parts if these assets are used by taxpayers not engaged in the assembly of finished motor vehicles.				
37.12	Motor vehicle manufacturing subsidiary assets:	2.5	3	3.5	12.5
	Includes assets defined as special tools, such as jigs, dies, fixtures, molds, patterns, gauges, and specialty transfer and shipping devices, owned by manufacturers of finished motor vehicles and used in qualified activities as defined in Class 37.11. Special tools are specifically designed for the production or processing of particular motor vehicle components and have no significant utilitarian value and cannot be adapted to further or different use after changes or improvements are made in the model design of the particular part produced by the special tools. Does not include general purpose small tools such as wrenches and drills, both hand and power-driven, and other general purpose equipment such as conveyors, transfer equipment, and materials handling devices.				
37.2	Manufacture of aerospace products:				
	Includes assets used in the production of aircraft, spacecraft, rockets, missiles and their components parts	6.5	8	9.5	7.5
37.3	Ship and boat building:				

ADR Classes and Guidelines *(continued)*

Asset guideline class	Description of assets included	Asset depreciation range (in years) Lower limit	Asset guideline period	Upper limit	Annual asset guideline repair allowance percentage
37.31	Ship and boat building machinery and equipment: Includes assets used in the manufacture and repair of ships, boats, caissons, drilling rigs and special fabrications not included in asset guideline class 37.32. Specifically includes all manufacturing and repairing machinery and equipment, including machinery and equipment used in the operation of assets included in asset guideline 37.32. Excludes buildings and their structural components	9.5	12	14.5	8.5
37.32	Ship and boat building dry docks and land improvements: Includes assets used in the manufacture and repair of ships, boats, caissons, drilling rigs and special fabrications not included in asset guideline class 37.31. Specifically includes floating and fixed dry docks, ship basins, graving docks, shipways, piers and all other land improvements such as water, sewer, and electric systems. Excludes buildings and their structural components	13	16	19	2.5
37.33	Ships and boat building—special tools: Includes assets defined as special tools such as dies, jigs, molds, patterns, fixtures, gauges, and drawings concerning such special tools used in the activities as defined in Classes 37.31 and 37.32. Special tools are specifically designed for the production or processing of particular machine components, products or parts, and have no significant utilitarian value and cannot be adopted to further or different use after changes or improvements are made in the model design of the particular part produced by the special tools, Does not include general purpose small tools such as wrenches and drills, both hand and power-driven, and other general purpose equipment such as conveyors, transfer equipment, and materials handling devices	5	6.5	8	0.5
37.4	Manufacture of railroad transportation equipment:				
37.41	Manufacture of locomotives: Includes assets used in building or rebuilding railroad locomotives (including mining and industrial locomotives). Does not include assets of railroad transportation companies or assets of companies which manufacture components of locomotives but do not manufacture finished locomotives	9	11.5	14	7.5
37.42	Manufacture of railroad cars: Includes assets used in building or rebuilding railroad freight or passenger cars (including rail transit cars). Does not include assets of railroad transportation com-				

ADR Classes and Guidelines *(continued)*

Asset guide-line class	*Description of assets included*	*Asset depreciation range (in years)* Lower limit	Asset guide-line period	Upper limit	*Annual asset guide-line repair allow-ance percent-age*
	panies or assets of companies which manufacture components of railroad cars but do not manufacture finished railroad cars	9.5	12	14.5	5.5
38.0	Manufacture of professional, scientific, and controlling instruments; photographic and optical goods; watches and clocks: Includes assets used in the manufacture of mechanical measuring, engineering, laboratory and scientific research instruments, optical instruments and lenses; surgical, medical and dental instruments, equipment and supplies; ophthalmic goods, photographic equipment and supplies; and watches and clocks	9.5	12	14.5	5.5
39.0	Manufacture of products not elsewhere classified: Includes assets used in the production of jewelry; musical instruments; toys and sporting goods; pens, pencils, office and art supplies. Also includes assets used in production of motor picture and television films and tapes; as waste reduction plants; and in the ginning of cotton	9.5	12	14.5	5.5
40.0	Railroad transportation: Includes the assets identified below and which are used in the commercial and contract carrying of passengers and freight by rail. Excludes any nondepreciable assets included in Interstate Commerce Commission accounts enumerated for this class. Excludes the transportation assets included in Class 00.2 above.				
40.1	Railroad machinery and equipment	11	14	17	10.5
	Includes assets classified in the following Interstate Commerce Commission accounts:				
	Road accounts:				
	(16) Station and office buildings (freight handling machinery and equipment only)				
	(25) TOFC/COFC terminals (freight handling machinery and equipment only)				
	(26) Communication systems				
	(27) Signals and interlockers				
	(37) Roadway machines				
	(44) Shop machinery				
	Equipment accounts:				
	(52) Locomotives				
	(53) Freight train cars				
	(54) Passenger train cars				
	(55) Highway revenue equipment				
	(57) Work equipment				
	(58) Miscellaneous equipment				

ADR Classes and Guidelines *(continued)*

Asset guide-line class	*Description of assets included*	*Asset depreciation range (in years)*			*Annual asset guide-line repair allow-ance percent-age*
		Lower limit	*Asset guide-line period*	*Upper limit*	
40.2	Railroad structures and similar improvements .... Includes assets classified in the following Interstate Commerce Commission road accounts: (6) Bridges, trestles, and culverts (7) Elevated structure (13) Fences, snowsheds, and signs (16) Station and office buildings (stations and other operating structures only) (17) Roadway buildings (18) Water stations (19) Fuel stations (20) Shops and enginehouses (25) TOFC/COFC terminals (operating structures only) (31) Power transmission systems (35) Miscellaneous structures (39) Public improvements construction	24	30	36	5.0
40.3	Railroad wharves and docks .... (23) Wharves and docks (24) Coal and ore wharves	16	20	24	5.5
40.5	Railroad power plant and equipment: Electric generating equipment:				
40.51	Hydraulic	40	50	60	1.5
40.52	Nuclear	16	20	24	3.0
40.53	Steam	22.5	28	33.5	2.5
40.54	Steam, compressed air, and other power plant equipment	22.5	28	33.5	7.5
41.0	Motor transport-passengers: Includes assets used in the urban and interurban commercial and contract carrying of passengers by road, except the transportation assets included in Class 00.2 above	6.5	8	9.5	11.5
42.0	Motor transport-freight: Includes assets used in the commercial and contract carrying of freight by road, except the transportation assets included in Class 00.2 above	6.5	8	9.5	11.0
44.0	Water transportation: Includes assets used in the commercial and contract carrying of freight and passengers by water except the transportation assets included in Class 00.2 above	16	20	24	8.0
45.0	Air transport: Includes assets used in the commercial and contract carrying of passengers and freight by air	5	6	7	14.0

ADR Classes and Guidelines *(continued)*

Asset guide-line class	Description of assets included	Asset depreciation range (in years) Lower limit	Asset guide-line period	Upper limit	Annual asset guide-line repair allow-ance percent-age
46.0	Pipeline transportation: Includes assets used in the private, commercial, and contract carrying of petroleum, gas, and other products by means of pipe conveyors. The trunk lines related storage facilities of integrated petroleum and natural gas producers are included in this class	17.5	22	26.5	3.0
48.0	Communication: Includes assets used in the furnishing of point-to-point communication services by wire or radio, whether intended to be received aurally or visually; and radio broadcasting and television.				
48.1	Telephone: Includes the assets identified below and which are used in the provision of commercial and contract telephonic services:				
48.11	Central office buildings: Assets intended to house central office equipment as defined in Federal Communications Commission Part 31 Account No. 212 whether section 1245 or section 1250 property	36	45	54	1.5
48.12	Central office equipment: Includes central office switching and related equipment as defined in Federal Communications Commission Part 31 Account No. 221	16	20	24	6.0
48.13	Station equipment: Includes such station apparatus and connections as teletypewriters, telephones, booths, private exchanges and comparable equipment as defined in Federal Communications Commission Part 31 Account Nos. 231, 232, and 234	8	10	12	10.0
48.14	Distribution plant: Includes such assets as pole lines, cable, aerial wire and underground conduits as are classified in underground conduits, and comparable equipment as defined in Federal Communications Commission Part 31 Account Nos. 241, 242.1, 242.2, 242.3, 242.4, 243, and 244	28	35	42	2.0
48.2	Radio and television broadcasting	5	6	7	10.0
48.3	Telegraph, ocean cable, and satellite communications: Includes communications-related assets used to provide domestic and international radio-telegraph, wire-telegraph, ocean-cable, and satellite communications services.				

ADR Classes and Guidelines *(continued)*

Asset guide-line class	Description of assets included	Asset depreciation range (in years) Lower limit	Asset guide-line period	Upper limit	Annual asset guide-line repair allow-ance percent-age
48.31	Electric power generating and distribution systems.......... Includes assets used in the provision of electric power by generation, modulation, rectification, channelization, control, and distribution. Does not include these assets when they are installed on customers' premises.	15.0	19.0	23.0	—
48.32	High frequency radio and microwave systems .... Includes assets such as transmitters and receivers, antenna supporting structures, antennas, transmission lines from equipment to antenna, transmitter cooling systems, and control and amplification equipment. Does not include cable and long-line systems.	10.5	13.0	15.5	—
48.33	Cable and long-line systems .... Includes assets such as transmission lines, pole lines, ocean cables, buried cable and conduit, repeaters, repeater stations, and other related assets. Does not include high frequency radio or microwave systems.	21.0	26.5	32.0	—
48.34	Central office control equipment................................ Includes assets for general control, switching, and monitoring of communications signals including electromechanical switching and channeling apparatus, multiplexing equipment, patching and monitoring facilities, in-house cabling, teleprinter equipment, and associated site improvements.	13.0	16.5	20.0	—
48.35	Computerized switching, channeling, and associated control Equipment .... Includes central office switching computers, interfacing computers, other associated specialized control equipment, and site improvements.	8.5	10.5	12.5	—
48.36	Satellite ground segment property .... Includes assets such as fixed earth station equipment, antennas, satellite communications equipment, and interface equipment. Does not include general purpose equipment or equipment used in satellite space segment property.	8.0	10.0	12.0	—
48.37	Satellite space segment property............................... Includes satellites and equipment used for telemetry, tracking, control, and monitoring.	6.5	8.0	9.5	—
48.38	Equipment installed on customer's premises................. Includes assets installed on customer's premises, such as computers, terminal equipment, power generation and distribution systems, private switching center, teleprinters, facsimile equipment, and other associated and related equipment.	8.0	10.0	12.0	—

ADR Classes and Guidelines *(continued)*

Asset guideline class	Description of assets included	Asset depreciation range (in years) Lower limit	Asset guideline period	Upper limit	Annual asset guideline repair allowance percentage
48.39	Support and service equipment. Includes assets used to support but not engage in communications. Includes store, warehouse, shop, tools, and test and laboratory assets.	11.0	13.5	16.0	
48.4	Cable television: Includes communications—related assets used to provide cable television (community antenna television) services. Does not include assets used to provide subscribers with two-way communications services.				
48.41	Headend. Includes assets such as towers, antennas, preamplifiers, converters, modulation equipment, and program non-duplication systems. Does not include headend buildings and program origination assets.	9	11	13	5
48.42	Subscriber connection and distribution systems. Includes assets such as trunk and feeder cable, connecting hardware, amplifiers, power equipment, passive devices, directional taps, pedestals, pressure taps, drop cables, matching transformers, multiple set connecter equipment, and converters.	8	10	12	5
48.43	Program origination. Includes assets such as cameras, film chains, video tape recorders, lighting, and remote location equipment excluding vehicles. Does not include buildings and their structural components.	7	9	11	9
48.44	Service and test. Includes assets such as oscilloscopes, field strength meters, spectrum analyzers, and cable testing equipment, but does not include vehicles.	7	8.5	10	2.5
48.45	Microwave systems. Includes assets such as towers, antennas, transmitting and receiving equipment and broad band microwave assets if used in the provision of cable television services. Does not include assets used in the provision of common carrier services.	7.5	9.5	11.5	2
49.0	Electric, gas and sanitary services:				
49.11	Electric utility hydraulic production plant: Includes assets used in the hydraulic power production of electricity for sale, related land improvements, dams, flumes, canals, and waterways	40	50	60	1.5
49.12	Electric utility nuclear production plant: Includes assets used in the nuclear power production of electricity for sale and related land improvements	16	20	24	3.0

ADR Classes and Guidelines *(continued)*

Asset guide-line class	Description of assets included	Asset depreciation range (in years) Lower limit	Asset guide-line period	Upper limit	Annual asset guide-line repair allow-ance percent-age
49.121	Nuclear fuel assemblies: Includes initial core and replacement core nuclear fuel assemblies (i.e., the composite of fabricated nuclear fuel and container) when used in a boiling water, pressurized water, or high temperature gas reactor used in the production of electricity. Does not include nuclear fuel assemblies used in breeder reactors	4.0	5.0	6.0	
49.13	Electric utility steam production plant: Includes assets used in the steam power production of electricity for sale, combustion turbines operated in a combined cycle with a conventional steam unit, and related land improvements	22.5	28	33.5	2.5
49.14	Electric utility transmission and distribution plant: Includes assets used in the transmission and distribution of electricity for sale and related land improvements	24	30	36	2.0
49.15	Electric utility combustion turbine production plant: Includes assets used in the production of electricity for sale by the use of such prime movers as jet engines, combustion turbines, diesel engines, gasoline engines and other internal combustion engines, their associated power turbines and/or generators, and related land improvements. Does not include combustion turbines operated in a combined cycle with a conventional steam unit	16	20	24	4.0
49.2	Gas utilities: Includes assets used in the production, transmission, and distribution of natural and manufactured gas for sale, including related land improvements and identified as:				
49.21	Distribution facilities: Including gas water heaters and gas conversion equipment installed by utility on customers' premises on a rental basis	28	35	42	2.0
49.22	Gas making facilities:				
49.221	Manufactured gas production plant: Includes assets used in the manufacture of gas having chemical and/or physical properties which do not permit complete interchangeability with domestic natural gas	24	30	36	2.0
49.222	Substitute natural gas (SNG) production plant (naphtha or lighter hydrocarbon feedstocks): Includes assets used in the catalytic conversion of feedstocks of naphtha or lighter hydrocarbons to a gaseous				

ADR Classes and Guidelines *(continued)*

Asset guide-line class	Description of assets included	Asset depreciation range (in years) Lower limit	Asset guide-line period	Upper limit	Annual asset guide-line repair allow-ance percent-age
	fuel which is completely interchangeable with domestic natural gas	11	14	17	4.5
49.23	Natural gas production plant	11	14	17	4.5
49.24	Trunk pipelines and related storage facilities	17.5	22	26.5	3.0
49.3	Water utilities: Includes assets used in the gathering, treatment, and commercial distribution of water	40	50	60	1.5
49.4	Central steam production and distribution: Includes assets used in the production and distribution of steam for sale	22.5	28	33.5	2.5
49.5	Industrial steam and electric generation and distribution systems: Includes assets used in the production and distribution of electricity with rated total capacity in excess of 500 kilowatts and/or assets used in the production and distribution of steam with rated total capacity in excess of 12,500 pounds per hour, for use by the taxpayer in his industrial manufacturing process or plant activity and not ordinarily available for sale to others. Assets used to generate or distribute electricity or steam of the type described above of lesser rated capacity are not included, but are included in the appropriate manufacturing equipment classes elsewhere specified	22.5	28	33.5	2.5
50.0	Wholesale and retail trade: Includes assets used in carrying out the activities of purchasing, assembling, sorting, grading, and selling of goods at both the wholesale and retail level. Also includes assets used in such activities as the operation of restaurants, cafes, coin-operated dispensing machines, and in brokerage of scrap metal	8	10	12	6.5
50.1	Wholesale and retail trade service assets: Includes assets such as glassware, silverware (including kitchen utensils), crockery (usually china) and linens (generally napkins, tablecloths and towels) used in qualified activities as defined in Class 50.0	2	2.5	3	—
65.0	Building services[3] Provision of the services of buildings, whether for use by others or for taxpayer's own account. Assets in the classes listed below include the structural shells of buildings and				

[3]This class is established for a three-year transition period in accordance with Section 109(e)(1) of the Revenue Act of 1971 (P.L. 92-178, CB 1972-1, 443) and will be in effect for the period beginning January 1, 1971 and ending January 1, 1974 or at such earlier date as of which asset classes incorporating the assets herein described are represcribed or modified. See Sections 1.167(a)-11(b)(3)(ii), 1.167(a)-11(b)(4)(i)(a), and 1.167(a)-11(b)(5)(vi) of the regulations for special rules relating to real property.

ADR Classes and Guidelines *(continued)*

Asset guideline class	*Description of assets included*	*Asset depreciation range (in years)* Lower limit	*Asset guideline period*	*Upper limit*	*Annual asset guideline repair allowance percentage*
	all integral parts thereof; equipment that services normal heating, plumbing, air conditioning, illumination, fire prevention, and power requirements; equipment for the movement of passengers and freight within the building; and any additions to buildings or their components, capitalized remodeling costs, and partitions both permanent and semipermanent. Structures, closely related to the equipment they house, which are section 38 property are not included. See section 1.48-1(e)(1) of the regulations. Such structures are included in asset guideline classes appropriate to the equipment to which they are related. Depreciation periods for assets used in the provision of the services of buildings and which are not specified below shall be determined according to the facts and circumstances pertinent to each asset, except in the case of farm buildings and other building structures for which a class has otherwise been designated.				
65.1	Shelter, space, and related building services for manufacturing and for machinery and equipment repair activities:				
65.11	Factories		45		
65.12	Garages		45		
65.13	Machine shops		45		
65.14	Loft buildings		50		
65.2	Building services for the conduct of wholesale and retail trade, includes stores and similar structures		50		
65.3	Building services for residential purposes:				
65.31	Apartments		40		
65.32	Dwellings		45		
65.4	Building services relating to the provision of miscellaneous services to businesses and consumers:				
65.41	Office buildings		45		
65.42	Storage:				
65.421	Warehouses		60		
65.422	Grain elevators		60		
65.43	Banks		50		
65.44	Hotels		40		
65.45	Theaters		40		
70.0	Services:				
70.1	Administrative Services:				
	Includes assets used in administering normal business transactions and the maintenance of business records, their retrieval and analysis, whether these services are performed for others or for taxpayer's own account				

ADR Classes and Guidelines *(continued)*

Asset guide-line class	Description of assets included	Asset depreciation range (in years): Lower limit	Asset guide-line period	Upper limit	Annual asset guide-line repair allow-ance percent-age
	and whether the assets are located in a single location or widely dispersed.				
70.11	Office furniture, fixtures, and equipment: Includes furniture and fixtures which are not a structural component of a building. Includes such assets as desks, files, safes, and communications equipment (not to include communications equipment which is included in other ADR classes)	8.0	10.0	12.0	2.0
70.12	Information systems: Includes computers and their peripheral equipment (does not include equipment that is an integral part of other capital equipment and which is included in other ADR classes of economic activity, i.e., computers used primarily for process or production control, switching and channeling)	5.0	6.0	7.0	7.5
	Information systems defined: 1) Computers: A computer is an electronically activated device capable of accepting information, applying prescribed processes to the information and supplying the results of these processes with or without human intervention. It usually consists of a central processing unit containing extensive storage, logic, arithmetic and control capabilities. Excluded from this category are adding machines, electronic desk calculators, etc. 2) Peripheral equipment consists of the auxiliary machines which may be placed under control of the central processing unit. Nonlimiting examples are Card readers, card punches, magnetic tape fees, high speed printers, optical character readers, tape cassettes, mass storage units, paper tape equipment, keypunches, data entry devices, teleprinters, terminals, tape drives, disc drives, disc files, disc packs, visual image projector tubes, card sorters, plotters, collators. Peripheral equipment may be used on-line or off-line.				
70.13	Data handling equipment, except computers: Includes typewriters, calculators, adding and accounting machines, copiers and duplicating equipment	5.0	6.0	7.0	15.0
70.2	Personal and professional services: Includes assets used in the provision of personal services such as those offered by hotels and motels, laundry and dry cleaning establishments, beauty and barber shops, photographic studios and mortuaries. Includes assets used in the provision of professional services such as those offered by doctors, dentists, lawyers. accountants, ar-				

ADR Classes and Guidelines *(continued)*

Asset guide-line class	*Description of assets included*	*Asset depreciation range (in years)* Lower limit	Asset guide-line period	Upper limit	*Annual asset guide-line repair allow-ance percent-age*
	classified in other ADR classes. Includes assets used in the provision of repair and maintenance services and those assets used in providing fire and burglary protection services and which are not classified in other ADR classes. Includes equipment or facilities used by cemetery organizations, news agencies, teletype wire services, plumbing contractors, frozen food lockers, research laboratories, hotels, and motels and which are not classified in other ADR classes	8	10	12	6.5
70.21	Personal and professional services—service assets: Includes assets such as glassware, silverware, crockery, and linens (generally sheets, pillowcases and bath towels) used in qualified activities as defined in Class 70.2......	2	2.5	3	
79.0	Recreation: Includes assets used in the provision of entertainment services on payment of a fee or admission charge, as in the operation of bowling alleys, billiard and pool establishments, theaters, concert halls, and miniature golf courses. Does not include amusement parks and assets which consist primarily of specialized land improvements or structures, such as golf courses, sports stadia, etc., and buildings which house the assets used in entertainment services	8	10	12	6.5
80.0	Theme and amusement parks: Includes assets used in the provision of rides, attractions, and amusements in activities defined as theme and amusement parks, and includes appurtenances associated with a ride, attraction, amusement or theme setting within the park such as ticket booths, facades, shop interiors, and props, special purpose structures, and buildings other than warehouses, administration buildings, hotels, and motels. Includes all land improvements for or in support of park activities, (e.g. parking lots, sidewalks, waterways, bridges, fences, landscaping, etc.) and support functions (e.g. food and beverage retailing, souvenir vending, and other nonlodging accommodations) if owned by the park and provided exclusively for the benefit of park patrons. This guidelines class is a composite of all assets used in this industry except transportation equipment (general purpose trucks, cars, airplanes, etc. which are included in asset guideline classes with the prefix 00.2), assets used in the provision of administrative services in asset guideline classes with the prefix 70.1, and warehouses, administration buildings, hotels, and motels	10	12.5	15	12.5

First-Year Convention Under Class Life Rules

If you elect to use ADR, you must also specify the "first-year convention" you intend to use. This is simply the method you choose for averaging the depreciation period for the first year in which assets are placed in service. This is necessary because not all the assets put in service in a given year are put into service at the same time.

There are two basic conventions you can use: the half-year convention and the modified half-year convention. There is also a short-year convention, but this is used only for election years shorter than 12 full months. Regardless of the convention adopted, all vintage accounts in a given year must use the same convention. However, accounts in subsequent years may use other conventions.

Depreciation of the vintage accounts for the first year under the two conventions is computed as follows:

Half-Year	*Modified Half-Year*
1. All property in the account is treated as having been placed in service on the first day of the second half of the taxable year.	1. All property in the account is treated as having been placed in service according to the table below.
2. All extraordinary retirements are treated as occurring on the first day of the second half of the taxable year.	2. All extraordinary retirements are treated as occurring in accordance with the table below.

Modified Half-Year Table

	Actual Date Placed in Service or Retired		*Treated as Placed in Service or Retired*
1(a)	Placed in service during first half of taxable year.	1(a)	First day of taxable year.
(b)	Retired during first half of year.	(b)	First day of year.
(c)	Retired during second half of year.	(c)	First day of second half of year.
2(a)	Placed in service during second half of taxable year.	2(a)	First day of the next taxable year.
(b)	Retired during first half of year.	(b)	First day of second half of year.
(c)	Retired during second half of year.	(c)	First day of the next year.

As can be seen, the half-year convention is better for you if you have actually placed most of the assets in service in the second half of the taxable year, and the modified half-year convention is better if you have actually placed most of the assets in service in the first half of the year.

First Year's Depreciation on Individual-Item Basis

Assume that you build a hotel and incur the costs given for each item. Based on the ADR useful lives and disregarding salvage value, the table below indicates the first year's depreciation for each item under straight-line and 150%-declining-balance depreciation methods.

Item	*Cost*	*Useful Life*	*S/L*	*First Year Depreciation 150% D/B*
Building & Improvements				
Building only	$500,000	40	$12,500	$18,750
Air Conditioning	45,000	8	5,625	8,433
Elevators:				
Freight (2)	25,000	12	2,083	3,125
Passenger (4)	40,000	12	3,333	5,000
Boiler & Oil Burner	30,000	8	3,750	5,625
Lighting System:				
Fixtures	15,000	8	1,875	2,813
Wiring	20,000	12	1,666	2,500
Plumbing:				
Bath tubs, etc.	12,500	12	1,042	1,563
Faucets, valves, etc.	7,500	12	625	938
Pipes:				
Cold water	12,500	12	1,042	1,563
Hot water	15,000	12	1,250	1,875
Roof—copper	25,000	12	2,083	3,125
Switchboards	5,000	8	625	938
Water tank—metal	10,000	8	1,250	1,875
Fire Alarm & Prevention Equipment	15,000	8	1,875	2,813
Total Building & Improvements	$777,500			
Furniture, Fixtures & Equipment				
Refrigeration System	11,000	8	1,375	2,063
Kitchen Equipment	20,000	8	2,500	3,750
Laundry Equipment	15,000	8	1,875	2,813
House Cleaning Equipment	10,000	8	1,250	1,875
Shades & Screens	10,000	8	1,250	1,875
Blankets & Spreads	6,000	8	750	1,125
Carpets & Rugs	12,000	8	1,500	2,250
Curtains, Draperies & Scarfs	6,000	8	750	1,125
Springs, Mattresses & Pillows	6,000	8	750	1,125
Furniture:				
Dining & Guest Rooms	24,000	8	3,000	4,500
Lobby	4,000	8	500	750
Total Furniture, Fixtures & Equipment	$124,000			
TOTAL	$901,500		$56,124	$84,187

Comparison of First-Year Depreciation Under Composite and Component Bases

Since the tax law limits you to 150%-declining-balance depreciation on new and straight-line on used commercial properties, you may be able to save tax dollars by figuring depreciation on a component basis rather than by using a composite rate. You might, for example, have separate accounts as follows:

	Useful Life	*Cost*
Building	40 years	$120,000
Wiring	12 years	20,000
Plumbing	12 years	12,000
Roof	12 years	8,000
Elevator	12 years	10,000
Paving	8 years	5,000
Air conditioning	8 years	20,000
Ceilings	8 years	9,000
Floor	8 years	10,000
		$214,000

This would result in first-year depreciation aggregating $19,000 using 150%-declining-balance.

If you were to use composite depreciation, the life of the composite building would be 26.88 years. Using this and 150%-declining-balance depreciation would give first-year depreciation of only $11,941.

If you had used the 200%-declining-balance method with the composite method, your first-year depreciation would still have been only $15,923.

Mortgage Interest and Amortization

The common practice is for mortgage payments to be called for on the constant payment plan under which periodic payments equal in amount and including both interest and amortization are made. While the total amount of each payment is equal (except, perhaps, the last), the portion of each payment which is allocated to interest decreases and the portion allocated to amortization increases as the payments go on and more and more of the mortgage debt is satisfied.

It is also common practice today to sell mortgages at a discount, thus increasing the yield to the purchaser.

The following tables are important planning tools to be used in connection with the common practices just noted. These tables are divided into four sections:

(1) The first section shows the constant annual combined amount of interest and amortization that has to be paid to liquidate a $1,000 mortgage over different periods of time and at different interest rates. The terms covered are 5, 10, 15, 20, 25, and 30 years. The interest rates covered are from 4% up.

(2) These tables may also be used for figuring the size of the balloon on a mortgage which is not completely self-liquidating, taking into account the borrower's ability to make payments of interest and principal, the rate of interest, and the rate of amortization. For example, assume a borrower is able to pay approximately 14% annually and the parties agree to a 7% interest rate. It will be seen that the 10-year term, 7% interest rate table comes closest to fulfilling the parties' needs. The balance shown in that table at any given year may be made the basis of the balloon. Thus, if payment is provided for at the rate of $11.62 monthly ($139.44 annually or approximately 14% of $1,000), the balloon at the end of 5 years would be $585.75 and at the end of 7 years, $375.08 for every $1,000 of principal debt originally owing.

(3) The second section consists of a table indicating the combined monthly interest and amortization which must be paid to liquidate a $1,000 mortgage over varying annual periods of time at differing interest rates.

Self-Liquidating Monthly Mortgage Payments—Annual Interest, Amortization, and Remaining Balance

The following tables are useful planning tools, helping you to determine quickly the constant monthly payments, the annual interest, the annual amortization payment and the remaining balance for self-liquidating mortgage loans at interest rates of 4% and up at payout terms of 5, 10, 15, 20, 25, and 30 years on each $1,000 of mortgage loan.

Note: The final payment shown in these tables usually is lower than the regular monthly payments, since, in the monthly payments, fractional sums are stated at the next higher cent.

Mortgages with Balloons: These tables may also be used in figuring the size of the balloon on a mortgage which is not completely self-liquidating. See the previous page for explanation of how to make this computation.

5-Year Term

	4% interest—$18.42 monthly payment			4½% interest—$18.65 monthly payment			5% interest—$18.88 monthly payment		
Year	*Interest*	*Amort.*	*Balance*	*Interest*	*Amort.*	*Balance*	*Interest*	*Amort.*	*Balance*
1	36.63	184.41	815.59	41.26	182.54	817.46	45.91	180.65	819.35
2	29.14	191.90	623.69	32.88	190.92	626.54	36.64	189.92	629.43
3	21.31	199.73	423.96	24.11	199.69	426.85	26.92	199.64	429.79
4	13.19	207.85	216.11	14.94	208.86	217.99	16.74	209.82	219.97
5	4.67	216.11	0	5.34	217.99	0	5.99	219.97	0

	5¼% interest—$18.99 monthly payment			5½% interest—$19.11 monthly payment			5¾% interest—$19.22 monthly payment		
Year	*Interest*	*Amort.*	*Balance*	*Interest*	*Amort.*	*Balance*	*Interest*	*Amort.*	*Balance*
1	48.23	179.65	820.35	50.53	178.79	821.21	52.85	177.79	822.21
2	38.55	189.33	631.02	40.44	188.88	632.33	42.37	188.27	633.94
3	28.37	199.51	431.51	29.79	199.53	432.80	31.26	199.38	434.56
4	17.65	210.23	221.28	18.58	210.74	222.06	19.47	211.17	223.39
5	6.33	221.28	0	6.63	222.06	0	7.00	223.39	0

	6% interest—$19.34 monthly payment			6¼% interest—$19.45 monthly payment			6½% interest—$19.57 monthly payment		
Year	*Ihterest*	*Amort.*	*Balance*	*Interest*	*Amort.*	*Balance*	*Interest*	*Amort.*	*Balance*
1	55.19	176.89	823.11	57.51	175.89	824.11	59.85	174.99	825.01
2	44.29	187.79	635.32	46.18	187.22	636.89	48.13	186.71	638.30
3	32.70	199.38	435.94	34.16	199.24	437.65	35.63	199.21	439.09
4	20.39	211.68	224.26	21.35	212.05	225.60	22.30	212.54	226.55
5	7.33	224.26	0	7.72	225.60	0	8.04	226.55	0

	6¾% interest—$19.69 monthly payment			7% interest—$19.81 monthly payment			7¼% interest—$19.92 monthly payment		
Year	*Interest*	*Amort.*	*Balance*	*Interest*	*Amort.*	*Balance*	*Interest*	*Amort.*	*Balance*
1	62.20	174.08	825.92	64.51	173.21	826.79	66.85	172.19	827.81
2	50.07	186.21	639.71	52.01	185.71	641.08	53.95	185.09	642.72
3	37.10	199.18	440.53	38.57	199.15	441.93	40.06	198.98	443.74
4	23.23	213.05	227.48	24.18	213.54	228.39	25.17	213.87	229.87
5	8.41	227.48	0	8.75	228.39	0	9.13	229.87	0

Self-Liquidating Mortgages—Annual Interest, Amortization, And Remaining Balance *(continued)*

5-Year Term *(continued)*

	7½% interest—$20.04 monthly payment			7¾% interest—$20.16 monthly payment			8% interest—$20.28 monthly payment		
Year	*Interest*	*Amort.*	*Balance*	*Interest*	*Amort.*	*Balance*	*Interest*	*Amort.*	*Balance*
1	69.18	171.30	828.70	71.54	170.38	829.62	73.87	169.49	830.51
2	55.89	184.59	644.11	57.83	184.09	645.53	59.81	183.55	646.96
3	41.58	198.90	445.21	43.08	198.84	446.69	44.56	198.80	448.16
4	26.12	214.36	230.85	27.08	214.84	231.85	28.06	215.30	232.86
5	9.45	230.85	0	9.85	231.85	0	10.21	232.86	0

	9% interest—$20.76 monthly payment			10% interest—$21.25 monthly payment			12⅜% interest—$22.43 monthly payment		
Year	*Interest*	*Amort.*	*Balance*	*Interest*	*Amort.*	*Balance*	*Interest*	*Amort.*	*Balance*
1	83.27	165.85	834.15	92.71	162.29	837.71	115.17	153.99	846.01
2	67.72	181.40	652.75	75.70	179.30	658.41	94.97	174.19	671.82
3	50.40	198.42	454.33	56.91	198.09	460.32	72.16	197.00	474.82
4	32.10	217.02	237.31	36.20	218.80	241.52	46.34	222.82	252.00
5	11.71	237.31	0	13.25	241.52	0	17.16	252.00	0

	12¾% interest—$22.63 monthly payment			13⅛% interest—$22.82 monthly payment			13½% interest—$23.01 monthly payment		
Year	*Interest*	*Amort.*	*Balance*	*Interest*	*Amort.*	*Balance*	*Interest*	*Amort.*	*Balance*
1	118.84	152.72	847.28	122.39	151.45	848.55	125.92	150.20	849.80
2	98.18	173.38	673.90	101.27	172.57	675.98	104.38	171.74	678.06
3	74.74	196.82	477.08	77.20	196.64	479.34	78.67	196.45	481.61
4	48.13	223.43	253.65	49.80	224.04	255.30	51.45	224.67	256.94
5	17.91	253.65	0	18.54	255.30	0	19.18	256.94	0

	13⅞% interest—$23.20 monthly payment			14¼% interest—$23.40 monthly payment			14⅝% interest—$23.59 monthly payment		
Year	*Interest*	*Amort.*	*Balance*	*Interest*	*Amort.*	*Balance*	*Interest*	*Amort.*	*Balance*
1	129.47	148.93	851.07	133.12	147.68	852.32	136.65	146.43	853.57
2	107.44	170.96	680.11	110.66	170.14	682.18	113.74	169.34	684.23
3	82.17	196.23	483.88	84.75	196.05	486.13	87.23	195.85	488.38
4	53.11	225.29	258.59	54.92	225.88	260.25	56.61	226.47	261.91
5	19.81	258.59	0	20.55	260.25	0	21.17	261.91	0

	15% interest—$23.79 monthly payment			15⅜% interest—$23.99 monthly payment			15¾% interest—$24.19 monthly payment		
Year	*Interest*	*Amort.*	*Balance*	*Interest*	*Amort.*	*Balance*	*Interest*	*Amort.*	*Balance*
1	140.29	145.19	854.81	143.92	143.96	856.04	147.54	142.74	857.26
2	116.94	168.54	686.27	120.16	167.72	688.32	123.37	166.91	690.35
3	89.85	195.63	490.64	92.48	195.40	492.92	95.09	195.19	495.16
4	58.41	227.07	263.57	60.19	227.69	265.23	62.03	228.25	266.91
5	21.91	263.57	0	22.65	265.23	0	23.37	266.91	0

Self-Liquidating Mortgages—Annual Interest, Amortization And Remaining Balance *(continued)*

Note: The tables for 10, 15, and 20 year terms are carried through 15¾% and the tables for 25 and 30 years terms are carried through 12%.

10-Year Term

	4% interest—$10.13 monthly payment			4½% interest—$10.37 monthly payment			5% interest—$10.61 monthly payment		
Year	*Interest*	*Amort.*	*Balance*	*Interest*	*Amort.*	*Balance*	*Interest*	*Amort.*	*Balance*
1	38.49	83.07	916.93	43.34	81.10	918.90	48.21	79.11	920.89
2	35.11	86.45	830.48	39.62	84.82	834.08	44.16	83.16	837.73
3	31.56	90.00	740.48	35.72	88.72	745.36	39.90	87.42	750.31
4	27.92	93.64	646.84	31.65	92.79	652.57	35.44	91.88	658.43
5	24.11	97.45	549.39	27.41	97.03	555.54	30.72	96.60	561.83
6	20.13	101.43	447.96	22.92	101.52	454.02	25.79	101.53	460.30
7	16.00	105.56	342.40	18.26	106.18	347.84	20.60	106.72	353.58
8	11.70	109.86	232.54	13.37	111.07	236.77	15.13	112.19	241.39
9	7.23	114.33	118.21	8.29	116.15	120.62	9.41	117.91	123.48
10	2.54	118.21	0	2.94	120.62	0	3.35	123.48	0

	5¼% interest—$10.73 monthly payment			5½% interest—$10.86 monthly payment			5¾% interest—$10.98 monthly payment		
Year	*Interest*	*Amort.*	*Balance*	*Interest*	*Amort.*	*Balance*	*Interest*	*Amort.*	*Balance*
1	50.64	78.12	921.88	53.08	77.24	922.76	55.50	76.26	923.74
2	46.43	82.33	839.55	48.72	81.60	841.16	51.01	80.75	842.99
3	42.01	86.75	752.80	44.11	86.21	754.95	46.24	85.52	757.47
4	37.35	91.41	661.39	39.24	91.08	663.87	41.19	90.57	666.90
5	32.43	96.33	565.06	34.11	96.21	567.66	35.85	95.91	570.99
6	27.25	101.51	463.55	28.68	101.64	466.02	30.20	101.56	469.43
7	21.79	106.97	356.58	22.96	107.36	358.66	24.20	107.56	361.87
8	16.04	112.72	243.86	16.89	113.43	245.23	17.83	113.93	247.94
9	9.98	118.78	125.08	10.49	119.83	125.40	11.12	120.64	127.30
10	3.58	125.08	0	3.71	125.40	0	3.98	127.30	0

	6% interest—$11.11 monthly payment			6¼% interest—$11.23 monthly payment			6½% interest—$11.36 monthly payment		
Year	*Interest*	*Amort.*	*Balance*	*Interest*	*Amort.*	*Balance*	*Interest*	*Amort.*	*Balance*
1	57.96	75.36	924.64	60.40	74.36	925.64	59.83	73.49	926.51
2	53.31	80.01	844.63	55.60	79.16	846.48	57.90	78.42	848.09
3	48.35	84.97	759.66	50.53	84.23	762.25	52.66	83.66	764.43
4	43.13	90.19	669.47	45.09	89.67	672.58	47.04	89.28	675.15
5	37.56	95.76	573.71	39.33	95.43	577.15	41.09	95.23	579.92
6	31.67	101.65	472.06	33.20	101.56	475.59	34.71	101.61	478.31
7	25.38	107.94	364.11	26.67	108.09	367.50	27.88	108.44	369.87
8	18.73	114.59	249.52	19.73	115.03	252.47	20.63	115.69	254.18
9	11.68	121.64	127.88	12.31	122.45	130.02	12.91	123.41	130.77
10	4.14	127.88	0	4.44	130.02	0	4.63	130.77	0

Self-Liquidating Mortgages—Annual Interest, Amortization And Remaining Balance *(continued)*

10-Year Term *(continued)*

	6¾% interest—$11.49 monthly payment			7% interest—$11.62 monthly payment			7¼% interest—$11.75 monthly payment		
Year	*Interest*	*Amort.*	*Balance*	*Interest*	*Amort.*	*Balance*	*Interest*	*Amort.*	*Balance*
1	65.29	72.59	927.41	67.73	71.71	928.29	70.18	70.82	929.18
2	60.23	77.65	849.76	62.55	76.89	851.40	64.86	76.14	853.04
3	54.81	83.07	766.69	57.01	82.44	768.97	59.14	81.86	771.18
4	49.04	88.84	677.85	51.02	88.41	680.55	53.02	87.98	683.20
5	42.85	95.03	582.82	44.64	94.80	585.75	45.43	94.57	588.63
6	36.23	101.65	481.17	37.79	101.65	484.10	39.36	101.64	486.99
7	29.17	108.71	372.46	30.42	109.02	375.08	31.73	109.27	377.72
8	21.59	116.29	256.17	22.55	116.89	258.19	23.50	117.50	260.22
9	13.50	124.38	131.79	14.12	125.32	132.87	14.71	126.29	133.93
10	4.82	131.79	0	5.06	132.87	0	5.27	133.93	0

	7½% interest—$11.88 monthly payment			7¾% interest—$12.01 monthly payment			8% interest—$12.14 monthly payment		
Year	*Interest*	*Amort.*	*Balance*	*Interest*	*Amort.*	*Balance*	*Interest*	*Amort.*	*Balance*
1	72.60	69.93	930.07	75.08	69.04	930.96	77.54	68.14	931.86
2	67.19	75.37	854.70	69.54	74.58	856.38	71.87	73.81	858.05
3	61.35	81.21	773.49	63.55	80.57	775.81	65.74	79.94	778.11
4	55.04	87.52	685.97	57.07	87.05	688.76	59.12	86.56	691.55
5	48.26	94.30	591.67	50.09	94.03	594.73	51.94	93.74	597.81
6	40.94	101.62	490.05	42.53	101.59	493.14	44.17	101.51	496.30
7	33.04	109.52	380.53	34.38	109.74	383.40	35.73	109.95	386.35
8	24.54	118.02	262.51	25.56	118.56	264.84	26.61	119.07	267.28
9	15.38	127.18	135.33	16.05	128.07	136.77	16.72	128.96	138.32
10	5.51	135.33	0	5.75	136.77	0	6.02	138.32	0

	8½% interest—$12.40 monthly payment			8¾% interest—$12.53 monthly payment			9% interest—$12.67 monthly payment		
Year	*Interest*	*Amort.*	*Balance*	*Interest*	*Amort.*	*Balance*	*Interest*	*Amort.*	*Balance*
1	82.46	66.34	933.66	84.91	65.45	934.55	87.36	64.68	935.32
2	76.59	72.21	861.45	78.95	71.41	863.14	81.31	70.73	864.59
3	70.21	78.59	782.86	72.45	77.91	785.23	74.65	77.39	787.20
4	63.27	85.53	697.32	65.35	85.01	700.22	67.40	84.64	702.56
5	55.71	93.09	604.23	57.61	92.75	607.47	59.46	92.58	609.98
6	47.48	101.32	502.91	49.16	101.20	506.27	50.78	101.26	508.72
7	38.52	110.28	392.63	39.94	110.42	395.85	41.30	110.74	397.98
8	28.78	120.02	272.61	29.89	120.47	275.38	30.90	121.14	276.84
9	18.17	130.63	141.98	18.92	131.44	143.94	19.56	132.48	144.36
10	6.63	142.17	0.18	6.94	143.42	0.52	7.10	144.36	0

Self-Liquidating Mortgages—Annual Interest, Amortization And Remaining Balance *(continued)*

10-Year Term *(continued)*

	9¼% interest—$12.80 monthly payment			9½% interest—$12.94 monthly payment			9¾% interest—$13.08 monthly payment		
Year	*Interest*	*Amort.*	*Balance*	*Interest*	*Amort.*	*Balance*	*Interest*	*Amort.*	*Balance*
1	89.84	63.76	936.23	92.31	62.97	937.03	94.76	62.20	937.80
2	83.68	69.92	866.32	86.06	69.22	867.81	88.42	68.54	869.26
3	76.93	76.67	789.65	79.19	76.09	791.71	81.43	75.53	793.74
4	69.53	84.07	705.51	71.64	83.64	708.07	73.73	83.23	710.51
5	61.42	92.18	613.40	63.34	91.94	616.13	65.25	91.71	618.79
6	52.52	101.08	512.33	54.21	101.07	515.06	55.89	101.07	517.73
7	42.77	110.83	401.50	44.18	111.10	403.97	45.59	111.37	406.36
8	32.07	121.53	279.97	33.16	122.12	281.85	34.23	122.73	283.63
9	20.34	133.26	146.72	21.04	134.24	147.61	21.72	135.24	148.38
10	7.48	146.12	0.60	7.72	147.56	0.05	7.93	149.03	0.64

	10% interest—$13.22 monthly payment			10¼% interest—$13.35 monthly payment			10½% interest—$13.49 monthly payment		
Year	*Interest*	*Amort.*	*Balance*	*Interest*	*Amort.*	*Balance*	*Interest*	*Amort.*	*Balance*
1	97.23	61.41	938.59	99.71	60.49	939.51	102.18	59.70	940.30
2	90.81	67.83	870.76	93.21	66.99	872.51	95.61	66.27	874.03
3	83.72	74.92	795.84	86.01	74.19	798.32	88.30	73.58	800.45
4	75.86	82.78	713.06	78.04	82.16	716.16	80.19	81.69	718.77
5	67.19	91.45	621.61	69.21	90.99	625.17	71.19	90.69	628.08
6	57.62	101.02	520.59	59.44	100.76	524.41	61.20	100.68	527.40
7	47.03	111.61	408.98	48.61	111.59	412.82	50.10	111.78	415.62
8	35.35	123.29	285.69	36.62	123.58	289.24	37.79	124.09	291.53
9	22.44	136.20	149.49	23.34	136.86	152.38	24.11	137.77	153.76
10	8.17	149.49	0	8.64	151.56	0.82	8.93	152.95	0.81

	10¾% interest—$13.63 monthly payment			11% interest—$13.77 monthly payment			11¼% interest—$13.92 monthly payment		
Year	*Interest*	*Amort.*	*Balance*	*Interest*	*Amort.*	*Balance*	*Interest*	*Amort.*	*Balance*
1	104.65	58.91	941.09	107.12	58.12	941.88	109.59	57.45	942.55
2	98.00	65.56	875.53	100.39	64.85	877.03	102.79	64.25	878.30
3	90.59	72.97	802.56	92.89	72.35	804.68	95.18	71.86	806.44
4	82.35	81.21	721.35	84.52	80.72	723.96	86.66	80.38	726.06
5	73.18	90.38	630.96	75.18	90.06	633.90	77.14	89.90	636.16
6	62.79	100.59	530.37	64.76	100.48	533.42	66.49	100.55	535.60
7	51.61	111.95	418.42	53.13	112.11	421.32	54.57	112.47	423.14
8	38.96	124.60	293.82	40.16	125.08	296.24	41.25	125.79	297.35
9	24.89	138.67	155.15	25.69	139.55	156.69	26.34	140.70	156.65
10	9.23	154.33	0.82	9.54	155.70	1.00	9.68	157.36	0.70

Self-Liquidating Mortgages—Annual Interest, Amortization And Remaining Balance *(continued)*

10-Year Term *(continued)*

	11½% interest—$14.06 monthly payment			11¾% interest—$14.20 monthly payment			12% interest—$14.35 monthly payment		
Year	*Interest*	*Amort.*	*Balance*	*Interest*	*Amort.*	*Balance*	*Interest*	*Amort.*	*Balance*
1	112.07	56.65	943.35	114.55	55.85	944.15	117.03	55.17	944.83
2	105.20	63.52	879.83	107.63	62.77	881.38	110.03	62.17	882.65
3	97.50	71.22	808.61	99.84	70.56	810.82	102.15	70.05	812.60
4	88.86	79.86	728.75	91.09	79.31	731.51	93.26	78.94	733.66
5	79.18	89.54	639.21	81.25	89.15	642.37	83.25	88.95	644.71
6	68.33	100.39	538.82	70.20	100.20	542.16	71.97	100.23	544.49
7	56.15	112.57	426.25	57.77	112.63	429.53	59.26	112.94	431.55
8	42.50	126.22	300.03	43.80	126.60	302.93	44.94	127.26	304.29
9	27.20	141.52	158.51	28.10	142.30	160.63	28.80	143.40	160.90
10	10.04	158.68	0	10.45	159.95	0.67	10.62	161.58	0

	12⅜% interest—$14.56 monthly payment			12¾% interest—$14.78 monthly payment			13⅛% interest—$15.00 monthly payment		
Year	*Interest*	*Amort.*	*Balance*	*Interest*	*Amort.*	*Balance*	*Interest*	*Amort.*	*Balance*
1	120.71	54.01	945.99	124.43	52.93	947.07	128.14	51.86	948.14
2	113.61	61.11	884.88	117.28	60.08	886.99	120.92	59.08	889.06
3	105.61	69.11	815.77	109.14	68.22	818.77	112.67	67.33	821.73
4	96.56	78.16	737.61	99.92	77.44	741.33	103.30	76.70	745.03
5	86.32	88.40	649.21	89.45	87.91	653.42	92.58	87.42	657.61
6	74.75	99.97	549.24	77.57	99.79	553.63	80.41	99.59	558.02
7	61.63	113.09	436.15	64.08	113.28	440.35	66.51	113.49	444.53
8	46.83	127.89	308.26	48.75	128.61	311.74	50.70	129.30	315.23
9	30.07	144.65	163.61	31.36	146.00	165.74	32.65	147.35	167.88
10	11.11	163.61	0	11.62	165.74	0	12.12	167.88	0

	13½% interest—$15.23 monthly payment			13⅞% interest—$15.45 monthly payment			14¼% interest—$15.68 monthly payment		
Year	*Interest*	*Amort.*	*Balance*	*Interest*	*Amort.*	*Balance*	*Interest*	*Amort.*	*Balance*
1	131.95	50.81	949.19	135.64	49.76	950.24	139.43	48.73	951.27
2	124.68	58.08	891.11	128.29	57.11	893.13	132.02	56.14	895.13
3	116.32	66.44	824.67	119.84	65.56	827.57	123.46	64.70	830.43
4	106.77	75.99	748.68	110.14	75.26	752.31	113.63	74.53	755.90
5	95.87	86.89	661.79	99.00	86.40	665.91	102.29	85.87	670.03
6	83.36	99.40	562.39	86.22	99.18	566.73	89.21	98.95	571.08
7	69.08	113.68	448.71	71.57	113.83	452.90	74.16	114.00	457.08
8	52.78	129.98	318.73	54.72	130.68	322.22	56.80	131.36	325.72
9	34.07	148.69	170.04	35.39	150.01	172.21	36.81	151.35	174.37
10	12.72	170.04	0	13.19	172.21	0	13.79	174.37	0

Self-Liquidating Mortgages—Annual Interest, Amortization And Remaining Balance *(continued)*

10-Year Term *(continued)*

	14⅝% interest—$15.90 monthly payment			15% interest—$16.13 monthly payment		
Year	*Interest*	*Amort.*	*Balance*	*Interest*	*Amort.*	*Balance*
1	143.08	47.72	952.28	146.83	46.73	953.27
2	135.62	55.18	897.10	139.32	54.24	899.03
3	126.97	63.83	833.27	130.59	62.97	836.06
4	116.99	73.81	759.46	120.49	73.07	762.99
5	105.45	85.35	674.11	108.73	84.83	678.16
6	92.10	98.70	575.41	95.10	98.46	579.70
7	76.64	114.16	461.25	79.26	114.30	465.40
8	58.78	132.02	329.23	60.89	132.67	332.73
9	38.22	152.58	176.65	39.58	153.98	178.75
10	14.15	176.65	0	14.81	178.75	0

	15⅜% interest—$16.36 monthly payment			15¾% interest—$16.60 monthly payment		
Year	*Interest*	*Amort.*	*Balance*	*Interest*	*Amort.*	*Balance*
1	150.57	45.75	954.25	154.41	44.79	955.21
2	143.02	53.30	900.95	146.82	52.38	902.83
3	134.22	62.10	838.85	137.95	61.25	841.58
4	123.95	72.37	766.48	127.57	71.63	769.95
5	112.04	84.28	682.20	115.44	83.76	686.19
6	98.10	98.22	583.98	101.26	97.94	588.25
7	81.90	114.42	469.56	84.66	114.54	473.71
8	63.01	133.31	336.25	65.66	133.54	339.77
9	41.01	155.31	180.94	42.58	156.62	183.15
10	15.38	180.94	0	16.05	183.15	0

Self-Liquidating Mortgages—Annual Interest, Amortization And Remaining Balance *(continued)*

15-Year Term

	4% interest—$7.40 monthly payment			4½% interest—$7.65 monthly payment			5% interest—$7.91 monthly payment		
Year	*Interest*	*Amort.*	*Balance*	*Interest*	*Amort.*	*Balance*	*Interest*	*Amort.*	*Balance*
1	39.10	49.70	950.30	44.04	47.76	952.24	48.96	45.96	954.04
2	37.06	51.74	898.56	41.83	49.97	902.27	46.62	48.30	905.74
3	34.99	53.81	844.75	39.53	52.27	850.00	44.13	50.79	854.95
4	32.77	56.03	788.72	37.12	54.68	795.32	41.54	53.38	801.57
5	30.49	58.31	730.41	34.62	57.18	738.14	38.80	56.12	745.45
6	28.10	60.70	669.71	31.99	59.81	678.33	35.94	58.98	686.47
7	25.65	63.15	606.56	29.26	62.54	615.79	32.92	62.00	624.47
8	23.07	65.73	540.83	26.39	65.41	550.38	29.74	65.18	559.29
9	20.38	68.42	472.41	23.36	68.44	481.94	26.41	68.50	490.79
10	17.63	71.17	401.24	20.22	71.58	410.36	22.91	72.01	418.78
11	14.71	74.09	327.15	16.94	74.86	335.50	19.22	75.70	343.08
12	11.69	77.11	250.04	13.49	78.31	257.19	15.35	79.57	263.51
13	8.54	80.26	169.78	9.89	81.91	175.28	11.28	83.64	179.87
14	5.27	83.53	86.25	6.14	85.66	89.62	7.02	87.90	91.97
15	1.86	86.25	0	2.20	89.62	0	2.50	91.97	0

	5¼% interest—$8.04 monthly payment			5½% interest—$8.18 monthly payment			5¾% interest—$8.31 monthly payment		
Year	*Interest*	*Amort.*	*Balance*	*Interest*	*Amort.*	*Balance*	*Interest*	*Amort.*	*Balance*
1	51.42	45.06	954.94	53.90	44.26	955.74	56.36	43.36	956.64
2	49.00	47.48	907.46	51.39	46.77	908.97	53.81	45.91	910.73
3	46.46	50.02	857.44	48.77	49.39	859.58	51.10	48.62	862.11
4	43.76	52.72	804.72	45.96	52.20	807.38	48.24	51.48	810.63
5	40.92	55.56	749.16	43.03	55.13	752.25	45.19	54.53	756.10
6	37.94	58.54	690.62	39.92	58.24	694.01	41.97	57.75	698.35
7	34.79	61.69	628.93	36.63	61.53	632.48	38.56	61.16	637.19
8	31.47	65.01	563.92	33.17	64.99	567.49	34.95	64.77	572.42
9	27.96	68.52	495.40	29.20	68.66	498.83	31.13	68.59	503.83
10	24.30	72.18	423.22	25.62	72.54	426.29	26.97	72.65	431.18
11	20.41	76.07	347.15	21.53	76.63	349.66	22.80	76.92	354.26
12	16.32	80.16	266.99	17.20	80.96	268.70	18.25	81.47	272.79
13	12.01	84.47	182.52	12.65	85.51	183.19	13.43	86.29	186.50
14	7.48	89.00	93.52	7.84	90.32	92.87	8.34	91.38	95.12
15	2.66	93.52	0	2.73	92.87	0	2.94	95.12	0

Self-Liquidating Mortgages—Annual Interest, Amortization And Remaining Balance *(continued)*

15-Year Term *(continued)*

	6% interest—$8.44 monthly payment			6¼% interest—$8.58 monthly payment			6½% interest—$8.72 monthly payment		
Year	*Interest*	*Amort.*	*Balance*	*Interest*	*Amort.*	*Balance*	*Interest*	*Amort.*	*Balance*
1	58.85	42.43	957.57	61.33	41.63	958.37	63.79	40.85	959.15
2	56.23	45.05	912.52	58.65	44.31	914.06	61.08	43.56	915.59
3	53.40	47.88	864.64	55.80	47.16	866.90	58.15	46.49	869.10
4	50.49	50.79	813.85	52.76	50.20	816.70	55.03	49.61	819.49
5	47.37	53.91	759.94	49.53	53.43	763.27	51.72	52.92	766.57
6	44.04	57.24	702.70	46.08	56.88	706.39	48.16	56.48	710.09
7	40.50	60.78	641.92	42.43	60.53	645.86	44.39	60.25	649.84
8	36.75	64.53	577.39	38.54	64.42	581.44	40.34	64.30	585.54
9	32.78	68.50	508.89	34.38	68.58	512.86	36.04	68.60	516.94
10	28.58	72.72	436.17	29.99	72.97	439.89	31.46	73.18	443.76
11	24.07	77.21	358.96	25.30	77.66	362.23	26.55	78.09	365.67
12	19.29	81.99	276.97	20.30	82.66	279.57	21.31	83.33	282.34
13	14.24	87.04	189.93	14.99	87.97	191.60	15.72	88.92	193.42
14	8.89	92.39	97.54	9.35	93.61	97.99	9.79	94.85	98.57
15	3.19	97.54	0	3.29	97.99	0	3.41	98.57	0

	6¾% interest—$8.85 monthly payment			7% interest—$8.99 monthly payment			7¼% interest—$9.13 monthly payment		
Year	*Interest*	*Amort.*	*Balance*	*Interest*	*Amort.*	*Balance*	*Interest*	*Amort.*	*Balance*
1	66.29	39.91	960.09	68.74	39.14	960.86	71.25	38.31	961.69
2	63.48	42.72	917.37	65.94	41.94	918.92	68.38	41.18	920.51
3	60.54	45.66	871.71	62.90	44.98	873.94	65.29	44.27	876.24
4	57.35	48.85	822.86	59.65	48.23	825.71	61.98	47.58	828.66
5	53.93	52.27	770.59	56.16	51.72	773.99	58.39	51.17	777.49
6	50.30	55.90	714.69	52.42	55.46	718.53	54.55	55.01	722.48
7	46.41	59.79	654.90	48.39	59.49	659.04	50.45	59.11	663.37
8	42.28	63.92	590.98	44.10	63.78	595.26	46.02	63.54	599.83
9	37.80	68.40	522.58	39.56	68.32	526.89	41.25	68.31	531.52
10	33.04	73.16	449.42	34.55	73.33	453.56	36.13	73.43	458.09
11	27.94	78.26	371.16	29.26	78.62	374.94	30.60	78.96	379.13
12	22.51	83.69	287.47	23.59	84.29	290.65	24.71	84.85	294.28
13	16.68	89.52	197.95	17.48	90.40	200.25	18.33	91.23	203.05
14	10.42	95.78	102.17	10.96	96.92	103.33	11.52	98.04	105.01
15	3.76	102.17	0	3.94	103.33	0	4.16	105.01	0

Self-Liquidating Mortgages—Annual Interest, Amortization And Remaining Balance *(continued)*

15-Year Term *(continued)*

	7½% interest—$9.28 monthly payment			7¾% interest—$9.42 monthly payment			8% interest—$9.56 monthly payment		
Year	*Interest*	*Amort.*	*Balance*	*Interest*	*Amort.*	*Balance*	*Interest*	*Amort.*	*Balance*
1	73.73	37.63	962.37	76.20	36.84	963.16	78.72	36.00	964.00
2	70.77	40.59	921.78	73.26	39.78	923.38	75.71	39.01	924.99
3	67.64	43.72	878.06	70.05	42.99	880.39	72.48	42.24	882.75
4	64.25	47.11	830.95	66.59	46.45	833.94	68.98	45.74	837.01
5	60.59	50.77	780.18	62.89	50.15	783.79	65.17	49.55	787.46
6	56.66	54.70	725.48	58.84	54.20	729.59	61.02	53.70	733.76
7	52.38	58.98	666.50	54.49	58.55	671.04	56.60	58.12	675.64
8	47.83	63.53	602.97	49.78	63.26	607.78	51.77	62.95	612.69
9	42.89	68.47	534.50	44.71	68.33	539.45	46.55	68.17	544.52
10	37.59	73.77	460.73	39.23	73.81	465.64	40.89	73.83	470.69
11	31.87	79.49	381.24	33.29	79.75	385.89	34.78	79.94	390.75
12	25.68	85.68	295.56	26.89	86.15	299.74	28.15	86.57	304.18
13	19.04	92.32	203.24	19.98	93.06	206.68	20.96	93.76	210.42
14	11.88	99.48	103.76	12.49	100.55	106.13	13.16	101.56	108.86
15	4.15	103.76	0	4.41	106.13	0	4.76	108.86	0

	8¼% interest—$9.70 monthly payment			8½% interest—$9.85 monthly payment			8¾% interest—$9.99 monthly payment		
Year	*Interest*	*Amort.*	*Balance*	*Interest*	*Amort.*	*Balance*	*Interest*	*Amort.*	*Balance*
1	81.19	35.22	964.79	83.68	34.53	965.48	86.17	33.72	966.29
2	78.18	38.23	926.56	80.63	37.58	927.90	83.10	36.79	929.51
3	74.90	41.51	885.06	77.31	40.90	887.01	79.75	40.14	889.38
4	71.34	45.07	840.00	73.69	44.52	842.49	76.10	43.79	845.59
5	67.48	48.93	791.07	69.76	48.45	794.05	72.11	47.78	797.82
6	63.29	53.12	737.96	65.48	52.73	741.32	67.76	52.13	745.69
7	58.74	57.67	680.29	60.82	57.39	683.93	63.01	56.88	688.81
8	53.80	62.61	617.68	55.74	62.47	621.47	57.83	62.06	626.75
9	48.43	67.98	549.71	50.22	67.99	553.48	52.17	67.72	559.04
10	42.61	73.80	475.91	44.21	74.00	479.49	46.00	73.89	485.15
11	36.28	80.13	395.79	37.67	80.54	398.96	39.27	80.62	404.54
12	29.42	86.99	308.80	30.55	87.66	311.30	31.93	87.96	316.59
13	21.96	94.45	214.36	22.81	95.40	215.90	23.92	95.97	220.62
14	13.87	102.54	111.82	14.37	103.84	112.07	15.18	104.71	115.91
15	5.08	111.33	0.50	5.20	113.01	0.94	5.65	114.25	1.66

Self-Liquidating Mortgages—Annual Interest, Amortization And Remaining Balance *(continued)*

15-Year Term *(continued)*

	9% interest—$10.15 monthly payment			9¼% interest—$10.29 monthly payment			9½% interest—$10.44 monthly payment		
Year	*Interest*	*Amort.*	*Balance*	*Interest*	*Amort.*	*Balance*	*Interest*	*Amort.*	*Balance*
1	88.66	33.14	966.86	91.16	32.33	967.68	93.65	31.64	968.37
2	85.55	36.25	930.61	88.04	35.45	932.23	90.51	34.78	933.60
3	82.14	39.66	890.95	84.62	38.87	893.36	87.06	38.23	895.37
4	78.43	43.37	847.58	40.86	42.63	850.74	83.27	42.02	853.35
5	74.34	47.46	800.12	76.75	46.74	804.00	79.10	46.19	807.17
6	69.92	51.88	748.24	72.24	51.25	752.76	74.51	50.78	756.39
7	65.03	56.77	691.97	67.29	56.20	696.56	69.47	55.82	700.58
8	59.72	62.08	629.39	61.87	61.62	634.94	63.93	61.36	639.23
9	53.90	67.90	561.49	55.92	67.57	567.38	57.85	67.44	571.79
10	47.53	74.27	487.22	49.40	74.09	493.29	51.15	74.14	497.66
11	40.57	81.23	405.99	42.25	81.24	412.06	43.79	81.50	416.17
12	32.92	88.88	317.11	34.41	89.08	322.98	35.71	89.58	326.59
13	24.59	97.21	219.90	25.81	97.68	225.30	26.82	98.47	228.12
14	15.50	106.30	113.60	16.38	107.11	118.19	17.04	108.25	119.88
15	5.51	113.60	0	6.04	117.45	0.75	6.30	118.99	0.89

	9¾% interest—$10.59 monthly payment			10% interest—$10.75 monthly payment			10¼% interest—$10.90 monthly payment		
Year	*Interest*	*Amort.*	*Balance*	*Interest*	*Amort.*	*Balance*	*Interest*	*Amort.*	*Balance*
1	96.15	30.94	969.07	98.62	30.38	969.62	101.14	29.67	970.34
2	92.99	34.10	934.97	95.46	33.54	936.08	97.95	32.86	937.48
3	89.51	37.58	897.40	91.95	37.05	899.03	94.42	36.39	901.09
4	85.68	41.41	856.00	88.06	40.94	858.09	90.51	40.30	860.80
5	81.46	45.63	810.38	83.78	45.22	812.87	86.18	44.63	816.17
6	76.81	50.28	760.10	79.04	49.96	762.91	81.38	49.43	766.75
7	71.68	55.41	704.70	73.81	55.19	707.72	76.07	54.74	712.02
8	66.03	61.06	643.65	68.03	60.97	646.75	70.19	60.62	651.40
9	59.81	67.28	576.37	61.64	67.36	579.39	63.68	67.13	584.28
10	52.95	74.14	502.23	54.30	74.40	504.99	56.46	74.35	509.93
11	45.38	81.71	420.53	46.79	82.21	422.78	48.48	82.33	427.61
12	37.05	90.04	330.50	38.18	90.82	331.96	39.63	91.18	336.43
13	27.87	99.22	231.28	28.70	100.30	231.66	29.83	100.98	235.46
14	17.75	109.34	121.95	18.20	110.80	120.86	18.98	111.83	123.64
15	6.61	120.48	1.47	6.57	120.86	0	6.97	123.84	0.20

Self-Liquidating Mortgages—Annual Interest, Amortization And Remaining Balance *(continued)*

15-Year Term *(continued)*

	10½% interest—$11.05 monthly payment			10¾% interest—$11.21 monthly payment			11% interest—$11.37 monthly payment		
Year	*Interest*	*Amort.*	*Balance*	*Interest*	*Amort.*	*Balance*	*Interest*	*Amort.*	*Balance*
1	103.64	28.97	971.04	106.13	28.40	971.61	108.63	27.82	972.19
2	100.44	32.17	938.88	102.93	31.60	940.01	105.41	31.04	941.16
3	96.90	35.71	903.17	99.36	35.17	904.85	101.82	34.63	906.53
4	92.97	39.64	863.53	95.38	39.15	865.71	97.81	38.64	867.90
5	88.60	44.01	819.53	90.96	43.57	822.14	93.34	43.11	824.80
6	83.75	48.86	770.67	86.04	48.49	773.66	88.36	48.09	776.71
7	78.36	54.25	716.43	80.57	53.96	719.70	82.79	53.66	723.06
8	72.39	60.22	656.21	74.47	60.06	659.65	76.58	59.87	663.19
9	65.75	66.86	589.35	67.69	66.84	592.81	69.66	66.79	596.40
10	58.38	74.23	515.13	60.14	74.39	518.42	61.93	74.52	521.89
11	50.20	82.41	432.73	51.73	82.80	435.63	53.30	83.15	438.74
12	41.12	91.49	341.24	42.38	92.15	343.49	43.68	92.77	345.98
13	31.04	101.57	239.68	31.97	102.56	240.94	32.95	103.50	242.48
14	19.85	112.76	126.92	20.39	114.14	126.80	20.97	115.48	127.01
15	7.42	125.19	1.74	7.50	127.03	0.23	7.61	128.84	1.83

	11¼% interest—$11.52 monthly payment			11½% interest—$11.68 monthly payment			11¾% interest—$11.84 monthly payment		
Year	*Interest*	*Amort.*	*Balance*	*Interest*	*Amort.*	*Balance*	*Interest*	*Amort.*	*Balance*
1	111.14	27.11	972.90	113.64	26.53	973.48	116.14	25.95	974.06
2	107.92	30.33	942.57	110.42	29.75	943.73	112.92	29.17	944.89
3	104.33	33.92	908.66	106.81	33.36	910.38	109.30	32.79	912.11
4	100.31	37.94	870.73	102.77	37.40	872.98	105.23	36.86	875.26
5	95.82	42.43	828.30	98.23	41.94	831.05	100.66	41.43	833.83
6	90.79	47.46	780.85	93.15	47.02	784.03	95.53	46.56	787.27
7	85.17	53.08	727.77	87.45	52.72	731.31	89.75	52.34	734.94
8	78.88	59.37	668.40	81.05	59.12	672.20	83.26	58.83	676.11
9	71.85	66.40	602.00	73.89	66.28	605.92	75.96	66.13	609.99
10	63.98	74.27	527.74	65.85	74.32	531.60	67.76	74.33	535.67
11	55.18	83.07	444.67	56.84	83.33	448.28	58.54	83.55	452.12
12	45.34	92.91	351.76	46.73	93.44	354.84	48.18	93.91	358.21
13	34.33	103.92	247.84	35.40	104.77	250.08	36.53	105.56	252.66
14	22.01	116.24	131.61	22.70	117.47	132.62	23.44	118.65	134.01
15	8.24	130.01	1.61	8.46	131.71	0.91	8.72	133.37	0.65

Self-Liquidating Mortgages—Annual Interest, Amortization And Remaining Balance *(continued)*

15-Year Term *(continued)*

	12% interest—$12.00 monthly payment			12⅜% interest—$12.24 monthly payment			12¾% interest—$12.49 monthly payment		
Year	*Interest*	*Amort.*	*Balance*	*Interest*	*Amort.*	*Balance*	*Interest*	*Amort.*	*Balance*
1	118.64	25.37	974.64	122.35	24.53	975.47	126.17	23.71	976.29
2	115.42	28.59	946.06	119.12	27.76	947.71	122.96	26.92	949.37
3	111.80	32.21	913.85	115.49	31.39	916.32	119.31	30.57	918.80
4	107.71	36.30	877.56	111.67	35.21	881.11	115.19	34.69	884.11
5	103.11	40.90	836.67	106.43	40.45	840.66	110.48	39.40	844.71
6	97.92	46.09	790.59	101.47	45.41	795.25	105.18	44.70	800.01
7	92.08	51.93	738.66	95.51	51.37	743.88	99.13	50.75	749.26
8	85.49	58.52	680.15	88.79	58.09	685.79	92.25	57.63	691.63
9	78.07	65.94	614.22	81.18	65.70	620.09	84.48	65.40	626.23
10	69.71	74.30	539.93	72.56	74.32	545.77	75.08	74.80	551.43
11	60.29	83.72	456.21	62.83	84.05	461.72	66.11	83.77	467.66
12	49.67	94.34	361.88	51.82	95.06	366.66	54.19	95.69	371.97
13	37.71	106.30	255.59	39.36	107.52	259.14	41.24	108.64	263.33
14	24.23	119.78	135.81	25.27	121.61	137.53	27.06	122.82	140.51
15	9.04	134.97	0.84	9.35	137.53	0	9.37	140.51	0

	13⅛% interest—$12.73 monthly payment			13½% interest—$12.98 monthly payment			13⅞% interest—$13.23 monthly payment		
Year	*Interest*	*Amort.*	*Balance*	*Interest*	*Amort.*	*Balance*	*Interest*	*Amort.*	*Balance*
1	129.85	22.91	977.09	133,62	22.14	977.86	136.93	21.38	978.62
2	126.65	26.11	950.98	130.45	25.31	952.55	134.22	24.54	954.08
3	123.01	29.75	921.23	126.81	28.95	923.60	130.59	28.17	925.91
4	118.87	33.89	887.34	122.65	33.11	890.49	126.42	32.34	893.57
5	114.13	38.63	848.71	117.90	37.86	852.63	121.64	37.12	856.45
6	108.75	44.01	804.70	112.44	43.32	809.31	116.14	42.62	813.83
7	102.61	50.15	754.55	106.22	49.54	759.77	109.86	48.90	764.93
8	95.63	57.13	697.42	99.13	56.63	703.14	102.60	56.16	708.77
9	87.65	65.11	632.31	90.96	64.80	638.34	93.41	64.45	644.32
10	78.58	74.18	558.13	81.66	74.10	564.24	84.77	73.99	570.33
11	68.23	84.53	473.60	71.02	84.74	479.50	73.82	84.94	485.39
12	56.44	96.32	377.28	58.84	96.92	382.58	61.25	97.51	387.88
13	43.01	109.75	267.53	44.93	110.83	271.75	46.84	111.92	275.96
14	27.72	125.04	142.49	28.99	126.77	144.98	30.29	128.47	147.49
15	10.27	142.49	0	10.78	144.98	0	11.27	147.49	0

Self-Liquidating Mortgages—Annual Interest, Amortization And Remaining Balance *(continued)*

15-Year Term *(continued)*

	14¼% interest—$13.49 monthly payment			14⅝% interest—$13.74 monthly payment			15% interest—$14.00 monthly payment		
Year	*Interest*	*Amort.*	*Balance*	*Interest*	*Amort.*	*Balance*	*Interest*	*Amort.*	*Balance*
1	141.24	20.64	979.36	144.95	19.93	980.07	148.76	19.24	980.76
2	138.09	23.79	955.57	141.84	23.04	957.03	145.67	22.33	958.43
3	134.47	27.41	928.16	138.21	26.67	930.36	142.08	25.92	932.51
4	130.31	31.57	896.59	134.06	30.82	899.54	137.91	30.09	902.42
5	125.50	36.38	860.21	129.23	35.65	863.89	133.08	34.92	867.50
6	119.97	41.91	818.30	123.67	41.21	822.68	127.46	40.54	826.96
7	113.58	48.30	770.00	117.20	47.68	775.00	120.95	47.05	779.91
8	106.23	55.65	714.35	109.74	55.14	719.86	113.38	54.62	725.29
9	97.76	64.12	650.23	101.21	63.67	656.19	104.61	63.39	661.90
10	88.02	73.86	576.37	91.05	73.83	582.36	94.41	73.59	588.31
11	76.76	85.12	491.25	79.60	85.28	497.08	82.59	85.41	502.90
12	63.82	98.06	393.19	66.27	98.61	398.47	68.55	99.45	403.45
13	48.88	113.00	280.19	50.82	114.06	284.41	53.21	114.79	288.66
14	31.69	130.19	150.00	33.00	131.88	152.53	34.40	133.60	155.06
15	11.88	150.00	0	12.35	152.53	0	12.94	155.06	0

	15⅜% interest—$14.25 monthly payment			15¾% interest—$14.51 monthly payment		
Year	*Interest*	*Amort.*	*Balance*	*Interest*	*Amort.*	*Balance*
1	152.43	18.57	981.43	156.20	17.92	982.08
2	149.38	21.62	959.81	153.18	20.94	961.14
3	145.80	25.20	934.61	149.62	24.50	936.64
4	141.63	29.37	905.24	145.48	28.64	908.00
5	136.80	34.20	871.04	140.62	33.50	874.50
6	131.14	39.86	831.18	134.95	39.17	835.33
7	124.58	46.42	784.76	128.31	45.81	789.52
8	116.90	54.10	730.66	120.56	53.56	735.96
9	107.98	63.02	667.64	111.48	62.64	673.32
10	97.57	73.43	594.21	100.88	73.24	600.08
11	85.46	85.54	508.67	88.46	85.66	514.42
12	71.33	99.67	409.00	73.96	100.16	414.26
13	54.89	116.11	292.89	57.00	117.12	297.14
14	35.73	135.27	157.62	37.15	136.97	160.17
15	13.38	157.62	0	13.95	160.17	0

Self-Liquidating Mortgages—Annual Interest, Amortization And Remaining Balance *(continued)*

20-Year Term

	4% interest—$6.06 monthly payment			4½% interest—$6.33 monthly payment			5% interest—$6.60 monthly payment		
Year	*Interest*	*Amort.*	*Balance*	*Interest*	*Amort.*	*Balance*	*Interest*	*Amort.*	*Balance*
1	39.49	33.32	966.68	44.34	31.62	968.38	49.33	29.87	970.13
2	38.03	34.69	931.99	42.90	33.06	935.32	47.79	31.41	938.72
3	36.66	36.06	895.93	41.38	34.58	900.74	46.19	33.01	905.71
4	35.15	37.57	858.36	39.80	36.16	864.58	44.50	34.70	871.01
5	33.62	39.10	819.26	38.12	37.84	826.74	42.71	36.49	834.52
6	32.04	40.68	778.58	36.40	39.56	787.18	40.83	38.37	796.15
7	30.38	42.34	736.24	34.58	41.38	745.80	38.90	40.30	755.85
8	28.64	44.08	692.16	32.68	43.28	702.52	36.84	42.36	713.49
9	26.85	45.87	646.29	30.68	45.28	657.24	34.66	44.54	668.95
10	24.99	47.73	598.56	28.61	47.35	609.89	32.39	46.81	622.14
11	23.05	49.67	548.89	26.44	49.52	560.37	29.99	49.21	572.93
12	21.01	51.71	497.18	24.16	51.80	508.57	27.47	51.73	521.20
13	18.90	53.82	443.36	21.78	54.18	454.39	24.80	54.40	466.80
14	16.72	56.00	387.36	19.29	56.67	397.72	22.09	57.11	409.69
15	14.43	58.29	329.07	16.70	59.26	338.46	19.13	60.07	349.62
16	12.06	60.66	268.41	13.95	62.01	276.45	16.05	63.15	286.47
17	9.59	63.13	205.28	11.14	64.82	211.63	12.81	66.39	220.08
18	7.01	65.71	139.57	8.13	67.83	143.80	9.42	69.78	150.30
19	4.36	68.36	71.21	5.02	70.94	72.86	5.85	73.35	76.95
20	1.56	71.21	0	1.76	72.86	0	2.10	76.95	0

	5¼% interest—$6.74 monthly payment			5½% interest—$6.88 monthly payment			5¾% interest—$7.03 monthly payment		
Year	*Interest*	*Amort.*	*Balance*	*Interest*	*Amort.*	*Balance*	*Interest*	*Amort.*	*Balance*
1	51.79	29.09	970.91	54.29	28.27	971.73	56.78	27.58	972.42
2	50.25	30.63	940.28	52.69	29.87	941.86	55.16	29.20	943.22
3	48.60	32.28	908.00	51.02	31.54	910.32	53.43	30.93	912.29
4	46.86	34.02	873.98	49.23	33.33	876.99	51.60	32.76	879.53
5	45.02	35.86	838.12	47.36	35.20	841.79	49.66	34.70	844.83
6	43.11	37.77	800.35	45.37	37.19	804.60	47.93	36.43	808.10
7	41.07	39.81	760.54	43.26	39.30	765.30	45.45	38.91	769.19
8	38.94	41.94	718.60	41.06	41.50	723.80	43.16	41.20	727.99
9	36.67	44.21	674.39	38.70	43.86	679.94	40.72	43.64	684.35
10	34.29	46.59	627.80	36.25	46.31	633.63	38.14	46.22	638.13
11	31.78	49.10	578.70	33.63	48.93	584.70	35.41	48.95	589.18
12	29.14	51.74	526.96	30.84	51.72	532.98	32.51	51.85	537.33
13	26.40	54.48	472.48	27.96	54.60	478.38	29.46	54.90	482.43
14	23.45	57.43	415.05	24.86	57.70	420.68	26.21	58.15	424.28
15	20.34	60.54	354.51	21.62	60.94	359.74	22.80	61.56	362.72
16	17.10	63.78	290.73	18.16	64.40	295.34	19.16	65.20	297.52
17	13.66	67.22	223.51	14.56	68.00	227.34	15.30	69.06	228.46
18	10.04	70.84	152.67	10.71	71.85	155.49	11.20	73.16	155.30
19	6.22	74.66	78.01	6.65	75.91	79.58	6.90	77.46	77.84
20	2.22	78.01	0	2.34	79.58	0	2.33	77.84	0

Self-Liquidating Mortgages—Annual Interest, Amortization And Remaining Balance *(continued)*

20-Year Term *(continued)*

	6% interest—$7.17 monthly payment			6¼% interest—$7.31 monthly payment			6½% interest—$7.46 monthly payment		
Year	*Interest*	*Amort.*	*Balance*	*Interest*	*Amort.*	*Balance*	*Interest*	*Amort.*	*Balance*
1	59.28	26.76	973.24	61.77	25.95	974.05	64.25	25.27	974.73
2	57.62	28.42	944.82	60.09	27.63	946.42	62.58	26.94	947.78
3	55.86	30.18	914.64	58.31	29.41	917.01	60.75	28.77	919.01
4	54.01	32.03	882.61	56.44	31.28	885.73	58.83	30.69	888.32
5	52.03	34.01	848.60	54.42	33.30	852.43	56.76	32.76	855.56
6	49.92	36.12	812.48	52.25	35.47	816.96	54.57	34.95	820.61
7	47.72	38.32	774.16	50.00	37.72	779.24	52.25	37.27	783.34
8	45.32	40.72	733.44	47.58	40.14	739.10	49.76	39.76	743.58
9	42.83	43.21	690.23	44.97	42.75	696.35	47.09	42.43	701.15
10	40.16	45.88	644.35	42.25	45.47	650.88	44.26	45.26	655.89
11	37.33	48.71	595.64	39.30	48.42	602.46	41.21	48.31	607.58
12	34.34	51.70	543.94	36.19	51.53	550.93	37.99	51.53	556.05
13	31.14	54.90	489.04	32.90	54.82	496.11	34.52	55.00	501.05
14	27.77	58.27	430.77	29.35	58.37	437.74	30.82	58.70	442.35
15	24.16	61.88	368.89	25.58	62.14	375.60	26.91	62.61	379.74
16	20.35	65.69	303.20	21.62	66.10	309.50	22.74	66.78	312.96
17	16.30	69.74	233.46	17.33	70.39	239.11	18.25	71.27	241.69
18	12.01	74.03	159.43	12.82	74.90	164.21	13.47	76.05	165.64
19	7.44	78.60	80.83	8.03	79.69	84.52	8.39	81.13	84.51
20	2.54	80.83	0	2.88	84.52	0	2.95	84.51	0

	6¾% interest—$7.61 monthly payment			7% interest—$7.76 monthly payment			7¼% interest—$7.91 monthly payment		
Year	*Interest*	*Amort.*	*Balance*	*Interest*	*Amort.*	*Balance*	*Interest*	*Amort.*	*Balance*
1	66.75	24.57	975.43	69.24	23.88	976.12	71.74	23.18	976.82
2	65.03	26.29	949.14	67.52	25.60	950.52	70.01	24.91	951.91
3	63.20	28.12	921.02	65.67	27.45	923.07	68.13	26.79	925.12
4	61.25	30.07	890.95	63.68	29.44	893.63	66.13	28.79	896.33
5	59.16	32.16	858.79	61.54	31.58	862.05	63.96	30.96	865.37
6	56.92	34.40	824.39	59.28	33.84	828.21	61.65	33.27	832.10
7	54.52	36.80	787.59	56.83	36.29	791.92	59.16	35.76	796.34
8	51.97	39.35	748.24	54.19	38.93	752.99	56.47	38.45	757.89
9	49.20	42.12	706.12	51.37	41.75	711.24	53.61	41.31	716.58
10	46.28	45.04	661.08	48.38	44.74	666.50	50.50	44.42	672.16
11	43.15	48.17	612.91	45.12	48.00	618.50	47.17	47.75	624.41
12	39.81	51.51	561.40	41.67	51.45	567.05	43.59	51.33	573.08
13	36.20	55.12	506.28	37.95	55.17	511.88	39.74	55.18	517.90
14	32.36	58.96	447.32	33.97	59.15	452.73	35.58	59.34	458.56
15	28.26	63.06	384.26	29.68	63.44	389.29	31.16	63.76	394.80
16	23.87	67.45	316.81	25.10	68.02	321.27	26.37	68.55	326.25
17	19.18	72.14	244.67	20.19	72.93	248.34	21.25	73.67	252.58
18	14.15	77.17	167.50	14.90	78.22	170.12	15.72	79.20	173.38
19	8.80	82.52	84.98	9.25	83.87	86.25	9.79	85.13	88.25
20	3.05	84.98	0	3.19	86.25	0	3.40	88.25	0

Self-Liquidating Mortgages—Annual Interest, Amortization And Remaining Balance *(continued)*

20-Year Term *(continued)*

	7½% interest—$8.06 monthly payment			7¾% interest—$8.21 monthly payment			8% interest—$8.37 monthly payment		
Year	*Interest*	*Amort.*	*Balance*	*Interest*	*Amort.*	*Balance*	*Interest*	*Amort.*	*Balance*
1	74.24	22.48	977.52	76.74	21.78	978.22	79.24	21.20	978.80
2	72.49	24.23	953.29	75.00	23.52	954.70	77.47	22.97	955.83
3	70.63	26.09	927.20	73.10	25.42	929.28	75.58	24.86	930.97
4	68.58	28.14	899.06	71.05	27.47	901.81	73.49	26.95	904.02
5	66.40	30.32	868.74	68.84	29.68	872.13	71.29	29.15	874.87
6	64.04	32.68	836.06	66.47	32.05	840.08	68.85	31.59	843.28
7	61.51	35.21	800.85	63.89	34.63	805.45	66.21	34.23	809.05
8	58.81	37.91	762.94	61.09	37.43	768.02	63.37	37.07	771.98
9	55.83	40.89	722.05	58.11	40.41	727.61	60.32	40.12	731.86
10	52.66	44.06	677.99	54.86	43.66	683.95	56.99	43.45	688.41
11	49.25	47.47	630.52	51.35	47.17	636.78	53.36	47.08	641.33
12	45.56	51.16	579.36	47.56	50.96	585.82	49.46	50.98	590.35
13	41.58	55.14	524.22	43.49	55.03	530.79	45.26	55.18	535.17
14	37.32	59.40	464.82	39.05	59.47	471.32	40.67	59.77	475.40
15	32.69	64.03	400.79	34.28	64.24	407.08	35.67	64.77	410.63
16	27.73	68.99	331.80	29.12	69.40	337.68	30.31	70.13	340.50
17	22.37	74.35	257.45	23.52	75.00	262.68	24.51	75.93	264.57
18	16.61	80.11	177.34	17.53	80.99	181.69	18.20	82.24	182.33
19	10.37	86.35	90.99	11.01	87.51	94.18	11.33	89.11	93.22
20	3.67	90.99	0	3.99	94.18	0	3.97	93.22	0

	8¼% interest—$8.52 monthly payment			8½% interest—$8.68 monthly payment			8¾% interest—$8.84 monthly payment		
Year	*Interest*	*Amort.*	*Balance*	*Interest*	*Amort.*	*Balance*	*Interest*	*Amort.*	*Balance*
1	81.74	20.51	979.50	84.24	19.93	980.08	86.74	19.35	980.66
2	79.98	22.27	957.24	82.48	21.69	958.40	84.98	21.11	959.56
3	78.08	24.17	933.07	80.56	23.61	934.79	83.06	23.03	936.53
4	76.01	26.24	906.83	78.48	25.69	909.10	80.96	25.13	911.40
5	73.76	28.49	878.34	76.21	27.96	881.15	78.67	27.42	883.99
6	71.32	30.93	847.42	73.73	30.44	850.71	76.17	29.92	854.07
7	68.67	33.58	813.84	71.04	33.13	817.59	73.45	32.64	821.44
8	65.79	36.46	777.38	68.12	36.05	781.55	70.47	35.62	785.83
9	62.66	39.59	737.80	64.93	39.24	742.31	67.23	38.86	746.97
10	59.27	42.98	694.83	61.46	42.71	699.61	63.69	42.40	704.58
11	55.59	46.66	648.17	57.69	46.48	653.13	59.83	46.26	658.32
12	51.59	50.66	597.52	53.58	50.59	602.55	55.62	50.47	607.85
13	47.25	55.00	542.52	49.11	55.06	547.49	51.02	55.07	552.79
14	42.54	59.71	482.82	44.24	59.93	487.57	46.00	60.09	492.70
15	37.42	64.83	417.99	38.95	65.22	422.35	40.53	65.56	427.15
16	31.87	70.38	347.62	33.18	70.99	351.37	34.56	71.53	355.62
17	25.84	76.41	271.21	26.91	77.26	274.11	28.04	78.05	277.57
18	19.29	82.96	188.25	20.08	84.09	190.02	20.93	85.16	192.42
19	12.18	90.07	98.19	12.65	91.52	98.51	13.17	92.92	99.51
20	4.46	97.79	0.40	4.56	99.61	1.10	4.71	101.38	1.87

Self-Liquidating Mortgages—Annual Interest, Amortization And Remaining Balance *(continued)*

20-Year Term *(continued)*

	9% interest—$9.00 monthly payment			9¼% interest—$9.16 monthly payment			9½% interest—$9.32 monthly payment		
Year	*Interest*	*Amort.*	*Balance*	*Interest*	*Amort.*	*Balance*	*Interest*	*Amort.*	*Balance*
1	89.24	18.76	981.24	91.75	18.18	981.83	94.25	17.60	982.41
2	87.47	20.53	960.71	89.99	19.94	961.89	92.51	19.34	963.07
3	85.56	22.44	938.27	88.07	21.86	940.04	90.59	21.26	941.81
4	83.45	24.55	913.72	85.96	23.97	916.07	88.48	23.37	918.45
5	81.14	26.86	886.86	83.65	26.28	889.79	86.16	25.69	892.76
6	78.64	29.36	857.50	81.11	28.82	860.98	83.61	28.24	864.52
7	75.83	32.17	825.33	78.33	31.60	829.38	80.81	31.04	833.48
8	72.85	35.15	790.18	75.28	34.65	794.73	77.73	34.12	799.36
9	69.56	38.44	751.74	71.93	38.00	756.74	74.34	37.51	761.86
10	65.96	42.04	709.70	68.27	41.66	715.08	70.62	41.23	720.63
11	62.01	45.99	663.71	64.25	45.68	669.40	66.52	45.33	675.31
12	57.70	50.30	613.41	59.84	50.09	619.31	62.03	49.82	625.49
13	52.97	55.03	558.38	55.00	54.93	564.39	57.08	54.77	570.73
14	47.80	60.20	498.18	49.70	60.23	504.16	51.65	60.20	510.53
15	42.19	65.81	432.37	43.89	66.04	438.13	45.67	66.18	444.36
16	35.99	72.01	360.36	37.51	72.42	365.71	39.11	72.74	371.62
17	29.20	78.80	281.56	30.52	79.41	286.31	31.89	79.96	291.66
18	21.86	86.14	195.42	22.86	87.07	199.24	23.95	87.90	203.76
19	13.76	94.24	101.18	14.45	95.48	103.77	15.23	96.62	107.15
20	4.93	101.18	0	5.24	104.69	0.91	5.64	106.21	0.94

	9¾% interest—$9.49 monthly payment			10% interest—$9.66 monthly payment			10¼% interest—$9.82 monthly payment		
Year	*Interest*	*Amort.*	*Balance*	*Interest*	*Amort.*	*Balance*	*Interest*	*Amort.*	*Balance*
1	96.75	17.14	982.87	99.25	16.67	983.33	101.76	16.09	983.92
2	95.01	18.88	963.99	97.49	18.43	964.90	100.04	17.81	966.11
3	93.08	20.81	943.19	95.59	20.33	944.57	98.12	19.73	946.39
4	90.96	22.93	920.26	93.44	22.48	922.09	96.00	21.85	924.55
5	88.62	25.27	895.00	91.09	24.83	897.26	93.66	24.19	900.36
6	86.04	27.85	867.16	88.51	27.41	869.85	91.06	26.79	873.57
7	83.21	30.68	836.48	85.62	30.30	839.55	88.18	29.67	843.90
8	80.08	33.81	802.67	82.45	33.47	806.08	84.99	32.86	811.05
9	76.63	37.26	765.42	78.94	36.98	769.10	81.46	36.39	774.66
10	72.83	41.06	724.36	75.08	40.84	728.26	77.55	40.30	734.36
11	68.64	45.25	679.12	70.81	45.11	683.15	73.22	44.63	689.74
12	64.03	49.86	629.26	66.07	49.85	633.30	68.42	49.43	640.31
13	58.95	54.94	574.32	60.86	55.06	578.24	63.11	54.74	585.58
14	53.34	60.55	513.78	55.11	60.81	517.43	57.23	60.62	524.97
15	47.17	66.72	447.07	48.71	67.21	450.22	50.72	67.13	457.84
16	40.37	73.52	373.55	41.68	74.24	375.98	43.51	74.34	383.50
17	32.87	81.02	292.53	33.90	82.02	293.96	35.52	82.33	301.18
18	24.61	89.28	203.25	25.32	90.60	203.36	26.67	91.18	210.00
19	15.50	98.39	104.87	15.83	100.09	103.27	16.87	100.98	109.03
20	5.47	108.42	3.55	5.35	103.27	0	6.02	111.83	2.79

Self-Liquidating Mortgages—Annual Interest, Amortization And Remaining Balance *(continued)*

20-Year Term *(continued)*

	10½% interest—$9.98 monthly payment			10¾% interest—$10.15 monthly payment			11% interest—$10.32 monthly payment		
Year	*Interest*	*Amort.*	*Balance*	*Interest*	*Amort.*	*Balance*	*Interest*	*Amort.*	*Balance*
1	104.27	15.50	984.51	106.78	15.03	984.98	109.29	14.56	985.45
2	102.57	17.20	967.31	105.08	16.73	968.26	107.60	16.25	969.20
3	100.67	19.10	948.22	103.19	18.62	949.64	105.72	18.13	951.08
4	98.57	21.20	927.02	101.09	20.72	928.93	103.62	20.23	930.86
5	96.23	23.54	903.49	98.75	23.06	905.87	101.28	22.57	908.29
6	93.64	26.13	877.36	96.15	25.66	880.21	98.67	25.18	883.12
7	90.76	29.01	848.35	93.25	28.56	851.66	95.76	28.09	855.04
8	87.56	32.21	816.15	90.02	31.79	819.87	92.51	31.34	823.70
9	84.01	35.76	780.40	86.43	35.38	784.50	88.88	34.97	788.74
10	80.07	39.70	740.70	82.44	39.37	745.13	84.84	39.01	749.73
11	75.70	44.07	696.64	77.99	43.82	701.32	80.32	43.53	706.21
12	70.84	48.93	647.71	73.04	48.77	652.55	75.29	48.56	657.66
13	65.45	54.32	593.40	67.53	54.28	598.28	69.67	54.18	603.48
14	59.46	60.31	533.09	61.40	60.41	537.87	63.40	60.45	543.04
15	52.82	66.95	466.15	54.58	67.23	470.65	56.41	67.44	475.60
16	45.44	74.33	391.82	46.98	74.83	395.82	48.60	75.25	400.35
17	37.25	82.52	309.31	38.53	83.28	312.55	39.89	83.96	316.40
18	28.16	91.61	217.70	29.13	92.68	219.87	30.18	93.67	222.74
19	18.06	101.71	116.00	18.66	103.15	116.72	19.34	104.51	118.23
20	6.85	112.92	3.08	7.01	114.80	1.92	7.25	116.60	1.64

	11¼% interest—$10.49 monthly payment			11½% interest—$10.66 monthly payment			11¾% interest—$10.84 monthly payment		
Year	*Interest*	*Amort.*	*Balance*	*Interest*	*Amort.*	*Balance*	*Interest*	*Amort.*	*Balance*
1	111.79	14.10	985.91	114.30	13.63	986.38	116.80	13.29	986.72
2	110.12	15.77	970.15	112.65	15.28	971.11	115.16	14.93	971.80
3	108.26	17.63	952.52	110.80	17.13	953.98	113.31	16.78	955.02
4	106.17	19.72	932.80	108.72	19.21	934.77	111.22	18.87	936.16
5	103.83	22.06	910.75	106.39	21.54	913.24	108.89	21.20	914.96
6	101.22	24.67	886.08	103.78	24.15	889.10	106.26	23.83	891.13
7	98.29	27.60	858.49	100.85	27.08	862.03	103.30	26.79	864.34
8	95.03	30.86	827.63	97.57	30.36	831.67	99.98	30.11	834.24
9	91.37	34.52	793.12	93.89	34.04	797.64	96.24	33.85	800.40
10	87.28	38.61	754.51	89.76	38.17	759.47	92.05	38.04	762.36
11	82.71	43.18	711.33	85.14	42.79	716.68	87.33	42.76	719.60
12	77.59	48.30	663.04	79.95	47.98	668.71	82.02	48.07	671.54
13	71.87	54.02	609.02	74.13	53.80	614.91	76.06	54.03	617.51
14	65.47	60.42	548.60	67.61	60.32	554.59	69.36	60.73	556.79
15	58.31	67.58	481.03	60.29	67.64	486.96	61.83	68.26	488.53
16	50.30	75.59	405.44	52.09	75.84	411.12	53.36	76.73	411.81
17	41.35	84.54	320.90	42.89	85.04	326.09	43.85	86.24	325.57
18	31.33	94.56	226.35	32.58	95.35	230.75	33.15	96.94	228.64
19	20.13	105.76	120.59	21.02	106.91	123.85	21.13	108.96	119.68
20	7.59	118.30	2.30	8.06	119.87	3.98	7.61	122.48	2.80

Self-Liquidating Mortgages—Annual Interest, Amortization And Remaining Balance *(continued)*

20-Year Term *(continued)*

	12% interest—$11.01 monthly payment			12⅜% interest—$11.27 monthly payment			12¾% interest—$11.54 monthly payment		
Year	*Interest*	*Amort.*	*Balance*	*Interest*	*Amort.*	*Balance*	*Interest*	*Amort.*	*Balance*
1	119.32	12.81	987.20	123.04	12.20	987.80	126.86	11.62	988.38
2	117.69	14.44	972.76	121.43	13.81	973.99	125.29	13.19	975.19
3	115.86	16.27	956.50	119.62	15.62	958.37	123.50	14.98	960.21
4	113.80	18.33	938.17	117.57	17.67	940.70	121.48	17.00	943.21
5	111.47	20.66	917.52	115.27	19.97	920.73	119.17	19.31	923.90
6	108.85	23.28	894.25	112.65	22.59	898.14	116.58	21.90	902.00
7	105.90	26.23	868.03	109.68	25.56	872.58	113.61	24.87	877.13
8	102.58	29.55	838.48	106.34	28.90	843.68	110.24	28.24	848.89
9	98.83	33.30	805.18	101.56	33.68	811.00	106.43	32.05	816.84
10	94.61	37.52	767.67	98.26	36.98	774.02	102.09	36.39	780.45
11	89.85	42.28	725.39	93.43	41.81	732.21	97.16	41.32	739.13
12	84.49	47.64	677.75	87.95	47.29	684.92	91.59	46.89	692.24
13	78.45	53.68	624.07	81.75	53.49	631.43	85.25	53.23	639.01
14	71.64	60.49	563.59	74.73	60.51	570.92	78.05	60.43	578.58
15	63.97	68.16	495.43	66.83	68.41	502.51	69.87	68.61	509.97
16	55.32	76.81	418.63	57.84	77.40	425.11	60.59	77.89	432.08
17	45.58	86.55	332.08	47.73	87.51	337.60	50.07	88.41	343.67
18	34.61	97.52	234.57	36.24	99.00	238.60	38.10	100.38	243.29
19	22.24	109.89	124.68	23.27	111.97	126.63	24.54	113.94	129.35
20	8.30	123.83	0.86	8.61	126.63	0	9.13	129.35	0

	13⅛% interest—$11.80 monthly payment			13½% interest—$12.07 monthly payment			13⅞% interest—$12.34 monthly payment		
Year	*Interest*	*Amort.*	*Balance*	*Interest*	*Amort.*	*Balance*	*Interest*	*Amort.*	*Balance*
1	130.54	11.06	988.94	134.31	10.53	989.47	138.07	10.01	989.99
2	129.00	12.60	976.34	132.82	12.02	977.45	136.60	11.48	978.51
3	127.24	14.36	961.98	131.08	13.76	963.69	134.90	13.18	965.33
4	125.25	16.35	945.63	129.10	15.74	947.95	132.94	15.14	950.19
5	122.95	18.65	926.98	126.85	17.99	929.96	130.71	17.37	932.82
6	120.36	21.24	905.74	124.25	20.59	909.37	128.13	19.95	912.87
7	117.40	24.20	881.54	121.29	23.55	885.82	125.20	22.88	889.99
8	114.03	27.57	853.97	117.93	26.91	858.91	121.80	26.28	863.71
9	110.17	31.43	822.54	114.04	30.80	828.11	117.92	30.16	833.55
10	105.80	35.80	786.74	109.62	35.22	792.89	113.45	34.63	798.92
11	100.81	40.79	745.95	104.57	40.27	752.62	108.33	39.75	759.17
12	95.11	46.49	699.46	98.77	46.07	706.55	102.44	45.64	713.53
13	88.63	52.97	646.49	92.17	52.67	653.88	95.71	52.37	661.16
14	81.25	60.35	586.14	84.59	60.25	593.63	87.96	60.12	601.04
15	72.83	68.77	517.37	75.93	68.91	524.72	79.05	69.03	532.01
16	62.89	78.71	438.66	66.03	78.81	445.91	68.85	79.23	452.78
17	52.67	88.93	349.73	54.72	90.12	355.79	57.13	90.95	361.83
18	39.87	101.73	248.00	41.76	103.08	252.71	43.68	104.40	257.43
19	25.68	115.92	132.08	26.96	117.88	134.83	28.22	119.86	137.57
20	9.52	132.08	0	10.01	134.83	0	10.51	137.57	0

Self-Liquidating Mortgages—Annual Interest, Amortization And Remaining Balance *(continued)*

20-Year Term *(continued)*

	14¼% interest—$12.62 monthly payment			14⅝% interest—$12.89 monthly payment			15% interest—$13.17 monthly payment		
Year	*Interest*	*Amort.*	*Balance*	*Interest*	*Amort.*	*Balance*	*Interest*	*Amort.*	*Balance*
1	141.93	9.51	990.49	145.64	9.04	990.96	149.45	8.59	991.41
2	140.48	10.96	979.53	144.23	10.45	980.51	148.07	9.97	981.44
3	138.81	12.63	966.90	142.58	12.10	968.41	146.46	11.58	969.86
4	136.89	14.55	952.35	140.70	13.98	954.43	144.61	13.43	956.43
5	134.68	16.76	935.59	138.51	16.17	938.26	142.45	15.59	940.84
6	132.13	19.31	916.28	135.99	18.69	919.57	139.94	18.10	922.74
7	129.19	22.25	894.03	133.05	21.63	897.94	137.03	21.01	901.73
8	125.79	25.65	868.38	129.67	25.01	872.93	133.65	24.39	877.34
9	121.90	29.54	838.84	125.85	28.83	844.10	129.74	28.30	849.04
10	117.41	34.03	804.81	121.14	33.54	810.56	125.18	32.86	816.18
11	112.22	39.22	765.59	116.00	38.68	771.88	119.91	38.13	778.05
12	106.26	45.18	720.41	109.95	44.73	727.15	113.47	44.57	733.48
13	99.37	52.07	668.34	102.94	51.74	675.41	106.95	51.09	682.39
14	91.45	59.99	608.35	94.86	59.82	615.59	98.39	59.65	622.74
15	82.33	69.11	539.24	85.50	69.18	546.41	88.80	69.24	553.50
16	71.81	79.63	459.61	74.66	80.02	466.39	77.68	80.36	473.14
17	59.68	91.76	367.85	62.16	92.52	373.87	64.76	93.28	379.86
18	45.73	105.71	262.14	47.67	107.01	266.86	49.76	108.28	271.58
19	29.64	121.80	140.34	30.94	123.74	143.12	32.35	125.69	145.89
20	11.11	140.34	0	11.56	143.12	0	12.15	145.89	0

	15⅜% interest—$13.45 monthly payment			15¾% interest—$13.73 monthly payment		
Year	*Interest*	*Amort.*	*Balance*	*Interest*	*Amort.*	*Balance*
1	153.24	8.16	991.84	157.01	7.75	992.25
2	151.90	9.50	982.34	155.70	9.06	983.19
3	150.33	11.07	971.27	154.17	10.59	972.60
4	148.48	12.92	958.35	152.37	12.39	960.21
5	146.38	15.02	943.33	150.27	14.49	945.72
6	143.88	17.52	925.81	147.82	16.94	928.78
7	141.00	20.40	905.41	144.95	19.81	908.97
8	137.62	23.78	881.63	141.59	23.17	885.80
9	133.71	27.69	853.94	137.67	27.09	858.71
10	129.13	32.27	821.67	133.09	31.67	827.04
11	123.81	37.59	784.08	127.71	37.05	789.99
12	117.60	43.80	740.28	121.44	43.32	746.67
13	110.37	51.03	689.25	114.11	50.65	696.02
14	101.96	59.44	629.81	105.52	59.24	636.78
15	92.13	69.27	560.54	95.48	69.28	567.50
16	80.70	80.70	479.84	83.76	81.00	486.50
17	67.39	94.01	385.83	70.04	94.72	391.78
18	51.86	109.54	276.29	53.99	110.77	281.01
19	33.79	127.61	148.68	35.23	129.53	151.48
20	12.72	148.68	0	13.28	151.48	0

Self-Liquidating Mortgages—Annual Interest, Amortization and Remaining Balance *(continued)*

25-Year Term

	4% interest—$5.28 monthly payment			4½% interest—$5.56 monthly payment			5% interest—$5.85 monthly payment		
Year	*Interest*	*Amort.*	*Balance*	*Interest*	*Amort.*	*Balance*	*Interest*	*Amort.*	*Balance*
1	39.56	23.80	976.20	44.54	22.18	977.82	49.54	20.66	979.34
2	38.60	24.76	951.44	43.54	23.18	954.64	48.48	21.72	957.62
3	37.57	25.79	925.65	42.44	24.28	930.36	47.36	22.84	934.78
4	36.55	26.81	898.84	41.35	25.37	904.99	46.19	24.01	910.77
5	35.45	27.91	870.93	40.18	26.54	878.45	44.98	25.22	885.55
6	34.31	29.05	841.88	38.97	27.75	850.70	43.67	26.53	859.02
7	33.13	30.23	811.65	37.70	29.02	821.68	42.30	27.90	831.12
8	31.89	31.47	780.18	36.34	30.38	791.30	40.87	29.33	801.79
9	30.61	32.75	747.43	34.98	31.74	759.56	39.39	30.81	770.98
10	29.28	34.08	713.35	33.53	33.19	726.37	37.81	32.39	738.59
11	27.91	35.45	677.90	31.96	34.76	691.61	36.16	34.04	704.55
12	26.45	36.91	640.99	30.38	36.34	655.27	34.41	35.79	668.76
13	24.94	38.42	602.57	28.71	38.01	617.26	32.59	37.61	631.15
14	23.38	39.98	562.59	26.96	39.76	577.50	30.66	39.54	591.61
15	21.75	41.61	520.98	25.14	41.58	535.92	28.65	41.55	550.06
16	20.05	43.31	477.67	23.22	43.50	492.42	26.52	43.68	506.38
17	18.29	45.07	432.60	21.23	45.49	446.93	24.27	45.93	460.45
18	16.46	46.90	385.70	19.14	47.58	399.35	21.93	48.27	412.18
19	14.54	48.82	336.88	16.97	49.75	349.60	19.46	50.74	361.44
20	12.55	50.81	286.07	14.66	52.06	297.54	16.86	53.34	308.10
21	10.49	52.87	233.20	12.28	54.44	243.10	14.15	56.05	252.05
22	8.32	55.04	178.16	9.77	56.95	186.15	11.57	58.93	193.12
23	6.10	57.26	120.90	7.15	59.57	126.58	8.24	61.96	131.16
24	3.73	59.63	61.27	4.44	62.28	64.30	5.07	65.13	66.03
25	1.31	61.27	0	1.56	64.30	0	1.75	66.03	0

	5¼% interest—$6.00 monthly payment			5½% interest—$6.15 monthly payment			5¾% interest—$6.30 monthly payment		
Year	*Interest*	*Amort.*	*Balance*	*Interest*	*Amort.*	*Balance*	*Interest*	*Amort.*	*Balance*
1	52.03	19.97	980.03	54.51	19.29	980.71	57.02	18.58	981.42
2	50.96	21.04	958.99	53.44	20.36	960.35	55.90	19.70	961.72
3	49.82	22.18	936.81	52.27	21.53	938.82	54.77	20.83	940.89
4	48.63	23.37	913.44	51.07	22.73	916.09	53.52	22.08	918.82
5	47.38	24.62	888.82	49.79	24.01	892.08	52.23	23.37	895.44
6	46.01	25.99	862.83	48.42	25.38	866.70	50.82	24.78	870.66
7	44.70	27.30	835.53	46.98	26.82	839.88	49.39	26.21	844.45
8	43.16	28.84	806.69	45.50	28.30	811.58	47.83	27.77	816.68
9	41.63	30.37	776.32	43.88	29.92	781.66	46.18	29.42	787.26
10	40.00	32.00	744.32	42.20	31.60	750.06	44.48	31.12	756.14
11	38.27	33.73	710.59	40.42	33.38	716.68	42.61	32.99	723.15
12	36.47	35.53	675.06	38.55	35.25	681.43	40.67	34.93	688.22
13	34.55	37.45	637.61	36.55	37.25	644.18	38.62	36.98	651.24
14	32.54	39.46	598.15	34.44	39.36	604.82	36.41	39.18	612.06
15	30.42	41.58	556.57	32.22	41.58	563.24	34.11	41.49	570.57

Self-Liquidating Mortgages—Annual Interest, Amortization and Remaining Balance *(continued)*

25-Year Term *(continued)*

	5¼% interest—$6.00 monthly payment			5½% interest—$6.15 monthly payment			5¾% interest—$6.30 monthly payment		
Year	*Interest*	*Amort.*	*Balance*	*Interest*	*Amort.*	*Balance*	*Interest*	*Amort.*	*Balance*
16	28.16	43.84	512.73	29.90	43.90	519.34	31.65	43.95	526.62
17	25.82	46.18	466.55	27.41	46.39	472.95	29.07	46.53	480.09
18	23.34	48.66	417.89	24.79	49.01	423.94	26.27	49.33	430.76
19	20.71	51.29	366.60	22.04	51.76	372.18	23.41	52.19	378.57
20	17.98	54.02	312.58	19.12	54.68	317.50	20.33	55.27	323.30
21	15.06	56.94	255.64	16.01	57.79	259.71	17.05	58.55	264.75
22	11.99	60.01	195.63	12.76	61.04	198.67	13.61	61.99	202.76
23	8.76	63.24	132.39	9.32	64.48	134.19	9.94	65.66	137.10
24	5.36	66.64	65.75	5.70	68.10	66.09	6.07	69.53	67.57
25	1.78	65.75	0	1.83	66.09	0	1.97	67.57	0

	6% interest—$6.45 monthly payment			6¼% interest—$6.60 monthly payment			6½% interest—$6.76 monthly payment		
Year	*Interest*	*Amort.*	*Balance*	*Interest*	*Amort.*	*Balance*	*Interest*	*Amort.*	*Balance*
1	59.52	17.88	982.12	62.01	17.19	982.81	64.50	16.62	983.38
2	58.41	18.99	963.13	60.91	18.29	964.52	63.41	17.71	965.67
3	57.24	20.16	942.97	59.73	19.47	945.05	62.21	18.91	946.76
4	55.99	21.41	921.56	58.48	20.72	924.33	60.95	20.17	926.59
5	54.66	22.74	898.82	57.17	22.03	902.30	59.58	21.54	905.05
6	53.23	24.17	874.65	55.73	23.47	878.83	58.14	22.98	882.07
7	51.78	25.62	849.03	54.22	24.98	853.85	56.62	24.50	857.57
8	50.20	27.20	821.83	52.61	26.59	827.26	54.97	26.15	831.42
9	48.53	28.87	792.96	50.89	28.31	798.95	53.23	27.89	803.53
10	46.74	30.66	762.30	49.09	30.11	768.84	51.37	29.75	773.78
11	44.84	32.56	729.74	47.14	32.06	736.78	49.34	31.78	742.00
12	42.84	34.56	695.18	45.08	34.12	702.66	47.22	33.90	708.10
13	40.72	36.68	658.50	42.88	36.32	666.34	44.98	36.14	671.96
14	38.44	38.96	619.54	40.54	38.66	627.68	42.54	38.58	633.38
15	36.05	41.35	578.19	38.06	41.14	586.54	39.95	41.17	592.21
16	33.50	43.90	534.29	35.42	43.78	542.76	37.21	43.91	548.30
17	30.80	46.60	487.69	32.64	46.56	496.20	34.26	46.86	501.44
18	27.93	49.47	438.22	29.60	49.60	446.60	31.12	50.00	451.44
19	24.87	52.53	385.69	26.40	52.80	393.80	27.17	53.34	398.10
20	21.62	55.78	329.91	23.03	56.17	337.63	24.19	56.93	341.17
21	18.18	59.22	270.69	19.41	59.79	277.84	20.40	60.72	280.45
22	14.53	62.87	207.82	15.56	63.64	214.20	16.32	64.80	215.65
23	10.64	66.76	141.06	11.46	67.74	146.46	12.00	69.12	146.53
24	6.53	70.87	70.19	7.10	72.10	74.36	7.34	73.78	72.75
25	2.17	70.19	0	2.48	74.36	0	2.40	72.75	0

Self-Liquidating Mortgages—Annual Interest, Amortization And Remaining Balance *(continued)*

25-Year Term *(continued)*

	6¾% interest—$6.91 monthly payment			7% interest—$7.07 monthly payment			7¼% interest—$7.23 monthly payment		
Year	*Interest*	*Amort.*	*Balance*	*Interest*	*Amort.*	*Balance*	*Interest*	*Amort.*	*Balance*
1	67.02	15.90	984.10	69.51	15.33	984.67	72.02	14.74	985.26
2	65.92	17.00	967.10	68.40	16.44	968.23	70.91	15.85	969.41
3	64.72	18.20	948.90	67.20	17.64	950.59	69.72	17.04	952.37
4	63.45	19.47	929.43	65.94	18.90	931.69	68.44	18.32	934.05
5	62.10	20.82	908.61	64.62	20.22	911.47	67.01	19.75	914.30
6	60.66	22.26	886.35	63.12	21.72	889.75	65.58	21.18	893.12
7	59.09	23.83	862.52	61.55	23.29	866.46	64.01	22.75	870.37
8	57.44	25.48	837.04	59.85	24.99	841.47	62.30	24.46	845.91
9	55.68	27.24	809.80	58.06	26.78	814.69	60.47	26.29	819.62
10	53.77	29.15	780.65	56.12	28.72	785.97	58.49	28.27	791.35
11	51.74	31.18	749.47	54.05	30.79	755.18	56.39	30.37	760.98
12	49.57	33.35	716.12	51.81	33.03	722.15	54.10	32.66	728.32
13	47.24	35.68	680.44	49.44	35.40	686.75	51.66	35.10	693.22
14	44.78	38.14	642.30	46.87	37.97	648.78	49.02	37.74	655.48
15	42.10	40.82	601.48	44.14	40.70	608.08	46.20	40.56	614.92
16	39.24	43.68	557.80	41.20	43.64	564.44	43.15	43.61	571.31
17	36.22	46.70	511.10	38.03	46.81	517.63	39.89	46.87	524.44
18	32.98	49.94	461.16	34.65	50.19	467.44	36.35	50.41	474.03
19	29.51	53.41	407.75	31.02	53.82	413.62	32.59	54.17	419.86
20	25.79	57.13	350.62	27.12	57.72	355.90	28.53	58.23	361.63
21	21.79	61.13	289.49	22.99	61.85	294.05	24.15	62.61	299.02
22	17.56	65.36	224.13	18.48	66.36	227.69	19.47	67.29	231.73
23	12.99	69.93	154.20	13.67	71.17	156.52	14.43	72.33	159.40
24	8.11	74.81	79.39	8.52	76.32	80.20	8.98	77.78	81.62
25	2.92	79.39	0	3.01	80.20	0	3.17	81.62	0

	7½% interest—$7.39 monthly payment			7¾% interest—$7.56 monthly payment			8% interest—$7.72 monthly payment		
Year	*Interest*	*Amort.*	*Balance*	*Interest*	*Amort.*	*Balance*	*Interest*	*Amort.*	*Balance*
1	74.52	14.16	985.84	77.02	13.70	986.30	79.53	13.11	986.89
2	73.42	15.26	970.58	75.92	14.80	971.50	78.43	14.21	972.68
3	72.23	16.45	954.13	74.72	16.00	955.50	77.26	15.38	957.30
4	70.96	17.72	936.41	73.45	17.27	938.23	75.99	16.65	940.65
5	69.54	19.14	917.27	72.06	18.66	919.57	74.58	18.06	922.59
6	68.11	20.57	896.70	70.57	20.15	899.42	73.10	19.54	903.05
7	66.48	22.20	874.50	68.95	21.77	877.65	71.49	21.15	881.90
8	64.77	23.91	850.59	67.19	23.53	854.12	69.72	22.92	858.98
9	62.92	25.76	824.83	65.30	25.42	828.70	67.83	24.81	834.17
10	60.93	27.75	797.08	63.28	27.44	801.26	65.76	26.88	807.29
11	58.78	29.90	767.18	61.05	29.67	771.59	63.52	29.12	778.17
12	56.44	32.24	734.94	58.67	32.05	739.54	61.11	31.53	746.64
13	53.94	34.74	700.20	56.10	34.62	704.92	58.50	34.14	712.50
14	51.23	37.45	662.75	53.29	37.43	667.49	55.67	36.97	675.53
15	48.33	40.35	622.40	50.31	40.41	627.08	52.59	40.05	635.48

Self-Liquidating Mortgages—Annual Interest, Amortization And Remaining Balance *(continued)*

25-Year Term *(continued)*

	7½% interest—$7.39 monthly payment			7¾% interest—$7.56 monthly payment			8% interest—$7.72 monthly payment		
Year	*Interest*	*Amort.*	*Balance*	*Interest*	*Amort.*	*Balance*	*Interest*	*Amort.*	*Balance*
16	45.21	43.47	578.98	47.06	43.66	583.42	49.26	43.38	592.10
17	41.83	46.85	532.08	43.57	47.15	536.27	45.68	46.96	545.14
18	38.20	50.48	481.60	39.77	50.95	485.32	41.76	50.88	494.26
19	34.28	54.40	427.20	35.69	55.03	430.29	37.57	55.07	439.19
20	30.05	58.63	368.57	31.26	59.46	370.83	32.98	59.66	379.53
21	25.51	63.17	305.40	26.51	64.21	306.62	28.03	64.61	314.92
22	20.59	68.09	237.31	21.33	69.39	237.23	22.65	69.99	244.93
23	15.30	73.38	163.93	15.72	75.00	162.23	16.85	75.79	169.14
24	9.59	79.09	84.84	9.74	80.98	81.25	10.53	82.11	87.03
25	3.47	84.84	0	3.22	81.25	0	3.74	87.03	0

	8¼% interest—$7.88 monthly payment			8½% interest—$8.05 monthly payment			8¾% interest—$8.22 monthly payment		
Year	*Interest*	*Amort.*	*Balance*	*Interest*	*Amort.*	*Balance*	*Interest*	*Amort.*	*Balance*
1	82.04	12.53	987.48	84.54	12.07	987.94	87.05	11.60	988.41
2	80.96	13.61	973.88	83.48	13.13	974.81	85.99	12.66	975.75
3	79.80	14.77	959.11	82.32	14.29	960.52	84.84	13.81	961.95
4	78.53	16.04	943.08	81.05	15.56	944.97	83.58	15.07	946.88
5	77.16	17.41	925.68	79.68	16.93	928.04	82.21	16.44	930.44
6	75.67	18.90	906.78	78.18	18.43	909.62	80.71	17.94	912.51
7	74.05	20.52	886.27	76.55	20.06	889.57	79.08	19.57	892.94
8	72.29	22.28	863.99	74.78	21.83	867.74	77.29	21.36	871.59
9	70.38	24.19	839.81	72.85	23.76	843.99	75.35	23.30	848.29
10	68.31	26.26	813.56	70.75	25.86	818.14	73.23	25.42	822.88
11	66.06	28.51	785.05	68.47	28.14	790.00	70.91	27.74	795.14
12	63.62	30.95	754.11	65.98	30.63	759.37	68.39	30.26	764.88
13	60.97	33.60	720.51	63.27	33.34	726.04	65.63	33.02	731.87
14	58.09	36.48	684.03	60.33	36.28	689.76	62.62	36.03	695.84
15	54.96	39.61	644.43	57.12	39.49	650.28	59.34	39.31	656.54
16	51.57	43.00	601.43	53.63	42.98	607.30	55.76	42.89	613.65
17	47.88	46.69	554.75	49.83	46.78	560.53	51.85	46.80	566.86
18	43.88	50.69	504.07	45.70	50.91	509.62	47.59	51.06	515.80
19	39.54	55.03	449.05	41.20	55.41	454.21	42.94	55.71	460.09
20	34.83	59.74	389.31	36.30	60.31	393.91	37.86	60.79	399.31
21	29.71	64.86	324.45	30.97	65.64	328.27	32.33	66.32	332.99
22	24.15	70.42	254.03	25.17	71.44	256.83	26.29	72.36	260.64
23	18.11	76.46	177.58	18.85	77.76	179.08	19.69	78.96	181.68
24	11.56	83.01	94.58	11.98	84.63	94.45	12.50	86.15	95.54
25	4.45	90.12	4.46	4.50	92.11	2.35	4.65	94.00	1.55

Self-Liquidating Mortgages—Annual Interest, Amortization And Remaining Balance *(continued)*

25-Year Term *(continued)*

	9% interest—$8.40 monthly payment			9¼% interest—$8.56 monthly payment			9½% interest—$8.74 monthly payment		
Year	*Interest*	*Amort.*	*Balance*	*Interest*	*Amort.*	*Balance*	*Interest*	*Amort.*	*Balance*
1	89.54	11.26	988.74	92.06	10.67	989.34	94.56	10.33	989.68
2	88.49	12.31	976.43	91.03	11.70	977.65	93.54	11.35	978.34
3	87.34	13.46	962.97	89.90	12.83	964.82	92.41	12.48	965.86
4	86.07	14.73	948.24	88.66	14.07	950.76	91.17	13.72	952.15
5	84.66	16.14	932.10	87.31	15.42	935.35	89.81	15.08	937.08
6	83.18	17.62	914.48	85.82	16.91	918.44	88.32	16.57	920.52
7	81.52	19.28	895.20	84.19	18.54	899.90	86.67	18.22	902.31
8	79.72	21.08	874.12	82.40	20.33	879.58	84.87	20.02	882.29
9	77.73	23.07	851.05	80.44	22.29	857.29	82.88	22.01	860.28
10	75.58	25.22	825.83	78.28	24.45	832.85	80.70	24.19	836.10
11	74.10	27.60	798.23	75.93	26.80	806.05	78.30	26.59	809.51
12	70.62	30.18	768.05	73.34	29.39	776.66	75.66	29.23	780.28
13	67.79	33.01	735.04	70.50	32.23	744.44	72.76	32.13	748.15
14	64.69	36.11	698.93	67.39	35.34	709.10	69.57	35.32	712.83
15	61.29	39.51	659.42	63.98	38.75	670.36	66.06	38.83	674.01
16	57.60	43.20	616.22	60.24	42.49	627.88	62.21	42.68	631.33
17	53.56	47.24	568.98	56.14	46.59	581.29	57.97	46.92	584.42
18	49.12	51.68	517.30	51.64	51.09	530.21	53.32	51.57	532.85
19	44.27	56.53	460.77	46.71	56.02	474.20	48.20	56.69	476.17
20	38.96	61.84	398.93	41.31	61.42	412.78	42.57	62.32	413.85
21	33.17	67.63	331.30	35.38	67.35	345.44	36.39	68.50	345.36
22	26.81	73.99	257.31	28.88	73.85	271.59	29.59	75.30	270.07
23	19.86	80.94	176.37	21.75	80.98	190.62	22.12	82.77	187.30
24	12.27	88.53	87.84	13.94	88.79	101.83	13.90	90.99	96.32
25	3.96	87.84	0	5.36	97.37	4.47	4.87	100.02	0

	9¾% interest—$8.91 monthly payment			10% interest—$9.09 monthly payment			10¼% interest—$9.26 monthly payment		
Year	*Interest*	*Amort.*	*Balance*	*Interest*	*Amort.*	*Balance*	*Interest*	*Amort.*	*Balance*
1	97.07	9.86	990.15	99.56	9.52	990.48	102.09	9.04	990.97
2	96.07	10.86	979.30	98.57	10.51	979.97	101.12	10.01	980.96
3	94.96	11.97	967.33	97.48	11.60	968.37	100.04	11.09	969.88
4	93.74	13.19	954.15	96.25	12.83	955.54	98.85	12.28	957.60
5	92.40	14.53	939.62	94.93	14.15	941.39	97.53	13.60	944.01
6	90.91	16.02	923.61	93.44	15.64	925.75	96.07	15.06	928.96
7	89.28	17.65	905.96	91.78	17.30	908.45	94.45	16.68	912.29
8	87.48	19.45	886.52	90.01	19.07	889.38	92.66	18.47	893.82
9	85.50	21.43	865.09	87.99	21.09	868.29	90.68	20.45	873.38
10	83.31	23.62	841.48	85.78	23.30	844.99	88.48	22.65	850.73
11	80.91	26.02	815.47	83.33	25.75	819.24	86.05	25.08	825.66
12	78.25	28.68	786.79	80.63	28.45	790.79	83.35	27.78	797.88
13	75.33	31.60	755.20	77.68	31.40	759.39	80.37	30.76	767.13
14	72.11	34.82	720.38	74.39	34.69	724.70	77.06	34.07	733.07
15	68.56	38.37	682.01	70.74	38.34	686.36	73.40	37.73	695.35

Self-Liquidating Mortgages—Annual Interest, Amortization And Remaining Balance *(continued)*

25-Year Term *(continued)*

	9¾% interest—$8.91 monthly payment			10% interest—$9.09 monthly payment			10¼% interest—$9.26 monthly payment		
Year	*Interest*	*Amort.*	*Balance*	*Interest*	*Amort.*	*Balance*	*Interest*	*Amort.*	*Balance*
16	64.64	42.29	639.73	66.74	42.34	644.02	69.35	41.78	653.57
17	60.33	46.60	593.14	62.29	46.79	597.23	64.86	46.27	607.31
18	55.58	51.35	541.80	57.39	51.69	545.54	59.89	51.24	556.08
19	50.35	56.58	485.22	51.96	57.12	488.42	54.39	56.74	499.34
20	44.58	62.35	422.87	46.01	63.07	425.35	48.29	62.84	436.50
21	38.22	68.71	354.16	39.37	69.71	355.64	41.54	69.59	366.92
22	31.21	75.72	278.45	32.09	76.99	278.65	34.06	77.07	289.85
23	23.49	83.44	195.02	24.06	85.02	193.63	25.78	85.35	204.50
24	14.98	91.95	103.07	15.13	93.95	99.68	16.61	94.52	109.99
25	5.61	101.32	1.75	5.29	99.68	0	6.45	104.68	5.31

	10½% interest—$9.44 monthly payment			10¾% interest—$9.62 monthly payment			11% interest—$9.80 monthly payment		
Year	*Interest*	*Amort.*	*Balance*	*Interest*	*Amort.*	*Balance*	*Interest*	*Amort.*	*Balance*
1	104.59	8.70	991.31	107.10	8.35	991.66	109.61	8.00	992.01
2	103.64	9.65	981.67	106.16	9.29	982.38	108.68	8.93	983.09
3	102.57	10.72	970.96	105.11	10.34	972.04	107.65	9.96	973.14
4	101.39	11.90	959.06	103.94	11.51	960.54	106.50	11.11	962.03
5	100.08	13.21	945.86	102.64	12.81	947.74	105.22	12.39	949.64
6	98.63	14.66	931.20	101.20	14.25	933.49	103.78	13.83	935.82
7	97.01	16.28	914.93	99.59	15.86	917.64	102.18	15.43	920.40
8	95.22	18.07	896.87	97.80	17.65	899.99	100.40	17.21	903.19
9	93.23	20.06	876.81	95.80	19.65	880.35	98.41	19.20	883.99
10	91.02	22.27	854.54	93.59	21.86	858.49	96.19	21.42	862.57
11	88.56	24.73	829.82	91.12	24.33	834.16	93.71	23.90	838.67
12	85.84	27.45	802.38	88.37	27.08	807.08	90.94	26.67	812.01
13	82.82	30.47	771.91	85.31	30.14	776.95	87.86	29.75	782.26
14	79.46	33.83	738.08	81.91	33.54	743.41	84.41	33.20	749.07
15	75.73	37.56	700.52	78.12	37.33	706.08	80.57	37.04	712.03
16	71.59	41.70	658.83	73.90	41.55	664.54	76.29	41.32	670.72
17	67.00	46.29	612.54	69.21	46.24	618.30	71.50	46.11	624.62
18	61.89	51.40	561.15	63.99	51.46	566.84	66.17	51.44	573.18
19	56.23	57.06	504.10	58.17	57.28	509.57	60.22	57.39	515.79
20	49.94	63.35	440.76	51.70	63.75	445.82	53.58	64.03	451.77
21	42.96	70.33	370.44	44.50	70.95	374.88	46.17	71.44	380.33
22	35.21	78.08	292.36	36.49	78.96	295.93	37.90	79.71	300.63
23	26.61	86.68	205.69	27.57	87.88	208.05	28.68	88.93	211.70
24	17.06	96.23	109.46	17.64	97.81	110.25	18.39	99.22	112.49
25	6.45	106.84	2.63	6.60	108.85	1.40	6.91	110.70	1.79

Self-Liquidating Mortgages—Annual Interest, Amortization And Remaining Balance *(continued)*

25-Year Term *(continued)*

	11¼% interest—$9.98 monthly payment			11½% interest—$10.16 monthly payment			11¾% interest—$10.35 monthly payment		
Year	*Interest*	*Amort.*	*Balance*	*Interest*	*Amort.*	*Balance*	*Interest*	*Amort.*	*Balance*
1	112.12	7.65	992.36	114.63	7.30	992.71	117.13	7.08	992.93
2	111.21	8.56	983.81	113.74	8.19	984.53	116.25	7.96	984.98
3	110.20	9.57	974.24	112.75	9.18	975.35	115.27	8.94	976.05
4	109.07	10.70	963.54	111.64	10.29	965.07	114.16	10.05	966.00
5	107.80	11.97	951.58	110.39	11.54	953.53	112.91	11.30	954.71
6	106.38	13.39	938.19	108.99	12.94	940.60	111.51	12.70	942.02
7	104.79	14.98	923.22	107.43	14.50	926.10	109.94	14.27	927.75
8	103.02	16.75	906.48	105.67	16.26	909.85	108.17	16.04	911.72
9	101.04	18.73	887.75	103.70	18.23	891.62	106.18	18.03	893.69
10	98.82	20.95	866.80	101.49	20.44	871.18	103.95	20.26	873.44
11	96.34	23.43	843.37	99.01	22.92	848.26	101.43	22.78	850.66
12	93.56	26.21	817.17	96.23	25.70	822.56	98.61	25.60	825.07
13	90.45	29.32	787.86	93.11	28.82	793.75	95.43	28.78	796.29
14	86.98	32.79	755.07	89.62	32.31	761.44	91.86	32.35	763.95
15	83.10	36.67	718.41	85.70	36.23	725.21	87.85	36.36	727.60
16	78.75	41.02	677.39	81.31	40.62	684.60	83.34	40.87	686.74
17	73.89	45.88	631.52	76.38	45.55	639.05	78.27	45.94	640.81
18	68.46	51.31	580.22	70.86	51.07	587.99	72.58	51.63	589.18
19	62.38	57.39	522.83	64.67	57.26	530.73	66.17	58.04	531.15
20	55.58	64.19	458.65	57.72	64.21	466.53	58.98	65.23	465.92
21	47.98	71.79	386.86	49.94	71.99	394.54	50.88	73.33	392.60
22	39.47	80.30	306.56	41.21	80.72	313.83	41.79	82.42	310.19
23	29.96	89.81	216.75	31.42	90.51	223.33	31.57	92.64	217.55
24	19.31	100.46	116.30	20.45	101.48	121.85	20.08	104.13	113.42
25	7.41	112.36	3.95	8.14	113.79	8.07	7.16	117.05	0

12% interest—$10.35 monthly payment

Year	*Interest*	*Amort.*	*Balance*	*Year*	*Interest*	*Amort.*	*Balance*
1	119.64	6.73	993.28	13	98.20	28.17	802.73
2	118.79	7.58	985.71	14	94.62	31.75	770.99
3	117.83	8.54	977.17	15	90.60	35.77	735.23
4	116,75	9.62	967.56	16	86.06	40.31	694.93
5	115.53	10.84	956.72	17	80.95	45.42	649.51
6	114.15	12.22	944.51	18	75.19	51.18	598.34
7	112.60	13.77	930.75	19	68.70	57.67	540.68
8	110.86	15.51	915.24	20	61.39	64.98	475.70
9	108.89	17.48	897.77	21	53.15	73.22	402.48
10	106.68	19.69	878.08	22	43.86	82.51	319.98
11	104.18	22.19	855.90	23	33.40	92.97	227.01
12	101.37	25.00	830.90	24	21.61	104.76	122.26
				25	8.32	118.05	4.22

Self-Liquidating Mortgages—Annual Interest, Amortization And Remaining Balance *(continued)*

30-Year Term

	4% interest—$4.77 monthly payment			4¼% interest—$4.92 monthly payment			4½% interest—$5.07 monthly payment		
Year	*Interest*	*Amort.*	*Balance*	*Interest*	*Amort.*	*Balance*	*Interest*	*Amort.*	*Balance*
1	39.69	17.56	982.45	42.18	16.87	983.14	44.67	16.18	983.83
2	38.97	18.28	964.17	41.45	17.60	965.54	43.93	16.92	966.92
3	38.23	19.02	945.15	40.69	18.36	947.18	43.15	17.70	949.23
4	37.45	19.80	925.36	39.89	19.16	928.03	42.34	18.51	930.73
5	36.64	20.61	904.76	39.06	19.99	908.04	41.49	19.36	911.37
6	35.80	21.45	883.32	38.19	20.86	887.19	40.60	20.25	891.13
7	34.93	22.32	861.00	37.29	21.76	865.44	39.67	21.18	869.96
8	34.02	23.23	837.78	36.35	22.70	842.74	38.70	22.15	847.81
9	33.08	24.17	813.61	35.36	23.69	819.06	37.68	23.17	824.65
10	32.09	25.16	788.46	34.34	24.71	794.35	36.62	24.23	800.42
11	31.07	26.18	762.28	33.27	25.78	768.57	35.51	25.34	775.08
12	30.00	27.25	735.03	32.15	26.90	741.67	34.34	26.51	748.58
13	28.89	28.36	706.68	30.98	28.07	713.61	33.12	27.73	720.86
14	27.73	29.52	677.17	29.77	29.28	684.33	31.85	29.00	691.86
15	26.53	30.72	646.45	28.50	30.55	653.79	30.52	30.33	661.54
16	25.28	31.97	614.49	27.17	31.88	621.92	29.13	31.72	629.82
17	23.98	33.27	581.23	25.79	33.26	588.67	27.67	33.18	596.64
18	22.62	34.63	546.60	24.35	34.70	553.97	26.14	34.71	561.94
19	21.21	36.04	510.57	22.85	36.20	517.78	24.55	36.30	525.64
20	19.75	37.50	473.07	21.28	37.77	480.01	22.88	37.97	487.68
21	18.22	39.03	434.04	19.64	39.41	440.61	21.14	39.71	447.97
22	16.63	40.62	393.43	17.94	41.11	399.50	19.31	41.54	406.44
23	14.97	42.28	351.15	16.15	42.90	356.61	17.41	43.44	363.00
24	13.25	44.00	307.16	14.30	44.75	311.86	15.41	45.44	317.57
25	11.46	45.79	261.37	12.36	46.69	265.17	13.32	47.53	270.05
26	9.59	47.66	213.72	10.33	48.72	216.46	11.14	49.71	220.34
27	7.65	49.60	164.13	8.22	50.83	165.64	8.86	51.99	168.35
28	5.63	51.62	112.51	6.02	53.03	112.61	6.47	54.38	113.98
29	3.53	53.72	58.79	3.72	55.33	57.29	3.97	56.88	57.10
30	1.34	55.91	2.89	1.32	57.73	0	1.36	59.49	0

Self-Liquidating Mortgages—Annual Interest, Amortization And Remaining Balance *(continued)*

30-Year Term *(continued)*

	4¾% interest—$5.22 monthly payment			5% interest—$5.37 monthly payment			5¼% interest—$5.52 monthly payment		
Year	*Interest*	*Amort.*	*Balance*	*Interest*	*Amort.*	*Balance*	*Interest*	*Amort.*	*Balance*
1	47.17	15.48	984.53	49.67	14.78	985.23	52.17	14.08	985.93
2	46.42	16.23	968.31	48.91	15.54	969.70	51.41	14.84	971.10
3	45.63	17.02	951.29	48.12	16.33	953.37	50.61	15.64	955.47
4	44.81	17.84	933.45	47.28	17.17	936.21	49.77	16.48	939.00
5	43.94	18.71	914.75	46.41	18.04	918.17	48.89	17.36	921.64
6	43.03	19.62	895.14	45.48	18.97	899.21	47.95	18.30	903.35
7	42.08	20.57	874.57	44.51	19.94	879.28	46.97	19.28	884.08
8	41.08	21.57	853.01	43.49	20.96	858.32	45.93	20.32	863.76
9	40.03	22.62	830.40	42.42	22.03	836.30	44.84	21.41	842.36
10	38.94	23.71	806.69	41.29	23.16	813.15	43.69	22.56	819.81
11	37.79	24.86	781.83	40.11	24.34	788.81	42.48	23.77	796.04
12	36.58	26.07	755.76	38.86	25.59	763.23	41.20	25.05	771.00
13	35.31	27.34	728.43	37.56	26.89	736.34	39.85	26.40	744.60
14	33.99	28.66	699.77	36.18	28.27	708.08	38.43	27.82	716.79
15	32.60	30.05	669.72	34.73	29.72	678.37	36.94	29.31	687.49
16	31.14	31.51	638.22	33.21	31.24	647.14	35.36	30.89	656.60
17	29.61	33.04	605.18	31.62	32.83	614.31	33.70	32.55	624.06
18	28.00	34.65	570.54	29.94	34.51	579.80	31.95	34.30	589.76
19	26.32	36.33	534.21	28.17	36.28	543.52	30.11	36.14	553.62
20	24.56	38.09	496.12	26.32	38.13	505.39	28.16	38.09	515.54
21	22.71	39.94	456.19	24.36	40.09	465.31	26.11	40.14	475.41
22	20.77	41.88	414.31	22.31	42.14	423.18	23.96	42.29	433.12
23	18.74	43.91	370.41	20.16	44.29	378.90	21.68	44.57	388.56
24	16.61	46.04	324.37	17.89	46.56	332.34	19.28	46.97	341.60
25	14.37	48.28	276.09	15.51	48.94	283.41	16.76	49.49	292.11
26	12.03	50.62	225.47	13.01	51.44	231.97	14.10	52.15	239.97
27	9.57	53.08	172.40	10.38	54.07	177.90	11.29	54.96	185.01
28	6.99	55.66	116.74	7.61	56.84	121.06	8.34	57.91	127.11
29	4.29	58.36	58.39	4.70	59.75	61.32	5.22	61.03	66.08
30	1.46	61.19	0	1.64	62.81	0	1.94	64.31	1.78

Self-Liquidating Mortgages—Annual Interest, Amortization And Remaining Balance *(continued)*

30-Year Term *(continued)*

	5½% interest—$5.68 monthly payment			5¾% interest—$5.84 monthly payment			6% interest—$6.00 monthly payment		
Year	*Interest*	*Amort.*	*Balance*	*Interest*	*Amort.*	*Balance*	*Interest*	*Amort.*	*Balance*
1	54.67	13.50	986.51	57.17	12.92	987.09	59.67	12.34	987.67
2	53.91	14.26	972.25	56.41	13.68	973.41	58.91	13.10	974.57
3	53.10	15.07	957.19	55.60	14.49	958.92	58.10	13.91	960.67
4	52.25	15.92	941.28	54.74	15.35	943.58	57.24	14.77	945.91
5	51.36	16.81	924.47	53.84	16.25	927.33	56.33	15.68	930.23
6	50.41	17.76	906.71	52.88	17.21	910.12	55.37	16.64	913.60
7	49.41	18.76	887.95	51.86	18.23	891.90	54.34	17.67	895.93
8	48.35	19.82	868.13	50.79	19.30	872.60	53.25	18.76	877.18
9	47.23	20.94	847.19	49.65	20.44	852.16	52.09	19.92	857.27
10	46.05	22.12	825.08	48.44	21.65	830.52	50.87	21.14	836.13
11	44.80	23.37	801.71	47.16	22.93	807.59	49.56	22.45	813.68
12	43.48	24.69	777.03	45.81	24.28	783.32	48.18	23.83	789.85
13	42.09	26.08	750.96	44.37	25.72	757.61	46.71	25.30	764.56
14	40.62	27.55	723.41	42.86	27.23	730.38	45.15	26.86	737.70
15	39.07	29.10	694.31	41.25	28.84	701.54	43.49	28.52	709.19
16	37.42	30.75	663.57	39.55	30.54	671.00	41.73	30.28	678.91
17	35.69	32.48	631.10	37.74	32.35	638.66	39.87	32.14	646.77
18	33.86	34.31	596.79	35.83	34.26	604.41	37.88	34.13	612.65
19	31.92	36.25	560.55	33.81	36.28	568.14	35.78	36.23	576.43
20	29.88	38.29	522.27	31.67	38.42	529.72	33.54	38.47	537.96
21	27.72	40.45	481.82	29.40	40.69	489.04	31.17	40.84	497.13
22	25.44	42.73	439.10	27.00	43.09	445.96	28.65	43.36	453.78
23	23.03	45.14	393.96	24.46	45.63	400.33	25.98	46.03	407.75
24	20.48	47.69	346.28	21.76	48.33	352.01	23.14	48.87	358.89
25	17.79	50.38	295.90	18.91	51.18	300.84	20.13	51.88	307.01
26	14.95	53.22	242.69	15.89	54.20	246.64	16.93	55.08	251.93
27	11.95	56.22	186.47	12.69	57.40	189.24	13.53	58.48	193.46
28	8.78	59.39	127.09	9.30	60.79	128.46	9.92	62.09	131.38
29	5.43	62.74	64.35	5.71	64.38	64.09	6.09	65.92	65.47
30	1.89	66.28	0	1.91	68.18	0	2.03	69.98	0

Self-Liquidating Mortgages—Annual Interest, Amortization And Remaining Balance *(continued)*

30-Year Term *(continued)*

	6¼% interest—$6.16 monthly payment			6½% interest—$6.32 monthly payment			6¾% interest—$6.49 monthly payment		
Year	*Interest*	*Amort.*	*Balance*	*Interest*	*Amort.*	*Balance*	*Interest*	*Amort.*	*Balance*
1	62.17	11.76	988.25	64.68	11.17	988.84	67.18	10.71	989.30
2	61.42	12.51	975.74	63.93	11.92	976.92	66.43	11.46	977.85
3	60.61	13.32	962.43	63.13	12.72	964.20	65.63	12.26	965.59
4	59.76	14.17	948.26	62.28	13.57	950.64	64.78	13.11	952.49
5	58.84	15.09	933.18	61.37	14.48	936.16	63.87	14.02	938.48
6	57.87	16.06	917.13	60.40	15.45	920.72	62.89	15.00	923.48
7	56.84	17.09	900.04	59.37	16.48	904.24	61.85	16.04	907.45
8	55.74	18.19	881.86	58.26	17.59	886.66	60.73	17.16	890.30
9	54.57	19.36	862.51	57.09	18.76	867.90	59.54	18.35	871.95
10	53.33	20.60	841.91	55.83	20.02	847.88	58.26	19.63	852.33
11	52.00	21.93	819.99	54.49	21.36	826.52	56.90	20.99	831.34
12	50.59	23.34	796.66	53.06	22.79	803.74	55.43	22.46	808.89
13	49.09	24.84	771.83	51.53	24.32	779.42	53.87	24.02	784.87
14	47.50	26.43	745.40	49.90	25.95	753.48	52.20	25.69	759.19
15	45.80	28.13	717.27	48.17	27.68	725.80	50.41	27.48	731.71
16	43.99	29.94	687.33	46.31	29.54	696.27	48.50	29.39	702.32
17	42.06	31.87	655.46	44.33	31.52	664.76	46.45	31.44	670.89
18	40.01	33.92	621.55	42.22	33.63	631.14	44.26	33.63	637.27
19	37.83	36.10	585.45	39.97	35.88	595.27	41.92	35.97	601.30
20	35.51	38.42	547.04	37.57	38.28	556.99	39.42	38.47	562.84
21	33.04	40.89	506.15	35.01	40.84	516.15	36.74	41.15	521.69
22	30.41	43.52	462.63	32.27	43.58	472.58	33.87	44.02	477.68
23	27.61	46.32	416.31	29.35	46.50	426.09	30.81	47.08	430.60
24	24.63	49.30	367.01	26.24	49.61	376.48	27.53	50.36	380.25
25	21.46	52.47	314.54	22.92	52.93	323.56	24.03	53.86	326.39
26	18.08	55.85	258.70	19.37	56.48	267.08	20.28	57.61	268.78
27	14.49	59.44	199.27	15.59	60.26	206.83	16.26	61.63	207.16
28	10.67	63.26	136.01	11.56	64.29	142.54	11.97	65.92	141.25
29	6.60	67.33	68.68	7.25	68.60	73.95	7.38	70.51	70.75
30	2.27	71.66	0	2.66	73.19	0.76	2.48	75.41	0

Self-Liquidating Mortgages—Annual Interest, Amortization And Remaining Balance *(continued)*

30-Year Term *(continued)*

	7% interest—$6.65 monthly payment			7¼% interest—$6.82 monthly payment			7½% interest—$6.99 monthly payment		
Year	*Interest*	*Amort.*	*Balance*	*Interest*	*Amort.*	*Balance*	*Interest*	*Amort.*	*Balance*
1	69.68	10.13	989.88	72.19	9.66	990.35	74.69	9.20	990.81
2	68.95	10.86	979.03	71.46	10.39	979.97	73.98	9.91	980.91
3	68.17	11.64	967.40	70.69	11.16	968.81	73.21	10.68	970.23
4	67.33	12.48	954.92	69.85	12.00	956.81	72.38	11.51	958.73
5	66.43	13.38	941.54	68.95	12.90	943.92	71.49	12.40	946.33
6	65.46	14.35	927.19	67.98	13.87	930.06	70.53	13.36	932.98
7	64.42	15.39	911.81	66.95	14.90	915.16	69.49	14.40	918.58
8	63.31	16.50	895.31	65.83	16.02	899.14	68.37	15.52	903.07
9	62.12	17.69	877.62	64.63	17.22	881.93	67.17	16.72	886.35
10	60.84	18.97	858.65	63.34	18.51	863.42	65.87	18.02	868.34
11	59.47	20.34	838.31	61.95	19.90	843.52	64.47	19.42	848.92
12	58.00	21.81	816.50	60.46	21.39	822.14	62.96	20.93	828.00
13	56.42	23.39	793.12	58.86	22.99	799.15	61.34	22.55	805.46
14	54.73	25.08	768.04	57.13	24.72	774.43	59.59	24.30	781.16
15	52.92	26.89	741.15	55.28	26.57	747.87	57.70	26.19	754.98
16	50.97	28.84	712.32	53.29	28.56	719.31	55.67	28.22	726.77
17	48.89	30.92	681.40	51.15	30.70	688.62	53.48	30.41	696.36
18	46.65	33.16	648.25	48.85	33.00	655.62	51.12	32.77	663.60
19	44.26	35.55	612.70	46.37	35.48	620.15	48.58	35.31	628.29
20	41.69	38.12	574.58	43.71	38.14	582.02	45.84	38.05	590.24
21	38.93	40.88	533.71	40.86	40.99	541.03	42.88	41.01	549.24
22	35.98	43.83	489.88	37.78	44.07	496.97	39.70	44.19	505.06
23	32.81	47.00	442.88	34.48	47.37	449.60	36.27	47.62	457.44
24	29.41	50.40	392.48	30.93	50.92	398.69	32.57	51.32	406.13
25	25.77	54.04	338.45	27.11	54.74	343.96	28.59	55.30	350.83
26	21.86	57.95	280.50	23.01	58.84	285.13	24.30	59.59	291.24
27	17.67	62.14	218.37	18.60	63.25	221.88	19.67	64.22	227.03
28	13.18	66.63	151.74	13.86	67.99	153.90	14.69	69.20	157.83
29	8.36	71.45	80.30	8.77	73.08	80.82	9.31	74.58	83.26
30	3.20	76.61	3.70	3.29	78.56	2.26	3.52	80.37	2.90

Self-Liquidating Mortgages—Annual Interest, Amortization And Remaining Balance *(continued)*

30-Year Term *(continued)*

	7¾% interest—$7.16 monthly payment			8% interest—$7.34 monthly payment			8¼% interest—$7.51 monthly payment		
Year	*Interest*	*Amort.*	*Balance*	*Interest*	*Amort.*	*Balance*	*Interest*	*Amort.*	*Balance*
1	77.20	8.73	991.28	79.70	8.39	991.62	82.21	7.92	992.09
2	76.50	9.43	981.85	79.01	9.08	982.54	81.53	8.60	983.50
3	75.74	10.19	971.67	78.25	9.84	972.71	80.80	9.33	974.17
4	74.92	11.01	960.67	77.44	10.65	962.06	80.00	10.13	964.04
5	74.04	11.89	948.78	76.55	11.54	950.53	79.13	11.00	953.04
6	73.09	12.84	935.94	75.60	12.49	938.04	78.19	11.94	941.10
7	72.05	13.88	922.07	74.56	13.53	924.52	77.16	12.97	928.14
8	70.94	14.99	907.09	73.44	14.65	909.87	76.05	14.08	914.07
9	69.74	16.19	890.90	72.22	15.87	894.00	74.85	15.28	898.79
10	68.44	17.49	873.41	70.90	17.19	876.82	73.54	16.59	882.20
11	67.03	18.90	854.52	69.48	18.61	858.21	72.12	18.01	864.19
12	65.52	20.41	834.11	67.93	20.16	838.06	70.57	19.56	844.64
13	63.88	22.05	812.06	66.26	21.83	816.24	68.90	21.23	823.41
14	62.11	23.82	788.24	64.45	23.64	792.60	67.08	23.05	800.36
15	60.19	25.74	762.51	62.49	25.60	767.01	65.10	25.03	775.34
16	58.13	27.80	734.71	60.36	27.73	739.28	62.96	27.17	748.17
17	55.89	30.04	704.68	58.06	30.03	709.26	60.63	29.50	718.68
18	53.48	32.45	672.23	55.57	32.52	676.75	58.10	32.03	686.65
19	50.87	35.06	637.18	52.87	35.22	641.53	55.36	34.77	651.89
20	48.06	37.87	599.32	49.95	38.14	603.40	52.38	37.75	614.14
21	45.02	40.91	558.41	46.78	41.31	562.10	49.14	40.99	573.16
22	41.73	44.20	514.22	43.36	44.73	517.37	45.63	44.50	528.67
23	38.18	47.75	466.48	39.64	48.45	468.93	41.82	48.31	480.36
24	34.35	51.58	414.90	35.62	52.47	416.46	37.68	52.45	427.92
25	30.21	55.72	359.19	31.27	56.82	359.65	33.19	56.94	370.98
26	25.73	60.20	299.00	26.55	61.54	298.11	28.31	61.82	309.16
27	20.90	65.03	233.97	21.45	66.64	231.48	23.01	67.12	242.05
28	15.68	70.25	163.72	15.91	72.18	159.30	17.26	72.87	169.18
29	10.03	75.90	87.83	9.92	78.17	81.14	11.02	79.11	90.07
30	3.94	81.99	5.85	3.44	84.65	0	4.24	85.89	4.19

Self-Liquidating Mortgages—Annual Interest, Amortization And Remaining Balance *(continued)*

30-Year Term *(continued)*

	8½% interest—$7.69 monthly payment			8¾% interest—$7.87 monthly payment			9% interest—$8.05 monthly payment		
Year	*Interest*	*Amort.*	*Balance*	*Interest*	*Amort.*	*Balance*	*Interest*	*Amort.*	*Balance*
1	84.71	7.58	992.43	87.22	7.23	992.78	89.73	6.88	993.13
2	84.05	8.24	984.20	86.56	7.89	984.90	89.08	7.53	985.60
3	83.32	8.97	975.23	85.84	8.61	976.29	88.37	8.24	977.37
4	82.52	9.77	965.47	85.06	9.39	966.91	87.60	9.01	968.37
5	81.66	10.63	954.84	84.20	10.25	956.67	86.76	9.85	958.52
6	80.72	11.57	943.28	83.27	11.18	945.50	85.83	10.78	947.75
7	79.70	12.59	930.70	82.25	12.20	933.31	84.82	11.79	935.97
8	78.59	13.70	917.00	81.14	13.31	920.01	83.72	12.89	923.08
9	77.38	14.91	902.09	79.93	14.52	905.49	82.51	14.10	908.99
10	76.06	16.23	885.87	78.61	15.84	889.66	81.19	15.42	893.57
11	74.63	17.66	868.21	77.17	17.28	872.38	79.74	16.87	876.71
12	73.06	19.23	848.99	75.59	18.86	853.53	78.16	18.45	858.26
13	71.37	20.92	828.07	73.88	20.57	832.96	76.43	20.18	838.09
14	69.52	22.77	805.30	72.00	22.45	810.52	74.54	22.07	816.02
15	67.50	24.79	780.52	69.96	24.49	786.03	72.47	24.14	791.88
16	65.31	26.98	753.55	67.73	26.72	759.31	70.20	26.41	765.48
17	62.93	29.36	724.20	65.29	29.16	730.16	67.73	28.88	736.60
18	60.34	31.95	692.25	62.64	31.81	698.36	65.02	31.59	705.01
19	57.51	34.78	657.47	59.74	34.71	663.65	62.05	34.56	670.46
20	54.44	37.85	619.63	56.58	37.87	625.79	58.81	37.80	632.67
21	51.09	41.20	578.43	53.13	41.32	584.47	55.27	41.34	591.33
22	47.45	44.84	533.60	49.37	45.08	539.39	51.39	45.22	546.11
23	43.49	48.80	484.80	45.26	49.19	490.21	47.15	49.46	496.66
24	39.18	53.11	431.69	40.78	53.67	436.54	42.51	54.10	442.56
25	34.48	57.81	373.89	35.89	58.56	377.99	37.43	59.18	383.39
26	29.37	62.92	310.98	30.56	63.89	314.10	31.88	64.73	318.67
27	23.81	68.48	242.50	24.74	69.71	244.39	25.81	70.80	247.87
28	17.76	74.53	167.98	18.39	76.06	168.33	19.17	77.44	170.44
29	11.17	81.12	86.86	11.46	82.99	85.34	11.91	84.70	85.74
30	4.00	88.29	0	3.90	90.55	0	3.96	92.65	0

Self-Liquidating Mortgages—Annual Interest, Amortization And Remaining Balance *(continued)*

30-Year Term *(continued)*

	9¼% interest—$8.23 monthly payment			9½% interest—$8.41 monthly payment			9¾% interest—$8.59 monthly payment		
Year	*Interest*	*Amort.*	*Balance*	*Interest*	*Amort.*	*Balance*	*Interest*	*Amort.*	*Balance*
1	92.23	6.54	993.47	94.74	6.19	993.82	97.25	5.84	994.17
2	91.60	7.17	986.31	94.13	6.80	987.02	96.65	6.44	987.74
3	90.91	7.86	978.46	93.45	7.48	979.55	96.00	7.09	980.65
4	90.15	8.62	969.84	92.71	8.22	971.33	95.28	7.81	972.84
5	89.32	9.45	960.40	91.89	9.04	962.30	94.48	8.61	964.23
6	88.41	10.36	950.04	91.00	9.93	952.38	93.60	9.49	954.75
7	87.41	11.36	938.69	90.01	10.92	941.47	92.63	10.46	944.30
8	86.31	12.46	926.24	88.93	12.00	929.47	91.57	11.52	932.78
9	85.11	13.66	912.59	87.74	13.19	916.29	90.39	12.70	920.09
10	83.79	14.98	897.62	86.43	14.50	901.79	89.10	13.99	906.10
11	82.35	16.42	881.20	84.99	15.94	885.86	87.67	15.42	890.69
12	80.77	18.00	863.20	83.41	17.52	868.35	86.10	16.99	873.71
13	79.03	19.74	843.46	81.67	19.26	849.09	84.37	18.72	854.99
14	77.12	21.65	821.82	79.76	21.17	827.93	82.46	20.63	834.37
15	75.03	23.74	798.09	77.66	23.27	804.67	80.36	22.73	811.64
16	72.74	26.03	772.07	75.35	25.58	779.10	78.04	25.05	786.60
17	70.23	28.54	743.53	72.82	28.11	750.99	75.49	27.60	759.00
18	67.48	31.29	712.25	70.03	30.90	720.09	72.67	30.42	728.58
19	64.46	34.31	677.94	66.96	33.97	686.13	69.57	33.52	695.07
20	61.15	37.62	640.32	63.59	37.34	648.79	66.15	36.94	658.14
21	57.51	41.26	599.07	59.88	41.05	607.75	62.39	40.70	617.44
22	53.53	45.24	553.83	55.81	45.12	562.63	58.24	44.85	572.59
23	49.17	49.60	504.24	51.33	49.60	513.04	53.66	49.43	523.16
24	44.38	54.39	449.85	46.41	54.52	458.52	48.62	54.47	468.70
25	39.13	59.64	390.21	41.00	59.93	398.60	43.07	60.02	408.68
26	33.37	65.40	324.82	35.05	65.88	332.73	36.95	66.14	342.55
27	27.06	71.71	253.12	28.51	72.42	260.32	30.20	72.89	269.66
28	20.14	78.63	174.49	21.33	79.60	180.72	22.77	80.32	189.35
29	12.55	86.22	88.28	13.43	87.50	93.22	14.58	88.51	100.84
30	4.23	94.54	0	4.74	96.19	0	5.55	97.54	3.31

Self-Liquidating Mortgages—Annual Interest, Amortization And Remaining Balance *(continued)*

30-Year Term *(continued)*

	10% interest—$8.78 monthly payment			10¼% interest—$8.96 monthly payment			10½% interest—$9.15 monthly payment		
Year	*Interest*	*Amort.*	*Balance*	*Interest*	*Amort.*	*Balance*	*Interest*	*Amort.*	*Balance*
1	99.75	5.62	994.39	102.26	5.27	994.74	104.77	5.04	994.97
2	99.16	6.21	988.19	101.70	5.83	988.91	104.21	5.60	989.37
3	98.52	6.85	981.34	101.07	6.46	982.46	103.60	6.21	983.16
4	97.80	7.57	973.78	100.38	7.15	975.31	102.91	6.90	976.27
5	97.01	8.36	965.42	99.61	7.92	967.40	102.15	7.66	968.62
6	96.13	9.24	956.18	98.76	8.77	958.63	101.31	8.50	960.12
7	95.16	10.21	945.98	97.82	9.71	948.92	100.37	9.44	950.69
8	94.10	11.27	934.71	96.77	10.76	938.17	99.33	10.48	940.21
9	92.92	12.45	922.26	95.62	11.91	926.26	98.18	11.63	928.59
10	91.61	13.76	908.51	94.34	13.19	913.07	96.90	12.91	915.68
11	90.17	15.20	893.31	92.92	14.61	898.47	95.47	14.34	901.35
12	88.58	16.79	876.53	91.35	16.18	882.30	93.89	15.92	885.44
13	86.82	18.55	857.99	89.61	17.92	864.39	92.14	17.67	867.77
14	84.88	20.49	837.50	87.69	19.84	844.55	90.19	19.62	848.16
15	82.74	22.63	814.87	85.56	21.97	822.58	88.03	21.78	826.39
16	80.37	25.00	789.88	83.20	24.33	798.26	85.63	24.18	802.22
17	77.75	27.62	762.26	80.58	26.95	771.31	82.97	26.84	775.39
18	74.86	30.51	731.75	77.69	29.84	741.48	80.01	29.80	745.60
19	71.66	33.71	698.05	74.48	33.05	708.43	76.73	33.08	712.52
20	68.13	37.24	660.82	70.93	36.60	671.84	73.09	36.72	675.80
21	64.24	41.13	619.69	67.00	40.53	631.31	69.04	40.77	635.04
22	59.93	45.44	574.25	62.64	44.89	586.43	64.55	45.26	589.78
23	55.17	50.20	524.06	57.82	49.71	536.73	59.56	50.25	539.53
24	49.91	55.46	468.61	52.48	55.05	481.69	54.02	55.79	483.75
25	44.11	61.26	407.35	46.57	60.96	420.73	47.87	61.94	421.82
26	37.69	67.68	339.68	40.02	67.51	353.22	41.05	68.76	353.06
27	30.61	74.76	264.92	32.76	74.77	278.46	33.47	76.34	276.73
28	22.78	82.59	182.34	24.73	82.80	195.66	25.06	84.75	191.98
29	14.13	91.24	91.11	15.83	91.70	103.97	15.72	94.09	97.90
30	4.58	100.79	0	5.98	101.55	2.42	5.35	104.46	0

Self-Liquidating Mortgages—Annual Interest, Amortization And Remaining Balance *(continued)*

30-Year Term *(continued)*

	10¾% interest—$9.33 monthly payment			11% interest—$9.52 monthly payment			11¼% interest—$9.71 monthly payment		
Year	*Interest*	*Amort.*	*Balance*	*Interest*	*Amort.*	*Balance*	*Interest*	*Amort.*	*Balance*
1	107.28	4.69	995.32	109.78	4.47	995.54	112.29	4.24	995.77
2	106.75	5.22	990.10	109.27	4.98	990.57	111.79	4.74	991.04
3	106.16	5.81	984.30	108.69	5.56	985.02	111.23	5.30	985.74
4	105.50	6.47	977.84	108.05	6.20	978.82	110.60	5.93	979.81
5	104.77	7.20	970.65	107.33	6.92	971.91	109.90	6.63	973.19
6	103.96	8.01	962.64	106.53	7.72	964.20	109.11	7.42	965.78
7	103.06	8.91	953.74	105.64	8.61	955.59	108.24	8.29	957.49
8	102.05	9.92	943.82	104.65	9.60	945.99	107.25	9.28	948.22
9	100.93	11.04	932.79	103.53	10.72	935.28	106.15	10.38	937.85
10	99.69	12.28	920.51	102.29	11.96	923.33	104.93	11.60	926.25
11	98.30	13.67	906.85	100.91	13.34	910.00	103.55	12.98	913.27
12	96.76	15.21	891.64	99.37	14.88	895.12	102.01	14.52	898.76
13	95.04	16.93	874.71	97.65	16.60	878.53	100.30	16.23	882.53
14	93.13	18.84	855.87	95.73	18.52	860.01	98.37	18.16	864.38
15	91.00	20.97	834.90	93.58	20.67	839.35	96.22	20.31	844.08
16	88.63	23.34	811.57	91.19	23.06	816.30	93.82	22.71	821.37
17	85.99	25.98	785.60	88.53	25.72	790.58	91.13	25.40	795.97
18	83.06	28.91	756.69	85.55	28.70	761.88	88.12	28.41	767.56
19	79.79	32.18	724.52	82.23	32.02	729.87	84.75	31.78	735.79
20	76.16	35.81	688.71	78.52	35.73	694.15	80.98	35.55	700.24
21	72.12	39.85	648.87	74.39	39.86	654.29	76.77	39.76	660.49
22	67.61	44.36	604.52	69.78	44.47	609.83	72.06	44.47	616.03
23	62.60	49.37	555.16	64.63	49.62	560.21	66.80	49.73	566.30
24	57.03	54.94	500.22	58.89	55.36	504.86	60.90	55.63	510.68
25	50.82	61.15	439.08	52.49	61.76	443.10	54.31	62.22	448.47
26	43.92	68.05	371.03	45.34	68.91	374.20	46.94	69.59	378.89
27	36.23	75.74	295.30	37.37	76.88	297.32	38.70	77.83	301.06
28	27.68	84.29	211.01	28.47	85.78	211.55	29.48	87.05	214.01
29	18.15	93.82	117.20	18.55	95.70	115.85	19.16	97.37	116.65
30	7.56	104.41	12.79	7.47	106.78	9.07	7.63	108.90	7.75

Self-Liquidating Mortgages—Annual Interest, Amortization And Remaining Balance *(continued)*

30-Year Term *(continued)*

	11½% interest—$9.90 monthly payment			11¾% interest—$10.09 monthly payment			12% interest—$10.29 monthly payment		
Year	*Interest*	*Amort.*	*Balance*	*Interest*	*Amort.*	*Balance*	*Interest*	*Amort.*	*Balance*
1	114.80	4.01	996.00	117.31	3.78	996.23	119.81	3.68	996.33
2	114.31	4.50	991.51	116.84	4.25	991.98	119.34	4.15	992.18
3	113.77	5.04	986.47	116.31	4.78	987.20	118.82	4.67	987.51
4	113.16	5.65	980.82	115.72	5.37	981.84	118.22	5.27	982.25
5	112.47	6.34	974.49	115.05	6.04	975.80	117.56	5.93	976.32
6	111.70	7.11	967.39	114.30	6.79	969.02	116.80	6.69	969.64
7	110.84	7.97	959.42	113.46	7.63	961.40	115.96	7.53	962.11
8	109.88	8.93	950.50	112.52	8.57	952.83	115.00	8.49	953.63
9	108.79	10.02	940.48	111.45	9.64	943.20	113.93	9.56	944.07
10	107.58	11.23	929.26	110.26	10.83	932.38	112.71	10.78	933.29
11	106.22	12.59	916.68	108.92	12.17	920.21	111.35	12.14	921.16
12	104.69	14.12	902.56	107.41	13.68	906.53	109.81	13.68	907.48
13	102.98	15.83	886.74	105.71	15.38	891.16	108.07	15.42	892.06
14	101.06	17.75	869.00	103.80	17.29	873.88	106.12	17.37	874.70
15	98.91	19.90	849.11	101.66	19.43	854.45	103.91	19.58	855.13
16	96.50	22.31	826.80	99.25	21.84	832.62	101.43	22.06	833.07
17	93.80	25.01	801.79	96.54	24.55	808.08	98.64	24.85	808.23
18	90.76	28.05	773.75	93.50	27.59	780.49	95.48	28.01	780.23
19	87.36	31.45	742.31	90.08	31.01	749.48	91.93	31.56	748.67
20	83.55	35.26	707.06	86.23	34.86	714.63	87.93	35.56	713.12
21	79.28	39.53	667.53	81.91	39.18	675.45	83.42	40.07	673.06
22	74.48	44.33	623.20	77.05	44.04	631.42	78.34	45.15	627.92
23	69.11	49.70	573.51	71.59	49.50	581.92	72.62	50.87	577.05
24	63.08	55.73	517.78	65.45	55.64	526.28	66.17	57.32	519.73
25	56.32	62.49	455.30	58.55	62.54	463.74	58.90	64.59	455.14
26	48.75	70.06	385.24	50.79	70.30	393.44	50.70	72.79	382.36
27	40.25	78.56	306.69	42.07	79.02	314.42	41.47	82.02	300.35
28	30.73	88.08	218.61	32.27	88.82	225.61	31.07	92.42	207.94
29	20.05	98.76	119.86	21.25	99.84	125.77	19.35	104.14	103.80
30	8.07	110.74	9.12	8.87	112.22	13.55	6.15	117.34	0

Self-Liquidating Mortgages—Constant Monthly Payment Table

The following table shows the constant monthly payment required to liquidate a mortgage loan of $1,000 running for any number of whole years between 5 and 40 years inclusive and at interest rates running from 4% through 12% at ¼% intervals. All fractions are rounded to the next higher cent, thus making the final payment slightly smaller than the others.

Interest Rate

Years of Loan	*4%*	*4¼%*	*4½%*	*4¾%*	*5%*	*5¼%*	*5½%*	*5¾%*	*6%*	*6¼%*	*6½%*
1	85.15	85.26	85.38	85.49	85.61	85.72	85.84	85.95	86.07	86.18	86.30
2	43.42	43.54	43.65	43.76	43.87	43.98	44.10	44.21	44.32	44.43	44.55
3	29.52	29.63	29.75	29.86	29.97	30.08	30.20	30.31	30.42	30.54	30.65
4	22.58	22.69	22.80	22.92	23.03	23.14	23.26	23.37	23.48	23.60	23.71
5	18.42	18.53	18.64	18.76	18.87	18.99	19.10	19.22	19.33	19.45	19.57
6	15.65	15.76	15.87	15.99	16.10	16.22	16.34	16.45	16.57	16.69	16.81
7	13.67	13.78	13.90	14.02	14.13	14.25	14.37	14.49	14.61	14.73	14.85
8	12.19	12.31	12.42	12.54	12.66	12.78	12.90	13.02	13.14	13.26	13.39
9	11.04	11.16	11.28	11.40	11.52	11.64	11.76	11.88	12.01	12.13	12.25
10	10.12	10.24	10.36	10.48	10.61	10.73	10.85	10.98	11.10	11.23	11.35
11	9.38	9.50	9.62	9.74	9.86	9.99	10.11	10.24	10.37	10.49	10.62
12	8.76	8.88	9.00	9.12	9.25	9.37	9.50	9.63	9.76	9.89	10.02
13	8.23	8.35	8.48	8.60	8.73	8.86	8.99	9.12	9.25	9.38	9.51
14	7.78	7.91	8.03	8.16	8.29	8.42	8.55	8.68	8.81	8.95	9.08
15	7.40	7.52	7.65	7.78	7.91	8.04	8.17	8.30	8.44	8.57	8.71
16	7.06	7.19	7.32	7.45	7.58	7.71	7.84	7.98	8.11	8.25	8.39
17	6.76	6.89	7.02	7.15	7.29	7.42	7.56	7.69	7.83	7.97	8.11
18	6.50	6.63	6.76	6.90	7.03	7.17	7.30	7.44	7.58	7.72	7.87
19	6.27	6.40	6.53	6.67	6.80	6.94	7.08	7.22	7.36	7.50	7.65
20	6.06	6.19	6.33	6.46	6.60	6.74	6.88	7.02	7.16	7.31	7.46
21	5.87	6.01	6.14	6.28	6.42	6.56	6.70	6.84	6.99	7.14	7.28
22	5.70	5.84	5.97	6.11	6.25	6.39	6.54	6.68	6.83	6.98	7.13
23	5.55	5.68	5.82	5.96	6.10	6.25	6.39	6.54	6.69	6.84	6.99
24	5.41	5.54	5.68	5.83	5.97	6.11	6.26	6.41	6.56	6.71	6.86
25	5.28	5.42	5.56	5.70	5.85	5.99	6.14	6.29	6.44	6.60	6.75
26	5.16	5.30	5.44	5.59	5.73	5.88	6.03	6.18	6.34	6.49	6.65
27	5.05	5.19	5.34	5.48	5.63	5.78	5.93	6.08	6.24	6.40	6.55
28	4.95	5.09	5.24	5.39	5.54	5.69	5.84	5.99	6.15	6.31	6.47
29	4.86	5.00	5.15	5.30	5.45	5.60	5.75	5.91	6.07	6.23	6.39
30	4.77	4.92	5.07	5.22	5.37	5.52	5.68	5.84	5.99	6.16	6.32
31	4.69	4.84	4.99	5.14	5.29	5.45	5.61	5.77	5.93	6.09	6.25
32	4.62	4.77	4.92	5.07	5.23	5.38	5.54	5.70	5.86	6.03	6.19
33	4.55	4.70	4.85	5.01	5.16	5.32	5.48	5.64	5.80	5.97	6.14
34	4.49	4.64	4.79	4.94	5.10	5.26	5.42	5.59	5.75	5.92	6.09
35	4.43	4.58	4.73	4.89	5.05	5.21	5.37	5.53	5.70	5.87	6.04
36	4.37	4.52	4.68	4.84	5.00	5.16	5.32	5.49	5.66	5.83	6.00
37	4.32	4.47	4.63	4.79	4.95	5.11	5.28	5.44	5.61	5.78	5.96
38	4.27	4.42	4.58	4.74	4.90	5.07	5.23	5.40	5.57	5.75	5.92
39	4.22	4.38	4.54	4.70	4.86	5.03	5.19	5.36	5.54	5.71	5.89
40	4.18	4.34	4.50	4.66	4.82	4.99	5.16	5.33	5.50	5.68	5.85

Self-Liquidating Mortgages—Constant Monthly Payment Table *(continued)*

Interest Rate

Years of Loan	*6¾%*	*7%*	*7¼%*	*7½%*	*7¾%*	*8%*	*8¼%*	*8½%*	*8¾%*	*9%*	*9¼%*
1	86.41	86.53	86.64	86.76	86.87	86.99	87.10	87.22	87.33	87.45	87.57
2	44.66	44.77	44.89	45.00	45.11	45.23	45.34	45.46	45.57	45.68	45.80
3	30.76	30.88	30.99	31.11	31.22	31.34	31.45	31.57	31.68	31.80	31.92
4	23.83	23.95	24.06	24.18	24.30	24.41	24.53	24.65	24.77	24.88	25.00
5	19.68	19.80	19.92	20.04	20.16	20.28	20.40	20.52	20.64	20.76	20.88
6	16.93	17.05	17.17	17.29	17.41	17.53	17.65	17.78	17.90	18.03	18.15
7	14.97	15.09	15.22	15.34	15.46	15.59	15.71	15.84	15.96	16.09	16.22
8	13.51	13.63	13.76	13.88	14.01	14.14	14.26	14.39	14.52	14.65	14.78
9	12.38	12.51	12.63	13.76	12.89	13.02	13.15	13.28	13.41	13.54	13.68
10	11.48	11.61	11.74	11.87	12.00	12.13	12.26	12.40	12.53	12.67	12.80
11	10.75	10.88	11.02	11.15	11.28	11.42	11.55	11.69	11.82	11.96	12.10
12	10.15	10.28	10.42	10.55	10.69	10.82	10.96	11.10	11.24	11.38	11.52
13	9.65	9.78	9.92	10.05	10.19	10.33	10.47	10.61	10.75	10.90	11.04
14	9.22	9.35	9.49	9.63	9.77	9.91	10.06	10.20	10.34	10.49	10.64
15	8.85	8.99	9.13	9.27	9.41	9.56	9.70	9.85	9.99	10.14	10.29
16	8.53	8.67	8.81	8.96	9.10	9.25	9.40	9.54	9.69	9.84	10.00
17	8.25	8.40	8.54	8.69	8.83	8.98	9.13	9.28	9.43	9.59	9.74
18	8.01	8.15	8.30	8.45	8.60	8.75	8.90	9.05	9.21	9.36	9.52
19	7.79	7.94	8.09	8.24	8.39	8.54	8.70	8.85	9.01	9.17	9.33
20	7.60	7.75	7.90	8.06	8.21	8.36	8.52	8.68	8.84	9.00	9.16
21	7.43	7.58	7.74	7.89	8.05	8.20	8.36	8.52	8.68	8.85	9.01
22	7.28	7.43	7.59	7.74	7.90	8.06	8.22	8.38	8.55	8.71	8.88
23	7.14	7.30	7.46	7.61	7.77	7.93	8.10	8.26	8.43	8.59	8.76
24	7.02	7.18	7.34	7.50	7.66	7.82	7.98	8.15	8.32	8.49	8.66
25	6.91	7.07	7.23	7.39	7.55	7.72	7.88	8.05	8.22	8.39	8.56
26	6.81	6.97	7.13	7.29	7.46	7.63	7.79	7.96	8.13	8.31	8.48
27	6.72	6.88	7.04	7.21	7.37	7.54	7.71	7.88	8.06	8.23	8.41
28	6.63	6.80	6.96	7.13	7.30	7.47	7.64	7.81	7.99	8.16	8.34
29	6.56	6.72	6.89	7.06	7.23	7.40	7.57	7.75	7.92	8.10	8.28
30	6.49	6.65	6.82	6.99	7.16	7.34	7.51	7.69	7.89	8.05	8.23
31	6.42	6.59	6.76	6.93	7.11	7.28	7.46	7.64	7.81	8.00	8.18
32	6.36	6.53	6.71	6.88	7.05	7.23	7.41	7.59	7.77	7.95	8.13
33	6.31	6.48	6.65	6.83	7.01	7.18	7.36	7.54	7.73	7.91	8.09
34	6.26	6.43	6.61	6.78	6.96	7.14	7.32	7.50	7.69	7.87	8.06
35	6.21	6.39	6.56	6.74	6.92	7.10	7.28	7.47	7.65	7.84	8.03
36	6.17	6.35	6.53	6.70	6.88	7.07	7.25	7.44	7.62	7.81	8.00
37	6.13	6.31	6.49	6.67	6.85	7.03	7.22	7.41	7.59	7.78	7.97
38	6.10	6.28	6.46	6.64	6.82	7.00	7.19	7.38	7.57	7.76	7.95
39	6.06	6.24	6.42	6.61	6.79	6.98	7.16	7.35	7.54	7.73	7.93
40	6.03	6.21	6.40	6.58	6.77	6.95	7.14	7.33	7.52	7.71	7.91

Self-Liquidating Mortgages—Constant Monthly Payment Table *(continued)*

Interest Rate

Years of Loan	*9½%*	*9¾%*	*10%*	*10¼%*	*10½%*	*10¾%*	*11%*	*11¼%*	*11½%*	*11¾%*	*12%*
1	87.68	87.80	87.92	88.03	88.15	88.27	88.38	88.50	88.62	88.73	88.85
2	45.91	46.03	46.14	46.26	46.38	46.49	46.61	46.72	46.84	46.96	47.07
3	32.03	32.15	32.27	32.38	32.50	32.62	32.74	32.86	32.98	33.10	33.21
4	25.12	25.24	25.36	25.48	25.60	25.72	25.85	25.97	26.09	26.21	26.33
5	21.00	21.12	21.25	21.37	21.49	21.62	21.74	21.87	21.99	22.12	22.24
6	18.27	18.40	18.53	18.65	18.78	18.91	19.03	19.16	19.29	19.42	19.55
7	16.34	16.47	16.60	16.73	16.86	16.99	17.12	17.25	17.39	17.52	17.65
8	14.91	15.04	15.17	15.31	15.44	15.57	15.71	15.84	15.98	16.12	16.25
9	13.81	13.94	14.08	14.21	14.35	14.49	14.63	14.76	14.90	15.04	15.18
10	12.94	13.08	13.21	13.35	13.49	13.63	13.78	13.92	14.06	14.20	14.35
11	12.24	12.38	12.52	12.66	12.80	12.95	13.09	13.24	13.38	13.53	13.68
12	11.66	11.81	11.95	12.10	12.24	12.39	12.54	12.68	12.83	12.98	13.13
13	11.19	11.33	11.48	11.63	11.78	11.92	12.08	12.23	12.38	12.53	12.69
14	10.78	10.93	11.08	11.23	11.38	11.54	11.69	11.85	12.00	12.16	12.31
15	10.44	10.59	10.75	10.90	11.05	11.21	11.37	11.52	11.68	11.84	12.00
16	10.15	10.30	10.46	10.62	10.77	10.93	11.09	11.25	11.41	11.57	11.74
17	9.90	10.05	10.21	10.37	10.53	10.69	10.85	11.02	11.18	11.35	11.51
18	9.68	9.84	10.00	10.16	10.32	10.49	10.65	10.82	10.98	11.15	11.32
19	9.49	9.65	9.81	9.98	10.14	10.31	10.47	10.64	10.81	10.98	11.15
20	9.32	9.48	9.65	9.82	9.98	10.15	10.32	10.49	10.66	10.84	11.01
21	9.17	9.34	9.51	9.68	9.85	10.02	10.19	10.36	10.54	10.71	10.89
22	9.04	9.21	9.38	9.55	9.73	9.90	10.07	10.25	10.42	10.60	10.78
23	8.93	9.10	9.27	9.44	9.62	9.79	9.97	10.15	10.33	10.51	10.69
24	8.83	9.00	9.17	9.35	9.52	9.70	9.88	10.06	10.24	10.42	10.60
25	8.74	8.91	9.09	9.26	9.44	9.62	9.80	9.98	10.16	10.35	10.53
26	8.66	8.83	9.01	9.19	9.37	9.55	9.73	9.91	10.10	10.28	10.47
27	8.58	8.76	8.94	9.12	9.30	9.49	9.67	9.85	10.04	10.23	10.41
28	8.52	8.70	8.88	9.06	9.25	9.43	9.61	9.80	9.99	10.18	10.37
29	8.46	8.64	8.82	9.01	9.19	9.38	9.57	9.75	9.94	10.13	10.32
30	8.41	8.59	8.78	8.96	9.15	9.33	9.52	9.71	9.90	10.09	10.29
31	8.36	8.55	8.73	8.92	9.11	9.30	9.48	9.68	9.87	10.06	10.25
32	8.32	8.50	8.69	8.88	9.07	9.26	9.45	9.64	9.84	10.03	10.22
33	8.28	8.47	8.66	8.85	9.04	9.23	9.42	9.61	9.81	10.00	10.20
34	8.25	8.44	8.63	8.82	9.01	9.20	9.39	9.59	9.78	9.98	10.18
35	8.22	8.41	8.60	8.79	8.98	9.18	9.37	9.56	9.76	9.96	10.16
36	8.19	8.38	8.57	8.76	8.96	9.15	9.35	9.54	9.74	9.94	10.14
37	8.16	8.35	8.55	8.74	8.94	9.13	9.33	9.53	9.72	9.92	10.12
38	8.14	8.33	8.53	8.72	8.92	9.11	9.31	9.51	9.71	9.91	10.11
39	8.12	8.31	8.51	8.70	8.90	9.10	9.30	9.50	9.70	9.90	10.10
40	8.10	8.30	8.49	8.69	8.89	9.08	9.28	9.48	9.68	9.88	10.08

Self-Liquidating Mortgages—Constant Monthly Payment Table *(continued)*

Interest Rate

Years of Loan	*12⅜%*	*12¾%*	*13⅛%*	*13½%*	*13⅞%*	*14¼%*	*14⅝%*	*15%*	*15⅜%*	*15¾%*
1	89.02	89.20	89.38	89.55	89.73	89.90	90.08	90.26	90.44	90.61
2	47.25	47.42	47.60	47.78	47.95	48.13	48.31	48.49	48.67	48.84
3	33.39	33.57	33.75	33.94	34.12	34.30	34.48	34.67	34.85	35.03
4	26.52	26.70	26.89	27.08	27.26	27.45	27.64	27.83	28.02	28.21
5	22.43	22.63	22.82	23.01	23.20	23.40	23.59	23.79	23.99	24.19
6	19.75	19.94	20.14	20.34	20.54	20.74	20.94	21.15	21.35	21.55
7	17.85	18.06	18.26	18.46	18.67	18.88	19.09	19.30	19.51	19.72
8	16.46	16.67	16.88	17.09	17.30	17.51	17.73	17.95	18.16	18.38
9	15.40	15.61	15.83	16.04	16.26	16.48	16.70	16.92	17.15	17.37
10	14.56	14.78	15.00	15.23	15.45	15.68	15.90	16.13	16.36	16.60
11	13.90	14.13	14.35	14.58	14.81	15.04	15.27	15.51	15.75	15.98
12	13.36	13.59	13.82	14.06	14.29	14.53	14.77	15.01	15.25	15.49
13	12.92	13.15	13.39	13.63	13.87	14.11	14.36	14.60	14.85	15.10
14	12.55	12.79	13.03	13.28	13.52	13.77	14.02	14.27	14.52	14.78
15	12.24	12.49	12.73	12.98	13.23	13.49	13.74	14.00	14.25	14.51
16	11.98	12.23	12.48	12.74	12.99	13.25	13.51	13.77	14.03	14.29
17	11.76	12.02	12.27	12.53	12.79	13.05	13.31	13.58	13.84	14.11
18	11.57	11.83	12.09	12.35	12.62	12.88	13.15	13.42	13.69	13.96
19	11.41	11.67	11.94	12.20	12.47	12.74	13.01	13.28	13.56	13.83
20	11.27	11.54	11.80	12.07	12.34	12.62	12.89	13.17	13.45	13.73

Federal Income Tax Rates

Single Person			*Head of Household*		
Taxable Income	*Rate on Excess*		*Taxable Income*	*Rate on Excess*	
$ - $ 500	$	14%	$ - $ 1,000	$	14%
500 - 1,000	70	15%	1,000 - 2,000	140	16%
1,000 - 1,500	145	16%	2,000 - 4,000	300	18%
1,500 - 2,000	225	17%	4,000 - 6,000	660	19%
2,000 - 4,000	310	19%	6,000 - 8,000	1,040	22%
4,000 - 6,000	690	21%	8,000 - 10,000	1,480	23%
6,000 - 8,000	1,110	24%	10,000 - 12,000	1,940	25%
8,000 - 10,000	1,590	25%	12,000 - 14,000	2,440	27%
10,000 - 12,000	2,090	27%	14,000 - 16,000	2,980	28%
12,000 - 14,000	2,630	29%	16,000 - 18,000	3,540	31%
14,000 - 16,000	3,210	31%	18,000 - 20,000	4,160	32%
16,000 - 18,000	3,830	34%	20,000 - 22,000	4,800	35%
18,000 - 20,000	4,510	36%	22,000 - 24,000	5,500	36%
20,000 - 22,000	5,230	38%	24,000 - 26,000	6,220	38%
22,000 - 26,000	5,990	40%	26,000 - 28,000	6,980	41%
26,000 - 32,000	7,590	45%	28,000 - 32,000	7,800	42%
32,000 - 38,000	10,290	50%	32,000 - 36,000	9,480	45%
38,000 - 44,000	13,290	55%	36,000 - 38,000	11,280	48%
44,000 - 50,000	16,590	60%	38,000 - 40,000	12,240	51%
50,000 - 60,000	20,190	62%	40,000 - 44,000	13,260	52%
60,000 - 70,000	26,390	64%	44,000 - 50,000	15,340	55%
70,000 - 80,000	32,790	66%	50,000 - 52,000	18,640	56%
80,000 - 90,000	39,390	68%	52,000 - 64,000	19,760	58%
90,000 - 100,000	46,190	69%	64,000 - 70,000	26,720	59%
Over $100,000	53,090	70%	70,000 - 76,000	30,260	61%
			76,000 - 80,000	33,920	62%
			80,000 - 88,000	36,400	63%
			88,000 - 100,000	41,440	64%
			100,000 - 120,000	49,120	66%
			120,000 - 140,000	62,320	67%
			140,000 - 160,000	75,720	68%
			160,000 - 180,000	89,320	69%
			Over $180,000	103,120	70%

Federal Income Tax Rates *(continued)*

Married Filing Joint Return; Surviving Spouse				*Married Individuals Filing Separately and Estates and Trusts*			
Taxable Income		*Rate on Excess*		*Taxable Income*		*Rate on Excess*	
$ -	$ 1,000	$	14%	-	$ 500	$	14%
1,000 -	2,000	140	15%	$ 500 -	1,000	70	15%
2,000 -	3,000	290	16%	1,000 -	1,500	145	16%
3,000 -	4,000	450	17%	1,500 -	2,000	225	17%
4,000 -	8,000	620	19%	2,000 -	4,000	310	19%
8,000 -	12,000	1,380	22%	4,000 -	6,000	690	22%
12,000 -	16,000	2,260	25%	6,000 -	8,000	1,130	25%
16,000 -	20,000	3,260	28%	8,000 -	10,000	1,630	28%
20,000 -	24,000	4,380	32%	10,000 -	12,000	2,190	32%
24,000 -	28,000	5,660	36%	12,000 -	14,000	2,830	36%
28,000 -	32,000	7,100	39%	14,000 -	16,000	3,550	39%
32,000 -	36,000	8,660	42%	16,000 -	18,000	4,330	42%
36,000 -	40,000	10,340	45%	18,000 -	20,000	5,170	45%
40,000 -	44,000	12,140	48%	20,000 -	22,000	6,070	48%
44,000 -	52,000	14,060	50%	22,000 -	26,000	7,030	50%
52,000 -	64,000	18,060	53%	26,000 -	32,000	9,030	53%
64,000 -	76,000	24,420	55%	32,000 -	38,000	12,210	55%
76,000 -	88,000	31,020	58%	38,000 -	44,000	15,510	58%
88,000 -	100,000	37,980	60%	44,000 -	50,000	18,990	60%
100,000 -	120,000	45,180	62%	50,000 -	60,000	22,590	62%
120,000 -	140,000	57,580	64%	60,000 -	70,000	28,970	64%
140,000 -	160,000	70,380	66%	70,000 -	80,000	35,190	66%
160,000 -	180,000	83,580	68%	80,000 -	90,000	41,790	68%
180,000 -	200,000	97,180	69%	90,000 -	100,000	48,590	69%
Over $200,000		110,980	70%	Over $100,000		55,490	70%

After-Tax Income Table

Example of use of this table: Find how much an unmarried man who is not head of household has left from a taxable income of $35,000.

Amount from the line $32,000-$38,000 under column for single persons...... $21,710
Percentage from that line (50%) times excess of $35,000 over $32,000 ($3,000) 1,500
After-tax income.. 23,210

Single Person			*Head of Household*		
Taxable Income	*After-Tax Income**	*Plus This % of Excess*	*Taxable Income*	*After-Tax Income**	*Plus This % of Excess*
$ - $ 500	–	86	$ - $ 1,000	–	86
500 - 1,000	430	85	1,000 - 2,000	860	84
1,000 - 1,500	855	84	2,000 - 4,000	1,700	82
1,500 - 2,000	1,275	83	4,000 - 6,000	3,340	81
2,000 - 4,000	1,690	81	6,000 - 8,000	4,960	78
4,000 - 6,000	3,310	79	8,000 - 10,000	6,520	77
6,000 - 8,000	4,900	76	10,000 - 12,000	8,060	75
8,000 - 10,000	6,410	75	12,000 - 14,000	9,560	73
10,000 - 12,000	7,910	73	14,000 - 16,000	11,020	72
12,000 - 14,000	9,370	71	16,000 - 18,000	12,460	69
14,000 - 16,000	10,790	69	18,000 - 20,000	13,840	68
16,000 - 18,000	12,170	66	20,000 - 22,000	15,200	65
18,000 - 20,000	13,490	64	22,000 - 24,000	16,500	64
20,000 - 22,000	14,770	62	24,000 - 26,000	17,880	63
22,000 - 26,000	16,010	60	26,000 - 28,000	19,020	59
26,000 - 32,000	18,410	55	28,000 - 32,000	20,200	58
32,000 - 38,000	21,710	50	32,000 - 36,000	22,520	55
38,000 - 44,000	24,710	45	36,000 - 38,000	25,720	52
44,000 - 50,000	27,410	40	38,000 - 40,000	25,760	49
50,000 - 60,000	29,810	38	40,000 - 44,000	26,740	48
60,000 - 70,000	33,610	36	44,000 - 50,000	28,660	45
70,000 - 80,000	37,210	34	50,000 - 52,000	31,360	44
80,000 - 90,000	40,610	32	52,000 - 64,000	32,240	42
90,000 - 100,000	43,810	31	64,000 - 70,000	37,280	41
Over $100,000	46,910	30	70,000 - 76,000	39,740	39
			76,000 - 80,000	42,080	38
			80,000 - 88,000	43,600	37
			88,000 - 100,000	46,560	36
			100,000 - 120,000	50,880	34
			120,000 - 140,000	57,680	33
			140,000 - 160,000	64,280	32
			160,000 - 180,000	70,680	31
			Over $180,000	76,880	30

*Lower Amount in First Column

After-Tax Income Table *(continued)*

Married Filing Joint Return; Surviving Spouse			*Married Individuals Filing Separately and Estates and Trusts*		
Taxable Income	*After-Tax Income**	*Plus This % of Excess*	*Taxable Income*	*After-Tax Income**	*Plus This % of Excess*
$ - $ 1,000	—	86	$ - $ 500	—	
1,000 - 2,000	860	85	500 - 1,000	430	85
2,000 - 3,000	1,710	84	1,000 - 1,500	855	84
3,000 - 4,000	2,550	83	1,500 - 2,000	1,275	83
4,000 - 8,000	3,380	81	2,000 - 4,000	1,690	81
8,000 - 12,000	6,620	78	4,000 - 6,000	3,310	78
12,000 - 16,000	9,740	75	6,000 - 8,000	4,870	75
16,000 - 20,000	12,740	72	8,000 - 10,000	6,370	72
20,000 - 24,000	15,620	68	10,000 - 12,000	7,810	68
24,000 - 28,000	18,340	64	12,000 - 14,000	9,170	64
28,000 - 32,000	20,900	61	14,000 - 16,000	10,450	61
32,000 - 36,000	23,340	58	16,000 - 18,000	11,670	58
36,000 - 40,000	25,660	55	18,000 - 20,000	12,830	55
40,000 - 44,000	27,860	52	20,000 - 22,000	13,930	52
44,000 - 52,000	29,940	50	22,000 - 26,000	14,970	50
52,000 - 64,000	33,940	47	26,000 - 32,000	16,970	47
64,000 - 76,000	39,580	45	32,000 - 38,000	19,790	45
76,000 - 88,000	44,980	42	38,000 - 44,000	22,490	42
88,000 - 100,000	50,020	40	44,000 - 50,000	25,010	40
100,000 - 120,000	54,820	38	50,000 - 60,000	27,410	38
120,000 - 140,000	62,420	36	60,000 - 70,000	31,210	36
140,000 - 160,000	69,620	34	70,000 - 80,000	34.810	34
160,000 - 180,000	76,420	32	80,000 - 90,000	38,210	32
180,000 - 200,000	82,820	31	90,000 - 100,000	41,410	31
Over $200,000	89,020	30	Over $100,000	44,510	30

*Lower Amount in First Column.

How Much $1 of Additional After-Tax Income Is Worth?

To get after-tax value from

Tax-free income, includes municipal bonds, life insurance return, special income earned abroad, etc.

Ordinary income, includes interest on taxable bonds, dividends (not considering the $100 exclusion), compensation, net rental income, etc.

Capital Gains: The returns indicated in this table are applicable only with respect to the first $50,000 of capital gains. The maximum tax on these gains is 25%. (The maximum tax on the amount in excess of $50,000 is 35% for taxable years beginning in 1972. It was 29.5% for 1970 and 32.5% for 1971.) The return also does not take into account any tax on capital gains as tax-preference income. If the tax applies, the return may be reduced by as much as 10%.

Taxable Income (thousands of dollars)						*How Much More Tax-Free Income Nets Over:*	
Single Individual	*Joint Return*	*Tax-Free Income*	*Long-Term Capital Gains*[1]	*Dividends or Interest*	*How Much More Capital Gain Nets Over Dividend and Interest*	*Capital Gains*	*Dividends & Interest*
$ 2-4	$ 4-8	$1.00	$.905	$.81	12%	10	23
4-6	8-12	1.00	.89	.78	14	12	28
6-8	12-16	1.00	.87½	.75	17	14	33
8-10	16-20	1.00	.86	.72	19	16	39
10-12	20-24	1.00	.84	.68	24	19	47
12-14	24-28	1.00	.82	.64	28	22	56
14-16	28-32	1.00	.805	.61	32	24	64
16-18	32-36	1.00	.79	.58	36	27	72
18-20	36-40	1.00	.78½	.55	41	28	78
20-22	40-44	1.00	.76	.52	46	29	82
22-26	44-52	1.00	.75	.50	50	32	92
26-32	52-64	1.00	.75	.47	60	33	100
32-38	64-76	1.00	.75	.45	67	33	113
38-44	76-88	1.00	.75	.42	79	33	122
44-50	88-100	1.00	.75	.40	88	33	138
50-60	100-120	1.00	.75	.38	97	33	150
60-70	120-140	1.00	.75	.36	108	33	163
70-80	140-160	1.00	.75	.34	121	33	194
80-90	160-180	1.00	.75	.32	134	33	213
90-100	180-200	1.00	.75	.31	142	33	223
100-150	200-300	1.00	.75	.30	150	33	233
150-200	300-400	1.00	.75	.30	150		
200 and over	400 and over	1.00	.75	.30	150		

[1]The return indicated in this table is applicable only with respect to the first $50,000 of capital gains. The maximum tax on these gains is 25%. Where a taxpayer has net long-term capital gains above $50,000, half of the gain is included in ordinary income and is taxed at a maximum 35%. Nor does it take into account the 10% tax on tax-preference income (which includes half of an individual's capital gains) in excess of $30,000 plus the amount of regular taxes.

Before-Tax Income Needed for Various Amounts of After-Tax Income (What Tax-Exempt Income Is Worth)

This table serves a dual purpose. On the one hand, it tells us how much before-tax income people in different tax brackets need to net them a certain amount. Thus, if a married man with taxable income of $52,000 desires an additional $500 after taxes, he must earn an additional $1,065. This sum is obtained by multiplying $500 by 8.51 (the figure at the $52,000, 4% line) and dividing by 4. The table can also be used to calculate the true worth of tax-free income.

Married Persons Taxable Income		*Tax-Exempt Yield*						
Separate Return	*Joint Return*	*4%*	*4.5%*	*5%*	*5.5%*	*6%*	*6.5%*	*7%*
$ 10,000	$ 20,000	5.88	7.61	7.36	8.09	8.82	9.56	10.29
12,000	24,000	6.25	7.03	7.82	8.59	9.37	10.16	10.94
14,000	28,000	6.56	7.38	8.20	9.02	9.84	10.66	11.48
16,000	32,000	6.90	7.76	8.62	9.48	10.35	11.21	12.07
18,000	36,000	7.27	8.18	9.08	10.00	10.91	11.82	12.73
20,000	40,000	7.69	8.65	9.62	10.58	11.54	12.50	13.46
22,000	44,000	8.00	9.00	10.00	11.00	12.00	13.00	14.00
26,000	52,000	8.51	9.57	10.64	11.70	12.77	13.63	14.89
32,000	64,000	8.89	10.00	11.12	12.22	13.33	14.44	15.56
38,000	76,000	9.52	10.71	11.90	13.10	14.28	15.48	16.67
44,000	88,000	10.00	11.25	12.50	13.75	15.00	16.25	17.50
50,000	100,000	10.53	11.84	13.16	14.47	15.79	17.11	18.42
60,000	120,000	11.11	12.49	13.88	15.28	16.67	18.06	19.44
70,000	140,000	11.76	13.23	14.70	16.18	17.64	19.12	20.59
80,000	160,000	12.50	14.06	15.62	17.19	18.75	20.31	21.87
90,000	180,000	12.90	14.52	16.12	17.74	[illegible]	[illegible]	22.58
100,000	200,000	13.33	15.00	16.66	18.33	20.00	21.67	23.33

Wealth Accumulator Table

Regular investment in sound ventures can be a sure road to wealth. The table below dramatically shows the wealth-accumulating power of regular investment at different buildup rates. If the buildup is taxable, only an approximation is possible. Take the actual rate of buildup and reduce it by your estimated average tax bracket over the period covered. Thus, if the actual return is 4% and your estimated average tax rate is 25%, your rate of buildup would be 3%.

A regular investment of $1,000 per year with a buildup at rate of:	*5 YRS*	*10 YRS*	*15 YRS*	*20 YRS*	*25 YRS*	*30 YRS*	*35 YRS*	*40 YRS*
3%	$ 5,468	$11,807	$19,156	$27,676	$ 37,553	$ 49,002	$ 62,275	$ 77,663
3½	5,550	12,141	19,971	29,269	40,313	53,429	69,007	87,509
4	5,632	12,486	20,824	30,969	43,311	58,328	76,598	98,826
4½	5,716	12,841	21,719	32,783	46,570	63,752	85,163	111,846
5	5,801	13,206	22,657	34,719	50,113	69,760	94,836	126,839
5½	5,888	13,583	23,641	36,786	53,965	76,419	105,765	144,118
6	5,975	13,971	24,672	38,992	58,156	83,801	118,120	164,047
6½	6,063	14,371	25,754	41,348	62,715	91,989	132,096	187,047
7	6,153	14,783	26,888	43,865	67,676	101,073	147,913	213,609
7½	6,244	15,208	28,077	46,552	73,076	111,154	165,820	244,300
8	6,335	15,645	29,324	49,422	78,954	122,345	186,102	279,781
8½	6,429	16,096	30,632	52,489	85,354	134,772	209,081	320,815
9	6,523	16,560	32,003	55,764	92,323	148,575	235,124	368,291
9½	6,618	17,038	33,441	59,263	99,914	163,907	264,648	423,239
10	6,715	17,531	34,949	63,002	108,181	180,943	298,126	486,851
11	6,912	18,561	38,189	71,265	126,998	220,913	379,164	645,826
12	7,115	19,654	41,753	80,698	149,333	270,292	483,463	859,142
13	7,322	20,814	45,671	91,469	175,850	331,315	617,749	1,145,485
14	7,535	22,044	49,980	103,768	207,332	406,737	790,672	1,529,908
15	7,753	23,349	54,717	117,810	244,711	499,956	1,013,345	2,045,953
20	8,929	31,150	86,442	224,025	566,377	1,418,257	3,538,009	8,812,629
25	10,258	41,566	137,108	428,680	1,318,488	4,033,967	12,320,951	37,610,819

After-Tax Cost of Interest Payments

The actual cost of interest payments to a real estate investor may be a lot less than he may think because: (1) When you finance a real estate deal by way of a long-term loan, you come in for a tax deduction for your interest payments on the loan. (2) You benefit from repaying the loan in relatively cheap inflation-devalued dollars—thus cutting the cost to you of the borrowed funds. (3) You have the prospect of substantial net after-tax returns from income-producing real estate. (4) With both income-producing property and residential property, you have the prospect of appreciation in value, an appreciation, by the way, which should cover both actual economic appreciation and dollar-value appreciation and for which you get long-term capital gain treatment when you cash in. (5) Income-producing property will give you depreciation deductions based on the total cost of the property—including borrowed funds.

You should remember, however, that if you pay enough interest to reduce your tax bracket, the amount of tax benefit decreases. For example, if your taxable income was $56,000, and you reduced it to $36,000 by paying $20,000 interest at 10%, the first $4,000 would cost you 4.7%; the next $8,000 would cost you 5%; the next $4,000, 5.2%; and the last $4,000, 5.5%. So, the actual after-tax cost of the $20,000 payment was $10,160, or 5.08%.

Also, individuals, partners, estates, and shareholders of Subchapter S corporations have to watch out for excess investment interest. This is defined as interest payments on investments which exceed $25,000 plus your investment income for the year plus your long-term capital gains for the year. The penalty for these excess interest payments is to disallow one-half of the interest deduction. Thus, if you paid $100,000 in investment interest, and you had investment income of $30,000 and no long-term capital gains, $45,000 of the interest payment would be excess, and you could only deduct one-half of it, or $22,500, for a total deduction of $77,500. However, you could carry over the $22,500 to your next tax year (see Internal Revenue Code § 163(d)(1) and (2)).

Taxable Income (thousands of dollars) Married Taxpayer		**Interest Rate**									
Separate Return	*Joint Return*	*6%*	*6½%*	*7%*	*7½%*	*8%*	*8½%*	*9%*	*9½%*	*10%*	*10½%*
$ 2-4	$ 4-8	4.86	5.26	5.67	6.07	6.48	6.89	7.29	7.70	8.10	8.51
4-6	8-12	4.68	5.07	5.46	5.85	6.24	6.63	7.02	7.41	7.80	8.19
6-8	12-16	4.50	4.88	5.25	5.63	6.00	6.38	6.75	7.13	7.50	7.88
8-10	16-20	4.32	4.68	5.04	5.40	5.76	6.12	6.48	6.84	7.20	7.56
10-12	20-24	4.08	4.42	4.76	5.10	5.44	5.88	6.12	6.46	6.80	7.14
12-14	24-28	3.84	4.16	4.48	4.80	5.12	5.44	5.76	6.08	6.40	6.72
14-16	28-32	3.66	3.97	4.27	4.58	4.88	5.19	5.49	5.80	6.10	6.41
16-18	32-36	3.48	3.77	4.06	4.35	4.64	4.93	5.22	5.51	5.80	6.09
18-20	36-40	3.30	3.58	3.85	4.13	4.40	4.68	4.95	5.23	5.50	5.78
20-22	40-44	3.12	3.38	3.64	3.90	4.16	4.42	4.68	4.94	5.20	5.46
22-26	44-52	3.00	3.25	3.50	3.75	4.00	4.25	4.50	4.75	5.00	5.25
26-32	52-64	2.82	3.06	3.29	3.53	3.76	4.00	4.23	4.47	4.70	4.94
32-38	64-76	2.70	2.93	3.15	3.38	3.60	3.83	4.05	4.28	4.50	4.73
38-44	76-88	2.52	2.73	2.94	3.15	3.36	3.57	3.78	3.99	4.20	4.41
44-50	88-100	2.40	2.60	2.80	3.00	3.20	3.40	3.60	3.80	4.00	4.20
50-60	100-120	2.28	2.47	2.66	2.85	3.04	3.23	3.42	3.61	3.80	3.99
60-70	120-140	2.16	2.34	2.52	2.70	2.88	3.06	3.24	3.42	3.60	3.78
70-80	140-160	2.04	2.21	2.38	2.55	2.72	2.89	3.06	3.23	3.40	3.57
80-90	160-180	1.92	2.08	2.24	2.40	2.56	2.72	2.88	3.04	3.20	3.36
90-100	180-200	1.86	2.02	2.17	2.33	2.48	2.64	2.79	2.95	3.10	3.26
100 and over	200 and over	1.80	1.95	2.10	2.25	2.40	2.55	2.70	2.85	3.00	3.15

After-Tax Cost of Interest Payments *(continued)*

Taxable Income (thousands of dollars) Married Taxpayer		Interest Rate								
Separate Return	*Joint Return*	*11%*	*11½%*	*12%*	*12½%*	*13%*	*13½%*	*14%*	*14½%*	*15%*
$ 2-4	$ 4-8	8.91	9.32	9.72	10.13	10.53	10.94	11.34	11.75	12.15
4-6	8-12	8.58	8.97	9.36	9.75	10.14	10.53	10.92	11.31	11.70
6-8	12-16	8.25	8.63	9.00	9.38	9.75	10.13	10.50	10.88	11.25
8-10	16-20	7.92	8.28	8.64	9.00	9.36	9.72	10.08	10.44	10.80
10-12	20-24	7.48	7.82	8.16	8.50	8.84	9.18	9.52	9.86	10.20
12-14	24-28	7.04	7.36	7.68	8.00	8.32	8.64	8.96	9.28	9.60
14-16	28-32	6.71	7.02	7.32	7.63	7.93	8.24	8.54	8.85	9.15
16-18	32-36	6.38	6.67	6.96	7.25	7.54	7.83	8.12	8.41	8.70
18-20	36-40	6.05	6.33	6.60	6.88	7.15	7.43	7.70	7.98	8.25
20-22	40-44	5.75	5.98	6.24	6.50	6.76	7.02	7.28	7.54	7.80
22-26	44-52	5.50	5.75	6.00	6.25	6.50	6.75	7.00	7.25	7.50
26-32	52-64	5.17	5.41	5.64	5.88	6.11	6.35	6.58	6.82	7.05
32-38	64-76	4.95	5.18	5.40	5.63	5.85	6.08	6.30	6.53	6.75
38-44	76-88	4.62	4.83	5.04	5.25	5.46	5.67	5.88	6.09	6.30
44-50	88-100	4.40	4.60	4.80	5.00	5.20	5.54	5.60	5.80	6.00
50-60	100-120	4.18	4.37	4.56	4.75	4.94	5.13	5.32	5.51	5.70
60-70	120-140	3.96	4.14	4.32	4.50	4.68	4.86	5.14	5.22	5.40
70-80	140-160	3.74	3.91	4.08	4.25	4.42	4.59	4.76	4.93	5.10
80-90	160-180	3.52	3.68	3.84	4.00	4.16	4.32	4.48	4.64	4.80
90-100	180-200	3.41	3.57	3.72	3.88	4.03	4.19	4.34	4.50	4.65
100 and over	200 and over	3.30	3.45	3.60	3.75	3.90	4.05	4.20	4.35	4.50

Investment Tax Credit

The investment tax credit is a special credit against the taxes due for the taxable year. The credit is granted where property subject to depreciation under Code § 167 is placed into service by a taxpayer after 8/15/71. (Special rules apply to property constructed or put into service before that date.) The credit applies to all new property, and used property, if ''purchased.'' The effect of the ''purchase'' requirement is to exclude used property acquired in tax-free transactions, for the most part, such as tax-free exchanges, inheritance, or from another member of a controlled group.

The credit applies at a flat rate of 7% of the ''qualified investment'' in the property. This means the cost or other basis if the property has a useful life of 7 years or more, but this is reduced as the following table indicates:

Life of Property	*Credit as % of Full Basis of Property*
7 years or more	7%
5 to 7 years	4-2/3%
3 to 5 years	2-1/3%

The credit is taken directly against the tax liability for the year without reference to the credit. However, it is limited to 50% of the tax liability as follows:

The credit for property put into service in the year, plus any unused credit from prior years, is limited to:

(1) the tax liability for the year or $25,000, whichever is less, or

(2) 50% of the tax liability for the year (without reference to the credit) in excess of $25,000.

Amounts of credit limited by this rule may be carried forward to later years.

Persons who claim the credit must file Form 3468 with their income tax returns for the year claimed.

This is only a brief outline of the workings of the investment tax credit. In an actual case, the Regs should be consulted.

Best Tax Salary

The best tax salary for an officer-stockholder is the one that will cost the least in taxes when the tax cost to employee and corporation are combined. It strikes a balance: Any increase will cost the employee more in taxes than the extra deduction will save the corporation; any decrease will cost the corporation more because of the reduced deduction than the reduction in tax will save the employee.

If earnings left in the corporation will not be withdrawn in the near future either as dividends or by liquidation and assuming that the stockholder-employee's other income equals his deductions and exemptions, there can be only one best salary taxwise.

Suppose a corporation has earnings of $100,000 before salary. It has a sole stockholder who is married. His best salary is between $40,000 and $44,000. If he were paid more than $44,000, the corporation would be saving taxes at a 48% rate, but sole stockholder would be paying taxes at a 50% rate. If he were paid less than $40,000, the corporation would be paying tax at a 48% rate, but the sole stockholder would be saving tax at a 45% rate.

Assuming the stockholder's other income equals his deductions and exemptions, here are the best salary levels for various corporate incomes.

Corporate Income Before Salary	*Single Taxpayer*	*Married Taxpayer* *Joint Return*	*Married Taxpayer* *Separate Return*
Less than $6,000	Full Corporate Income		
$6,000 to $12,000	$ 6,000	Full Corporate Income	$ 6,000
$12,000 to $31,000	$ 6,000	$12,000	$ 6,000
$31,000 to $47,000	Full Corporate Income Less $25,000		
$47,000 to $57,000	Full Corporate Income Less $25,000		$22,000
$57,000 to $69,000	$32,000	Full Corporate Income Less $25,000	$22,000
Over $69,000	$32,000	$44,000	$22,000

Table of Building Expenditures Showing Expensed and Capitalized Items

Whether an item is a repair or a capital improvement is of vital importance for tax purposes. Costs of repairs are deductible currently; capital improvement costs are recoverable over the life of the improvement via depreciation. Hence, taxpayers prefer to have their expenses deemed repairs.

The question whether a building expenditure will be regarded, for income tax purposes, as a fully deductible repair item or whether it must be treated as a capital investment subject to annual depreciation deductions spread over the useful life of the asset cuts across all classifications of a real estate ownership and operation. There is no clear-cut rule of thumb that provides an infallible answer to every expenditure. The following table sets forth the tax treatment of basic real estate building expenditure types.

Item	*Expense*	*Capital*
Floors - patching	X	
Floors - new		X
Foundation - new		X
Foundation - repair	X	
Fire escapes - new		X
Fire escapes - rails replaced		X
Stairway supports - new	X	
Roof - repair	X	
Roof - reshingling		X
Roof - replacement		X
Ratproofing of building		X
Plastering	X	
Papering	X	
Painting building	X	
Painting - inside	X	
Leaks - mending	X	
Electric wiring - new		X
Electric wiring - defectives replaced	X	
Pipes - iron replaced by brass		X
Office - layout temporarily changed	X	
Heating - permanent conversion		X
Termite control	X	
Residence - converting upper floor for rental		X
Front - new		X
Furnace - relining		X
Furnace - enameling	X	
Commissions or fees paid for negotiating a lease or sale		X
Conforming property to a taxpayer's different use		X
Casualties - repairs arising from	X	
Insulating	X	
Plumbing - defective replaced	X	
Alteration - building		X
Architect fee - building addition		X
Wells - cleaning out and repairing	X	
Damaged property - restored to normal operating condition	X	
Damaged property - restoration resulting in something different or better - deemed replacement		X
Maintenance of property - good housekeeping	X	
Restoration of property purchased in rundown condition		X
Alterations conforming property to taxpayer's use		X
Repairs and improvements - part of general plan of betterment		X
Assessments for local improvements		X

Present Worth Valuation Tables

Leases and mortgages provide for regular periodic payments over the term. In handling a real estate transaction, it often becomes necessary to translate these future payments into their present worth. When an office building is sold, for example, the present value of the assigned leases (the expected future savings) may be determined by the following tables. Similarly, a seller taking back a purchase money mortgage must be covered with the present value of the mortgage.

A brief explanation of the present worth tables will be helpful. Essentially, obtaining present worth is a discounting process in which the future payments receivable are discounted for interest. There are two recognized mathematical approaches to obtaining present value, the Hoskold Sinking Fund valuation premise and the Inwood Coefficient. Each of these methods gives a present worth but founded on different premises. The Hoskold process assumes that the portion of each payment representing a return of capital is set aside in a sinking fund and the entire capital then returned in full at the end of the period. The Inwood Premise assumes that each year the portion of the return representing capital is actually paid over to the owner and the outstanding investment thereby reduced. Thus, under the Inwood process, since the outstanding investment becomes less each year, the treatment is similar to a mortgage which is being amortized regularly. The Hoskold process, however, treats the capital investment as a straight (nonamortized) mortgage note which is repaid in one lump sum at maturity.

Present Worth of $1 per Annum (Hoskold Sinking Fund Valuation Premise)

Problem: Find the present worth of a net income of $1,000 per year, for 20 years with interest on the investment at 7%. This assumes that the portion of the annual return ($1,000) which represents the return of the capital invested can be safely invested at 7% compounded annually, so that at the end of 20 years the full amount of the original investment can be withdrawn from the compound interest account, thus returning the investment in one lump sum at the end of the term.

Answer: In table under 7% and opposite 20 years, we find the factor 9.327, meaning that $1 per year for 20 years under the above assumptions has a present worth of $9.327. Then, $1,000 × 9.327 = $9,327.

Speculative Interest Rates

Years	*5%*	*6%*	*7%*	*8%*	*9%*	*10%*	*12%*	*15%*
1	0.952	0.943	0.935	0.926	0.917	0.909	0.893	0.870
2	1.843	1.810	1.777	1.746	1.716	1.687	1.632	1.556
3	2.677	2.607	2.541	2.478	2.418	2.361	2.255	2.112
4	3.460	3.344	3.236	3.134	3.039	2.950	2.785	2.570
5	4.195	4.026	3,871	3.726	3.592	3.468	3.243	2.955
6	4.888	4.660	4.452	4.263	4.088	3.928	3.642	3.283
7	5.540	5.249	4.987	4.750	4.535	4.338	3.992	3.565
8	6.155	5.799	5.481	5.196	4.939	4.707	4.302	3.810
9	6.737	6.312	5.937	5.604	5.307	5.039	4.578	4.025
10	7.287	6.792	6.360	5.980	5.642	5.341	4.825	4.215
11	7.808	7.242	6.753	6.326	5.950	5.615	5.048	4.384
12	8.301	7.665	7.119	6.646	6.232	5.866	5.250	4.536
13	8.770	8.063	7.461	6.943	6.492	6.096	5.434	4.672
14	9.214	8.437	7.780	7.219	6.733	6.308	5.601	4.796
15	9.637	8.790	8.080	7.476	6.956	6.503	5.755	4.908
16	10.039	9.123	8.360	7.715	7.163	6.684	5.896	5.010
17	10.422	9.438	8.624	7.939	7.355	6.851	6.026	5.103
18	10.786	9.736	8.872	8.149	7.535	7.007	6.146	5.189
19	11.134	10.019	9.106	8.346	7.703	7.152	6.257	5.268
20	11.466	10.286	9.327	8.531	7.861	7.288	6.361	5.341
21	11.782	10.540	9.535	8.705	8.008	7.414	6.457	5.409
22	12.085	10.782	9.733	8.869	8.147	7.533	6.547	5.472
23	12.374	11.011	9.919	9.024	8.277	7.644	6.631	5.530
24	12.651	11.230	10.096	9.170	8.400	7.749	6.709	5.585
25	12.915	11.438	10.264	9.309	8.516	7.848	6.783	5.636
26	13.169	11.636	10.423	9.439	8.625	7.940	6.852	5.684
27	13.411	11.825	10.575	9.563	8.729	8.028	6.917	5.729
28	13.644	12.006	10.719	9.681	8.827	8.111	6.979	5.771
29	13.867	12.178	10.856	9.793	8.919	8.189	7.037	5.810
30	14.081	12.343	10.987	9.899	9.007	8.263	7.091	5.847
31	14.286	12.500	11.111	10.000	9.091	8.333	7.143	5.882
32	14.483	12.651	11.230	10.096	9.170	8.400	7.192	5.915
33	14.672	12.795	11.343	10.188	9.246	8.463	7.238	5.947
34	14.854	12.933	11.452	10.275	9.318	8.524	7.282	5.976
35	15.029	13.065	11.555	10.358	9.386	8.581	7.324	6.005
36	15.197	13.192	11.654	10.438	9.451	8.635	7.364	6.031
37	15.358	13.313	11.749	10.514	9.514	8.687	7.401	6.056
38	15.514	13.430	11.840	10.587	9.573	8.737	7.437	6.080
39	15.663	13.542	11.927	10.656	9.630	8.784	7.471	6.103
40	15.807	13.650	12.010	10.722	9.684	8.829	7.504	6.125
41	15.946	13.753	12.090	10.786	9.736	8.872	7.535	6.146
42	16.079	13.852	12.167	10.847	9.785	8.913	7.565	6.165
43	16.208	13.947	12.240	10.905	9.833	8.953	7.593	6.184
44	16.332	14.039	12.311	10.961	9.878	8.990	7.620	6.202
45	16.451	14.127	12.378	11.015	9.922	9.026	7.646	6.219
46	16.567	14.212	12.444	11.066	9.964	9.061	7.671	6.236
47	16.678	14.294	12.506	11.116	10.004	9.094	7.695	6.251
48	16.785	14.372	12.566	11.163	10.042	9.126	7.717	6.266
49	16.888	14.448	12.624	11.209	10.079	9.156	7.739	6.281
50	16.988	14.521	12.680	11.253	10.115	9.186	7.760	6.295

Compound Interest Annuity Table (Inwood Coefficient)

By this table the present worth of an annuity of $1,000 each year payable for 20 years, discounted at 4% interest is $13,590. To translate this into a practical situation: if you were now to pay $13,590 for the right to receive $1,000 annually for the next 20 years you would be receiving 4% on your investment and, in addition, a portion of your investment would be returned to you each year.

A new application of this table can be found for lessees who pay a bonus to buy an existing lease. Where you buy a lease, you can write off its cost over the lease term. Suppose, however, the lease contains renewal options. In 1958, Congress passed a law that said, in effect, that in the usual case you would write off the cost of the lease over the remaining initial term of the lease if at least 75% of the cost of acquiring the lease is attributable to the lease term without taking into account renewal options. Under Treasury Regulations, it points out that in determining whether the 75% test has been met, all the facts and circumstances of the case must be taken into account. It then goes on to show that in appropriate cases an annuity approach can be used.

Example: Assume Wilson pays $100,000 for a lease on unimproved property. There are 21 years remaining in the original term with two 21-year renewal options. A uniform rent is provided for during the initial and renewal terms. Assuming that 5% is the appropriate interest rate to use, by applying tables (Inwood) to find the present value of an annuity of $1 per year for 21 years, we come up with a factor of 12.821. For a 63-year period, the factor is 19.075. Multiplying the fraction 12.821/19.075 by $100,000 gives us a cost of the initial term of the lease of $67,210, or 67.21%. Thus, in this case, the 75% test is not met. And unless the taxpayer can show that it is more probably that the lease will not be renewed than it will be renewed, the $100,000 cost will have to be spread over the full 63 years. But, each year, the probabilities can be reviewed (Reg. §1.178-1(b)(2), (5)).

Speculative Interest Rates

Years	*5%*	*5½%*	*6%*	*7%*	*8%*	*9%*	*10%*	*12%*	*15%*
1	0.952	0.948	0.943	0.935	0.926	0.917	0.909	0.893	0.870
2	1.859	1.846	1.833	1.808	1.783	1.759	1.736	1.690	1.625
3	2.723	2.698	2.673	2.624	2.577	2.531	2.487	2.402	2.283
4	3.546	3.505	3.465	3.387	3.312	3.240	3.170	3.037	2.855
5	4.329	4.270	4.212	4.100	3.993	3.890	3.791	3.605	3.352
6	5.076	4.996	4.917	4.766	4.623	4.486	4.355	4.111	3.785
7	5.786	5.683	5.582	5.389	5.206	5.033	4.868	4.564	4.160
8	6.463	6.334	6.210	5.971	5.747	5.535	5.335	4.968	4.487
9	7.108	6.952	6.802	6.515	6.247	5.995	5.759	5.328	4.772
10	7.722	7.538	7.360	7.024	6.710	6.418	6.145	5.650	5.019
11	8.306	8.093	7.887	7.499	7.139	6.805	6.495	5.938	5.234
12	8.863	8.618	8.384	7.943	7.536	7.161	6.814	6.194	5.421
13	9.394	9.117	8.853	8.358	7.904	7.487	7.103	6.424	5.583
14	9.899	9.590	9.295	8.745	8.244	7.786	7.367	6.628	5.724
15	10.380	10.038	9.712	9.108	8.559	8.061	7.606	6.811	5.847
16	10.838	10.462	10.106	9.447	8.851	8.313	7.824	6.974	5.954
17	11.274	10.865	10.477	9.763	9.122	8.544	8.022	7.120	6.047
18	11.690	11.246	10.828	10.059	9.372	8.756	8.201	7.250	6.128
19	12.085	11.608	11.158	10.336	9.604	8.950	8.365	7.366	6.198
20	12.462	11.950	11.470	10.594	9.818	9.128	8.514	7.469	6.259
21	12.821	12.275	11.764	10.835	10.017	9.292	8.649	7.562	6.312
22	13.163	12.583	12.042	11.061	10.201	9.442	8.772	7.645	6.359
23	13.489	12.875	12.303	11.272	10.371	9.580	8.883	7.718	6.399
24	13.799	13.152	12.550	11.469	10.529	9.707	8.985	7.784	6.434
25	14.094	13.414	12.783	11.654	10.675	9.823	9.077	7.843	6.464

Compound Interest Annuity Table (Inwood Coefficient) *(continued)*

Speculative Interest Rates

Years	*5%*	*5½%*	*6%*	*7%*	*8%*	*9%*	*10%*	*12%*	*15%*
26	14.375	13.662	13.003	11.826	10.810	9.929	9.161	7.896	6.491
27	14.643	13.898	13.210	11.987	10.935	10.026	9.237	7.943	6.513
28	14.898	14.121	13.406	12.137	11.051	10.116	9.307	7.984	6.534
29	15.141	14.333	13.591	12.278	11.158	10.198	9.370	8.022	6.551
30	15.372	14.534	13.765	12.409	11.258	10.274	9.427	8.055	6.566
31	15.593	14.724	13.929	12.532	11.350	10.343	9.479	8.085	6.579
32	15.803	14.904	14.084	12.647	11.435	10.406	9.526	8.112	6.590
33	16.002	15.075	14.230	12.754	11.514	10.464	9.569	8.135	6.600
34	16.193	15.237	14.368	12.854	11.587	10.518	9.609	8.157	6.609
35	15.374	15.390	14.498	12.948	11.655	10.567	9.644	8.176	6.617
36	16.547	15.536	14.621	13.035	11.717	10.612	9.676	8.193	6.623
37	16.711	15.674	14.737	13.117	11.775	10.653	9.704	8.207	6.629
38	16.868	15.805	14.846	13.193	11.829	10.691	9.733	8.221	6.634
39	17.017	15.929	14.949	13.265	11.879	10.726	9.757	8.233	6.638
40	17.159	16.046	15.046	13.332	11.925	10.757	9.779	8.244	6.642
41	17.294	16.157	15.138	13.394	11.967	10.786	9.799	8.253	6.645
42	17.423	16.263	15.224	13.452	12.007	10.815	9.817	8.262	6.648
43	17.546	16.363	15.306	12.043	10.838	9.834	9.834	8.270	6.650
44	17.663	16.458	15.383	13.558	12.077	10.861	9.849	8.276	6.652
45	17.774	16.548	15.456	13.605	12.108	10.881	9.863	8.283	6.654
46	17.880	16.633	15.524	13.650	12.137	10.900	9.875	8.288	6.656
47	17.981	16.714	15.589	13.692	12.164	10.918	9.887	8.293	6.657
48	18.077	16.790	15.650	13.730	12.189	10.933	9.897	8.297	6.659
49	18.169	16.863	15.708	13.767	12.212	10.948	9.906	8.301	6.660
50	18.256	16.931	15.762	13.801	12.233	10.962	9.915	8.305	6.661
51	18.339	16.997	15.813	13.832	12.253	10.974	9.923	8.308	6.661
52	18.418	17.058	15.861	13.862	12.271	10.985	9.930	8.310	6.662
53	18.493	17.117	15.907	13.890	12.288	10.996	9.936	8.313	6.663
54	18.565	17.173	15.950	13.916	12.304	11.005	9.942	8.315	6.663
55	18.633	17.225	15.990	13.940	12.319	11.014	9.947	6.317	6.664
56	18.698	17.275	16.029	13.963	12.332	11.022	9.952	8.319	6.664
57	18.760	17.322	16.065	13.984	12.344	11.029	9.956	8.320	6.664
58	18.819	17.367	16.099	14.003	12.356	11.036	9.960	8.322	6.665
59	18.876	17.410	16.131	14.022	12.367	11.042	9.964	8.323	6.665
60	18.929	17.450	16.161	14.039	12.377	11.048	9.967	8.324	6.665
61	18.980	17.488	16.190	14.055	12.386	11.053	9.970	8.325	6.665
62	19.029	17.524	16.217	14.070	12.394	11.058	9.973	8.326	6.666
63	19.075	17.558	16.242	14.084	12.402	11.062	9.975	8.327	6.666
64	19.119	17.591	16.266	14.098	12.409	11.066	9.978	8.327	6.666
65	19.161	17.622	16.289	14.110	12.416	11.070	9.980	8.328	6.666
66	19.201	17.651	16.310	14.121	12.422	11.073	9.981	8.329	6.666
67	19.239	17.679	16.331	14.132	12.428	11.077	9.983	8.329	6.666
68	19.275	17.705	16.350	14.142	12.433	11.079	9.985	8.329	6.666
69	19.310	17.730	16.368	14.152	12.438	11.082	9.986	8.330	6.666
70	19.343	17.753	16.384	14.160	12.443	11.084	9.987	8.330	6.666

Discounted Value of $1 Due at a Given Future Time

This table shows the present or discounted value of $1 due at a given future time. For example, assume property which will revert to a lessor in 10 years will then be worth $1,000. The present value of this reversion, computed at an assumed rate of 4% on the investment, if sound by finding the factor on the 10-year line in the 4% column. The factor .6756 is multiplied by 1000 to obtain the answer of $675.60.

Interest Rate

Number of Years	*3%*	*3½%*	*4%*	*4½%*	*5%*	*6%*	*7%*	*8%*
1	0.9709	0.9662	0.9615	0.9569	0.9524	0.9434	0.9346	0.9259
2	0.9426	0.9335	0.9246	0.9157	0.9070	0.8900	0.8734	0.8573
3	0.9151	0.9019	0.8890	0.8763	0.8638	0.8396	0.8163	0.7938
4	0.8885	0.8714	0.8548	0.8386	0.8227	0.7921	0.7629	0.7350
5	0.8626	0.8420	0.8219	0.8025	0.7835	0.7473	0.7130	0.6806
6	0.8375	0.8135	0.7903	0.7679	0.7462	0.7050	0.6663	0.6302
7	0.8131	0.7860	0.7599	0.7348	0.7107	0.6651	0.6227	0.5835
8	0.7894	0.7594	0.7307	0.7032	0.6768	0.6274	0.5820	0.5403
9	0.7664	0.7337	0.7026	0.6729	0.6446	0.5919	0.5439	0.5002
10	0.7441	0.7089	0.6756	0.6439	0.6139	0.5584	0.5083	0.4632
11	0.7224	0.6849	0.6496	0.6162	0.5847	0.5268	0.4751	0.4289
12	0.7014	0.6618	0.6246	0.5897	0.5568	0.4970	0.4440	0.3971
13	0.6810	0.6394	0.6006	0.5643	0.5303	0.4688	0.4150	0.3677
14	0.6611	0.6178	0.5775	0.5400	0.5051	0.4423	0.3878	0.3405
15	0.6419	0.5969	0.5553	0.5167	0.4810	0.4173	0.3624	0.3152
16	0.6232	0.5767	0.5339	0.4945	0.4581	0.3936	0.3387	0.2919
17	0.6050	0.5572	0.5134	0.4732	0.4363	0.3714	0.3166	0.2703
18	0.5874	0.5384	0.4936	0.4528	0.4155	0.3503	0.2959	0.2502
19	0.5703	0.5202	0.4746	0.4333	0.3957	0.3305	0.2765	0.2317
20	0.5537	0.5026	0.4564	0.4146	0.3769	0.3118	0.2584	0.2145
21	0.5375	0.4856	0.4388	0.3968	0.3589	0.2942	0.2415	0.1987
22	0.5219	0.4692	0.4220	0.3797	0.3418	0.2775	0.2257	0.1839
23	0.5067	0.4533	0.4057	0.3634	0.3256	0.2618	0.2109	0.1703
24	0.4919	0.4380	0.3901	0.3477	0.3101	0.2470	0.1971	0.1577
25	0.4776	0.4231	0.3751	0.3327	0.2953	0.2330	0.1842	0.1460
26	0.4637	0.4088	0.3607	0.3184	0.2812	0.2198	0.1722	0.1352
27	0.4502	0.3950	0.3468	0.3047	0.2678	0.2074	0.1609	0.1252
28	0.4371	0.3817	0.3335	0.2916	0.2551	0.1956	0.1504	0.1159
29	0.4243	0.3687	0.3207	0.2790	0.2429	0.1846	0.1406	0.1073
30	0.4120	0.3563	0.3083	0.2670	0.2314	0.1741	0.1314	0.0994
31	0.4000	0.3442	0.2965	0.2555	0.2204	0.1643	0.1228	0.0920
32	0.3883	0.3326	0.2851	0.2445	0.2099	0.1550	0.1147	0.0852
33	0.3770	0.3213	0.2741	0.2340	0.1999	0.1462	0.1072	0.0789
34	0.3660	0.3105	0.2636	0.2239	0.1904	0.1379	0.1002	0.0730
35	0.3554	0.3000	0.2534	0.2143	0.1813	0.1301	0.0937	0.0676
36	0.3450	0.2898	0.2437	0.2050	0.1727	0.1227	0.0875	0.0626
37	0.3350	0.2800	0.2343	0.1962	0.1644	0.1158	0.0818	0.0580
38	0.3252	0.2706	0.2253	0.1877	0.1566	0.1092	0.0765	0.0536
39	0.3158	0.2614	0.2166	0.1797	0.1491	0.1031	0.0715	0.0497
40	0.3066	0.2526	0.2083	0.1719	0.1420	0.0972	0.0668	0.0460

Discounted Value of $1 Due at a Given Future Time *(continued)*

Interest Rate

Number of Years	*9%*	*10%*	*11%*	*12%*	*13%*	*14%*	*15%*
1	0.9174	0.9091	0.9009	0.8929	0.8850	0.8772	0.8696
2	0.8417	0.8264	0.8116	0.7972	0.7831	0.7695	0.7561
3	0.7722	0.7513	0.7312	0.7118	0.6931	0.6750	0.6575
4	0.7084	0.6830	0.6587	0.6355	0.6133	0.5921	0.5718
5	0.6499	0.6209	0.5935	0.5674	0.5428	0.5194	0.4972
6	0.5963	0.5645	0.5346	0.5066	0.4803	0.4556	0.4323
7	0.5470	0.5132	0.4816	0.4523	0.4251	0.3996	0.3759
8	0.5019	0.4665	0.4339	0.4039	0.3762	0.3506	0.3269
9	0.4604	0.4241	0.3909	0.3606	0.3329	0.3075	0.2843
10	0.4224	0.3855	0.3522	0.3220	0.2946	0.2697	0.2472
11	0.3875	0.3505	0.3173	0.2875	0.2607	0.2366	0.2149
12	0.3555	0.3186	0.2858	0.2567	0.2307	0.2076	0.1869
13	0.3262	0.2897	0.2575	0.2292	0.2042	0.1821	0.1625
14	0.2992	0.2633	0.2320	0.2046	0.1807	0.1597	0.1413
15	0.2745	0.2394	0.2090	0.1827	0.1599	0.1401	0.1229
16	0.2519	0.2176	0.1883	0.1631	0.1415	0.1229	0.1069
17	0.2311	0.1978	0.1696	0.1456	0.1252	0.1078	0.0929
18	0.2120	0.1799	0.1528	0.1300	0.1108	0.0946	0.0808
19	0.1945	0.1635	0.1377	0.1161	0.0981	0.0829	0.0703
20	0.1784	0.1486	0.1240	0.1037	0.0868	0.0728	0.0611
21	0.1637	0.1351	0.1117	0.0926	0.0768	0.0638	0.0531
22	0.1502	0.1228	0.1007	0.0826	0.0680	0.0560	0.0462
23	0.1378	0.1117	0.0907	0.0738	0.0601	0.0491	0.0402
24	0.1264	0.1015	0.0817	0.0660	0.0532	0.0431	0.0349
25	0.1160	0.0923	0.0736	0.0588	0.0471	0.0378	0.0304
26	0.1064	0.0829	0.0663	0.0525	0.0417	0.0331	0.0264
27	0.0976	0.0763	0.0597	0.0470	0.0369	0.0291	0.0230
28	0.0895	0.0693	0.0538	0.0420	0.0326	0.0255	0.0200
29	0.0822	0.0630	0.0485	0.0374	0.0289	0.0224	0.0174
30	0.0754	0.0573	0.0437	0.0334	0.0256	0.0196	0.0151
31	0.0691	0.0521	0.0394	0.0298	0.0226	0.0172	0.0131
32	0.0634	0.0474	0.0354	0.0266	0.0200	0.0151	0.0114
33	0.0582	0.0431	0.0319	0.0238	0.0177	0.0132	0.0099
34	0.0534	0.0391	0.0288	0.0212	0.0157	0.0116	0.0086
35	0.0490	0.0356	0.0259	0.0189	0.0139	0.0102	0.0075
36	0.0449	0.0323	0.0234	0.0169	0.0123	0.0089	0.0065
37	0.0412	0.0294	0.0210	0.0151	0.0109	0.0078	0.0057
38	0.0378	0.0267	0.0189	0.0135	0.0096	0.0069	0.0049
39	0.0347	0.0243	0.0171	0.0120	0.0085	0.0060	0.0043
40	0.0318	0.0221	0.0154	0.0107	0.0075	0.0053	0.0037

Compound Interest Table

Example of use of this table:

Find how much $1,000 now in bank will grow to in 14 years at 4% interest.
From table 14 years at 4% 1.7317
Value in 14 years of $1,000 $1,731.70

Interest Rate

Number of Years	*3%*	*3½%*	*4%*	*4½%*	*5%*	*6%*	*7%*	*8%*
1	1.0300	1.0350	1.0400	1.0450	1.0500	1.0600	1.0700	1.0800
2	1.0609	1.0712	1.0816	1.0920	1.1025	1.1236	1.1449	1.1664
3	1.0927	1.1087	1.1249	1.1412	1.1576	1.1910	1.2250	1.2597
4	1.1255	1.1475	1.1699	1.1925	1.2155	1.2624	1.3107	1.3604
5	1.1593	1.1877	1.2167	1.2462	1.2763	1.3332	1.4025	1.4693
6	1.1941	1.2293	1.2653	1.3023	1.3401	1.4135	1.5007	1.5868
7	1.2299	1.2723	1.3159	1.3609	1.4071	1.5030	1.6057	1.7138
8	1.2668	1.3168	1.3686	1.4221	1.4775	1.5938	1.7181	1.8509
9	1.3048	1.3629	1.4233	1.4861	1.5513	1.6894	1.8384	1.9990
10	1.3439	1.4106	1.4802	1.5530	1.6289	1.7908	1.9671	2.1589
11	1.3842	1.4600	1.5395	1.6229	1.7103	1.8982	2.1048	2.3316
12	1.4258	1.5111	1.6010	1.6959	1.7959	2.0121	2.2521	2.5181
13	1.4685	1.5640	1.6651	1.7722	1.8856	2.1329	2.4098	2.7196
14	1.5126	1.6187	1.7317	1.8519	1.9799	2.2609	2.5785	2.9371
15	1.5580	1.6753	1.8009	1.9353	2.0789	2.3965	2.7590	3.1721
16	1.6047	1.7340	1.8730	2.0224	2.1829	2.5403	2.9521	3.4259
17	1.6528	1.7947	1.9479	2.1134	2.2920	2.6927	3.1588	3.7000
18	1.7024	1.8575	2.0258	2.2085	2.4066	2.8543	3.3799	3.9960
19	1.7535	1.9225	2.1068	2.3079	2.5270	3.0255	3.6165	4.3157
20	1.8061	1.9898	2.1911	2.4117	2.6533	3.2075	3.8696	4.6609
21	1.8603	2.0594	2.2788	2.5202	2.7860	3.3995	4.1405	5.0338
22	1.9161	2.1315	2.3699	2.6337	2.9253	3.6035	4.4304	5.4365
23	1.9736	2.2061	2.4647	2.7522	3.0715	3.8197	4.7405	5.8714
24	2.0328	2.2833	2.5633	2.8760	3.2251	4.0489	5.0723	6.3411
25	2.0938	2.3632	2.6658	3.0054	3.3864	4.2918	5.4274	6.8484
26	2.1566	2.4460	2.7725	3.1407	3.5557	4.5493	5.8073	7.3963
27	2.2213	2.5316	2.8834	3.2820	3.7335	4.8223	6.2138	7.9880
28	2.2879	2.6202	2.9987	3.4297	3.9201	5.1116	6.6488	8.6271
29	2.3566	2.7119	3.1187	3.5840	4.1161	5.4183	7.1142	9.3172
30	2.4273	2.8068	3.2434	3.7453	4.3219	5.7434	7.6122	10.5582
31	2.5001	2.9050	3.3731	3.9139	4.5380	6.0881	8.1451	10.8676
32	2.5751	3.0067	3.5081	4.0900	4.7649	6.4533	8.7152	11.7370
33	2.6523	3.1119	3.6484	4.2740	5.0032	6.8408	9.3253	12.6760
34	2.7319	3.2209	3.7943	4.4664	5.2533	7.2510	9.9781	13.6901
35	2.8139	3.3336	3.9461	4.6673	5.5160	7.6860	10.6765	14.7853
36	2.8983	3.4503	4.1039	4.8774	5.7918	8.1479	11.4239	15.9681
37	2.9852	3.5710	4.2681	5.0969	6.0814	8.6360	12.2236	17.2456
38	3.0748	3.6960	4.4388	5.3262	6.3855	9.1542	13.0792	18.6252
39	3.1670	3.8254	4.6164	5.5659	6.7048	9.7035	13.9948	20.1152
40	3.2620	3.9593	4.8010	5.8164	7.0400	10.2857	14.9744	21.7245

Compound Interest Table *(continued)*

Interest Rate

Number of Years	*9%*	*10%*	*11%*	*12%*	*13%*	*14%*	*15%*	*20%*
1	1.0900	1.1000	1.1100	1.1200	1.1300	1.1400	1.1500	1.2000
2	1.1881	1.2100	1.2321	1.2544	1.2769	1.2996	1.3225	1.4400
3	1.2950	1.3310	1.3576	1.4049	1.4428	1.4815	1.5208	1.7280
4	1.4115	1.4647	1.5180	1.5735	1.6304	1.6389	1.7490	2.0736
5	1.5386	1.6105	1.6350	1.7623	1.8424	1.9254	2.0113	2.4883
6	1.6771	1.7715	1.8704	1.9738	2.0819	2.1949	2.3130	2.9859
7	1.8230	1.9487	2.0761	2.2106	2.3526	2.5022	2.6600	3.5831
8	1.9925	2.1435	2.3045	2.4759	2.6584	2.8525	3.0590	4.2998
9	2.1718	2.3579	2.5580	2.7730	3.0040	3.2519	3.5178	5.1597
10	2.3673	2.5937	2.8394	3.1058	3.3945	3.7072	4.0455	6.1917
11	2.5804	2.8531	3.1517	3.4785	3.8358	4.2262	4.6523	7.4300
12	2.8126	3.1384	3.4984	3.8959	4.3345	4.8179	5.3502	8.9161
13	3.0658	3.4522	3.8832	4.3634	4.8980	5.4924	6.1527	10.6993
14	3.3417	3.7974	4.3104	4.8871	5.5347	6.2613	7.0757	12.8391
15	3.6424	4.1772	4.7845	5.4735	6.2542	7.1379	8.1370	15.4070
16	3.9703	4.5949	5.3108	6.1303	7.0673	8.1372	9.3576	18.4884
17	4.3276	5.0544	5.8950	6.8660	7.9860	9.2764	10.7612	22.1861
18	4.7171	5.5599	6.5435	7.6899	9.0242	10.5751	12.3754	26.6233
19	5.1416	6.1159	7.2633	8.6127	10.1974	12.0556	14.2317	31.9479
20	5.6044	6.7274	8.0623	9.6462	11.5230	13.7434	16.3665	38.3375
21	6.1088	7.4002	8.9491	10.8038	13.0210	15.6675	18.8215	46.0051
22	6.6586	8.1402	9.9335	12.1003	14.7138	17.8610	21.6447	55.2061
23	7.2578	8.9543	11.0262	13.5523	16.6266	20.3615	24.8914	66.2473
24	7.9110	9.8497	12.2391	15.1786	18.7880	23.2122	28.6251	79.4968
25	8.6230	10.8347	13.5854	17.0000	21.2305	26.4619	32.9189	95.3962
26	9.3991	11.9181	15.0793	19.0400	23.9905	30.1665	37.8567	114.4754
27	10.2450	13.1099	16.7386	21.3248	27.1092	34.3899	43.5353	137.3705
28	11.1671	14.4209	18.5799	23.8838	30.6334	39.2044	50.0656	164.8446
29	12.1721	15.8630	20.6236	26.7499	34.6158	44.6931	57.5754	197.8135
30	13.2676	17.4494	22.8922	29.9599	39.1158	50.9501	66.2117	237.3763
31	14.4617	19.1943	25.4104	33.5551	44.2009	58.0831	76.1435	284.8515
32	15.7633	21.1137	28.2055	37.5817	49.9470	66.2148	87.5650	341.8218
33	17.1820	23.2251	31.3082	42.0915	56.4402	75.4849	100.6998	410.1862
34	18.7284	25.5476	34.7521	47.1425	63.7774	86.0527	115.8048	492.2235
35	20.4139	28.1024	38.5748	52.7996	72.0685	98.1001	133.1755	590.6682
36	22.2512	30.9128	42.8180	59.1355	81.4374	111.8342	153.1518	708.8018
37	24.2538	34.0039	47.5280	66.2318	92.0242	127.4909	176.1246	850.5622
38	26.4366	37.4048	52.7561	74.1796	103.9874	145.3397	202.5433	1020.6746
39	28.8159	41.1447	58.5593	83.0812	117.5057	165.6872	232.9248	1224.8096
40	31.4094	45.2592	65.0008	93.0509	132.7815	188.8835	267.8635	1469.7715

Rent Prorating Table

Not infrequently, in commencing or terminating tenancies, it becomes necessary to calculate daily rent charges for short periods. This table may be used where only the annual rental is known. Note that the table indicates daily rental for both 30-day and 31-day months.

Rent per Year	*Rent per Month*	*Rent per Day (30 days)*	*Rent per Day (31 days)*	*Rent per Year*	*Rent per Month*	*Rent per Day (30 days)*	*Rent per Day (31 days)*
$ 1	$ .09	$ .003	$ .0029	$ 725	$ 60.42	$ 2.01	$ 1.950
2	.17	.0056	.0054	750	62.50	2.084	2.017
3	.25	.0083	.008	775	64.59	2.153	2.084
4	.34	.011	.01	800	66.67	2.223	2.151
5	.42	.014	.013	825	68.75	2.292	2.218
6	.50	.016	.016	850	70.84	2.361	2.286
7	.59	.019	.019	875	72.92	2.431	2.352
8	.67	.022	.021	900	75.00	2.50	2.420
9	.75	.025	.024	925	77.09	2.57	2.487
10	.84	.028	.027	950	79.17	2.639	2.554
20	1.67	.056	.054	975	81.25	2.708	2.621
25	2.09	.070	.068	1,000	83.34	2.778	2.689
30	2.50	.084	.081	1,025	85.42	2.847	2.756
40	3.34	.111	.108	1,050	87.50	2.917	2.823
50	4.17	.139	.134	1,075	89.59	2.986	2.880
60	5.00	.166	.161	1,100	91.67	3.056	2.958
70	5.84	.195	.189	1,125	93.75	3.125	3.025
75	6.25	.208	.202	1,150	95.84	3.195	3.092
80	6.67	.222	.215	1,175	97.92	3.264	3.159
90	7.50	.25	.242	1,200	100.00	3.334	3.226
100	8.34	.278	.269	1,300	108.34	3.611	3.495
125	10.42	.347	.336	1,400	116.67	3.889	3.764
150	12.50	.417	.403	1,500	125.00	4.167	4.033
175	14.59	.486	.470	1,600	133.34	4.445	4.301
200	16.67	.556	.538	1,700	141.67	4.723	4.570
225	18.75	.625	.605	1,800	150.00	5.00	4.84
250	20.84	.695	.672	1,900	158.34	5.278	5.108
275	22.92	.764	.740	2,000	166.67	5.56	5.377
300	25.00	.834	.807	3,000	250.00	8.334	8.065
325	27.09	.903	.874	4,000	333.34	11.111	10.753
350	29.17	.972	.941	5,000	416.67	13.889	13.441
375	31.25	1.042	1.009	6,000	500.00	16.667	16.13
400	33.34	1.112	1.076	7,000	583.34	19.445	18.818
425	35.42	1.181	1.143	8,000	666.67	22.223	21.506
450	37.50	1.25	1.21	9,000	750.00	25.00	24.194
475	39.59	1.32	1.277	10,000	833.34	27.778	26.882
500	41.67	1.389	1.344	11,000	916.67	30.556	29.57
525	43.75	1.458	1.412	12,000	1,000.00	33.34	29.889
550	45.84	1.528	1.479	13,000	1,083.34	36.111	34.947
575	47.92	1.598	1.546	14,000	1,166.67	38.889	37.635
600	50.00	1.667	1.613	15,000	1,250.00	41.667	40.323
625	52.09	1.737	1.68	16,000	1,333.34	44.445	43.811
650	54.17	1.806	1.748	17,000	1,416.67	47.223	44.690
675	56.25	1.875	1.815	18,000	1,500,00	50.00	48.387
700	58.34	1.945	1.882	19,000	1,583.34	52.778	50.070

Land Value Per Square Foot

The following table converts value per square foot into both value for a lot 25′ x 100′ and value for an acre of land.

Value per Sq. Ft. of Land	*Value of a Lot 25′ x 100′*	*Value of an Acre*	*Value per Sq. Ft. of Land*	*Value of a Lot 25′ x 100′*	*Value of an Acre*
$.01	$ 25.00	$ 435.60	$ .51	$1,275.00	$22,215.60
.02	50.00	871.20	.52	1,300.00	22,651.20
.03	75.00	1,306.80	.53	1,325.00	23,086.80
.04	100.00	1,742.40	.54	1,350.00	23,522.40
.05	125.00	2,178.00	.55	1,375.00	23,958.00
.06	150.00	2,613.60	.56	1,400.00	24.393.60
.07	175.00	3,049.20	.57	1,425.00	24,829.20
.08	200.00	3,484.80	.58	1,450.00	25,264.80
.09	225.00	3,920.40	.59	1,475.00	25,700.40
.10	250.00	4,356.00	.60	1,500.00	26,136.00
.11	275.00	4,791.60	.61	1,525.00	26,571.60
.12	300.00	5,227.20	.62	1,550.00	27,007.20
.13	325.00	5,662.80	.63	1,575.00	27,442.80
.14	350.00	6,098.40	.64	1,600.00	27,878.40
.15	375.00	6,534.00	.65	1,625.00	28,314.00
.16	400.00	6,969.60	.66	1,650.00	28,749.60
.17	425.00	7,405.20	.67	1,675.00	29,185.20
.18	450.00	7,840.80	.68	1,700.00	29,620.80
.19	475.00	8,276.40	.69	1,725.00	30,056.40
.20	500.00	8,712.00	.70	1,750.00	30,492.00
.21	525.00	9,147.60	.71	1,775.00	30,927.60
.22	550.00	9,583.20	.72	1,800.00	31,363.20
.23	575.00	10,018.80	.73	1,825.00	31,798.80
.24	600.00	10,454.40	.74	1,850.00	32,234.40
.25	625.00	10,890.00	.75	1,875.00	32,670.00
.26	650.00	11,325.60	.76	1,900.00	33,105.60
.27	675.00	11,761.20	.77	1,925.00	33,541.20
.28	700.60	12,196.80	.78	1,950.00	33,976.80
.29	725.00	12,632.40	.79	1,975.00	34,412.40
.30	750.00	13,068.00	.80	2,000.00	34,848.00
.31	775.00	13,503.60	.81	2,025.00	35,283.60
.32	800.00	13,939.20	.82	2,050.00	35,719.20
.33	825.00	14.374.80	.83	2,075.00	36,154.80
.34	850.00	14,810.40	.84	2,100.00	36,590.40
.35	875.00	15,246.00	.85	2,125.00	37,026.00
.36	900.00	15,681.60	.86	2,150.00	37,461.60
.37	925.00	16,117.20	.87	2,175.00	37,897.20
.38	950.00	16,552.80	.88	2,200.00	38,332.80
.39	975.00	16,988.40	.89	2,225.00	38,768.40
.40	1,000.00	17,424.00	.90	2,250.00	39.204.00
.41	1,025.00	17,859.60	.91	2,275.00	39,639.60
.42	1,050.00	18,295.20	.92	2,300.00	40,075.20
.43	1,075.00	18,730.80	.93	2,325.00	40,510.80
.44	1,100.00	19,166.40	.94	2,350.00	40,946.40
.45	1,125.00	19,602.00	.95	2,375.00	41,382.00
.46	1,150.00	20,037.60	.96	2,400.00	41,817.60
.47	1,175.00	20,473.20	.97	2,425.00	42,253.20
.48	1,200.00	20.908.80	.98	2,450.00	42,688.80
.49	1,225.00	21,344.40	.99	2,475.00	43,124.40
.50	1,250.00	21,780.00	1.00	2,500.00	43,560.00

Real Estate Investor's Tax Evaluator

	Deal #1	*Deal #2*
Rental Income	$______	$______
Expenses:		
Interest	$______	$______
Amortization	______	______
Real estate taxes	______	______
Other taxes (including income taxes)	______	______
Insurance	______	______
Payroll costs	______	______
Repairs	______	______
Other expenses	______	______
Total Expenses	$______	$______
Depreciation:		
Present basis for depreciation	$______	$______
Method of depreciation	______	______
(a) 200%-declining-balance	______	______
(b) 150%-declining-balance	______	______
(c) Sum-of-the-digits	______	______
(d) Straight-line	______	______
Investment Credit:	$______	$______
Taxable Income: Income less expenses (not including amortization) and depreciation using alternate methods		
(a)______	$______	$______
(b)______	______	______
(c)______	______	______
(d)______	______	______
Income Taxes:		
Sole proprietorship	$______	$______
Partnership	______	______
Corporation	______	______

INDEX

References are to Paragraph [¶] Numbers